Nancy E. Lewis

MODERN SHAKESPEAREAN CRITICISM

edited by
Alvin B. Kernan
Yale University

Harcourt, Brace & World, Inc.
New York / Chicago / San Francisco / Atlanta

Essays on Style, Dramaturgy, and the Major Plays

MODERN SHAKESPEAREAN CRITICISM
Essays on Style, Dramaturgy, and the Major Plays

edited by Alvin B. Kernan

Library of Congress Catalog Card Number: 71-97863

Printed in the United States of America

PREFACE

This book aims to provide students of Shakespeare with a basic, single-volume collection of the best modern Shakespearean criticism. The twenty-six essays reprinted here deal with crucial elements of Shakespeare's poetic style and dramaturgy and with his major plays.

Part I, Shakespeare's Dramatic Universe, contains eight essays that discuss the type of world Shakespeare regularly creates in his plays, various aspects of his verbal and dramatic style, and his management of plots and methods of characterization and "character grouping." Several of the essays in this part, such as John Russell Brown's "Verbal Drama," are among those in the book that will make students aware of the additional effects and meanings that emerge when the plays are actually produced on the stage rather than read.

The essays in Part II, The Intellectual and Theatrical Setting, provide information about the intellectual milieu in which Shakespeare wrote and the theatrical conditions that helped to shape his plays. In "Shakespeare's Sonnets and the 1590's" Patrick Cruttwell uses Shakespeare's sonnet sequence to trace in the poetry and plays of the time the gradual movement from conventional subject matter and style to a much more complex and questioning view of reality and the human condition. R. A. Foakes's "The Profession of Playwright" is a remarkable condensation of all that is presently known with any certainty about the theater during the last years of Elizabeth Tudor's reign—the make-up of the professional acting companies, the physical structure of the theater, the nature of the audience, the relationship of players and playwrights, finances, costumes, props, and stage effects. This single essay provides all the theatrical background students need in order to understand the plays.

The remainder of the book is divided into five parts that deal chronologically and by genre with the major phases of Shakespeare's career as a playwright: the early comedies, the histories, the Elizabethan tragedies, the Jacobean tragedies, and the late plays and the romances. Several essays provide general theories about the genres in which Shakespeare worked. Northrop Frye's "The Argument of Comedy" sketches quickly and impressively the nature of the comic impulse and the form in which it is usually expressed, and relates Shakespeare's particular brand of comedy to the comic tradition. Maynard Mack's "The Jacobean Shakespeare" not only provides a brilliant summation of Shakespeare's major tragedies but develops implicitly a theory of the nature of tragedy in general and of Shakespearean tragedy in particular. My essay on the history plays and D. A. Traversi's on the romances, though intended primarily to explicate a number of plays, treat these plays as groups and thus develop theories about the nature of the Shakespearean history play and about the handling of the themes and conventions of romance.

Essays dealing with the individual plays were chosen with several criteria in mind. Excellence, of course, was a prime consideration, but I also sought works that would perform at least two other functions: (1) provide a coherent and complete view of an entire play and (2) serve as a model for the use of some particular critical technique. I selected essays that attempt a reading of an entire play rather than essays that provide insights into particular aspects of a play, in order that students may feel after reading an essay that they have at least one large view of what that play is about and how its subject is presented. I do not mean to imply that each of the essays reprinted here tells the whole truth about the play it deals with. In several cases there is so much more to say that I was tempted to add qualifying footnotes to point out other views; but I confined my editorial changes, all clearly indicated by brackets, to the modification of references in footnotes that would otherwise have been obscure and to the correction or clarification of a very few words in the texts.

Each essay on a play, then, grapples with an interpretation of the whole and tries to see how the beginning relates to the end, how the individual parts fit together to create a unity, how the smaller pieces reflect the larger creation. At the same time, each provides a lesson in the ways in which various critical methods can be used to enhance our understanding of the plays. Harry Levin's "Form and Formality in *Romeo and Juliet*" analyzes the way in which Shakespeare used rhetoric and certain conventional devices of phrasing to build up a conception of character and action. Helen Gardner, in her essay on *As You Like It,* offers a fine discussion of tragedy and comedy and then interprets the play in terms of her distinction between these genres. Cleanth Brooks in "The Naked Babe and the Cloak of Manliness" opens the question of the presence of images in drama and demonstrates the insight that can be gained from taking imagery seriously and tracing the instances and placement of imagery in a play. In *"King Lear* or *Endgame"* Jan Kott explores the advantages of comparing Shakespeare's work with the modern Theater of the Grotesque. My essay on *Othello* uses the device of "the world of the play" in an attempt to organize an understanding of the relationship of the play's parts. David Young's analysis of *A Midsummer Night's Dream* serves as a model of what it means to seek the structure of a play. C. L. Barber's discussion of *The Merchant of Venice* relates the play to the myths and social festivals to which it is analogous.

The essays on Shakespearean style and dramaturgy can be supplemented in various ways by the essays and parts of essays that are directed primarily toward the explication of particular plays. For example, a reading of Clemen or Downer on imagery can lead directly into Brooks's tracing of the imagery in *Macbeth;* a reading of L. C. Knights on the symbolic rather than realistic nature of the plays can be supported by Jan Kott's discussion of why romantic and realistic productions of *King Lear* were unsatisfactory.

Indeed, for all their variety of method and approach, the critics represented in this volume are in remarkable agreement about the fundamental tenets of Shakespearean criticism, about the ways in which the plays are to be approached and understood. It is this agreement, and not the fact that all the essays included here were written in the last forty years, that makes the term "modern" a meaningful adjective in the context of this collection. In the largest and crudest terms, what these critics share is a belief that Shakespeare's plays are most usefully and properly approached, not as realistic imitations of human nature and affairs, but as symbolic structures, elaborately intertwined and interworking parts that combine to create, not a photographic representation of the world, but an image of reality as it is perceived by the imagination. It is only fitting, then, that this book should begin with G. Wilson Knight's essay "On the Principles of Shakespeare Interpretation," published in 1930, in which the implications of this insight were first fully projected and used to illuminate the nature of poetic drama and Shakespeare's plays.

ALVIN B. KERNAN

CONTENTS

V. THE ELIZABETHAN TRAGEDIES

The Earlier Tragic Form and Subject Matter

VI. TRAGIC FORM AND THE JACOBEAN TRAGEDIES

The Structure of the Later Tragedies

Shakespeare's Later Tragedies

VII. THE LATE PLAYS AND THE ROMANCES

The Last of the Great Tragedies

The Romances

I

SHAKESPEARE'S DRAMATIC UNIVERSE

THE SYMBOLIC WORLD OF THE PLAYS

On the Principles of Shakespeare Interpretation

G. Wilson Knight

. . . To receive the whole Shakespearian vision into the intellectual consciousness demands a certain and very definite act of mind. One must be prepared to see the whole play in space as well as in time. It is natural in analysis to pursue the steps of the tale in sequence, noticing the logic that connects them, regarding those essentials that Aristotle noted: the beginning, middle, and end. But by giving supreme attention to this temporal nature of drama we omit what, in Shakespeare, is at least of equivalent importance. A Shakespearian tragedy is set spatially as well as temporally in the mind. By this I mean that there are throughout the play a set of correspondences which relate to each other independently of the time-sequence which is the story: such are the intuition-intelligence opposition active within and across *Troilus and Cressida,* the death-theme in *Hamlet,* the nightmare evil of *Macbeth*. This I have sometimes called the play's 'atmosphere'. In interpretation of *Othello* it has to take the form of an essential relation, abstracted from the story, existing between the Othello, Desdemona, and Iago conceptions. Generally, however, there is unity, not diversity. Perhaps it is what Aristotle meant by 'unity of idea'. Now if we are prepared to see the whole play laid out, so to speak, as an area, being simultaneously aware of these thickly-scattered correspondences in a

---

single view of the whole, we possess the unique quality of the play in a new sense. 'Faults' begin to vanish into thin air. Immediately we begin to realize necessity where before we saw irrelevance and beauty dethroning ugliness. For the Shakespearian person is intimately fused with this atmospheric quality; he obeys a spatial as well as a temporal necessity. Gloucester's mock-suicide, Malcolm's detailed confession of crimes, Ulysses' long speech on order, are cases in point. But because we, in our own lives and those of our friends, see events most strongly as a time-sequence—thereby blurring our vision of other significances—we next, quite arbitrarily and unjustly, abstract from the Shakespearian drama that element which the intellect most easily assimilates; and, finding it not to correspond with our own life as we see it, begin to observe 'faults'. This, however, is apparent only after we try to rationalize our impressions; what I have called the 'spatial' approach is implicit in our imaginative pleasure to a greater or a less degree always. It is, probably, the ability to see larger and still larger areas of a great work spatially with a continual widening of vision that causes us to appreciate it more deeply, to own it with our minds more surely, on every reading; whereas at first, knowing it only as a story, much of it may have seemed sterile, and much of it irrelevant. A vivid analogy to this Shakespearian quality is provided by a fine modern play, *Journey's End.* Everything in the play gains tremendous significance from war. The story, which is slight, moves across a stationary background: if we forget that background for one instant parts of the dialogue fall limp; remember it, and the most ordinary remark is tense, poignant—often of shattering power. To study *Measure for Measure* or *Macbeth* without reference to their especial 'atmospheres' is rather like forgetting the war as we read or witness *Journey's End;* or the cherry orchard in Tchehov's famous play. There is, however, a difference. In *Journey's End* the two elements, the dynamic and static, action and background, are each firmly actualized and separated except in so far as Stanhope, rather like Hamlet, bridges the two. In *The Cherry Orchard* there is the same division. But with Shakespeare a purely spiritual atmosphere interpenetrates the action, there is a fusing rather than a contrast; and where a direct personal symbol growing out of the dominating atmosphere is actualized, it may be a supernatural being, as the Ghost, symbol of the death-theme in *Hamlet,* or the Weird Sisters, symbols of the evil in *Macbeth.*

Since in Shakespeare there is this close fusion of the temporal, that is, the plot-chain of event following event, with the spatial, that is, the omnipresent and mysterious reality brooding motionless over and within the play's movement, it is evident that my two principles thus firmly divided in analysis are no more than provisional abstractions from the poetic unity. But since to make the first abstraction with especial crudity, that is, to analyse the sequence of events, the 'causes' linking dramatic motive to action and action to result in time, is a blunder instinctive to the human intellect, I make no apology for restoring balance by insistence on the other. My emphasis is justified, in that it will be seen to clarify many difficulties. It throws neglected beauties into strong relief, and often resolves the whole play with a sudden revelation. For example, the ardour of Troilus in battle against the Greeks at the close of *Troilus and Cressida,* Mariana's lovely prayer for Angelo's life, the birth of love in Edmund at the close of *King Lear,* and the stately theme of Alcibiades' revenge in *Timon of Athens*—all these cannot be properly understood without a clear knowledge of the general themes which vitalize the action of those plays.

These dual elements seem perfectly harmonized in *Troilus and Cressida, Measure for Measure, Macbeth,* and *King Lear.* In *Hamlet* the spatial element is mainly confined to the theme of Hamlet and the Ghost, both sharply contrasted with their environment: thus the play offers a less unified statement as a whole, and interpretation is rendered difficult and not wholly satisfactory. With *Othello,* too, there is difficulty. Unless the play is to be considered as purely a sequence of events, if we are to find a spatial reality, we must view the qualities of the three chief persons together and in their essential relation to each other expect to find the core of the metaphysical significance: for the primary fact of the play is not, as in *Macbeth* and *King Lear,* a blending, but rather a differentiating, a demarcation, and separation, of essence from essence. In *Timon of Athens* both elements appear, but the temporal predominates in that the imaginative atmosphere itself changes with the play's progress: which fact here seems to reflect the peculiar clarity and conscious mastery of the poet's mind. With the poet, as with the reader, the time-sequence will be uppermost in consciousness, the pervading atmosphere or static background tending to be unconsciously apprehended or created, a half-realized significance, a vague all-inclusive deity of the dramatic universe. In respect of this atmospheric suggestion we find a sense of mystery in *King Lear* which cannot be found in *Othello;* and, in so far as the Shakespearian play lacks mystery, it seems, as a rule, to lack profundity. But in *Timon of Athens* the mystery of *King Lear* is, as it were, mastered, and yet re-expressed with the clarity of *Othello.* Here the poet explicates the atmospheric quality of former plays in a philosophic tragedy whose dominant temporal quality thus mirrors the clarity, in no sense the sterility, of the poet's vision. The spatial, that is, the spiritual, quality uses the temporal, that is, the story, lending it dominance in order to express itself the more clearly: *Timon of Athens* is essentially an allegory or parable. My suggestion as to the poet's 'consciousness' must, however, be considered as either pure hazard or useful metaphor, illuminating the play's nature and perhaps hitting the truth of Shakespeare's mind in composition. Certainly Hazlitt thought that in *Timon of Athens* the poet was of all his plays the most 'in earnest'. But elsewhere I am not concerned with the poet's 'consciousness', or 'intentions'. Nor need the question arise; but, since a strong feeling exists that no subtlety or profundity can be born from a mind itself partly unconscious of such things, and since Shakespeare's life appears not to have been mainly concerned with transcendental realities—except in that he was born, loved, was ambitious, and died—it will be as well to refer briefly to the matter of 'intentions'. This I shall do next, and will afterwards deal with two other critical concepts which, with 'intentions', have helped to work chaos with our understanding of poetry.

There is a maxim that a work of art should be criticized according to the artist's 'intentions': than which no maxim could be more false. The intentions of the artist are but clouded forms which, if he attempt to crystallize them in consciousness, may prefigure a quite different reality from that which eventually emerges in his work,

> not answering the aim
> And that unbodied figure of the thought
> That gave't surmised shape.

In those soliloquies where Brutus and Macbeth try to clarify their own motives into clean-cut concepts, we may see good examples of the irrelevance born by 'intentions' to the instinctive power which is bearing the man towards his fate: it is the same with the poet. Milton's puritanical 'intentions' bear little relevance to his Satan. 'Intentions' belong to the plane of intellect and memory: the swifter consciousness that awakens in poetic composition touches subtleties and heights and depths unknowable by intellect and intractable to memory. That consciousness we can enjoy at will when we submit ourselves with utmost passivity to the poet's work; but when the intellectual mode returns it often brings with it a troop of concepts irrelevant to the nature of the work it thinks to analyse, and, with its army of 'intentions', 'causes', 'sources', and 'characters', and its essentially ethical outlook, works havoc with our minds, since it is trying to impose on the vivid reality of art a logic totally alien to its nature. In interpretation we must remember not the facts but the quality of the original poetic experience; and, in translating this into whatever concepts appear suitable, we find that the facts too fall into place automatically when once the qualitative focus is correct. Reference to the artist's 'intentions' is usually a sign that the commentator—in so far as he is a commentator rather than a biographer—has lost touch with the essentials of the poetic work. He is thinking in terms of the time-sequence and causality, instead of allowing his mind to be purely receptive. It will be clear, then, that the following essays say nothing new as to Shakespeare's 'intentions'; attempt to shed no light directly on Shakespeare the man; but claim rather to illuminate our own poetic experiences enjoyed whilst reading, or watching, the plays. In this sense, they are concerned only with realities, since they claim to interpret what is generally admitted to exist: the supreme quality of Shakespeare's work.

Next as to 'sources'. This concept is closely involved with that of 'intentions'. Both try to explain art in terms of causality, the most natural implement of intellect. Both fail empirically to explain any essential whatsoever. There is, clearly, a relation between Shakespeare's plays and the work of Plutarch, Holinshed, Vergil, Ovid, and the Bible; but not one of these, nor any number of them, can be considered a cause of Shakespeare's poetry and therefore the word 'source', that is, the origin whence the poetic reality flows, is a false metaphor. In Shakespeare's best known passage of aesthetic philosophy we hear that the poet's eye glances 'from heaven to earth, from earth to heaven', and the poet's pen turns to 'shapes' the 'forms of things unknown'. It 'gives to airy nothing a local habitation and a name'. That is, the source of poetry is rooted in the otherness of mental or spiritual realities; these, however, are a 'nothing' until mated with earthly shapes. Creation is thus born of a union between 'earth' and 'heaven', the material and the spiritual. Without 'shapes' the poet is speechless; he needs words, puppets of the drama, tales. But the unknown 'forms' come first. In another profound but less known passage (*Richard II,* V.v.6) we hear that in creation the brain is 'the female to the soul'. The spiritual then is the masculine, the material the feminine, agent in creation. The 'source' of *Antony and Cleopatra,* if we must indeed have a 'source' at all, is the transcendent erotic imagination of the poet which finds its worthy bride in an old world romance. It seems, indeed, that the great poet must, if he is to forgo nothing of concreteness and humanity, lose himself in contemplation of an actual tale or an actual event in order to find himself in supreme vision; otherwise he will tend to philosophy, to the divine element unmated to the earthly. Therefore 'sources', as usually understood, have their use for the poet: they have little value for the interpreter. The tale of Cleopatra married to a Hardy's imagination would have given birth to a novel very different from Shakespeare's play: the final poetic result is always a mystery. That result, and not vague hazards as to its 'source', must be the primary object of our attention. It should further be observed that, although the purely 'temporal' element of Shakespearian drama may sometimes bear a close relation to a tale probably known by Shakespeare, what I have called the 'spatial' reality is ever the unique child of his mind; therefore interpretation, concerned, as in the following essays, so largely with that reality, is clearly working outside and beyond the story alone. Now, whereas the spatial quality of these greater plays is different in each, they nearly all turn on the same plot. It is therefore reasonable to conclude that the poet has chosen a series of tales to whose life-rhythm he is spontaneously attracted, and has developed them in each instance according to his vision.

And finally, as to 'character'. [In the present essay] the term is refused, since it is so constantly entwined with a false and unduly ethical criticism. So often we hear that 'in *Timon of Athens* it was Shakespeare's intention to show how a generous but weak character may come to ruin through an unwise use of his wealth'; that 'Shakespeare wished in *Macbeth* to show how crime inevitably brings retribution'; that 'in *Antony and Cleopatra* Shakespeare has given us a lesson concerning the dangers of an uncontrolled passion'. These are purely imaginary examples, coloured for my purpose, to indicate the type of ethical criticism to which I refer. It continually brings in the intention-concept, which our moral-philosophy, rightly or wrongly, involves. Hence, too, the constant and fruitless search for 'motives' sufficient to account for Macbeth's and Iago's actions: since the moral critic feels he cannot blame a 'character' until he understands his 'intentions', and without the opportunity of praising and blaming he is dumb. It is not, indeed, possible to avoid ethical considerations; nor is it advisable. Where one person within the drama is immediately apparent as morally good and another as bad, we will note the difference: but we should follow our dramatic intuitions. A person in the drama may act in such a way that we are in no sense antagonized but are aware of beauty and supreme interest only; yet the analogy to that same action may well be intolerable to us in actual life. When such a divergence occurs the commentator must be true to his artistic, not his normal, ethic. Large quantities of Shakespeare criticism have wrecked themselves on the teeth of this dualism. In so far as moral values enter into our appreciation of the poetic work, they will tend to be instinctive to us: Shakespeare here, as in his other symbols, speaks our own language. I mean, it is as natural to us to like Cordelia better than Goneril with a liking which may be said to depend partly on moral values as it is for us to recognize the power of Shakespeare's tempest-symbol as suggesting human tragedy, or his use of jewel-metaphors to embody the costly riches of love. In ages hence, when perhaps tempests are controlled by science and communism has replaced wealth, then the point of Shakespeare's symbolism may need explanation; and then it may, from a new ethical view-point, be necessary to analyse at length the moral values implicit in the Cordelia and Edmund conceptions. But in these matters Shakespeare speaks almost the same language as we, and ethical terms, though they must frequently occur in interpretation, must only be allowed in so far as they are used in absolute obedience to the dramatic and aesthetic significance: in which case they cease to be ethical in the usual sense.

This false criticism is implied by the very use of the word 'character'. It is impossible to use the term without any tinge of a morality which blurs vision. The term, which in ordinary speech often denotes the degree of moral control exercised by the individual over his instinctive passions, is altogether unsuited to those persons of poetic drama whose life consists largely of passion unveiled. *Macbeth* and *King Lear* are created in a soul-dimension of primal feeling, of which in real life we may be only partly conscious or may be urged to control by a sense of right and wrong. In fact, it may well seem that the more we tend away from the passionate and curbless life of poetic drama, the stronger we shall be as 'characters'. And yet, in reading *Macbeth* or *King Lear* we are aware of strength, not weakness. We are not aware of failure:

rather we 'let determined things to destiny hold unbewailed their way'. We must observe, then, this paradox: the strong protagonist of poetic drama would probably appear a weakling if he were a real man; and, indeed, the critic who notes primarily Macbeth's weakness is criticizing him as a man rather than a dramatic person. Ethics are essentially critical when applied to life; but if they hold any place at all in art, they will need to be modified into a new artistic ethic which obeys the peculiar nature of art as surely as a sound morality is based on the nature of man. From a true interpretation centred on the imaginative qualities of Shakespeare, certain facts will certainly emerge which bear relevance to human life, to human morals: but interpretation must come first. And interpretation must be metaphysical rather than ethical. We shall gain nothing by applying to the delicate symbols of the poet's imagination the rough machinery of an ethical philosophy created to control the turbulences of actual life. Thus when a critic adopts the ethical attitude, we shall generally find that he is unconsciously lifting the object of his attention from his setting and regarding him as actually alive. By noting 'faults' in Timon's 'character' we are in effect saying that he would not be a success in real life: which is beside the point, since he, and Macbeth, and Lear, are evidently dramatic successes. Now, whereas the moral attitude to life is positive and dynamic and tells us what we ought to do, that attitude applied to literature is invariably negative and destructive. It is continually thrusting on our attention a number of 'failures', 'mistakes', and 'follies' in connexion with those dramatic persons from whom we have consistently derived delight and a sense of exultation. Even when terms of negation, such as 'evil', necessarily appear—as with *Hamlet* and *Macbeth*—we should so employ them that the essence they express is felt to be something powerful, autonomous, and grand. Our reaction to great literature is a positive and dynamic experience. Crudely, sometimes ineffectually, interpretation will attempt to translate that experience in a spirit also positive and dynamic.

To do this we should regard each play as a visionary whole, close-knit in personification, atmospheric suggestion, and direct poetic-symbolism: three modes of transmission, equal in their importance. Too often the first of these alone receives attention: whereas, in truth, we should not be content even with all three, however clearly we have them in our minds, unless we can work back through them to the original vision they express. Each incident, each turn of thought, each suggestive symbol throughout *Macbeth* or *King Lear* radiates inwards from the play's circumference to the burning central core without knowledge of which we shall miss their relevance and necessity: they relate primarily, not directly to each other, nor to the normal appearances of human life, but to this central reality alone. The persons of Shakespeare have been analysed carefully in point of psychological realism. But in giving detailed and prolix attention to any one element of the poet's expression, the commentator, starting indeed from a point on the circumference, instead of working into the heart of the play, pursues a tangential course, riding, as it were, on his own life-experiences farther and farther from his proper goal. Such is the criticism that finds fault with the Duke's decisions at the close of *Measure for Measure:* if we are to understand the persons of Shakespeare we should consider always what they do rather than what they might have done. Each person, event, scene, is integral to the poetic statement: the removing, or blurring, of a single stone in the mosaic will clearly lessen our chance of visualizing the whole design.

Too often the commentator discusses Shakespeare's work without the requisite emotional sympathy and agility of intellect. Then the process of false criticism sets in: whatever elements lend themselves most readily to analysis on the analogy of actual life, these he selects, roots out, distorting their natural growth; he then praises or blames according to their measure of correspondence with his own life-experiences, and, creating the plaster figures of 'character', searches everywhere for 'causes' on the analogy of human affairs, noting that Iago has no sufficient reason for his villainy, executing some strange transference such as the statement that Lady Macbeth would have done this or that in Cordelia's position; observing that there appears to have been dull weather on the occasion of Duncan's murder. But what he will not do is recapture for analysis his own original experience, concerned, as it was, purely with a dramatic and artistic reality: with Iago the person of motiveless and instinctive villainy, with Cordelia known only with reference to the *Lear* universe, with the vivid extravagant symbolism of abnormal phenomena in beast and element and the sun's eclipse which accompanies the unnatural act of murder. These, the true, the poetic, realities, the commentator too often passes over. He does not look straight at the work he would interpret, is not true to his own imaginative reaction. My complaint is, not that such a commentator cannot appreciate the imaginative nature of Shakespeare—that would be absurd and unjustifiable—but that he falsifies his own experience when he begins to criticize. Part of the play—and that the less important element of story—he tears out ruthlessly for detailed analysis on the analogy of human life: with a word or two about 'the magic of poetry' or 'the breath of genius' he dismisses the rest. Hence the rich gems of Shakespeare's poetic symbolism have been left untouched and unwanted, whilst Hamlet was being treated in Harley Street. Hence arises the criticism discovering faults in Shakespeare. But when a right interpretation is offered it will generally be seen that both the fault and the criticism which discovered it are without meaning. The older critics drove psychological analysis to unnecessary lengths: the new school of 'realistic' criticism, in finding faults and explaining them with regard to Shakespeare's purely practical and financial 'intentions', is thus in reality following the wrong vision of its predecessors. Both together trace the process of my imaginary critic, who, thinking to have found an extreme degree of realism in one place, ends by complaining that he finds too little in another. Neither touch the heart of the Shakespearian play.

Nor will a sound knowledge of the stage and the especial theatrical technique of Shakespeare's work render up its imaginative secret. True, the plays were written as plays, and meant to be acted. But that tells us nothing relevant to our purpose. It explains why certain things cannot be found in Shakespeare: it does not explain why the finest things, the fascination of *Hamlet,* the rich music of *Othello,* the gripping evil of *Macbeth,* the pathos of *King Lear,* and the gigantic architecture of *Timon of Athens* came to birth. Shakespeare wrote in terms of drama, as he wrote in English. In the grammar of dramatic structure he expresses his vision: without that, or some other, structure he could not have expressed himself. But the dramatic nature of a play's origin cannot be adduced to disprove a quality implicit in the work itself. True, when there are any faults to be explained, this particular pursuit and aim of Shakespeare's poetry may well be noted to account for their presence. Interpretation, however, tends to resolve all but minor difficulties in connexion with the greater plays: therefore it is not necessary in the following essays to remember, or comment on, the dramatic structure of their expression, though from another point of view such comment and analysis may well be interesting. It illuminates one facet of their surface: but a true philosophic and imaginative interpretation will aim at cutting below the surface to reveal that burning core of mental or spiritual reality from which each play derives its nature and meaning.

That soul-life of the Shakespearian play is, indeed, a thing of divine worth. Its perennial fire is as mysterious, as near and yet as far, as that of the sun, and, like the sun, it burns on while generations pass. If interpretation attempts to split the original beam into different colours for inspection and analysis it does not claim, any more than will the scientist, that its spectroscope reveals the whole reality of its attention. It discovers something: exactly what it discovers, and whether that discovery be of ultimate value, cannot easily be demonstrated. But, though we know the sun better in the spring fields than in the laboratory, yet we might remember that the spectroscope discovered Helium first in the solar ray, which chemical was after sought and found on earth. So, too, the interpretation of poetic vision may have its use. And if it seems sometimes to bear little relevance to its original, if its mechanical joints creak and its philosophy lumber clumsily in attempt to follow the swift arrow-flight of poetry, it is, at least, no less rational a pursuit than that of the mathematician who writes a rhythmic curve in the stiff symbols of an algebraic equation.

I shall now shortly formulate what I take to be the main principles of right Shakespearian interpretation:

(i) Before noticing the presence of faults we should first regard each play as a visionary unit bound to obey none but its own self-imposed laws. To do this we should attempt to preserve absolute truth to our own imaginative reaction, whithersoever it may lead us in the way of paradox and unreason. We should at all costs avoid selecting what is easy to understand and forgetting the superlogical.

(ii) We should thus be prepared to recognize what I have called the 'temporal' and the 'spatial' elements: that is, to relate any given incident or speech either to the time-sequence of story or the peculiar atmosphere, intellectual or imaginative, which binds the play. Being aware of this new element we should not look for perfect verisimilitude to life, but rather see each play as an expanded metaphor, by means of which the original vision has been projected into forms roughly correspondent with actuality, conforming thereto with greater or less exactitude according to the demands of its own nature. It will then usually appear that many difficult actions and events become coherent and, within the scope of their universe, natural.

(iii) We should analyse the use and meaning of direct poetic symbolism—that is, events whose significance can hardly be related to the normal processes of actual life. Also the minor symbolic imagery of Shakespeare, which is extremely consistent, should receive careful attention. Where certain images continually recur in the same associative connexion, we can, if we have reason to believe that this associative force is strong enough, be ready to see the presence of the associative value when the images occur alone. Nor should we neglect the symbolic value of aural effects such as the discharge of canon in *Hamlet* and *Othello* or the sound of trumpets in *Measure for Measure* and *King Lear*.

(iv) The plays from *Julius Caesar* (about 1599) to *The Tempest* (about 1611) when properly understood fall into a significant sequence. This I have called 'the Shakespeare Progress'. Therefore in detailed analysis of any one play it may sometimes be helpful to have regard to its place in the sequence, provided always that thought of this sequence be used to illuminate, and in no sense be allowed to distort, the view of the play under analysis. Particular notice should be given to what I have called the 'hate-theme', which is turbulent throughout most of these plays: an especial mode of cynicism toward love, disgust at the physical body, and dismay at the thought of death; a revulsion from human life caused by a clear sight of its limitations—more especially limitations imposed by time. This progress I have outlined in *Myth and Miracle*, being concerned there especially with the Final Plays.

Planes of Reality[1]

S. L. Bethell

There is no need to summarise what is known of the structure and physical conditions of the Elizabethan theatre, since this has been well done by a number of writers. It is necessary, however, to stress certain relevant factors.[2] As galleries ran all round the theatre, even above the back of the stage, the actors could be seen from every direction, as in a circus. Below them, in the roofless yard, groundlings crowded close on three sides of the projecting 'apron'; whilst even more embarrassing was the proximity of those young men of fashion who, hiring stools upon the stage itself, displayed their own rich costume in competition with the company's wardrobe. Even with the abundance of make-up, scenery, and properties in use to-day, it would have been impossible for actors so closely beset with audience, to create and sustain an illusion of actual life, especially as they performed in broad daylight. In Shakespeare's time painted scenery was, in fact, used hardly at all; and as the 'act drop' was still unknown, stools, benches, and other properties must have been carried on and off in full sight of the audience; beds, we know, were directed to be 'thrust out' on to the stage, complete with occupant. A small set might be prepared on the 'inner stage' behind a drawn curtain; but this was possible only for scenes of small dimension, such as the Capulets' tomb, or Belarius' cave in *Cymbeline*. In these circumstances, much of the 'business' was necessarily conventional: a siege was represented by an attack upon the tiring house, with scaling ladders erected against the gallery above. There was some crude realism, and a scene of violent death might be rendered more convincing by pricking a bladder of vinegar (presumably beneath the victim's shirt), as is directed in the pre-Shakespearean *Cambises:* Shake-

---

From S. L. Bethell, *Shakespeare and the Popular Dramatic Tradition.* Reprinted by permission of Duke University Press.

[1] I have taken this term, and with it a valuable suggestion, from *Shakespeare's Last Plays,* by E. M. W. Tillyard (Chatto & Windus, 1938).

[2] My facts are taken from E. K. Chambers: *The Elizabethan Stage,* 4 vols. (Clarendon Press, 1923), from *Shakespeare and the Theatre,* and from [M. C. Bradbrook: *Elizabethan Stage Conditions* (New York: Macmillan, 1932) and *Themes and Conventions of Elizabethan Tragedy* (New York: Macmillan, 1935)].

speare himself seems to have discarded such obvious methods after his early experimental plays. The sort of realism represented by a fully furnished drawing-room set in Ibsen or Pinero was, of course, unattainable, and seems hardly to have been desired. The Elizabethans relied on their poetry for much that is nowadays left to the producer. Though more subtly efficient than our modern stage-mechanism in securing the appropriate responses, the use of verse marks in itself a further remove from naturalism. Verse goes with conventionalism, whilst naturalism logically implies a colloquial prose. This accounts for the inappropriateness of Victorian productions of Shakespeare, where naturalistic settings conflicted with the subtler atmospheric suggestions of the verse.

The inability of the Elizabethan theatre to produce an illusion of actuality was wholly to the good, as modern experimental theatres have shown. At a standard presentation of Ibsen, the audience remain passively receptive, whilst in another, two-dimensional world, beyond the orchestra-pit, within a picture-frame and behind footlights, the actors create a vivid illusion of actual life. In the Elizabethan, or the modern experimental theatre, there is no illusion of actual life; but the audience are vividly aware of acting in progress, and the communication, through their cooperative goodwill, of a work of dramatic art. If the one type of production is more realistic, the other is essentially more real.

Shakespeare, despite an occasional grumble at the inadequacy of his 'wooden O' (*Henry V,* Prologue, l. 13), wisely accepted the situation as it was, and turned it to good. Perhaps he would have welcomed the resources at Ibsen's command, but fortunately he was safe from temptation. I do not suggest that he had any conscious insight into the advantages of his own position; indeed, its strength lay partly in the unconscious acceptance, by both playwright and audience, of conditions as they found them. But Shakespeare did not merely acquiesce in those limitations which the physical conditions of his theatre placed upon dramatic illusion; he actually exploited them, so that conventions in production are integrally related to conventions in the treatment of history, in the presentation of character, and in the verse. Moreover, he even draws attention to the play as play, overtly, in the dialogue itself, emphasising verbally what the manner of production already implied: the co-existence of play-world and real world in the minds of his audience. Perhaps when characters within a play referred to plays and players, or noted that 'All the world's a stage' (*As You Like It,* II.vii.139), a certain piquancy in the situation may have been all that forced itself into conscious attention. As they had never experienced naturalistic drama, the Elizabethans would not appreciate, as we do to-day, the nature of their own drama in distinction from it; just as it is impossible to appreciate a state of physical well-being, until suffering has supplied us with a standard of comparison. But this double consciousness of play-world and real world has the solid advantage of 'distancing' a play, so that the words and deeds of which it consists may be critically weighed in the course of its performance. An Ibsen drama, attended to passively, is discussed afterwards in abstract terms; but in a Shakespearean play, criticism is an integral part of apprehension, and apprehension thereby becomes an activity of the whole mind. This is, of course, due mainly to the fact that the verse must be understood for a proper appreciation of the action; but the detachment necessary for attention to the verse is gained by insisting on the essential artificiality of the play-world, and thus holding play-world and real world before the mind simultaneously yet without confusion. Such an attitude has the advantage of accepting and exploiting the situation as it really is, whereas naturalism must engage in a constant effort to delude the audience into taking for actuality what they are bound to know, in their moments of critical alertness, to be only a stage performance. To gain a hearing, naturalism destroys the critical awareness necessary for appreciation: it is hardly surprising that a method thus divided against itself has produced little of permanent value.

When Malvolio appears before Olivia's household, cross-gartered and in 'the trick of singularity' (*Twelfth Night,* II.v.164), Signor Fabian has an interesting comment:

> If this were played upon a stage now, I could condemn it as an improbable fiction.
>
> (III.iv.140)

It is, of course, an improbable fiction, and Shakespeare is employing a common enough literary device to cope with it. There are a great many novelists whose characters exclaim: 'Why, it's just like a novel!' This sort of remark carries more than one layer of suggestion. Superficially it makes an improbable situation more plausible. If the characters displayed no consciousness of its improbability we should be left with a rankling doubt; but since they react as we do to the situation, we are able to accept its improbability, and incorporate it into the world of fiction. At the same time, whatever illusion may have been created has now been broken through: Shakespeare's mention of 'playing upon a stage' forcibly reminds his audience of the nature of the spectacle before them. A naturalistic writer plays with fire when he attempts this sort of thing; but in the Elizabethan theatre, with an audience continually aware of the two worlds of fiction and reality side by side, the effect is at the same time to justify an improbable situation, and to underline the essential unreality of the play-world. This latter function is much the more important: Shakespeare was not sufficiently concerned for probability and consistency to have inserted Fabian's comment merely for the sake of verisimilitude. It occurs at a significant juncture, when the baiting of Malvolio is about to be carried to extremes. The passage continues:

> SIR TOBY His very genius hath taken the infection of the device, man.

MARIA Nay, pursue him now, lest the device take air and taint.
FABIAN Why, we shall make him mad indeed.
MARIA The house will be the quieter.
SIR TOBY Come, we'll have him in a dark room and bound. . . .
(III.iv.142)

The Victorians, who sympathised with Malvolio's sufferings to the extent of creating him a tragic hero, and who disdained the Elizabethan crudity which could enjoy Sir Toby's horseplay, failed to perceive that the Elizabethans were not in the habit of mistaking their comedies for real life. Shakespeare erected, through Fabian, a plain enough notice for his audience, and for the Victorians too, if they had taken trouble over his text. We are reminded that the play is only a play, just when the reminder is needed to enable us to enjoy the comedy of Malvolio's imprisonment. The original audience would take such a hint unconsciously, but the Victorians, cut off from the popular tradition, preferred to discover the tragedy which Shakespeare was so careful not to write.

This explanation of Shakespeare's deeper—and surely unconscious—intention may seem far-fetched, and would never have occurred to me had I considered only the passage from *Twelfth Night*. But elsewhere there are similar reminders of the play as play, without any ostensible design of rendering plausible an improbable incident. Indeed, in *Love's Labour's Lost,* the immediate intention is diametrically opposite: to excuse a naturalistic departure from the normal theatrical habit of ending a light comedy with wedding bells. *Love's Labour's Lost* is the most artificial of Shakespeare's comedies; the only note of ungarbled seriousness occurs at the end, when Biron is condemned to 'jest a twelvemonth in an hospital' (*Love's Labour's Lost,* V.ii.881), as a cure for levity and a preliminary to marriage. The unusual task imposed by Rosalind upon her knight breaks incongruously into the abstract gaiety of a simplified play-world, bearing a sharp reminder of suffering and sorrow, ingredients of the real world hitherto unheeded through five acts of artificial wit-combat. This bitter reminder of the real world is underlined and at the same time distanced by the ensuing remarks of Biron and the King:

BIRON Our wooing doth not end like an old play;
Jack hath not Jill: these ladies' courtesy
Might well have made our sport a comedy.
KING Come, sir, it wants a twelvemonth and a day,
And then 'twill end.
BIRON That's too long for a play.
(V.ii.884)

The young Shakespeare, commenting in public on his technique, reinforces the dual consciousness of play-world and real world in the minds of his audience. A play so artificial may end quite appropriately with a reference from within to its own true nature. But, coming immediately after the hospital theme, this passage serves a more delicate purpose. With its reminder of reality, as distinguished from the play-world, it underlines the reference to human suffering by taking us back to the real world where it is to be encountered. At the same time, by making explicit the nature of the play as play, it preserves a threatened poise: we remember that it is a stage personage only who is to 'jest a twelvemonth in an hospital' and that personal sympathy would be misplaced. The intellectual position of the comedy has been strengthened, whilst its 'artificiality' has been satisfactorily restored.

In plot and setting, *As You Like It* is every whit as artificial as *Love's Labour's Lost*. There is the same movement of lovers in patterned pairs (with two temporary triangles as an added complication in the later play); and the Masque of Hymen completes a general, if superficial, resemblance to the modern 'musical comedy'. The dialogue is easy and relatively mature: Rosalind's prose in the Forest of Arden is so natural-seeming that as a character she 'comes alive' mainly by this means; but Shakespeare is the more careful to provide a balance of artificiality in his verse, and to indicate through his verse-technique the varying degrees of actuality to which we are expected to adjust ourselves. This explains the antiphonal echoing of phrases between Orlando and Duke Senior, when the former bursts in upon the exiles with his demand for hospitality:

ORLANDO . . . .
If ever you have look'd on better days,
If ever been where bells have knoll'd to church,
If ever sat at any good man's feast,
If ever from your eyelids wiped a tear
And know what 'tis to pity and be pitied,

. . . .

DUKE SENIOR True is it that we have seen better days,
And have with holy bell been knoll'd to church
And sat at good men's feasts and wiped our eyes
Of drops that sacred pity hath engender'd:

. . . .

(*As You Like It,* II.vii.113)

This careful pattern of question and answer distances and tones down a scene where otherwise emotion might run too high. The tendency throughout is to pass lightly over whatever has the potentiality of heightened emotion, in order, presumably, to keep the intellect unclouded and to concentrate serious attention upon certain themes: court *versus* country, literary pastoral and the clod-hopping rustic, tradition and innovation in rural economy. And so the love-tangle resolves itself at a level of actuality similar to the average Gilbert and Sullivan opera. The lovers' repetitive phrases have the effect of 'Three little maids from school':

SILVIUS It is to be all made of sighs and tears;
And so am I for Phebe.
PHEBE And I for Ganymede.
ORLANDO And I for Rosalind.
ROSALIND And I for no woman.
(V.ii.90)

In the next scene, the lovers pair off appropriately, and Rosalind is reunited to her father mostly in rhyme and as an integral part of the Masque of Hymen.

Apart from such obvious instances in which verse-technique is used to distance the dramatic experience, it would be possible to grade all the verse in an ascending scale of artificiality, from the broken, vigorous dialogue of Duke Frederick, to the near-burlesque of Silvius and Phebe. Duke Frederick has the sort of verse which develops in the tragedies:

She is too subtle for thee; and her smoothness,
Her very silence and her patience
Speak to the people, and they pity her.
Thou art a fool: she robs thee of thy name;
And thou wilt show more bright and seem more virtuous
When she is gone. Then open not thy lips:
Firm and irrevocable is my doom
Which I have passed upon her; she is banish'd.
(III.v.1)

Contrast:

SILVIUS Sweet Phebe, do not scorn me; do not, Phebe;
Say that you love me not, but say not so
In bitterness. The common executioner,
Whose heart the accustom'd sight of death makes hard,
Falls not the axe upon the humbled neck
But first begs pardon: will you sterner be
Than he that dies and lives by bloody drops?
(III.v.1)

This is rhythmically more regular; the fourth and sixth lines have the pointless inversions of a strained 'poetic' style; and the conceit has a certain obvious ingenuity typically Petrarchan. Between the extremes that I have quoted lies a wide range of delicately perceptible differences in style, all indicating degrees of remoteness from actuality. At this time Shakespeare seems to have been serious in prose—there is more prose than verse in *As You Like It*—and to have used verse mainly to emphasise the conventional. This view of the matter is borne out in a significant remark of Jaques. Orlando enters and addresses Rosalind, who, as Ganymede, has been effectively ridiculing Jaques' melancholy:

ORLANDO Good day and happiness, dear Rosalind!
JAQUES Nay, then, God be wi' you, an you talk in blank verse.
(IV.i.30)

The incident is, I suppose, explicable in naturalistic terms: Orlando utters an involuntary blank verse line, and the cynical Jaques seizes upon it to make his escape with an implied sneer against the lover. But, in any event, the mention of blank verse by a character draws attention to the play as play, in the same way as the remarks of Fabian and Biron, already discussed. Jaques' Parthian shot goes farther, however, by associating blank verse with the conventions of fashionable wooing, and thus suggesting that the play's artificiality is especially constituted by the verse. We have seen that this is, in fact, true of *As You Like It.*

Deliberate emphasis upon the unreality of the play-world is uncommon nowadays. It is still, however, an habitual device of the Marx brothers, those excellent Hollywood comedians, who combine the wildest nonsense with a delicate satirical probing of the defective values in our modern civilisation. Their methods are purely conventional, and they require above everything an alert audience, ready to grasp at every word and each significant gesture. It would be fatal for their purpose, if the audience were to become emotionally involved in the thin line of romantic story which holds their performance together. In their best film, *Animal Crackers,* which appeared some years ago, there are two direct reminders of the film as film. Groucho forgets the name of the character he represents, and turning to the audience, demands a programme: this is complicated by the reference back from film to 'legitimate' stage, since programmes are not provided in the cinema. At another point in the film, he reminds us after a feeble pun, that 'You can't expect all the jokes to be good'. I do not know whether the Marx brothers are consciously aware, any more than Shakespeare is likely to have been, that this type of joke has an important effect upon the relationship of actors and audience. They have continued to employ it in more recent films with remarkable consistency, and this indicates at least a strong instinctive sense of its usefulness. In *The Marx Brothers Go West* we were told as (I think) the engine-driver was being gagged, 'This is the best gag in the picture,' and in *The Big Store,* when the villain is finally unmasked, Groucho exclaims, echoing the average comment from the stalls: 'I could have told you in the first reel he was a crook.' The effect is the same as in Shakespeare; it reinforces the double consciousness of play-world and real world and at the same time it distances the play as play, and produces intimacy with the audience for the actor as actor rather than as character.

It has already been observed that the acting of female parts by boys was further complicated by the frequency with which the story demanded a male disguise. It is usually said that the boy would welcome relief for a time from the embarrassment of his unaccustomed garments, and would probably act the better for being unencumbered. Since the investigation of Elizabethan theatrical conditions opened a new field of conjecture, 'practical' explanations of this kind have been carried to excess. A boy would soon learn to manage his skirts without thinking of them: girls do, and the talent is unlikely to be inherited.

It is better to seek explanations in the nature of Shakespeare's sources, and in the psychology of an audience to which the principle of multi-consciousness applies. Probably the situation of 'boy playing girl playing boy' pleased in its suggestion of multiple planes of reality. It would, of course, be a pleasure entirely dependent upon the dual consciousness of play-world and real world. I have seen, at a concert-party performance, a female impersonator (i.e. a man who habitually plays women's parts) playing the part of a woman in man's clothes. A popular audience clearly recognised and enjoyed the unusual situation. Cleopatra's objection to a Roman triumph:

> . . . I shall see
> Some squeaking Cleopatra boy my greatness
> I' the posture of a whore,
> (*Antony and Cleopatra,* V.ii.219)

effects through dialogue a precisely similar complication in the planes of reality. Also, as a direct reference to acting, it performs the same function as the other passages I have considered, bringing forcibly to mind the duality of play-world and real world. This passage is especially remarkable, since it occurs in a tragedy and at a moment of great emotional intensity. Moreover, *Antony and Cleopatra* comes at the end of the tragic period, when Shakespeare has learnt all there is to learn about his art. An alert and critically detached audience is implied, and an attitude to tragedy very different from that to which we are accustomed.

Children are always fascinated by the notion of infinite regression. I remember a certain biscuit-tin which always gave me, as a small boy, a distinct sense of the 'numinous'. It had on it a picture of a boy holding a tin just like the real one, and on the tin the boy held was another picture of a boy holding a tin. The childish question 'And who made God?' betrays a similar interest. The concern of Shakespeare and the Elizabethans with 'planes of reality', shows, not, of course, their childishness, but a healthy preoccupation with the questions men naturally ask when undeterred by the advances of civilisation. The 'play-within-the-play', as in *A Midsummer Night's Dream* and *Hamlet,* or the device by which the main play is presented before a stage audience, as in *The Taming of the Shrew* or Kyd's *Spanish Tragedy,* further illustrates the same preoccupation. An audience watches a stage audience watching a play, and so becomes simultaneously aware of three planes of reality. Shakespeare carries the matter farther by his frequent metaphorical use of play and players. To Jaques 'All the world's a stage . . .' (*As You Like It,* II.vii.139), and to Macbeth

> Life's but a walking shadow, a poor player
> That struts and frets his hour upon the stage
> And then is heard no more.
> (*Macbeth,* V.v.24)

Contemplation of regression, which produced the parlour-games of Viola-Cesario and Hamlet's Mousetrap, has here assumed philosophical significance. The solidity of the first plane of reality, the plane of our terrestrial life, is seen to be illusory. It is significant that in the last fully Shakespearean play, the planes of reality appear with most complexity. Prospero says of his Masque of Ceres:

> These our actors,
> As I foretold you, were all spirits and
> Are melted into air, into thin air.
> (*The Tempest,* IV.i.148)

'On the actual stage', observes Dr. Tillyard, 'the masque is executed by players pretending to be spirits, pretending to be real actors, pretending to be supposed goddesses and rustics.' [3] And immediately after the revels end, Prospero reminds us that, as his spirit actors have vanished, so

> The cloud-capp'd towers, the gorgeous palaces,
> The solemn temples, the great globe itself,
> Yea, all which it inherit, shall dissolve
> And, like this insubstantial pageant faded,
> Leave not a rack behind. We are such stuff
> As dreams are made on, and our little life
> Is rounded with a sleep.
> (IV.i.152)

The world is seen as transient, and therefore insubstantial, whilst a reference to the dream-world adds a further complication. It seems as if Shakespeare had deliberately crowded into a few moments of his last play all that can suggest the manifold mystery of experience. Both Jaques and Macbeth employed the play metaphor to express an attitude of cynicism: in Jaques, the cynicism which was a recognised ingredient of contemporary fashionable melancholy; in Macbeth, the cynicism of a hardened sinner, who, having rejected the laws of God and man, cut off from all sympathetic contact with the world outside himself, has become incapable of apprehending meaning in that world. But Prospero's speech begins:

> You do look, my son, in a moved sort,
> As if you were dismay'd: be cheerful, sir.
> (IV.i.146)

To Prospero, whose 'beating mind' (IV.i.163) achieves at this moment an insight into reality, the transitoriness of this world is matter for cheerfulness. We are therefore justified in pushing the parallel far-

---

[3] *Shakespeare's Last Plays,* p. 80.

ther, and remembering that, though the actors have faded, as invisible spirits they still exist; and that from sleep there is awakening. Sleep, in Shakespeare, is always regarded as remedial:

> Sleep that knits up the ravell'd sleave of care,
> The death of each day's life, sore labour's bath,
> Balm of hurt minds, great nature's second course,
> Chief nourisher in life's feast. . . .
>
> (*Macbeth*, II.ii.37)

If, as seems likely, Prospero in his great speech voices Shakespeare's own conclusions, then this passage, far from proclaiming the agnosticism of a world-weary artist, clearly asserts, at the culmination of a life-long and unique poetic experience, the existence of an eternal order behind the relatively trivial and impermanent phenomenal world, as the 'real' world exists in comparative stability behind the shadow world of the theatre. The survival of human persons after their sleep of death is incidentally implied. The final organisation of Shakespeare's experience is thus functionally related to the dual consciousness of play-world and real world, characteristic of Elizabethan playhouse psychology. If Shakespeare put the whole of life into his plays, he reciprocally interpreted life in terms of the theatre.

VERBAL AND DRAMATIC IMAGERY

The Development of Shakespeare's Imagery: Introduction

Wolfgang Clemen

Anyone who will take the trouble to compare the imagery in *Antony and Cleopatra* with the imagery in *Henry VI* or in the *Two Gentlemen of Verona* cannot but be greatly impressed by the vast difference between them. They lie so far apart that a connection, a transition between these two styles seems scarcely possible. But if one delves deeper into Shakespeare's dramas, and if one examines each of the plays in turn, from the earlier works to the late tragedies, it will become apparent that in the former, this art is prepared for, step by step. Here we stand before an amazing and unique development of an element of poetic expression, an evolution so striking and of such compass as is difficult to find in any other poet. It is the aim of this book to describe this in its separate phases and forms and to show its connection with Shakespeare's general development.

Anyone who has occupied himself with Shakespeare at all has at least some conception of the general development of his art. If, however, we are to study this evolution more in detail and if we are to become fully conscious of what we at first feel in a vague and general way, we shall be constrained to return again and again to the individual, concrete fact; we must fix our gaze upon separate courses of development in order to grasp the more comprehensive and the more general. Thus, for example, similar scenes and situations in the various plays must

---

Reprinted by permission of the publishers from Wolfgang Clemen, *The Development of Shakespeare's Imagery,* Cambridge, Mass.: Harvard University Press, and by permission of Methuen & Company, Ltd.

be compared with one another; we must investigate how Shakespeare manages his plot, how he characterizes his men and women, and how his description of nature, his technique of exposition, his method of preparing for a crisis, and his manner of resolving a conflict undergo changes and attain to perfection. Only from such individual investigations can we gain a definite picture of what one may term the general development of Shakespeare's art. By investigating the special development of a very important element of Shakespeare's style, this book would seek to help towards a more distinct conception of the history of Shakespeare's art in its entirety.

It must be remembered, to be sure, that every investigation of an individual development carries with it the danger of overlooking the connection of this element with the play as an organic whole. Only too easily do we forget that the distinction which we make between different elements of dramatic art is at bottom an artificial one. Delineation of character, plot, atmosphere and dramatic structure of a play do not, in fact, exist as independent spheres, distinct one from the other. Only one thing really exists: the play as a whole, as a totality. Everything else is simply an aspect which *we* detach from the whole in order to facilitate our investigation and make it feasible. Herein lies the final difficulty which is responsible for the problematical character of all literary investigation concerned with poetic development. It is only by means of the individual study of such isolated aspects that the total development can become tangible and clear to us. But it is just this method of isolating and cutting out that may easily destroy the living organism of the work of poetry.

Hence it must be our aim to reduce to the minimum errors due to isolating the "imagery" from the other elements of the dramatic work. This study seeks to show how manifold and various are the conditions and qualifications determining the form and nature of each image, and how many factors are to be considered in order to grasp fully the real character of the imagery of a play. It is very tempting to examine a passage from Shakespeare by itself, and it often gives us great aesthetic pleasure. But it is a method suitable only in a few definite cases. In most cases it is deceptive, because we examine the given passage from a viewpoint which does not coincide with Shakespeare's own intention. When Shakespeare wrote this passage, he wrote it for a certain particular situation, for a particular moment of his play. The special circumstances involved in this situation he kept before his mind's eye, and of them he thought while composing the passage. Sometimes, he sought by means of the imagery to lend enhanced expression to the feeling of the character concerned; at other times, it might have been his intent to give the audience a hint towards understanding what was still to come, or perhaps to provide a counterpoint to one of the central themes of the play. Before we can claim to appreciate and appraise rightly an image or a sequence of images, we must first know what particular purpose this image serves where it occurs.

An isolated image, an image viewed outside of its context, is only half the image. Every image, every metaphor gains full life and significance only from its context. In Shakespeare, an image often points beyond the scene in which it stands to preceding or following acts; it almost always has reference to the whole of the play. It appears as a cell in the organism of the play, linked with it in many ways.

It is the aim of this book to investigate these relations and connections, in order to arrive at a truly organic method of understanding the images. There are certain important questions which naturally follow from this angle of approach.

We must first of all consider the immediate context in which the image stands. How is the image, the metaphor related to the train of thought? How does it fit into the syntax of the text? Are there criteria by which we may distinguish between degrees of connection?

The further question arises, whether certain forms of dramatic speech, the monologue or the dialogue, have an influence upon the nature of the image.

As a dramatic situation, a specific motive or inducement, stands behind every image, the following questions arise: What motives are especially productive of images, out of what situations do most images grow? What is the relationship of the images to their occasion?

Each image is used by an individual character. Is the use of imagery different for each character, can any relation be discerned between the nature of Shakespeare's men and women and the way they use imagery? Are characters to be found in Shakespeare which are especially marked by speaking in images?

All these relationships point, each in its own way, to the fundamental fact that the image is rooted in the totality of the play. It has grown in the air of the play; how does it share its atmosphere or contribute to its tenor? To what degree is the total effect of the play enhanced and coloured by images? For the distribution of the images in the whole play is often very striking, and leads to an investigation of the relationships between dramatic structure and the use of imagery.

Thus imagery necessarily suggests to us the fundamental problems lying beneath the complex construction of a play. Swinburne has already pointed out "That the inner and the outer qualities of a poet's work are of their very nature indivisible" . . . and emphasized that "criticism which busies itself only with the outer husk or technical shell of a great artist's work taking no account of the spirit or the thought which informs it, cannot have even so much value as this. . . ."[1] One should go even a step further and say that it is not possible to interpret stylistic peculiarities before being perfectly clear about this "thought which informs the artist's work". Style is a word of many meanings, and hence is subject to the most varied interpretation. In the past few

[1] Swinburne, *A Study of Shakespeare,* 1902, pp. 7, 8.

years there has been no dearth of attempts to raise the concept of style to a higher plane and to interpret it in a way that illuminates its real significance.[2] Shakespeare's style has not long ago been happily defined as "the product of the characters, the passions, the situations, which in fact are the living, driving forces behind and determining the style".[3] This book, too, attempts to view the imagery in this way and to discover the forces determining it.

The answer to all these questions will only be found when the problem is considered as one of evolution. The power to associate the imagery with the very fabric of the play, at first a mere potentiality, develops and extends, step by step, with Shakespeare's development. In Shakespeare's early plays we miss many of the functions of which the images in later plays are capable. Only little by little did Shakespeare discover the possibilities which imagery offers to the dramatist. In his hands metaphors gradually develop into more and more effective instruments: at first fulfilling only a few simple functions, they later often serve several aims at one and the same time and play a decisive part in the characterization of the figures in the play and in expressing the dramatic theme. The image eventually becomes the favourite mode of expression of the later Shakespeare. This fact, well known to the majority of Shakespeare's readers, deserves, however, investigation and explanation. Why does Shakespeare, especially in the greatest plays, repeatedly replace the direct statement by a metaphorical phrase? Why does the later Shakespeare say the deepest and wisest things through an image instead of in "plain language"? It is a superficial and unsatisfying explanation to declare that metaphorical language is "more poetical". We must seek better answers.

As a rule, too little attention is paid to the fact that images in a play require quite another mode of investigation than, say, images in a lyric poem.[4] We are able to comprehend a lyric poem—like a painting or a statue—almost at one single glance, "immediately"; a drama, on the other hand, we can understand only through a series of impressions, "successively". This holds equally true of the essential nature of the epic poem or of the novel, but in the case of the drama, the sequence of time, the process of the successive exposition, plays a far more important rôle.[5] For the action of the drama unfolds itself in one

---

[2] Cf. Middleton Murry, *The Problem of Style,* London, 1925; Owen Barfield, *Poetic Diction,* London, 1928; Henry W. Wells, *Poetic Imagery,* New York, 1924; Stephen J. Brown, *The World of Imagery,* London, 1927; C. Day Lewis, *The Poetic Image,* London, 1947; Rosemond Tuve, *Elizabethan and Metaphysical Imagery,* University of Chicago Press, 1948.

[3] Oliver Elton, *Style in Shakespeare,* British Academy Lecture, 1936.

[4] A clear recognition and appreciation of the particular functions of imagery in drama is to be found in Una Ellis-Fermor's book on *The Frontiers of Drama,* London, 1945 (Chapter V, "The Functions of Imagery in Drama").

[5] J. Dover Wilson says of the Elizabethan play, "Above all it was action in motion, a work of art which, unlike that of architecture, sculpture, painting, or lyrical

evening, visibly and audibly, before the eyes and ears of the audience; its effect depends largely upon how far the audience can be brought under the spell of this sequence of events in time, how far it experiences with the characters the course of the dramatic happenings, and lives in it during the actual performance. The dramatist himself shapes everything in his play according to this immanent law of the succession of time. His art, as Dover Wilson once put it, is one of "progressive revelation".

In every epic poem and in every novel, we find sections which can be taken by themselves, which lose none of their significance even when we do not know their connection with the temporal course of the events. The novelist can allow himself digressions, broad descriptive passages and historical or sociological explanations; he often brings in something that has no significance for what is to come and likewise much that did not necessarily result from what preceded. Time, the progress of things and events, often seems to stand still in the novel and the epic poem; a protracted lingering occurs at some point without our being able to detect any advance. In the drama, which is subject to entirely different laws, this would be utterly impossible. The texture of the drama is of a much closer web, and the necessity of an inner continuity, of a mutual cooperation and connection of all parts, is greater in the drama than in the epic poem or the novel. This becomes clearer if we look at a play of a great dramatist (dramatists of lesser rank naturally often fail to fulfil these conditions) and examine the often apparently insignificant details which he introduces. Almost every single detail is used later on, reappears suddenly at an important point. Individual touches which seemed insignificant when they were introduced for the first time, acquire real meaning with the progress of events. In a truly great drama nothing is left disconnected, everything is carried on. The dramatist is continuously spinning threads which run through the whole play and which he himself delivers into our hand in order that, by their aid, we may understand what follows, and accompany it with greater tension and keener participation. It is one of the artistic achievements of the great dramatist to prepare in the mind of the audience a whole net of expectations, intuitions and conjectures so that each new act, each new scene, is approached with a definite predisposition. This unobtrusive preparation of our mind for what is to come is one of the most important preliminary conditions necessary for a powerful dramatic effect. For the climax of the drama does not come

---

poetry, was not to be apprehended in all its parts at one and the same moment, but conveyed the intentions of its creator through a series of impressions, each fleeting as the phases of a musical symphony, each deriving tone and colour from all that had gone before and bestowing tone and colour on all that came after, and each therefore contributing to the cumulative effect which was only felt when the play was over" (*What Happens in Hamlet,* 1935, p. 230).

suddenly; we ourselves have gone the whole way and have followed the separate threads which led up to the climax.

It has been necessary to emphasize this peculiar feature of dramatic art because certain conclusions that are important for the examination of the images in a play result from it. Just as every detail has its proper place in that dramatic structure, and is only to be understood when this has been examined, so, too, each image, each metaphor, forms a link in the complicated chain of the drama. This progress of dramatic action must, therefore, be understood in order to appreciate the function of the image.

Since Aristotle men have thought and discussed again and again the nature of metaphor; what forms of thought find expression in it, what types of metaphorical expression there are and what kinds of application. Even in recent years this subject, which cannot be further pursued here, has been dealt with from widely differing angles.[6] We must refrain from applying any one of these definitions or one of the conventional systems of classification to Shakespeare's images. Such classification is alien to the vital, organic quality of Shakespeare's language. A separate treatment of comparison, simile, personification, metaphor and metonymy, would only be illuminating if there were a definite and regularly recurring relationship between these formal types and the imagery—e.g. if from the fact that an image appears in the guise of comparison, specific and similar conclusions could be drawn as to the nature and the function of the image. But that is not the case; the same formal type has manifold possibilities of application, and it is solely the context in which the image stands that can offer any information about what a particular formal type may signify "just here".

It is an odd fact that our critical endeavours are generally satisfied when we have succeeded in classifying and cataloguing something. We believe that our perceptive faculties have reached their goal when we have divided and subdivided phenomena of poetry and history into a system of pigeon-holes and have pasted a label on to everything. That is a curious error. Often enough such a rigid schematic system of classification destroys a living feeling both for the unity and for the many-hued iridescent richness of the poetical work. This is especially true of Shakespeare's style, which is of an incomparable variety and elasticity. The principal source of error in the statistical method of approach is that a set of statistics gives us the illusion that all the phenomena encompassed by it are equal among themselves. In reality, however, this is only seldom the case. If, for example, we state that in a certain play there are three sea-images as opposed to eight garden-metaphors, the statistical statement itself is still of very little help and may indeed be misleading. The three sea-images may be comprehensive,

---

[6] Cf. Middleton Murry, *The Problem of Style,* London, 1925; "Metaphor" in *Countries of the Mind,* 2nd series (1931); Hermann Pongs, *Das Bild in der Dichtung,* Marburg, 1927; Stephen J. Brown, *The World of Imagery,* London, 1927; C. Day Lewis, *The Poetic Image,* London, 1947.

they may stand at important points and may have a far greater significance for the drama than the eight metaphors from the garden. The statistical method can never tell us anything about the relevancy, the degree of significance of the individual image; under the same heading it lists unimportant, mere "padding"-images together with images of the greatest dramatic import. Is it not true that everywhere great poetic art seems to begin just where statistics end—where no measuring of things is any longer possible and numbers no longer have anything to tell us? Neither the statistical method nor the systematic classification of all the images is suited for the plan and the purpose of this study. In order not to lose sight of the general line of development it has proved necessary to make selections and to offer typical illustrations instead of detailed lists. With regard to the plays to be treated, it has also been necessary to make a selection. The point of view varies with the different plays; it is naturally impossible to investigate in all the dramas all of the questions outlined above. In each case one aspect which appears especially clearly in the drama under consideration, will be discussed—the rest will be merely touched upon.

The examination of Shakespeare's imagery under the aspect of development and of the factors determining it is, of course, by no means the only approach to this extensive theme. Shakespeare's images in their total effect may also bear witness to the wealth of the things he knew, loved and hated. In the human world of the dramas, these images form, as it were, a second world. What is not conjured up and evoked by them—animals and plants, heavenly bodies and elements, callings and trades, arts and sciences, innumerable details of the Elizabethan world even down to the humble utensils of everyday life! The main task which Professor Caroline Spurgeon set herself in her book, *Shakespeare's Imagery,* was to exhibit this world in all its comprehensiveness and to use it as a means of discovering Shakespeare's personality, his "senses, tastes, interests" and, of course, his views. To attain such a goal the systematic classification of all the images is naturally indispensable; it was carried out by Professor Spurgeon for the first time with the greatest accuracy. The second part of her book deals with "The Function of the Imagery as Background and Undertone in Shakespeare's Art". Every student of Shakespeare's dramatic art can learn a great deal from these chapters. The present study is much indebted to Professor Spurgeon's pioneer work in this field that had found little attention before her book was published.[7] The main difference, however, between Professor Spurgeon's method and that of the present study lies in the fact that she is primarily interested in the *content* of the images.[8] But a study which aims at describing the development of

[7] Msgr. F. C. Kolbe's book, *Shakespeare's Way,* London, 1930, seems to be the only book previous to Miss Spurgeon's study to examine Shakespeare's imagery in detail.

[8] Cf. Spurgeon, *Shakespeare's Imagery,* p. 8.

the language of imagery and its functions must of necessity investigate the form of the images and their relation to the context. This accounts for a fundamental difference of approach and point of view, notwithstanding the fact that, in many respects, points of contact will be seen to exist.

The Life of Our Design: The Function of Imagery in the Poetic Drama

Alan S. Downer

Why, there you touch'd the life of our design.
(*Troilus and Cressida,* II.ii.194)

In discussing poetic drama one has to begin with a number of negative generalizations: there is no such thing; there once was such a thing; it is a lost art, though not necessarily a dead one. Perhaps it is dormant because it has been defined as if it were a joining of two elements, poetry and drama, when actually it is only one: poetic drama. That is, it will not be resurrected by a poet, like Byron or Stephen Phillips, writing a play, or by a playwright, like Sheridan Knowles or Maxwell Anderson, trying to write a poem. Poetic drama must be written by dramatic poets. If the truism is chiastic, truth yet lies in the figure.

But if the definition of poetic drama is schismatic, so too is its criticism and analysis. In Miss Bradby's fascinating and infuriating little anthology of *Shakespeare Criticism,* 1919–1935, the critical lines are drawn: on the one side is the Shakespeare-as-a-dramatist brigade commanded by Granville-Barker and J. Isaacs; on the other, Shakespeare-as-a-poet, better equipped and manned, and officered by Spurgeon and Murry and G. Wilson Knight. The strange thing about this general confrontation of critical armies is that although the roll is taken on

---

From *The Hudson Review,* Vol. II, No. 2 (Summer, 1949). First published in *The Hudson Review.* Reprinted by permission of Alan S. Downer.

each side, and all are present and as fully armed as possible, no attempt seems to be made to join battle. Mr. Barker will occasionally take issue in a footnote with Professor Bradley, and a junior officer like Eric Bentley speak a few ill-mannered words about the enemy, but nothing conclusive ever happens. Not a shot is fired, not an attempt is made to storm the barricades, or on the other hand to sign a treaty of friendship and mutual aid. It is as if each side felt that something too precious to risk might be involved in either engagement or compromise. As a consequence, both sides are impoverished, and the neutrals uneasily trade with both at once in a state of utter uncertainty. Yet Union is possible with Honor and without Compromise; and it could stem from a recognition of the true nature of poetic drama.

The drama is a unique form of expression in that it employs living actors to tell its story; its other aspects—setting, characters, dialogue, action and theme—it shares with other forms of communication. But the fact that the dramatist is not dealing with characters merely, but with three-dimensional persons is paralleled by the fact that he is not dealing with a setting verbally described but three-dimensionally realized, with action that actually occurs in time and space, with dialogue which is spoken by human voices for the human ear: so many tools, so many tribulations. One of the very real problems of the dramatist is just this, that he, unlike the poet, must deal with the thingness of things; to him a mossy stone must be a mossy stone and a ship tossed on an ocean a ship tossed on an ocean, not a synonym for *peace* or *turmoil*. But the point is, surely, that for the poetic dramatist the stone is more than a stone without ever losing its stoniness, and the tempest may be a highly symbolic one without losing its reality. So, although the drama in general makes considerable use of physical objects—"props"—to tell its story, the higher drama transmutes the physical prop into a symbol, gaining richer meaning without expansion. The poetic drama relates the dramatic symbol to the poetic image, intensifying the unity of the work, and gaining still greater richness without greater bulk, compression being the ever-present necessity of the form.

It is my present purpose to examine the function of imagery in poetic drama, the language of poetry, and its relation to the essentially dramatic devices which might be similarly named the language of props, the language of setting, and the language of action. In the interests of communication I have chosen most of my illustrations from Shakespeare.

The more perceptive of the poetic critics have recognized the existence of this dramatic language, if they have refused to see its true relation to the verbal. Coleridge, for example: "Shakespeare as a poet was providing in images a substitute for that visual language which in his dramatic works he got from his actors." The definition of action as visual language is so illuminating that one wonders why Coleridge did not see by its flash the limitation of the earlier portion of his statement.

In the same chapter of the *Biographia Literaria* he gives the cue to most of his successors: the poetic power, he declares, consists in part of "reducing multitude into unity of effect, and modifying a series of thoughts by some one predominant thought or feeling." In particular this inspired Caroline Spurgeon in her counting and analysis of Shakespeare's images to determine, where possible, the "iterative images" of the plays. Using *image* broadly to cover every kind of simile and metaphor, she produced a documented and be-graphed volume which is the happy hunting ground of the anti-theatrical critics. Miss Spurgeon, however, felt that the results of her study could be used as a more general tonic. In her estimation the iterative image is a revelation of the writer's personality, temperament and quality of mind, and it throws fresh light on individual plays by serving as Background and Undertone, raising and sustaining emotion, providing atmosphere, and emphasizing a theme. It reminds one of the old patent medicines which cured everything from sterility to toothache. From her analysis, for instance, Miss Spurgeon concludes that Shakespeare was more sensitive to the horror of bad odors than to the allure of fragrant ones, and to the loathsomeness of bad cooking than to appreciation of delicate and good, presumably because he had "more opportunity of experiencing the one than the other." There is no other evidence that Miss Spurgeon had a sense of humor.

On the other hand, her extended discussion of the martlet image in *Macbeth* very nearly penetrates to the heart of Shakespeare's dramatic technique. The martlet is a foolish bird and Banquo notices him on Macbeth's castle:

> no jutty, frieze,
> Buttress, nor coign of vantage, but this bird
> Hath made his bed and procreant cradle.

Martlet was a slang word for dupe, like the word gull; that is, a metaphor. But in the *Macbeth* scene the bird is imagined to be present as part of the "setting," and therefore becomes, not a poetic image, but a dramatic symbol, of the "guest who is to be 'fooled.' " Into dramatic symbolism, even when it is so intimately linked with the poetic imagery of the play, Miss Spurgeon will not go. She is, for instance, rather annoyed at the gardener's scene in *Richard II* because "no human gardeners ever discoursed like these," though she recognizes its importance in, as she says, "gathering up, focussing and pictorially presenting," the leading theme of the play.

The other school of modern interpretation of Shakespeare is perhaps best represented by Granville-Barker's essay on *King Lear*, in which he restores the play to the stage and demonstrates that it is essentially theatrical. "The whole scheme and method of its writing is a contrivance for its effective acting. The contrast and reconciliation of grandeur and simplicity, this setting of vision in terms of actuality, this inarticulate passion which breaks now and again into memorable phrases—does not even the seeming failure of expression give us a sense of the helplessness of humanity pitted against higher powers? All the magnificent art of this is directed to one end; the play's acting in a theater." The reactions to this kind of statement are violent and equally dogmatic—mere theatricalism, declared one reviewer.

It is surely too late to go around saying that *King Lear* is not adapted to theatrical representation. Is it not also too late to declare that poetic drama cannot reveal its meaning and depth and implications on the stage as fully as any other work of art in its own medium?

In seeing Shakespeare on the modern stage, we take immediate pleasure in the story and a secondary pleasure in the characterization. But certain critical writers have suggested that there is a third and more important pleasure—the meaning as interpreted by the interplay of images. Since we are reasonably deaf to spoken poetry, it would seem that this is a pleasure reserved, as the critics suggest, for the study. Aside from the fact that this makes Shakespeare look a little foolish, like a composer who writes a quartet to be performed by a one-armed violinist, is it true? I believe that it is not; that Shakespeare, if he began as two characters, the Poet and the Playwright, managed to unite them somehow as the Poetic Dramatist; if he began by using the language of action *and* the language of poetry he soon learned to use the language of *imagery in action* which is the major characteristic of poetic drama.

Perhaps the theatricalist and the reader of poetry can find common ground in a consideration of dramatic symbolism. At any rate, in this subject there is less excuse for the automatic or reflex sneer at the other's expense, since symbolism is as basic to drama as imagery is to poetry.

Symbolism grows naturally out of the materials of drama. The successful unravelling of the plot dilemma in a Greek tragedy or a Roman comedy frequently depended upon the manipulation of some physical object, some prop, a piece of cloth, a footprint, a birthmark, a chest. In the more intricate popular drama of the last century, a cache of gold, a missent letter, a list of conspirators might be the mainspring of the action. In such plays, however, one tires very quickly of the mere ingenuity by which the eventual discovery of the gold, or arrival of the letter is held off.

It was a considerable step up the ladder of dramatic interest and intensity in the nineteenth century when Ibsen discovered that the game of "pistol-pistol-who's-got-the-pistol" could not only make a fascinating plot but could suggest the relation of the action to some aspect of the experience of the audience. When Hedda Gabler produces a case of pistols at the beginning of her play, it is basic dramatic economy that she should give one to Lövborg to commit suicide with, and use the other to put an end to her own wretched life. Further, it is nicely ironic. But when the point is carefully made that these pistols are her sole material heritage from General Gabler, a parallel avenue of suggestion is opened. She has inherited her personal characteristics from the old general, and the pistols are symbols, not only of the spiritual heritage but of the order which shaped it—the empty, decadent life of the military caste. At the end of the play it is clear that Hedda's environment and heredity shaped all her actions, drove her to urge Lövborg's suicide and finally caused her own death. The pistols are not merely the means of the action, but the meaning of the action.

Lest it be objected that such an interpretation of a dramatic symbol stems from the study rather than the stage, a current example may be added. One of the earliest and sturdiest of the successes of the 1947–48 season on Broadway was William Wister Haines's *Command Decision.* There is no pretense about this play: it is a tightly constructed, efficient product, intended for the open market. Yet despite its employment of stereotypes, conventions, and elements of melodrama, the audience is caught up in the movement of the play: we who have usually been asked to worry only about the problems of the doughboy and GI Joe, are suddenly emotionally involved in the problems of majors and brigadier-generals, hitherto satirized or portrayed as villains.

The action takes place in a Nissen hut, headquarters of an air-force command in England. The setting is narrow: the back wall, only a few feet from the footlights, is papered with a huge geodetic survey map of Western Europe. Throughout most of the performance, this map is covered, the curtains being withdrawn only when it is necessary to explain current operations. At such times the audience sees the major target cities to be destroyed and the pitifully short arc of fighter cover. The decision, which the title reflects, is whether the destruction of the targets warrants the certain loss of American soldiers.

These soldiers, whose lives are at stake, and who would be the main concern of the conventional war play or film, we never see. We see only the men whose responsibility it is to send them out and who are popularly supposed to die in bed. Yet humanity is never remote. The whole world of the action is brought into the Nissen hut; each revelation of the map creates increasing tension. At its first showing, it is merely expository: this is where we must operate. At its second, it begins to become symbolic: this is the awful dilemma which presses upon the leading character. Finally, it symbolizes the underlying meaning of the play; the desperate nature of any decision for any man under competing pressures. The map as symbol enables the audience to participate in the emotional tension of the play, serves as a unifying force, and reveals the deeper significance of what might all too easily have been a routine piece of theatrical journalism. It is, further, the best kind of dramatic symbol in that it is never obtrusive, being equally germane to the action and the theme.

It may very well be that Mr. Haines stumbled upon this dramatic symbol quite unconsciously. There is nothing in his work as a novelist to indicate that he is particularly concerned with form in that medium.

His experience in Hollywood working with a medium which deals largely and conventionally in visual symbols may have led him unawares to the device. The point is that the device is there for the use of the most prosaic dramatist and it serves to enrich his work by requiring the mechanical aspects of the play to do double duty.

This "language of props" is equivalent to the simpler uses of imagery in poetry, but it can become highly complex in the poetic drama. For the sake of familiarity, if for no other reason, one turns to Shakespeare for illustration. Since it is, however, somewhat unfair to the authors of both works to juxtapose *Richard II* and *Command Decision,* a contemporary of Shakespeare's may be used as bridge and buffer. The simpler uses of dramatic symbolism in the poetic drama are clearly exhibited in the first part of Marlowe's *Tamburlaine.* The Scythian tyrant is obsessed with the idea of power as symbolized in the "sweet fruition of an earthly crown." It is not surprising that the crown—a commonplace symbol, wholly apart from its use in the drama—figures largely in the action.

In the first scene, Cosroe is crowned emperor. In the second act, foolish Mycetes rushes on stage seeking to hide his crown in a simple hole. Tamburlaine overtakes him:

> TAMBURLAINE Is this your crown? (*Taking it*)
> MYCETES Ay, didst thou ever see a fairer? (*Relinquishing it*)
> TAMBURLAINE (*Ironically*) You will not sell it, will you?
> MYCETES Such another word and I will have thee executed.
> Come, give it me!
> TAMBURLAINE No, I took it prisoner.
> MYCETES You lie; I gave it you.
> TAMBURLAINE Then, 'tis mine.
> MYCETES No, I mean I let you keep it.
> TAMBURLAINE Well, I mean you shall have it again.
> Here, take it for a while: I lend it thee,
> Till I may see thee hemmed with armed men;
> Then shalt thou see me pull it from thy head:
> Thou art no match for mighty Tamburlaine.

Later, as Cosroe dies, Tamburlaine puts on his crown; a banquet of crowns is introduced; and the play ends with the triumphant crowning of Zenocrate. Throughout all this action, the symbol remains as simple as possible—verbalized, the crown stands for "perfect bliss" and "sole felicity," its

> virtues carry with it life and death;
> To ask and have, command and be obeyed.

The crown is the symbol of the king's rank, the ruler's god-like power.

The crown which is handled so dramatically in the deposition scene of *Richard II* is, to be sure, the symbol of the king's rank. But it is not simply the sole felicity in which Tamburlaine displayed such interest. It is the symbol of the condition of England, as in the words of Gaunt:

> A thousand flatterers sit within thy crown
> Whose compass is no bigger than thy head;
> And yet, incaged in so small a verge,
> The waste is no whit lesser than thy land.

And Northumberland proposes to "redeem from broking pawn the blemish'd crown." Further, it is the symbol of Richard as actor:

> within the hollow crown
> That rounds the mortal temples of a king
> Keeps death his court; and there the antic sits,
> Scoffing his state and grinning at his pomp;
> Allowing him a breath, a little scene,
> To monarchize. . . .

It is a symbol of that "divinity doth hedge a king":

> For every man that Bolingbroke hath press'd
> To lift shrewd steel against our golden crown
> God for his Richard hath in heavenly pay
> A glorious angel. . . .

The divinity which the crown symbolizes is strengthened by a second image, the king as the sun:

> knowst thou not
> That when the searching eye of heaven is hid
> Behind the globe, that lights the lower world,
> Then thieves and robbers range abroad unseen. . . .
> But when from under this terrestrial ball
> He fires the proud tops of the Eastern pines. . . .
> Then murthers, treasons and detested sins,
> The cloak of night being pluck'd from off their backs,
> Stand bare and naked, trembling at themselves?
> So when this thief, this traitor Bolingbroke,
> Who all this while hath revell'd in the night
> Whilst we were wand'ring in th'Antipodes,
> Shall see us rising in our throne, the East,
> His treasons will sit blushing in his face,
> Not able to endure the sight of day,
> But self-affrighted tremble at his sin.

The image is extended and explicit. Even the dullest in the audience must have been impressed by it. At any rate, Bolingbroke is not slow to seize upon it:

> See, see, King Richard doth himself appear,
> As doth the blushing discontented sun
> From out the fiery portal of the east. . . .

At this moment (III.3) Richard is standing upon the walls of Flint Castle, which is to say the upper stage, and Bolingbroke is on the ground. At the end of the scene in response to his opponent's demands, Richard descends to the main stage, with still another reference to the sun image:

> Down, down I come like glist'ring Phaeton,
> Wanting the manage of unruly jades. . . .

He sees himself no longer as king, but an unsuccessful pretender to the title.

The climax of the action of the play, in which the complexity of the image is finally revealed, is the deposition of Richard. In the drama, the whole Parliament is assembled, with the lords and bishops of England providing not only a larger audience for the display of Richard's theatrical talents, but a more impressive background for the action. When the great moment comes, Richard makes the most of it, in a scene which should be compared with Tamburlaine's taking and returning of Mycetes' crown.

> Give me the crown. Here, cousin, seize the crown.
> (*As Bolingbroke hesitates*) Here, cousin,
> (*A pause; Bolingbroke steps to him, and Richard holds the crown between them*)
> On this side my hand, and on that side yours.
> Now is this golden crown like a deep well
> That owes two empty buckets,

and so on. How carefully Shakespeare has pointed the action here; not simply a passing of the crown from one hand to the other, but a tableau, and an extended simile to illustrate it. So the visual symbolic exchange of the crown, to quote Miss Spurgeon's words on another matter, "gathers up, focusses and pictorially presents" the downfall of a man whose nature was ill-suited to kingship, and who has to some extent come to realize the fact.

There are striking uses of this "language of props," the realization of the verbal image in dramatic terms, in later Shakespearean tragedy. For example, in *Macbeth* Miss Spurgeon found repeated iteration in the dialogue of the idea of ill-fitting clothes. Mr. Cleanth Brooks has related the image somewhat more closely to the play by seeing it as an interpretation of Macbeth's position as usurper: he is uncomfortable in garments not his own. Actually, the image suggests disguise. Macbeth is an unhappy hypocrite who declares before the murder of Duncan, "False face must hide what the false heart doth know," and before the murder of Banquo, "We must . . . make our faces vizards to our hearts, disguising what they are."

But the image is more than a mere verbal one. It is *realized,* made visual in the action of the play.

The first four scenes are various moments during and after a battle. In them, Macbeth will naturally be wearing his warrior's costume, his armor, as much a symbol of his nature and achievements as is Duncan's crown. When he defeats Norway, for instance, he is "lapped in proof," but when Ross and Angus greet him as Thane of Cawdor, he protests, "Why do you dress me in borrowed robes?" The image continues, verbally, as Banquo observes, half-jesting,

> New honors come upon him
> Like our strange garments, cleave not to their mold
> But with the aid of use.

Under pressure from his wife, however, he resolves to seize the kingship, to cover his warrior's garments and the golden opinions that went with them with the clothing that was properly Duncan's. The murder is committed with constant reference in the dialogue to the clothing image (skilfully interpreted by Mr. Brooks) and the scene as marked in the Folio ends with the flight of Macbeth and his Lady from the crime as she urges him to

> Get on thy nightgown, lest occasion call us
> And show us to be watchers.

When next Macbeth enters he is wearing his dressing gown, and if the actor is wise it will be such a gown as calls attention to itself, for at this point the change in costume, the disguising of the armor, dramatizes both the change in Macbeth's nature and the iterated poetic image. From now until nearly the end of the play, Macbeth is cowardly, melancholic, suspicious, and unhappy; the reverse of all the qualities that had made him the admired warrior of the early scenes. He cannot buckle his distempered cause within the belt of rule; and Macduff's fear is prophetic, "Adieu, lest our old robes sit easier than our new," prophetic not only for the unhappy Scots, but for Macbeth himself.

One of the achievements of this highly skilful play is the maintaining of interest in, if not sympathy for, the central figure; assassin, evil governor, usurper, and murderer. Shakespeare maintains this interest not merely by portraying Macbeth as a man in the control of wyrd, or too susceptible to uxorial suggestion, but, I think, by making us constantly aware of the armor—the honest warrior's nature—under the loosely hanging robes of a regicide. Until Act II, scene iii, Macbeth is quite possibly dressed as a warrior. From that point, until Act V, scene iii, he is dressed in his borrowed robes. But in the latter scene, with his wife eliminated as a motivating force, and with the English army moving against him, he begins to resume some of his former virtues: his courage returns, his forthrightness, his manliness. "Give me my armour," he cries, and in a lively passage with the Doctor, he makes grim jests about the power of medicine as Seyton helps him into his warrior's dress. He is all impatience to be back at the business he understands as he does not understand government:

> MACBETH Give me my armour.
> SEYTON 'Tis not needed yet.
> MACBETH Give me my armour.
> Send out moe horses, skirr the country round;
> Hang those that talk of fear. Give me mine armour. . . .
> Throw physic to the dogs, I'll none of it!—
> Come put mine armour on. Give me my staff.—
> Seyton, send out.—Doctor, the thanes fly from me.—
> Come, sir, despatch.—If thou couldst, doctor, cast
> The water of my land, find her disease,
> And purge it to a sound and pristine health,
> I would applaud thee to the very echo,
> That should applaud again.—Pull't off, I say.—

The tragic fall of this good man is dramatically underlined in his attempts to resume his old way of life. His infirmity of purpose cannot be more strongly presented than in his donning and doffing of the armor, and his bragging exit, with the equally revealing order:

> Bring it after me!

This is not an isolated, but only a more complex use of costume as symbol in poetic drama. For subtlety it might be contrasted with the costume changes of Tamburlaine, who appearing first in his shepherd's weeds, casts them off contemptuously at his first triumph:

> Lie here ye weeds that I disdain to wear!
> This complete armour and this curtle axe
> Are adjuncts more beseeming Tamburlaine;

and who later wears in sequence white, scarlet, and black armor to indicate the stiffening of his attitude towards his victims. This is a simple dramatic device. In *Macbeth* the costume change is related to the iterated image to make concrete Macbeth's state of mind, and related also to the larger problem, the power of evil to corrupt absolutely, with which the play is concerned.

Without insisting too strongly on this kind of relation of image and symbol to clothe the idea of the play in reality, a few familiar instances may make the process clearer. *Hamlet,* for example, establishes in its opening scene, with the ghost, and the references to decay and unwholesomeness, what Mr. Knight calls "the embassy of death." The hand of death is upon the play from the very start and references to it are constantly reiterated. However, it is death of a particular sort, not just Hamlet's musings upon the possibilities of suicide. Hamlet speaks of the sun breeding "maggots in a dead dog," the king compares his nephew to a foul disease, and describes his subjects as "muddied, / Thick and unwholesome in their thoughts and whispers." The idea is repeated over and over in the play which has been made explicit at the very start, "Something is rotten in the state of Denmark."

But if we have missed it through insensitivity, Shakespeare presents his symbol of the state of Denmark dramatically, in terms of the theater, before our eyes: *Enter two clowns,* who discourse learnedly of death and suicide and toss skulls and bones about the stage remarking on the pocky corpses they now must deal with; "Faith, if 'a be not rotten before 'a die," catches up the very word Marcellus had used earlier to describe the condition of the state.

It is this same kind of symbolism that Miss Spurgeon noticed with some surprise in the Gardener's scene of *Richard II,* in which the "leading theme . . . (is) gathered up, focussed, and pictorially presented." As she points out, this could hardly be missed by any careful reader. The lines of the play are larded with images of nature gone awry, the ugly clouds flying in the fair and crystal sky, the flourishing branch cracked and hacked down, and the summer leaves faded; there is a fearful tempest, a flood tide;

> The bay trees in our country all are withered,
> And meteors fright the fixed stars of heaven;
> The pale-faced moon looks bloody on the earth . . . ;

an unseasonable stormy day causes rivers to flood. But where the other characters of the play refer to the disordered political conditions in England in terms of unkempt nature, the Gardener reverses them by comparing the task of ordering his garden to the task of the governor of a commonwealth.

> O what pity it is
> That he had not so trimm'd and dress'd his land
> As we this garden!

Miss Spurgeon declares the scene to have been "deliberately inserted at the cost of any likeness to nature, for no human gardeners ever discoursed like these." To demand verisimilitude in what is obviously a poetic device is to apply to Shakespeare the standards of David Belasco. Probably even the most theatrical of theatricalists would be willing to grant the rightness and the effectiveness of the device, for it does realize dramatically and visually in terms of character and action the theme of the play. On reconsideration it may seem over-deliberate, super-imposed, introducing as it does two totally new characters for the sole purpose of the device, but Shakespeare had not yet learned dramatic economy. In *Hamlet,* the gravediggers belong to the plot as well as to the imagery.

The repeated pictures of natural conditions in *Richard II* introduce a second important function of the image in Elizabethan poetic drama. We are all convinced, I suppose, that the dramatist was forced to work without the benefit or encumbrance of representational scenery, and that the formal nature of the background of the Globe is the excuse for so many of those

> Barkloughly Castle call they this at hand

speeches, and such more extended and always (on the modern stage) intrusive passages in which we are informed,

> The grey-eyed morn smiles on the frowning night,
> Check'ring the Eastern clouds with streaks of light,

together with other meteorological data. But perhaps the Elizabethan playwright was more fortunate than his cabined, cribbed and confined successor. Not only could he shift his scene at will, or indeed not bother with a "scene" at all, but he could in his images create a world for his action more complete than any producer could provide, and uniquely adapted to the needs of both his play and his theme.

In *Richard,* for example, the action transpires not before painted seacoasts and cardboard castles, but in an envelope which is at once scenic and emotional. The cumulative effect of the nature images is not merely to suggest the political condition of England, but the kind of world in which such a conflict as that between Bolingbroke and Richard could take place. The device is not very skillfully used, perhaps, for *Richard* is close to being an apprentice play. In the later works, the setting as an emotional envelope is more artfully handled.

Lear is a case in point and a particularly striking contrast to *Richard.* Instead of giving magnitude to his action (as in the other tragedies) by relating the struggles of the protagonist to affairs of state, in England, Rome, or Denmark, Shakespeare creates a world of his own, a special world of King Lear, and he creates it by means of imagery.

It is the worst of all possible worlds. The animals which inhabit it are dragons, curs, rats, geese, kites, wolves, vultures, tigers. It is a world of disease, of plagues, carbuncles, boils. Whatever happens in this world happens in the most violent manner, wrenched, beaten, pierced, stung, scourged, flayed, gashed, scalded, tortured, broken on the rack. All this has been noted before by Miss Spurgeon and others. The world of Lear is a world of torment, a world unfriendly to man. In such a world the events of the play are entirely natural, possible, logical. The imagery, better than any possible stage setting, provides a background for the action, enriching the language of the play and serving to unify its execution.

For what, strangely enough, does not seem to have been commented on is the realization of this metaphorical world in the action of the play, in the tempest which runs through its center and in the torturing and blinding of Gloucester. Both scenes have come in for critical attack as incapable of presentation or too horrible for effective use. But it is clear that both are as essential to the play's action as to its theme, and that the blinding of Gloucester—detailed as it is—is made as horrible as possible for a purpose. If we experience an emotion of disgust, or terror, it is because both elements are present, not simply in the action, but in the world of the play. It is the dramatization of the image which makes the meaning of the play evident. If Richard's crown is the "language of props," Lear's tempest is the "language of setting."

The most difficult of the dramatist's devices to appreciate in the study is his primary device, the "language of action." Our modern playwrights are at some pains to render the action clear in extended stage directions, separated from the dialogue by italics and parentheses. Now Shakespeare resorts to a stage direction only rarely, most of the movement in his plays being implicit in the poetry. The significance of this lies less in the freedom of interpretation permitted the actor than in the indication of a further unity between the devices of poetry and the theater in the poetic drama.

For a simple and clear instance of this we may again turn to *Richard II*. The plot of this play, the conflict between Richard and Bolingbroke, might be diagrammed by tracing the letter X and letting the downward stroke stand for the king, the upward for the usurper, and the point of crossing the deposition scene. It is curious to note how the dominance of first the king and then the usurper is symbolized in their positions on the stage as well as in the imagery and the plot line. For three acts, Richard is in the ascendant. Whatever Bolingbroke's activities, Richard maintains his position as king. This is indeed symbolized by his appearance "on the walls" of Flint Castle, while Bolingbroke and his followers remain below. His descent to Bolingbroke's level is accompanied by a punning speech:

> Base court, where kings grow base,
> To come at traitors' calls and do them grace;

but his recognition of the true state of affairs is indicated as Bolingbroke kneels and Richard raises him up. In the deposition scene the shift in positions is completed, and verbalized by Richard in a final allusion to the sun image:

> O that I were a mockery king of snow,
> Standing before the sun of Bolingbroke
> To melt myself away in water drops.

It is a sign of the maturing artist that as his skill increases in each of the dramatic forms he elects to try, Shakespeare relies more and more upon the essentially dramatic materials available to him, the actors, their movements and physical relationships. In the most perfect of the histories, for instance, *1 Henry IV,* he has involved himself in a highly complex plot, the handling of which is a constant source of wonder and admiration. Ostensibly, Shakespeare is relating the events of a portion of the reign of Henry IV, a revolt engineered by the Percy family, and the waywardness of the Prince of Wales. But the two problems confronting the king are brought into significant relationship to one another, and the facts of history are made to serve the purposes of art. The subject of the play is not English history, but the general education of princes. Events have been so modified that the play actually confronts two ways of life—Hotspur's and Falstaff's—and presents the dilemma of Hal in choosing between them. Although a good deal of ink has been spilled over the character of Falstaff, and a number of romantic female tears over Percy, Shakespeare's intention is clear from his manipulation of the characters in a crucial scene. In Act V, Scene iv, Douglas enters, challenges Henry IV, they fight and, "the King being in danger, enter Prince of Wales." One must perhaps visualize the scene in the Elizabethan theater—a broad platform projecting into the audience with entrance doors on each side at the rear. Douglas and the Prince fight, and "Douglas flieth" through one of the doors. As the King goes to join his troops, enter, through the opposite door, Hotspur. The two youths exchange challenges; "They fight."

> *Enter Falstaff.*
> FALSTAFF Well said, Hal! to it, Hal! Nay you shall find no boy's play here, I can tell you.
> *Enter Douglas. He fighteth with Falstaff, who falls down as if he were dead.* (*Exit Douglas.*) *The Prince killeth Percy.*

Percy dies, still prating romantically of his honor and his proud titles which now accrue to Hal; Hal speaks his eulogy and turns from the body to go to the nearest door. But on his way, "He spieth Falstaff on the ground." As in *Richard II* the positions of the characters in the scene are symbolic. Hal has, seemingly, been presented with a choice between the way of life represented by Hotspur and the way of life represented by Falstaff. And here they are, two (apparent) corpses on the ground, one on either side of him. The choice is to make, and he chooses—neither. Having bid farewell to Percy, he now bids farewell to Jack, confirming the promise of his first soliloquy and anticipating the rejection of Falstaff at the end of Part II.

Significant illustrations of this "language of action" could be chosen from nearly any of the plays. Indeed, nearly all the most familiar, most memorable scenes involve some kind of symbolic action. Not merely in tragedy, with Lear buffeted by the tempest, or Hamlet leaping into the grave of Ophelia, but in comedy, with Titania fondly caressing the hairy snout of ass-headed Bottom, or Feste torturing Malvolio into a realization of his humanity. The very essence of the tragic idea of

Hamlet and *Lear* and the comic idea of *A Midsummer Night's Dream* and *Twelfth Night* is contained in those moments of action. This is not to say that the poetry is superfluous. These are further instances of the complete welding of the elements of poetry and the elements of theater which constitute successful poetic drama.

CHARACTER AND STRUCTURE

How Many Children Had Lady Macbeth?

L. C. Knights

PART I

I

For some years there have been signs of a re-orientation of Shakespeare criticism. The books that I have in mind have little in common with the majority of those that have been written on Shakespeare, but they are likely to have a decisive influence upon criticism in the future. The present, therefore, is a favourable time in which to take stock of the traditional methods, and to inquire why so few of the many books that have been written are relevant to our study of Shakespeare as a poet. The inquiry involves an examination of certain critical presuppositions, and of these the most fruitful of irrelevancies is the assumption that Shakespeare was pre-eminently a great 'creator of characters'. So extensive was his knowledge of the human heart (so runs the popular opinion) that he was able to project himself into the minds of an infinite variety of men and women and present them 'real as life' before us. Of course, he was a great poet as well, but the poetry is an added grace which gives to the atmosphere of the plays a touch of 'magic' and which provides us with the thrill of single memorable lines and lyric passages.

This assumption that it is the main business of a writer—other than

---

From L. C. Knights, *Explorations*. Reprinted by permission of Chatto and Windus, Ltd.

the lyric poet—to create characters is not, of course, confined to criticism of Shakespeare, it long ago invaded criticism of the novel. 'Character creation', says Mr. Logan Pearsall Smith, 'is regarded as the very essence of English fiction, the *sine qua non* of novel writing.' And in a recent book of extracts from Scott, Mr. Hugh Walpole writes:

> The test of a character in any novel is that it should have existed before the book that reveals it to us began and should continue after the book is closed. . . . These are our friends for life—but it is the penalty of the more subconscious school of modern fiction that, when the book is closed, all that we have in our hands is a boot-button, a fragment of tulle, or a cocktail shaker. We have dived, it seems, so very deep and come to the surface again with so little in our grasp. . . . But (he continues) however gay, malicious, brilliant and amusing they [modern novels] may be, this hard business of creating a world for us, a world filled with people in whom we may believe, whom we may know better than we know our friends, is the gift of the very few.[1]

It should be obvious that a criterion for the novel by which we should have to condemn *Wuthering Heights, Heart of Darkness, Ulysses, To the Lighthouse* and the bulk of the work of D. H. Lawrence does not need to be very seriously considered.

There is no need to search for examples in the field of Shakespeare criticism. In the latest book on Shakespeare that has come to hand, we read: 'His creations are not *ideas* but *characters*—real men and women, fellow humans with ourselves. We can follow their feelings and thoughts like those of our most intimate acquaintances.' [2] The case is even better illustrated by Ellen Terry's recently published *Lectures on Shakespeare.* To her the characters are all flesh and blood and she exercises her ingenuity on such questions as whether Portia or Bellario thought of the famous quibble, and whether it was justified.[3] And how did the Boy in *Henry V* learn to speak French? 'Robin's French is quite fluent. Did he learn to speak the lingo from Prince Hal, or from Falstaff in London, or did he pick it up during his few weeks in France with the army?'[4] Ellen Terry of course does not represent critical Authority; the point is not that she could write as she did, but that the book was popular. Most of the reviewers were enthusiastic. The *Times Literary Supplement* said that the book showed 'the insight of a genius', and the reviewer in the *Times,* speaking of her treatment of Falstaff's page, declared, 'To Ellen Terry, Robin was as alive and as real as could be; and we feel as if she had given us a new little friend to laugh with and be sorry for'.

---

[1] *The Waverly Pageant,* pp. 38–40.
[2] Ranjee G. Shahani, *Shakespeare Through Eastern Eyes,* p. 177.
[3] *Four Lectures on Shakespeare,* pp. 119–120.
[4] *Op. cit.,* p. 49.

And if we wish for higher authority we have only to turn to the book by Mr. Logan Pearsall Smith, *On Reading Shakespeare*. Mr. Smith demands respect as the author of *Words and Idioms,* in which he showed the kind of interest in language needed for the critical approach to Shakespeare. But there is nothing of that interest in the present essay. Here Shakespeare is praised because he provides 'the illusion of reality', because he puts 'living people' upon the stage, because he creates characters who are 'independent of the work in which they appear . . . and when the curtain falls they go on living in our imaginations and remain as real to us as our familiar friends'.—'Those inhabitants of the world of poetry who, in our imagination, lead their immortal lives apart.'[5]

The most illustrious example is, of course, Dr. Bradley's *Shakespearean Tragedy*. The book is too well known to require much descriptive comment, but it should be observed that the Notes, in which the detective interest supersedes the critical, form a logical corollary to the main portions of the book. In the Lectures on *Macbeth* we learn that Macbeth was 'exceedingly ambitious. He must have been so by temper. The tendency must have been greatly strengthened by his marriage.' But 'it is difficult to be sure of his customary demeanour'. And Dr. Bradley seems surprised that 'This bold ambitious man of action has, within certain limits, the imagination of a poet'. These minor points are symptomatic. It is assumed throughout the book that the most profitable discussion of Shakespeare's tragedies is in terms of the characters of which they are composed.—'The centre of the tragedy may be said with equal truth to lie in action issuing from character, or in character issuing in action. . . . What we feel strongly, as a tragedy advances to its close, is that the calamities and catastrophe follow inevitably from the deeds of men, and that the main source of these deeds is character. The dictum that, with Shakespeare, "character is destiny" is no doubt an exaggeration . . . but it is the exaggeration of a vital truth.' It is this which leads Dr. Bradley to ask us to imagine Posthumus in the place of Othello, Othello in the place of Posthumus, and to conjecture upon Hamlet's whereabouts at the time of his father's death.

The influence of the assumption is pervasive. Not only are all the books of Shakespeare criticism (with a very few exceptions) based upon it, it invades scholarship (the notes to the indispensable Arden edition may be called in evidence), and in school children are taught to think they have 'appreciated' the poet if they are able to talk about the characters—aided no doubt by the neat summaries provided by Mr. Verity which they learn so assiduously before examinations.

---

[5] Mr. Smith reminds us that, 'There are other elements too in this draught of Shakespeare's brewing—in the potent wine that came to fill at last the great jewelled cup of words he fashioned, to drink from which is one of the most wonderful experiences life affords.'

In the mass of Shakespeare criticism there is not a hint that 'character'—like 'plot', 'rhythm', 'construction' and all our other critical counters—is merely an abstraction from the total response in the mind of the reader or spectator, brought into being by written or spoken words; that the critic therefore—however far he may ultimately range—begins with the words of which a play is composed. This applies equally to the novel or any other form of art that uses language as its medium. 'A Note on Fiction' by Mr. C. H. Rickword in *The Calendar of Modern Letters* expresses the point admirably with regard to the novel: 'The form of a novel only exists as a balance of response on the part of the reader. Hence schematic plot is a construction of the reader's that corresponds to an aspect of the response and stands in merely diagrammatic relation to the source. Only as precipitates from the memory are plot or character tangible; yet only in solution have either any emotive valency.'[6]

A Shakespeare play is a dramatic poem. It uses action, gesture, formal grouping and symbols, and it relies upon the general conventions governing Elizabethan plays. But, we cannot too often remind ourselves, its end is to communicate a rich and controlled experience by means of words—words used in a way to which, without some training, we are no longer accustomed to respond. To stress in the conventional way character or plot or any of the other abstractions that can be made, is to impoverish the total response. 'It is in the total situation rather than in the wrigglings of individual emotion that the tragedy lies.'[7] 'We should not look for perfect verisimilitude to life,' says Mr. Wilson Knight, 'but rather see each play as an expanded metaphor, by means of which the original vision has been projected into forms roughly correspondent with actuality, conforming thereto with greater or less exactitude according to the demands of its nature. . . . The persons, ultimately, are not human at all, but purely symbols of a poetic vision.'[8]

It would be easy to demonstrate that this approach is essential even when dealing with plays like *Hamlet* or *Macbeth* which can be made to yield something very impressive in the way of 'character'. And it is the only approach which will enable us to say anything at all relevant about plays like *Measure for Measure* or *Troilus and Cressida* which have consistently baffled the critics. And apart from Shakespeare, what are we to say of *Tamburlaine, Edward II, The Revenger's Tragedy* or *The Changeling* if we do not treat them primarily as poems?

---

[6] *The Calendar,* October 1926. In an earlier review, Mr. Rickword wrote: 'Mere degree of illusion provides no adequate test: novelists who can do nothing else are able to perform the trick with ease, since "nothing is easier than to create for oneself the idea of a human being, a figure and a character, from glimpses and anecdotes".' (*The Calendar,* July 1926; both pieces are reprinted in *Towards Standards of Criticism,* Wishart.)

[7] M. C. Bradbrook, *Elizabethan Stage Conditions,* p. 102.

[8] G. Wilson Knight, *The Wheel of Fire,* p. 16.

Read with attention, the plays themselves will tell us how they should be read. But those who prefer another kind of evidence have only to consider the contemporary factors that conditioned the making of an Elizabethan play, namely the native tradition of English drama descending from the morality plays, the construction of the playhouse and the conventions depending, in part, upon that construction, and the tastes and expectations of the audience. I have not space to deal with any of these in detail. Schücking has shown how large a part was played in the Elizabethan drama by 'primitive technique', but the full force of the morality tradition remains to be investigated. It is, I think, impossible to appreciate *Troilus and Cressida* on the one hand, or the plays of Middleton (and even of Ben Jonson) on the other, without an understanding of the 'morality' elements that they contain. As for the second factor, the physical peculiarities of the stage and Elizabethan dramatic conventions, I can only refer to Miss Bradbrook's *Elizabethan Stage Conditions*. We can make a hasty summary by saying that each of these factors determined that Elizabethan drama should be non-realistic, conditioned by conventions that helped to govern the total response obtained by means of the language of each play. A consideration of Shakespeare's use of language demands a consideration of the reading and listening habits of his audience. Contrary to the accepted view that the majority of these were crude and unlettered, caring only for fighting and foolery, bombast and bawdry, but able to *stand* a great deal of poetry, I think there is evidence (other than the plays themselves) that very many of them had an educated interest in words, a passionate concern for the possibilities of language and the subtleties of poetry. At all events they were trained, by pamphlets, by sermons and by common conversation, to listen or to read with an athleticism which we, in the era of the *Daily Mail* and the Best Seller, have consciously to acquire or do our best to acquire. And all of them shared the speech idiom that is the basis of Shakespeare's poetry.[9]

II

We are faced with this conclusion: the only profitable approach to Shakespeare is a consideration of his plays as dramatic poems, of his use of language to obtain a total complex emotional response. Yet the bulk of Shakespeare criticism is concerned with his characters, his heroines, his love of Nature or his 'philosophy'—with everything, in short, except with the words on the page, which it is the main business of the critic to examine. I wish to consider as briefly as possible

---

[9] I have presented some of the evidence in an essay on 'Education and the Drama in the Age of Shakespeare,' *The Criterion,* July 1932.

how this paradoxical state of affairs arose. To examine the historical development of the kind of criticism that is mainly concerned with 'character' is to strengthen the case against it.

A start must be made towards the end of the seventeenth century, and it is tempting to begin with Thomas Rymer. If Rymer is representative his remarks on *Othello*[10] show how completely the Elizabethan tradition had been lost. Of one of the storm speeches (II.i), important both as symbol and ironic commentary, he says, 'Once in a man's life, he might be content at *Bedlam* to hear such a rapture. In a Play one should speak like a man of business.' He had no conception of the function of rhetoric on the Elizabethan stage; of Othello's speech,

> O now, for ever
> Farewell the Tranquill minde; farewell Content;

he says, 'These lines are recited here, not for any thing Poetical in them, besides the sound, that pleases'. Combining a demand for realistic verisimilitude with an acceptance of the neo-classic canons he has no difficulty in ridiculing the play:

> The moral, sure, of this Fable is very instructive.
>
> First, This may be a caution to all Maidens of Quality how, without their Parents consent, they run away with Blackamoors.
>
> Secondly, This may be a warning to all good Wives that they look well to their Linnen.
>
> Thirdly, This may be a lesson to Husbands that before their Jealousie be Tragical the proofs may be Mathematical.

And so on to the triumphant conclusion:

> What can remain with the Audience to carry home with them from this sort of Poetry for their use and edification? how can it work, unless (instead of settling the mind and purging our passions) to delude our senses, disorder our thoughts, addle our brain, pervert our affections, hair our imaginations, corrupt our appetite, and fill our head with vanity, confusion, *Tintamarre,* and Jingle-jangle, beyond what all the Parish Clarks of *London* with their *Old Testament* farces and interludes, in *Richard* the second's time, could ever pretend to? . . . The tragical part is plainly none other than a Bloody Farce, without salt or savour.[11]

---

[10] In *A Short View of Tragedy* (1693).

[11] I cannot understand Mr. Eliot's remark that he has 'never seen a cogent refutation of Thomas Rymer's objections to *Othello*' (*Selected Essays,* p. 141). A narrow sensibility, a misunderstanding of the nature of dramatic conventions, and the command of a few debating tricks (e.g. the description of the play in terms of the external plot, which would make any tragedy look ridiculous) are sufficient to account for his objections. A point by point refutation is possible but hardly necessary.

But perhaps Rymer is not sufficiently representative for his work to be called as evidence. He had a following which included such critics as Gildon and Dennis, and even Pope was influenced by him, but he was censured by Dryden, Addison and Rowe, amongst others, and the rules he stood for never gained anything like a complete ascendancy in the criticism of the eighteenth century. For evidence of the kind that we require we must turn to Dryden, who was not only 'a representative man' but also an enthusiastic admirer of Shakespeare, and if he was not 'the father of English criticism', he was at least a critic whose opinions must be reckoned with. When Rymer says of the Temptation scene in *Othello,* 'Here we see a known Language does wofully encumber and clog the operation, as either forc'd, or heavy, or trifling, or incoherent, or improper, or most what improbable', it is permissible to disregard him; but when we find that Dryden makes similar remarks of other plays of Shakespeare, it is obvious not only that ways of thought and feeling have changed sufficiently since the Elizabethan period to demand a different idiom, but that the Shakespearean idiom is, for the time being, out of the reach of criticism. In the Preface to his version of *Troilus and Cressida* (1679) Dryden says: 'Yet it must be allowed to the present age, that the tongue in general is so much refined since Shakespeare's time that many of his words, and more of his phrases, are scarce intelligible. And of those which we understand, some are ungrammatical, others coarse; and his whole style is so pestered with figurative expressions, that it is as affected as it is obscure.' And of *Troilus and Cressida:* 'I undertook to remove that heap of rubbish under which many excellent thoughts lay wholly buried . . . I need not say that I have refined the language, which before was obsolete.' [12]

Not only the idiom but the Elizabethan conventions were now inaccessible. In the *Defence of the Epilogue* (1672) Dryden takes exception to *The Winter's Tale, Love's Labour's Lost* and *Measure for Measure,* 'which were either grounded on impossibilities, or at least so meanly written, that the comedy neither moved your mirth, nor the serious part your concernment'. And he proceeds to criticize Fletcher in the true spirit of William Archer.

The implications of Dryden's remarks became the commonplaces of criticism for the succeeding generations. It was permissible to speak of Shakespeare's 'Deference paid to the reigning Barbarism' (Theo-

[12] Later he remarks: 'I will not say of so great a poet that he distinguished not the blown puffy style from true sublimity; but I may venture to maintain that the fury of his fancy often transported him beyond the bounds of judgment, either in coining of new words and phrases, or racking words which were in use into the violence of a catachresis. It is not that I would explode the use of metaphors from passion, for Longinus thinks 'em necessary to raise it: but to use 'em at every word, to say nothing without a metaphor, a simile, an image, or description, is, I doubt, to smell a little too strongly of the buskin.'—The force of Elizabethan language springs from its metaphorical life.

bald), and 'The vicious taste of the age' (Hanmer), and to write, 'The Audience was generally composed of the meaner sort of people' (Pope), and 'The publick was gross and dark. . . . Those to whom our author's labours were exhibited had more skill in pomps or processions than in poetical language' (Johnson). In his *Preface* (1747) Warburton writes:

> The Poet's hard and unnatural construction . . . was the effect of mistaken Art and Design. The Public Taste was in its Infancy; and delighted (as it always does during that state) in the high and turgid; which leads the writer to disguise a vulgar expression with hard and forced constructions, whereby the sentence frequently becomes cloudy and dark . . . an obscurity that ariseth, not from the licentious use of a single Term, but from the unnatural arrangement of a whole sentence. . . . Not but in his best works (he continues), we must allow, he is often so natural and flowing, so pure and correct, that he is even a model for style and language.

Of all the eighteenth-century critics only Johnson (an exception we have often to make) at times transcended the limitations of conventional Shakespeare criticism. He censures Hanmer, who in his edition of Shakespeare 'is solicitous to reduce to grammar what he could not be sure that his author intended to be grammatical', and he writes admirably of 'a style which never becomes obsolete. . . . This style is probably to be sought in the common intercourse of life, among those who speak only to be understood, without ambition of elegance.' But he stops short at that. This 'conversation above grossness and below refinement, where propriety resides' is where Shakespeare 'seems to have gathered his *comick* dialogue'. But it is in Shakespeare's tragedies that his style is most vividly idiomatic and full bodied, and Johnson was capable of writing, 'His comedy pleases by the thoughts and language, and his tragedy for the greater part by incident and action'. Johnson's great virtues as a critic did not include an understanding of Shakespeare's idiom. For him, 'The style of Shakespeare was in itself ungrammatical, perplexed and obscure', and many passages remained 'obscured by obsolete phraseology or by the writer's unskilfulness and affectation'. We remember also how he could 'scarcely check his risibility' at the 'blanket of the dark' passage in *Macbeth*.

It should not be necessary to insist that I do not wish to deny the achievements of the Augustan age in poetry and criticism. But an age of which the commonplaces of criticism were that 'Well placing of words, for the sweetness of pronunciation, was not known till Mr. Waller introduced it',[13] and that Pope's *Homer* 'tuned the English tongue';[14] an age which produced the *Essay on Criticism* and the

[13] Dryden, *Defence of the Epilogue.*
[14] Johnson, *Life of Pope.*

Satires of Dr. Donne Versified, and which consistently neglected the Metaphysical poets and the minor Elizabethans, such an age was incapable of fully understanding Shakespeare's use of words. Since the total response to a Shakespeare play can only be obtained by an exact and sensitive study of the quality of the verse, of the rhythm and imagery, of the controlled associations of the words and their emotional and intellectual force, in short by an exact and sensitive study of Shakespeare's handling of language, it is hardly reasonable to expect very much relevant criticism of Shakespeare in the eighteenth century. What can be expected is criticism at one remove from the plays, that is, of every aspect that can be extracted from a play and studied in comparative isolation; of this kind of criticism an examination of 'characters' is the most obvious example.

A significant passage occurs in Shaftesbury's *Advice to an Author,* published in 1710:

> Our old dramatick Poet, Shakespeare, may witness for our good Ear and manly Relish. Notwithstanding his natural Rudeness, his unpolish'd style, his antiquated Phrase and Wit, his want of Method and Coherence, and his Deficiency in almost all the Graces and Ornaments of this kind of Writings; yet by the Justness of his *Moral,* the Aptness of many of his *Descriptions,* and the plain and natural Turn of several of his *Characters,* he pleases his Audience, and often gains their Ear, without a single Bribe from Luxury or Vice.

We see here the beginning of that process of splitting up the indivisible unity of a Shakespeare play into various elements abstracted from the whole. If a play of Shakespeare's could not be appreciated as a whole, it was still possible to admire and to discuss his moral sentiments, his humour, his poetic descriptions and the life-likeness of his characters. Thus, Warburton mentions '. . . the Author's Beauties . . . whether in Style, Thought, Sentiment, Character, or Composition'.

The intensive study of Shakespeare's characters was not fully developed until the second half of the eighteenth century. Dryden had remarked that 'No man ever drew so many characters, or generally distinguished 'em from one another, excepting only Jonson', and Pope observed, 'His *Characters* are so much Nature herself, that 'tis a sort of injury to call them by so distant a name as copies of her. . . . Every single character in Shakespeare is as much an Individual as those in Life itself; it is as impossible to find any two alike'; and Theobald echoed him in a lyrical passage,—'If we look into his Characters, and how they are furnished and proportion'd to the Employment he cuts out for them, how are we taken up with the Mastery of his Portraits! What draughts of Nature! What variety of Originals, and how differing each from the other!' [15] But in the second half of the century character

[15] Pope adds: 'Had all the speeches been printed without the very names of the Persons, I believe one might have apply'd them with certainty to every speaker.'

study became one of the main objects of Shakespeare criticism. This is sufficiently indicated by the following titles: *A Philosophical Analysis and Illustration of some of Shakespeare's Remarkable Characters* (Richardson, 1774), *An Essay on the Character of Hamlet* (Pilon, 1777), *Essays on Shakespeare's Dramatic Characters* (Richardson, 1784), *Remarks on some of the Characters of Shakespeare* (Whately, 1785), *Shakespeare's Imitation of Female Characters* (Richardson, 1789), and so on.

Of the essays of this kind, the most famous is Maurice Morgann's *Essay on the Dramatic Character of Sir John Falstaff* (1777). The pivot of Morgann's method is to be found in one of his footnotes:

> The reader must be sensible of something in the composition of *Shakespeare's* characters, which renders them essentially different from those drawn by other writers. The characters of every Drama must indeed be grouped, but in the groups of other poets the parts which are not seen do not in fact exist. But there is a certain roundness and integrity in the forms of *Shakespeare,* which give them an independence as well as a relation, insomuch that we often meet with passages which, tho' perfectly felt, cannot be sufficiently explained in words, without unfolding the whole character of the speaker. . . . The reader will not now be surprised if I affirm that those characters in Shakespeare, which are seen only in part, are yet capable of being unfolded and understood in the whole; every part being in fact relative, and inferring all the rest. It is true that the point of action or sentiment, which we are most concerned in, is always held out for our special notice. But who does not perceive that there is a peculiarity about it, which conveys a relish of the whole? And very frequently, when no particular point presses, he boldly makes a character act and speak from those parts of the composition which are *inferred* only, and not distinctly shown. This produces a wonderful effect; it seems to carry us beyond the poet to nature itself, and gives an integrity and truth to facts and character, which they could not otherwise obtain. And this is in reality that art in *Shakespeare* which, being withdrawn from our notice, we more emphatically call *nature.* A felt propriety and truth from causes unseen, I take to be the highest point of Poetic composition. If the characters of *Shakespeare* are thus *whole,* and as it were original, whilst those of almost all other writers are mere imitation, *it may be fit to consider them rather as Historic than Dramatic beings; and, when occasion requires, to account for their conduct from the* WHOLE *of character, from general principles, from latent motives, and from policies not avowed.*[16]

It is strange how narrowly Morgann misses the mark. He recognized what can be called the full-bodied quality of Shakespeare's work—it

[16] These last italics are mine.

came to him as a feeling of 'roundness and integrity'. But instead of realizing that this quality sprang from Shakespeare's use of words, words which have 'a network of tentacular roots, reaching down to the deepest terrors and desires', he referred it to the characters' 'independence' of the work in which they appeared, and directed his exploration to 'latent motives and policies not avowed'. Falstaff's birth, his early life, his association with John of Gaunt, his possible position as head of his family, his military service and his pension are all examined in order to determine the grand question, 'Is Falstaff a constitutional coward?' [17]

In the Essay, of course, 'Falstaff is the word only. Shakespeare is the theme', and several admirable things are said incidentally. But more than any other man, it seems to me, Morgann has deflected Shakespeare criticism from the proper objects of attention by his preposterous references to those aspects of a 'character' that Shakespeare did not wish to show. He made explicit the assumption on which the other eighteenth-century critics based their work, and that assumption has been pervasive until our own time. In 1904 Dr. Bradley said of Morgann's essay, 'There is no better piece of Shakespeare criticism in the world'.[18]

I have already suggested the main reason for the eighteenth-century approach to Shakespeare via the characters, namely an inability to appreciate the Elizabethan idiom and a consequent inability to discuss Shakespeare's plays as poetry. And of course the Elizabethan dramatic tradition was lost, and the eighteenth-century critics in general were ignorant of the stage for which Shakespeare wrote.[19] But other factors should also be considered; for instance, the neo-classic insistence upon the moral function of art (before you can judge a person in a play he must have more or less human 'motives'), and the variations of meaning covered by the term 'nature' from the time of Pope to the time of Wordsworth. Literary psychologizing also played a part; Kames and William Richardson[20] both found Shakespeare's persons useful illustrations of psychological theories, and Samuel Richardson fostered an interest in introspective analysis, so that Macbeth's soliloquies were assumed to have something in common with the introspections of Clarissa. Finally (and Richardson serves to remind us) 'the sentimental age set in early in the eighteenth century'. If we consider any of the

[17] I have discussed Falstaff's dramatic function—the way in which he helps to define Shakespeare's total attitude towards the matter in hand—in *Determinations,* edited by F. R. Leavis (Chatto and Windus).

[18] *The Scottish Historical Review,* Vol. I, p. 291.

[19] 'Shakespeare's plays were to be acted in a paltry tavern, to an unlettered audience, just emerging from barbarity.'—Mrs. Montagu, *Essay on the Writings and Genius of Shakespeare* (Fifth Edition, 1785), p. 13.

[20] [In a note Knights supplies a number of good examples of the psychologizing of late eighteenth-century critics, particularly the *Essays on Some of Shakespeare's Dramatic Characters* (5th ed., 1797) of William Richardson.]

Character writers of the seventeenth century, Earle, Overbury or Hall, we find that they preserve a distance from their subjects which the eighteenth-century creators of characters do not. The early Characters have a frame round them, whereas the Vicar of Wakefield, Beau Tibbs, and even Sir Roger de Coverley make a more direct appeal to human sympathy and emotion. The 'human' appeal ('These are our friends for life . . .') which has made the fortune of Best Sellers, is an intrusion which vitiated, and can only vitiate, Shakespeare criticism.

One form of the charge against eighteenth-century Shakespeare criticism is that it made the approach too easy. In Pope's edition, 'Some of the most shining passages are distinguish'd by commas in the margin', and Warburton also marked what he considered particularly beautiful passages. From this it was but a step to collect such passages into anthologies. The numerous editions of the collections of *Beauties* show how popular this method of reading Shakespeare had become by the end of the century. This is an obvious method of simplification, but it is only part of the process whereby various partial (and therefore distorted) responses were substituted for the full complex response demanded by a Shakespeare play—a process that was fatal to criticism.[21]

There is no need, even if it were possible, to discuss nineteenth-century Shakespeare criticism in detail, partly because it is more familiar, partly because—as Mr. Nichol Smith and Mr. Babcock have helped us to realize—the foundations of modern Shakespeare criticism were laid in the eighteenth century. In the nineteenth century the word 'poetry' changed its significance, but preconceptions about 'the poetic' derived from reading Keats (or Tennyson) did not increase understanding of seventeenth-century poetry. And everything combined to foster that kind of interest in Shakespeare that is represented at certain levels by Mrs. Jameson's *Shakespeare's Heroines* and Mary Cowden Clarke's *Girlhood of Shakespeare's Heroines*. In so far as the word 'romantic' has other than an emotive use, it serves to distinguish individualist qualities as opposed to the social qualities covered by 'classical'. One of the main results of the Romantic Revival was the stressing of 'personality' in fiction. At the same time, the growth of the popular novel, from Sir Walter Scott and Charlotte Brontë to our own Best Sellers, encouraged an emotional identification of the reader with hero or heroine (we all 'have a smack of Hamlet' nowadays).[22] And

---

[21] For the collections of Shakespeare's Beauties see R. W. Babcock, *The Genesis of Shakespeare Idolatry,* pp. 115–118. The most famous of these anthologies, William Dodd's *Beauties of Shakespeare,* first published in 1752, not only went through many editions in the eighteenth century, but was frequently reprinted in the nineteenth.

[22] See the letters to popular novelists quoted on p. 58 of Q. D. Leavis's *Fiction and the Reading Public:* 'Your characters are so human that they live with me as friends', etc.

towards the end of the century the influence of Ibsen was responsible for fresh distortions which can best be studied in Archer's *The Old Drama and the New*.

In Shakespeare criticism from Hazlitt to Dowden we find the same kind of irrelevance. Hazlitt says of Lady Macbeth:

> She is a great bad woman, whom we hate, but whom we fear more than we hate.

And of the Witches:

> They are hags of mischief, obscene panders to iniquity, malicious from their impotence of enjoyment, enamoured of destruction, because they are themselves unreal, abortive, half-existences—who become sublime from their exemption from all human sympathies and contempt for all human affairs, as Lady Macbeth does by the force of passion! Her fault seems to have been an excess of that strong principle of self-interest and family aggrandisement, not amenable to the common feelings of compassion and justice, which is so marked a feature in barbarous nations and times.

What has this to do with Shakespeare? And what the lyric outburst that Dowden quotes approvingly in his chapter on *Romeo and Juliet?*

> Who does not recall those lovely summer nights, in which the forces of nature seem eager for development, and constrained to remain in drowsy languor? . . . The nightingale sings in the depths of the woods. The flower-cups are half-closed.

And so on.

Wherever we look we find the same reluctance to master the words of the play, the same readiness to abstract a character and treat him (because he is more manageable that way) as a human being. When Gervinus says that the play *Hamlet* 'transports us to a rude and wild period from which Hamlet's whole nature recoils, and to which he falls a sacrifice because by habit, character and education he is alienated from it, and like the boundary stone of a changing civilization touches a world of finer feeling', he exhibits the common fault. In this instance Hamlet is wrenched from his setting and violently imported into the society described by Saxo Grammaticus. Criticism is not all so crass as Sir Herbert Tree's remark that 'We must interpret Macbeth, before and at the crisis, by his just and equitable character as a king that history gives him'.[23] But there are enough modern instances to show that the advice that Hartley Coleridge gave in *Blackwood's* needed no arguing. 'Let us', he said, 'for a moment, put Shakespeare out of the question,

---

[23] *Illustrated London News,* September 9, 1911.

and consider Hamlet as a real person, a recently deceased acquaintance.' [24]

The habit of regarding Shakespeare's persons as 'friends for life' or, maybe, 'deceased acquaintances', is responsible for most of the vagaries that serve as Shakespeare criticism. It accounts for the artificial simplifications of the editors ('In a play one should speak like a man of business'). It accounts for the 'double time' theory for *Othello*. It accounts for Dr. Bradley's Notes. It is responsible for all the irrelevant moral and realistic canons that have been applied to Shakespeare's plays, for the sentimentalizing of his heroes (Coleridge and Goethe on Hamlet) and his heroines. And the loss is incalculable. Losing sight of the *whole* dramatic pattern of each play, we inhibit the development of that full complex response that makes our experience of a Shakespeare play so very much more than an appreciation of 'character'—that is, usually, of somebody else's 'character'. That more complete, more intimate possession can only be obtained by treating Shakespeare primarily as a poet.

PART II

I

Since everyone who has written about Shakespeare probably imagines that he has 'treated him primarily as a poet', some explanation is called for. How should we read Shakespeare?

We start with so many lines of verse on a printed page which we read as we should read any other poem. We have to elucidate the meaning (using Dr. Richards's fourfold definition[25]) and to unravel ambiguities; we have to estimate the kind and quality of the imagery and determine the precise degree of evocation of particular figures; we have to allow full weight to each word, exploring its 'tentacular roots', and to determine how it controls and is controlled by the rhythmic movement of the passage in which it occurs. In short, we have to decide exactly why the lines 'are so and not otherwise'.

As we read other factors come into play. The lines have a cumulative effect. 'Plot', aspects of 'character' and recurrent 'themes'—all 'precipitates from the memory'—help to determine our reaction at a given point. There is a constant reference backwards and forwards. But the work of detailed analysis continues to the last line of the last act. If the razor-edge of sensibility is blunted at any point we cannot claim to have read what Shakespeare wrote, however often our eyes may have

---

[24] *Blackwood's Magazine*, Vol. XXIV (1828), p. 585.
[25] *Practical Criticism*, pp. 181–183.

travelled over the page. A play of Shakespeare's is a precise particular experience, a poem—and precision and particularity are exactly what is lacking in the greater part of Shakespeare criticism, criticism that deals with *Hamlet* or *Othello* in terms of abstractions that have nothing to do with the unique arrangement of words that constitutes these plays.

Obviously what is wanted to reinforce the case against the traditional methods is a detailed examination of a particular play. Unfortunately anything approaching a complete analysis is precluded by the scope of the present essay. The following remarks on one play, *Macbeth,* are, therefore, not offered as a final criticism of the play; they merely point to factors that criticism must take into account if it is to have any degree of relevance, and emphasize the kind of effect that is necessarily overlooked when we discuss a Shakespeare play in terms of characters 'copied from life', or of 'Shakespeare's knowledge of the human heart'.

Even here there is a further reservation to be made. In all elucidation there is an element of crudity and distortion. 'The true generalization', Mr. Eliot reminds us, 'is not something superposed upon an accumulation of perception; the perceptions do not, in a really appreciative mind, accumulate as a mass, but form themselves as a structure; and criticism is the statement in language of this structure; it is a development of sensibility.' [26] Of course, the only *full* statement in language of this structure is in the exact words of the poem concerned; but what the critic can do is to aid 'the return to the work of art with improved perception and intensified, because more conscious, enjoyment'. He can help others to 'force the subject to expose itself', he cannot fully expose it in his own criticism. And in so far as he paraphrases or 'explains the meaning' he must distort. The main difference between good and bad critics is that the good critic points to something that is actually contained in the work of art, whereas the bad critic points away from the work in question; he introduces extraneous elements into his appreciation—smudges the canvas with his own paint. With this reservation I should like to call the following pages an essay in elucidation.

II

Macbeth is a statement of evil. I use the word 'statement' (unsatisfactory as it is) in order to stress those qualities that are 'non-dramatic', if drama is defined according to the canons of William Archer or Dr. Bradley. It also happens to be poetry, which means that the apprehension of the whole can only be obtained from a lively attention to the parts, whether they have an immediate bearing on the main action or 'illustrate character', or not. Two main themes, which can only be

---

[26] *The Sacred Wood* (Second Edition, 1928), p. 15. See also p. 11, *op. cit.,* and *Selected Essays,* p. 205.

separated for the purpose of analysis, are blended in the play—the themes of the reversal of values and of unnatural disorder. And closely related to each is a third theme, that of the deceitful appearance, and consequent doubt, uncertainty and confusion. All this is obscured by false assumptions about the category 'drama'; *Macbeth* has greater affinity with *The Waste Land* than with *The Doll's House*.[27]

Each theme is stated in the first act. The first scene, every word of which will bear the closest scrutiny, strikes one dominant chord:

> Faire is foule, and foule is faire,
> Hover through the fogge and filthie ayre.

It is worth remarking that 'Hurley-burley' implies more than 'the tumult of sedition or insurrection'. Both it and 'when the Battaile's lost, and wonne' suggest the kind of metaphysical pitch-and-toss that is about to be played with good and evil. At the same time we hear the undertone of uncertainty: the scene opens with a question, and the second line suggests a region where the elements are disintegrated as they never are in nature; thunder and lightning are disjoined, and offered as alternatives. We should notice also that the scene expresses the same movement as the play as a whole: the general crystallizes into the immediate particular ('Where the place?'—'Upon the Heath.'—'There to meet with Macbeth.') and then dissolves again into the general presentment of hideous gloom. All is done with the greatest speed, economy and precision.

The second scene is full of images of confusion. It is a general principle in the work of Shakespeare and many of his contemporaries that when A is made to describe X, a minor character or event, the description is not merely immediately applicable to X, it helps to determine the way in which our whole response shall develop. This is rather crudely recognized when we say that certain lines 'create the atmosphere' of the play. Shakespeare's power is seen in the way in which details of this kind develop, check, or provide a commentary upon the main interests that he has aroused.[28] In the present scene the description

---

[27] See the Arden Edition, p. xxii: 'The scenes (Act IV, scenes ii and iii) seem to have been composed with evident effort, as if Shakespeare felt the necessity of stretching out his material to the ordinary length of a five-act tragedy, and found lack of *dramatic* material, which was certainly wanting in his authority, Holinshed. *Hence* his introduction in Act V of the famous "sleep-walking scene" . . . and the magnificently *irrelevant* soliloquies of the great protagonist himself.' The italics are mine. There is something wrong with a conception of 'the dramatic' that leads a critic to speak of Macbeth's final soliloquies as 'irrelevant' even though 'magnificent'. I deal with the dramatic function of Act IV, scene ii and Act IV, scene iii below.

[28] Cf. Coleridge, *Lectures on Shakespeare, etc.* (Bohn Edition), p. 406: 'Massinger is like a Flemish painter, in whose delineations objects appear as they do in nature, have the same force and truth, and produce the same effect upon the

—Doubtfull it stood,
As two spent Swimmers, that doe cling together,
And choake their Art—

applies not only to the battle but to the ambiguity of Macbeth's future fortunes. The impression conveyed is not only one of violence but of unnatural violence ('to bathe in reeking wounds')

Where the Norweyan Banners flowt the Skie,
And fanne our people cold.

(These lines alone should be sufficient answer to those who doubt the authenticity of the scene.) When Duncan says, 'What he hath lost, Noble *Macbeth* hath wonne', we hear the echo,

So from that Spring, whence comfort seem'd to come,
Discomfort swells,

—and this is not the only time the Captain's words can be applied in the course of the play. Nor is it fantastic to suppose that in the account of Macdonwald Shakespeare consciously provided a parallel with the Macbeth of the later acts when 'The multiplying Villanies of Nature swarme upon him'. After all, everybody has noticed the later parallel between Macbeth and Cawdor ('He was a Gentleman, on whom I built an absolute Trust').

A poem works by calling into play, directing and integrating certain interests. If we really accept the suggestion, which then becomes revolutionary, that *Macbeth* is a poem, it is clear that the impulses aroused in Act I, scenes i and ii, are part of the whole response, even if they are not all immediately relevant to the fortunes of the protagonist. If these scenes are 'the botching work of an interpolator', he botched to pretty good effect.

In Act I, scene iii, confusion is succeeded by uncertainty. The Witches

looke not like th' Inhabitants o' th' Earth,
And yet are on't.

Banquo asks Macbeth,

Why doe you start, and seeme to feare
Things that doe sound so faire?

He addresses the Witches,

---

spectator. But Shakespeare is beyond this;—he always by metaphors and figures involves in the thing considered a universe of past and possible experiences.'

You should be women,
And yet your Beards forbid me to interprete
That you are so. . . .
. . . i' th' name of truth
Are yet fantasticall, or that indeed
Which outwardly ye shew?

When they vanish, 'what seem'd corporall' melts 'as breath into the Winde'. The whole force of the uncertainty of the scene is gathered into Macbeth's soliloquy,

This supernaturall solliciting
Cannot be ill; cannot be good . . .

which with its sickening see-saw rhythm completes the impression of 'a phantasma, or a hideous dream'.[29] Macbeth's echoing of the Witches' 'Faire is foule' has often been commented upon.

In contrast to the preceding scenes, Act I, scene iv suggests the natural order which is shortly to be violated. It stresses: natural relationships—'children', 'servants', 'sons' and 'kinsmen'; honourable bonds and the political order—'liege', 'thanes', 'service', 'duty', 'loyalty', 'throne', 'state' and 'honour'; and the human 'love' is linked to the natural order of organic growth by images of husbandry. Duncan says to Macbeth,

I have begun to plant thee, and will labour
To make thee full of growing.

When he holds Banquo to his heart Banquo replies,

There if I grow,
The Harvest is your owne.

Duncan's last speech is worth particular notice,

. . . in his commendations, I am fed:
It is a Banquet to me.

---

[29] The parallel with *Julius Caesar,* Act II, scene i, 63–69, is worth notice:

Between the acting of a dreadfull thing,
And the first motion, all the Interim is
Like a Phantasma, or a hideous Dreame . . .

Macbeth speaks of 'the Interim', and his 'single state of Man' echoes Brutus'

The state of man,
Like to a little Kingdome, suffers then
The nature of an Insurrection.

The rhythm of Macbeth's speech is repeated in Lady Macbeth's

What thou would'st highly,
That would'st thou holily, etc.

At this point something should be said of what is meant by 'the natural order'. In *Macbeth* this comprehends both 'wild nature'—birds, beasts and reptiles—and humankind since 'humane statute purg'd the gentle Weale'. The specifically human aspect is related to the concept of propriety and degree,—

communities,
Degrees in Schooles and Brother-hoods in Cities,
Peacefull Commerce from dividable shores,
The primogenitive, and due of byrth,
Prerogative of Age, Crownes, Scepters, Lawrels.

In short, it represents society in harmony with nature, bound by love and friendship, and ordered by law and duty. It is one of the main axes of reference by which we take our emotional bearings in the play.

In the light of this the scene of Duncan's entry into the castle gains in significance. The critics have often remarked on the irony. What is not so frequently observed is that the key words of the scene are 'loved', 'wooingly', 'bed', 'procreant Cradle', 'breed, and haunt', all images of love and procreation, supernaturally sanctioned, for the associations of 'temple-haunting' colour the whole of the speeches of Banquo and Duncan.[30] We do violence to the play when we ignore Shakespeare's insistence on what may be called the 'holy supernatural' as opposed to the 'supernaturall solliciting' of the Witches. I shall return to this point. Meanwhile it is pertinent to remember that Duncan himself is 'The Lords anoynted Temple' (II.iii.70).[31]

The murder is explicitly presented as unnatural. After the greeting of Ross and Angus, Macbeth's heart knocks at his ribs 'against the use of Nature'. Lady Macbeth fears his 'humane kindnesse'; she wishes herself 'unsexed', that she may be troubled by 'no compunctious visitings of Nature', and invokes the 'murth'ring Ministers' who 'wait on Natures Mischiefe'. The murder is committed when

Nature seemes dead, and wicked Dreames abuse
The Curtain'd sleepe,

and it is accompanied by portents 'unnaturall, even like the deed that's done'. The sun remains obscured, and Duncan's horses 'Turn'd wilde in nature'. Besides these explicit references to the unnatural we notice the violence of the imagery—

---

[30] See F. R. Leavis, *How to Teach Reading* (now reprinted as an appendix to *Education and the University*), for a more detailed analysis of these lines.

[31] Later, Macduff says to Malcolm:

Thy Royall Father
Was a most Sainted King.
(IV.iii.108)

I have given Sucke, and know
How tender 'tis to love the Babe that milkes me,
I would, while it was smyling in my Face,
Have pluckt my Nipple from his Bonelesse Gummes,
And dasht the Braines out. . . .

Not only are the feelings presented unnatural in this sense, they are also strange—peculiar compounds which cannot be classified by any of the usual labels—'fear', 'disgust', etc. Macbeth's words towards the end of Act II, scene i serve to illustrate this:

Thou sowre [sure] and firme-set Earth
Heare not my steps, which way they walke, for feare
Thy very stones prate of my where-about,
And take the present horror from the time,
Which now sutes with it.

The first three lines imply a recognition of the enormity of the crime; Macbeth asks that the earth ('sure and firme-set' contrasted with the disembodied 'Murder' which 'moves like a Ghost') shall not hear his steps, for if it does so the very stones will speak and betray him—thereby breaking the silence and so lessening the horror. 'Take' combines two constructions. On the one hand, 'for fear they take the present horror from the time' expresses attraction, identification with the appropriate setting of his crime. But 'take' is also an imperative, expressing anguish and repulsion. 'Which now sutes with it' implies an acceptance of the horror, willing or reluctant according to the two meanings of the previous line. The unusual sliding construction (unusual in ordinary verse, there are other examples in Shakespeare, and in Donne) expresses the unusual emotion which is only crudely analysed if we call it a mixture of repulsion and attraction fusing into 'horror'.

'Confusion now hath made his Master-peece', and in the lull that follows the discovery of the murder, Ross and an Old Man, as chorus, echo the theme of unnatural disorder. The scene (and the Act) ends with a 'sentence' by the Old Man:

Gods benyson go with you, and with those
That would make good of bad, and Friends of Foes.

This, deliberately pronounced, has an odd ambiguous effect. The immediate reference is to Ross, who intends to make the best of a dubious business by accepting Macbeth as king. But Macduff also is destined to 'make good of bad' by destroying the evil. And an overtone of meaning takes our thoughts to Macbeth, whose attempt to make good of bad by restoring the natural order is the theme of the next movement; the tragedy lies in his inevitable failure.

A key is found in Macbeth's words spoken to the men hired to murder Banquo (III.i.91–100). When Dr. Bradley is discussing the possibility that *Macbeth* has been abridged he remarks ('very aptly' according to the Arden editor), 'surely, anyone who wanted to cut the play down would have operated, say, on Macbeth's talk with Banquo's murderers, or on Act III, scene vi, or on the very long dialogue of Malcolm and Macduff, instead of reducing the most exciting part of the drama'.[32] No, the speech to the murderers is not very 'exciting' —but its function should be obvious to anyone who is not blinded by Dr. Bradley's preconceptions about 'drama'. By accepted canons it is an irrelevance; actually it stands as a symbol of the order that Macbeth wishes to restore. In the catalogue,

> Hounds, and Greyhounds, Mungrels, Spaniels, Curres,
> Showghes, Water-Rugs, and Demy-Wolves

are merely 'dogs', but Macbeth names each one individually; and

> the valued file
> Distinguishes the swift, the slow, the subtle,
> The House-keeper, the Hunter, every one
> According to the gift, which bounteous Nature
> Hath in him clos'd.

It is an image of order, each one in his degree. At the beginning of the scene, we remember, Macbeth had arranged 'a feast', 'a solemn supper', at which 'society' should be 'welcome'. And when alone he suggests the ancient harmonies by rejecting in idea the symbols of their contraries—'a fruitlesse Crowne', 'a barren Scepter', and an 'unlineall' succession. But this new 'health' is 'sickly' whilst Banquo lives, and can only be made 'perfect' by his death. In an attempt to re-create an order based on murder, disorder makes fresh inroads. This is made explicit in the next scene (III.ii). Here the snake, usually represented as the most venomous of creatures, stands for the natural order which Macbeth has 'scotched' but which will 'close, and be her selfe'.[33]

At this point in the play there is a characteristic confusion. At

---

[32] *Shakespearean Tragedy,* p. 469. *Macbeth,* Arden Edition, pp. xxi–xxii. I discuss the importance to Act III, scene vi, and of the Malcolm-Macduff dialogue later.

[33] The murder of Banquo, like the murder of Duncan, is presented as a violation of natural continuity and natural order. Macbeth will 'cancell and teare to pieces that great Bond' which keeps him pale. 'Bond' has a more than general significance. The line is clearly associated with Lady Macbeth's 'But in them, Natures Coppie's not eterne', and the full force of the words is only brought out if we remember that when Shakespeare wrote them, copyholders formed numerically the largest land-holding class in England whose appeal was always to 'immemorial antiquity' and 'times beyond the memory of man'. The Macbeth-Banquo opposition is emphasized when we learn that Banquo's line will 'stretch out to the cracke of Doome' (IV.i.117). Macbeth is cut off from the natural sequence, 'He has no children' (IV.iii.217) he is a 'Monster' (V.vii.54). Macbeth's isolation is fully brought out in the last Act.

the end of Act III, scene ii, Macbeth says, 'Things bad begun, make strong themselves by ill', that is, all that he can do is to ensure his physical security by a second crime, although earlier (III.i.106–107) he had aimed at complete 'health' by the death of Banquo and Fleance, and later he says that the murder of Fleance would have made him

> perfect,
> Whole as the Marble, founded as the Rocke.
> (III.iv.21–22)

The truth is only gradually disentangled from this illusion.

The situation is magnificently presented in the banquet scene. Here speech, action and symbolism combine. The stage direction *'Banquet prepar'd'* is the first pointer. In Shakespeare, as Mr. Wilson Knight has remarked, banquets are almost invariably symbols of rejoicing, friendship and concord. Significantly, the nobles sit in due order.

> MACBETH You know your owne degrees, sit downe:
> At first and last, the hearty welcome.
> LORDS Thankes to your Majesty.
> MACBETH Our selfe will mingle with Society,
> And play the humble Host:
> Our Hostesse keepes her State, but in best time
> We will require her welcome.
> LADY MACBETH Pronounce it for me Sir, to all our Friends,
> For my heart speakes, they are welcome.
> *Enter first Murderer.*

There is no need for comment. In a sense the scene marks the climax of the play. One avenue has been explored; 'Society', 'Host', 'Hostesse', 'Friends' and 'Welcome' repeat a theme which henceforward is heard only faintly until it is taken up in the final orchestration, when it appears as 'Honor, Love, Obedience, Troopes of Friends'. With the disappearance of the ghost, Macbeth may be 'a man againe', but he has, irretrievably,

> displac'd the mirth,
> Broke the good meeting, with most admir'd disorder.

The end of the scene is in direct contrast to its beginning.

> Stand not upon the order of your going,
> But go at once

echoes ironically, 'You know your owne degrees, sit downe'.

Before we attempt to disentangle the varied threads of the last Act, two more scenes call for particular comment. The first is the scene in Macduff's castle. Almost without exception the critics have stressed the pathos of young Macduff, his 'innocent prattle', his likeness to Arthur, and so on—reactions appropriate to the work of Sir James Barrie which obscure the complex dramatic function of the scene.[34] In the first place, it echoes in different keys the theme of the false appearance, of doubt and confusion. At its opening we are perplexed with questions: —Is Macduff a traitor? If so, to whom, to Macbeth or to his wife? Was his flight due to wisdom or to fear? Ross says,

> But cruell are the times, when we are Traitors
> And do not know our selves: when we hold Rumor
> From what we feare, yet know not what we feare.

Lady Macduff says of her son,

> Father'd he is,
> And yet hee's Father-lesse.[35]

She teases him with riddles, and he replies with questions.

Secondly, the scene shows the spreading evil. As Fletcher has pointed out, Macduff and his wife are 'representatives of the interests of loyalty and domestic affection'.[36] There is much more in the death of young Macduff than 'pathos'; the violation of the natural order is completed by the murder. But there is even more than this. That the tide is about to turn against Macbeth is suggested both by the rhythm and imagery of Ross's speech:

> But cruell are the times, when we are Traitors
> And do not know our selves: when we hold Rumor
> From what we feare, yet know not what we feare,
> But floate upon a wilde and violent Sea
> Each way, and move—[37]

The comma after 'way', the complete break after 'move', give the rhythm of a tide, pausing at the turn. And when Lady Macduff answers the Murderer's question, 'Where is your husband?'

> I hope in no place so unsanctified,
> Where such as thou may'st find him

---

[34] Dr. Bradley says of this and the following scene: 'They have a technical value in helping to give the last stage of the action the form of a conflict between Macbeth and Macduff. But their chief function is of another kind. It is to touch the heart with a sense of beauty and pathos, to open the springs of love and of tears.'—*Shakespearean Tragedy*, p. 391, see also p. 394.

[35] Compare the equivocation about Macduff's birth.

[36] Quoted by Furness, p. 218. The whole passage from Fletcher is worth attention.

[37] The substitution of a dash for the full stop after 'move' is the only alteration that seems necessary in the Folio text. The other emendations of various editors ruin both the rhythm and the idiom. Ross is in a hurry and breaks off; he begins the next line, 'Shall not be long', omitting 'I' or 'it'—which some editors needlessly restore. In the Folio a colon is used to indicate the breaking off of a sentence in Act V, scene iii, 20.

we recall the associations set up in Act III, scene vi, a scene of choric commentary upon Macduff's flight to England, to the 'Pious Edward', 'the Holy King'.

Although the play moves swiftly, it does not move with a simple directness. Its complex subtleties include cross-currents, the ebb and flow of opposed thoughts and emotions. The scene in Macduff's castle, made up of doubts, riddles, paradoxes and uncertainties, ends with an affirmation, 'Thou ly'st thou shagge-ear'd Villaine'. But this is immediately followed, not by the downfall of Macbeth, but by a long scene which takes up once more the theme of mistrust, disorder and evil.

The conversation between Macduff and Malcolm has never been adequately explained. We have already seen Dr. Bradley's opinion of it. The Clarendon editors say, 'The poet no doubt felt this scene was needed to supplement the meagre parts assigned to Malcolm and Macduff'. If this were all, it might be omitted. Actually the Malcolm-Macduff dialogue has at least three functions. Obviously Macduff's audience with Malcolm and the final determination to invade Scotland help on the story, but this is of subordinate importance. It is clear also that Malcolm's suspicion and the long testing of Macduff emphasize the mistrust that has spread from the central evil of the play.[38] But the main purpose of the scene is obscured unless we realize its function as choric commentary. In alternating speeches the evil that Macbeth has caused is explicitly stated, without extenuation. And it is stated impersonally.

Each new Morne,
New Widdowes howle, new Orphans cry, new sorowes
Strike heaven on the face, that it resounds
As if it felt with Scotland, and yell'd out
Like Syllable of Dolour.

Our Country sinkes beneath the yoake,
It weepes, it bleeds, and each new day a gash
Is added to her wounds.

Not in the Legions
Of horrid Hell, can come a Divell more damn'd
In evils, to top Macbeth.
I grant him Bloody,
Luxurious, Avaricious, False, Deceitfull,
Sodaine, Malicious, smacking of every sinne
That has a name.

---

[38] As an example of the slight strands that are gathered into the pattern of the play consider the function of the third Murderer in Act III, scene iii. It seems that Macbeth has sent him 'to make security doubly sure'. Only after some doubt do the first two decide that the third 'needs not our mistrust'.

With this approach we see the relevance of Malcolm's self-accusation. He has ceased to be a person. His lines repeat and magnify the evils that have already been attributed to Macbeth, acting as a mirror wherein the ills of Scotland are reflected. And the statement of evil is strengthened by contrast with the opposite virtues, 'As Justice, Verity, Temp'rance, Stablenesse'.

There is no other way in which the scene can be read. And if dramatic fitness is not sufficient warrant for this approach, we can refer to the pointers that Shakespeare has provided. Macbeth is 'luxurious' and 'avaricious', and the first sins mentioned by Malcolm in an expanded statement are lust and avarice. When he declares,

> Nay, had I powre, I should
> Poure the sweet Milke of Concord, into Hell,
> Uprore the universall peace, confound
> All unity on earth,

we remember that this is what Macbeth has done.[39] Indeed Macduff is made to answer,

> These Evils thou repeat'st upon thy selfe,
> Hath banish'd me from Scotland.[40]

Up to this point at least the impersonal function of the speaker is predominant. And even when Malcolm, once more a person in a play, announces his innocence, it is impossible not to hear the impersonal overtone:

> For even now
> I put my selfe to thy Direction, and
> Unspeake mine owne detraction. Heere abjure
> The taints, and blames I laide upon my selfe,
> For strangers to my Nature.

He speaks for Scotland, and for the forces of order. The 'scotch'd Snake' will 'close, and be herselfe'.

There are only two alternatives; either Shakespeare was a bad dramatist, or his critics have been badly misled by mistaking the *dramatis personae* for real persons in this scene. Unless of course the ubiquitous Interpolator has been at work upon it.

---

[39] For a more specific reference see Act IV, scene i, 50–61,—

> Though the treasure
> Of Natures Germaine tumble altogether,
> Even till destruction sicken . . .

[40] 'Hath' is third person plural. See Abbott, *Shakespearian Grammar,* §334. I admit the lines are ambiguous but they certainly bear the interpretation I have given them. Indeed most editors print, 'upon thyself / Have banished . . .'

I have called *Macbeth* a statement of evil; but it is a statement not of a philosophy but of ordered emotion. This ordering is of course a continuous process (hence the importance of the scrupulous analysis of each line), it is not merely something that happens in the last Act corresponding to the dénouement or unravelling of the plot. All the same, the interests aroused are heightened in the last Act before they are finally 'placed', and we are given a vantage point from which the whole course of the drama may be surveyed in retrospect. There is no formula that will describe this final effect. It is no use saying that we are 'quietened', 'purged' or 'exalted' at the end of *Macbeth* or of any other tragedy. It is no use taking one step nearer the play and saying we are purged, etc., because we see the downfall of a wicked man or because we realize the justice of Macbeth's doom whilst retaining enough sympathy for him or admiration of his potential qualities to be filled with a sense of 'waste'. It is no use discussing the effect in abstract terms at all; we can only discuss it in terms of the poet's concrete realization of certain emotions and attitudes.

At this point it is necessary to return to what I have already said about the importance of images of grace and of the holy supernatural in the play. For the last hundred years or so the critics have not only sentimentalized Macbeth—ignoring the completeness with which Shakespeare shows his final identification with evil—but they have slurred the passages in which the positive good is presented by means of religious symbols. In Act III the banquet scene is immediately[41] followed by a scene in which Lennox and another Lord (both completely impersonal) discuss the situation; the last half of their dialogue is of particular importance. The verse has none of the power of, say, Macbeth's soliloquies, but it would be a mistake to call it undistinguished; it is serenely harmonious, and its tranquillity contrasts with the turbulence of the scenes that immediately precede it and follow it, as its images of grace contrast with their 'toile and trouble'. Macduff has fled to 'the Pious Edward', 'the Holy King', who has received Malcolm 'with such grace'. Lennox prays for the aid of 'some holy Angell',

> that a swift blessing
> May soone returne to this our suffering Country,
> Under a hand accurs'd.

---

[41] If we omit Act III, scene v where for once the editors' 'spurious' may be allowed to stand. I thought at first that Shakespeare intended to portray the Witches at this point as rather shoddy creatures, thereby intensifying the general irony. Certainly the rhythm of Hecate's speech is banal—but so is the obvious rhythm of *Sweeney Agonistes*, and it does provide a contrast with the harmony of the verse in the next scene. Certainly also Shakespeare did not intend to portray the Witches as in any way 'dignified' ('Dignified, impressive, sexless beings, ministers of fate and the supernatural powers . . . existing in the elemental poetry of wind and storm'—*Macbeth,* Arden Edition, p. xlii). But the verse is too crude to serve even this purpose.

And the 'other Lord' answers, 'Ile send my Prayers with him'. Many of the phrases are general and abstract—'grace', 'the malevolence of Fortune', 'his high respect'—but one passage has an individual particularity that gives it prominence:

> That by the helpe of these (with him above
> To ratifie the Worke) we may againe
> Give to our Tables meate, sleepe to our Nights:
> Free from our Feasts, and Banquets bloody knives;
> Do faithful Homage, and receive free Honors,
> All which we pine for now.

Food and sleep, society and the political order are here, as before, represented as supernaturally sanctioned. I have suggested that this passage is recalled for a moment in Lady Macduff's answer to the Murderer (IV.ii.80), and it is certainly this theme which is taken up when the Doctor enters after the Malcolm-Macduff dialogue in Act IV, scene iii; the reference to the King's Evil may be a compliment to King James, but it is not merely that. We have only to remember that the unseen Edward stands for the powers that are to prove 'the Med'cine of the sickly Weale' of Scotland to see the double meaning in

> there are a crew of wretched Soules
> That stay his Cure. . . .

Their disease 'is called the Evill'. The 'myraculous worke', the 'holy Prayers', 'the healing Benediction', Edward's 'vertue', the 'sundry Blessings . . . that speake him full of Grace' are reminders not only of the evil against which Malcolm is seeking support, but of the positive qualities against which the evil and disorder must be measured. Scattered notes ('Gracious England', 'Christendome', 'heaven', 'gentle Heavens') remind us of the theme until the end of the scene, when we know that Macbeth (the 'Hell-Kite', 'this Fiend of Scotland')

> Is ripe for shaking, and the Powers above
> Put on their Instruments.

The words quoted are not mere formalities; they have a positive function, and help to determine the way in which we shall respond to the final scenes.

The description of the King's Evil (IV.iii.141–159) has a particular relevance; it is directly connected with the disease metaphors of the last Act;[42] and these are strengthened by combining within themselves the ideas of disorder and of the unnatural which run throughout the

[42] The original audience would be helped to make the connexion if, as is likely, the Doctor of Act IV, scene iii, and the Doctor of Act V were played by the same actor, probably without any change of dress. We are not meant to think of two Doctors in the play (Dr. A. of Harley Street and Dr. B. of Edinburgh) but simply, in each case, of 'a Doctor'.

play. Lady Macbeth's sleep-walking is a 'slumbry agitation', and 'a great perturbation in Nature'. Some say Macbeth is 'mad'. We hear of his 'distemper'd cause', and of his 'pester'd senses' which

> recoyle and start,
> When all that is within him, do's condemne
> It selfe, for being there.

In the play general impressions are pointed by reference to the individual and particular (cf. Act IV, scene iii, where 'the general cause is given precision by the 'Fee-griefe due to some single breast'); whilst at the same time particular impressions are reflected and magnified. Not only Macbeth and his wife but the whole land is sick. Caithness says,

> Meet we the Med'cine of the sickly Weale,
> And with him poure we in our Countries purge,
> Each drop of us.

And Lennox replies,

> Or so much as it needes,
> To dew the Soveraigne Flower, and drowne the Weeds
> (V.ii.27–30)

—an admirable example, by the way, of the kind of fusion already referred to, since we have not only the weed-flower opposition, but a continuation of the medical metaphor in 'Soveraigne', which means both 'royal' and 'powerfully remedial'.[43] And the images of health and disease are clearly related to moral good and evil. The Doctor says of Lady Macbeth,

> More needs she the Divine, than the Physitian:
> God, God forgive us all.

Macbeth asks him,

---

[43] Macbeth himself says:

> If thou could'st, Doctor, cast
> The Water of my Land, finde her Disease,
> And purge it to a sound and pristine Health,
> I would applaud thee to the very Eccho.

And he continues:

> What Rubarb, Senna, or what Purgative drugge
> Would scowre these English hence?
> (V.iii.50–56)

The characteristic reversal (the English forces being represented as an impurity which has to be 'scoured') need not surprise us since Macbeth is the speaker.

> Can'st thou not Minister to a minde diseas'd,
> Plucke from the Memory a rooted Sorrow,
> Raze out the written troubles of the Braine,
> And with some sweet Oblivious Antidote
> Cleanse the stufft bosome, of that perillous stuffe
> Which weighes upon the heart?

There is terrible irony in his reply to the Doctor's 'Therein the Patient must minister to himselfe': 'Throw Physicke to the Dogs, Ile none of it.'

We have already noticed the association of the ideas of disease and of the unnatural in these final scenes—

> unnatural deeds
> Do breed unnatural troubles,

and there is propriety in Macbeth's highly charged metaphor,

> My way of life
> Is falne into the Seare, the yellow Leafe.

But the unnatural has now another part to play, in the peculiar 'reversal' that takes place at the end of *Macbeth.* Hitherto the agent of the unnatural has been Macbeth. Now it is Malcolm who commands Birnam Wood to move, it is 'the good Macduff' who reveals his unnatural birth, and the opponents of Macbeth whose 'deere causes' would 'excite the mortified man'. Hitherto Macbeth has been the deceiver, 'mocking the time with fairest show'; now Malcolm orders,

> Let every Souldier hew him downe a Bough,
> And bear't before him, thereby shall we shadow
> The numbers of our Hoast, and make discovery
> Erre in report of us.

Our first reaction is to make some such remark as 'Nature becomes unnatural in order to rid itself of Macbeth'. But this is clearly inadequate; we have to translate it and define our impressions in terms of our response to the play at this point. By associating with the opponents of evil the ideas of deceit and of the unnatural, previously associated solely with Macbeth and the embodiments of evil, Shakespeare emphasizes the disorder and at the same time frees our minds from the burden of the horror. After all, the movement of Birnam Wood and Macduff's unnatural birth have a simple enough explanation.

There is a parallel here with the disorder of the last Act. It begins with Lady Macbeth sleep-walking—a 'slumbry agitation'—and the remaining scenes are concerned with marches, stratagems, fighting, suicide, and death in battle. If we merely read the play we are liable to overlook the importance of the sights and sounds which are obvious on the stage. The frequent stage directions should be observed—*Drum and Colours, Enter Malcolm . . . and Soldiers Marching, A Cry within of Women*—and there are continuous directions for *Alarums, Flourishes,* and fighting. Macduff orders,

> Make all our Trumpets speak, give them all breath,
> Those clamorous Harbingers of Blood, and Death,

and he traces Macbeth by the noise of fighting:

> That way the noise is: Tyrant shew thy face.
> . . . There thou should'st be,
> By this great clatter, one of greatest note
> Seemes bruited.

There are other suggestions of disorder throughout the Act. Macbeth

> cannot buckle his distemper'd cause
> Within the belt of Rule.

He orders, 'Come, put mine Armour on', and almost in the same breath, 'Pull't off I say'. His 'Royal Preparation' is a noisy confusion. He wishes 'th' estate o' th' world were now undon', though the tone is changed now since he bade the Witches answer him,

> Though bladed Corne be lodg'd and Trees blown downe,
> Though Castles topple on their Warders heads:
> Though Pallaces, and Pyramids do slope
> Their heads to their Foundations.

But all this disorder has now a positive tendency, towards the good which Macbeth had attempted to destroy, and which he names as 'Honor, Love, Obedience, Troopes of Friends'. At the beginning of the battle Malcolm says,

> Cosins, I hope the dayes are neere at hand
> That Chambers will be safe,

and Menteith answers, 'We doubt it nothing'. Siward takes up the theme of certainty as opposed to doubt:

> Thoughts speculative, their unsure hopes relate,
> But certaine issue, stroakes must arbitrate,
> Towards which, advance the warre.

And doubt and illusion are finally dispelled:

> Now neere enough:
> Your leavy Skreenes throw downe,
> And shew like those you are.

By now there should be no danger of our misinterpreting the greatest of Macbeth's final speeches.

> To morrow, and to morrow, and to morrow,
> Creepes in this petty pace from day to day,
> To the last syllable of Recorded time.
> And all our yesterdays, have lighted Fooles
> The way to dusty death. Out, out, breefe Candle.
> Life's but a walking Shadow, a poore Player,
> That struts and frets his houre upon the Stage,
> And then is heard no more. It is a Tale
> Told by an Ideot, full of sound and fury
> Signifying nothing.

The theme of the false appearance is revived—with a difference. It is not only that Macbeth sees life as deceitful, but the poetry is so fine that we are almost bullied into accepting an essential ambiguity in the final statement of the play, as though Shakespeare were expressing his own 'philosophy' in the lines. But the lines are 'placed' by the tendency of the last Act (order emerging from disorder, truth emerging from behind deceit), culminating in the recognition of the Witches' equivocation ('And be these Jugling Fiends no more believ'd . . .'), the death of Macbeth, and the last words of Siward, Macduff and Malcolm (V.vii.64–105).

This tendency has behind it the whole weight of the positive values which Shakespeare has already established, and which are evoked in Macbeth's speech—

> My way of life
> Is falne into the Seare, the yellow Leafe,
> And that which should accompany Old-Age,
> As Honor, Love, Obedience, Troopes of Friends,
> I must not looke to have: but in their stead,
> Curses, not lowd but deepe, Mouth-honor, breath
> Which the poore heart would faine deny, and dare not.

Dr. Bradley claims, on the strength of this and the 'To-morrow, and to-morrow' speech, that Macbeth's 'ruin is never complete. To the end he never totally loses our sympathy. . . . In the very depths a gleam of his native love of goodness, and with it a tinge of tragic grandeur, rests upon him.' But to concentrate attention thus on the *personal* implications of these lines is to obscure the fact that they have an even more important function as the keystone of the system of values that gives emotional coherence to the play. Certainly those values are likely to remain obscured if we concentrate our attention upon 'the two great terrible figures, who dwarf all the remaining characters of the drama', if we ignore the 'unexciting' or 'undramatic' scenes, or if conventional 'sympathy for the hero' is allowed to distort the pattern of the whole.

I must repeat that I have no illusions about the adequacy of these remarks as criticism; they are merely pointers. But if we follow them our criticism at least will not be deflected, by too great a stress upon 'personality', into inquiries into 'latent motives and policies not avowed', or into pseudo-critical investigations that are only slightly parodied by the title of this essay.

CHARACTER GROUPING AND PLOT

The Nature of Plot in Drama

Una Ellis-Fermor

If we approach the play by way of plot instead of by way of character, we shall reach similar conclusions. For since character, plot, imagery, language, verbal music are only aspects of the indivisible whole which is the play, whatever we discover in one of them to be essential to the whole will reveal itself also in others. We separate them by virtue of an agreed convention. But in relation to the whole and to each other they are inseparable; each may in fact appear at times to be an aspect of another, since their territories are ultimately indivisible. And just as what drama presents to our imagination as character differs from what life presents, so is it with plot, which is not identical with a series of actual events or even with the groups of events that sometimes seem to emerge in life. Each has a similar relation to its counterpart in what we call the actual world in that in each the artist's imagination has selected from the raw material on which his inspiration worked and revealed a pattern inherent in it. And the nature of this imaginative selection is determined by the mode of the dramatist, so that in every aspect of the technique we may trace a corresponding pattern in harmony with the form of the whole to which it contributes.[1] Each aspect of the technique, then, plays its part in revealing the dramatist's apprehension of life, but plot may fitly follow character here since they merge naturally into each other through the continuous interplay between individual character and even within a given play.

From Una Ellis-Fermor, *Shakespeare the Dramatist.* Reprinted by permission of Methuen & Company, Ltd.

[1] On the nature of the patterns defined by selection see [Ellis-Fermor, *Shakespeare the Dramatist* (London: Methuen, 1961), Chapter III].

Plot, indeed, whether simple or complex, single or multiple, may be said to have two aspects, the spatial, which is concerned with character-grouping, and the temporal, which has regard to the order and relation of events.[2] The first, like a picture or a statuary group, may be thought of (if we adopt Lessing's distinction)[3] as static in time and extended in space and in studying it we consider the characters not in terms of their experience or of their effect upon the plot, but in terms of the illumination we receive from their juxtaposition and their relative positions in the composition. The other approach to plot shows it as extended in time and gives us the ordered sequence of causally related events. This again appears, upon closer inspection, to have two strands, the inner and the outer plot or drama, both moving continuously forward in time, both intermittently revealed and inseparably related.[4] The differences in mode that we have already observed may be traced in both these aspects of the plot and in both levels of the second.

Thus, in the spatial aspect a dramatist of one kind will use a design which itself seems to demonstrate some theme or argument, a logical, expository grouping that constitutes an explanation or furnishes a key to some problems, reminding us sometimes of the Victorian narrative school of painting in which the picture 'told a story'. Another, having no demonstrable theme, problem, or thesis, having no palpable design upon his drama and no purpose but the artist's fundamental purpose of making a work of art, will reveal wholly different implications through the composition of his picture.

The first will present a carefully planned range of characters that balance each other as in Ibsen's *Ghosts,*[5] where the five are so selected that each contributes to the central idea of the play one part of the final, composite effect. The dead hand of convention and obligation has subdued to its purposes Pastor Manders, who has thus become its vehicle and its exponent, but it has driven Mrs Alving to rebellion and so to emancipation of thought. Modifying the contrasted positions of these two are three others who show the workings of the compulsion upon related, yet differing, types of mind and character. Each is a variation on the central theme and the whole group indicates the salient effects, and in representative proportions: Regine has rebelled without thought or heart-searching and has suffered the degeneration that comes of rejecting the good and the bad alike in a given social

[2] The intimacy of the relationship between character and plot again becomes clear when we consider that the groupings of character may be regarded either as the structural aspect of character or the spatial aspect of plot. Upon the spatial aspect of plot, see G. Wilson Knight, *The Wheel of Fire,* Chap. I.

[3] See *Laokoon,* Chaps. XV–XVIII. 'Es bleibt dabei: die Zeitfolge ist das Gebiet des Dichters, so wie der Raum das Gebiet des Malers.' (Chap. XVIII.)

[4] The relations of these two levels of plot within the time continuum admit obviously of wide variety in kind and spacing.

[5] [See Ellis-Fermor, *op. cit.,* p. 143.]

code; her 'father', Engstrand, as immoral as she but more shrewd, has cunningly observed the workings of the system and found his account in playing upon its victims; Osvald has escaped psychological harm only to be destroyed by the physical consequences from which nothing could save him. Each bears mute or articulate testimony to the weight of this dead hand and their relationship demonstrates the operation of the curse; a Laocoon group, figures still imprisoned or too late emancipated to maintain valid life.

But another dramatist may relate his characters in such a way that, instead of a close-locked group, itself the image of the operation of a force, with each member sustaining an essential part of the whole in strict relation of contrast and likeness to the others, we find characters widely differing as individuals or as groups, and so placed that our imaginations are induced to supply, it may be [all] unawares, intermediate and background figures or moods that complete a harmony of wide range and complexity, suggesting to our minds not a clear-cut image or a dominant theme, but the breadth of life and of humanity. We recognize that without such subtlety of relationship between the figures in the picture there would be no harmony, but only a scattering of portraits, vivid it might be and even varied, but giving no significance to the content of the play. Somewhere in the dramatist's way of relating them lies the stimulus to which our imaginations respond; here we may find secret impressions conveyed by the grouping itself. Shakespeare in as early a play as *A Midsummer Night's Dream* already prompts us by the spatial aspect of his plot alone to the 'generation of still breeding thoughts' by which we 'people this little world'.

And what a range this world has! Our first glance shows us princes and their subjects, townsfolk, peasants, and craftsmen; lovers, parents, and children; the wide variety of personality which ranges from the judicial magnanimity of Theseus to the crabbed Egeus, the unmoral fairy world, the childish egotism of the young lovers and the hearty freedom of the peasants. But delicate threads of relationship join these figures or groups into a more complex and subtle pattern. Theseus and Hippolyta are princes, but so also are Oberon and Titania; even Bottom is the born ruler of his village community. Hermia, Helena, Lysander, and Demetrius are lovers after one fashion, but so, after another and a better, are Theseus and Hippolyta, and so in their strange way are Oberon and Titania. Not only are there the human relations of parent and child, lover and lover, but also a wide range of age, from the old Egeus and the mature Theseus to the four young lovers, all made significant by the constant presence of the ageless, immortal fairies. At the centre still is Theseus, the responsible father of his people, at once submitting to and upholding the social order of his dukedom; but the individualists Bottom and Puck are there too, each absorbed, in delighted preoccupation, with fantasies humdrum or exquisite of his own creating. And so the network spreads, linking, each to each, characters in all else disparate and seemingly unrelated. Each figure in a play whose spatial structure is of this kind is like an illuminated point, independent and set at a distance from each of the others; yet seemingly endless patterns now suggest themselves by linking each to several others and the central figure to all. There is here no palpable intention of suggesting by the disposal of the characters the multitudinous complexity of life, still less of laying upon each the task of sustaining its share of an emergent idea. But the imaginary line that flashes from one corner to another of the picture passes through (and gathers up by its passing) many who are not present in the play. Prince, townsman, peasant, craftsman, reveal when we link them the invisible presence of intermediate 'occupations' and 'trades'. And the fairies, creatures of yet another kind, set off and illuminate by contrast the human groups and their organisation. Age, maturity, youth suggest between them the span of human life, but the ageless fairies reveal by their timelessness the significance of time which determines human life. And what our imaginations receive is an impression not of a theme or of an idea but of a world and a life in which every individual is essentially itself and not primarily a part of a thematic design, but in which, nevertheless, each is related to others by contrast or likeness of age, sex, function, or temperament, so that none can be thought of for long in isolation. But it is the secret impressions that have given us the sense of this; the imaginary lines which linked light to light and drew out from their background of invisibility those hidden figures whose momentary and imagined presence made up the world in which the people of the play lived and were at home. The function of the dramatic mode here is to enrich, fill out, and if need be modify the image of the world that surrounds and reveals itself through the characters.[6] Just so, when we considered these as individuals, it was seen to reveal the fuller world within each character.

. . .

But in the plays of Shakespeare's maturity, we perceive a third dimension, akin to the depth given by perspective to a painting; in dimensions

---

[6] The nature of this kind of spatial structure becomes clearer still if we set beside it yet another play of Ibsen, *The Pillars of the Community*, whose character grouping might appear at first glance to resemble that of *A Midsummer Night's Dream*. The relations between the many strands of action and the direct links between the numerous characters reveal to a careful inspection the fact that the most seemingly detached of these strands are related to at least three or four others. But there is a palpable purpose behind this only less evident than that behind the statuesque grouping of the characters in *Ghosts*. Again, the characters are related to certain problems and responsible for revealing them. They are so placed not so much to imply a world of men as to contribute to a balance of forces. Through them all runs the dominant theme of Bernicks' conversion, the progress of his soul through crime and punishment to redemption. Ibsen gathers up and puts into Bernick's hands all the threads of the plot and consequently all the responsibility. We assist throughout the play at an inevitable progress to a triumphant demonstration. But the function of the spatial aspect is to contribute to our understanding of the emergent theme, rather than to extend the implication of the play.

and tone alike the characters retreat successively from the foreground towards a background where they reach a virtual vanishing point.[7] In the play of *Antony and Cleopatra* the magnitude of the issues, the grandeur of the chief characters, the multiplicity of figures and events witness to the vastness of its design and the cosmic imagery leads the imagination on to a universe beyond, into which the immediate world

---

[7] This technique in painting is, of course, common and elementary knowledge. But even at the risk of offering a naïve comment, I should like to describe those aspects which appear relevant also to the study of drama. This footnote should obviously be passed over by those who know the elements of the technique of painting and, even more obviously, by those who paint.

The familiar ways of conveying the impression of distance are by the perspective of line and of colour; in line by diminution of size in identical objects and in colour by diminution of tone or change of line. Thus, both in nature and in painting, we observe fewer distinctive characteristics as objects become more distant and, as a corollary, they make less claim on the attention. This does not imply that they appear less real. A tree at a distance does not normally appear unreal; it is merely, by reason of its position, less individualized than a tree in the foreground. We can see the pattern of the window-curtain in the house across the road; we cannot distinguish even the windows in a farm near Calais seen from Dover Beach. But we accept both as houses. Moreover, in both the trees and the houses, loss of size has been accompanied by loss of tone (or brilliance of hue). When the atmosphere does not contribute a colour of its own, grey, blue, purple, increasing in proportion to the distance, we are able to observe pure loss of tone with distance. This can conveniently be done in, for instance, the Painted Desert of Arizona, where objects eighty miles away will be found surprisingly to retain some of their colour, but to retain it in diluted form. This may perhaps be regarded as a case of pure colour perspective, since nothing has been added by 'veils' of atmosphere. Even when atmosphere does interfere, there is still a true relationship between line and colour perspective, though it may sometimes take a fantastic form; when one is painting a tree in a London fog, the furthest branch may be reduced to a pale grey, while the nearest is dark and vivid and hardly any linear perspective is noticed. The law is ultimately the same: with increasing distance there must be both reduction of size and dilution of colour; though the one may have its maximum effect and the other its minimum, in any given scene there must be a consistent relationship between the two. What is essential is the diminishing potency of the object in the picture. The loss of tone also accounts for the loss of detail; the main patches of colour are themselves diluted, the shadows grow paler, the highlights dimmer until there is, at a sufficient distance, no distinction between the three. Anyone who attempts to paint mountain or desert scenery recognizes this regressive loss of tone, its contribution to the sense of distance and the relative inability of linear perspective to achieve this by itself.

Just as certain painters (Cuyp, Van Goyen, Capelle, Hendrik Avercamp) achieve the effect of great distance and depth of scene by continuous and simultaneous perspective of line and colour, so, too, certain dramatists use a corresponding technique in the spatial structure of their plays.

Nor, as we have said, does this recession from the foreground of the play rob the characters or episodes of reality, but only of distinction in detail. The essential reality of the minor figures remains up to the verge of visibility (at which point a sentry's only speech may be 'My Lord?'). Here, admittedly, it is hard to find individuality and it would be an ill-constructed drama in which we could, for a dramatist, though aware of the reality of even the least of his minors, will nevertheless reduce him to an almost invisible figure if his function in the play sets him in the far distant background.

of the play seems limitlessly extended. The spatial structure too plays its own, considerable part in this final impression. The spatial relations of the characters may be traced as they were in *A Midsummer Night's Dream* and the amplitude of the later play is then seen to embrace the whole known world. But just as in a painting the sense of vastness may be given not only by the spread of the foreground, but also by depth and distance,[8] so, in a play, the relative proportions in function and the relative vividness in personality complete that impression of extent already made upon us by greatness of scope, character, and event. In the greatest plays, moreover, distance itself gives prominence to the chief characters; the attention of the subordinate agents is focused upon them, investing them with significance which draws some of its potency from their spatial relations. A whole universe, it seems, is intent upon the action of those foreground figures and their power in turn reaches to the uttermost bounds of the world, to figures upon the very border of invisibility. The dramatic function of perspective in *Antony and Cleopatra* is to evoke, by this secret impression, the sense at once of vastness, of coherence, and of significance.

When we attempt to group in the mind's eye the figures in this play, we are struck at once by the operation of a simple law; those that are most vivid in personality are also those that have the most important functions. A character of relatively minor importance who makes a brief appearance in an early scene and with no evident or immediate promise of a greater part to play later, yet stirs the imagination and remains vividly in our minds, will almost invariably appear again in a later scene when his function will be graver or weightier. The marks of such a character may be of various kinds; the language he speaks, his imagery, or a noticeable habit of syntax; the attention he draws to himself from other characters; a peculiar relation to one of the main characters, even if it is only our own emotional response to him; some light thrown upon him by the attitude of that other or by some comment drawn from him. This, which we may describe as the colour or tone initially given to a minor character, will be found to correspond, when the whole play is before us, with the function assigned him, with his ultimate position in the plot. Characters, on the other hand, whose initial speeches seem curiously colourless in view of the number of scenes in which they promise to appear, turn out to have in fact little function beyond that of frequently standing on the stage; they do not speak much or contribute much; they are found to be as limited in their ultimate function as they are in their initial colour. There is thus,

---

[8] Frith's *Ramsgate Sands* is a long, crowded ribbon of figures that gives little sense of distance, but Hendrik Avercamp's *Winter* (a far smaller canvas) is a wide and melancholy plain of ice, its distances defined by diminishing figures, progressively smaller and fainter. The element of continuous regression, found in many Dutch landscapes with figures, is of vital importance to the impression of depth and distance.

it would appear, a consistent relation between what, reverting to our pictorial image, we may call colour and size and as scene succeeds scene in the temporal plot of the play it tends to reveal the same tonal relation between the characters in it as does the total spatial plot.

Setting aside then the main characters, whose prominence no one proposes to question, we may fairly expect to discover continuous regression in the spatial grouping of the minor figures. And it is upon continuity in regression that a great part of the depth of the play's focus depends. Behind the first ten or twelve figures, who themselves recede and diminish in size and colour from Antony and Cleopatra to Maecenas, Agrippa, and Alexas, come those of further diminishing proportions, Scarus, Dolabella, Menecrates, Mardian, Canidius, with behind them again, Ventidius, Thyreus, the clown, the Soothsayer, Dercetas, Diomed. In all these, function and colour, though growing ever slighter and fainter, are still distinct, while behind them range a number of figures, growing steadily less distinct, servants, messengers, soldiers, guards, some thirty-five or -six of them, the ultimate horizon being represented by the virtually invisible Taurus (of III.viii.21) whose total contribution to the play is the line 'My Lord?'

Now it is somewhere within this range, from Scarus to Taurus, that the principle of continuous regression in character grouping will finally be revealed, for it is these minor figures who between them define the furthest depths of the scene. Scarus appears in three scenes,[9] though he only speaks in the first two and has only ten speeches, some twenty-five lines, in all. But the five speeches in III.viii are full of rich and memorable imagery, part comic, part poetic, the vehement language and syntax of wrath and abuse. We recognize the clear colours of the character; an experienced officer involved in a defeat, a brave, high-hearted soldier. He stands out at once from the background of soldiers, guards and messengers who appear once and then disappear and in the second and third scenes his function grows to match the vividness with which his character was first drawn. He supports and encourages Antony helping to turn the tide of war, and is then drawn forward out of the background by the warmth and understanding of Antony's words to Cleopatra. The sharpness of colour which caught the eye in his first three or four short speeches was, then, a true index of his position and of a function ultimately greater than we should have expected.

Behind him again are more figures who belong to the ever receding background and mark its depth by their ever decreasing colour and magnitude. The soldier who bears the news of Enobarbus's desertion[10] has but five speeches so brief that they total only about seven lines; something of his character is allowed to appear, sturdy, loyal, uncompromising, even provocative. And this degree of individuality is war-

---

[9] III.viii; IV.vii; IV.viii.
[10] IV.v.

ranted by his function; he is the means of revealing the gentleness of Antony on the eve of a great battle and calls forth the expression of the General's generous understanding of Enobarbus. The slight figure of this soldier is thus so placed and so coloured that it illuminates one side of Antony's character. Of corresponding dimensions and tone are the soldier who in III.vi bears Enobarbus's treasure to him from Antony, the messenger of I.iii and Silius in III.i. And close to them in the grouping, but diminished and paler, are the soldier of III.vii and Diomed in IV.xii and V.i.

At a little further distance we come upon figures such as Seleucus, the Messenger of I.ii, the two servants of II.vii, and the guard of V.ii. The few lines of Seleucus (he has only three, divided between three speeches) contain more colour than their brevity might suggest, but the function of the disloyal servant has a moment's sharp significance and so the colour of his speech, for the moment too matches it, slight though both are.

We are approaching the vanishing point now, where Taurus disappears with his two-word speech, but to the very edge of visibility the figures maintain their simultaneous diminution of function and tone. The four soldiers who in IV.iii listen to the mysterious music on the eve of Antony's defeat, being charged with the function of heightening, in their short scene, the effect of anticipation and of revealing the perilous psychological balance of Antony's troops, have yet just enough individual tone to be distinguishable from each other and the first, with his nine short speeches contained in seven lines, is the leader; he can hear the music and shows some initiative in investigating it. The second, more imaginative and apprehensive, hazards an interpretation. The anxiety of the third only echoes the other speakers point by point and the fourth shows a steady if imaginative optimism. The last three share between them fourteen speeches in about as many lines, but the faint indications of character can still be seen. Behind them and fainter yet are Varrius, the second and third soldiers of IV.ix, the three guards of IV.xii, the messenger of I.ii, Demetrius, the Egyptian of V.i, and the messenger of III.vii. The last two are as nearly colourless and functionless as it is possible to be while yet serving some purpose in the background of the play and are only slightly removed from the invisibility of the vanishing-point. But their function is nevertheless indispensable, for they define the last positions in that continuous regression which has given depth and distance to the spatial aspect of the play and completed the impression of its magnitude.

If we look at the temporal aspects of that ordered sequence of events that we call the plot, we find that this also is affected by the mode of the dramatist; one will present a logically articulated series and the other reveal what the poet has divined by inducing a continuing or developing experience in the mind of reader or audience. The first is the counterpart of the self-explanatory characters and the demonstrative spatial plot that we have just described. The other is associated with the process that reveals or modifies character by half-hidden signs and plots by leaving our imaginations to supply (it may be all unawares) the events needed to complete the full graph by linking together crucial events or scenes.

The coherence given to the first kind of plot by the logic of event serves a philosopher dramatist to emphasize his underlying idea and is indeed almost inseparable from his mode of writing. It is found in its finest form in the middle work of Ibsen, where the architectural power of the master building governs the relation of events, the indication of cause and effect by a precise articulation of the details of the plot. Each episode, each piece of setting, each section of dialogue, by its content, by its timing and by its placing, contributes directly to a design whose purpose is to set before us an interlocking series of events such as shall leave us no conclusion but the one Ibsen intends us to draw. The opening passages of these plays often fulfil four or five functions simultaneously, all directly or indirectly connected with the elucidation and the disengaging of the theme. This flawless, economical integration of the parts with the whole and with each other gives its own impression of inevitability; the sequence of events constitutes a demonstration. This is the natural way for him to use structure to demonstrate his theme. A usual but not an inseparable consequence of this compact and coherent plotting is the brevity of its dramatic time. The ultimate causes of the events presented to us lie far back in the past and Ibsen must bring them before our eyes by some form of recollection or reminiscence, but the occasion or immediate cause of word, deed, or event within the play is followed closely by its consequence and the final stages of the demonstration are before us in detail. So full is this detail that it may mislead us into thinking that the dramatist has given us the fulness of life itself.[11]

This logical and coherent ordering of the sequence of events, though only used in the drama of high seriousness by the philosophical dramatist has been understood from relatively early times by dramatists with other purposes. Even if the dramatist has no theme for the demonstrative technique to define by the three means we have already described, he may yet take a purely artistic delight in its design. The relations of cause and effect within each subsidiary plot and more still the relation between them, take on, in the hands of some dramatists of superlative skill, the beauty that always belongs to subtly related rhythms and curves of movement, such as those of a corps de ballet or a flock of seagulls in spring. In such cases, the content of the play is usually

[11] This specific artistic discipline was one that could be learnt by Ibsen's successors and its influence may be traced in the work of Galsworthy and Granville-Barker in England and of Brieux in France. Few clearer instances could be found than Galsworthy's *Strife*, a play in which the addition of symmetry in the two subsidiary plots which combine to form the whole plot gives an almost euclidian finality to the demonstration. Barker's *Voysey Inheritance,* though less economical and less compact, belongs to the same family. It continues to appear in varying degree in many of the dramatists concerned with social problems; *Hindle Wakes, Chains,* and *Jane Clegg* all appear to owe something to it.

comic; the finest comedy of intrigue is of this kind and Terence and Plautus mastered it long ago. Sometimes a mind of musical or it may be of mathematical bent will design a complex plot the intricate relations and variations of whose curves are themselves a delight to us and, we must presume, to him. Perhaps no dramatist has ever touched Ben Jonson in this special domain. He did not use it in his tragedies, but in the near-tragedy of *Volpone* and in the bitter satire of *The Alchemist* we find a comedy whose rhythms hold strange commerce with 'The laws that keep / The planets in their radiant courses.' But there is no theme here to be served and the only 'precepts deep' we are like to meet at the hands of Ben Jonson's rascals are curiously congruous with those of Praed's worthy vicar. The strength, swiftness, and precision of Ben Jonson's draughtsmanship carry the technique of this particular kind of plot to achievements it does not usually reach, except in the process of demonstrating a theme. But it must be admitted that in the humbler domain of farce many a play has been saved from worthlessness by the taut, athletic movements and the logic (it may be fantastic) of its plot; by a strict disposal of the relations of cause and effect the more noticeable perhaps in that this is the only kind of artistic virtue farce is free to practise.

Now Shakespeare's mode which reveals the character of Coriolanus and the magnitude of the spatial design in *Antony and Cleopatra* by secret impressions made upon our imaginations makes an utterly different disposal of the ordered sequence of events that constitute the temporal aspect of the plot. These are not now compact, nor, on the plane of actual event, closely coherent. There are wide gaps in the sequence, to be leapt by the imagination, and these spaces or intervals have not a merely negative but a positive function. This becomes clear when we consider what is in fact omitted in some of the greatest of his plays from the material he might have used, material that a lesser dramatist would have considered suitable or even highly effective in its theatrical or rhetorical effects.

If we look at some dozen of such potential scenes that find no place in *Macbeth* we notice at once that not only is the logical continuity of event set aside in some cases but that it is superseded in order that a profound reality may thereby have the greater power to evoke an imaginative response. At the risk of seeming to speak frivolously, I will name some of these, because I think that each one on my list would have been seized on as valuable theatrical material by some Elizabethan dramatist (even if we have to go as low as Chettle to find him), and that some of them have counterparts easily recognized in the work of the major Jacobeans. Some of these could take the form predominantly of spectacle, some of poetic or rhetorical soliloquy; some again could be built into effective episodes presented through the dialogue.

Shakespeare gives us nothing of the turbulent emotions that must have occupied Macbeth's mind during that ride from Forres to Inverness (between I.iv and I.v) when, with murder in his heart, he rode ahead to provide for Duncan's coming; nor of Lady Macbeth's when, a prey to the same nightmare thoughts, she presided at the supper of Duncan between I.vi and I.vii. Shakespeare does not present the murder of Duncan between II.i and II.ii, nor the coronation of Macbeth between II.iii and III.i. Nor, though he makes clear that there is an interval, does he give us any episode to illustrate the first stages of Macbeth's assumption of power, any soliloquy in which Macbeth should decide upon the murder of Banquo (that crucial decision which separates him from Lady Macbeth), nor that other soliloquy which would have disclosed Macbeth's growing sense of insecurity, so clearly acknowledged in III.i. We have no scene in which he orders the murder of Lady Macduff, comparable to III.i in which he arranges that of Banquo. And when we pass into the later part of the play we find that we have seen nothing of the many further incidents of Macbeth's tyrannous and uneasy reign which are commonplaces to Malcolm and Macduff in IV.iii. Neither have we any picture of Lady Macbeth's mental progress between the banquet of III.iv and the sleepwalking of V.i; during three scenes she has not appeared at all. There is no record of the mustering of the English forces between IV.iii and V.ii, nor of the simultaneous rising of the Scots, and again no revelation of Macbeth's inner experience between IV.i and V.ii, when during three scenes he himself does not appear.

Now I submit that none of these are impracticable in the theatre. The Elizabethan soliloquy was equal to the revelation of any thought or emotion and though certain of the scenes suggested would have repeated the form of others already in the play, there are contemporaries of Shakespeare who would not have been deterred by this from a fine piece of theatrical effect; any skilled dramatist knows how to vary his repetitions and even to snatch a cumulative effect from them. Furthermore, five at least of these are scenes that few working theatre-men who were not great artists would have been likely to resist: the murder of Duncan, the coronation of Macbeth, the haunting of Lady Macbeth's mind by the crimes she has known or guessed at, the mustering of the English army, and the rising of the Scots to join them. It would have been a strangely different play if we had had these instead of or as well as what we have. But it is evident that the scenes that are there must have some superior power of carrying the action from point to point so as to stimulate our imaginations to conceive the whole.

The art of the dramatist has been engaged not in presenting a closely locked and logically coherent action that points irresistibly to a certain deduction, but in selecting those fragments of the whole that stimulate our imaginations to an understanding of the essential experience, to the perception of a nexus of truths too vast to be defined as themes, whose enduring power disengages a seemingly unending series of perceptions and responses.

It would seem that the imagination of audience or reader is thrown forward, by the immense impact of such scenes, upon a track of emotional experience, to come to rest upon the next scene, at the moment in its curving flight at which it can alight without interference or loss of momentum, to be projected again upon another movement, there to be similarly received, diverted, and flung out again upon its track of discovery. And this proceeds with economy and harmony as do the forces of gravitation at work upon the movements of the bodies in a solar system.

May we attempt, despite the presumption of the act, to consider, by looking at what goes before and what follows, why Shakespeare does not give us the murder of Duncan? Our imaginations have been engaged first by the fortunes of Macbeth through the initial meeting with the witches and his rapid rise to favour and power and then by the terrible conflict in his mind as temptation lays holds upon it and the vision of murder 'shakes so [his] single state of man that function is smothered in surmise'. From this point we identify ourselves with Macbeth; we have looked into his mind by one of those shafts of illumination which are the glory of the evocative technique in the revelation of character. The meeting with Lady Macbeth at once releases and directs the full force of those elemental powers of evil which lead him forward towards the crime he dreads and desires. From the moment at which he sees the air-drawn dagger he is in a state of suspended life in which time and place and fact have lost their customary relations, in which he sees only 'the future in the instant'. In that world of his imagination, and of ours identified with his, the murder is already done; the act itself is a piece of automatism, a kind of sleepwalking, the mere embodying in deed of what his will and resolution had already accomplished. There is no interim between this and the revulsion and horror which follow immediately after it; almost we may believe that that recoil would have followed if the deed had been imagined only and prevented of actual achievement. In this flight from one point of experience to another there is no room for pause; the presentation of the deed itself would have been a disastrous and irrelevant interruption, breaking the curve of the essential experience. For the act itself which is for Macbeth a timeless interim, a suspension of the faculties, could not have been so for us, the audience. We should have had perforce to subject our imaginations to that scene and in so doing change the swift forward movement of our minds. Even if the dramatist had presented to us a Macbeth who himself moved like a sleepwalker, it would still have been a fatal interruption. And in fact he could hardly have done this if he had lifted the scene into the dominant position it must occupy if it is to be presented at all. For Macbeth in this trancelike frenzy of resolution to have spoken would have been impossible; the silence of suspended consciousness does not speak, even in soliloquy. And yet no such scene as this could have been trusted to dumb show. All other possible stage treatments our fancy can devise lead us but to the same conclusion, that the essential, inner experience which is the essence of the play's action here must move swift as thought from the moment when the bell invites him to the moment when he heard 'a noise' 'as [he] descended'. From the middle of I.iv to the end of II.ii is a 'hideous storm of terror' from which there must be no respite for the audience until, dazed and horror-stricken, we come to rest to hear the intrusion of the everyday world as the porter grumbles his way to the door on which the knocking still resounds.

Such, I would suggest, is the process at work as the action of great poetic drama is embodied in a sequence of events ordered not by demonstrative but by poetic logic. So great is its evocative power that our imagination can bridge a gap which in lesser drama and in common life would contain the crucial event of Macbeth's career. This or a like process will be found to indicate not merely the gaps and the omissions but the functional relations of the moments by which the artist leads us, from point to point, to an apprehension of the essential action of the play which the presentation of outward fact not only could not give us but would in certain instances destroy.

This seemingly arbitrary selection of crucial situations was the customary foundation of Elizabethan drama; the finest tragic dramatists, Marlowe, Webster, Middleton, Ford, all seem to be feeling their way to the same kind of plot as we find in Shakespeare and sometimes triumphantly if intermittently achieving it. The succession of disconnected crises that we sometimes find even in the major and usually in the minor dramatists points to a failure of artistic imagination in them, an imperfect hold upon the action (in Aristotle's sense) by whose direction Shakespeare's plots were unfolded.

We spoke at the beginning of this chapter of the inner and outer aspects of the plot and though the distinction is dangerous if it is used arbitrarily, it has a certain value. Some of the events in the plot belong to the surface and we are aware of them at once as deeds or speeches that visibly determine its direction. If we could imagine a sequence of outer events that formed a coherent series in a play we could speak of an outer plot, and if we could be made aware of the corresponding sequence of inner events we could similarly speak of the inner plot. In fact we cannot do either, for we cannot imagine a series sufficiently coherent to form by itself a plot or a strand of a plot, but it is evident that the two processes are at work in every play which is a work of art and that their relative proportions and the interplay between them go far to determine the nature of the play. A play which discloses the deeper levels of experience in the minds of the characters is to that extent concerned with an inner level of plot and one which shows us principally the effects of these experiences is concerned primarily with an outer plot; if Kyd's *Hamlet* had survived (always supposing it to have existed) it would, we may suppose, be found to have treated the story in such a way that the proportions and relations of these two aspects of its plot were like those of *The Spanish Tragedy*. But these are not the proportions or the relations of Shakespeare's *Hamlet*.

A plot which leaves upon our minds the impression that it is logical, argumentative, or demonstrative will be found to be so at its outer as at its inner level and a play whose structure is evocative will be so at both levels also. I have already suggested[12] that in *Macbeth* an event or series of events may evoke in our imaginations other intervening events, so that we pass from one to another without the sense of hiatus or space and end with a sense of the continuity of the whole, ordered sequence. Just so, the revelation of inner event may proceed in this way, whether by soliloquy or by dialogue. Macbeth's soliloquy 'If it were done when 'tis done', although it begins as an attempt to think out his position, is filled with thick-coming fancies and terrifying images that seem to leave his argument where it began. But we who have heard him know that a long phase of experience has been lived through and the very pauses, changes of direction, or inconsistencies have but shown us the journeying mind coming momentarily into sight. They have evoked in our imaginations the experience through which he has travelled; but it is an experience of which much is left undescribed, even in soliloquy. So it is with Hamlet when he sets out to debate whether to be or not to be. Our imaginations leap the gaps with his. The inner plot here uses its own special medium of revelation, the soliloquy, but the mode is still evocative, even within the soliloquy itself. The progress of a mind intent upon its inner experience may be revealed to us by just such a stirring of our imaginations when Lear speaks to the Fool in Act I, scene v. We no longer see the same man at the end of that short passage of dialogue as we did at the beginning; we have followed the slender but sufficient clues through a wilderness of experience and self-discovery.

In the same way, we may recognize the contrary mode; the logical treatment of plot that we find in *The Alchemist* or *Strife* may be discovered also at the inner level whenever the experience of a character is revealed systematically, step by step; so that, whatever its relation to the events that belong primarily to the outer aspect of the plot, we recognize a piece of continuous disclosure or self-discovery going on beneath that surface. This is comparatively rare in drama, but we may find it in Racine's *Bérénice* or *Athalie* and we find it again in Ibsen's *Rosmersholm* or *John Gabriel Borkman*. Rebekka West, like Mrs Alving, has made a great part of her pilgrimage before the play opens, but *Rosmersholm,* unlike *Ghosts,* is mainly concerned with the final stages of her interpretation, with her assessment of her past conduct, and her deliberate translation of her final decision into action. And her mind, despite the strength of her emotions, works as clearly upon the true meaning of her past and the dilemma it has created in the present as if she were examining the motives and conduct of another person. Our imagination is required to follow her steps, but not to leap chasms with her.

---

[12] [Pp. 86–87.]

Some indication of the variety possible to the inter-relations of these different levels of plot may be seen when we look at Ibsen's play bearing in mind such a play as *Hamlet* where also the inner aspect is concerned with exploration, a measure of self-discovery and integration. In *Hamlet,* the events in the world that surrounds him continually affect and are in turn affected by his inward progression; neither escapes for long the influence of the other. But in plays such as *Rosmersholm* the events that make up the surface become a mere vehicle for the significant succession of inner events. Moreover, this drama arises primarily not from the effect of tragic or catastrophic event upon the surface level of the play or from entirely new experience offered by this to the character, but from exploration and revaluation of the past in the light of these events, of fresh situations and changing relations. The material for an Elizabethan domestic tragedy does indeed lie behind the play; a long history of mingled events upon both levels, of interesting deeds, thoughts and decisions has brought the characters to the point at which they now stand. But the substance of the play itself is the recollection of that history and the re-assessment both of it and of the present to which Rebekka is prompted by the slight and relatively colourless surface events of the play.[13]

Some relation between these levels, between that which lies upon the surface and that which lies at varying depths beneath it, reveals itself then as surely in a play's structure as in the dramatist's revelation of character. But equally surely the mode of the essential dramatist distinguishes itself in both from that of the philosophic dramatist. And the mark of the evocative mode is, even here, its generic power, while the mark of the other is its logical demonstration. Even in so great a play as *Rosmersholm,* where the poetry of Ibsen's thought creates high imaginative drama, the logic of inner event is still to be found in the process of the mind which is revealed at the inner level of the plot.

From the linking and proportioning of these two levels comes, as I have suggested, the balance of the play's content. From their separation many significant implications derive. One of these in Elizabethan drama is the impression of the fluidity of time and of the different nature which it may assume at different moments. Our sense of multiple time-schemes within a play such as *Othello* comes in part from this difference of the tempo, the inner life proceeding with a swiftness perfectly consistent with common experience, the succession of outer events occupying meanwhile a brief space of solar time. The systole and diastole of

---

[13] The unfailing tact of the Greek drama leads to its special rendering by the aid of the Chorus of the relationship between the levels of event. The disclosure of the characters' motives and reflections gives us the origins of their actions, but the acts themselves are banished from the stage. Thus we have a drama which lays emphasis upon the inner aspect of plot in the midst of tragic and catastrophic outward events. These events are withdrawn into the background and the causes and responses within the human soul are given their true supremacy.

many plays may be traced to the same cause; two separate and equally true ways of measuring time, implied by the two different levels, may reveal at the heart of a play a hint of the mystery of the two lives led by every man, of the mystery, that is, of incarnation.

THE MULTIPLE PLOT

Emotion of Multitude

William Butler Yeats

I have been thinking a good deal about plays lately, and I have been wondering why I dislike the clear and logical construction which seems necessary if one is to succeed on the Modern Stage. It came into my head the other day that this construction, which all the world has learned from France, has everything of high literature except the emotion of multitude. The Greek drama has got the emotion of multitude from its chorus, which called up famous sorrows, long-leaguered Troy, much-enduring Odysseus, and all the gods and heroes to witness, as it were, some well-ordered fable, some action separated but for this from all but itself. The French play delights in the well-ordered fable, but by leaving out the chorus it has created an art where poetry and imagination, always the children of far-off multitudinous things, must of necessity grow less important than the mere will. This is why, I said to myself, French dramatic poetry is so often a little rhetorical, for rhetoric is the will trying to do the work of the imagination. The Shakespearean Drama gets the emotion of multitude out of the subplot which copies the main plot, much as a shadow upon the wall copies one's body in the firelight. We think of *King Lear* less as the history of one man and his sorrows than as the history of a whole evil time. Lear's shadow is in Gloster, who also has ungrateful children, and the mind goes on imagining other shadows, shadow beyond shadow till it has pictured the world. In *Hamlet,* one hardly notices, so subtly

---

is the web woven, that the murder of Hamlet's father and the sorrow of Hamlet are shadowed in the lives of Fortinbras and Ophelia and Laertes, whose fathers, too, have been killed. It is so in all the plays, or in all but all, and very commonly the subplot is the main plot working itself out in more ordinary men and women, and so doubly calling up before us the image of multitude. Ibsen and Maeterlinck have on the other hand created a new form, for they get multitude from the Wild Duck in the Attic, or from the Crown at the bottom of the Fountain, vague symbols that set the mind wandering from idea to idea, emotion to emotion. Indeed all the great Masters have understood that there cannot be great art without the little limited life of the fable, which is always the better the simpler it is, and the rich, far-wandering, many-imaged life of the self-seen world beyond it. There are some who understand that the simple unmysterious things living as in a clear noonlight are of the nature of the sun, and that vague many-imaged things have in them the strength of the moon. Did not the Egyptian carve it on emerald that all living things have the sun for father and the moon for mother, and has it not been said that a man of genius takes the most after his mother?

THE LANGUAGE OF STAGE AND ACTOR

Verbal Drama

John Russell Brown

Opening Shakespeare's *Works* every reader is liable to attend to the words only; they are cunning and wonderful, and absorb immediate interest. Our minds can be pleasurably entangled, at any point, in a subtle net of ambiguities, complexities and levels of meaning, of word-music and allusiveness; and having caught us in one segment, the whole play, or several plays, can be animated by our efforts to understand. Shakespeare's verbal art is, in fact, a trap; it can prevent us from inquiring further.

Perhaps rhetorical passages are the strongest barriers. Figurative argument marching vigorously within a metrical form towards some culminating statement both convinces and arrests as we read: so in *Henry the Fifth:*

> Therefore doth heaven divide
> The state of man in divers functions,
> Setting endeavour in continual motion;
> To which is fixed as an aim or butt
> Obedience; for so work the honey bees,
> Creatures that by a rule in nature teach
> The act of order to a peopled kingdom.
> They have a king, and officers of sorts,
> Where some like magistrates correct at home;

From John Russell Brown, *Shakespeare's Plays in Performance.* Reprinted by permission of John Russell Brown and Edward Arnold (Publishers), Ltd.

Others like merchants venture trade abroad;
Others like soldiers, armed in their stings,
Make boot upon the summer's velvet buds,
Which pillage they with merry march bring home
To the tent-royal of their emperor; . . .
(I.ii.183 ff.)

And further traps are hidden even here, for we must keep alert if we are to remember the whole argument when the next two lines catch us with their euphony, allusiveness, and completeness:

Who, busied in his majesty, surveys
The singing masons building roofs of gold, . . .

The 'singing masons . . .' draws our attention away from neighbouring lines, becoming independent of the immediate context; our imagination feeds fully, and other business seems impertinent.

Or a conceit can dominate our thoughts by its mere elaboration; so in *Much Ado,* Hero sends Margaret to Beatrice:

. . . say that thou overheard'st us;
And bid her steal into the pleached bower,
Where honeysuckles, ripened by the sun,
Forbid the sun to enter—like favourites,
Made proud by princes, that advance their pride
Against that power that bred it. There will she hide her
To listen our propose.
(III.i.6–12)

At first we may be puzzled by unnecessary decoration—'Why not identify the bower simply?' we ask; but then the words claim our further consideration, and literary criticism and historical research occupy our thoughts. Yes: *steal* and *honeysuckles* are appropriate to the close, sweet yet familiar entanglement that will follow. *Ripened by the sun* is a contrast to Beatrice's earlier, 'Thus goes every one to the world but I, and I am sunburnt' (II.i.286–7).

The *honeysuckles* on the pleached bower are also *proud;* and so Hero, again contrasting natural growth, will soon arraign Beatrice:

But nature never fram'd a woman's heart
Of prouder stuff than that of Beatrice.
Disdain and scorn ride sparkling in her eyes,
Misprising what they look on; and her wit
Values itself so highly that to her
All matter else seems weak. She cannot love, . . .
(III.i.49–54)

The *honeysuckles, ripened by the sun,* are like Beatrice in denying the full nature of the *power* that made them *favourites.* Nor must we miss the topicality of this decorative conceit: favourites *were* powerful at the court of Elizabeth I in 1598–9—when *Much Ado* was written. The great Lord Burghley died on 13 September 1598, and for some years his son, Robert, had been rising to influence challenged by the more military and handsome Earl of Essex. Francis Bacon warned the Earl not to force the issue:

> My Lord, these courses be like to hot waters, they will help at a pang: but if you use them, you shall spoil the stomach, and you shall be fain still to make them stronger and stronger, and yet in the end they will lose their operation.

And there were lesser favourites like Sir Christopher Hatton—'a mere vegetable of the Court, that sprung up at night'—Sir Walter Raleigh, or the Queen's godson, Sir John Harington. Power could suddenly be lost: when Harington returned from Ireland knighted by Essex, the Queen exclaimed, 'By God's Son! I am no Queen; that man is above me' and banished the comparatively innocent godson from Court. When Hero likens honeysuckles to proud favourites her words draw our attention until we observe the whole play in little: pride *versus* nature, in Beatrice, Benedick, Don John and Dogberry ('I am a wise fellow; and, which is more, . . . as pretty a piece of flesh as any is in Messina . . .'); a reminder of the impermanence of pride, and honeysuckles and favourites.

One decorative passage can send us to more words, to the course of the play's action, and back again to words; we stay fascinated in the verbal contrivance and have little leisure to ask how important this steeplechase is for the comedy as a whole. Books have been filled with accounts of these pursuits: Shakespeare's use of language and his imagery, his themes perceived in the 'poetic texture' of the dialogue. While none of these studies would claim to be inclusive or final, all suggest that a careful study of words reveals a coherent 'attitude to life' which is a hidden, unifying influence on the structure and substance of the plays.

In the eighteenth century, before literary criticism grew subtle and hardworking, a fascination with Shakespeare's words led to numerous collections of the 'beauties of Shakespeare'. So when the poet, Pope, prepared an edition of the plays he helped his readers and showed his own discrimination by marking with asterisks the finest passages. Now that we no longer quote a splendid passage and leave its wings unmeasured by criticism, we are still liable to be held by the words and pride ourselves on showing the relevance and complexity of any highly wrought passage.

But there are many other elements in a drama that must be appreciated—those which are not so easily reached through the printed page—and the very words themselves can be fully known only if they are considered in their dramatic contexts. They must be heard in sequence, supported by actors' impersonations, related to the physical and visual elements of performance; and so, perhaps, revalued.

For example, theatre history reminds us of numerous lines that would yield a lean harvest to literary investigation, but have inspired successive audiences to wonder and applause. Notable in the earlier plays is Richard III's 'A horse! a horse! my kingdom for a horse!' (V.v.7), or Petruchio's response to the Shrew's last speech, 'Why, there's a wench! Come on, and kiss me, Kate.' (V.ii.180); dramatic considerations of physical action and bearing, intonation and emphasis, a new simplicity and weight of utterance, carry these moments. In *Henry the Fourth, Part II* the crucial moment in the last long interview between the dying king and Prince Hal is the simple, incomplete verse-line, 'O my son' (IV.iv.178), which every actor of the role in my experience has made more affecting than the other hundred and fifty lines of the duologue. *Hamlet* has many such lines: 'Go on; I'll follow thee' to the Ghost, and 'O God!', 'Murder!', 'My uncle!' (I.iv.79 and 86, and I.v.24 ff.). When Hamlet first calls the Ghost 'father' many actors have found that the text asks for particular emphasis:

> Kean, we are told, was no longer frightened. Booth 'dropped on one knee . . . and bowed his head, not in terror, but in awe and love.' At the sight of the spirit, Salvini's face was 'illumined with an awe-struck joy'; and his Hamlet, 'spontaneously, and one would almost say unconsciously, uncovers his head.' [1]

The theatrical fact of the silent Ghost meeting Hamlet is large and, in ways that the reader might never guess, the text grows in performance to answer it. Later, Hamlet's first words in his mother's closet, 'Now, mother, what's the matter?' and, near the end of the same scene, his repeated 'Good night, mother.' (III.iv.8 and 159 ff.) are powerful beyond literary analysis. Such uncomplicated, forceful lines are in the comedies too, in Rosalind's 'And so am I for no woman' (*As You Like It,* V.ii.81 ff.) or Benedick's 'This can be no trick' (*Much Ado About Nothing,* II.iii.201). All these live only in their dramatic context, nourished by timing, surprise, repetition, change of dramatic idiom, physical performance, mood, grouping.

In the greatest tragedies Shakespeare seems especially concerned to build theatrical intensity and revelation with the barest verbal material. Obviously, Lady Macbeth's sleep-walking scene verbally echoes important themes and introduces staggering images and juxtapositions of ideas, but its full power is not easily revealed by literary analysis. According to the Doctor and Gentlewoman her 'Oh, oh, oh!' (V.i.49) is the emotional climax revealing a heart 'sorely charg'd': her fullest suffering lies beneath the words that somnambulism releases. For a literary analyst, Macbeth's last couplet:

---

[1] A. C. Sprague, *Shakespeare and the Actors* (1948), p. 140.

> Lay on Macduff;
> And damn'd be him that first cries 'Hold, enough!'
> (V.viii.33–34)

has a metrical obviousness and traces of fustian; it gains stature and meaning only in enactment, by a physical resurgence and concentration. Here is a report of Irving's Macbeth in *The Academy* of 2 October 1875:

> What one finds so good in his Fifth Act, is not only the gradations of abjectness and horror, as evil news follow on evil news, but the self-control that has long deserted him, gathered together at last; and the end, whatever the end may be, accepted with some return of the old courage, only more reckless and wild; for it is the last chance and a poor one . . .
>
> Mr. Irving's fight with Macduff illustrates quite perfectly, in its savage and hopeless wildness, the last temper of Macbeth.

There are effects that are supported by the text but can be realised only in performance.

King Lear alone could provide weighty evidence of the need to pass beyond literary analysis: 'Come, boy' and 'I shall go mad!' to the fool —the 'tone in which Garrick uttered' these last words 'absolutely thrilled' his audience;[2] and:

> I will say nothing.

> Didst thou give all to thy daughters?

> Come, unbutton here.

> Give me thy arm;
> Poor Tom shall lead thee.

> Then kill, kill, kill, kill, kill, kill!

> Come, come; I am a king,
> My masters, know you that.

> Then there's life in't. Nay, an you get it, you shall get it by running. Sa, sa, sa, sa.

> Do not laugh at me;
> For, as I am a man, I think this lady
> To be my child Cordelia.
> And so I am, I am.

[2] W. Clark Russell, *Representative Actors* (n.d.), p. 110.

Thou'lt come no more,
Never, never, never, never, never.
Pray you undo this button. Thank you, sir.
Do you see this? Look on her. Look, her lips.
Look there, look there! [3]

Words like *laugh* and *man, my child* and *I am,* or *never, see* and *look* and even *button* will yield to literary analysis and show something of the relevance of these passages; and so will their syntax and metre. But Cordelia's 'And so I am, I am' or Lear's 'Look there, look there!' demand theatrical criticism to explain the rightness, delicacy and overwhelming intensity of feeling that accompanies the monosyllables in performance. These are the moments that stay with the audience long after the play is finished.

A dramatic text is spoken and heard; some words may be, as it were, in capital letters, some may be written very small indeed, some almost illegibly—quite different from the uniform scale of a printed page. In non-dramatic forms of writing such effects may sometimes be managed, but for a play in performance they are necessary, and greatly magnified. Listen to anyone's speech: the words 'I will' spoken very quickly have a different meaning and are almost opposite in aural effect compared with the same words spoken very slowly and quietly. Or coming after a long sentence and complicated interplay of syntax and metre, they will sound differently and mean differently from the same words in a nimble prose exchange. (Alterations of pitch or stress, or of tone and texture, also modify them.) In such ways the literary meaning and metrical effect of a printed text develop through performance into something far more complicated.

The first rule for reading the text of a play is to remember that dramatic energy is dynamic not static, that the dramatist has tried to control the tempo of performance in the smallest detail, to prepare, sustain and release moments of large emotion and alternately lead forward and hold back the audience's attention. The second rule is to remember the actor, whose sensibility and physical performance support the words, and the other actors on stage with him.

Short but sustained speech will illustrate the dynamic qualities of theatrical writing; for example, Oberon's reply to Puck just before day comes to the wood outside Athens in *A Midsummer Night's Dream:*

But we are spirits of another sort:
I with the Morning's love have oft made sport;
And, like a forester, the groves may tread
Even till the eastern gate, all fiery red,
Opening on Neptune with fair blessed beams,

---

[3] I.v.47; II.iv.285; III.ii.38; III.iv.48 and 107; IV.i.79–80; IV.vi.188 and 201–5; IV.viii.68–70; V.iii.307–11.

Turns into yellow gold his salt green streams.
But, notwithstanding, haste, make no delay;
We may effect this business yet ere day.
(III.ii.388–95)

The plot is scarcely forwarded by the information of the first six lines, but much else is accomplished. Time and the general situation are established with talk of the 'eastern gate, all fiery red.' And the gold and fiery light of the sun in opposition to cold water, repeats an important theme in the play, echoing earlier references to a 'cold fruitless moon', 'salt tears', 'the moon, the governess of floods, / Pale in her anger', or the sea's 'contagious fogs'. But to understand its theatrical effect enactment must be considered as well: these ideas are not neatly defined, but placed and imaged so that the warmth and yellow radiance transfigure the salt and green sea; the sun overpowers the sea with the long, tidal reach of syntax, so making the green one gold. When the actor speaks the lines this metrical effect is inescapable; rhythm, pitch, stress and phrase ensure its communication. So, too, the character Oberon grows, the long, controlled sound of his speech giving him an authority which he has no need to claim—often a main consideration in the balance of an acted scene. The control is astonishing: after the quick descriptive clause of 'like a forester', another adverbial clause follows and within that yet another with 'Opening on Neptune with fair blessed beams'; he has leisure, even, for the double epithet of 'fair blessed' at its close, before the strong and simple verb of the main clause is supplied in 'Turns'. The impression of controlled power in Oberon depends largely on temporal and musical means and on the clarity of performance; and because these are usually unrecognised in operation by the audience, they work with seeming inevitability—this, again, is part of their effect, giving an impression of reserved power.

The influence of these six lines extends beyond the time in which they are spoken. They accentuate, by contrast, the renewed speed of Oberon's concluding couplet when he leaves without doubting Puck's response, and the energy, compactness and outspokenness of Puck left alone on the stage:

Up and down, up and down,
I will lead them up and down . . .

Their reverberations continue when the lovers enter, for the young men's unsustained rhythms in asserting power, by contrast with both Puck and Oberon, will sound shallow and insecure:

Where art thou, proud Demetrius? Speak thou now . . .

Out of dramatic context, both rhythm and vocabulary might be called direct and efficient, but theatrical enactment must revalue this.

When we progress beyond the meaning of words and our own appreciation of rhythm and texture, to their enactment, we move quickly from the printed page to the whole stage, from variations of tempo and emphasis to physical movement, silence, posture, grouping, the potential surprise of an entrance or exit, emotional performances. We must continue to ask 'What is the effect?' in preference to 'What is the meaning?' When at last we ask the second question we have to account for impressions which quotation of the text alone can never represent.

The dynamic nature of theatrical energy ensures that a dramatist must be specially concerned with metre and prose rhythms. (The lameness of translated plays is some indication of the importance of an author's time-control through speech.) Someone who did not understand a word of English could hear Cordelia's answer to Lear in performance and gain some impression of her physical involvement and the extremity, purity and strength of her feeling. The rhythms of her short speech must answer and satisfy the rhythms of his longer speech:

> Do not laugh at me;
> For, as I am a man, I think this lady
> To be my child Cordelia.
> And so I am, I am.

To manage the proper rhythmic balance, the two impersonators of these roles must be closely and silently attuned to each other's performance and, therefore, they will communicate a shared, delicate and intuitive sympathy; how this reaches the audience is not easily explained, but it is an effect good actors can command in such a context. Metre and syntax instigate, and release, the physical and emotive elements of performance.

In Shakespeare's day this generative power of words in a theatrical context could be controlled surely by virtue of the firm metrical base of blank-verse. When he began to write, the iambic beat was over-assertive; in his preface to *Menaphon* (1589), Thomas Nashe criticised dramatists who indulged the 'spacious volubility of a drumming decasyllabon.' But other writers besides William Webbe, in his *Discourse of English Poetry* (1586), judged that the 'natural course of most English verses seemeth to run upon the old iambic stroke',[4] and most sought to refine rather than replace its 'measure' or 'certain frame'.

By accepting a far more regular metre than would be tolerated to-day, the Elizabethans discovered a manner of speech that was both forcible and subtle. As Sir Philip Sidney put it, each syllable could be 'peysed', or weighed:

> The Senate of Poets hath chosen verse as their fittest raiment . . . not speaking (table-talk fashion or like men in a dream) words as they chanceably fall from the mouth, but peysing each syllable of each word by just proportion according to the dignity of the subject.[5]

[4] *Elizabethan Critical Essays,* ed. G. G. Smith (1904), i. 273.
[5] *Idem,* i. 160.

For play-writing, metre was almost universal: Hamlet asks the players for 'temperance' and 'smoothness' even in the 'very torrent, tempest, and, as I may say, whirlwind of your passion' (III.ii.6–8) and this implies rigorous verbal accomplishment for both actor and author. Joseph Hall's *Virgidemiarum* (1598) pictures some dramatists watching a play and following the actors in a manuscript as if it were a musical score:

> Meanwhile our poets in high parliament,
> Sit watching every word, and gesturement,
> Like curious censors of some doughty gear,
> Whispering their verdict in their fellow's ear.
> Woe to the word whose margent in their scroll
> Is noted with a black condemning coal.
> But if each period might the synod please—
> Ho! bring the ivy boughs, and bands of bays.
> (I.iii.45–53)

Blank verse gives the necessary control, power and coherence for physical enactment to grow out of the speaking of the text. The control comes by 'peysing' each syllable and varying the interplay of syntax and metre. Impressions of emotion grow by breaking a regular confinement, or by extending over many lines a single unit of rhythmic design. And coherence derives from the regularity sustained beneath all manner of irregularities, the now discreet and scarcely heard 'drumming' of the iambic pentameters. Metre enables a dramatic poet to influence the dynamics of production and the actors' performances.

In *Romeo and Juliet* Friar Lawrence enters the play alone, carrying a basket:

> The gray-ey'd morn smiles on the frowning night,
> Check'ring the eastern clouds with streaks of light;
> And fleckel'd darkness like a drunkard reels
> From forth day's path and Titan's fiery wheels.
> Now, ere the sun advance his burning eye
> The day to cheer and night's dank dew to dry,
> I must up-fill this osier cage of ours
> With baleful weeds and precious-juiced flowers.
> (II.iii.1–8)

Thematically the soliloquy is significant. In the previous scene the sun had been associated with Juliet as Romeo exclaims:

> What light through yonder window breaks?
> It is the east, and Juliet is the sun.
> (II.ii.2–3)

Later Juliet is to call Romeo 'thou day in night', a light so fine that it will draw worship away from the 'garish sun' (III.ii.17–25). At the end of the play, the Prince also speaks of the dawn:

> A glooming peace this morning with it brings,
> The sun for sorrow will not show his head.
> (V.iii.304–5)

The night, too, recurs as an image throughout the play, in Romeo's foreboding and Juliet's invocation of 'gentle night' and 'loving black-brow'd night', and repeatedly in Romeo's dying speech in the 'palace of dim night' when Juliet's

> beauty makes
> This vault a feasting presence full of light.
> (V.iii.74–120)

Here then, with his first entry, the Friar is presented verbally, as if he willingly accepts the alternation of night and day and of good and evil: thematically a position of strength. But by temporal effects his soliloquy means much more. Its antitheses fit neatly into the metrical line-units, and the rhyme. The iambics of the first couplet are regular except for the easy reversal in the first foot of the second line—'Check'ring'—and the stronger reversal in the first line: 'The gray-ey'd morn *smiles* on the frowning night'. Notice how well-contained the 'frowning night' is, at the metrically regular end of the line; and how the potential threat is then dispersed in the belittling 'Check'ring' placed strongly in the first reversed foot of the next line. By all these means, the couplet is a stage-direction: Friar Lawrence's movements have a regular pace; he is neat; he is smoothly and pleasantly optimistic; he is gentle. The next line gives more power to darkness by comparing it with a 'drunkard' reeling, but still this reaction is not developed; here the notion is reduced in scale by 'fleckel'd' and quenched by the overwhelming metrical strength of 'From forth day's path' at the beginning of the next line, and by the additional description in 'Titan's fiery wheels'. The image of a drunkard being almost run over by a chariot is potentially brutal; but the 'drunkard' is lost from consciousness in considering the course of the sun, and the Friar immediately veers to another aspect of his concerns, introduced with a regular pentameter without the trace of a caesura which earlier had contributed to an impression of neatness: 'Now ere the sun advance his burning eye'. 'Burning eye' suggests some danger but this is turned to favour and to prettiness in the double antitheses and early caesura of the next line: 'The day to cheer and night's dank dew to dry.' Here is an indication of thought and feeling that must suggest physical bearing; the Friar's temperament is nervous but habitually controlled by an easy intellectual optimism; he recognises danger but dismisses it from his consideration by thoughts of the good. His posture, facial expressions, tone of voice expressing all this will add to the theatrical effect, especially as he is a new character alone on the large open stage, an object of intense scrutiny. So in performance, the Friar's acceptance of the 'alternation of night and day, and of good and evil' is not the position of strength the printed text might suggest: he is, also, somewhat shallow and petty.

In the Ball Scene of *Romeo and Juliet,* Act I Scene v, metrical variety indicates the individual bearing of the actors and also major elements in stage-management. It starts with grumbling and emphatic prose for the servants suggesting a Breughel-like detail and scale. Then comes the more sustained but short-phrased, almost puffing, emphasis of Capulet managing his guests; he is largely monosyllabic, directly physical in detail, repetitive and, for a time, alliterative:

> Welcome, gentlemen! Ladies that have their toes
> Unplagu'd with corns will have a bout with you.
> Ah ha, my mistresses! which of you all
> Will now deny to dance? She that makes dainty,
> She I'll swear hath corns; am I come near ye now?
> Welcome, gentlemen!

and then he retires into the longer phrases of personal reminiscence. Romeo's question to a nameless servant:

> What lady's that which doth enrich the hand
> Of yonder knight?

is smoothly sustained in image and rhythm; the simple reply, 'I know not, sir', does not deflect him; he modifies his image, and rhymes with his own last word:

> O, she doth teach the torches to burn bright!

Metrical regularity is emphasised by alliteration and then a more powerful irregularity with 'burn bright!' at the end of the line. His imagery changes again, but in sustained response and guided by the rhymed couplets. Tybalt interjects in another rhythm, sharp and athletic:

> This, by his voice, should be a Montague.
> Fetch me my rapier, boy, What, dares the slave. . . .

He changes from soliloquy to dialogue without embarrassment, and his speech builds quickly in emphatic statement. When he is questioned by Capulet his anger is sustained largely by repetition; he then becomes more brief and leaves with new, incisive threats.

The following dialogue between Romeo and Juliet is in complete contrast: they share a sonnet, its rhymes, form and images. The two lovers are strangely singled out from the other dancers and the sonnet, with its dominant image of worship, is their own predestined dance—impelled, gentle, mutual and awed; it requires a separation from the scene's ordinary pace—its blank verse and couplets—which they alone know. Through its verbal exchanges they move towards their kisses, first palm-to-palm and then lip-to-lip. Without such a presentation these intimate actions would have been lost in the crowded, animated scene, or might have been exaggerated by the actors in an effort to give them dramatic forcefulness; as Shakespeare directs through his metrical dialogue, the kisses have their own silence because our attention waits upon them for the completion of the sonnet. Even the words are revalued by their metrical setting: if the lovers did not have to share the rhythms and form of the sonnet, their conceits might ring too keenly; but, secure in the privacy of the sonnet, the wit can sound tender and contented as, perhaps, off-stage only intimate love-talk can be.

Similes, metaphors and other figures of speech, when read in conjunction with the rhythm and tempo of speech, can indicate physical performance. The Friar's changing imagery suggests a timorous nature, Romeo's sustained imagery an absorption in a single feeling. But, perhaps more powerfully, images also display a general, overall excitement, a state of being in which fantasy becomes real.

When we read a printed text we pick our way slowly through the conceits—as we have attended to Hero's talk of honeysuckles. But the actor has assimilated all this—or should have done—so that in speaking the difficulties disappear and excitement takes their place. Hero is a young girl in love, about to talk of love and to give thoughts of love to her cousin, who has derided love; lightly spoken her speech is alive with feeling as well as thought.[6] (The metre helps, too; notice the way in which 'like favourites' starts its new, energetic development at the end of a line after the period had seemed to be complete.) In Anthony Mundy's *Zelauto* (1580), a novel which Shakespeare almost certainly read while preparing to write *The Merchant of Venice,* a young man becomes satisfied that his lady is concerned for him; he is said to look 'smug' and then:

> his conceits began to come so nimbly together, that he now rolled in his rhetoric, like a flea in a blanket.
>
> (Sig. P3)

However complex Shakespeare's imagery can seem, and however long a reader may pour over the words, from the stage it is often a wide-spreading vigour and enjoyment that is the dominant impression communicated to the audience.

Two testimonies are useful here. First Bernard Shaw inveighing against academic critics and elocution teachers:

> Powerful among the enemies of Shakespear are the commentator and the elocutionist: the commentator because, not knowing Shakespear's language, he sharpens his reasoning faculty . . . in-

---

[6] [See Brown, *Shakespeare's Plays in Performance* (New York: St. Martin's Press, 1967), pp. 171–72.]

> stead of sensitizing his artistic faculty to receive the impression of moods and inflexions of feeling conveyed by word-music; the elocutionist because . . . he devotes his life to the art of breaking up verse in such a way as to make it sound like insanely pompous prose. The effect of this on Shakespear's earlier verse, which is full of the naïve delight of pure oscillation, to be enjoyed as an Italian enjoys a barcarolle, or a child a swing, or a baby a rocking-cradle, is destructively stupid.
>
> (Review of *All's Well, Saturday Review,* 2 Feb., 1895)

The second is from the publishers of the first edition of *Troilus and Cressida* in 1609 who wrote in their preface that Shakespeare had:

> such a dexterity, and power of wit, that the most displeased with plays are pleas'd with his comedies. And all such dull and heavy-witted wordlings, as were never capable of the wit of a comedy, coming by report of them to his representations have found that wit there, that they never found in themselves, and have parted better witted than they came; feeling an edge of wit set upon them, more than ever they dream'd they had brain to grind it on. So much and such savoured salt of wit is in his comedies, that they seem (for their height of pleasure) to be born in that sea that brought forth Venus.

Alive in performance, Shakespeare's most conceited and obscure passages can represent enjoyment or vigour or confidence or sexual excitement—all powerful over an audience; they may also suggest sensitivity, gentleness, deep involvement—the kind of feelings which do not startle an audience but affect them slowly. The reader misses all this because he does not assimilate the conceits and rhetoric as an actor does, nor hear them as one part of the actor's performance.

II

THE INTELLECTUAL AND THEATRICAL SETTING

THE AGE AND ITS EFFECT ON LITERARY STYLE

Shakespeare's Sonnets and the 1590's

Patrick Cruttwell

The 1590's are the crucial years. In the Elizabethan *fin-de-siècle* there occurred a change, a shift of thought and feeling, which led directly to the greatest moment in English poetry: the "Shakespearean moment", the opening years of the seventeenth century, in which were written all the supreme Shakespearean dramas. The 1590's brought about that deep change of sensibility which marks off the later from the earlier Elizabethans, which alters the climate from that of *Arcadia* and *The Faerie Queene* to that which welcomed *Hamlet,* which probably demanded the Shakespearean rewriting of that drama from its crude original blood-and-thunder Kyd, and which found its other great poet in the person of Donne. To think of the Elizabethan age as a solid, unchanging unity is utterly misleading. Within it there were two generations and (roughly corresponding to those generations) two mentalities. In the 1590's the one "handed over" to the other. Such a statement is, of course, the grossest simplification; in the realms of the mind and the imagination things do not happen as neatly as that. And in fact, the 1590's are intensely confused, precisely because the "handing over" was then taking place; new and old were deeply entangled, and all generalizations must be loaded with exceptions. But there *was* an old, and there *was* a new, and the task of criticism is to analyse and distinguish.

Of all the poetry then written, none shows better what was really happening than the Sonnets of Shakespeare. They deal with far more

---

From Patrick Cruttwell, *The Shakespearean Moment.* Reprinted by permission of Chatto and Windus, Ltd.

than the personal events which make up their outward material; they show an intensely sensitive awareness of the currents and cross-currents of the age. They have hardly received the properly critical attention that they deserve; real criticism, it may be, has fought shy of them because of the fatal and futile attraction they have exercised on the noble army of cranks, who are far too busy identifying the young man, the dark lady, the rival poet, and William Shakespeare, to bother about the quality of the poetry. But the Sonnets are, in their own right, and quite apart from external "problems", poems of great and intriguing interest, as well as of beauty; they are much more subtle and varied than a casual reading reveals. The sweet and unchanging smoothness of their form is extremely deceptive; and it is partly this—the contrast between spirit and form—which makes them, of all the works of the 1590's, the best adapted to help us to a comprehension of the age's development in poetry. For what they show is a blending of new and old, the new *in* the old, and the new growing through the old; they use a form (the sonnet-sequence) which was above all the chosen form of the old, and in that form they say something completely at odds with the old, and destined to conquer it. On the surface they are fashionable and conventional, for the 1590's was the great age of the sonnet-sequence; below the surface, they are radically original.

If the word "fact" be given its proper meaning, our external knowledge concerning the Sonnets is limited to three facts, three dates. The first is the well-known reference, in Francis Meres's *Palladis Tamia,* to Shakespeare's "sugard sonnets among his private friends". The date of this is 1598, in which year Shakespeare was thirty-four. The second is the printing of two of the sonnets (the 138th and 144th) in *The Passionate Pilgrim* in 1599. The third is the publication of the whole in 1609. All else is conjecture, ranging from the rational through the plausible to the certifiable. From Meres's remark it would not be safe to conclude that *all* the Sonnets had been written by 1598, but it does seem reasonable to conclude that a good many of them had been; he would hardly have included them, as he does, in a list of Shakespeare's productions, if there had been only a handful. "Among his private friends" gives the kind of public they were written for, the target they were aimed at: that semi-private manuscript circulation so common in Renaissance literature. The fact that Francis Meres, who was a very obscure scribbler, had heard of them, probably read them himself, shows that this sort of privacy was hardly leak-proof. There is nothing surprising in their having stayed in manuscript for at least eleven years; Donne's love-poetry remained unprinted for nearly forty, but was very widely known. The printing (almost certainly unauthorized) of the two sonnets in *The Passionate Pilgrim* tells us one thing of value. These two happen to be among the most savage of those addressed to the lady, in a style and with a content one is (rightly) inclined to think of as approaching the mature Shakespearean; we know, then, that he *was* writing in this manner in the 1590's.

The first impression which a quick, unprejudiced reading of these 154 sonnets must give is that they are not a unity. There is no coherent plot or dominant theme; mood and style vary enormously, the changes are often abrupt and the connections obscure. Within this miscellany can be seen some groups which hold together. The first seventeen, for instance, are all addressed to a beautiful young nobleman, urging him to hurry up and marry in order to perpetuate his beauty in offspring. This is followed by a longer group, still addressed to the young man (or *a* young man—it might not be the same), announcing that it is in the poet's verse that his beauty will stay immortal. There are indications of a separation and a return, a quarrel and a reconcilement; there is a hint that the relationship has lasted for three years. The young man, as the sequence proceeds, seems to be looked on as a patron no less than as a lover; a rival poet, more successful than the writer at winning the patron's favour, enters on the scene, together with a good deal of self-depreciation and contempt for his own poetry on the part of the writer. The dark lady makes her appearance; first, it would seem, she was the writer's mistress, then the young man's, and by her fickleness she poisons the relations between them. Running through these stories—we can call them that whether we look on them as fiction or autobiography—are other themes: disgust at the dirty job of being a popular playwright and actor, bitterness at growing old, envy of other writers more up-to-date, intellectual, and highbrow, anger and disillusion with the state of society, uneasiness about the writer's own place in it, disgust with the whole business of love and sex.

Such are the contents. The first decision which has to be made is how we are to take them: as an exercise in fictional sonnetteering, such as the Elizabethans produced as from an assembly-line, or as personal and closely autobiographical. The probabilities seem overwhelmingly in favour of the latter. For one thing, there is the general "feel" of the poems; then there are the many correspondencies between themes in the Sonnets and in the plays of Shakespeare's middle period: that is, round about 1600. Moreover, if Shakespeare had set out to make an objective sequence with a fictional story, he would surely have made a far better job of it, have produced something more coherent and clearer, something nearer to *Venus and Adonis* and *The Rape of Lucrece;* and it seems unlikely, since he was by the 1590's fully launched as a writer of plays, that his dramatic faculty would have wanted to express itself in another form: it was busy enough in the theatre. The Sonnets he probably looked on as a totally different kind of writing, something outside his professional career, aimed at a different audience. They were, perhaps, part of his early campaign to win recognition in another world from that of the London theatres, in the world of the Court, the aristocracy, and the classical highbrows who tended to despise the popular drama. The two long poems, and *Love's Labour's Lost,* are evidence of this effort; to understand it we must forget our own perception that the supreme glory of the Elizabethan age was the achievement of the London theatres, and remember that in the 1590's and earlier virtually all the forces most likely to impress and attract a young writer, almost all that was socially most glittering and culturally most imposing, regarded those theatres and all they had so far produced with a contempt both social and intellectual. This contempt we are apt to regard with indulgent pity—"how ridiculously wrong they were!" —we forget how biting and humiliating it must have been to a sensitive and struggling contemporary. We are apt also to imagine that it died sooner than it did, that it was confined to the earlier, Sidneyan part of the Elizabethan age and limited to courtly snobs or academic pedants; but Hall's satire will prove that it was still pervasive, still powerful, in the 1590's, and Hall was neither courtier nor pedant. The third satire of his first book (*Virgidemiarum,* published in 1597) expresses the highbrow contempt for the popular drama. That drama, says Hall, is full of rant—"graced with huf-cap termes and thundring threats"; its language is tasteless and incongruous—"termes Italianate, Big-sounding sentences, and words of state"; it is "a goodly *hotch-potch*" of clownish gagging and tragedy (a criticism which, as we know from *Hamlet,* Shakespeare himself agreed with); it caters for the low and vulgar, and it is thoroughly mercenary:

> Shame that the Muses should be bought and sold,
> For every peasants Brasse, on each scaffold . . .
> Too popular is *Tragick Poesie,*
> Strayning his tip-toes for a farthing fee.

What we, in fact, regard with envious admiration—the power of the Elizabethan drama to appeal to all levels—a very considerable number of very respectable Elizabethans regarded with shocked disgust. And Shakespeare's 111th sonnet expresses a self-loathing agreement with this contempt:

> O for my sake doe you with fortune chide,
> The guiltie goddesse of my harmful deeds,
> That did not better for my life provide,
> Then publick meanes which publick manners breeds.
> Thence comes it that my name receives a brand,
> And almost thence my nature is subdu'd
> To what it workes in, like the Dyers hand,
> Pitty me then, and wish I were renu'de . . .

The imagery of staining shows a sense of more than intellectual degradation, of something which infects his whole being, a moral contagion. That impression is reinforced by the 110th, which makes a confession of deviations in love, of seeking (and finding) unworthy substitutes, and makes it through the image of the actor's life, the touring, self-exhibiting, posturing clown:

> Alas, 'tis true, I have gone here and there,
> And made my selfe a motley to the view,
> Gor'd mine own thoughts, sold cheap what is most deare,
> Made old offences of affections new.
> Most true it is, that I have lookt on truth
> Asconce and strangely . . .

A moral degradation, it would seem to be felt as: and also a social one. The 100th sonnet is evidence of that:

> Where art thou Muse that thou forgetst so long,
> To speake of that which gives thee all thy might?
> Spendst thou thy furie on some worthless songe,
> Darkning thy powre to lend *base* subiects light.
> Returne forgetfull Muse, and straight redeeme,
> In *gentle* numbers time so idely spent . . .

Base and *gentle* are epithets which, in Elizabethan English, had associations far more precisely social than they have to-day. The Muse is being urged to return to themes not only artistically more elevating but also socially more elevated. In his mingling of social and literary condemnation, Shakespeare on his own occupation is not so far from Hall.

If, then, the Sonnets derive from an episode in Shakespeare's life in which he made some sort of contact with the world of elegance and aristocracy, the next problem is to find the nature of that experience. The Sonnets, as we said, are not a unity; the experience they present was neither simple nor single, but complex and changing. Although there is no evidence at all that the printed arrangement of the poems was Shakespeare's—no evidence, indeed, that there ever *was* an arrangement—still, one can trace a certain logical development, and the development is from simplicity to complexity.

The early sonnets—that is, to speak more exactly, those which come first in the printed text, though it seems very likely that they were also the earliest—show the simple sensibility of the early Renaissance. There is a vast deal of words to very little matter; the method is that of constant variations on the same theme. The language is smooth and mellifluous,[1] the imagery clear and unsurprising. Ideas are few, simple, and in a sense artificial: marry and beget children so that your beauty

[1] "Smooth", "mellifluous", "honey-tongued", etc., seem to have been the stock-epithets for the contemporary praise of Shakespeare's early writings: for examples—

> 'Honie-tong'd Shakespeare' (John Weever: *Epigrammes,* 1599).
> 'Mellifluous & hony-tongued S.' (Meres: *Palladis Tamia,* 1598).
> 'And S. thou, whose hony-flowing Vaine' (Richard Barnfeild: *Poems in Divers Humors,* 1598).
> 'O sweet Mr. S.' (Anon.: *Return from Parnassus, c.* 1600).

It is not irrelevant to remember that when Ophelia recalls the unspoiled love of Hamlet, his romantic and chivalrous courtship, she remembers how she "suck'd the Honie of his Musicke Vowes".

may outlive you, your beauty will survive your death in my verse. There is no need to think that these ideas were held insincerely, but they do come from the common stock of Renaissance poetry; they lack the force of a theme which has a particular value. Of these poems one may sometimes feel, what one could never feel of the later ones, that some other writer could have produced them.

The love that these early sonnets celebrates is a simple unqualified adoration; neither it nor its object is questioned, criticized, or analysed. The object is a young man who is in no way characterized, or rendered with a sense of individual reality; he seems to be rather the ideal youth of the Renaissance, beautiful, highborn, wilful, and irresistible. He is regarded with a curious sexual ambiguity, as in the 53rd:

> Describe *Adonis* and the counterfet,
> Is poorely immitated after you,
> On *Hellens* cheeke all art of beautie set,
> And you in *Grecian* tires are painted new.

The symbols of male and female beauty are taken as interchangeable. The 20th sonnet makes that ambiguity more apparent:

> A Womans face with natures owne hand painted,
> Hast thou the Master Mistris of my passion . . .
> And for a woman wert thou first created,
> Till nature as she wrought thee fell a dotinge,
> And by addition me of thee defeated,
> By adding one thing to my purpose nothing.
> But since she prickt thee out for womens pleasure,
> Mine be thy love and thy loves use their treasure.

There is there, perhaps, a slight feeling of frustration, a sense that this sort of love is hardly satisfying, which comes to the surface in the wry punning jest of "prickt". Primarily, it means "marked thee in the list of males"—as Falstaff tells Shallow ("prick him") to mark down his recruits. But it also had a very current sexual meaning: as a verb, "to copulate", and as a noun, "the male sexual organ"—as in Mercutio's "the bawdy hand of the Dyall is now upon the pricke of Noone". This obscene jest in the 20th sonnet seems the first appearance in the sequence of a feeling and meaning not altogether simple; but in general, these first sonnets are quite at home in the climate of Renaissance "homosexual"[2] feeling, which was in part an aesthetic affectation, based perhaps on Hellenism, imitation of the Greeks, in part a quite genuine emotion, compounded from love of beauty, worship of noble birth, and an elegiac tenderness for youth. The 37th sonnet sums up the nature of the young man's attractiveness; it opens with a simile which likens Shakespeare to a "decrepit Father" who "takes delight / To see his active childe doe deedes of youth", and then lists the qualities of his

---

[2] The word is to be taken with no implications of abnormality.

charm: "beautie, birth, or wealth, or wit." The homosexual feeling that undoubtedly exists in the Sonnets has a certain un-physical remoteness; it is never explicit and aggressive, as it is in Marlowe. But then Marlowe was a tough individual and a *mauvais sujet,* while Shakespeare appears to have been a respectable gentleman. There is, of course, no need to evoke the climate of the Renaissance in order to explain how a middle-aged, middle-class, provincial poet, sensuous and sensitive to his finger-tips, conceived a passionate adoration for a young, highborn and courtly Adonis; there is no need, in fact, to go further back than Oscar Wilde and Lord Alfred Douglas. (No *literary* comparison intended.) The insistence that the loved one should get married is certainly curious; one can only explain it on the usual terms, that these first seventeen sonnets were "commissioned". But it does at least demonstrate that the quality of this love was neither physical nor possessive.

As the sequence proceeds, the texture of the poems, though the subject remains the young man, shows a slow thickening, an increasing complexity. They become much more introspective; the interest is often far more on the writer's general state of mind than on the object of his love or even the love itself. In the 29th, for instance ("When in disgrace with Fortune and mens eyes"), the real concentration of intensity falls on the sense of utter failure that fills the writer's being; the conclusion, which affirms that this failure is redeemed by his love, is weak and unconvincing by comparison. This pattern is followed in many sonnets; often, the real weight of the poem, which is thoroughly pessimistic, introspective, and not concerned at all with love, is feebly opposed by the final couplet alone. Of these the most striking is the 66th ("Tir'd with all these, for restfull death I cry"), in which the long piling Hamlet-like list of the world's iniquities utterly overwhelms the protesting little line at the end—"save that to dye, I leave my Love alone." In these poems and many more, an all-inclusive self-examination replaces or reinforces the narrow theme of love; self-disgust, self-contempt, self-reproach are the usual tones of this introspection, and even the rare moments of satisfaction are qualified and brushed aside at once:

> Sinne of selfe-love possesseth al mine eie,
> And all my soule, and al my every part;
> And for this sinne there is no remedie,
> It is so grounded inward in my heart.
> Me thinkes no face so gracious is as mine,
> No shape so true, no truth of such account,
> And for my selfe mine owne worth do define,
> As I all other in all worths surmount.
> But when my glasse shewes me my selfe indeed
> Beated and chopt with tand antiquitie,
> Mine owne selfe love quite contrary I read;
> Selfe, so selfe loving were iniquity . . .
>
> (62)

Bitterness at the thought of age, as here, is one of the points on which this self-hatred is focussed; but another, more particular, and also, it would seem, more deeply felt, is the conviction of failure as a poet. This is hinted at in some of the early sonnets, as for example in the 32nd:

> If thou survive my well contented daie,
> When that churle death my bones with dust shall cover
> And shalt by fortune once more re-survay
> These poore rude lines of thy deceased Lover;
> Compare them with the bett'ring of the time,
> And though they be out-stript by every pen,
> Reserve them for my love, not for their rime,
> Exceeded by the hight of happier men . . .

—but there seems no great bitterness there: it sounds like polite and conventional modesty, and just where the failure lies is not yet defined. It is defined later, with great and bitter precision, stimulated, it seems, by the coming of the more successful rival. His own verse has got into a rut; it is now old-fashioned and monotonous:

> Why write I still all one, ever the same,
> And keepe invention in a noted weed,
> That every word doth almost tel my name,
> Shewing their birth, and where they did proceed?
> (76)

The 78th particularizes further; the failure is seen as a lack of artistic grace and a deficiency in learning:

> In others workes thou doost but mend the stile,
> And Arts with thy sweete graces graced be.
> But thou art all my art, and doost advance
> As high as learning, my rude ignorance.[3]

What this sense of poetic failure means in Shakespeare's literary career, and in relation to the time when the Sonnets were written, will be looked into later.

The poems, as they proceed, then, move away from a simple and single contemplation and adoration of the young Adonis. They widen in scope, till every interest of the writer's life is brought within their reach: his dreams of social success and bitterness at social failure, the problems and rivalries of his career as an author, his perceptions of the evils and injustices in society, his private anguish at growing old

[3] It is interesting to see, so early and in Shakespeare himself, a recognition of what was to become the critical commonplace: that he "wanted art" (as Jonson put it) and was unlearned.

and his private fear of death. The young man is still the centre, but he too is involved in the growing complexity. For now he is looked on with a critical eye, as a fallible individual and not as a symbol that cannot be questioned. The obsequious adoration which some of the sonnets award him—"my soverayne", "your servant", "your slave", "your vassal"—is qualified by hints of rebuke:

> No more bee greev'd at that which thou hast done,
> Roses have thornes, and silver fountaines mud,
> Cloudes and eclipses staine both Moone and Sunne,
> And loathsome canker lives in sweetest bud.
> (35)

A contrast is felt between his outward beauty and inward corruption:

> O what a Mansion have those vices got
> Which for their habitation chose out thee.
> (95)

And now he is looked at through the eyes of others:

> That tongue that tells the story of thy daies,
> (Making lascivious comments on thy sport)
> Cannot dispraise, but in a kinde of praise,
> Naming thy name, blesses an ill report.
> (95)

He is, as it were, becoming dramatized: seen in the round, seen and felt as a real human being, in the context of society and under the scrutiny of an observant though still loving mind.

When the dark lady makes her delayed but most effective entry (she does not effectively appear till the 127th sonnet[4]—one would almost think that Shakespeare's theatrical cunning had something to do with it), the process we have already traced continues, at a faster tempo and with ever-increasing intensity. These sonnets which deal with the lady (127 to 152) contain most of the greatness and most of the maturity in the whole sequence; they can be taken as a single poem, in the way in which (for instance) Donne's nineteen *Holy Sonnets* are a single poem. The lady is depicted with a familiar equality, a bitter and bawdy ferocity, such as are never accorded to the young man even at his naughtiest. His goings-on are excused and even admired; hers are neither. Her promiscuity is described in language of tough and "unpoetic" realism; and this too the young man never receives:

> If eyes corrupt by over-partiall lookes,
> Be anchord in the baye where all men ride,
> Why of eyes falsehood hast thou forged hookes,

[4] Sonnets 40–42 hint at her.

Whereto the judgement of my heart is tide?
Why should my heart thinke that a severall plot,
Which my heart knowes the wide worlds common place?
(137)

The first of these images has an indecent pun on "ride", one of the commonest of Elizabethan verbs for describing male sexual activity (the jestings of the Frenchmen, before Agincourt, about the Dauphin's horse, for example); the last is derived from the contemporary enclosures of common land ("severall plot" meaning "privately-owned piece of land"), and its play with the sexual meaning of the word ("promiscuous") was also a favourite Elizabethan jest. The language, when the lady is the subject, comes much nearer to that of common speech—and of the drama—and much farther from the lyrically "poetical", than when the young man is dealt with.

From this perception that the lady is a whore, comes a moral tone far fiercer and deeper, and a self-examination more searching, than anything before. There is not only the famous 129th sonnet on lust, there is also the 146th, which is one of the very few passages in Shakespeare explicitly and traditionally theological, in its conflict between body and soul ("poore soul the centre of my sinfull earth"), its advice to the soul to thrive by denying the body, and its Donne-like ending:

So shalt thou feede on death, that feedes on men,
And death once dead, there's no more dying then

—which is very close to the last line of Donne's tenth Holy Sonnet:

And death shall be noe more; death, thou shalt dye.

Of these sonnets' introspection, the dominant theme is that of a self-divided personality, of a love which exists in spite of the judgment of reason, in spite of a moral perception of its wrongness and of its object's worthlessness, even in spite of the senses' recognition that she is not particularly beautiful. Others do not find her so, and the others are probably right:

If that be faire whereon my false eyes dote,
What meanes the world to say it is not so?
If it be not, then love doth well denote,
Loves eye is not so true as all mens . . .
(148)

There is an utter disintegration of the personality: senses, wits, and heart are at strife ("but my five wits, nor my five senses can / Diswade one foolish heart from serving thee" [5]); the whole self is at odds with

---

[5] 141.

the love which it cannot resist ("when I against my selfe with thee pertake").[6] It is not only self-division; it is also a perverted craving for self-deception, a deception that does not deceive. He asks to be cheated; but of course the mere asking implies that the cheat is already detected:

> If I might teach thee witte better it were,
> Though not to love, yet love to tell me so,
> As testie sick-men when their deaths be neere,
> No newes but health from their Phisitions know.
> (140)

Behind this is a conviction that the whole relationship is wrong, is false in itself and founded on falsehood—in the sonnets devoted to the lady, the words "false" and "falsehood" occur nine times, "lie" or "belied" six times—and if all is false, then why should the parts be true? This comes to a climax in what is perhaps the most terrible poem of the whole sequence, the 138th: the most terrible, and also the nakedest, since it confesses things that are not easily confessed:

> When my love sweares that she is made of truth,
> I do beleeve her though I know she lyes,
> That she might thinke me some untuterd youth,
> Unlearned in the worlds false subtilties.
> Thus vainely thinking that she thinkes me young,
> Although she knowes my dayes are past the best,
> Simply I credit her false speaking tongue,
> On both sides thus is simple truth supprest:
> But wherefore sayes she not she is unjust?
> And wherefore say not I that I am old?
> O loves best habit is in seeming trust,
> And age in love, loves not t' have yeares told.
> Therefore I lye with her, and she with me,
> And in our faults by lyes we flattered be.

Of this climactic poem the last couplet, with its pun on "lye", is the very apex. The pun's grim seriousness is quite in the mature Shakespearean manner, like the remarkable triple pun in *The Winter's Tale* —Leontes raving with jealousy to his son:

> Goe play (Boy) play: thy Mother playes, and I
> Play too; but so disgrac'd a part, whose issue
> Will hisse me to my Grave . . .

—in which *play* means, first, the innocent childish play of the boy; next, the adulterous sexual sport of the wife; finally, the playing of an

---

[6] 149.

actor, in the shameful role of the cuckold. The pun in the sonnet forces together the physical union and its context, as it were, its whole surrounding universe, of moral defilement and falsehood. It says, in fact, what the opening of the 129th sonnet says:

> The expence of Spirit in a waste of shame
> Is lust in action . . .

and it says it with the same union of moral power and physical precision. "The expence of spirit," for the modern reader, has only emotional force; it is in fact a piece of contemporary sexual physiology. From the heart to the sexual organs, was believed to go a vein, bearing in it the "spirit generative". "Expence" means "expenditure": what the phrase refers to is the loss of the "spirit generative" in the act of sex.

This love that is known to be wrong, and is yet persisted in, leads at last to a total reversal of the moral order. Good becomes bad in this love, and bad becomes good: "When all my *best* doth worship thy *defect*"—"that in my minde thy *worst* all *best* exceeds." "Fair" is equivocated against "foul", "bright" against "black":

> Or mine eyes seeing this, say this is not,
> To put faire truth upon so foule a face
> (137)

—which reminds one of the way in which the witches of *Macbeth* juggle and equivocate "fair" against "foul"; and there too the meaning is that the moral order is reversed. Clearest of all is the final couplet of 150:

> If thy unworthinesse raisd love in me,
> More worthy I to be belov'd of thee

—he has loved her for her unworthiness, this in turn has infected him, has made him unworthy, and hence his unworthiness makes him "worthy" of her. This hell is the exact antithesis of the Baudelairian heaven in *Moesta et Errabunda*—"oú tout ce que l'on aime est digne d'être aimé." Substitute *indigne* for *digne,* and Baudelaire's meaning would be identical with Shakespeare's.

The sonnet which follows this (151) shows a slight change of tone, a relaxing of the moral struggle; it reads like a resigned sardonic acceptance of the utter wrongness of the whole business. It admits, in terms unusually religious for Shakespeare, that his love is betraying his soul:

> For thou betraying me, I doe betray
> My nobler part to my gross bodies treason

but the phrases addressed to her—"gentle cheater", "sweet selfe"—have an air of tired and tolerant affection. Two rogues together, might as well have some fun—the spirit is not unlike that of Villon in the *Ballade de la Grosse Margot:*

> Ie suis paillard, la paillarde me suit.
> Lequel vault mieux? chascun bien s'entresuit.
> L'ung l'aultre vault; c'est a mau chat mau rat.

And the rest of the sonnet carries on in that spirit with an almost cheerful obscenity, with an elaborate and thoroughly Donne-like conceit on male sexuality; the final couplet:

> No want of conscience hold it that I call
> Her love, for whose deare love I rise and fall

is exactly in the manner of the lines in Donne's nineteenth *Elegie:*

> We easly know
> By this these Angels from an evil sprite,
> Those set our hairs, but these our flesh upright.

We have come a long way from the lyrical idealism of the opening sonnet—

> From fayrest creatures we desire increase,
> That thereby beautie's Rose might never dye

—to reach a poem as complex as this, which in fourteen lines can range from religious solemnity to bawdy mockery. We have come, in fact, from Spenser to Donne.

The way that the Sonnets go is also the way of their age. The 1590's, as said above, was the golden age of sonnetteering; as also of amorous pastoral. They darkened the air; they emerged by their thousands. And if we are honest, we must admit that almost all of them are unbearably tedious; what life they ever had has long since departed. "The sweete sobs of Sheepheardes and Nymphes", "the drery abstracts of my endless cares"—Webbe and Drayton, respectively, describe with an all-too-faithful if unmeant precision the nature and effect of this verse:[7] always sweet, always lachrymose, always unreal. If we read through Spenser's *Amoretti*[8]—it is fairer to choose an example from a true poet than

[7] The first of these phrases is from William Webbe's *Discourse of English Poetrie* (1586); the second from the first sonnet of Michael Drayton's *Ideas Mirrour* (1594).
[8] Published in 1595; probably written two or three years earlier.

from one of the countless poetasters who practised the *genre*—the final impression is monotony. For, first, there is a desperate narrowness of subject; these sonnets *are* really "all about love", which is not true, as we have seen, of Shakespeare's. Then, within this subject, the number of attitudes is strictly limited, and entirely conventional. The Lady is cruel as a tigress, dealing out death with her eyes; the lover despairing and moribund. The loved one is never analysed and never individualized; she is worshipped with the language of religion—"my sweet saynt", "her temple fayre", "my thoughts lyke sacred Priests". As the moods are few and the tone unchanging, so is the language narrow in scope. "Fair", for example, is an epithet-of-all-work; it occurs some sixty times in these 88 sonnets. The particular and the physical are very far away—the 77th sonnet, for example:

> Was it a dreame, or did I see it playne?
> A goodly table of pure yvory,
> All spred with juncats fit to entertayne
>
> The greatest Prince with pompous roialty;
> Mongst which, there in a silver dish did ly
> Two golden apples of unvalewd price;
> Far passing those which Hercules came by,
> Or those which Atalanta did entice . . .

—we need the explanation which the last lines give us, that this is the lady's breast. The 15th has a similar quality, and a curious anticipation of Donne (he may have remembered it when he wrote *The Sunne Rising*); but the contrast between them enforces the point:

> Ye tradefull Merchants, that with weary toyle
> Do seeke most pretious things to make your gaine,
> And *both the Indias* of their treasure spoile;
> What needeth you to seek so farre in vaine?
> For loe, my Love doth in her selfe containe
> All this worlds riches that may far be found . . .
>
> Looke, and tomorrow late, tell mee,
> Whether *both th' India's* of spice and Myne
> Be where thou leftst them, or lie here with mee . . .

Spenser's "love" is a far-away abstraction; the rest of the sonnet goes off into conceits which build up the idealized, unindividualized "fair one" (sapphire eyes, ruby lips, pearly teeth, ivory forehead, golden hair, silver hands). Donne has the bedroom reality of "lie here with mee", which two lines later is made even more concrete by "all here in one bed lay". When Spenser does try to give a physical force to his abstract verse, it is clear at once that he is outside his proper range; the hackneyed antithesis of ice and fire ("my Love is lyke to yse, and I to fyre") topples to the ludicrous with "but that I burne much more in boyling sweat".

To look at one such sonnet-sequence is to look at them all; there can never have been, before or since, such a standardized and derivative poetry. Drayton's *Ideas Mirrour* (to take just one more example) has all the elements which we have found in Spenser and could find in a hundred others. The religious language: "receave the incense which I offer here . . . My soules oblations to thy sacred name." The murderous cruelty:

> O thou unkindest fayre, most fayrest shee,
> In thine eyes tryumph murthering my poore hart . . .

The uncritical adoration:

> So may he grace all these in her alone,
> Superlative in all comparison.

Smoothness and standardization, abstractness and unreality, utter lack of criticism or analysis: these are the marks of the lyrical verse which, in the last years of the sixteenth century, was brought against something new. At the centre of the new thing were a spreading and a sharpening of the spirit of criticism. That Shakespeare both shared in this spirit and shared in it consciously—was aware of its existence—his Sonnets show more than one sign. There is the line in the 38th—"if my slight Muse doe please these curious daies": "curious" means, exactly, "critical". There is that in the 32nd—"had my friend's Muse grown with this growing age":[9] he is clearly aware of a ferment and development around him. But most explicit is the 130th ("My Mistres eyes are nothing like the Sunne"), which goes one by one through the commonplaces of the conventional lyric and points out, in the name of reality and commonsense, that they are so much nonsense. Not much reading is required in Elizabethan poetastery to find these platitudes, to appreciate just how exact and pointed is the satire of this sonnet. The seventh poem of Thomas Watson's 'ΕΚΑΤΟΜΠΑΘΙΑ or *Passionate Centurie of Love* ("published at the request of certain Gentlemen his very frendes" in 1582), contains in its eighteen lines all but one of the platitudes that Shakespeare makes fun of. Watson on the left, Shakespeare's comments on the right:

Her yellow lockes exceede the beaten goulde	If haires be wiers, black wiers grow on her head
Her sparkling eies in heav'n a place deserve	My Mistres eyes are nothing like the Sunne

[9] The "friend" is Shakespeare himself: the line is put into the mouth of the beloved.

Her wordes are musicke all of silver sounde	I love to hear her speake, yet well I know, / That musick hath a far more pleasing sound
On either cheeke a *Rose* and *Lillie* lies	I have seene Roses damaskt, red and white, / But noe such Roses see I in her cheekes
Her breath is sweet perfume, or hollie flame	And in some perfumes is there more delight / Then in the breath that from my Mistres reekes
Her lips more red then any *Corall* stone	*Currall* is far more red then her lips red
Her necke more white then aged Swans that mone; / her brest transparent is, like Christall rocke	If Snow be white, why then her Brests are dunne

The modern reader, if he feels inclined to dismiss as turgid nonsense the great bulk of Elizabethan sonnetteering and amorous versifying, is in good company. Shakespeare thought the same. What he is here writing is literary satire, and what he is satirizing is something not so remote from some of the sonnets which he himself had written in praise of the young Adonis. There was, in fact, in these years, a tremendous outbreak of satirical writing, and one of the favourite targets of this satire was the amorous sonnetteer. Both the fashion and its antidote arose almost simultaneously.[10]

Donne, Hall, and Marston are the most notable of the verse satirists of the 1590's. Their satires have a good deal in common, though Donne's are by far the best and stand apart from the others not only by their finer quality; but the precise nature of the literary *genre* they all practise—its descent from Roman satire, notably Juvenal and Persius, and its convention of "roughness"—matters a good deal less than the mood which created it and which it expressed. The disillusioned man, the unsparing critic, the embittered railer, the Plain Dealer (Wycherley's character is in the tradition): these are the satirist's poses. He is immensely indignant with everyone and everything; indignation is emphatically the making of *his* verses. Society is utterly rotten; all is degenerate, all is corrupt; and he applies himself with fervent and reforming zeal to the "lashing" of the age. The metaphor of flagellation is extraordinarily frequent (these examples are some of many):

---

[10] Cf. J. B. Leishman's introduction to his edition of the *Three Parnassus Plays* (Nicholson & Watson, 1949).

Quake, guzzel dogs, that live on putrid slime,
Skud from the lashes of my yerking rhyme.

. . . whilst I securely let him overslip,
Nere yerking him with my satiric whip.

Hold out ye guiltie, and ye galled hides,
And meet my far-fetch'd stripes with waiting sides.

Al these and more, deserve some blood-drawne lines:
But my sixe Cords beene of too loose a twine.[11]

(None of these satirical zealots appears to have had the common-sense of Swift's observation in the *Tale of a Tub:* "Now, if I know anything of mankind, these gentlemen might very well spare their reproof and correction; for there is not, through all nature, another so callous and insensible a member as the world's posteriors, whether you apply to it the toe or the birch.")

The mood, then, is one of unqualified railing and thorough-going criticism. Directed at what? At everything: this satire does not pick and choose, but assaults in all directions—indiscriminate rage, at times on the edge of hysteria, possesses it. It works in much the same way, though with incomparably less terseness and control, as Shakespeare's 66th sonnet; it makes its indictment by sheer piling-up. This wholesale railing enters Shakespeare's drama from the 1600's onwards; it begins in lightweight style with Jaques—"wee two will raile against our Mistris the world, and *all* our miserie", "Ile raile against *all* the first borne of Egypte"—this being the exact equivalent of the (also lightweight) railing of Donne's second Satire: "Sir; though (I thanke God for it) I do hate Perfectly *all* this towne"—and when it has developed to the depth and ferocity of Hamlet and Timon and Lear, universality is still its keynote and "all" the word which signals it:

How weary, stale, flat, and unprofitable
Seemes to me *all* the uses of this world?

Who dares? who dares
In puritie of Manhood stand upright
And say, this mans a Flatterer. If one be,
So are they *all:* for everie grize of Fortune
Is smooth'd by that below. The Learned pate
Duckes to the Golden Foole. *All's* oblique:
There's nothing levell in our cursed Natures
But direct villanie. Therefore be abhorr'd,
All Feasts, Societies, and Throngs of men.

---

[11] These four quotations are from: Marston's *Scourge of Villanie,* proemium ad librum primum, 1598; ibid., Satire III; Hall's *Virgidemiarum,* conclusion to first three books, 1597; ibid., Book IV, Satire I.

Plague *all,*
That your Activitie may defeat and quell
The sourse of *all* Erection. There's more Gold,
Do you damne others, and let this damne you,
And ditches grave you *all.*

And thou *all*-shaking Thunder,
Strike flat the thicke Rotundity o' th' world,
Cracke Natures moulds, *all* germaines spill at once
That makes ingratefull Man.[12]

The end of this railing—as the two last quotations indicate—was a thoroughgoing hatred of life, of the very source of life; its beginning was an individualist criticism, a questioning of assumptions that had gone unquestioned. The curious cult of Melancholy—itself another fashion of the 1590's—was perhaps its beginning, at least one of its earliest symptoms; for melancholy went with solitariness, it was at once the pride and the curse of the man who went off by himself, to criticize what others accepted. Jaques is a lightweight melancholiac, as also a lightweight critical railer; the melancholy-satirical connection is there also in Marston:

Thou musing Mother of faire Wisdom's lore,
Ingenuous Melancholy, I implore
Thy grave assistance; take thy gloomie seate,
Enthrone thee in my bloud, let me intreate
Stay his quick jocund skippes, and force him runne
A sad-paced course, until my whippes are done.[13]

And just as Shakespeare thought of the age as penetrated with the spirit of criticism ("if my slight Muse can please these curious daies"), so did Hall, in the same spirit and with the same word:

> I well foresee in the timely publication of these my concealed Satyres, I am set upon the racke of many mercilesse and peremptorie censures; which sith the calmest and most plausible writer is almost fatally subject unto *in the curiositie of these nicer times,* how may I hope to be exempted upon the occasion of so busy and stirring a subject?[14]

This wholesale railing, which has its place and its force when it is only a part of the whole, as it is in Shakespeare's drama, is more than

[12] *Hamlet,* I.2; *Timon,* IV.2; ibid.; *Lear,* III.2.
[13] *Scourge of Villanie:* proemium ad librum primum.
[14] *Virgidemiarum:* postscript. There is also Samuel Daniel, who talks of "these more curious times" in *Musophilus* (1601). The phrase seems to have been a cliché, as, according to Swift, its modern equivalent was in the early eighteenth century: " 'Tis grown a word of Course for Writers to say, This Critical Age, as Divines say, This Sinful Age." (*Thoughts on Various Subjects.*)

a little disagreeable—even worse, more than a little incredible—when the satirists present it as a total attitude to life. Shakespeare digested and used it, as he did all things; Donne and Hall went beyond it to better things (great poetry and a Deanery for Donne, silence and a Bishopric for Hall); Marston stayed—to become surely the most tediously forcible-feeble of all Jacobean dramatists. The particular criticisms of the satirists are of greater inherent interest than their universal invectives; and for our purpose the most relevant is their criticism of the amorous sonnetteer. They note and deride exactly what wearies a modern reader. They satirise the adoration of the mistress's perfections:

> Do not I put my mistress in before,
> And piteously her gracious aid implore?
> Do not I flatter, call her wondrous fair,
> Virtuous, divine, most debonair?[15]

They deal faithfully with the lover's conscientious misery:

> For when my ears receiv'd a fearful sound
> That he was sick, I went, and there I found
> Him laid of love, and newly brought to bed
> Of monstrous folly, and a frantic head.
> His chamber hang'd about with elegies,
> With sad complaints of his love's miseries;
> His windows strew'd with sonnets, and the glass
> Drawn full of loveknots. I approach'd the ass,
> And straight he weeps, and sighs some sonnet out
> To his fair love . . .[16]

And above all, their central point of attack is just that which we have seen was Shakespeare's in the 130th sonnet: insincerity and unreality:

> Nor list I sonnet of my Mistresse face,
> To paint some Blowesse with a borrowed grace.

> Then poures he forth in patched *Sonettings*
> His love, his lust, and loathsome flatterings . . .
> Then can he terme his durtie ill-fac'd bride
> Lady and Queene, and virgin deifide:
> Be shee all sootie-blacke, or bery-browne,
> Shees white as morrows milk, or flaks new blowne.[17]

Satire implies irony, however crude; and irony implies the ability to see and to feel more than one thing at once, and to feel one's own

---

[15] Marston: "The Author in praise of his precedent Poem"— i.e., *Metamorphosis of Pygmalion,* 1598.
[16] Marston: Satire III, 1598.
[17] Hall: *Virgidemiarum,* Book I, Satire I; ibid., Satire VII.

self as multiple. The single- and simple-minded cannot achieve it. And hence that sense of a multiple and divided personality, which exists so strongly in those of Shakespeare's sonnets which deal with the lady, is also a vital part, deep and widespread, of the new spirit of the age. Civil war—war inside the individual—is a favourite image, one that Shakespeare carries with him from the Sonnets themselves ("such civill warre is in my love and hate")[18] to the plays which he wrote round the turn of the century, the plays which emerged from the crisis. Brutus uses it, tormented by uncertainty:

> Since *Cassius* first did whet me against *Caesar,*
> I have not slept.
> Betweene the acting of a dreadfull thing,
> And the first motion, all the *Interim* is
> Like a *Phantasma,* or a hideous Dreame;
> The *Genius,* and the mortall Instruments
> Are then in councell; and the state of man,
> Like to a little Kingdome, suffers then
> The nature of an Insurrection.
>
> (II.i)

Hamlet uses it, describing to Horatio his restless broodings on the ship which is taking him to England:

> Sir, in my heart there was a kinde of fighting,
> That would not let me sleepe . . .
>
> (V.ii)

And—nearest in subject and spirit to the Sonnets—Troilus uses it, shocked and hysterical at Cressida's faithlessness:

> This she? no, this is *Diomeds Cressida:*
> If beautie have a soule, this is not she:
> If soules guide vowes, if vowes are sanctimonies;
> If sanctimonie be the gods delight:
> If there be rule in unitie it selfe,
> This is not she: O madnesse of discourse!
> That cause sets up, with, and against thy selfe,
> Bi-fold authoritie:[19] where reason can revolt
> Without perdition, and losse assume all reason,
> Without revolt. This is, and is not *Cressid:*
> Within my soule, there doth conduce a fight
> Of this strange nature, that a thing inseperate,
> Divides more wider then the skie and earth.
>
> (V.ii)

---

[18] 35.

[19] The Folio's reading is "by foule authoritie." This is the Quarto's: spelling modernized from "by-fould" for the sake of clarity.

This speech, and the scene it is set in, objectify in terms of drama, and divide among the characters, the elements which in the Sonnets are involved and internal. What Troilus is shocked *out of,* is the lyrical ideal love—"if beautie have a soule", "if vowes be sanctimonies" (the language of the "religion" of love); what he is shocked *into,* is an anarchy of the personality and a chaos of all perceptions. "This is, and is not *Cressid*"—the hysterical denial of reality—has its parallel in the 137th sonnet:

> Thou blinde fool Love, what doost thou to mine eies,
> That they behold, and see not what they see? . . .
> Or mine eies seeing this, say this is not . . .

And in another of the plays written in the early 1600's, *Measure for Measure,* we find the same response to the same kind of situation: a sudden, overbalancing moral shock. Angelo, immediately after Isabella's first visit to him and his first perception of his own desire, asks himself: "What dost thou? or what art thou *Angelo?*"

The collapse of reason's authority, which Troilus feels in himself, is in the 147th sonnet:

> My reason the Phisition to my love,
> Angry that his Prescriptions are not kept,
> Hath left me, and I desperate now approve,
> Desire is death, which physick did except.
> Past cure I am, now reason is past care . . .

The tough commonsense and astringent bawdy, which in the Sonnets are the means of preserving control (certainly for the poetry, perhaps for the poet), are there in the drama: in the dry mockery of Ulysses—"What hath *she* done Prince, that can soyle our mothers?"—and the rant-reducing bathos of Thersites:

> TROILUS Not the dreadfull spout,
> Which Shipmen doe the Hurricano call,
> Constring'd in masse by the almightie Fenne,
> Shall dizzie with more clamour Neptunes eare,
> In his discent; then shall my prompted sword,
> Falling on *Diomed.*
> THERSITES Heele tickle it for his concupie.

Only a poetry which is complex in itself, the expression of complex conditions, could thus be turned into drama. The simple poetry and single personality of the lyrical sonnetteers denied them the dramatic quality; few of them were dramatists at all, none was a dramatist of living power. From their verse those elements are absent of which, in the play, Ulysses and Thersites are the spokesmen; and this gives a wider relevance to what was noted in the Sonnets, that as they move from uncritical adoration and mellifluous simplicity, from a poetry, that is, not unlike the poetry of the sonnetteers, so their object is dramatized, "seen in the round".

This difference in literary and personal qualities was reinforced by a social difference, a difference in the kind of acceptance which the writers strove for. The simple, lyrical, undramatic appealed to, and wrote for, the courtly Renaissance world and the taste which grew from it, whose attraction, as we have seen, the young Shakespeare felt strongly; the multiple, critical, dramatic was alien to that world, its true home was the London theatre. For the former world, poetry was an elegant accomplishment, something you pleased your friends with ("among his private friends"). Publication was deprecated; the "common reader" (or common spectator) was outside the circle. "Onely he may show (his writings) to a friend", advises Castiglione's *Courtier,* the Bible of the courtly Renaissance: "let him be circumspect in keeping them close."[20] Even when they published, which of course they usually did, eventually, being "obliged", like Thomas Watson, by "request of friends" if not by "hunger", they aimed at a one-level audience and a one-level acceptance. There is, in fact, only one way in which a Spenserian or Sidneyan sonnet can be "taken": if not in that way, it is not taken at all. Thus the multiple personality of the dramatists reflected (both caused, and was caused by) the nature of the public he wrote for; thus Shakespeare's complaint that his nature had been "stained" by his bread-winning at the playhouse was true in a way which perhaps he did not know: in his raid on the world of politeness and "gentility" and essential simplicity, he took over with him—he could not help it—the complex ironies of the professional dramatist. The gulf was bridged later, at least in part, when the theatre's creations had achieved a prestige they had never had in the earlier days; it was bridged by men like Jonson and Donne—and Shakespeare himself: but the Sonnets prove how great had been the effort and the strain, what feelings of shame and unworthiness and "not belonging" a popular dramatist had to overcome if he entered the alien world. He was right, in a sense: right, at least, to feel that he did not "belong". At first: but later, he did.

---

[20] George Pettie protests against this kind of thing:

> Those which mislike that a Gentleman should publish the fruits of his learning, and some curious Gentlemen, who thinke it most commendable in a Gentleman, to cloake his art and skill in everie thing, and to seeme to doe all things of his own mother with, as it were. . . (*A Petite Pallace,* etc., 1576).

Pettie's sarcastic repetition of "Gentleman" indicates the snobbish element in the anti-printing convention. A later protest came from Drayton, in the preface to the first eighteen books of *Poly-Olbion* (published in 1612):

> In publishing this my poem, there is this great disadvantage against me, that it cometh out at this time, when verses are wholly deducted to chambers, and nothing esteemed in this lunatic age, but what is kept in cabinets, and must only pass by transcription.

This multiple personality is a prey to uncertainty; his values are never secure. It is this insecurity that makes the "problem-plays" problematical; there seems in their author (and it spreads to his readers) a radical doubt of his ultimate purpose. The doubt appears in all fields which the dramas touch: in politics for one. In such "political" plays as *Henry VI, Julius Caesar, Henry IV,* and *Henry V*—plays which do not have the particular "atmosphere" of the problem-plays, whatever their dates—there seems no questioning of the basic Elizabethan political assumptions, even when these are dissected and discussed in dramatic terms. "Honour" (martial glory) in *Henry IV,* for instance. Hotspur, Falstaff, and the Prince divide it dramatically between them: Hotspur giving the one extreme, chivalrous, out-of-date bellicosity, Falstaff supplying the other, cynical earthy realism, and the Prince representing the mean, the reasonable honour which is finally victorious, over the opposition of the first and the temptation of the second. All three views are given with an undistorted calmness; each has its full value. One feels that Shakespeare enjoys and appreciates all of them, without worrying over which is "right". So with the presentation of the "mob" in *Henry VI* and *Julius Caesar:* the conventional view of it as the irrational unstable many-headed monster—the medieval view, as in Chaucer's *Clerk's Tale*—is vigorously and unambiguously upheld. Each of these plays has a brief episode, identical in tone and feeling—in *Henry VI,* the killing of the man who, in all innocence, has failed to address Cade as "Mortimer", and in *Julius Caesar* the tearing to pieces of the poet Cinna because he shares his name with one of the conspirators—which exposes with grim farce the brutal irresponsible stupidity of the mob and its leaders. But in *Troilus and Cressida* one wonders, and feels that Shakespeare is wondering. Honour is debated in that play also: Hector, speaking for reason, would have Helen returned and the war ended; Troilus, for honour, would have her retained. But the debate is curiously unconvincing and inconclusive; it ends with a sudden and quite unmotivated conversion of Hector, a lapse from his subtle and sensible arguing:

> But value dwels not in particular will,
> It holds his estimate and dignitie
> As well, wherein 'tis precious of it selfe,
> As in the prizer: 'Tis mad Idolatrie,
> To make the service greater then the God . . .
> (II.ii)

—to a bellicose ranting quite out of character—if the former was "in" it:

> I am yours,
> You valiant off-spring of great *Priamus,*
> I have a roisting challenge sent among'st
> The dull and factious nobles of the Greekes,
> Will strike amazement to their drowsie spirits . . .
> (*Ibid.*)

And so with the mob's representative in this play. Thersites is foul-mouthed, vile, "low" in every sense; but the heroes he rails at are presented in such a way that one cannot but feel some agreement with his railings. So, later, in *Coriolanus:* there, too, the mob and its leaders receive no quarter—but what of the hero, the mob's enemy? He is surely shown to be just as uncontrollable, just as unpredictable, just as much at the mercy of his emotions and prejudices. The critical spirit has spread, from areas where it had always been permitted to areas hitherto comparatively sacrosanct. The new spirit of the 1590's was becoming incapable of the earlier, idealizing worship of the Queen (in her later years she seems to have been positively unpopular); it was losing that strange poetic adoration of Elizabeth which turns her to a blend of lover's mistress, lay Madonna, and medieval Lady of the tourney. Spenser is of course its supreme representative, as in these lines from *The Shepheardes Calender* (April):

> Of fair Elisa be your silver song,
> That blessed wight,
> The flowre of virgins: may she florish long
> In princely plight!
> For she is *Syrinx* daughter without spotte,
> Which *Pan* the shepheardes god, of her begotte:
> So sprong her grace
> Of heavenlie race,
> No mortall blemish may her blotte . . .
>
> Tell me, have ye seene her angelike face,
> Like *Phoebe* fayre?
> Her heavenlie haveour, her princely grace,
> Can ye well compare?
> The redde rose medled with the white yfere
> In either cheeke depeincten lively chere:
> Her modest eye,
> Her majestie,
> Where have you seene the like but there?

These lines show how close was such adoration of Gloriana to the sonnetteers' eulogies on their ladies: the critical scepticism which could no longer swallow the one must inevitably reject the other.

Thus from both ends, from the Queen at the apex to the mob at the base, uncertainty spreads, to embrace the whole world of government and authority. In *Measure for Measure,* Isabella's "drest in a little brief authoritie" and Claudio's "the demy-god (Authoritye)" remind one of the 66th sonnet's "art made tonguetide by Authoritie". The note is one of puzzlement rather than a firmbased denunciation: Shakespeare was no revolutionary—indeed, if one had to label his political "position", it would be that of a natural conservative whom the stress of events, internal and external, had driven to the edge of anarchism. Puzzlement is the note: Claudio, again, is utterly baffled to explain his own condemnation:

Whether it be the fault and glimpse of newnes
Or whether that the body publique, be
A horse whereon the Governor doth ride,
Who newly in the Seate, that it may know
He can command; lets it straight feele the Spur:
Whether the Tirranny be in his place,
Or in his Eminence that fills it up
I stagger in . . .

(I.ii)

"I stagger in": indeed, everyone in the play is baffled by Angelo's behaviour—Angelo included. His own bewilderment ("What dost thou? or what art thou *Angelo?*") we have already noted. The others can only conclude that he is abnormal: it is not only the bawdy Lucio who describes him as inhumanly cold in sex, the Duke also refers to him as one who "scarce confesses that his blood flowes". Yet the Duke admires him too—"a man of stricture and firme abstinence"—and this attitude, half-critical, half-admiring, wholly uncertain, is exactly that of the magnificent 94th sonnet:

They that have power to hurt and will doe none,
That do not do the thing, they most do showe,
Who mooving others, are them selves as stone,
Unmooved, colde, and to temptation slowe . . .

—it might be a description of Angelo (the betrayer of Mariana) before he met Isabella—

They rightly do inherit heavens graces

—is that "rightly" ironic or not? What is the exact tone of the superb line which follows—

They are the lords and owners of their faces

—again, ironic or not? Lytton Strachey, quoting these lines in *Eminent Victorians* (apropos of Cromer in Egypt), decided they were simple condemnation: in them, he thought, Shakespeare described a kind of man "whom he did not like". But they are not by any means so simple: they are balanced between a deep envy, a reluctant admiration, and a suppressed distaste, and their net effect is of utter bewilderment: how *can* there be people who feel so little, attract so greatly, are so perfectly successful—and inflict such pain?

Shakespeare reduces all things—as he had to, being a dramatist, and as he was impelled to, being a born dramatist—to terms of human beings; politics, for him, mean the behaviour of individuals. Between the fields of politics, morals and psychology, he, like his age, made no clear divisions. Hence the uncertainty which we are analysing appears with equal clarity in the latter two, as well as in the first, of these fields. In the speech from *Troilus* already cited (when Troilus has realized Cressida's faithlessness) the inner confusion goes much deeper than the simple, traditional antithesis of reason versus passion, as rendered, for example, in the great lines from Fulke Greville's *Mustapha* (probably written in the 1590's):

> Oh wearisome Condition of Humanity!
> Borne under one Law, to another bound:
> Vainely begot, and yet forbidden vanity,
> Created sicke, commanded to be sound:
> What meaneth Nature by these diverse Lawes?
> Passion and Reason, selfe-division cause.

Greville's simpler mind feels the "self-division" which is a feature of the age; but his values are still secure and his terms orthodox, he is still sure what reason stands for and what it should do, even if it fails to do it. Troilus is not; the "authority" within him (which is, or should be, reason) is "bi-fold", it has become interchangeable with what ought to be its clear-cut opposites, "loss" and "revolt": and that is why the "fight" within him is not merely desperate, but also "strange"—something which he cannot understand. So, too, in Angelo's crisis, the twist of bewilderment is supplied by the fact that moral causes are not having their expected moral effects; on the contrary, the effects are the opposites of what they should be. It is Isabella's goodness that tempts him—"corrupt with vertuous season". The oxymoron which expresses this chaos is repeated again and again, in a circling movement which itself represents the speaker's bewilderment:

> Can it be,
> That Modesty may more betray our Sence
> Then womans lightnesse? . . .
> Dost thou desire her *fowly,* for those things
> That make her *good?* . . .
> Oh cunning enemy, that to catch a Saint,
> With Saints dost bait thy hooke: most dangerous
> Is that temptation, that doth goad us on
> To *sinne,* in loving *vertue.*
>
> (II.ii)

Here again Shakespeare is turning into drama the material of the Sonnets; for this is exactly the moral anarchy we have already seen there, in the complex interplay of "foul" and "fair" and in his "unworthiness" which makes him "worthy" of her.

Maturity and complexity are not attained without losses; the works they beget may win the admiration of posterity, but to their possessors they are apt to come unsought and unwelcomed: matters for regret, even for shame, more than for rejoicing. In the age we are considering, a recurrent feeling is a sad looking back to a past idealized out of all reality, when life and love, society and individuals, were simpler and better. To construct an idealized Middle Ages is no Romantic or Victorian invention; the Middle Ages, indeed, seem to have become "romantic" almost as soon as they came to an end. The Elizabethans were just as prone as later ages to "Gothick" fantasies, and their motive was the same—to express by contrast their sense of the wrongness of their own times. There seems a curious paradox here. Modern research has undoubtedly shown how deeply medieval, in all spheres of life, the Elizabethans still were; but if we think that *they* saw themselves as such, we shall see them wrong. *They* thought they were very different from the men of the Middle Ages: thought it, and regretted it. To this feeling, Drayton's stanzas in *Piers Gaveston* (1593) give a thorough representative expression.—

His (sc. Edward I's) court a schoole, where artes were daily red,
And yet a campe where armes were exercised,
Vertue and learning here were nourished,
And stratagems by souldiers still devised:
  Heere skilfull schoolmen were his counsaylors,
  Schollers his captaines, captaines *Senators*.

Here sprang the roote of true gentilitie,
Vertue was clad in gold and crownd with honor,
Honor intitled to Nobilitie,
Admired so of all that looked on her:
  Wisedome, not wealth, possessed wisemens roomes,
  Unfitting base insinuating groomes.

Then Machivels were loth'd as filthie toades,
And good men as rare pearles were richely prized,
The learned were accounted little Gods,
The vilest Atheist as the plague despised:
  Desert then gaynd, that virtues merit craves,
  And artles Pesants scorn'd as basest slaves.

Pride was not then, which all things overwhelms,
Promotion was not purchased with gold,
Men hew'd their honor out of steeled helms:
In those dayes fame with bloud was bought and sold,
  No petti-fogger pol'd the poore for pence,
  These dolts, these dogs, as traytors banisht hence.

Then was the Souldier prodigall of bloud,
His deedes eternizd by the Poets pen:
Who would not dye to doe his countrey good,
When after death his fame yet liv'd to men?
  Then learning liv'd with liberalitie,
  And men were crowned with immortalitie.

(lines 61–90)

The contrasts, of course, are directed against his own age; the same spirit fills the lines of *As You Like It* (*c.* 1599) in which Orlando sees the faithful old Adam as typical figure of "the constant service of the antique world, / When service sweate for dutie, not for meade"; and Greene's pamphlet *A Quip for an Upstart Courtier* (1593) laments in similar strain:

> Then charity flourished in the court, and young courtiers strove to exceede one an other in vertue, not in bravery; they rode, not with fans to ward their faces from the winde, but with burgant to resist the stroke of a battle-axe; they could then better exhort a soldier to armor, then court a lady with amorets; they caused the trumpette to sound them pointes of warre, not poets to write them wanton eligies of love; they soght after honorable fame, but hunted not after fading honor.[21]

The attraction of this dream was perhaps intensified by the fact that the Elizabethan age did still contain, in its outward trappings at least, some of the elements of medieval chivalry: contained them, and imagined them embodied in certain of its own men. In Sidney, of course, and later in Essex:

> The household of Robert Earl of Essex perhaps provides the last example of a military service in which a complete career could be envisaged within the retinue of a single powerful subject. Around the Devereux there clustered those gentlemen who still felt that their own knightly rank was only strengthened by the fact that they served Lord Essex in a brotherhood of the sword.[22]

If this is so, if Essex really presented to his contemporaries the last enchantments of feudal chivalry, we can understand why he exercised such a fascination over the writers of the age (both Spenser and Shakespeare celebrate him, the former as a "faire branch of honor, flower of chevalrie") and why, when he fell, he fell amid such sympathy for himself and such revulsion against the Queen. He stood for the "good old days": hateful modernity had killed him. He died because he was out-of-date. His fate, and Sidney's, are in significant contrast: Sidney dying, in 1586, universally honoured; Essex in 1601, on the scaffold.

---

[21] The same pamphlet complains, in what will strike modern readers as a comically twentieth century manner, that good old honest workmanship has vanished from the land:

> Now every trade hath his sleight, to slubber up his work to the eie, and to make it good to the sale, howsoever it proves in the wearing. The shoomaker cares not if his shoes hold the drawing on: The taylor sowes with hot needle and burnt thred. Tush[,] pride has banisht conscience, and velvet-breeches honestie.

English craftsmanship, like English beer, is never what it was.

[22] David Mathew: *Social Structure in Caroline England* (Oxford, 1948).

Now, whatever may have been the identity, or the fate, of "Mr. W. H.", there is no doubt that he, the young man of the Sonnets, embodied for Shakespeare this dream of a beautiful past:

> Thus is his cheeke the map of daies out-worne,
> When beauty liv'd and dy'd as flowers do now . . .
>
> In him those holy antique houres are seene,
> Without all ornament, itself, and true.
>
> (68)

Not only the past, but more precisely the past of medieval chivalry, the past which Drayton lamented:

> When in the Chronicle of wasted time,
> I see discriptions of the fairest wights,
> And beautie making beautifull old rime,
> In praise of Ladies dead, and lovely Knights,
> Then in the blazon of sweet beauties best,
> Of hand, of foote, of lip, of eye, of brow,
> I see their antique pen would have exprest
> Even such a beautie as you maister now.
>
> (106)

This world was already, by the end of the sixteenth century, invested with an air of picturesque antiquity—"old rime", "antique Pen"—and it is in this world, and not in the world of to-day, that the young man's beauty is at home. Of that unreal, regretted, lost simplicity, he is almost a symbol, as the dark lady of its opposite: of the complex, tortured reality which has taken its place. Her very beauty is doubtful —it is only on the young man that "beauty" and "beautiful" are lavished with Spenserian confidence. *Her* beauty, if beauty it be, is distinctively, and disturbingly, modern:

> In the ould age blacke was not counted faire,
> Or if it weare it bore not beauties name.
>
> (127)

She is an individual, and her style of attractiveness is individual. She is flesh and blood—"my Mistres when shee walkes treads on the ground".[23] In this profound and widespread storm, of which she would appear to have been, for Shakespeare, the personal centre, a

---

[23] This is exactly in the spirit and manner, the jaunty knowing commonsensical manner, of Donne's

> Love's not so pure, and abstract, as they use
> To say, which have no Mistresse, but their muse

—as also of Iago's remark to Roderigo—"the Wine she drinkes is made of grapes."

vast deal of junk, early Renaissance and belated medieval, was cast overboard in the name of reality and commonsense; and among it, that standardized international model of feminine beauty—the golden-haired, fair-skinned, blue-eyed lady of Spenser and Botticelli, the imaginary lady of imaginary knights, whose behaviour was as predictable as her looks. But nowadays women use make-up ("fairing the foule with Arts faulse borrow'd face" [24]), and they wear false hair ("ere beauties dead fleece made another gay" [25]), and such things are the outward and trivial signs of the central fact, that love in these modern days is difficult and treacherous. The feeling was shared by Donne, as *Loves Deity* demonstrates:

> Sure, they which made him (sc. Love) god, meant not so much,
> Nor he, in his young godhead practis'd it;
> But when an even flame two hearts did touch,
> His office was indulgently to fit
> Actives to passives. Correspondencie
> Only his subject was; It cannot bee
> Love, till I love her, that loves mee.

Lost innocence, lost simplicity, lost certainty, all symbolized in a lost and regretted past: these themes, strong both in the Sonnets and in the age when they were written, are equally strong in the plays which Shakespeare wrote round the turn of the century. A great deal of *Hamlet* is a lament for these losses. Hamlet envies in Fortinbras the simple decisive man of action, who can *do things* for childish reasons, whose certainty and simplicity of values Hamlet himself can no longer subscribe to: for he criticizes even while he envies—it is only "for an egg shell" that the hero is heroic, he finds honour "in a straw", he dies "for a fantasy, a trick of fame". Similarly, Hamlet's repudiation of Ophelia is a rejection of a simple romantic love which cannot survive in the stress of what has come later; the letter he sends her is a savage parody (sane or insane, it does not matter) of that early uncritical adoration, and incidentally of the kind of poetry which expressed it ("To the Celestiall, and my Soules Idoll, the most beautified Ophelia"—"an ill phrase, a vile phrase", says the critical Polonius); and her description of him, as he had been before the storm blew up, is a description of the ideal youth of the Renaissance court, the unspoiled unreal beauty of Castiglione's Courtier, the Adonis of the Sonnets, in fact—

> That unmatch'd Forme and Feature of blowne youth.

The Sonnets, then, give us the perfect text through which to see what really happened to the minds of men in this crucial decade,

---

[24] Sonnet 127.
[25] Sonnet 68.

and especially to the poetry which expressed those happenings. We may well feel inclined to shrink from the "subjective" reading of the Sonnets, which sees them as the record of the crisis (or *a* crisis, at least) in their author's personal life, when we remember the sentimental extravaganzas such a reading has so often given rise to—and always will, for the Frank Harrises and Ivor Browns will always be with us; but it does seem justifiable to a degree which would not be permissible in a reading of the plays. Justifiable, but inadequate: for the Sonnets record much else. Perhaps this is always the case with any writer whose life and work are unified: the crisis was all-involving. It was personal and emotional; it was social, and touched its victim's professional career and his attitude towards his career; it involved his art, and drove him, both as a result of it and in order to express it, into a change of style; and it was his own microcosmic reproduction of the change and crisis of the time. It brought him towards a new relationship with his medium, the language, and a new use of it; that use remains, in essentials, permanent—the method of his maturity. The Sonnets are a sort of embryo, in which the essential evolution of the whole of Shakespeare is carried out in miniature.

THE CONDITIONS OF THE THEATER

The Profession of Playwright

R. A. Foakes

When Shakespeare came to London between 1584 and 1592, he must often have heard the trumpets sound to announce a performance at a playhouse, and seen the crowds flock to it. Dukes and ambassadors, gentlemen and captains, citizens and apprentices, ruffians and harlots, 'Tailers, Tinkers, Cordwayners, Saylers, olde Men, yong Men, Women, Boyes, Girles, and such like' were likely to be among that audience, gathering to watch a spectacle that held something for each of them. Here was a splendid world of delight and instruction, offering poetry for the cultured, shows and a strong plot for the citizen, clowning and bawdy for the illiterate; and for everyone it brought to life, as no other medium then could, history, mythology, biblical story, and a whole range of earlier literature. Playwrights ransacked, as Stephen Gosson alleged, 'the Palace of Pleasure, the Golden Asse, the Oethiopian historie, Amadis of Fraunce, the Rounde Table, baudie Comedies in Latine, French, Italian and Spanish' to provide ever some new attraction. The Theatre was at once courtly and plebeian, aristocratic and popular, witty and vulgar, refined and ribald; it was a universal theatre, a meeting-place of all sorts of people, and a focus for all sorts of talent. It offered the writer a versatile stage, and actors who could sing, dance, tumble and fence as readily as they delivered their lines; and it gave scope to many kinds of writing. It challenged the popular compiler of chronicle plays to attempt poetic richness, and encouraged the sophisticated author, who knew his Terence and Plautus, to throw in a song or two, and some clowning, something for the crowd.

From *Early Shakespeare,* Stratford-upon-Avon Studies, Vol. III, ed. John Russell Brown and Bernard Harris. Reprinted by permission of R. A. Foakes and Edward Arnold (Publishers), Ltd.

[Foakes's chronology of the Elizabethan theater and his selected bibliography appear on pp. 160–61 at the end of the essay.]

The stage was not only exciting in itself, but had a special prominence as the centre of a controversy between, on the one side, the church and civic governors of London, on the other side the court and aristocracy. If the actors seemed in their splendour to be kings indeed to the people, they were emissaries of the devil to puritan divines, who grew bitter as the churches emptied: 'Wyll not a fylthy playe, wyth the blast of a Trumpette sooner call thyther a thousande, than an houres tolling of a Bell bring to the Sermon a hundred?', complained a preacher at St. Paul's in 1578. Fulminations against the theatre as 'Satan's synagogue' or 'the nest of the Devil' did not affect its popularity, and the church tried what it could do to restrain play-acting; so the Bishop of London, advising Sir William Cecil to prohibit plays for a year in 1564, added dryly, 'and if it wer for ever, it wer nott amisse'. The church had the support of the Mayor and Aldermen of the City of London, who were continually seeking injunctions against 'common plaiers of interludes'. They complained that the actors drew large assemblies to view plays, and crowds were dangerous as tending to vice and disorder, and as liable to spread infection, especially in time of plague. Their pressure was successful to the extent that the public theatres were built in suburbs to the north of the city, or south of the River Thames on Bankside, in areas that were out of the jurisdiction of the city authorities.

Against these, the actors had powerful allies at Court, where Queen Elizabeth liked to see a play or two on festive occasions, especially at Christmas, when it was usual for one or more companies to be called to perform before her. Their chief protectors, however, were the lords whose name and livery they took to give them prestige and good standing in an age when players not 'belonging to any Baron of the Realme' were condemned in the statutes as rogues and vagabonds. The relationship between a company and their patron may not always have been very close, but he could intervene strongly on their behalf, as the Lord Admiral and Lord Chamberlain did through Privy Council for their companies in 1598, causing a third company to be suppressed. What the actors gained by such patronage may be glimpsed in a letter written by James Burbage and five others to the Earl of Leicester in 1572, in which they ask him to

> vouchsaffe to reteyne us at this present as your houshold Servaunts and daylie wayters, not that we meane to crave any further stipend or benefite at your Lordshippes handes but our Lyveries as we have had, and also your honors License to certifye that we are your household Servaunts when we shall have occasion to travayle amongst our frendes as we do usuallye once a yere, and as other noble-mens Players do and have done in tyme past.

So in attacking or protecting the stage, the highest authorities were involved, Bishops, Mayors of London, the Queen and great lords who could exercise some control through Privy Council. The profession of acting or of writing plays had a special prominence because of this, and held its own risks. Plagues or disturbances might cause all playing to be prohibited, and force actors to travel far into the provinces; the city authorities might find some new means of harassing them, such as forcing them to contribute to the upkeep of the poor; but also the most benevolently inclined lords and the Queen herself were susceptible to the influence plays might have on the public, and were liable suddenly to become the stage's worst enemy if they suspected a play of engaging in political or religious matters. Actors and authors would then be disciplined, playing suppressed, and authors perhaps committed to prison, as, among others, Ben Jonson and John Marston were later to suffer imprisonment in this way. At the same time, to be an actor, author, or, as was not uncommon, both, was to engage in a profession capable of bringing glamour, prestige, popularity, and wealth. A letter-writer lamented in 1587, 'Yt is a wofull sight to see two hundred proude players jett in their silkes, wheare five hundred pore people sterve in the streets'; but many must have found the players a fine sight. Shakespeare became one of them, wore the livery of several lords, and eventually took his place at the head of the list of actors granted four yards of red cloth for liveries to walk in the coronation procession through London in 1604. He had reason to be proud.

During Shakespeare's early years, great developments were taking place in play-acting. There was a long tradition of playing by adult companies of men, performing in inn-yards, on scaffolds, or in halls and private houses; and an equally long tradition of acting by schoolboys, especially by the boys of the schools of St. Paul's Cathedral and the Chapel Royal. Before the 1570s there seem to have been performances on Sundays and holidays, perhaps without any settled regularity. Frequent regulations forbidding playing during time of divine service or the late afternoon show that plays were commonly staged on Sundays, chiefly in 'great Innes, havinge Chambers and secret places adjoyninge to their open stages and gallyries', as one order puts it. As early as 1545 a proclamation speaks of plays being 'commonly & besylye set foorthe', and the city regulations extended in 1566 to forbidding Robert Fryer, a goldsmith, from staging plays for the public in his house before 4 on Sundays and festivals. The presentation of plays was evidently widespread, but, except for private performances in the houses of the great, or at Court, was confined to non-working days.

The first building constructed for dramatic performances was erected by James Burbage, an actor, in 1576; he called it, simply, The Theatre. It was a structure developed from the inn-yard or from the arenas long used to exhibit bear-baiting, with tiers of galleries extending round a central area and stage exposed to the open sky. In the same year, Richard Farrant, new master of the Children of the Chapel, leased a part of the old priory of Blackfriars, and converted it into an indoor theatre, where his boys proceeded to perform before the public. He seems to have done this to compete with the Children of Paul's, whose vicar choral, Sebastian Westcote, had been cited by the Court of Aldermen in the previous year because, as they said, he 'kepethe playes and resorte of the people to great gaine'; his boys perhaps acted in buildings of the school. A little later, about 1577, another public theatre was built, the Curtain.

These events mark the beginning of a full-scale professionalism in the theatre. Its further development over the next twenty years falls into three phases, and Shakespeare emerges as a fledged actor-dramatist in the third phase. The first extended through the 1580s. During this period the standing of the adult players was enhanced when a group of actors was selected in 1583 to form a company under the Queen's patronage; this new company took prominence because of the talents of its leading players, especially Richard Tarleton, the great clown. The children's companies were active until 1584, when the Children of Paul's seem to have ceased playing for a time. The Children of the Chapel appeared occasionally after this date until 1592, and then vanished until 1600. In 1587, however, the Children of Paul's returned to playing for three years. It is doubtful if plays were as yet given on more than two or three days a week, but performances certainly were offered on days other than holidays. Already in 1578 John Stockwood spoke with horror in a sermon of 'the gaine that is reaped of eighte ordinarie places in the Citie whiche I knowe, by playing but once a weeke (whereas many times they play twice and sometimes thrice) it amounteth to 2000 pounds by the yeare'; and in 1583 the licence for the Queen's Men permitted them to play at two inns, the Bull and the Bell, on holidays, Wednesdays and Saturdays.

Tarleton died in 1588, a jester much loved and much mourned; and this blow to the Queen's Men was followed by another when the company became involved in the Martin Marprelate controversy in 1589. The actors seem to have become too vehement in their attack on the puritans, who had begun the affair with a series of anonymous pamphlets purporting to be written by Martin and denouncing episcopacy. Playing was prohibited in November, because the actors had dealt with 'matters of Divinytie and of State unfitt to be suffred', as the Privy Council minute puts it. Thereafter the Queen's Men are traceable in the provinces, with only an occasional appearance in London; and in May 1594, Philip Henslowe noted in his *Diary* that the company 'broke & went into the contrey to playe'. The Children of Paul's were also involved in this controversy through the writings of their principal dramatist, John Lyly, and their acting was suppressed altogether in 1590.

There is not much evidence of the repertory of the Queen's Men during these years, but it included chronicle plays, classical romance, and pseudo-moralities like the two extant plays by Robert Wilson, an actor in the company; one important dramatist, Robert Greene, sold much of his work to them. It was probably a more popular repertory than that of the boys' companies, for their chief draw, Tarleton, was famous for his ability to play 'knave and foole'. The children, acting in indoor theatres, charging higher entrance fees, and drawing a narrower and more select audience, had thrown up no outstanding actors, but gave scope to the scholarly talents of university-trained writers like John Lyly, who produced witty comedies on classical themes. Lyly was writing by 1584, and may be referred to in Stephen Gosson's *School of Abuse* (1579) as the author of 'two prose books played at the Belsavage, where you shall find never a word without wit, never a line without pith, never a letter placed in vain'; certainly this is an apt comment on those plays of his which remain. He was the major dramatist of the decade, and Shakespeare studied his work with great profit. Nevertheless, it would be wrong to draw too simple a contrast between the sophistication of the children's companies, and the crude vigour of the adult players, between the expensive 'private' theatres and the cheaper 'public' playhouses.[1] The tastes of the audiences at these were not so different as to prevent authors like George Peele and Christopher Marlowe from writing for both; and, in addition, all the companies had enough in common to be welcome at Court to play before the most select audience in the realm, and to be able to entertain in the provinces audiences that were probably less sophisticated than any in London.

The decay of the Queen's Men and the suppression of the Children of Paul's coincided with the ascendancy of other adult companies, marking a second phase in the growth of a full-scale professional theatre. Two of these companies were to emerge quickly as outstanding. First were the Lord Admiral's Men, who played under the patronage of the Lord High Admiral, Lord Howard; they appeared as a group in 1585, and Edward Alleyn, who was then a member and had acted earlier, acquired a major share in the control of the company in 1589. Alleyn seems to have been one of the great actors of the English stage, a man praised by Thomas Nashe in 1592 as the finest ever: 'Not *Roscius* nor *Aesope,* those admyred tragedians that have lived ever since before Christ was borne, could ever performe more in action than famous *Ned Allen.*' The second company was the group known as Lord Strange's Men, who played under the patronage of Ferdinando Stanley, later Earl of Derby. Their early history is obscure, but possibly by 1588, certainly from 1590 to 1594, they were working in liaison with the Admiral's Men, at times as one combined company. In 1594, after

---

[1] Such a contrast is often drawn, most fully in A. Harbage's *Shakespeare and the Rival Traditions* (1952). He argues that there were 'two distinct theatrical traditions in England, signalized by two distinct kinds of theatre', the public and private theatres; these, he claims, had different repertories, at the public theatres, 'romantic, idealistic, positive, and often patriotic and religious' plays being in vogue, while at the private theatres satirical comedy prevailed. Most of his evidence relates to the period after 1600, when the children began to play again, and though he once acknowledges that there was 'probably' no private theatre operating between 1590 and 1599, he ignores this in his general argument. The lists of 'the known repertories of all companies until 1613' given in an appendix should not be relied on; they do not include, for instance, the lost plays recorded by Henslowe. G. Wickham's *Early English Stages, I, 1300–1576* (1959) helps to put Harbage's account into a fuller historical perspective.

the death of Lord Derby, the companies separated, many of the former Strange's Men taking the patronage of the Lord Chamberlain, Lord Hunsdon. Richard Burbage, a slightly younger man than Alleyn, was their leading player: he may have acted in the 1580s, but first comes to notice in 1590, when he was probably with the Admiral's Men. It would be pleasant to think that he learned his craft from Alleyn, whose standing as the leading actor of the age he inherited in the first decades of the seventeenth century, after Alleyn, still not forty years old, retired finally from the stage about 1605.

These two companies seem to have had the main use of the true theatres, as distinct from inn-yards and the like, available in London. James Burbage (father of Richard), a poor actor in the early 1570s, married a wealthy woman and used her money to build the first theatre. After 1585, the Curtain, operated by a Henry Laneman, was used as an 'easer' to the Theatre by an agreement between the proprietors who pooled and equally divided the profits. By 1586, possibly much earlier, a theatre at Newington Butts was in use. Then in 1587, Philip Henslowe, who seems, like Burbage, to have acquired money by marriage, contracted with a grocer, John Cholmley, to build what was to become the Rose Theatre. This was erected by 1588, and by 1592 had passed into the sole ownership of Henslowe. As James Burbage saw his son become a leading actor and sharer in the Chamberlain's Men before he died in 1597, so Philip Henslowe saw his stepdaughter, Joan Woodward, marry Edward Alleyn in 1592, and from that time on Alleyn became a son to him. The close relationship between the leading actor and sharer in the company's stock and the theatre owner may have been a stabilizing factor in the history of these two companies. During their period of association, the Strange's and Admiral's Men played at the Curtain, the Rose, and, for a brief period in June 1594, at Newington Butts, which by then may have come into Henslowe's control.

Other companies were active during these years. The Earl of Pembroke's Men, who were ruined by the great plague of 1593 which stopped all playing in London between February and December, the Earl of Sussex's Men, who seem to have broken up in 1594, and the Queen's Men, before their removal to the provinces, all had some connection with the activities of the Admiral's and Strange's Men. Plays belonging to Pembroke's Men seem to have passed to Sussex's Men, who acted briefly with the Queen's Men in April 1594 before both companies broke up. Some of their plays came into the repertory of the newly formed Chamberlain's Men in 1594, among them *Titus Andronicus, The Taming of a Shrew* and a version of *Hamlet,* while others were taken over by the Admiral's Men, like *The Jew of Malta,* and *Friar Bacon and Friar Bungay*. From this year, 1594, which marks the end of the second phase of development, the Admiral's and Chamberlain's Men dominated the London stage, at any rate until the turn of the century.

Of these two companies, the Admiral's Men had a longer continuity and fame at this time, largely through Edward Alleyn, but also, perhaps, because most of the plays of the best writers of 1587–92 were written for them, or passed into their repertory—plays by Marlowe, Kyd, Peele, Lodge and Greene. Marlowe wrote one play for the Children of the Chapel, and so did George Peele, but the rest of their work was sold to adult companies, usually to the Admiral's Men; Greene wrote mainly for the Queen's Men, but his plays came into the repertory of Strange's Men or the Admiral's Men by about 1592. The new writing talent of the so-called 'University Wits' was thus chiefly deployed for the adult companies that rose in the decay of the Queen's Men and the Children's companies. These men, who, except for Thomas Kyd, were graduates, wrote for the stage perhaps partly because they lacked patronage, or could not scrape a living by poetry, but also because the emergent companies of the late 1580s were competing for plays. Robert Greene seems to describe how he came to write plays in his pamphlet *Francesco's Fortunes* (1590), where, in the person of Francesco, he tells how he 'fell in amongst a company of players, who persuaded him to try his wit in writing', and so he wrote a comedy, 'which so generally pleased the audience that happy were those actors in short time, that could get any of his works'. These 'sweet Gentlemen', who, in the words of Thomas Nashe writing in 1589, 'vaunted their pens in private devices, and tricked up a company of taffata fooles with their feathers', brought to their craft a new poetic energy and command of language, a new maturity of design and power of thought, and a new insight into character. They brought also an academic training to their work, which is as sophisticated in its kind as Lyly's is in his own vein. Their plays, especially those of Marlowe, are the earliest English plays which are still widely read and occasionally revived on the stage.

The plays of these writers had their greatest theatrical success while Edward Alleyn, who played Orlando in Greene's *Orlando Furioso,* Tamburlaine, Doctor Faustus, and Barabas in *The Jew of Malta,* was at the height of his powers. Well before Alleyn retired from the stage for some years in 1597, Greene (1592), Marlowe (1593), Kyd (1594) and Peele (1596) were all dead. It was during their great burst of creative activity that Shakespeare appeared as an actor and playwright. The first certain allusions to him and his writings are found in pamphlets of 1592. In that year Thomas Nashe referred in his *Pierce Penniless* to the character of Talbot in *Henry VI;* Robert Greene misquoted a line from *3 Henry VI* in his *Greene's Groat's-Worth of Wit,* and complained of Shakespeare as an 'upstart Crow', a man who had pilfered the writings of others, or who had presumed equality with established authors, or who was a mere actor pretending that he could 'bombast out a blanke verse' as well as university-educated poets—several interpretations of Greene's doubtful words are possible; and finally, Henry Chettle defended Shakespeare as 'excellent in the quality he professes'. Such testimony from his contemporaries establishes that he had 'arrived' by this time.

In the same year, 1592, Philip Henslowe began to record his share of the daily takings at his theatres, and to list the plays performed, in his account-book, better known as his *Diary,* which is now in the library of Dulwich College. Among the plays he noted as performed by Strange's Men early in 1592 were a *Henry VI,* probably new on 3 March 1592, 'tittus and vespacia', and *The Jealous Comedy,* probably new on 5 January 1593. The Earl of Sussex's Men, acting at the end of 1593, performed a *Buckingham* and 'titus & ondronicus'; and the Admiral's and Chamberlain's Men, acting together briefly in June 1594, are recorded as staging 'andronicous', *Hamlet,* and *The Taming of a Shrew.* In 1594 also, a quarto of *Titus Andronicus* was published, its title-page reading, 'As it was Plaide by the Right Honourable the Earle of Darbie, Earle of Pembrooke, and Earl of Sussex their Servants'. In the same year a quarto of *The Taming of a Shrew* as played by Pembroke's Men appeared, and in 1597 *The True Tragedy of Richard Duke of York,* a play now thought to be a bad version of *3 Henry VI,* was ascribed to the same company. The relationship of *Titus and Vespasia* to *Titus Andronicus* is not known, and that between *The Taming of a Shrew* and *The Taming of the Shrew,* though close, remains indeterminate; *The Jealous Comedy* may have no connection with *The Comedy of Errors,* and *Buckingham* may have nothing to do with *Richard III;* but there is left enough evidence to show that Shakespeare was at work at the very latest by the beginning of 1592, and probably for some time before that. It also seems likely that his progress to the Chamberlain's Men was via Pembroke's and Sussex's Men. Through a connection, perhaps as actor and writer, with these companies he would have come into association with Strange's Men, who were acting a part of *Henry VI* in 1592, and with the Admiral's Men. Then, when Strange's and Admiral's separated after playing as a combined group in June 1594, he joined the new company that succeeded Strange's Men and took the patronage of the Lord Chamberlain, Lord Hunsdon.

So Shakespeare, coming to London as the old style of adult playing by the Queen's Men, referred to as 'Vetus Comoedia' already in 1589, was in decay, and as the boys, after achieving their finest work in acting Lyly's plays, were suppressed, attached himself to a company that soon brought him into connection with the prominent Strange's and Admiral's Men. These, financed by the only builders who had established their own theatres in close connection with a company, and possessing the leading actors in Alleyn and Burbage, were the inheritors of the achievement of the adult and boys' companies of the 1580s; and after 1594, their wealth and their talent stabilized in family relationships, they came to have something of a monopoly. Shakespeare came to maturity in the third phase of development from the building of the Theatre in 1576, the post-Marlovian phase, after emerging in 1594 to work with the up-and-coming Richard Burbage in the Chamberlain's Men.

During the next six years the Admiral's and Chamberlain's Men had little serious competition to face; no Children's companies or 'private' theatres were operating, and not much is heard of other adult companies. A new theatre, the Swan, was built in about 1596 on Bankside by Francis Langley, who drew a number of the Admiral's Men, and a few actors probably from the Chamberlain's Men, to play there as the Earl of Pembroke's Men in 1597. But the venture was short-lived, for the Privy Council prohibited all playing after a performance at the Swan of a lost play by Nashe, *The Isle of Dogs,* in July 1597; it was apparently a play 'contanynge very seditious and sclanderous matter'. Langley's company promptly returned to the Rose to play in Henslowe's theatre, and were absorbed into the Admiral's Men again. Henslowe quickly obtained a licence to start playing again, but Langley did not, and an order of Privy Council in February 1598 calling for the suppression of a third company may show that he staged plays for a time without permission. This order of the Privy Council shows that the Admiral's Men and the Chamberlain's Men were the only companies licensed to perform plays at this time. Their predominance is reflected in the way they took turns in appearances at Court in connection with the Queen's Christmas festivities until 1600, when an Earl of Derby's company also played there. It is reflected also in the prosperity which brought to each company a new theatre. Cuthbert Burbage, the elder son of James, took over, on the death of his father in 1597, a troublesome dispute with the owner of the ground on which the Theatre was built, and solved it by taking down the building, transporting it from Shoreditch piece by piece across the river, and setting it up again on Bankside, presumably with much renovation. This new, or renewed, theatre was called the Globe, and its appearance near the Rose, which was also south of the river, caused Henslowe and Alleyn to plan a new stage for their company. In 1600 they opened the splendid new Fortune theatre in Finsbury; they had moved across the river in the opposite direction to the Chamberlain's Men, instructing their builder to copy the Globe in many details, and clearly setting out to match their rivals.

The two main companies competed not only in their theatres, but also in their repertories. They each inherited part of the stock of the old Sussex's, Pembroke's and Queen's Men, and until 1594 they played the same kinds of play, as Henslowe's records confirm. It is probable that they continued to do so, though not much is known about the repertory of the Chamberlain's Men apart from Shakespeare's plays, whereas Henslowe's lists provide a great deal of information about that of the Admiral's Men. However, Shakespeare's plays reveal some evidence of competition. At first he seems to have built on the work of his contemporaries and predecessors, trying his hand at chronicle-history, at Senecan tragedy, and at various forms of comedy, and imitating now Marlowe, now Lyly or Greene. After 1594, when his status as a leading member of his company is confirmed by his acting, together with Richard Burbage, and the famous clown William Kemp, as payee for Court performances, he continued to write several different kinds of play, sometimes in response to successes at the Rose. His creation of Shylock may have been provoked by a revival of *The Jew of Malta* by the Admiral's in 1595–6. They had a play on the theme of *Julius Caesar,* a *Henry V,* and a *Troilus and Cressida* before Shakespeare wrote his; and they replied to his *Henry IV,* or rather to his portrait of Falstaff, with their *Sir John Oldcastle.* The rivalry of the companies extended even to personal oppositions, as revealed by Henslowe's records of loans to discharge Thomas Dekker from arrest by the Chamberlain's Men in 1599, and to enable William Bird to pursue a lawsuit against Thomas Pope, a member of Shakespeare's company.

The affairs of the two companies may have differed a good deal in detail, and after the building of the Globe, they had a different organization. But before 1599 both companies consisted of a number of sharers, who each owned a share in the joint stock of plays, properties, costumes, and the like; they employed other actors, possibly some with a high standing as master actors, some hired men, some boys. They worked in a theatre owned by a financier, James Burbage or Philip Henslowe, who took half of the receipts in the galleries at each performance as his perquisite. Relations between owner and company were doubtless close, and Henslowe came to act as banker, moneylender, and general helper to the Admiral's Men. However, this company lost its family link with the owner when Alleyn retired from the stage in 1597. Although he returned to it from 1600 to about 1605, he devoted himself more and more to his properties, taking a large share with Henslowe in ownership; they built the Fortune as partners. The Chamberlain's Men kept and strengthened the link between owner and players. Richard Burbage, who continued to act until his death in 1619, and his brother Cuthbert, the inheritor of the Theatre, made a new arrangement with the company when they built the Globe. They kept only a half share in the lease and profits of the playhouse for themselves, and admitted five leading players, one of them Shakespeare, to equal shares in the other half. So a body of the sharers of the acting company obtained an interest in the ownership of the theatre itself; and this no doubt contributed to the strength of Shakespeare's company during the later part of his career.

Nevertheless, Henslowe's accounts contain much that is relevant to a consideration of Shakespeare as an actor and dramatist. Most plays of this period are lost; many were never printed, or were printed anonymously, and few authors seem to have troubled about the publication of the plays they wrote after they had sold them to a company. Ben Jonson was the first to gather his works together and oversee their printing in 1616; Shakespeare's plays had to wait for some of his fellows to bring them out seven years after his death. It is doubtful whether all printed texts survive, and certainly most manuscripts do not; they remained in the company stock until destroyed by time or the decay of the theatres, or, often, by some accident, such as the fire which burnt down the Fortune in 1621, reducing to ashes playbooks and costumes. There would be little evidence even of the titles of missing plays if Henslowe's *Diary* had not survived, to show how men wrote for the Admiral's company, singly or in collaboration, to show what they wrote (the *Diary* indicates that Michael Drayton was the author of *Sir John Oldcastle,* printed anonymously in 1599, and had a hand in 23 other plays now lost), and to offer the only proof that some men wrote at all (Charles Massey is an example). It is useful to cite the *Diary* here because the early association and later rivalry of the Admiral's Men and Chamberlain's Men make it probable that their repertory systems of presentation and their methods of obtaining plays were roughly similar.[2]

Henslowe's lists show that the Admiral's Men played a daily repertory, probably excepting Sundays, and with longer breaks during Lent, when acting was forbidden, and in summer, during the long vacation, when the company sometimes travelled in the country. Performances were in the afternoon, and there was normally a change of play every day. Even a very successful play, like George Chapman's *Humorous Day's Mirth* (*Comedy of Humours*), first acted in May 1597, was not performed more than twice in one week. No play received more than thirty-two performances in all, and twelve to fifteen indicate a respectable success. This meant a huge turnover of plays: between June and December 1594, fifteen new plays entered the repertory, and another fifteen during the following year. Not many of these remained in the repertory for as much as a year, though some were revived after a lapse of time. A dramatist sold his work outright to the company for comparatively little, £5 being a typical figure in the 1590s, and the company seems to have withheld plays from publication, as more of an asset unprinted, at least until their first run was over, and often for a much longer period. In such conditions, playwrights multiplied, and collaboration was common. Among the authors who wrote for Henslowe at this time were Chapman, Dekker, Henry Chettle, John Day, Samuel

---

[2] W. W. Greg branded Henslowe as 'an illiterate moneyed man . . . who regarded art as a subject for exploitation' (*Henslowe's Diary,* ii. 112–13); and E. K. Chambers modified this view only slightly, calling Henslowe a 'capitalist' as if this marked him and his company off as inferior to the Chamberlain's Men. Greg went on to argue that 'the financial arrangements which we find obtaining in the groups of companies under Henslowe's control were the exception rather than the rule' (p. 113). There is no evidence for this claim, prior to 1598–9 when the Burbages admitted actors to a share in the Globe; and James Burbage may have been as illiterate as Henslowe who could read, write and keep accounts, even if he spelt words oddly. Also, Burbage was as much a capitalist as Henslowe, or, for that matter, Shakespeare. Greg influenced R. B. Sharpe, who attempted in his *The Real War of the Theatres* to show that Henslowe's company made a 'proletarian appeal' to a lower-class audience, whereas the Chamberlain's Men played to a superior, fashionable audience, and that their plays were correspondingly different. His argument is unwarranted, for it is based on a comparison of repertories, and while that of the Admiral's Men is fully documented in Henslowe's *Diary,* we know little of the Chamberlain's Men's plays apart from the few, principally Shakespeare's, which have been preserved. See also T. W. Baldwin, *The Organization and Personnel of the Shakespearean Company* (1927), pp. 1–45, and *Henslowe's Diary,* edited by R. A. Foakes and R. T. Rickert (1961), pp. xxv–xxxiii.

Rowley, Michael Drayton, Thomas Heywood, Henry Porter and Ben Jonson. Some, like Rowley, Jonson and Heywood, were also actors; and some other actors in the company, like Charles Massey and John Singer, wrote an occasional piece for the stage. Many seem to have written loyally for the Admiral's Men, but Ben Jonson changed allegiances several times, Chapman went over to writing for the Children's companies when these were revived after 1600, and it seems that authors were free to sell to whom they pleased. At the same time, it was natural for actors like Samuel Rowley or Shakespeare, who had a stake in one company, to write mainly for their own group.

The repertory of the Admiral's Men shows an enormous variety of plays, on British history, real and mythical, on recent French history, comedies set in Greece, France and Italy, plays on biblical themes, the new comedies of 'humours' of Chapman and Jonson, romantic comedies like Dekker's *Shoemakers Holiday,* a 'pastoral tragedy', and tragedies on themes ranging from *Agamemnon* to *Cox of Cullompton.* It also included a fair number of plays, presumably comedies, with titles like *Crack me this Nut, The Fountain of New Fashions, Christmas Comes but Once a Year, What Will Be Shall Be,* and *As Merry as May Be,* some of which are reminiscent of Shakespearian titles, *Twelfth Night or What You Will, As You Like It, Much Ado about Nothing.* The range is remarkable, and reflects another feature common to this company and the Chamberlain's Men, that they were able to perform all kinds of plays, and entertain all kinds of audiences; it also points to the mixed character of the audience at the public theatres in the 1590s. Both companies might be called on to play in private at the house of some lord; for instance, Henslowe recorded a payment in March 1598 to 'the carman for caryinge and bryngyn of the stufe back agayne when they playd in fleatstreat pryvat', and the Chamberlain's Men acted *Henry IV* before the Flemish ambassador in private in 1600; perhaps on each occasion they had already acted on the public stage before an audience ranging from gallant to groundling during the afternoon of the day concerned. Both companies were accustomed to acting at Court, and both knew what it was to travel in the country, and amble, as Dekker put it, writing of Ben Jonson, 'in leather pilch by a play-wagon, in the high-way'.

Wherever they performed, much of the attraction of the actors and their plays no doubt lay in their flamboyance, in the richness and splendour of fine costumes, hangings, and stages that were already in 1592, according to Thomas Nashe, 'stately furnisht'. There is plenty of evidence for the splendid appearance of the players and stage in Elizabethan theatres, which have so often been regarded as 'bare'.[3] Henslowe

[3] Some popular handbooks on Shakespeare keep alive the notion of a 'bare platform' within 'the bare framework of the theatre', where 'the absence of stage-scenery meant that Shakespeare had to create it in the verse he wrote', so that even a backcloth now looks 'garish and absurd' against the splendour of the

noted frequent expenses for very elaborate costumes for plays, and among other documents left by him and Edward Alleyn are lists of properties and costumes in the stock of the Admiral's Men in 1598. The items include a hell-mouth, two steeples, Phaeton's chariot, a tree of golden apples, various tombs, an altar, a canopy, two mossy banks, a dragon, a lion, a great horse, a frame for beheading, and the cauldron used in Marlowe's *Jew of Malta.* The lists also mention the city of Rome and the cloth of the sun and moon, perhaps both painted cloths for hanging at the rear of the stage. The theatres themselves presented an attractive appearance. The stage façade was richly ornamented ('painted' was the word used by Gabriel Harvey and Edmund Spenser), with its gallery or balcony over the stage, doors on either side, and canopy supported on two columns over part of the great platform area extending into the middle of the arena, where the groundlings stood to watch and listen. The columns supporting the canopy were marbled, or perhaps gold at some theatres, if we may trust the testimony of Thomas Heywood in his translation of Ovid's *Art of Love* (?1600), who speaks of

> The golden ensignes yonder spreading fare,
> Which wafts them to the gorgeous Theater:
> See what thin leaves of gold foile guild the wood,
> Making the columns seeme all massie good.

The canopy itself was painted on the underside like a sky, 'nail'd up with many a star' as Thomas Middleton said, a 'heaven' to match the 'hell' under the stage. The mainposts of the framework supporting the three tiers of galleries surrounding the stage area, and the columns bearing the canopy, were, at the Fortune Theatre, adorned with figures of satyrs. The stage itself was hung with an arras or painted cloth; so Ben Jonson testifies in his Children's play for court-presentation, *Cynthia's Revels* (1600), in which a boy walks on the stage in the Induction pretending to be a gentleman come to watch the play, and speaks with other children acting as stage-hands,

> Slid, the boy takes me for a piece of *perspective* (I hold my life) or some silk cortaine come to hang the stage here! sir cracke, I am none of your fresh pictures, that use to beautifie the decaied dead arras at a publike theatre.

---

verse (J. D. Wilson, *The Essential Shakespeare* (1932), pp. 31–2). The evidence for the visual richness of the Elizabethan theatres has in fact long been available, and is well emphasized in W. M. Merchant, *Shakespeare and the Artist* (1959), Chapter I, and in A. M. Nagler, *Shakespeare's Stage,* pp. 32–7; see also *Shakespeare Survey* (1959), especially the articles by C. W. Hodges, 'The Lantern of Taste', pp. 8–14, and R. Southern, 'On Reconstructing a Practicable Elizabethan Public Playhouse', pp. 22–34.

In addition to elaborate properties, painted cloths, splendid costumes, and a richly decorated stage façade, it is known that special hangings were used to mark, for instance, a tragedy, as in the Induction to *A Warning for Fair Women* (1599), a play belonging to the Chamberlain's Men, History says

> The stage is hung with blacke: and I perceive
> The Auditors preparde for *Tragedie.*

It would be surprising, then, if part of the attraction of the theatre was not its spectacle; the stage itself must have seemed magnificent to the groundlings, but the plays too might provide much visual splendour. So in *The Trumpet of War* (1598), Stephen Gosson describes how 'in publike Theaters, when any notable shew passeth over the stage, the people arise up out of their seates, & stand upright with delight and eagernesse to view it well'. The plays of the public theatres have numerous shows and processions, often quite elaborate, like the following, from the successful *Old Fortunatus* by Dekker, played by the Admiral's Men before the Queen, probably over Christmas 1598–9; Fortunatus lies under a tree, and there enter

> a *Carter,* a *Sailor,* a *Monke,* a *Shepheard* all crown'd, a *Nimph* with a Globe, another with *Fortunes* wheele, then *Fortune:* After her fowre *Kings* with broken Crownes and Scepters, chained in silver Gyves and led by her. The foremost come out singing. Fortune takes her Chaire, the Kings lying at her feete, shee treading on them as shee goes up.

Such a lavish show was not to be seen in all plays, but most have processions, council-scenes, battle-scenes, duels, a play within the play (like *The Spanish Tragedy* and *A Midsummer Night's Dream*), a trial, a dance or masque, or a display of some kind.

The large, open stage projecting into the arena was suitable for such shows, and in addition to this area, the dramatist had a balcony, at least two doors, a central curtain, tent or alcove, the exact nature of which is not yet certainly established, and the two pillars supporting the canopy to use if he wished. The 'hell' under the stage could also be employed to good effect with the aid of trapdoors, as in *Hamlet,* where the Ghost speaks from under the stage. But for all its splendour, its possibilities of spectacle and of effects like fireworks, or descents from the 'heavens' (Henslowe installed a throne there in 1595), the stage was basically a simple one, with a permanent, largely neutral, background, the interior façade of the theatre itself. There was no proscenium arch to the stage, and the greater part of the acting-space could not be curtained off; so one scene followed another with no break in performances that took place in open daylight. The main visual effects were embodied in the appearance and movements of actors or managed by portable properties; further dimensions of visual splendour might be suggested by a poet's verse, which, as Shakespeare supposes in the prologue to *Henry V,* could piece out the imperfections of the stage, and tempt an audience to think their 'wooden O' transformed into 'the vasty fields of France'. In general, plays were sufficiently independent of scenery and machinery to be staged readily elsewhere than in the theatre, as at Court, or within a private house.

The characteristics of their theatres helped to make possible the adaptability and the wide range of repertory of the Admiral's and Chamberlain's Men. Their daily repertory must have given the actors hard work, and their labour was not always rewarded; a play might prove unpopular and be hissed off the stage, and on occasion Henslowe's gallery receipts dropped to a few shillings. The players also had to adjust themselves to the developments in the theatre and the drama in the 1580s and 1590s, to a continual refining and experimentation, to subtler conceptions of character, freer verse rhythms, new modes of play, like the 'humour' comedies that Jonson and Chapman made fashionable in 1597–8. As part of this adjustment, they developed new styles of acting. At the end of the 1590s the style of the period of Kyd and Marlowe was being parodied, by Jonson in *Poetaster,* by Shakespeare in the person of Pistol, by Marston in his *Antonio's Revenge*. Hieronimo and Tamburlaine became symbols of rant, as in *Histriomastix* (?1598–9), where some soldiers who have seized a group of players address them with the words,

> Sirha, is this you would rend and teare the Cat
> Upon a Stage, and now march like a drownd rat?
> Looke up and play the *Tamburlaine*.

Indeed, in Thomas Middleton's *Black Book,* a pamphlet published in 1604, a 'villanous lieutenant' is described as having a 'head of haire like one of my devils in *Doctor Faustus,* when the old theatre cracked and frighted the audience'. *Doctor Faustus,* like Shakespeare's *Richard III,* remained a popular play, but the new theatres built in the late 1590s, the Globe and Fortune, mark the success of a new drama, and, no doubt, of a new and more refined style of acting than that of Tarleton, or the ranting manner required of Alleyn for parts like Tamburlaine and Orlando. The distance between the styles of 1590 and of 1600 or so may be gauged by the contrast between the texture of the players' speeches delivered at the court of Elsinore, and the texture of *Hamlet* itself; for here Shakespeare deliberately recalled a manner he had long outgrown, and used it as a dramatic device to mark off the play within the play.

The external evidence as to how the actors played their parts is not very trustworthy, since much of it is found in the writings of prejudiced men attacking or defending the stage; it is also difficult to interpret, since the same vocabulary was used of oratory and of acting. However, the puritans constantly complained that the actors were too lifelike, with their 'effeminate gestures, to ravish the sence; and wanton speache, to whet desire to inordinate lust', as Stephen Gosson phrased it in 1579. One of their usual epithets to describe acting was 'lively', in the sense displayed in a passage from J. Rainoldes, *Th'overthrow of Stage-Playes* (1600), where he speaks of 'the *actors,* in whom the earnest care of lively representing the lewd demeanour of bad persons doeth worke a great impression of waxing like unto them'. The defenders of the stage also tended to emphasize this ability of the actors to represent people, to 'appeare to you to be the selfe same men' they impersonated, to cite a commendatory poem in Thomas Heywood's *Apology for Actors* (1612). This does not mean that acting was naturalistic, only that the best acting always then seemed true to life.[4] The frequent gibes at country-players, or at rant and 'forced passion', together with the parody of Kyd's manner, suggest that by the end of the 1590s the notion of truth to life had changed; certainly the dramatist could make greater demands of his actors, as Shakespeare developed, for instance, the women's roles played by boys to the scale of Portia, Gertrude and Beatrice, and enlarged the traditional ranting part of the tragic hero to embrace the alternate brooding and passionate activity, the humour and irony of Hamlet.

However successful the actors were in keeping pace with dramatic developments, they could not expect to please their severer critics among the audience. The most substantial and judicious part of them probably sat in the galleries, which would account for a writer in 1600 comparing himself to 'a Player that in speaking an Epilogue makes love to the two-pennie-roume for a *plaudit*'. There might be sitting not only gentlemen and citizens, but also the author of the play, or perhaps a group of poets. In his third satire in *Virgidemiarum* (1598), Joseph Hall remarks how in a theatre

---

[4] There has been much controversy about the nature of Elizabethan acting. B. L. Joseph argued in his *Elizabethan Acting* (1951) that an actor's gestures and delivery were formalized on the pattern of those practised by an orator, and set forth in manuals of speaking. He was anticipated in this view by Harbage, 'Elizabethan Acting', *PMLA* (1939), 685–708, and has restated it in 'The Elizabethan Stage and the Art of Elizabethan Drama', *Shakespeare-Jahrbuch* (1955), 145–60. Several writers have attacked his conclusions, taking evidence from Elizabethan comments on the stage, or from plays themselves, and have claimed that acting was naturalistic, or that actors tried to be lifelike, or, alternatively, that there was a mixture of formal and naturalistic acting. The whole question turns on what the Elizabethans thought was natural, and this we cannot know for certain. See in this connection S. L. Bethell, 'Shakespeare's Actors', *Review of English Studies* (1950), 193–205; J. R. Brown, 'On the Acting of Shakespeare's Plays', *Quarterly Journal of Speech* (1953), 477–84; R. A. Foakes, 'The Player's Passion', *Essays and Studies* (1954), 62–77; and M. Rosenberg, 'Elizabethan Actors: Men or Marionetts?', *PMLA* (1954), 915–27. One question that receives scant attention by most of the writers on acting is the degree of change that took place between 1580 and 1642, when the theatres were closed; I think that there was rapid change before 1600 from stylization towards a greater truth to life and subtlety of presentation.

> our Poets in high Parliament
> Sit watching every word, and gesturement,
> Like curious Censors of some doughtie geare,
> Whispering their verdit in their fellowes eare.

Ben Jonson is specifically attacked by Dekker in *Satiromastix* (1602) for behaving in this way, and Horace, the character representing him, is told, 'you shall not sit in a Gallery, when your comedies and Enterludes have entred their Actions, and there make vile and bad faces at everie lyne, to make Gentlemen have an eye to you, and to make Players afraide to take your part'. No doubt authors were often glad to take their share of applause, as John Day indicates in his *Isle of Gulls* (1606), where one character asks, 'Doe Poets use to bespeake their Auditory', and is answered by another, 'The best in grace doe, and but for that some that I know had never had their grace in Poetry till this day'; but they did not spare the actors.

Perhaps an actor-playwright like Shakespeare was less likely to sit in judgment than the scholarly Ben Jonson, but even he put some authorial advice to actors into the mouth of Hamlet. Thomas Dekker, writing in 1607 of the Fortune Theatre, said that he had not listened to his plays being acted ('mine eare stood not within the reach of their Larums'), but this did not prevent him from making a very sharp complaint about the players,

> that in such Consorts, many of the Instruments are for the most part out of tune, And no marvaile; for let the Poet set the note of his Nombers, even to Apolloes owne lyre, the Player will have his owne Crochets, and sing false notes, in dispite of all the rules of Musick.

Such an attitude on the part of a working dramatist is not surprising if his heritage is borne in mind; for the influence of the university-trained men, Greene, Marlowe and others, who had set up new poetic and intellectual standards for public theatre plays at the end of the 1580s, continued to be felt. It was they who developed the main medium of the later drama, blank verse, into an admirable form for Shakespeare to perfect, and the steady continuance of verse plays throughout this period shows more than that the audience was used to listening, as to sermons, and could relish spoken styles in a way that it is hard for us to recapture fully; it illustrates also that the authors, and many among the audiences, had a concern for literary values. This may be reflected in the common term for playwright, the word used by Dekker, for instance, which was, simply, poet.

If Dekker, a popular dramatist and steady writer for the Admiral's Men, could chide actors strongly, as in the passage cited above, it is hardly remarkable that others are critical. The most extreme form of this criticism is found in the universities, which had their own long tradition of occasional productions of satirical or scholarly plays, mostly written in Latin. The antagonism of the scholar-poet and the actor is illustrated in the trio of plays, *The Pilgrimage to Parnassus,* and the two parts of *The Return from Parnassus,* acted in Cambridge between 1598 and 1602. In the first of these a clown is drawn on by a rope, in a caustic accusation that the public theatres dragged a clown into every play; and in the third, Burbage and Kemp of the Chamberlain's Men are impersonated as illiterate, and as practising the 'basest trade'. The comment of the character Philomusus here on actors, as

> those leaden spouts,
> That nought doe vent but what they do receive,

echoes the frequent remarks of a similar tone made by Greene and Nashe especially among the 'University Wits' ten years previously. In one of his kinder moments, Greene said of an actor, 'what sentence thou utterest on the stage, flowes from the censure of our wittes, and what sentence or conceipte of the invention the people applaud for excellent, that comes from the secrets of our knowledge. I graunt your action, though it be a kind of mechanical labour.'

This attitude stemmed not merely from a natural tension between an author conscious of his play as poetry, and actors for whom any one play was part of a changing repertory; it arose in large part from the scholar's sense of getting a poor reward for his labour, receiving merely a few pounds for a play. This grievance is also voiced in *2 Return from Parnassus,* where Studioso says,

> Better it is mongst fidlers to be chiefe,
> Then at a plaiers trencher beg reliefe.
> But ist not strange these mimick apes should prize
> Unhappy Schollers at a hireling rate?
> Vile world, that lifts them up to hye degree,
> And treads us downe in groveling misery.
> *England* affordes those glorious vagabonds,
> That carried earst their fardels on their backes,
> Coursers to ride on through the gazing streetes,
> Sooping [sweeping] it in their glaring Satten sutes,
> And pages to attend their maisterships:
> With mouthing words that better wits have framed
> They purchase lands, and now Esquiers are namde.

However much they might abuse the actors, university men continued to write for the public stages. Among the regular writers for the Admiral's Men in the late 1590s were at least two graduates, John Day and Thomas Heywood, besides the learned Ben Jonson, who worked with them for a time, and George Chapman. Indeed, writers could not afford to be too hostile to the stage, since, as Francis Meres says in his *Palladis Tamia* (1598), poets lacked patronage, and were 'soly or chiefly maintained, countenanced and patronized' by 'our witty Comedians and stately Tragedians (the glorious and goodlie representers of all fine witte, glorified phrase and queint action)', that is to say, the actors.

The poet who turned to the theatre in order to earn money had to be prolific in his output of plays if he wished to make any sort of a living out of his writing, and the scholar's complaint of poverty helps to put into focus the advantages of working as a dramatist from within the company. A number of men were actor-dramatists, and several of the sharers in the Admiral's Men wrote plays, among them for a time Ben Jonson; but most of them wrote occasionally, and must have drawn their main income from their share in the theatre profits, or their pay as actors. Jonson, for instance, seems to have had a hand in six or seven plays between 1597 and 1600, and Sam Rowley, another sharer in the Admiral's Men, probably wrote or contributed to no more than eight or ten plays during a career lasting well into the seventeenth century. By contrast, Henry Chettle, a writer making a living out of his plays, wrote two and collaborated in fourteen during the single year 1598; in the same year Dekker also had a hand in at least sixteen plays. Until 1598 or so, Shakespeare was in the position of an actor-sharer, who could take time over his plays, and his output, though large by modern standards, was slender in comparison with Dekker's. After 1598, when he took a share in the new Globe, his position was still more privileged; an interest in the property and in the acting company was enough to give him a good income, and he had a unique position as a dramatist. He had the best conditions for writing, possessing an intimate knowledge of the company he worked for, the leisure of one who did not need to make a living by writing, and the authority of a superior status in the company. It is not surprising that he had the major share in that process of refinement whereby the drama was transmuted in the 1590s and brought to full maturity.

[William Shakespeare's] dramatic and literary success in the 1590s was based on the development of a regular professional theatre and a professional drama drawing on the best talents of the time, and uniting in the work of the two companies, the Admiral's and Chamberlain's Men, an inheritance of a scholarly drama, often on classical themes as represented in the plays of the Children's companies, and an inheritance of a popular, vigorous drama, as represented in the plays of the Queen's Men. These traditions, brought together and given new life by the University Wits, sustained the public theatres which, prior to 1600, were the only theatres operating in London, and which drew their audience from all classes of society. In this way the development of a rich drama which might appeal to everyone at some level was ensured. Many dramatists of considerable power became productive during this decade, and helped to give a context and stimulus to Shakespeare, who had the genius to make the most of the possibilities offered to him by his theatre. He learned how to write to please at once the aristocrat (*A Midsummer Night's Dream* was probably written for private performance to celebrate a nobleman's wedding), the scholar, the citizen and the groundling; and from his success and enormous prestige by 1600, it is apparent that, more than any of his contemporaries, he fulfilled Dekker's pattern of a perfect poet, as one who

> Can call the *Banish'd Auditor* home, And tye
> His Eare (with golden chaines) to his Melody:
> Can draw with *Adamantine Pen* (even Creatures
> Forg'de out of the *Hammer,*) on tiptoe, to *Reach*-up,
> And (from *Rare silence*) clap their *Brawny hands,*
> T'*Applaud,* what their *charmd* soule scarce understands.

Selected Dates and Facts

1576	James Burbage built the Theatre in Shoreditch, a northern suburb of London. Richard Farrant converted part of the old Blackfriars priory into an indoor playhouse for the Children of the Chapel Royal.
?1577	The Curtain Theatre opened, also in Shoreditch.
1583	Players selected from the adult companies to form the Queen's Men.
1585	Admiral's Men established by this date, with Edward Alleyn among them.
?1587/8	Philip Henslowe built the Rose Theatre, on Bankside, a southern suburb of London, south of the Thames.
?1588	Richard Tarleton, leading actor of the Queen's Men, died. Lord Strange's Men established by this date.
1590	Richard Burbage first mentioned as an actor. The children's companies suppressed.
1590–4	Lord Strange's Men and the Admiral's Men probably working in association or in combination.
1592	Shakespeare established as actor and playwright, working probably for Pembroke's and Sussex's Men. Henslowe began to make entries in his *Diary*. Robert Greene died.
1593	Plague closed the theatres for most of the year. Pembroke's Men broke up. Christopher Marlowe died.
1594	Queen's Men and Sussex's Men broke up, their stock passing to Admiral's and Strange's Men. These two companies separated after June, some members of Strange's re-forming as the Lord Chamberlain's Men, who were joined by Shakespeare. Thomas Kyd died.
?1596	The Swan Theatre built by Francis Langley on Bankside.
1597	Some players of Admiral's and Chamberlain's Men seceded to form a new group at the Swan, where their performance of Nashe's *Isle of Dogs* caused acting to be prohibited.
1598	The Admiral's Men, reinforced by the Swan group who returned to the Rose, and the Chamberlain's Men were the only companies licensed to act.

1599 The Globe Theatre built on Bankside; Shakespeare admitted to a share in its ownership.

1600 The Fortune Theatre built by Henslowe and Edward Alleyn in Finsbury, a northern suburb of London. The Children's companies begin playing again in indoor theatres.

Scholarship: the standard reference books are E. K. Chambers, *The Elizabethan Stage* (1923), 4 vols., and *William Shakespeare: a Study of Facts and Problems* (1930), 2 vols. W. W. Greg edited *Henslowe's Diary* (1904–7) and *Henslowe Papers* (1908).

J. C. Adams' *The Globe Playhouse* (1943) contains much information, but many scholars believe that Adams was not sufficiently rigorous in selecting evidence and approached his subject with strong, unrecognized prejudices (see especially a review by G. F. Reynolds in *JEGP* for 1943). C. W. Hodges' *The Globe Restored* (1953) is balanced and well illustrated. A full study of theatrical conditions and traditions is G. Wickham's *Early English Stages,* of which the first of two volumes has appeared (1959). A short yet comprehensive book is A. M. Nagler, *Shakespeare's Stage* (1958).

Shakespeare's public is considered in A. Harbage, *Shakespeare's Audience* (1941) and *Shakespeare and the Rival Traditions* (1952), and more general manifestations of taste in C. J. Sisson, *Le Goût Public et le Théâtre Élisabethain* (Dijon, 1922) and L. B. Wright, *Middle-Class Culture in Elizabethan England* (1935).

Specialized aspects of the theatrical scene are studied in H. N. Hillebrand, *The Child Actors* (1926) and R. B. Sharpe, *The Real War of the Theatres* (1935).

A. Nicoll has written a retrospective account of the study of Elizabethan theatres in *Shakespeare Survey* (1948).

III

COMIC THEORY AND THE EARLY COMEDIES

A THEORY OF COMEDY

The Argument of Comedy

Northrop Frye

The Greeks produced two kinds of comedy, Old Comedy, represented by the eleven extant plays of Aristophanes, and New Comedy, of which the best known exponent is Menander. About two dozen New Comedies survive in the work of Plautus and Terence. Old Comedy, however, was out of date before Aristophanes himself was dead; and today, when we speak of comedy, we normally think of something that derives from the Menandrine tradition.

New Comedy unfolds from what may be described as a comic Oedipus situation. Its main theme is the successful effort of a young man to outwit an opponent and possess the girl of his choice. The opponent is usually the father (*senex*), and the psychological descent of the heroine from the mother is also sometimes hinted at. The father frequently wants the same girl, and is cheated out of her by the son, the mother thus becoming the son's ally. The girl is usually a slave or courtesan, and the plot turns on a *cognitio* or discovery of birth which makes her marriageable. Thus it turns out that she is not under an insuperable taboo after all but is an accessible object of desire, so that the plot follows the regular wish-fulfillment pattern. Often the central Oedipus situation is thinly concealed by surrogates or doubles of the main characters, as when the heroine is discovered to be the hero's sister, and has to be married off to his best friend. In Congreve's *Love*

From *English Institute Essays 1948,* ed. D. A. Robertson, New York: Columbia University Press, 1949, pp. 58–73. Reprinted by permission of Columbia University Press.

for Love, to take a modern instance well within the Menandrine tradition, there are two Oedipus themes in counterpoint: the hero cheats his father out of the heroine, and his best friend violates the wife of an impotent old man who is the heroine's guardian. Whether this analysis is sound or not, New Comedy is certainly concerned with the maneuvering of a young man toward a young woman, and marriage is the tonic chord on which it ends. The normal comic resolution is the surrender of the *senex* to the hero, never the reverse. Shakespeare tried to reverse the pattern in *All's Well That Ends Well,* where the king of France forces Bertram to marry Helena, and the critics have not yet stopped making faces over it.

New Comedy has the blessing of Aristotle, who greatly preferred it to its predecessor, and it exhibits the general pattern of Aristotelian causation. It has a material cause in the young man's sexual desire, and a formal cause in the social order represented by the *senex,* with which the hero comes to terms when he gratifies his desire. It has an efficient cause in the character who brings about the final situation. In classical times this character is a tricky slave; Renaissance dramatists often use some adaptation of the medieval "vice"; modern writers generally like to pretend that nature, or at least the natural course of events, is the efficient cause. The final cause is the audience, which is expected by its applause to take part in the comic resolution. All this takes place on a single order of existence. The action of New Comedy tends to become probable rather than fantastic, and it moves toward realism and away from myth and romance. The once romantic (originally mythical) feature in it, the fact that the hero or heroine turns out to be freeborn or someone's heir, is precisely the feature that trained New Comedy audiences tire of most quickly.

The conventions of New Comedy are the conventions of Jonson and Molière, and a fortiori of the English Restoration and the French rococo. When Ibsen started giving ironic twists to the same formulas, his startled hearers took them for portents of a social revolution. Even the old chestnut about the heroine's being really the hero's sister turns up in *Ghosts* and *Little Eyolf.* The average movie of today is a rigidly conventionalized New Comedy proceeding toward an act which, like death in Greek tragedy, takes place offstage, and is symbolized by the final embrace.

In all good New Comedy there is a social as well as an individual theme which must be sought in the general atmosphere of reconciliation that makes the final marriage possible. As the hero gets closer to the heroine and opposition is overcome, all the right-thinking people come over to his side. Thus a new social unit is formed on the stage, and the moment that this social unit crystallizes is the moment of the comic resolution. In the last scene, when the dramatist usually tries to get all his characters on the stage at once, the audience witnesses the birth of a renewed sense of social integration. In comedy as in life the regular expression of this is a festival, whether a marriage, a dance, or a feast. Old Comedy has, besides a marriage, a *komos,* the processional dance from which comedy derives its name; and the masque, which is a by-form of comedy, also ends in a dance.

This new social integration may be called, first, a kind of moral norm and, second, the pattern of a free society. We can see this more clearly if we look at the sort of characters who impede the progress of the comedy toward the hero's victory. These are always people who are in some kind of mental bondage, who are helplessly driven by ruling passions, neurotic compulsions, social rituals, and selfishness. The miser, the hypochondriac, the hypocrite, the pedant, the snob: these are humors, people who do not fully know what they are doing, who are slaves to a predictable self-imposed pattern of behavior. What we call the moral norm is, then, not morality but deliverance from moral bondage. Comedy is designed not to condemn evil, but to ridicule a lack of self-knowledge. It finds the virtues of Malvolio and Angelo as comic as the vices of Shylock.

The essential comic resolution, therefore, is an individual release which is also a social reconciliation. The normal individual is freed from the bonds of a humorous society, and a normal society is freed from the bonds imposed on it by humorous individuals. The Oedipus pattern we noted in New Comedy belongs to the individual side of this, and the sense of the ridiculousness of the humor to the social side. But all real comedy is based on the principle that these two forms of release are ultimately the same: this principle may be seen at its most concentrated in *The Tempest.* The rule holds whether the resolution is expressed in social terms, as in *The Merchant of Venice,* or in individual terms, as in Ibsen's *An Enemy of the People.*

The freer the society, the greater the variety of individuals it can tolerate, and the natural tendency of comedy is to include as many as possible in its final festival. The motto of comedy is Terence's "Nothing human is alien to me." This may be one reason for the traditional comic importance of the parasite, who has no business to be at the festival but is nevertheless there. The spirit of reconciliation which pervades the comedies of Shakespeare is not to be ascribed to a personal attitude of his own, about which we know nothing whatever, but to his impersonal concentration on the laws of comic form.

Hence the moral quality of the society presented is not the point of the comic resolution. In Jonson's *Volpone* the final assertion of the moral norm takes the form of a social revenge on Volpone, and the play ends with a great bustle of sentences to penal servitude and the galleys. One feels perhaps that the audience's sense of the moral norm does not need so much hard labor. In *The Alchemist,* when Lovewit returns to his house, the virtuous characters have proved so weak and the rascals so ingenious that the action dissolves in laughter. Whichever is morally the better ending, that of *The Alchemist* is more concentrated comedy. *Volpone* is starting to move toward tragedy, toward the vision of a greatness which develops *hybris* and catastrophe.

The same principle is even clearer in Aristophanes. Aristophanes is the most personal of writers: his opinions on every subject are written all over his plays, and we have no doubt of his moral attitude. We know that he wanted peace with Sparta and that he hated Cleon, and when his comedy depicts the attaining of peace and the defeat of Cleon we know that he approved and wanted his audience to approve. But in *Ecclesiazusae* a band of women in disguise railroad a communistic scheme through the Assembly, which is a horrid parody of Plato's *Republic,* and proceed to inaugurate Plato's sexual communism with some astonishing improvements. Presumably Aristophanes did not applaud this, yet the comedy follows the same pattern and the same resolution. In *The Birds* the Peisthetairos who defies Zeus and blocks out Olympus with his Cloud-Cuckoo-Land is accorded the same triumph that is given to the Trygaeus of the *Peace* who flies to heaven and brings a golden age back to Athens.

Comedy, then, may show virtue her own feature and scorn her own image—for Hamlet's famous definition of drama was originally a definition of comedy. It may emphasize the birth of an ideal society as you like it, or the tawdriness of the sham society which is the way of the world. There is an important parallel here with tragedy. Tragedy, we are told, is expected to raise but not ultimately to accept the emotions of pity and terror. These I take to be the sense of moral good and evil, respectively, which we attach to the tragic hero. He may be as good as Caesar, and so appeal to our pity, or as bad as Macbeth, and so appeal to terror, but the particular thing called tragedy that happens to him does not depend on his moral status. The tragic catharsis passes beyond moral judgment, and while it is quite possible to construct a moral tragedy, what tragedy gains in morality it loses in cathartic power. The same is true of the comic catharsis, which raises sympathy and ridicule on a moral basis, but passes beyond both.

Many things are involved in the tragic catharsis, but one of them is a mental or imaginative form of the sacrificial ritual out of which tragedy arose. This is the ritual of the struggle, death, and rebirth of a God-Man, which is linked to the yearly triumph of spring over winter. The tragic hero is not really killed, and the audience no longer eats his body and drinks his blood, but the corresponding thing in art still takes place. The audience enters into communion with the body of the hero, becoming thereby a single body itself. Comedy grows out of the same ritual, for in the ritual the tragic story has a comic sequel. Divine men do not die; they die and rise again. The ritual pattern behind the catharsis of comedy is the resurrection that follows the death, the epiphany or manifestation of the risen hero. This is clear enough in Aristophanes, where the hero is treated as a risen God-Man, led in triumph with the divine honors of the Olympic victor, rejuvenated, or hailed as a new Zeus. In New Comedy, the new human body is, as we have seen, both a hero and a social group. Aristophanes is not only closer to the ritual pattern, but contemporary with Plato;

and his comedy, unlike Menander's, is Platonic and dialectic: it seeks not the entelechy of the soul but the Form of the Good, and finds it in the resurrection of the soul from the world of the cave to the sunlight. The audience gains a vision of that resurrection whether the conclusion is joyful or ironic, just as in tragedy it gains a vision of a heroic death whether the hero is morally innocent or guilty.

Two things follow from this: first, that tragedy is really implicit or uncompleted comedy; second, that comedy contains a potential tragedy within itself. With regard to the latter, Aristophanes is full of traces of the original death of the hero which preceded his resurrection in the ritual. Even in New Comedy the dramatist usually tries to bring his action as close to a tragic overthrow of the hero as he can get it, and reverses this movement as suddenly as possible. In Plautus the tricky slave is often forgiven or even freed after having been threatened with all the brutalities that a very brutal dramatist can think of, including crucifixion. Thus the resolution of New Comedy seems to be a realistic foreshortening of a death-and-resurrection pattern, in which the struggle and rebirth of a divine hero has shrunk into a marriage, the freeing of a slave, and the triumph of a young man over an older one.

As for the conception of tragedy as implicit comedy, we may notice how often tragedy closes on the major chord of comedy: the Aeschylean trilogy, for instance, proceeds to what is really a comic resolution, and so do many tragedies of Euripides. From the point of view of Christianity, too, tragedy is an episode in that larger scheme of redemption and resurrection to which Dante gave the name of *commedia.* This conception of *commedia* enters drama with the miracle-play cycles, where such tragedies as the Fall and the Crucifixion are episodes of a dramatic scheme in which the divine comedy has the last word. The sense of tragedy as a prelude to comedy is hardly separable from anything explicitly Christian. The serenity of the final double chorus in the St. Matthew Passion would hardly be attainable if composer and audience did not know that there was more to the story. Nor would the death of Samson lead to "calm of mind all passion spent" if Samson were not a prototype of the rising Christ.

New Comedy is thus contained, so to speak, within the symbolic structure of Old Comedy, which in its turn is contained within the Christian conception of *commedia.* This sounds like a logically exhaustive classification, but we have still not caught Shakespeare in it.

It is only in Jonson and the Restoration writers that English comedy can be called a form of New Comedy. The earlier tradition established by Peele and developed by Lyly, Greene, and the masque writers, which uses themes from romance and folklore and avoids the comedy of manners, is the one followed by Shakespeare. These themes are largely medieval in origin, and derive, not from the mysteries or the moralities or the interludes, but from a fourth dramatic tradition. This is the drama of folk ritual, of the St. George play and the mummers' play, of the feast of the ass and the Boy Bishop, and of all the dramatic activity that punctuated the Christian calendar with the rituals of an immemorial paganism. We may call this the drama of the green world, and its theme is once again the triumph of life over the waste land, the death and revival of the year impersonated by figures still human, and once divine as well.

When Shakespeare began to study Plautus and Terence, his dramatic instinct, stimulated by his predecessors, divined that there was a profounder pattern in the argument of comedy than appears in either of them. At once—for the process is beginning in *The Comedy of Errors* —he started groping toward that profounder pattern, the ritual of death and revival that also underlies Aristophanes, of which an exact equivalent lay ready to hand in the drama of the green world. This parallelism largely accounts for the resemblances to Greek ritual which Colin Still has pointed out in *The Tempest.*

The Two Gentlemen of Verona is an orthodox New Comedy except for one thing. The hero Valentine becomes captain of a band of outlaws in a forest, and all the other characters are gathered into this forest and become converted. Thus the action of the comedy begins in a world represented as a normal world, moves into the green world, goes into a metamorphosis there in which the comic resolution is achieved, and returns to the normal world. The forest in this play is the embryonic form of the fairy world of *A Midsummer Night's Dream,* the Forest of Arden in *As You Like It,* Windsor Forest in *The Merry Wives of Windsor,* and the pastoral world of the mythical sea-coasted Bohemia in *The Winter's Tale.* In all these comedies there is the same rhythmic movement from normal world to green world and back again. Nor is this second world confined to the forest comedies. In *The Merchant of Venice* the two worlds are a little harder to see, yet Venice is clearly not the same world as that of Portia's mysterious house in Belmont, where there are caskets teaching that gold and silver are corruptible goods, and from whence proceed the wonderful cosmological harmonies of the fifth act. In *The Tempest* the entire action takes place in the second world, and the same may be said of *Twelfth Night,* which, as its title implies, presents a carnival society, not so much a green world as an evergreen one. The second world is absent from the so-called problem comedies, which is one of the things that makes them problem comedies.

The green world charges the comedies with a symbolism in which the comic resolution contains a suggestion of the old ritual pattern of the victory of summer over winter. This is explicit in *Love's Labor's Lost.* In this very masque-like play, the comic contest takes the form of the medieval debate of winter and spring. In *The Merry Wives of Windsor* there is an elaborate ritual of the defeat of winter, known to folklorists as "carrying out Death," of which Falstaff is the victim; and Falstaff must have felt that, after being thrown into the water, dressed up as a witch and beaten out of a house with curses, and finally supplied with a beast's head and singed with candles while he said, "Divide me like a brib'd buck, each a haunch," he had done about all that could reasonably be asked of any fertility spirit.

The association of this symbolism with the death and revival of human beings is more elusive, but still perceptible. The fact that the heroine often brings about the comic resolution by disguising herself as a boy is familiar enough. In the Hero of *Much Ado About Nothing* and the Helena of *All's Well That Ends Well,* this theme of the withdrawal and return of the heroine comes as close to a death and revival as Elizabethan conventions will allow. The Thaisa of *Pericles* and the Fidele of *Cymbeline* are beginning to crack the conventions, and with the disappearance and revival of Hermione in *The Winter's Tale,* who actually returns once as a ghost in a dream, the original nature-myth of Demeter and Proserpine is openly established. The fact that the dying and reviving character is usually female strengthens the feeling that there is something maternal about the green world, in which the new order of the comic resolution is nourished and brought to birth. However, a similar theme which is very like the rejuvenation of the *senex* so frequent in Aristophanes occurs in the folklore motif of the healing of the impotent king on which *All's Well That Ends Well* is based, and this theme is probably involved in the symbolism of Prospero.

The conception of a second world bursts the boundaries of Menandrine comedy, yet it is clear that the world of Puck is no world of eternal forms or divine revelation. Shakespeare's comedy is not Aristotelian and realistic like Menander's, nor Platonic and dialectic like Aristophanes', nor Thomist and sacramental like Dante's, but a fourth kind. It is an Elizabethan kind, and is not confined either to Shakespeare or to the drama. Spenser's epic is a wonderful contrapuntal intermingling of two orders of existence, one the red and white world of English history, the other the green world of the Faerie Queene. The latter is a world of crusading virtues proceeding from the Faerie Queene's court and designed to return to that court when the destiny of the other world is fulfilled. The fact that the Faerie Queene's knights are sent out during the twelve days of the Christmas festival suggests our next point.

Shakespeare too has his green world of comedy and his red and white world of history. The story of the latter is at one point interrupted by an invasion from the comic world, when Falstaff *senex et parasitus* throws his gigantic shadow over Prince Henry, assuming on one occasion the role of his father. Clearly, if the Prince is ever to conquer France he must reassert the moral norm. The moral norm is duly reasserted, but the rejection of Falstaff is not a comic resolution. In comedy the moral norm is not morality but deliverance, and we certainly do not feel delivered from Falstaff as we feel delivered from Shylock with his absurd and vicious bond. The moral norm does not carry with it the vision of a free society: Falstaff will always keep a bit of that in his tavern.

Falstaff is a mock king, a lord of misrule, and his tavern is a Saturnalia. Yet we are reminded of the original meaning of the Saturnalia, as a rite intended to recall the golden age of Saturn. Falstaff's world is not a golden world, but as long as we remember it we cannot forget that the world of *Henry V* is an iron one. We are reminded too of another traditional denizen of the green world, Robin Hood, the outlaw who manages to suggest a better kind of society than those who make him an outlaw can produce. The outlaws in *The Two Gentlemen of Verona* compare themselves, in spite of the Italian setting, to Robin Hood, and in *As You Like It* Charles the wrestler says of Duke Senior's followers: "There they live like the old Robin Hood of England: they say many young gentlemen flock to him every day, and fleet the time carelessly, as they did in the golden world."

In the histories, therefore, the comic Saturnalia is a temporary reversal of normal standards, comic "relief" as it is called, which subsides and allows the history to continue. In the comedies, the green world suggests an original golden age which the normal world has usurped and which makes us wonder if it is not the normal world that is the real Saturnalia. In *Cymbeline* the green world finally triumphs over a historical theme, the reason being perhaps that in that play the incarnation of Christ, which is contemporary with Cymbeline, takes place offstage, and accounts for the halcyon peace with which the play concludes. From then on in Shakespeare's plays, the green world has it all its own way, and both in *Cymbeline* and in *Henry VIII* there may be suggestions that Shakespeare, like Spenser, is moving toward a synthesis of the two worlds, a wedding of Prince Arthur and the Faerie Queene.

This world of fairies, dreams, disembodied souls, and pastoral lovers may not be a "real" world, but, if not, there is something equally illusory in the stumbling and blinded follies of the "normal" world, of Theseus' Athens with its idiotic marriage law, of Duke Frederick and his melancholy tyranny, of Leontes and his mad jealousy, of the Court Party with their plots and intrigues. The famous speech of Prospero about the dream nature of reality applies equally to Milan and the enchanted island. We spend our lives partly in a waking world we call normal and partly in a dream world which we create out of our own desires. Shakespeare endows both worlds with equal imaginative power, brings them opposite one another, and makes each world seem unreal when seen by the light of the other. He uses freely both the heroic triumph of New Comedy and the ritual resurrection of its predecessor, but his distinctive comic resolution is different from either: it is a detachment of the spirit born of this reciprocal reflection of two illusory realities. We need not ask whether this brings us into a higher order of existence or not, for the question of existence is not relevant to poetry.

We have spoken of New Comedy as Aristotelian, Old Comedy as Platonic and Dante's *commedia* as Thomist, but it is difficult to suggest a philosophical spokesman for the form of Shakespeare's comedy. For Shakespeare, the subject matter of poetry is not life, or nature, or reality, or revelation, or anything else that the philosopher builds on, but poetry itself, a verbal universe. That is one reason why he is both the most elusive and the most substantial of poets.

SHAKESPEARE'S EARLY COMEDIES

"A Midsummer Night's Dream": Structure

David P. Young

"The Iron Tongue of Midnight Hath Told Twelve"

The structure of *A Midsummer Night's Dream* involves, among other things, its time scheme, long considered a problem. The difficulties are well known; temporal references in the play are, like the references to the moon, inconsistent. Theseus and Hippolyta, at the beginning of the play, expect to wait four days until their marriage ceremony; count as they will, however, commentators are able to account for only three. There are various ways in which this discrepancy may be explained. It can be argued that Theseus and Hippolyta succumb to their impatience and move things up one day, or that everyone is anxious to seal the bonds between the quartet of lovers while they are harmoniously arranged. It is also quite possible that the occasion of the original performance was, in fact, four days before the wedding of the couple honored by the play and that Shakespeare never bothered to readjust this actual reference to the details of the plot. The discrepancies in the time scheme have also been used to support theories of revision. But the most sensible reaction is that of Kittredge:

> The time scheme of the drama has worried the critics a good deal and has helped them in spinning tenuous theories of revision. We need only observe that the four days and four nights contemplated by Hippolyta in I.i.7–11, are not fully spanned. . . . No audience would note the discrepancy, for the night in the enchanted forest is long enough to bewilder the imagination.[1]

---

[1] Kittredge Edition, p. ix.

Hippolyta supports this when she says:

> Four days will quickly steep themselves in night;
> Four nights will quickly dream away the time.
> (I.i.7–8)

The time in this play is indeed "dreamed away," so that undue concern about its exact chronology is a little like the mechanicals' anxious consultation of the almanac.

The temporal patterning of the play is more profitably examined in terms of its effect on the audience. What they witness is a movement from daytime in the city to nighttime in the woods, which then swings back to day again. All of this is controlled by the dramatist in a way that leaves no confusion about the time of day or night at any given moment in the play.[2] We are carefully prepared for the nocturnal scenes first by the planning of the lovers, then by the rehearsal arrangements of the clowns. In the first night-scene at the opening of the second act, we are brought gradually to an awareness of night which is very like the gathering of dusk on a summer evening. There are oblique references in the opening lines to the moon, night, and starlight; these are balanced by visual images that do not suggest darkness. Puck next describes himself as a "wanderer of the night" and sketches two indoor nocturnal scenes. With Oberon's entrance and opening line—"Ill met by moonlight, proud Titania"—we have come to full night, but it is and will remain, for the most part, the peculiarly "glimmering" night which Oberon mentions a few lines later.

Similarly, we begin to anticipate the arrival of daylight long before it comes. "Cock crow" has been mentioned before the end of the second act. The end of the third act brings Puck's "this must be done with haste" speech and Oberon's reply, which fully prepares us for dawn. We have one more scene, however, before daybreak, that between Bottom and Titania. Then, with all the necessary magic performed, the fairies "hear the morning lark" and leave the stage; a horn blows, and Theseus and Hippolyta enter, bringing with them full daylight. This day-night-day pattern is all the audience knows and all it needs to know.

Almost all, one should say, for the play takes one more turn back to darkness again, and the pattern becomes day-night-day-night. We are vaguely aware of this throughout the fifth act because Theseus has mentioned the need to while away the space between "after-supper and bedtime," a matter of some three hours. The "tedious brief" scene of Pyramus and Thisby, as if to make its oxymoron come true, takes up this time, for as it ends Theseus announces that it is past midnight. This is an excellent example of Shakespeare's illusory use of time for

---

[2] Cf. the discussion of scene-setting techniques in this play in Arthur Colby Sprague, *Shakespeare and His Audience: A Study in the Technique of Exposition* (Cambridge, Mass., 1935), pp. 56 f.

dramatic effect. It may not be credible to the scrupulous commentator that "Pyramus and Thisby" could occupy three hours, but it is perfectly credible to the audience, even though Theseus' announcement comes as something of a jolt. The jolt has a dramatic function, for the audience has nearly forgotten the fairies and their world. The lovers may think that they are out of the woods and free for good of their midsummer madness, but the audience is to be reminded that error, illusion, and mystery still exist. Theseus unwittingly aids this final twist by announcing that it is "almost fairy time." Then, as the mortals leave the stage, Puck replaces them with his superb nocturnal litany and all the fairies troop in to bless the marriages. By coming round to "fairy time" again, the play asserts the validity and constancy of both its worlds, day and night, reason and imagination. By returning from night to day it completes a circle; by reintroducing night it performs a figure eight.

Perhaps the most noticeable fact about time in *A Midsummer Night's Dream* is its minimization. In other Shakespearean plays it has a significant role in the workings of the plot. It untangles the knots of *Twelfth Night,* defeats the lovers in *Romeo and Juliet,* and appears before the curtain to divide *The Winter's Tale* in half. In *A Midsummer Night's Dream,* however, it neither starts nor finishes the action. The events in the woods are a suspension of reality, and their resolution, like their initiation, is extra-temporal. We know that one night has been passed in the woods. But what matters about Bottom's dream (as well as Titania's and the four lovers') is not when it happened or how long it lasted, but that its victim was somehow "translated," was absent from his usual self, another person in another place. In his own thick-witted way, Bottom touches on this when he says that his dream "hath no bottom." He is speaking of it in spatial terms, and such terms seem to be appropriate. Because of the minimization of time in *A Midsummer Night's Dream,* most discussions of its structure tend to emphasize spatial aspects—positioning of character groups, levels of awareness, spheres of action. It is these aspects of the play that we turn to next.

"By Some Illusion See Thou Bring Her Here"

There are two worlds in *A Midsummer Night's Dream*—the kingdom of Theseus and the kingdom of Oberon, the one an orderly society, the other a confusing wilderness. The action of the play moves between the two, as two groups of characters from the real and reasonable world find themselves temporarily lost in the imaginary and irrational world. This pattern of action corresponds closely both to the religious morality and the romance, where the respective heroes often move on a narrative line that can be schematized as follows:[3]

---

[3] I owe this schematization to a suggestion in David M. Bevington, *From Mankind to Marlowe* (Cambridge, Mass., 1962), p. 190.

Morality:

fall from grace	/	temporary prosperity of evil	/	divine reconciliation

Romance:

separation	/	wandering	/	reunion

As the secular drama came to supersede the religious, it branched out, and one of the variations, based on the pastoral ideal, presented the movement through bad fortune to good fortune in spheres of action already familiar from the romance:

Pastoral Romance:

society	/	wilderness	/	an improved society

The purest examples of this pattern in Shakespeare are *As You Like It* and the late romances, *Cymbeline, The Winter's Tale,* and *The Tempest,* but it may be found at work in plays as diverse as *Two Gentlemen* and *King Lear.* In *A Midsummer Night's Dream* it is present at its most comic pitch: the danger which initially sends the central characters into the wilderness is less severe than in, say, *As You Like It,* and the corresponding need for some sort of social reform is slight. The wilderness, as a result, comes to play a more dominant role. In the pastoral romances, it is usually a pseudo-ideal and a temporary haven. In *A Midsummer Night's Dream,* as personified in the fairies, it governs most of the action and controls most of the characters, recalling the more powerful forces of disruption at work in the midsection of both morality and romance.

It will be noted that the spheres of action in these traditional narrative patterns do not alter significantly. It is the characters and, by imaginative extension, ourselves who alter as we move through the worlds in question, discovering their interaction. In *A Midsummer Night's Dream,* this process of discovery reveals that the opposing worlds seem to form concentric circles. At first, following the characters from Athens to the woods, we may feel that the two areas are simply adjacent, but as Theseus and daylight reenter the play, we realize that it is possible to enter the woods and reemerge on the other side into human society. Thus, Theseus and his world seem to envelop the world of the woods. But Oberon and Titania, as we learn early in the play and are reminded directly at the end, are not the subjects of Theseus. Their awareness exceeds his, and their world is larger, enveloping his; he is their unconscious subject. Thus we discover another and larger circle, enclosing the first two. Then comes Puck's epilogue, which reminds us that everything we have been watching is a play, an event in a theater with ourselves as audience. Here is a still larger circle, enveloping all the others. The process stops there, but the discovery of ever more comprehensive circles inevitably suggests that there is another one still to be discovered. This is not merely a trick or a display of artistic ingenuity; treating us as it does to an expansion of consciousness and a series of epistemological discoveries, it suggests that our knowledge of the world is less reliable than it seems.

Thus it is that the concentric circles described above can also be used to depict the spectrum of awareness formed by the characters in the play. These are more usually depicted as levels on a kind of rising ladder of intelligence and consciousness,[4] but the very action by which we learn of the differences, that of one character standing aside to watch characters who are less aware of a given situation, suggests the enclosing image of a circle or sphere. In the inmost circle are the mechanicals, and at their center stands Bottom, supremely ignorant of all that is happening. All of the humor derived from Bottom depends on his absolute lack of awareness joined to the absolute confidence with which he moves through the play. If this makes him amusing, it also makes him sympathetic, as if we unconsciously recognized his kinship not only with the other characters but with ourselves. The difference, after all, is one of degree.

In the next circle belong the lovers; they are not much better off than the clowns, but the fact that they are largely victims of enchantment rather than native stupidity gives them claim to a fuller awareness, since Bottom's enchantment never alters his behavior or his nature. The circle beyond belongs to Theseus and Hippolyta, who oversee the action from a distance and are not victimized by the fairies. Hippolyta deserves the further station, on the basis of her conversation with Theseus at the beginning of the fifth act. The fairies occupy the next circle, Titania first, because she is tricked by her husband, then Oberon and Puck. Even these two, however, are not at all times fully aware of the course of events, and we, the audience, watch them as they watch the others. The furthest circle, then, belongs to us. Or is it the furthest? Does not the playwright belong still further out, overseeing not only the events of the play but our reaction to them, enchanting us as Puck enchants the lovers?

The four groups into which the characters of *A Midsummer Night's Dream* fall present us with another spatial aspect of construction. The effect is like that of a fugue, in which we are simultaneously aware of several lines of movement and thus of position and interaction. Each of the four groups in the play has its own set of experiences. Since we know that these are occurring simultaneously, we are conscious of the location of each group and the ways in which the various actions impinge upon one another. This consciousness is essentially spatial; it requires harmonious resolution just as does the temporal action. If for no other reason, the fairies' entrance in the fifth act would be necessary

---

[4] This is the way they are described in an excellent analysis by Bertrand Evans in his *Shakespeare's Comedies* (Oxford, 1960), pp. 33–46.

as the final step in the series of group positionings. The other three groups have gathered there; the arrival of the fairies completes the choreography.

A large part of our interest in the comedy is directed to the way in which the four groups are handled. Their introduction, for example, is formal and at the same time intriguing enough to capture our interest as we gradually realize how the strands of action are to be divided. We meet each group in turn with whatever is necessary in the way of individual and group characterization as well as the details of exposition required to start each action. Theseus and Hippolyta begin the parade with their mood of revelry and a few key details about their wedding. Egeus bustles in, changing the tone and introducing the lovers' plot, with three of the four lovers present. The stage is then cleared for some conventional love dialogue, the plans which will initiate the action in the woods, and the introduction of the fourth lover. In the next scene, we meet the mechanicals and are treated to a full characterization of Bottom. The exposition prepares us for complications in the woods, but it also looks forward, as did that of Theseus, to the final events of the play. For the masque-like introduction of the fairy group, we shift to the second sphere of action. As the last details necessary to the exposition fall into place, Demetrius and Helena enter and the interwoven adventures of three of the groups begin, with Theseus and Hippolyta held in the background for the duration of the night.

It is clear by the time these four groups of characters have been introduced that we are witnessing an art that divides our attention among a number of subjects. The four groups are not unrelated. By the end of the exposition, all have been shown to have the royal wedding as a point of contact: it is the deadline set for Hermia by Theseus, the occasion for the clown's performance, and the reason for the presence of the fairies. Other linkings and encounters will follow. Nonetheless, each group has a set of common characteristics and each will undergo a particular set of experiences.

The division of interest through multiplication of plots and characters is typical of Elizabethan drama, which has often been called an art of multiplicity.[5] As Madelaine Doran has shown, it originated in medieval practices of narration and staging and continued to be valued in the Renaissance even by those critics who were theoretically committed to the unities.[6] Those dramatists who practiced it risked chaos, since the traditional means of dramatic unification were not open to them. *A*

---

[5] Madelaine Doran, *Endeavors of Art* (Madison, Wis., 1954), quotes from Heinrich Wölfflin, *Principles of Art History* (London, 1932), p. 166, and discusses the concept in her first chapter. G. K. Hunter also uses it in his *Lyly*, p. 137 and n. He says the term is used by Rossiter in *English Drama from Early Times to the Elizabethans*. I have not found it there, but Rossiter discusses the concept on pp. 72 f. and in his Epilogue.

[6] See Doran, pp. 258–94.

Midsummer Night's Dream risks more than most. Not only does it avoid a single action, it has no central character to whom the various events are unmistakably related. Furthermore, it cannot even be said to have a single theme; its dispersal of interest among various groups and settings is a dispersal, in part, of subject matter as well. Yet Shakespeare achieves unity, partly through careful control of tone and setting and partly through his handling of the groups, a spatial organization which is almost geometrical in its order and which involves relationships within each group as well as among the four.

Our sense of the lovers' permutations, for example, is distinctly spatial; almost any discussion of them is apt to resort to diagrammatic figures.[7] We begin the play with a triangle, Lysander-Hermia-Demetrius, but we soon realize, as Helena's presence and importance is established, that it is in fact a quadrangle, with Helena the neglected corner. In the second act, Lysander's allegiance is suddenly switched, so that we have "cross-wooing," each man pursuing the wrong woman. We also have, as Baldwin points out,[8] a circle, since each of the four parties is pursuing another: Hermia is looking for Lysander; he is wooing Helena; she continues to love Demetrius; and he is still enamored of Hermia. This is the quadrangle at its most disrupted state, and two steps are necessary to repair it. The first of these comes in the third act, when Demetrius is restored to Helena. This reverses the original triangle, and Hermia becomes the neglected party. The fourth act finds the quadrangle in its proper state, each man attached to the right woman, restoring a situation which predates the beginning of the play.

These permutations are further complicated by the question of friendship. Each member of the quadrangle has, potentially, one love and two friends therein, but the shifting of love relationships disrupts the friendships as well. Lysander and Hermia are at the outset alienated from Demetrius but friends of Helena, so much so that they tell her their secret. When Lysander falls in love with Helena, their friendship is of course destroyed; she thinks he is making fun of her. The next alteration, Demetrius' restoration to Helena, destroys the Hermia-Helena friendship: Hermia thinks Helena is somehow responsible; Helena thinks everyone is mocking her. Thus, the restoration of the proper love relationships also restores the friendships of all four; even Lysander and Demetrius, who were ready to fight to the death, are friends again at the end of the play.

The lovers' quadrangle is set within another calmer quadrangle involving the royal couples. We learn of its existence when Oberon and Titania meet. She immediately charges him with love of Hippolyta, "Your buskin'd mistress and your warrior love," and he counters:

---

[7] The most extensive analysis of this kind is by Baldwin, *Literary Genetics*, pp. 476 f.

[8] Ibid.

> How canst thou thus, for shame, Titania,
> Glance at my credit with Hippolyta,
> Knowing I know thy love to Theseus?
> (II.i.74–76)

There are cross-purposes, it appears, within this group as well. They do not, however, lead to the complications that beset the lovers. Theseus and Hippolyta are unaware of the fairies' marital difficulties. Moreover, the true occasion of the quarrel is the changeling boy, so that Oberon's practicing on Titania is all that is needed to restore the quadrangle to harmony and enable the fairies to join forces for the ritual blessing at the end.

Oberon solves his problems with Titania by finding her an absurd lover, thus creating a sort of mock triangle with Bottom as the oblivious third party. But Bottom is also a lover in his role of Pyramus and is part of another absurd triangle in which he plays not the intruding beast, lion or ass, but the rightful mate.

These geometrical figures are of course illusory, but by use of the analogy to which they point, we see more clearly the constant interaction among the four character groups, the collisions and entanglements which make their separate adventures interdependent. The lovers begin and end the play with an attachment to the court of Theseus and the revels surrounding his wedding. In between, they are the victims of their journey to the woods and consequent involvement with the fairies. The fairies, who have arrived to bless the royal wedding, are finally able to arrange two more and to solve their own difficulties through an involvement with the mechanicals. The mechanicals, intent on entertaining Theseus, unwittingly entertain Oberon and Puck as well. Their involvement with the lovers is more subtle. It is true that their entertainment finally has the four lovers as audience, but Bottom's adventures, as well as the play he stars in, provide a good deal of indirect comment on the lovers, most of it in the form of parody. This kind of relationship belongs to Shakespeare's practice of "mirroring," a spatial technique which deserves a section of its own.

The Wat'ry Glass

Shakespeare's device of using scenes, characters, and speeches to point up thematic relationships by means of reflection has only recently begun to receive critical attention.[9] The term "mirroring" is a useful one, re-

---

[9] Hereward T. Price, "Mirror-Scenes in Shakespeare," in *J. Q. Adams Memorial Studies* (Washington, D.C., 1948), pp. 101–13; Reuben A. Brower, *The Fields of Light* (New York, 1951, pp. 95–122); Maynard Mack, "The Jacobean Shakespeare: Some Observations on the Construction of the Tragedies," in *Jacobean Theatre*, Stratford-upon-Avon Studies, Vol. I (New York, 1960), pp. 11–41.

calling as it does Hamlet's remarks about art. To say that art mirrors nature is to suggest more than mere imitation; the process of reflection sends the image back to its origin and, presumably, stimulates thought. Ulysses and Achilles discuss the same notion in *Troilus and Cressida,* using Plato as a springboard. Before Ulysses turns the idea to Achilles' waning reputation, Achilles himself gives it a general application:

> For speculation turns not to itself,
> Till it hath travell'd and is mirror'd there
> Where it may see itself. This is not strange at all.
> (III.iii.109–11)

Mirroring, then, while it may heighten mood and unify action, can also breed speculation. There is a good deal of evidence to indicate that Shakespeare used it specifically for "the parallel advancement of plot and idea." [10]

This function betrays the origins of mirroring; there had been dramatic devices with the same function and with reasonably similar techniques for some time. The parallel and simultaneous actions of medieval drama sometimes employed reflecting scenes and characters.[11] Medieval drama moves between the realistic and the allegorical so easily and frequently that we are not perhaps inclined to see sequential scenes as mirrors; it would be difficult at times to say which is primary and which reflective. Nonetheless, the fact that these dramas present scenes and characters that are different in kind and thematically alike relates them to the more sophisticated practices which were to follow. After all, *Gorboduc,* which uses allegorical dumb shows to reflect moral and philosophical content, is not very different and not much more sophisticated. Shakespeare's own eventual finesse with the technique in plays like *Lear* and *Hamlet* was the outgrowth of such painful and emblematic beginnings as the fly-killing scene in *Titus* and the dunghill and father-son scenes in the *Henry VI* cycle.

Mirroring in the comedies, less noticed than in the tragedies and histories, has a life and validity of its own. While Shakespeare uses it for the same purposes as in more serious plays, he also employs it concomitantly for comic effect. Perhaps its use as a comic device has distracted attention from its other functions, but mimicry, parody, and exaggeration can mean as much as more serious forms of imitation. The image returned by a fun-house mirror may provoke thought as well as laughter.

We have already noticed the paired characters in *A Midsummer*

---

[10] Price, p. 103.

[11] See, for instance, the Digby *Mary Magdalene* (in J. Q. Adams, *Chief Pre-Shakespearean Dramas,* pp. 225–42) in which realistic scenes are followed by scenes on separate allegorical stages which mirror the moral crises in the main action.

Night's Dream and noted how they lend symmetry to the plot. Shakespeare also takes advantage of them to set up reflections which underline key dramatic ideas. Thus, the near-identity of the lovers is used to stress the inadequacy of that kind of love which yields itself to irrationality and the consequent heavy demands upon both personality and intelligence. Demetrius and Lysander address the women they woo in the same conventional vocabulary of exaggerated praise, each mirroring the other's inadequacy. The women expose one another in similar fashion. Hermia has no sooner sworn her love by Cupid's bow and arrow and by "all the vows that ever men have broke" than Helena is on stage for her soliloquy, talking of winged Cupid and Demetrius' broken oaths in the same way. Thus, the two women who think themselves so different—one lucky in love, the other rejected—are shown to have an identity which, incidentally, foreshadows the events to come. Later on, in the woods, Helena herself employs the image of a mirror. Speaking of her earlier desire to be like Hermia, she accounts herself a failure:

> What wicked and dissembling glass of mine,
> Made me compare with Hermia's sphery eyne?
> (II.ii.98–99)

It is at precisely this moment that Lysander wakes up and falls in love with her. "Transparent Helena," he shouts, not seeing in her the image of his folly. He too goes on to insist that she and Hermia are completely different. Throughout the night, the four lovers will peer at each other and always fail to see what the playwright makes so clear to us, their likenesses.

Much the same thing can be said about the royal pairs. It is appropriate that Theseus, as representative of daylight and right reason, should have subdued his bride-to-be to the rule of his masculine will. That is the natural order of things.[12] It is equally appropriate that Oberon, as king of darkness and fantasy, should have lost control of his wife, and that the corresponding natural disorder described by Titania should ensue. All the details in these dual situations have the same function. Both royal pairs love panoramas, but the landscapes they see are appropriately different. The means that each king employs to establish rule in his kingdom are significantly opposed. Even the Masters of the Revels of each monarchy, Philostrate and Puck, serve to strengthen the sense of contrast within likeness.

What we have here differs from the mirroring found in the tragedies. There, the tragic hero occupies the center of attention, while surrounding characters reflect him, as Horatio, Laertes, and Fortinbras mirror Hamlet, or while alternate scenes reflect his dilemma, as do the

[12] This point is extensively discussed in Olson, "*A Midsummer Night's Dream* and the Meaning of Court Marriage," pp. 101 ff. He cites the Theseus of *The Two Noble Kinsmen* as a more explicit example.

Gloucester scenes in *Lear*. In these plays, mirroring works mostly one way. Even the standard mirror device found in earlier comedies, the servant subplot, has this characteristic. Since *A Midsummer Night's Dream* cannot be said to have a central character, however, or even a central group of characters, any mirroring that takes place is necessarily reflexive or retroactive, throwing as much meaning on one scene, group, or character as on another. This is another illustration of the way in which diffusion marks this play, as well, I believe, as other Shakespearean comedies, where mirroring has the same two-way effect. If we could accept this, we would stop speaking of plot and subplot in Shakespearean comedy and recognize the uniqueness of its form. Nor need we be afraid of admitting to disunity. The continually rebounding reflections constantly strengthen identity, suggesting that everything we see is an aspect of the same situation and bringing to the play a startlingly organic unity. Again I think it accurate to stress the germinal role of *A Midsummer Night's Dream* in the development of this technique; while there are hints of it in *Love's Labour's Lost,* it was not until *A Midsummer Night's Dream* that Shakespeare found the means to use it fully.

If any group of characters in the play may be said to exist primarily for purposes of reflection, it is the mechanicals. This does not subordinate them in importance; they could easily claim supreme position as the busiest glasses in this comedy of reflection. What is more, they bring to the climax of the play its biggest and funniest mirror. Their reflective function is worth examining in some detail.

The mechanicals' first scene gives us hints of the echo and parody we are to have from them through the rest of the play. Their concern for an orderly handling of their task catches the theme Theseus has just sounded and will continue to sound throughout the play. Their respect for hierarchy recalls the issue raised by the entrance of Egeus and the lovers,[13] and their plans for rehearsal echo the plans of Demetrius and Hermia. Their confused use of language (e.g. "I will aggravate my voice") presents an aspect of the confusion that will later reign in the woods, and the paradoxes they blunder into, "lamentable comedy," "monstrous little voice," hint at the doubts about familiar categories—dreaming and waking, reason and imagination—with which the play will eventually leave us. The interlude about true love thev plan to perform promises to mock the lovers we have just seen. Finally, Bottom's enthusiastic confidence that he can perform any role—tyrant, lover, maiden, or lion—amusingly introduces us to the theme of metamorphosis, the activity which will dominate all experience in the woods.

---

[13] "These common life characters . . . furnish a rule of ignorant common sense against which the vagaries of their superiors may be measured. So the first act closes by showing the persistence of order in the lower segment of society" (Ibid., p. 106).

All of these echoes, or pre-echoes, it should be added, are those that remain within the context of the play's events. Others, directed at the knowing audience, have already begun to parody such "outside" targets as bad plays, whining poetry, and court fashion. These mirrorings prepare the audience for the subtler parodies involved in the lovers' plot and dialogue, bring it into a closer relationship with the play, and open the way for some of the insights into the nature of dramatic illusion which the play ultimately provides.

Once in the woods, the clowns keep up a continuous comic counterpoint to the adventures of the lovers. When Hermia rushes off in search of errant Lysander ("Either death or you I'll find immediately"), the cast of "Pyramus and Thisby" troops on ("Are we all met?") to rehearse another story of desperate love. By virtue of its versification, their language is more mechanical than what we have just heard from Lysander and will soon hear from Demetrius, but the vocabulary and tone are similar. Like Lysander and Demetrius, Bottom, playing the role of a faithful lover, finds himself the victim of a sudden transformation. The other clowns flee, but Bottom as Ass stays on to become the paramour of the fairy queen. Their beauty and beast tableaux alternate with the comings and goings of the lovers, each reflecting the absurdity of the other.

Verbal echoes strengthen the mirror relationships. Lysander swears to Helena that reason brings him to her:

> The will of man is by his reason sway'd;
> And reason says you are the worthier maid.
> Things growing are not ripe until their season;
> So I, being young, till now not ripe to reason;
> And touching now the point of human skill,
> Reason becomes the marshal to my will
> And leads me to your eyes.
>
> (II.ii.115–21)

Bottom echoes him more sensibly when Titania first admits that she has fallen in love at first sight:

> Methinks, mistress, you should have little reason for that. And yet, to say the truth, reason and love keep little company together now-a-days. The more the pity that some honest neighbours will not make them friends.
>
> (III.i.145–50)

Demetrius, once in the woods, thinks his problem is to find Hermia:

> Thou told'st me they were stol'n unto this wood;
> And here am I, and wood within this wood
> Because I cannot greet my Hermia.
>
> (II.i.191–93)

The problem, as Bottom suggests, is much simpler than that:

> If I had wit enough to get out of this wood, I have enough to serve mine own turn.
>
> (III.i.153–54)

Stupid as he may be, Bottom is not the victim of love's madness and so, throughout the night of errors, conducts himself with greater dignity and common sense. The distortive mirror can also serve as a corrective.

As object of Titania's affection, Bottom mirrors not only the Athenians, but the fairy queen's earlier loves as well. He is a kind of mock-Oberon, a role he tries valiantly to play, sending the fairies off on appropriate errands just as Oberon has sent Puck for the little Western flower, but of course his asshood keeps betraying him into unkingly needs:

> Methinks I have a great desire to a bottle of hay.
> Good hay, sweet hay, hath no fellow.
>
> (IV.i.35–36)

Titania has also been, and will again be, in love with Theseus, and she has led him, as she leads Bottom, through "the glimmering night." Theseus has put such experiences behind him. He would probably agree with Quince that "A paramour is (God bless us!) a thing of naught" (IV.ii.13–14). But Bottom's adventures offer a farcical reminder of events in Theseus' past. Thus, a clown's dream becomes one of the key mirrors in the play, reflecting almost all of the male characters in one way or another. Bottom is not the successful actor he had hoped to be, but he gets his chance to play a number of roles—not just lover and tyrant, but several kinds of lover and one or two kinds of tyrant; not lion, but a beast at least as interesting if not nearly as frightening.

"Pyramus and Thisby" is the climax of the mechanicals' reflective career. If it does not succeed in holding the mirror up to nature, it holds it up to almost everything else. "The best in this kind are but shadows," says Theseus. Shadows of what? Of the events and characters of *A Midsummer Night's Dream,* but the audience of "Pyramus and Thisby" may be partially pardoned for not recognizing their own images. The lovers, back from the woods and safely married, need not compare their experiences with those of Pyramus and Thisby in a less accommodating wood. Nor can they be expected so soon to recognize in the poetry of the play the inadequate language of their own vocabulary of love. Theseus and Hippolyta, too, have put their pasts behind them; nothing about this play is able to provoke their memories. The mechanicals, as with the other effects of the drama, fail in this function too; "speculation turns not to itself."

Not, that is, among the characters of the play. But we are also the audience of "Pyramus and Thisby" and have many comparisons to make. The resemblance between the "fond pageant" in the woods and the "tragical mirth" in the palace does not escape us, nor do the references to at least some of the other plays and the various dramatic and poetic conventions which the playwright finds hard to admire. Beyond these reflections we begin to discern an even larger one. Perhaps it is begun by Theseus' remarks about the poet, but it is the kind of insight that ought to be provoked by any play within a play, a mirror for the audience-drama relationship if ever there was one. Shakespeare exploits it thoroughly. Within a play about love written for a wedding, he puts a play about love written for a wedding. If "Pyramus and Thisby" is inept, it is also well-meaning and deserving of charity; so is *A Midsummer Night's Dream.* If Bottom and his fellows can expect sixpence a day for life as their reward, so perhaps does Shakespeare's company deserve generous remuneration. But there are contrasts too. Where the mechanicals fail at dramatic illusion, unity, and appropriateness, *A Midsummer Night's Dream* succeeds. The playwright manages to exploit the contrast as a kind of mild reminder that he knows his business; he can even afford to parody himself (assuming that this play follows *Romeo and Juliet*). This is perhaps what gave Max Beerbohm the impression that in this play, "we have the Master, confident in his art, at ease with it as a man in his dressing-gown, kicking up a loose slipper and catching it on his toe." [14]

The discerning audience will finally find in the mirror of the mechanicals' performance one more image—its own. They are bound to notice that "Pyramus and Thisby" does not have a very perceptive audience. Not that it deserves one, but as *A Midsummer Night's Dream* is superior to "Pyramus and Thisby," so, the playwright seems to hope, will its audience be superior. Elizabethan audiences, we know, were not always as attentive or polite as the actors and playwrights might wish. Perhaps they were being asked in this comedy, as well as in *Love's Labour's Lost,* to recognize their image and reform it altogether. Certainly they are given a chance to behave more astutely than the audience of "Pyramus and Thisby," to see to it that they are not quite as condescending as Theseus, as inconsistent as Hippolyta, as oblivious, when faced with their own images, as the lovers. The playwright, by placing them higher than any of the characters in the play, gives them every opportunity. If they should fail, they have only themselves to blame. There is just a hint of mockery in Puck's epilogue:

> If we shadows have offended,
> Thinke but this, and all is mended—
> That you have but slumb'red here
> While these visions did appear.
> And this weak and idle theme,
> No more yielding but a dream.
> (V.i.430–35)

---

[14] Quoted in the New Cambridge Edition, p. xix.

Anyone who is willing to admit that he has slept through this performance cannot claim to be very alert. In fact, he must inevitably be compared to those characters in the play who are willing to think that they have "dreamed" it, dismissing events which exposed them significantly. Shakespeare gives us our choice. We may remain within the outer circles of consciousness with Oberon, Puck, and himself, or we may doze off and fall inward toward the condition of Bottom and the lovers. In the mirror of *A Midsummer Night's Dream,* the spectator may find, even if he does not recognize, his very form and pressure.

If we now draw back to summarize the various stylistic and structural devices exhibited in the preceding pages, we will begin to discover how closely they are related, how much a part of a single, overarching artistic purpose. The multiplicity of this drama, its division of interest, is revealed in its characterizations and groupings, in the exposition and careful counterpointing of the several plots, in the diversity of styles which support all this diffusion, and in those stylistic and structural devices which emphasize spaciousness and abundance. But Shakespeare's is an art that divides to reunite. The multiple activities and beings we see belong to a single panorama. The devices that bring them together range from the schematized relationships of the plot to the extremely subtle interplay of reflections in language and action. The sharing of likenesses among the most diverse and unlikely elements of the play serves to unite them even as it functions to surprise and amuse us. Finally, when it has accomplished its miraculous union of materials, the play calls attention to itself as an artistic entity, inviting us to muse, as we return to reality, on the nature and significance of illusion. This last touch, expressed with humility, has behind it a certain bravado, the confidence of a master artist. It is almost as though a magician had revealed the deceptions on which his art depended, confident that our credulity would put us back in his hands when it came time for the next trick. This is to suggest not that Shakespeare thought his art false or misleading, but that he was strongly aware of its techniques and effects at this point and equally conscious of the discrepancy between his own knowledge and that of his audience.

What, finally, may be said of the relation of *A Midsummer Night's Dream* to the development of Shakespeare's dramaturgy? Facile comparisons are impossible. Shakespeare was not an artist to repeat himself, so we do not discover startling parallels of character and situation between this play and later ones. To demonstrate the exact position of *A Midsummer Night's Dream* in Shakespeare's development would require an exhaustive comparison both of earlier and later plays which is not possible here. My method must be to claim little but hopefully suggest much. I will content myself with two specific observations. First, as indicated above, I believe that Shakespeare developed a comedy of multiple interest in which he achieved organic unity not by subordination of one element to another (as continued to be partly the case in his tragedies) but by a careful thematic control through which diverse elements were shown to be facets of the same idea. He developed this kind of comedy from Lyly's comedies of debate, gradually shifting the emphasis from debate to action and character.[15] *Love's Labour's Lost* is his first try, and the unification by debate is still very prominent. In *A Midsummer Night's Dream,* however, in which I maintain that he first mastered the form to his own satisfaction, the debate subjects have receded into the background. They are still there for those who wish to discern them—daylight and reason versus moonlight and imagination—but they are expressed through character and event rather than by argument. I think that it could be shown that later comedies —including the late romances—employ this same structure and are most profitably analyzed in this light. It should be noted, moreover, that Shakespeare's use of the technique is not strictly limited to his comic practice. Whenever he had diverse elements to unify, he was apt to resort not to unity of time, place, or event, but to unity of idea, achieved by the devices that first came to full fruition in *A Midsummer Night's Dream.*

The second point has to do with the relation of plot to poetry and of structure, to use the terms of this chapter, to style. It is generally said or implied in discussions of Shakespeare's development that he began with an imperfect union of these two aspects of his art and gradually learned to integrate them. Just when he mastered the problem is not a matter of general agreement. Many critics have professed to see in *A Midsummer Night's Dream* the disjunction of style and structure characteristic of Shakespeare's earliest work. If this chapter has achieved its purpose, it has shown that the poetry of this play is completely wedded to the needs and demands of the multiple plot. In fact, this discussion has imposed a division which does not really exist. The moments of stylistic bravura, we have seen, are an integral part of the play's structure, and the constant use of mirroring is just as much a stylistic device as a technique for achieving unity of form. *A Midsummer Night's Dream,* then, can be seen as a solution to the playwright's problem of uniting poetry and plot, one of the earliest in his canon.

---

[15] It is to Hunter's discussion of Lyly's structuring techniques that I owe the idea of unification around a debate topic.

"As You Like It"

Helen Gardner

As its title declares, this is a play to please all tastes. It is the last play in the world to be solemn over, and there is more than a touch of absurdity in delivering a lecture, particularly on a lovely summer morning, on this radiant blend of fantasy, romance, wit and humor. The play itself provides its own ironic comment on anyone who attempts to speak about it: "You have said; but whether wisely or no, let the forest judge."

For the simple, it provides the stock ingredients of romance: a handsome, well-mannered young hero, the youngest of three brothers, two disguised princesses to be wooed and wed, and a banished, virtuous Duke to be restored to his rightful throne. For the more sophisticated, it propounds, in the manner of the old courtly literary form of the *débat,* a question which is left to us to answer: Is it better to live in the court or the country? "How like you this shepherd's life, Master Touchstone?", asks Corin, and receives a fool's answer: "Truly, shepherd, in respect of itself, it is a good life; but in respect that it is a shepherd's life, it is naught. In respect that it is solitary, I like it very well; but in respect that it is private, it is a very vile life." Whose society would you prefer, Le Beau's or Audrey's? Would you rather be gossiped at in the court or gawped at in the country? The play has also the age-old appeal of the pastoral, and in different forms. The pastoral romance of princesses playing at being a shepherd boy and his sister is combined with the pastoral love-eclogue in the wooing of Phoebe, with the burlesque of this in the wooing of Audrey, and with the tradition of the moral eclogue, in which the shepherd is the wise man, in Corin. For the learned and literary this is one of Shakespeare's most allusive plays, uniting old traditions and playing with them lightly. Then there are the songs—the forest is full of music—and there is spectacle: a wrestling match to delight lovers of sport, the procession with the deer, which goes back to old country rituals and folk plays, and finally the masque of Hymen, to end the whole

---

with courtly grace and dignity. This is an image of civility and true society, for Hymen is a god of cities, as Milton knew:

> There let *Hymen* oft appear
> In Saffron robe, with Taper clear,
> And pomp, and feast, and revelry,
> With mask, and antique Pageantry.
> [*L'Allegro,* ll. 125–28]

The only thing the play may be said to lack, when compared with Shakespeare's other comedies, is broad humor, the humor of gross clowns. William makes only a brief appearance. The absence of clowning may be due to an historic reason, the loss of Kempe, the company's funny man. But if this was the original reason for the absence of pure clowning, Shakespeare has turned necessity to glorious gain and made a play in which cruder humors would be out of place. *As You Like It* is the most refined and exquisite of the comedies, the one which is most consistently played over by a delighted intelligence. It is Shakespeare's most Mozartian comedy.

The basic story is a folk tale. The ultimate sources for the plots of Shakespeare's greatest tragedy and his most unflawed comedy are stories of the same kind. The tale of the old king who had three daughters, of whom the elder two were wicked and the youngest was good, belongs to the same primitive world of the imagination as the tale of the knight who had three sons, the eldest of whom was wicked and robbed the youngest, who was gallant and good, of his inheritance. The youngest son triumphed, like Jack the Giant Killer, over a strong man, a wrestler, joined a band of outlaws in the forest, became their king, and with the aid of an old servant of his father, the wily Adam Spencer, in the end had his revenge on his brother and got his rights. Lodge retained some traces of the boisterous elements of this old story; but Shakespeare omitted them. His Orlando is no bully, threatening and blustering and breaking down the doors to feast with his boon companions in his brother's house. He is brave enough and quick-tempered; but he is above all gentle. On this simple story Lodge grafted a pastoral romance in his *Rosalynde*. He made the leader of the outlaws a banished Duke, and gave both exiled Duke and tyrant usurper only daughters, as fast friends as their fathers are sworn enemies. The wrestling match takes place at the tyrant's court and is followed by the banishment of Rosalynde and the flight of the two girls to the forest, disguised as shepherd and shepherdess. There the shepherd boy is wooed by the gallant hero, and arouses a passion of lovesickness in a shepherdess who scorns her faithful lover. The repentance of the wicked brother and his flight to the forest provide the necessary partner for the tyrant's good daughter, and all ends happily with marriages and the restoration of the good Duke. Shakespeare added virtually nothing to the plot of Lodge's novel. There is no comedy in which, in one sense, he invents so little. He made the two Dukes into brothers. Just as in *King Lear* he put together two stories of good and unkind children, so here he gives us two examples of a brother's unkindness. This adds to the fairy-tale flavor of the plot, because it turns the usurping Duke into a wicked uncle. But if he invents no incidents, he leaves out a good deal. Besides omitting the blusterings of Rosader (Orlando), he leaves out a final battle and the death in battle of the usurping Duke, preferring to have him converted offstage by a chance meeting with a convenient and persuasive hermit. In the same way he handles very cursorily the repentance of the wicked brother and his good fortune in love. In Lodge's story, the villain is cast into prison by the tyrant who covets his estates. In prison he repents, and it is as a penitent that he arrives in the forest. Shakespeare also omits the incident of the attack on Ganymede and Aliena by robbers, in which Rosader is overpowered and wounded and Saladyne (Oliver) comes to the rescue and drives off the assailants. As has often been pointed out, this is both a proof of the genuineness of his repentance and a reason, which many critics of the play have felt the want of, for Celia's falling in love. Maidens naturally fall in love with brave young men who rescue them. But Shakespeare needs to find no "reasons for loving" in this play in which a dead shepherd's saw is quoted as a word of truth: "Whoever lov'd that lov'd not at first sight." He has far too much other business in hand at the center and heart of his play to find time for mere exciting incidents. He stripped Lodge's plot down to the bare bones, using it as a kind of frame, and created no subplot of his own. But he added four characters. Jaques, the philosopher, bears the same name as the middle son of Sir Rowland de Boys—the one whom Oliver kept at his books—who does not appear in the play until he turns up casually at the end as a messenger. It seems possible that the melancholy Jaques began as this middle son and that his melancholy was in origin a scholar's melancholy. If so, the character changed as it developed, and by the time that Shakespeare had fully conceived his cynical spectator he must have realized that he could not be kin to Oliver and Orlando. The born solitary must have no family: Jaques seems the quintessential only child. To balance Jaques, as another kind of commentator, we are given Touchstone, critic and parodist of love and lovers and of court and courtiers. And, to make up the full consort of pairs to be mated, Shakespeare invented two rustic lovers, William and Audrey, dumb yokel and sluttish goat-girl. These additional characters add nothing at all to the story. If you were to tell it you would leave them out. They show us that story was not Shakespeare's concern in this play; its soul is not to be looked for there. If you were to go to *As You Like It* for the story you would, in Johnson's phrase, "hang yourself."

In an essay called "The Basis of Shakespearian Comedy"[1] Professor

---

[1] *Essays and Studies* (English Association: John Murray, 1950).

Nevill Coghill attempted to "establish certain things concerning the nature of comic form, as it was understood at Shakespeare's time." He pointed out that there were two conceptions of comedy current in the sixteenth century, both going back to grammarians of the fourth century, but radically opposed to each other. By the one definition a comedy was a story beginning in sadness and ending in happiness. By the other it was, in Sidney's words, "an imitation of the common errors of our life" represented "in the most ridiculous and scornefull sort that may be; so that it is impossible that any beholder can be content to be such a one." Shakespeare, he declared, accepted the first; Jonson, the second. But although *As You Like It,* like *A Midsummer Night's Dream,* certainly begins in sadness and ends with happiness, I do not feel, when we have said this, that we have gone very far toward defining the play's nature, and I do not think that the plot in either of these two lovely plays, or in the enchanting early comedy *Love's Labor's Lost,* which indeed has hardly any plot at all, can be regarded as the "soul" or animating force of Shakespeare's most original and characteristic comedies. Professor Coghill's formula fits plays which we feel rather uneasy about, *The Merchant of Venice* and *Measure for Measure.* It is precisely the stress on the plot which makes us think of these as being more properly described as tragicomedies than comedies. Neither of them is a play which we would choose as a norm of Shakespeare's genius in comedy. In *As You Like It* the plot is handled in the most perfunctory way. Shakespeare crams his first act with incident in order to get everyone to the forest as soon as he possibly can and, when he is ready, he ends it all as quickly as possible. A few lines dispose of Duke Frederick, and leave the road back to his throne empty for Duke Senior. As for the other victim of a wicked brother, it is far more important that Orlando should marry Rosalind than that he should be restored to his rights.

Mrs. Suzanne Langer, in her brilliant and suggestive book *Feeling and Form,*[2] has called comedy an image of life triumphing over chance. She declares that the essence of comedy is that it embodies in symbolic form our sense of happiness in feeling that we can meet and master the changes and chances of life as it confronts us. This seems to me to provide a good description of what we mean by "pure comedy," as distinct from the corrective or satirical comedy of Jonson. The great symbol of pure comedy is marriage by which the world is renewed, and its endings are always instinct with a sense of fresh beginnings. Its rhythm is the rhythm of the life of mankind, which goes on and renews itself as the life of nature does. The rhythm of tragedy, on the other hand, is the rhythm of the individual life which comes to a close, and its great symbol is death. The one inescapable fact about every human being is that he must die. No skill in living, no sense of life, no inborn grace or acquired wisdom can avert this

[2] Routledge, 1953.

individual doom. A tragedy, which is played out under the shadow of an inevitable end, is an image of the life pattern of every one of us. A comedy, which contrives an end which is not implicit in its beginning, and which is, in itself, a fresh beginning, is an image of the flow of human life. The young wed, so that they may become in turn the older generation, whose children will wed, and so on, as long as the world lasts. Comedy pictures what Rosalind calls "the full stream of the world." At the close of a tragedy we look back over a course which has been run: "the rest is silence." The end of a comedy declares that life goes on: "Here we are all over again." Tragic plots must have a logic which leads to an inescapable conclusion. Comic plots are made up of changes, changes and surprises. Coincidences can destroy tragic feeling: they heighten comic feeling. It is absurd to complain in poetic comedy of improbable encounters and characters arriving pat on their cue, of sudden changes of mind and mood by which an enemy becomes a friend. Puck, who creates and presides over the central comedy of *A Midsummer Night's Dream,* speaks for all comic writers and lovers of true comedy when he says:

> And those things do best please me
> That befall preposterously.

This aspect of life, as continually changing and presenting fresh opportunities for happiness and laughter, poetic comedy idealizes and presents to us by means of fantasy. Fantasy is the natural instrument of comedy, in which plot, which is the "soul" of tragedy, is of secondary importance, an excuse for something else. After viewing a tragedy we have an "acquist of true experience" from a "great event." There are no "events" in comedy; there are only "happenings." Events are irreversible and comedy is not concerned with the irreversible, which is why it must always shun the presentation of death. In adapting Lodge's story Shakespeare did not allow Charles the wrestler to kill the Franklin's sons. Although they are expected to die, we may hope they will recover from their broken ribs. And he rejected also Lodge's ending in which the wicked Duke was killed in battle, preferring his improbable conversion by a hermit. But why should we complain of its improbability? It is only in tragedy that second chances are not given. Comedy is full of purposes mistook, not "falling on the inventor's head" but luckily misfiring altogether. In comedy, as often happens in life, people are mercifully saved from being as wicked as they meant to be.

Generalization about the essential distinctions between tragedy and comedy is called in question, when we turn to Shakespeare, by the inclusiveness of his vision of life. In the great majority of his plays the elements are mixed. But just as he wrote one masterpiece which is purely tragic, dominated by the conception of Fate, in *Macbeth,* so he wrote some plays which embody a purely comic vision. Within the general formula that "a comedy is a play with a happy ending," which can, of course, include tragicomedies, he wrote some plays in which the story is a mere frame and the essence of the play lies in the presentation of an image of human life, not as an arena for heroic endeavor but as a place of encounters.

Tragedy is presided over by time, which urges the hero onward to fulfill his destiny. In Shakespeare's comedies time goes by fits and starts. It is not so much a movement onward as a space in which to work things out: a midsummer night, a space too short for us to feel time's movement, or the unmeasured time of *As You Like It* or *Twelfth Night*. The comedies are dominated by a sense of place rather than of time. In Shakespeare's earliest comedy it is not a very romantic place: the city of Ephesus. Still, it is a place where two pairs of twins are accidentally reunited, and their old father, in danger of death at the beginning, is united to his long-lost wife at the close. The substance of the play is the comic plot of mistakings, played out in a single place on a single day. The tragicomic story of original loss and final restoration provides a frame. In what is probably his second comedy, *The Two Gentlemen of Verona,* Shakespeare tried a quite different method. The play is a dramatization of a *novella,* and it contains no comic place of encounters where time seems to stand still. The story begins in Verona, passes to Milan, and ends in a forest between the two cities. None of these places exerts any hold upon our imaginations. The story simply moves forward through them. In *Love's Labor's Lost,* by contrast, Shakespeare went as far as possible in the other direction. The whole play is a kind of ballet of lovers and fantastics, danced out in the King of Navarre's park. Nearby is a village where Holofernes is the schoolmaster, Nathaniel the curate, and Dull the constable. In this play we are given, as a foil to the lords and ladies, not comic servants, parasitic on their masters, but a little comic world, society in miniature, going about its daily business while the lovers are engaged in the discovery of theirs. Shakespeare dispensed with the tragicomic frame altogether here. There is no sorrow at the beginning, only youthful male fatuity; and the "putting right" at the close lies in the chastening of the lords by the ladies. The picture of the course of life as it appears to the comic vision, with young men falling in love and young women testing their suitors, and other men "laboring in their vocations" to keep the world turning and to impress their fellows, is the whole matter of the play. Much more magical than the sunlit park of the King of Navarre is the wood near Athens where Puck plays the part of chance. Shakespeare reverted here to the structural pattern of his earliest comedy, beginning with the cruel fury of Egeus against his daughter, the rivalry of Lysander and Demetrius and the unhappiness of the scorned Helena, and ending with Theseus's overriding of the father's will and the proper pairing of the four lovers. But here he not only set his comic plot of mistakings within a frame of sorrow turning to joy, he also set his comic place of encounters apart from the real world, the palace where the play begins and ends. All the center of the play takes place in the moonlit wood where lovers immortal and mortal quarrel, change partners, are blinded, and have their eyes purged.

Having created a masterpiece, Shakespeare, who never repeated a success, went back in his next play to tragicomedy, allowing the threat of terrible disaster to grow through the play up to a great dramatic fourth act. *The Merchant of Venice* has what *The Two Gentlemen of Verona* lacks, an enchanted place. Belmont, where Bassanio goes to find his bride, and where Lorenzo flees with Jessica, and from which Portia descends like a goddess to solve the troubles of Venice, is a place apart, "above the smoke and stir." But it is not, like the wood near Athens, a place where the changes and chances of our mortal life are seen mirrored. It stands too sharply over against Venice, a place of refuge rather than a place of discovery. *Much Ado About Nothing* reverts to the single place of *The Comedy of Errors* and *Love's Labor's Lost;* and its tragicomic plot, which also comes to a climax in a dramatic scene in the fourth act, is lightened not by a shift of scene but by its interweaving with a brilliant comic plot, and by all kinds of indications that all will soon be well again. The trouble comes in the middle of this play; at the beginning, as at the end, all is revelry and happiness. A sense of holiday, of time off from the world's business, reigns in Messina. The wars are over, peace has broken out, and Don Pedro and the gentlemen have returned to where the ladies are waiting for them to take up again the game of love and wit. In the atmosphere created by the first act Don John's malice is a cloud no bigger than a man's hand. And although it grows as the play proceeds, the crisis of the fourth act is like a heavy summer thundershower which darkens the sky for a time but will, we know, soon pass. The brilliant lively city of Messina is a true place of mistakings and discoveries, like the park of the King of Navarre; but, also like the park of the King of Navarre, it lacks enchantment. It is too near the ordinary world to seem more than a partial image of human life. In *As You Like It* Shakespeare returned to the pattern of *A Midsummer Night's Dream,* beginning his play in sorrow and ending it with joy, and making his place of comic encounters a place set apart from the ordinary world.

The Forest of Arden ranks with the wood near Athens and Prospero's island as a place set apart, even though, unlike them, it is not ruled by magic. It is set over against the envious court ruled by a tyrant, and a home which is no home because it harbors hatred, not love. Seen from the court it appears untouched by the discontents of life, a place where "they fleet the time carelessly, as they did in the golden age," the gay greenwood of Robin Hood. But, of course, it is no such Elysium. It contains some unamiable characters. Corin's master is churlish and Sir Oliver Martext is hardly sweet-natured; William is a dolt and Audrey graceless. Its weather, too, is by no means always sunny. It has a bitter winter. To Orlando, famished with hunger and supporting the fainting Adam, it is "an uncouth forest" and a desert where the air is bleak. He is astonished to find civility among men who

> in this desert inaccessible,
> Under the shade of melancholy boughs,
> Lose and neglect the creeping hours of time.

In fact Arden does not seem very attractive at first sight to the weary escapers from the tyranny of the world. Rosalind's "Well, this is the forest of Arden" does not suggest any very great enthusiasm; and to Touchstone's "Ay, now I am in Arden; the more fool I: when I was at home, I was in a better place: but travelers must be content," she can only reply "Ay, be so, good Touchstone." It is as if they all have to wake up after a good night's rest to find what a pleasant place they have come to. Arden is not a place for the young only. Silvius, forever young and forever loving, is balanced by Corin, the old shepherd, who reminds us of that other "penalty of Adam" beside "the seasons' difference": that man must labor to get himself food and clothing. Still, the labor is pleasant and a source of pride: "I am a true laborer: I earn that I eat, get that I wear, owe no man hate, envy no man's happiness, glad of other men's good, content with my harm; and the greatest of my pride is to see my ewes graze and my lambs suck." Arden is not a place where the laws of nature are abrogated and roses are without their thorns. If, in the world, Duke Frederick has usurped on Duke Senior, Duke Senior is aware that he has in his turn usurped upon the deer, the native burghers of the forest. If man does not slay and kill man, he kills the poor beasts. Life preys on life. Jaques, who can suck melancholy out of anything, points to the callousness that runs through nature itself as a mirror of the callousness of men. The herd abandons the wounded deer, as prosperous citizens pass with disdain the poor bankrupt, the failure. The race is to the swift. But this is Jaques's view. Orlando, demanding help for Adam, finds another image from nature:

> Then but forbear your food a little while,
> Whiles, like a doe, I go to find my fawn
> And give it food. There is a poor old man,
> Who after me hath many a weary step
> Limp'd in pure love: till he be first suffic'd,
> Oppress'd with two weak evils, age and hunger,
> I will not touch a bit.

The fact that they are both derived ultimately from folk tale is not the only thing that relates *As You Like It* to *King Lear*. Adam's somber line, "And unregarded age in corners thrown," which Quiller-Couch said might have come out of one of the greater sonnets, sums up the fate of Lear:

> Dear daughter, I confess that I am old;
> Age is unnecessary: on my knees I beg
> That you'll vouchsafe me raiment, bed, and food.

At times Arden seems a place where the same bitter lessons can be learned as Lear has to learn in his place of exile, the blasted heath. Corin's natural philosophy, which includes the knowledge that "the property of rain is to wet," is something which Lear has painfully to acquire:

> When the rain came to wet me once and the wind to make me chatter, when the thunder would not peace at my bidding, there I found 'em, there I smelt 'em out. Go to, they are not men o' their words: they told me I was everything; 'tis a lie, I am not ague-proof.

He is echoing Duke Senior, who smiles at the "icy fang and churlish chiding of the winter's wind," saying:

> This is no flattery: these are counselors
> That feelingly persuade me what I am.

Amiens's lovely melancholy song:

> Blow, blow, thou winter wind,
> Thou art not so unkind
> As man's ingratitude. . . .
>
> Freeze, freeze, thou bitter sky,
> That dost not bite so nigh
> As benefits forgot. . . ,

is terribly echoed in Lear's outburst:

> Blow, winds, and crack your cheeks! rage! blow!
> . . .
> Rumble thy bellyful! Spit, fire! spout, rain!
> Nor rain, wind, thunder, fire, are my daughters:
> I tax not you, you elements, with unkindness;
> I never gave you kingdom, call'd you children. . . .

And Jaques's reflection that "All the world's a stage" becomes in Lear's mouth a cry of anguish:

> When we are born, we cry that we are come
> To this great stage of fools.

It is in Arden that Jaques presents his joyless picture of human life, passing from futility to futility and culminating in the nothingness of senility—"sans everything"; and in Arden also a bitter judgment on human relations is lightly passed in the twice repeated "Most friendship is feigning, most loving mere folly." But then one must add that hard on the heels of Jaques's melancholy conclusion Orlando enters with Adam in his arms, who, although he may be "sans teeth" and at the end of his usefulness as a servant, has, beside his store of virtue and his peace of conscience, the love of his master. And the play is full of signal instances of persons who do not forget benefits: Adam, Celia, Touchstone—not to mention the lords who chose to leave the court and follow their banished master to the forest. In a recent number of the *Shakespeare Survey* Professor Harold Jenkins has pointed out how points of view put forward by one character find contradiction or correction by another, so that the whole play is a balance of sweet against sour, of the cynical against the idealistic, and life is shown as a mingling of hard fortune and good hap. The lords who have "turned ass," "leaving their wealth and ease a stubborn will to please," are happy in their gross folly, as Orlando is in a lovesickness which he does not wish to be cured of. What Jaques has left out of his picture of man's strange eventful pilgrimage is love and companionship, sweet society, the banquet under the boughs to which Duke Senior welcomes Orlando and Adam. Although life in Arden is not wholly idyllic, and this place set apart from the world is yet touched by the world's sorrows and can be mocked at by the worldly wise, the image of life which the forest presents is irradiated by the conviction that the gay and the gentle can endure the rubs of fortune and that this earth is a place where men can find happiness in themselves and in others.

The Forest of Arden is, as has often been pointed out, a place which all the exiles from the court, except one, are only too ready to leave at the close. As, when the short midsummer night is over, the lovers emerge from the wood, in their right minds and correctly paired, and return to the palace of Theseus; and, when Prospero's magic has worked the cure, the enchanted island is left to Caliban and Ariel, and its human visitors return to Naples and Milan; so the time of holiday comes to an end in Arden. The stately masque of Hymen marks the end of this interlude in the greenwood, and announces the return to a court purged of envy and baseness. Like other comic places, Arden is a place of discovery where the truth becomes clear and where each man finds himself and his true way. This discovery of truth in comedy is made through errors and mistakings. The trial and error by which we come to knowledge of ourselves and of our world is symbolized by the disguisings which are a recurrent element in all comedy, but are particularly common in Shakespeare's. Things have, as it were, to become worse before they become better, more confused and farther from the proper pattern. By misunderstandings men come to understand, and by lies and feignings they discover truth. If Rosalind, the princess, had attempted to "cure" her lover Orlando, she might have succeeded. As Ganymede, playing Rosalind, she can try him to the limit in perfect safety, and discover that she cannot mock or flout him out of his "mad humor of love to a living humor of madness," and drive him "to forswear the full stream of the world, and to live in a nook merely monastic." By playing with him in the disguise of a boy, she discovers when she can play no more. By love of a shadow, the mere image of a charming youth, Phoebe discovers that it is better to love than to be loved and scorn one's lover. This discovery of truth by feigning, and of what is wisdom and what folly by debate, is the center of *As You Like It*. It is a play of meetings and encounters, of conversations and sets of wit: Orlando versus Jaques, Touchstone versus Corin, Rosalind versus Jaques, Rosalind versus Phoebe, and above all Rosalind versus Orlando. The truth discovered is, at one level, a very "earthy truth": Benedick's discovery that "the world must be peopled." The honest toil of Corin, the wise man of the forest, is mocked at by Touchstone as "simple sin." He brings "the ewes and the rams together" and gets his living "by the copulation of cattle." The goddess Fortune seems similarly occupied in this play: "As the ox hath his bow, the horse his curb, and the falcon her bells, so man hath his desires; and as pigeons bill, so wedlock would be nibbling." Fortune acts the role of a kindly bawd. Touchstone's marriage to Audrey is a mere coupling. Rosalind's advice to Phoebe is brutally frank: "Sell when you can, you are not for all markets." The words she uses to describe Oliver and Celia "in the very wrath of love" are hardly delicate, and after her first meeting with Orlando she confesses to her cousin that her sighs are for her "child's father." Against the natural background of the life of the forest there can be no pretense that the love of men and women can "forget the He and She." But Rosalind's behavior is at variance with her bold words. Orlando has to prove that he truly is, as he seems at first sight, the right husband for her, and show himself gentle, courteous, generous and brave, and a match for her in wit, though a poor poet. In this, the great coupling of the play, there is a marriage of true minds. The other couplings run the gamut downward from it, until we reach Touchstone's image of "a she-lamb of a twelvemonth" and "a crooked-pated, old, cuckoldy ram," right at the bottom of the scale. As for the debate as to where happiness is to be found, the conclusion come to is again, like all wisdom, not very startling or original: that "minds innocent and quiet" can find happiness in court or country:

> Happy is your Grace,
> That can translate the stubbornness of fortune
> Into so quiet and so sweet a style.

And, on the contrary, those who wish to can "suck melancholy" out of anything, "as a weasel sucks eggs."

In the pairing one figure is left out. "I am for other than for dancing measures," says Jaques. Leaving the hateful sight of reveling and pastime, he betakes himself to the Duke's abandoned cave, on his way to the house of penitents where Duke Frederick has gone. The two commentators of the play are nicely contrasted. Touchstone is the parodist, Jaques the cynic. The parodist must love what he parodies. We know this from literary parody. All the best parodies are written by those who understand, because they love, the thing they mock. Only poets who love and revere the epic can write mock-heroic and the finest parody of classical tragedy comes from Housman, a great scholar. In everything that Touchstone says and does gusto, high spirits and a zest for life ring out. Essentially comic, he can adapt himself to any situation in which he may find himself. Never at a loss, he is life's master. The essence of clowning is adaptability and improvisation. The clown is never baffled and is marked by his ability to place himself at once *en rapport* with his audience, to be all things to all men, to perform the part which is required at the moment. Touchstone sustains many different roles. After hearing Silvius's lament and Rosalind's echo of it, he becomes the maudlin lover of Jane Smile; with the simple shepherd Corin he becomes the cynical and worldly-wise man of the court; with Jaques he is a melancholy moralist, musing on the power of time and the decay of all things; with the pages he acts the lordly amateur of the arts, patronizing his musicians. It is right that he should parody the rest of the cast, and join the procession into Noah's ark with his Audrey. Jaques is his opposite. He is the cynic, the person who prefers the pleasures of superiority, cold-eyed and cold-hearted. The tyrannical Duke Frederick and the cruel Oliver can be converted; but not Jaques. He likes himself as he is. He does not wish to plunge into the stream, but prefers to stand on the bank and "fish for fancies as they pass." Sir Thomas Elyot said that dancing was an image of matrimony: "In every daunse, of a most auncient custome, there daunseth together a man and a woman, holding eche other by the hande or the arme, which betokeneth concorde." There are some who will not dance, however much they are piped to, any more than they will weep when there is mourning. "In this theater of man's life," wrote Bacon, "it is reserved only for God and angels to be lookers on." Jaques arrogates to himself the divine role. He has opted out from the human condition.

It is characteristic of Shakespeare's comedies to include an element that is irreconcilable, which strikes a lightly discordant note, casts a slight shadow, and by its presence questions the completeness of the comic vision of life. In *Love's Labor's Lost* he dared to allow the news of a death to cloud the scene of revels at the close, and, through Rosalind's rebuke to Berowne, called up the image of a whole world of pain and weary suffering where "Mirth cannot move a soul in agony." The two comedies whose main action is motivated by hatred end with malice thwarted but not removed. In *The Merchant of Venice* and *Much Ado About Nothing*, Shakespeare asks us to accept the fact that the human race includes not only a good many fools and rogues but also some persons who are positively wicked, a fact which comedy usually ignores. They are prevented from doing the harm they wish to do. They are not cured of wishing to do harm. Shylock's baffled exit and Don John's flight to Messina leave the stage clear for lovers and well-wishers. The villains have to be left out of the party at the close. At the end of *Twelfth Night* the person who is left out is present. The impotent misery and fury of the humiliated Malvolio's last words, "I'll be reveng'd on the whole pack of you," call in question the whole comic scheme by which, through misunderstandings and mistakes, people come to terms with themselves and their fellows. There are some who cannot be "taught a lesson." In Malvolio pride is not purged; it is fatally wounded and embittered. It is characteristic of the delicacy of temper of *As You Like It* that its solitary figure, its outsider, Jaques, does nothing whatever to harm anyone, and is perfectly satisfied with himself and happy in his melancholy. Even more, his melancholy is a source of pleasure and amusement to others. The Duke treats him as virtually a court entertainer, and he is a natural butt for Orlando and Rosalind. Anyone in the play can put him down and feel the better for doing so. All the same his presence casts a faint shadow. His criticism of the world has its sting drawn very early by the Duke's rebuke to him as a former libertine, discharging his filth upon the world, and he is to some extent discredited before he opens his mouth by the unpleasant implication of his name. But he cannot be wholly dismissed. A certain sour distaste for life is voided through him, something most of us feel at some time or other. If he were not there to give expression to it, we might be tempted to find the picture of life in the forest too sweet. His only action is to interfere in the marriage of Touchstone and Audrey; and this he merely postpones. His effect, whenever he appears, is to deflate: the effect does not last and cheerfulness soon breaks in again. Yet as there is a scale of love, so there is a scale of sadness in the play. It runs down from the Duke's compassionate words:

> Thou seest we are not all alone unhappy:
> This wide and universal theater
> Presents more woeful pageants than the scene
> Wherein we play in,

through Rosalind's complaint "O, how full of briers is this working-day world," to Jaques's studied refusal to find anything worthy of admiration or love.

One further element in the play I would not wish to stress, because though it is pervasive it is unobtrusive: the constant, natural and easy reference to the Christian ideal of loving-kindness, gentleness, pity and humility and to the sanctions which that ideal finds in the commands and promises of religion. In this fantasy world, in which the world of our experience is imaged, this element in experience finds a place with others, and the world is shown not only as a place where we may find happiness, but as a place where both happiness and sorrow may be hallowed. The number of religious references in *As You Like It* has often been commented on, and it is striking when we consider the play's main theme. Many are of little significance and it would be humorless to enlarge upon the significance of the "old religious man" who converted Duke Frederick, or of Ganymede's "old religious uncle." But some are explicit and have a serious, unforced beauty: Orlando's appeal to outlawed men,

> If ever you have look'd on better days,
> If ever been where bells have knoll'd to church . . . ;

Adam's prayer,

> He that doth the ravens feed,
> Yea, providently caters for the sparrow,
> Be comfort to my age!

and Corin's recognition, from St. Paul, that we have to find the way to heaven by deeds of hospitality. These are all in character. But the God of Marriage, Hymen, speaks more solemnly than we expect and his opening words with their New Testament echo are more than conventional:

> Then is there mirth in heaven,
> When earthly things made even
> Atone together.

The appearance of the god to present daughter to father and to bless the brides and grooms turns the close into a solemnity, an image of the concord which reigns in Heaven and which Heaven blesses on earth. But this, like much else in the play, may be taken as you like it. There is no need to see any more in the god's appearance with the brides than a piece of pageantry which concludes the action with a graceful spectacle and sends the audience home contented with a very pretty play.

The Merchants and the Jew of Venice: Wealth's Communion and an Intruder

C. L. Barber

Should I go to church
And see the holy edifice of stone
And not bethink me straight of dangerous rocks,
Which, touching but my gentle vessel's side,
Would scatter all her spices on the stream,
Enrobe the roaring waters with my silks,
And, in a word, but even now worth this,
And now worth nothing?

When Nashe, in *Summer's Last Will and Testament,* brings on a Christmas who is a miser and refuses to keep the feast, the kill-joy figure serves, as we have noticed,[1] to consolidate feeling in support of holiday. Shakespeare's miser in *The Merchant of Venice* has the same sort of effect in consolidating the gay Christians behind Portia's "The quality of mercy is not strained." The comic antagonist as we get him in Nashe's churlish Christmas, uncomplicated by such a local habitation as Shakespeare developed for Shylock, is a transposed image of the pageant's positive spokesmen for holiday. Summer reminds him, when he first comes on, of the role he ought to play, and his miserliness is set off against the generosity proper to festivity:

SUMMER Christmas, how chance thou com'st not as the rest,
Accompanied with some music, or some song?
A merry carol would have grac'd thee well;
Thy ancestors have us'd it heretofore.

CHRISTMAS Aye, antiquity was the mother of ignorance: this latter world, that sees but with her spectacles, hath spied a pad in those sports more than they could.

---

[1] [Barber, *Shakespeare's Festive Comedy,* p. 60.]

SUMMER What, is't against thy conscience for to sing?

CHRISTMAS No, nor to say, by my troth, if I may get a good bargain.

SUMMER Why, thou should'st spend, thou should'st not to care to get. Christmas is god of hospitality.

CHRISTMAS So will he never be of good husbandry. I may say to you, there is many an old god that is now grown out of fashion. So is the god of hospitality.

SUMMER What reason canst thou give he should be left?

CHRISTMAS No other reason, but that Gluttony is a sin, and too many dunghills are infectious. A man's belly was not made for a powdering beef tub: to feed the poor twelve days, and let them starve all the year after, would but stretch out the guts wider than they should be, and so make famine a bigger den in their bellies than he had before. . . .

AUTUMN [Commenting on Christmas]
A fool conceits no further than he sees,
He hath no sense of aught but what he feels.

CHRISTMAS Aye, aye, such wise men as you come to beg at such fool's doors as we be.

AUTUMN Thou shut'st thy door; how should we beg of thee? . . .

CHRISTMAS *Liberalitas liberalitate perit;* . . . our doors must have bars, our doublets must have buttons. . . . Not a porter that brings a man a letter, but will have his penny. I am afraid to keep past one or two servants, lest, hungry knaves, they should rob me: and those I keep, I warrant I do not pamper up too lusty; I keep them under with red herring and poor John all the year long. I have damned up all my chimnies. . . .[2]

Here is the stock business about denying food and locking up which appears also in Shylock's part, along with a suggestion of the harsh ironical humor that bases itself on "the facts"—"aye, such wise men as you come to beg at such fool's doors as we be"—and also a moment like several in *The Merchant of Venice* where the fangs of avarice glint naked—"if I may get a good bargain." Shylock, moreover, has the same attitude as Nashe's miser about festivity:

What, are there masques? Hear you me, Jessica.
Lock up my doors; and when you hear the drum
And the vile squealing of the wry-neck'd fife,
Clamber not you up to the casements then,
Nor thrust your head into the public street
To gaze on Christian fools with varnish'd faces;
But stop my house's ears—I mean my casements.
Let not the sound of shallow fopp'ry enter
My sober house.

(II.v.28–36)

[2] Lines 1627–1710 in McKerrow, *Nashe,* III, 284–287.

Lorenzo's enterprise in stealing Jessica wins our sympathy partly because it is done in a masque, as a merriment:

> BASSANIO . . . put on
> Your boldest suit of mirth, for we have friends
> That purpose merriment . . .
> (II.ii.210–212)

> LORENZO Nay, we will slink away at supper time,
> Disguise us at my lodging, and return
> All in an hour.
> GRATIANO We have not made good preparation.
> SALERIO We have not spoke us yet of torchbearers.
> SOLANIO 'Tis vile, unless it may be quaintly ordered. . . .
> (II.iv.1–6)

The gallants are sophisticated, like Mercutio, about masquerade; but this masque *is* "quaintly ordered," because, as Lorenzo confides to Gratiano,

> Fair Jessica shall be my torchbearer.
> (II.iv.40)

The episode is another place where Shakespeare has it come true that nature can have its way when people are in festive disguise. Shylock's "tight" opposition, "fast bind, fast find" (II.v.54) helps to put us on the side of the "masquing mates," even though what they do, soberly considered, is a gentlemanly version of raiding the Lombard quarter or sacking bawdy houses on Shrove Tuesday.[3]

Making Distinctions About the Use of Riches

The Merchant of Venice as a whole is not shaped by festivity in the relatively direct way that we have traced in *Love's Labour's Lost* and *A Midsummer Night's Dream.* The whirling away of daughter and ducats is just one episode in a complex plot which is based on story materials and worked out with much more concern for events, for what happens next, than there is in the two previous comedies. This play was probably written in 1596, at any rate fairly early in the first period of easy mastery which extends from *Romeo and Juliet, A Midsummer Night's Dream,* and *Richard II* through the Henry IV and V plays and *As You Like It* to *Julius Caesar* and *Twelfth Night.* At the opening of this period, the two comedies modeled directly on festivities represent a new departure, from which Shakespeare returns

[3] [See Barber, *op. cit.,* p. 38.]

in *The Merchant of Venice* to write a comedy with a festive emphasis, but one which is rather more "a kind of history" and less "a gambold." The play's large structure is developed from traditions which are properly theatrical; it is not a theatrical adaptation of a social ritual. And yet analogies to social occasions and rituals prove to be useful in understanding the symbolic action. I shall be pursuing such analogies without suggesting, in most cases, that there is a direct influence from the social to the theatrical form. Shakespeare here is working with autonomous mastery, developing a style of comedy that makes a festive form for feeling and awareness out of all the theatrical elements, scene, speech, story, gesture, role which his astonishing art brought into organic combination.

Invocation and abuse, poetry and railing, romance and ridicule—we have seen repeatedly how such complementary gestures go to the festive celebration of life's powers, along with the complementary roles of revellers and kill-joys, wits and butts, insiders and intruders. What is mocked, what kind of intruder disturbs the revel and is baffled, depends on what particular sort of beneficence is being celebrated. *The Merchant of Venice,* as its title indicates, exhibits the beneficence of civilized wealth, the something-for-nothing which wealth gives to those who use it graciously to live together in a humanly knit group. It also deals, in the role of Shylock, with anxieties about money, and its power to set men at odds. Our econometric age makes us think of wealth chiefly as a practical matter, an abstract concern of work, not a tangible joy for festivity. But for the new commercial civilizations of the Renaissance, wealth glowed in luminous metal, shone in silks, perfumed the air in spices. Robert Wilson, already in the late eighties, wrote a pageant play in the manner of the moralities, *Three Lords and Three Ladies of London,* in which instead of Virtues, London's Pomp and London's Wealth walked gorgeously and smugly about the stage.[4] Despite the terrible sufferings some sections of society were experiencing, the 1590's were a period when London was becoming conscious of itself as wealthy and cultivated, so that it could consider great commercial Venice as prototype. And yet there were at the same time traditional suspicions of the profit motive and newly urgent anxieties about the power of money to disrupt human relations.[5] Robert Wilson also wrote, early in the eighties, a play called *The Three Ladies of London,* where instead of London's Wealth and Pomp we have Lady Lucar and the attitude towards her which her name implies. It was in expressing and so coping with these anxieties about money that

[4] Printed together with *The Three Ladies of London* in Robert Dodsley, *A Select Collection of Old Plays,* ed. W. C. Hazlett (London, 1874–76), Vol. VI.

[5] A very useful background for understanding *The Merchant of Venice* is provided by L. C. Knights' *Drama and Society in the Age of Jonson* (London, 1937) and by the fundamental social history which Mr. Knights used as one point of departure, R. H. Tawney's *Religion and the Rise of Capitalism* (New York, 1926).

Shakespeare developed in Shylock a comic antagonist far more important than any such figure had been in his earlier comedies. His play is still centered in the celebrants rather than the intruder, but Shylock's part is so fascinating that already in 1598 the comedy was entered in the stationer's register as "a book of the Merchant of Venice, or otherwise called the Jew of Venice." Shylock's name has become a byword because of the superb way that he embodies the evil side of the power of money, its ridiculous and pernicious consequences in anxiety and destructiveness. In creating him and setting him over against Antonio, Bassanio, Portia, and the rest, Shakespeare was making distinctions about the use of riches, not statically, of course, but dynamically, as distinctions are made when a social group sorts people out, or when an organized social ritual does so. Shylock is the opposite of what the Venetians are; but at the same time he is an embodied irony, troublingly like them. So his role is like that of the scapegoat in many of the primitive rituals which Frazer has made familiar, a figure in whom the evils potential in a social organization are embodied, recognized and enjoyed during a period of licence, and then in due course abused, ridiculed, and expelled.

The large role of the antagonist in *The Merchant of Venice* complicates the movement through release to clarification: instead of the single outgoing of *A Midsummer Night's Dream,* there are two phases. Initially there is a rapid, festive movement by which gay youth gets something for nothing, Lorenzo going masquing to win a Jessica gilded with ducats, and Bassanio sailing off like Jason to win the golden fleece in Belmont. But all this is done against a background of anxiety. We soon forget all about Egeus' threat in *A Midsummer Night's Dream,* but we are kept aware of Shylock's malice by a series of interposed scenes. Will Summer said wryly about the Harvest merrymakers in *Summer's Last Will and Testament,* "As lusty as they are, they run on the score with George's wife for their posset." [6] We are made conscious that running on the score with Shylock is a very dangerous business, and no sooner is the joyous triumph accomplished at Belmont than Shylock's malice is set loose. It is only after the threat he poses has been met that the redemption of the prodigal can be completed by a return to Belmont.

The key question in evaluating the play is how this threat is met, whether the baffling of Shylock is meaningful or simply melodramatic. Certainly the plot, considered in outline, seems merely a prodigal's dream coming true: to have a rich friend who will set you up with one more loan so that you can marry a woman both beautiful and rich, girlishly yielding and masterful; and on top of that to get rid of the obligation of the loan because the old moneybags from whom your friend got the money is proved to be so villainous that he does

---

[6] Lines 943–944 in McKerrow, *Nashe,* III, 263.

not deserve to be paid back! If one adds humanitarian and democratic indignation at anti-semitism, it is hard to see, from a distance, what there can be to say for the play: Shylock seems to be made a scapegoat in the crudest, most dishonest way. One can apologize for the plot, as Middleton Murry and Granville-Barker do, by observing that it is based on a fairy-story sort of tale, and that Shakepeare's method was not to change implausible story material, but to invent characters and motives which would make it acceptable and credible, moment by moment, on the stage.[7] But it is inadequate to praise the play for delightful and poetic incoherence. Nor does it seem adequate to say, as E. E. Stoll does, that things just do go this way in comedy, where old rich men are always baffled by young and handsome lovers, lenders by borrowers.[8] Stoll is certainly right, but the question is whether Shakespeare has done something more than merely appeal to the feelings any crowd has in a theater in favor of prodigal young lovers and against old misers. As I see it, he has expressed important things about the relations of love and hate to wealth. When he kept to old tales, he not only made plausible protagonists for them, but also, at any rate when his luck held, he brought up into a social focus deep symbolic meanings. Shylock is an ogre, as Middleton Murry said, but he is the ogre of money power. The old tale of the pound of flesh involved taking literally the proverbial metaphors about money-lenders "taking it out of the hide" of their victims, eating them up. Shakespeare keeps the unrealistic literal business, knife-sharpening and all; we accept it, because he makes it express real human attitudes:

> If I can catch him once upon the hip,
> I will feed fat the ancient grudge I bear him.[9]
> (I.iii.47–48)

So too with the fairy-story caskets at Belmont: Shakespeare makes Bassanio's prodigal fortune meaningful as an expression of the triumph of human, social relations over the relations kept track of by accounting. The whole play dramatizes the conflict between the mechanisms of wealth and the masterful, social use of it. The happy ending, which abstractly considered as an event is hard to credit, and the treatment of Shylock, which abstractly considered as justice is hard to justify, *work*

---

[7] John Middleton Murry, *Shakespeare* (New York, 1936), pp. 154–157; Harley Granville-Barker, *Prefaces to Shakespeare* (Princeton, 1946–47), I, 335–336.

[8] *Shakespeare Studies* (New York, 1927), pp. 293–295.

[9] It is striking that, along with the imagery of the money-lender feeding on his victims, there is the complementary prohibition Shylock mentions against eating with Christians; Shakespeare brings alive a primitive anxiety about feasting *with* people who might feast *on* you. And when Shylock violates his own taboo ("But yet I'll go in hate, to feed upon / The prodigal Christian." II.v.14–15) it is he who is caught upon the hip!

as we actually watch or read the play because these events express relief and triumph in the achievement of a distinction.

To see how this distinction is developed, we need to attend to the tangibles of imaginative design which are neglected in talking about plot. So, in the two first scenes, it is the seemingly incidental, random talk that establishes the gracious, opulent world of the Venetian gentlemen and of the "lady richly left" at Belmont, and so motivates Bassanio's later success. Wealth in this world is something profoundly social, and it is relished without a trace of shame when Salerio and Salanio open the play by telling Antonio how rich he is:

> Your mind is tossing on the ocean;
> There where your argosies with portly sail—
> Like signiors and rich burghers on the flood,
> Or, as it were, the pageants of the sea—
> Do overpeer the petty traffickers,
> That curtsy to them, do them reverence,
> As they fly by them with their woven wings.
> (I.i.8–14)

Professor Venezky points out that Elizabethan auditors would have thought not only of the famous Venetian water ceremonies but also of "colorfully decorated pageant barges" on the Thames or of "pageant devices of huge ships which were drawn about in street shows." [10] What is crucial is the ceremonial, social feeling for wealth. Salerio and Salanio do Antonio reverence just as the petty traffickers of the harbor salute his ships, giving way to leave him "with better company" when Bassanio and Gratiano arrive. He stands at ease, courteous, relaxed, melancholy (but not about his fortunes, which are too large for worry), while around him moves a shifting but close-knit group who "converse and waste the time together" (III.iv.12), make merry, speak "an infinite deal of nothing" (I.i.114), propose good times: "Good signiors, both, when shall we laugh? say, when?" (I.i.66). When Bassanio is finally alone with the royal merchant, he opens his mind with

> To you, Antonio,
> I owe the most, in money and in love.
> (I.i.130–131)

Mark Van Doren, in his excellent chapter on this play, notes how these lines summarize the gentleman's world where "there is no incompatibility between money and love." [11] So too, one can add, in this community there is no conflict between enjoying Portia's beauty

---

[10] Venezky, *Pageantry,* p. 172.
[11] *Shakespeare* (New York, 1939), p. 96.

and her wealth: "her sunny locks / Hang on her temples like a golden fleece." When, a moment later, we see Portia mocking her suitors, the world suggested is, again, one where standards are urbanely and humanly social: the sad disposition of the county Palatine is rebuked because (unlike Antonio's) it is "unmannerly." Yet already in the first scene, though Shylock is not in question yet, the anxiety that dogs wealth is suggested. In the lines which I have taken as an epigraph for this chapter, Salerio's mind moves from attending church—from safety, comfort and solidarity—through the playful association of the "holy edifice of stone" with "dangerous rocks," to the thought that the sociable luxuries of wealth are vulnerable to impersonal forces:

> rocks,
> Which, touching but my gentle vessel's side,
> Would scatter all her spices on the stream,
> Enrobe the roaring waters with my silks . . .
> (I.i.31–34)

The destruction of what is cherished, of the civic and personal, by ruthless impersonal forces is sensuously immediate in the wild waste of shining silk on turbulent water, one of the magic, summary lines of the play. Earlier there is a tender, solicitous suggestion that the vessel is the more vulnerable because it is "gentle"—as later Antonio is gentle and vulnerable when his ships encounter "the dreadful touch / Of merchant-marring rocks" (III.ii.270–271) and his side is menaced by a "stony adversary" (IV.i.4).

When Shylock comes on in the third scene, the easy, confident flow of colorful talk and people is checked by a solitary figure and an unyielding speech:

> SHYLOCK Three thousand ducats—well.
> BASSANIO Ay, sir, for three months.
> SHYLOCK For three months—well.
> BASSANIO For the which, as I told you, Antonio shall be bound.
> SHYLOCK Antonio shall become bound—well.
> BASSANIO May you stead me? Will you pleasure me? Shall I know your answer?
> SHYLOCK Three thousand ducats for three months, and Antonio bound.
> (I.iii.1–10)

We can construe Shylock's hesitation as playing for time while he forms his plan. But more fundamentally, his deliberation expresses the impersonal logic, the mechanism, involved in the control of money. Those *well's* are wonderful in the way they bring bland Bassanio up short. Bassanio assumes that social gestures can brush aside such consideration:

SHYLOCK Antonio is a good man.
BASSANIO Have you heard any imputation to the contrary?
SHYLOCK Ho, no, no, no, no! My meaning in saying he is a good man, is to have you understand me that he is sufficient.
(I.iii.12–17)

The laugh is on Bassanio as Shylock drives his hard financial meaning of "good man" right through the center of Bassanio's softer social meaning. The Jew goes on to calculate and count. He connects the hard facts of money with the rocky sea hazards of which we have so far been only picturesquely aware: "ships are but boards"; and he betrays his own unwillingness to take the risks proper to commerce: "and other ventures he hath, squand'red abroad."

. . . I think I may take his bond.
BASSANIO Be assur'd you may.
SHYLOCK I will be assur'd I may; and, that I may be assured, I will bethink me.
(I.iii.28–31)

The Jew in this encounter expresses just the things about money which are likely to be forgotten by those who have it, or presume they have it, as part of a social station. He stands for what we mean when we say that "money is money." So Shylock makes an ironic comment—and *is* a comment, by virtue of his whole tone and bearing—on the folly in Bassanio which leads him to confuse those two meanings of "good man," to ask Shylock to dine, to use in this business context such social phrases as "Will you *pleasure* me?" When Antonio joins them, Shylock (after a soliloquy in which his plain hatred has glittered) becomes a pretender to fellowship, with an equivocating mask:

SHYLOCK This is kind I offer.
BASSANIO This were kindness.
SHYLOCK This kindness will I show.
(I.iii.143–144)

We are of course in no doubt as to how to take the word "kindness" when Shylock proposes "in a merry sport" that the penalty be a pound of Antonio's flesh.

In the next two acts, Shylock and the accounting mechanism which he embodies are crudely baffled in Venice and rhapsodically transcended in Belmont. The solidarity of the Venetians includes the clown, in whose part Shakespeare can use conventional blacks and whites about Jews and misers without asking us to take them too seriously:

To be ruled by my conscience, I should stay with the Jew my master, who (God bless the mark) is a kind of devil. . . . My master's a very Jew.
(II.ii.24–25, 111)

Even the street urchins can mock Shylock after the passion which "the dog Jew did utter in the streets":

> Why, all the boys in Venice follow him,
> Crying his stones, his daughter, and his ducats.
> (II.viii.23–24)

Transcending Reckoning at Belmont

The simplest way to describe what happens at Belmont is to say that Bassanio is lucky; but Shakespeare gives a great deal of meaning to his being lucky. His choosing of the casket might be merely theatrical; but the play's handling of the age-old story motif makes it an integral part of the expression of relations between people and possessions. Most of the argument about gold, silver, and lead is certainly factitious, even tedious. It must necessarily be so, because the essence of a lottery is a discontinuity, something hidden so that the chooser cannot get from here to there by reasoning. Nerissa makes explicit a primitive notion of divination:

> Your father was ever virtuous; and holy men at their death have good inspirations. Therefore the lott'ry that he hath devised in these three chests of gold, silver, and lead, whereof who chooses his meaning chooses you, will no doubt never be chosen by any rightly but one who shall rightly love.
> (I.ii.30–36)

The elegant phrasing does not ask us to take the proposition very seriously, but Nerissa is pointing in the direction of a mystery. Part of the meaning is that love is not altogether a matter of the will, however willing. Portia recognizes this even when her heart is in her mouth as Bassanio is about to choose:

> Away then! I am lock'd in one of them.
> If you do love me, you will find me out.
> Nerissa and the rest, stand all aloof.
> Let music sound while he doth make his choice . . .
> (III.ii.40–43)

The song, "Tell me, where is fancy bred," serves to emphasize the break, the speechless pause while Bassanio chooses. The notion that it serves as a signal to warn Bassanio off gold and silver is one of those busy-body emendations which eliminate the dramatic in seeking to elaborate it. The dramatic point is precisely that there is no signal: "Who chooseth me must give and hazard all he hath" (II.vii.16).

If we look across for a moment at Shylock, thinking through opposites as the play's structure invites us to do, his discussion with Antonio about the "thrift" of Jacob and the taking of interest proves to be relevant to the luck of the caskets. Antonio appeals to the principle that interest is wrong because it involves no risk:

> This was a venture, sir, that Jacob serv'd for;
> A thing not in his power to bring to pass,
> But sway'd and fashion'd by the hand of heaven.
> (I.iii.92–94)

One way to get a fortune is to be fortunate: the two words fall together significantly at the conclusion of the opening scene:

> BASSANIO O my Antonio, had I but the means
> To hold a rival place with one of them,
> I have a mind presages me such thrift
> That I should questionless be fortunate!
> ANTONIO Thou know'st that all my fortunes are at sea . . .
> (I.i.173–177)

Antonio's loan is venture capital. It fits with this conception that Bassanio, when at Belmont he goes "to my fortune and the caskets," turns away from money, from "gaudy gold, / Hard food for Midas," and from silver, the "pale and common drudge / 'Tween man and man" (III.ii.101–104). Money is not used to get money; that is the usurer's way:

> ANTONIO Or is your gold and silver ewes and rams?
> SHYLOCK I cannot tell; I make it breed as fast.
> (I.iii.96–97)

Instead Bassanio's borrowed purse is invested in life—including such lively things as the "rare new liveries" (II.ii.117) that excite Launcelot, and the "gifts of rich value" which excite Nerissa to say

> A day in April never came so sweet
> To show how costly summer was at hand
> As this fore-spurrer comes before his lord.
> (II.ix.93–95)

With the money, Bassanio invests *himself,* and so risks losing himself—as has to be the case with love. (Antonio's commitment of his body for his friend is in the background.) It is a limitation of the scene where he makes his choice that the risk has to be conveyed largely by the poetry, since the outward circumstances are not hazardous. Portia describes Bassanio as

> young Alcides when he did redeem
> The virgin tribute paid by howling Troy
> To the sea monster. . . .
> Go, Hercules!
> Live thou, I live.
> (III.ii.55–61)

Of course we know that these are lover's feelings. But the moment of choice is expressed in terms that point beyond feelings to emphasize discontinuity; they convey the experience of being lost and giddily finding oneself again in a new situation. The dramatic shift is all the more vividly rendered in the language since gesture here can do little. Portia speaks of an overwhelming ecstasy of love when "all the other passions fleet to air" (III.ii.108). Bassanio likens himself to an athlete

> Hearing applause and universal shout,
> Giddy in spirit, still gazing in a doubt
> Whether those peals of praise be his or no.
> (III.ii.143–145)

He describes in a wonderful way the experience of being disrupted by joy:

> Madam, you have bereft me of all words,
> Only my blood speaks to you in my veins;
> And there is such confusion in my powers
> As, after some oration fairly spoke
> By a beloved prince, there doth appear
> Among the buzzing pleased multitude,
> Where every something, being blent together,
> Turns to a wild of nothing, save of joy,
> Express'd and not express'd.
> (III.ii.175–183)

This poetry is remarkable for the conscious way that it describes being carried beyond expression, using words to tell of being beyond them. The lines in which Portia gives herself and her possessions to Bassanio make explicit, by an elaborate metaphor of accounting, that what is happening sets the accounting principle aside:

> You see me, Lord Bassanio, where I stand,
> Such as I am. Though for myself alone
> I would not be ambitious in my wish
> To wish myself much better, yet for you
> I would be trebled twenty times myself,
> A thousand times more fair, ten thousand times more rich,
> That, only to stand high in your account,
> I might in virtues, beauties, livings, friends,
> Exceed account. But the full sum of me
> Is sum of nothing, which, to term in gross,
> Is an unlesson'd girl, unschool'd, unpractic'd. . . .
> (III.ii.149–159)

This is extravagant, and extravagantly modest, as fits the moment; but what is telling is the way the lines move from possessions, through the paradox about sums, to the person in the midst of them all, "where I stand," who cannot be added up. It is she that Bassanio has won, and with her a way of living for which his humanity, breeding, and manhood can provide a center:

> Happiest of all is that her gentle spirit
> Commits itself to yours to be directed,
> As from her lord, her governor, her king.
> (III.ii.163–165)

The possessions *follow* from this human, social relation.

Comical/Menacing Mechanism in Shylock

But the accounting mechanism which has been left behind by Bassanio and Portia has gone on working, back at Venice, to put Antonio at Shylock's mercy, and the anxiety it causes has to be mastered before the marriage can be consummated,

> For never shall you lie by Portia's side
> With an unquiet soul.
> (III.ii.305–306)

Historical changes in stock attitudes have made difficulties about Shylock's role as a butt, not so much in the theater, where it works perfectly if producers only let it, but in criticism, where winds of doctrine blow sentiments and abstractions about. The Elizabethans almost never saw Jews except on the stage, where Marlowe's Barabas was familiar. They did see *one,* on the scaffold, when Elizabeth's unfortunate physician suffered for trumped-up charges of a poisoning plot. The popular attitude was that to take interest for money was to be a loan shark—though limited interest was in fact allowed by law. An aristocrat who like Lord Bassanio ran out of money commanded sympathy no longer felt in a middleclass world. Most important of all, suffering was not an absolute evil in an era when men sometimes embraced it deliberately, accepted it as inevitable, and could watch it with equanimity. Humanitarianism has made it necessary for us to be much more thoroughly insulated from the human reality of people if we are to laugh at their discomfiture or relish their suffering. During the romantic period, and sometimes more recently, the play was presented as a tragi-comedy, and actors vied with one another in making Shylock a figure of pathos. I remember a very moving scene, a stock feature of romantic productions, in which George Arliss came home after Bassanio's party, lonely and tired and old, to knock in vain at the door of the house left empty by Jessica. How completely unhistorical the romantic treatment was, E. E. Stoll demonstrated overwhelmingly in his essay on Shylock in 1911, both by wide-ranging comparisons of Shylock's role with others in Renaissance drama and by analysis of the *optique du théâtre*.[12]

To insert a humanitarian scene about Shylock's pathetic homecoming prevents the development of the scornful amusement with which Shakespeare's text presents the miser's reaction in Solanio's narrative:

> I never heard a passion so confus'd,
> So strange, outrageous, and so variable,
> As the dog Jew did utter in the streets.
> "My daughter! O my ducats! O my daughter!
> Fled with a Christian! O my Christian ducats! . . ."
> (II.viii.12–16)

Marlowe had done such a moment already with Barabas hugging in turn his money bags and his daughter—whom later the Jew of Malta poisons with a pot of porridge, as the Jew of Venice later wishes that Jessica "were hears'd at my foot, and the ducats in her coffin" (III.i.93–94). But the humanitarian way of playing the part develops suggestions that are *also* in Shakespeare's text:

> I am bid forth to supper, Jessica.
> There are my keys. But wherefore should I go?
> I am not bid for love; they flatter me.
> But yet I'li go in hate, to feed upon
> The prodigal Christian.
> (II.v.11–15)

Shakespeare's marvelous creative sympathy takes the stock role of Jewish usurer and villain and conveys how it would feel to be a man living inside it. But this does not mean that he shrinks from confronting the evil and the absurdity that go with the role; for the Elizabethan age, to understand did not necessarily mean to forgive. Shylock can be a thorough villain and yet be allowed to express what sort of treatment has made him what he is:

> You call me misbeliever, cutthroat dog,
> And spet upon my Jewish gaberdine,
> And all for use of that which is mine own.
> (I.iii.112–114)

We can understand his degradation and even blame the Antonios of Venice for it; yet it remains degradation:

> Thou call'dst me dog before thou hadst a cause;
> But, since I am a dog, beware my fangs.
> (III.iii.6–7)

---

[12] In *Shakespeare Studies.*

Shylock repeatedly states, as he does here, that he is only finishing what the Venetians started. He can be a drastic ironist, because he carries to extremes what is present, whether acknowledged or not, in their silken world. He insists that money is money—and they cannot do without money either. So too with the rights of property. The power to give freely, which absolute property confers and Antonio and Portia so splendidly exhibit, is also a power to refuse, as Shylock so logically refuses:

> You have among you many a purchas'd slave,
> Which, like your asses and your dogs and mules,
> You use in abject and in slavish parts,
> Because you bought them. Shall I say to you,
> "Let them be free, marry them to your heirs! . . ."
> You will answer,
> "The slaves are ours." So do I answer you.
> The pound of flesh which I demand of him
> Is dearly bought, 'tis mine, and I will have it.
> (IV.i.90–100)

At this point in the trial scene, Shylock seems a juggernaut that nothing can stop, armed as he is against a pillar of society by the principles of society itself: "If you deny me, fie upon your law! . . . I stand for judgement. Answer. Shall I have it?" Nobody does answer him here, directly; instead there is an interruption for Portia's entrance. To answer him is the function of the whole dramatic action, which is making a distinction that could not be made in direct, logical argument.

Let us follow this dramatic action from its comic side. Shylock is comic, so far as he is so, because he exhibits what should be human, degraded into mechanism. The reduction of life to mechanism goes with the miser's wary calculation, with the locking up, with the preoccupation with "that which is mine own." Antonio tells Bassanio that

> My purse, my person, my extremest means
> Lie all unlock'd to your occasions.
> (I.i.138–139)

How open! Antonio has to live inside some sort of rich man's melancholy, but at least he communicates with the world through outgoing Bassanio (and, one can add, through the commerce which takes his fortunes out to sea). Shylock, by contrast, who breeds barren metal, wants to keep "the vile squeeling of the wry-neck'd fife" out of his house, and speaks later, in a curiously revealing, seemingly random illustration, of men who "when the bagpipe sings i'th'nose, / Cannot contain their urine" (V.i.49–50). Not only is he closed up tight inside himself, but after the first two scenes, we are scarcely allowed by his lines to feel with him. And we never encounter him alone; he regularly comes on to join a group whose talk has established an outside point of view towards him. This perspective on him does not exclude a potential pathos. There is always potential pathos, behind, when drama makes fun of isolating, anti-social qualities. Indeed, the process of *making fun of* a person often works by exhibiting pretensions to humanity so as to show that they are inhuman, mechanical, not validly appropriate for sympathy. With a comic villain such as Shylock, the effect is mixed in various degrees between our responding to the mechanism as menacing and laughing at it as ridiculous.

So in the great scene in which Salanio and Salerio taunt Shylock, the potentiality of pathos produces effects which vary between comedy and menace:

> SHYLOCK You knew, none so well, none so well as you, of my daughter's flight.
> SALERIO That's certain. I, for my part, knew the tailor that made the wings she flew withal.
>
> (III.i.27–30)

Shylock's characteristic repetitions, and the way he has of moving ahead through similar, short phrases, as though even with language he was going to use only what was his own, can give an effect of concentration and power, or again, an impression of a comically limited, isolated figure. In the great speech of self-justification to which he is goaded by the two bland little gentlemen, the iteration conveys the energy of anguish:

> —and what's his reason? I am a Jew. Hath not a Jew eyes? Hath not a Jew hands, organs, dimensions, senses, affections, passions? fed with the same food, hurt with the same weapons, subject to the same diseases, healed by the same means, warmed and cooled by the same winter and summer as a Christian is? If you prick us, do we not bleed? If you tickle us, do we not laugh? If you poison us, do we not die? And if you wrong us, shall we not revenge? If we are like you in the rest, we will resemble you in that.
>
> (III.i.60–71)

Certainly no actor would deliver this speech without an effort at pathos; but it is a pathos which, as the speech moves, converts to menace. And the pathos is qualified, limited, in a way which is badly falsified by humanitarian renderings that open all the stops at "Hath not a Jew hands, etc. . . ." For Shylock thinks to claim only a *part* of humanness, the lower part, physical and passional. The similar self-pitying enumeration which Richard II makes differs significantly in going from "live with bread like you" to social responses and needs, "Taste grief, / Need friends" (*Richard II,* III.ii.175–176). The passions in Shylock's speech are conceived as reflexes; the parallel clauses draw them all towards the level of "tickle . . . laugh." The same assumption, that the passions and social responses are mechanisms on a par with a nervous tic, appears in the court scene when Shylock defends his right to follow his "humor" in taking Antonio's flesh:

> As there is no firm reason to be rend'red
> Why he cannot abide a gaping pig,
> Why he a harmless necessary cat,
> Why he a woollen bagpipe—but of force
> Must yield to such inevitable shame
> As to offend himself, being offended;
> So can I give no reason, nor I will not,
> More than a lodg'd hate and a certain loathing
> I bear unto Antonio . . .
>
> (IV.i.52–61)

The most succinct expression of this assumption about man is Shylock's response to Bassanio's incredulous question:

> BASSANIO Do all men kill the things they do not love?
> SHYLOCK Hates any man the thing he would not kill?
>
> (IV.i.66–67)

There is no room in this view for mercy to come in between "wrong us" and "shall we not revenge?" As Shylock insists, there is Christian example for him: the irony is strong. But the mechanism of stimulus and response is only a part of the truth. The reductive tendency of Shylock's metaphors, savagely humorous in Iago's fashion, goes with this speaking only the lower part of the truth. He is not cynical in Iago's aggressive way, because as an alien he simply doesn't participate in many of the social ideals which Iago is concerned to discredit in self-justification. But the two villains have the same frightening, ironical power from moral simplification.

Shylock becomes a clear-cut butt at the moments when he is himself caught in compulsive, reflexive responses, when instead of controlling mechanism he is controlled by it: "O my daughter! O my ducats!" At the end of the scene of taunting, his menace and his pathos become ridiculous when he dances like a jumping jack in alternate joy and sorrow as Tubal pulls the strings:

> TUBAL Yes, other men have ill luck too. Antonio, as I heard in Genoa—
>
> SHYLOCK What, what, what? Ill luck, ill luck?
>
> TUBAL Hath an argosy cast away coming from Tripolis.
>
> SHYLOCK I thank God, I thank God!—Is it true? is it true?
>
> TUBAL I spoke with some of the sailors that escaped the wrack.
>
> SHYLOCK I thank thee, good Tubal. Good news, good news! Ha, ha! Where? in Genoa?
>
> TUBAL Your daughter spent in Genoa, as I heard, one night fourscore ducats.

SHYLOCK Thou stick'st a dagger in me. I shall never see my gold again. Fourscore ducats at a sitting! Fourscore ducats!

TUBAL There came divers of Antonio's creditors in my company to Venice that swear he cannot choose but break.

SHYLOCK I am very glad of it. I'll plague him; I'll torture him. I am glad of it.

TUBAL One of them show'd me a ring that he had of your daughter for a monkey.

SHYLOCK Out upon her! Thou torturest me, Tubal. It was my turquoise; I had it of Leah when I was a bachelor. I would not have given it for a wilderness of monkeys.

TUBAL But Antonio is certainly undone.

SHYLOCK Nay, that's true, that's very true.

(III.i.102–130)

This is a scene in the dry manner of Marlowe, Jonson, or Molière, a type of comedy not very common in Shakespeare: its abrupt alternations in response convey the effect Bergson describes so well in *Le Rire,* where the comic butt is a puppet in whom motives have become mechanisms that usurp life's self-determining prerogative. Some critics have left the rhythm of the scene behind to dwell on the pathos of the ring he had from Leah when he was a bachelor. It is like Shakespeare once to show Shylock putting a gentle sentimental value on something, to match the savage sentimental value he puts on revenge. There *is* pathos; but it is being fed into the comic mill and makes the laughter all the more hilarious.

The Community Setting Aside Its Machinery

In the trial scene, the turning point is appropriately the moment when Shylock gets caught in the mechanism he relies on so ruthlessly. He narrows everything down to his roll of parchment and his knife: "Till thou canst rail the seal from off my bond . . ." (IV.i.139). But two can play at this game:

as thou urgest justice, be assur'd
Thou shalt have justice more than thou desir'st.
(IV.i.315–316)

Shylock's bafflement is comic, as well as dramatic, in the degree that we now see through the threat that he has presented, recognizing it to have been, in a degree, unreal. For it is unreal to depend so heavily on legal form, on fixed verbal definition, on the mere machinery by which human relations are controlled. Once Portia's legalism has broken through his legalism, he can only go on the way he started, weakly asking "Is that the law?" while Gratiano's jeers underscore the comic symmetry:

> A Daniel still say I, a second Daniel!
> I thank thee, Jew, for teaching me that word.
> (IV.i.340–341)

The turning of the tables is not, of course, simply comic, except for the bold, wild and "skipping spirit" of Gratiano. The trial scene is a species of drama that uses comic movement in slow motion, with an investment of feeling such that the resolution is in elation and relief colored by amusement, rather than in the evacuation of laughter. Malvolio, a less threatening kill-joy intruder, is simply laughed out of court, but Shylock must be ruled out, with jeering only on the side lines. The threat Shylock offers is, after all, drastic, for legal instruments, contract, property are fundamental. Comic dramatists often choose to set them hilariously at naught; but Shakespeare is, as usual, scrupulously responsible to the principles of social order (however factitious his "law" may be literally). So he produced a scene which exhibits the limitations of legalism. It works by a dialectic that carries to a more general level what might be comic reduction to absurdity. To be tolerant, because we are all fools; to forgive, because we are all guilty—the two gestures of the spirit are allied, as Erasmus noted in praising the sublime folly of following Christ. Shylock says before the trial "I'll not be made a soft and dull-ey'd fool" by "Christian intercessors" (III.iii.14–15). Now when he is asked how he can hope for mercy if he renders none, he answers: "What judgement shall I dread, doing no wrong?" As the man who will not acknowledge his own share of folly ends by being more foolish than anyone else, so Shylock, who will not acknowledge a share of guilt, ends by being more guilty—and more foolish, to judge by results. An argument between Old Testament legalism and New Testament reliance on grace develops as the scene goes forward. (Shylock's references to Daniel in this scene, and his constant use of Old Testament names and allusions, contribute to the contrast.) Portia does not deny the bond—nor the law behind it; instead she makes such a plea as St. Paul made to his compatriots:

> Therefore, Jew,
> Though justice be thy plea, consider this—
> That, in the course of justice, none of us
> Should see salvation. We do pray for mercy,
> And that same prayer doth teach us all to render
> The deeds of mercy.
> (IV.i.97–102)

Mercy becomes the word that gathers up everything we have seen the Venetians enjoying in their reliance on community. What is on one side an issue of principles is on the other a matter of social solidarity: Shylock is not one of the "we" Portia refers to, the Christians who say in the Lord's Prayer "Forgive us our debts as we forgive our debtors." All through the play the word Christian has been repeated, primarily in statements that enforce the fact that the Jew is outside the easy bonds of community. Portia's plea for mercy is a sublime version of what in less intense circumstances, among friends of a single communion, can be conveyed with a shrug or a wink:

> Dost thou hear, Hal? Thou knowest in the state of innocency Adam fell; and what should poor Jack Falstaff do in the days of villainy?
>
> (*1 Henry IV,* III.iii.185–188)

Falstaff, asking for an amnesty to get started again, relies on his festive solidarity with Hal. Comedy, in one way or another, is always asking for amnesty, after showing the moral machinery of life getting in the way of life. The machinery as such need not be dismissed—Portia is very emphatic about not doing that. But social solidarity, resting on the buoyant force of a collective life that transcends particular mistakes, can set the machinery aside. Shylock, closed off as he is, clutching his bond and his knife, cannot trust this force, and so acts only on compulsion:

> PORTIA Do you confess the bond?
> ANTONIO I do.
> PORTIA Then must the Jew be merciful.
> SHYLOCK On what compulsion must I? Tell me that.
> PORTIA The quality of mercy is not strain'd;
> It droppeth as the gentle rain from heaven
> Upon the place beneath. It is twice blest—
> It blesseth him that gives, and him that takes.
>
> (IV.i.181–187)

It has been in giving and taking, beyond the compulsion of accounts, that Portia, Bassanio, Antonio have enjoyed the something-for-nothing that Portia here summarizes in speaking of the gentle rain from heaven.

Sharing in the Grace of Life

The troth-plight rings which Bassanio and Gratiano have given away are all that remain of plot to keep the play moving after the trial. It is a slight business, but it gives the women a teasing way to relish the fact that they have played the parts of men as they give up the liberty of that disguise to become wives. And the play's general subject is continued, for in getting over the difficulty, the group provides one final demonstration that human relationships are stronger than their outward signs. Once more, Bassanio expresses a harassed perplexity about obligations in conflict; and Portia gayly pretends to be almost a Shylock about this lover's bond, carrying the logic of the machinery to absurd lengths before showing, by the new gift of the ring, love's power to set debts aside and begin over again.

No other comedy, until the late romances, ends with so full an expression of harmony as that which we get in the opening of the final scene of *The Merchant of Venice.* And no other final scene is so completely without irony about the joys it celebrates. The ironies have been dealt with beforehand in baffling Shylock; in the moment of relief after expelling an antagonist, we do not need to look at the limitations of what we have been defending. So in *Summer's Last Will and Testament,* when Summer is confronted by a miserly Christmas, he comes out wholeheartedly for festivity, whereas elsewhere, confronting spokesmen for festivity, he is always wry about it. He dismisses Christmas with

> Christmas, I tell thee plain, thou art a snudge,
> And wer't not that we love thy father well,
> Thou shouldst have felt what 'longs to Avarice.
> It is the honor of nobility
> To keep high days and solemn festivals—
> Then to set their magnificence to view,
> To frolic open with their favorites,
> And use their neighbors with all courtesy,
> When thou in hugger-mugger spend'st thy wealth.
> Amend thy manners, breathe thy rusty gold:
> Bounty will win thee love, when thou art old.[13]

The court compels Shylock to breathe his gold and give bounty to Lorenzo. He is plainly told that he is a snudge—and we are off to noble magnificence and frolic at Belmont. No high day is involved, though Shakespeare might easily have staged the solemn festival due after Portia's wedding. Instead Lorenzo and Jessica feel the harmony of the universe and its hospitality to life in a quiet moment of idle talk and casual enjoyment of music. There is an opening out to experience in their exquisite outdoor poetry which corresponds to the openness stressed by Nashe in contrast to miserly hugger-mugger.

> The moon shines bright. In such a night as this,
> When the sweet wind did gently kiss the trees
> And they did make no noise—in such a night
> Troilus methinks mounted the Troyan walls
> And sigh'd his soul towards the Grecian tents,
> Where Cressid lay that night.
>
> (V.i.1–6)

The openness to experience, the images of reaching out towards it, or of welcoming it, letting music "creep in our ears," go with the perception of a gracious universe such as Portia's mercy speech invoked:

---

[13] McKerrow, *Nashe,* III, 287, ll. 1722–32.

How sweet the moonlight sleeps upon this bank!
Here will we sit and let the sounds of music
Creep in our ears. Soft stillness and the night
Become the touches of sweet harmony.
Sit, Jessica. Look how the floor of heaven
Is thick inlaid with patens of bright gold.
There's not the smallest orb which thou behold'st
But in his motion like an angel sings . . .
(V.i.54–61)

Lorenzo is showing Jessica the graciousness of the Christian world into which he has brought her; and it is as richly golden as it is musical! Jessica is already at ease in it, to the point of being able to recall the pains of famous lovers with equanimity, rally her lover on his vows and turn the whole thing off with "I would out-night you did no body come, / But hark, I hear the footing of a man." That everybody is so perfectly easy is part of the openness:

LORENZO Who comes so fast in silence of the night?
MESSENGER A friend.
LORENZO A friend? What friend? Your name, I pray you, friend? . . .
Sweet soul, let's in, and there expect their coming.
And yet no matter. Why should we go in?
. . . bring your music forth into the air.
(V.i.25–27, 51–54)

As the actual music plays, there is talk about its Orphic power, and we look back a moment towards Shylock

The man that hath no music in himself
Nor is not mov'd with concord of sweet sounds,
Is fit for treasons, stratagems, and spoils . . .
(V.i.82–84)

A certain contemplative distance is maintained by talking *about* perception, *about* harmony and its conditions, even while enjoying it. Portia comes on exclaiming how far the candle throws its beams, how much sweeter the music sounds than by day. There are conditions, times and seasons, to be observed; but the cosmological music, which cannot be heard directly at all, is behind the buoyant decorum of the people:

How many things by season season'd are
To their right praise and true perfection!
Peace ho! The moon sleeps with Endymion
And would not be awak'd.
(V.i.107–110)

At the end of the play, there is Portia's news of Antonio's three argosies richly come to harbor, and the special deed of gift for Lorenzo

—"manna in the way / Of starved people." Such particular happy events are not sentimental because Shakespeare has floated them on an expression of a tendency in society and nature which supports life and expels what would destroy it.

I must add, after all this praise for the way the play makes its distinction about the use of wealth, that *on reflection,* not when viewing or reading the play, but when thinking about it, I find the distinction, as others have, somewhat too easy. While I read or watch, all is well, for the attitudes of Shylock are appallingly inhuman, and Shakespeare makes me feel constantly how the Shylock attitude rests on a lack of faith in community and grace. But when one thinks about the Portia-Bassanio group, not in opposition to Shylock but alone (as Shakespeare does not show them), one can be troubled by their being so very very far above money:

> What, no more?
> Pay him six thousand, and deface the bond.
> Double six thousand and then treble that . . .
> (III.ii.298–300)

It would be interesting to see Portia say no, for once, instead of always yes: after all, Nashe's miser has a point, "*Liberalitas liberalitate perit.*" One can feel a difficulty too with Antonio's bland rhetorical question:

> when did friendship take
> A breed of barren metal of his friend?
> (I.iii.134–135)

Elizabethan attitudes about the taking of interest were unrealistic: while Sir Thomas Gresham built up Elizabeth's credit in the money market of Antwerp, and the government regulated interest rates, popular sentiment continued on the level of thinking Antonio's remark reflects. Shakespeare's ideal figures and sentiments are open here to ironies which he does not explore. The clown's role just touches them when he pretends to grumble

> We were Christians enow before, e'en as many as could well live by one another. This making of Christians will raise the price of hogs.
> (III.v.23–26)

In *As You Like It* [there is] a more complete confronting of ironies, which leaves, I feel, a cleaner aftertaste. Shakespeare could no doubt hav gone beyond the naïve economic morality of Elizabethan popular culture, had he had an artistic need. But he did not, because in the antithetical sort of comic form he was using in this play, the ironical function was fulfilled by the heavy contrasts embodied in Shylock.

About Shylock, too, there is a difficulty which grows on reflection, a difficulty which may be felt too in reading or performance. His part fits perfectly into the design of the play, and yet he is so alive that he raises an interest beyond its design. I do not think his humanity spoils the design, as Walter Raleigh and others argued,[14] and as was almost inevitable for audiences who assumed that to be human was to be ipso facto good. But it is true that in the small compass of Shylock's three hundred and sixty-odd lines, Shakespeare provided material that asks for a whole additional play to work itself out. Granville-Barker perceptively summarizes how much there is in the scene, not sixty lines long, in which Shylock is seen at home:

> The parting with Launcelot: he has a niggard liking for the fellow, is even hurt a little by his leaving, touched in pride, too, and shows it childishly.
>
> Thou shalt not gormandize
> As thou hast done with me . . .
>
> . . . The parting with Jessica, which we of the audience know to be a parting indeed; that constant calling her by name, which tells us of the lonely man! He has looked to her for everything, has tasked her hard, no doubt; he is her jailer, yet he trusts her, and loves her in his extortionate way. Uneasy stranger that he is within these Venetian gates; the puritan, who, in a wastrel world, will abide by law and prophets![15]

To have dramatized "he has looked to her for everything, has tasked her hard, no doubt," would have taken Shakespeare far afield indeed from the prodigal story he was concerned with—as far afield as *King Lear*. Yet the suggestion is there. The figure of Shylock is like some secondary figure in a Rembrandt painting, so charged with implied life that one can forget his surroundings. To look sometimes with absorption at the suffering, raging Jew alone is irresistible. But the more one is aware of what the play's whole design is expressing through Shylock, of the comedy's high seriousness in its concern for the grace of community, the less one wants to lose the play Shakespeare wrote for the sake of one he merely suggested.

---

[14] *Shakespeare* (London, 1923, first published 1907), pp. 149–151.
[15] *Prefaces*, I, 355.

"Twelfth Night" and the Morality of Indulgence

John Hollander

I

To say that a play is "moral" would seem to imply that it represents an action which concretizes certain ethical elements of human experience, without actually moralizing at any point, and without having any of the characters in it state univocally a dogma, precept, or value that would coincide completely with the play's own moral intention. It was just this univocal didacticism, however, which characterized what was becoming in 1600 a prevailing comic tradition. The moral intent of the Jonsonian "comedy of humours" was direct and didactic; its purpose was to show

> the times deformitie
> Anatomiz'd in euery nerue and sinnew
> With constant courage, and contempt of feare.[1]

For moral purposes, a humour is an identifying emblem of a man's moral nature, graven ineradicably onto his physiological one. In the world of a play, a humour could be caricatured to such a degree that it would practically predestine a character's behavior. It was made to

> . . . so possesse a man, that it doth draw
> All his affects, his spirits and his powers,
> In their conflux, all to runne one way,
> This may be truly said to be a Humour.

The emblematic character of the humour, and the necessity for its use, were affirmed even more directly by Sidney, whose dramatic theory Jonson seems to have greatly admired:

From *The Sewanee Review*, Vol. LXVIII, No. 2 (1959). First published in *The Sewanee Review*.

[1] Ben Jonson, *Every Man Out of His Humour* (1599), Induction, II.120–122.

> Now, as in Geometry the oblique must bee knowne as wel as the right, and in Arithmeticke the odde as well as the euen, so in the actions of our life who seeth not the filthiness of euil wanteth a great foile to perceiue the beauty of vertue. This doth the Comedy handle so in our priuate and domestical matters, as with hearing it we get as it were an experience, what is to be looked for of a nigardly *Demea,* of a crafty *Dauus,* of a flattering *Gnato,* of a vaine glorious *Thraso,* and not onely to know what effects are to be expected, but to know who be such, by the signifying badge giuen them by the Comedian.

Now *Every Man In His Humour* was first acted in 1598, and it is known that Shakespeare appeared in it. He seems in *Twelfth Night* (for which I accept the traditional date of 1600–1601) to have attempted to write a kind of moral comedy diametrically opposed to that of Jonson, in which "the times deformitie" was not to be "anatomiz'd," but represented in the core of an action. For a static and deterministic Humour, Shakespeare substituted a kinetic, governing Appetite in the action, rather than in the bowels, of his major characters. In his plot and language, he insists continually on the fact and importance of the substitution. Characters in a comedy of humours tend to become caricatures, and caricatures tend to become beasts, inhuman personifications of moral distortions that are identified with physiological ones. I believe that it was Shakespeare's intention in *Twelfth Night* to obviate the necessity of this dehumanization by substituting what one might call a moral process for a moral system. While it is true that the play contains quite a bit of interesting discussion of humours as such, and that there is some correspondence between appetites and humours, it is equally true that the only person in the play who believes in the validity of humourous classifications, who, indeed, lives by them, is himself a moral invalid. I will have more to say about this later. At this point I merely wish to suggest that the primary effective difference between Shakespeare's and Jonson's techniques in making moral comedy is the difference between what is merely a display of anatomy, and a dramatization of a metaphor, the difference between a Pageant and an Action.

II

The Action of *Twelfth Night* is indeed that of a Revels, a suspension of mundane affairs during a brief epoch in a temporary world of indulgence, a land full of food, drink, love, play, disguise and music. But parties end, and the reveller eventually becomes satiated and drops heavily into his worldly self again. The fact that plays were categorized as "revells" for institutional purposes may have appealed to Shakespeare; he seems at any rate to have analyzed the dramatic and moral nature of feasting, and to have made it the subject of his play. His analysis is schematized in Orsino's opening speech.

The essential action of a revels is: To so surfeit the Appetite upon excess that it "may sicken and so die." It is the Appetite, not the whole Self, however, which is surfeited: the Self will emerge at the conclusion of the action from where it has been hidden. The movement of the play is toward this emergence of humanity from behind a mask of comic type.

Act I, Scene i, is very important as a statement of the nature of this movement. Orsino's opening line contains the play's three dominant images:

> If music be the food of love, play on.
> Give me excess of it, that, surfeiting,
> The appetite may sicken, and so die.
> (I.i.1–3)

Love, eating, and music are the components of the revelry, then. And in order that there be no mistake about the meaning of the action, we get a miniature rehearsal of it following immediately:

> That strain again! It had a dying fall.
> Oh, it came o'er my ear like the sweet sound
> That breathes upon a bank of violets
> Stealing and giving odor! Enough, no more.
> 'Tis not so sweet now as it was before.
> O spirit of love, how quick and fresh art thou!
> That, notwithstanding thy capacity
> Receiveth as the sea, naught enters there,
> Of what validity and pitch soe'er,
> But falls into abatement and low price,
> Even in a minute! So full of shapes is fancy
> That it alone is high fantastical.
> (I.i.4–15)

A bit of surfeiting is actually accomplished here; what we are getting is a proem to the whole play, and a brief treatment of love as an appetite. The substance of a feast will always fall into "abatement and low price" at the conclusion of the feasting, for no appetite remains to demand it. We also think of Viola in connection with the "violets / Stealing and giving odor," for her actual position as go-between-turned-lover is one of both inadvertent thief and giver. The Duke's rhetoric is all-embracing, however, and he immediately comments significantly upon his own condition.

> Oh, when mine eyes did see Olivia first,
> Methought she purged the air of pestilence!
> That instant was I turned into a hart,
> And my desires, like fell and cruel hounds,
> E'er since pursue me.
> (I.i.19–23)

Like Actaeon, he is the hunter hunted; the active desirer pursued by his own desires. As embodying this overpowering appetite for romantic love, he serves as a host of the revels.[2]

The other host is Olivia, the subject of his desire. We see almost at once that her self-indulgence is almost too big to be encompassed by Orsino's. Valentine, reporting on the failure of his mission, describes her state as follows:

> So please my lord, I might not be admitted,
> But from her handmaid do return this answer:
> The element itself, till seven years' heat,
> Shall not behold her face at ample view;
> But, like a cloistress, she will veiled walk
> And water once a day her chamber round
> With eye-offending brine—all this to season
> A brother's dead love, which she would keep fresh
> And lasting in her sad remembrance.
>
> (I.i.24–32)

"To season a brother's dead love": she is gorging herself on this fragrant herb, and though she has denied herself the world, she is no true anchorite, but, despite herself, a private glutton. The Duke looks forward to the end of her feast of grief,

> . . . when liver, brain, and heart,
> These sovereign thrones, are all supplied, and filled
> Her sweet perfections with one self king!
>
> (I.i.37–39)

The trinitarian overtone is no blasphemy, but a statement of the play's teleology. When everyone is supplied with "one self king," the action will have been completed.

The first three scenes of the play stand together as a general prologue, in which the major characters are introduced and their active natures noted. Viola is juxtaposed to Olivia here; she is not one to drown her own life in a travesty of mourning. It is true that she is tempted to "serve that lady" (as indeed she does, in a different way). But her end in so doing would be the whole play's action in microcosm; the immersion in committed self-indulgence would result in the revelation of her self:

> And might not be delivered to the world
> Till I had made mine own occasion mellow,
> What my estate is.
>
> (I.ii.42–44)

---

[2] See the extremely provocative commentary on the Duke's opening lines in Kenneth Burke, *The Philosophy of Literary Form* (Baton Rouge, 1941), pp. 344–349.

She will serve the Duke instead, and use her persuasive talents to accomplish the ends to which his own self-celebrating rhetoric can provide no access. "I can sing," she says, "and speak to him in many sorts of music." Her sense of his character has been verified; the Captain tells her that his name is as his nature. And "what is his name?" she asks. "Orsino," answers the Captain. Orsino—the bear, the ravenous and clumsy devourer. Her own name suggests active, affective music; and the mention of Arion, the Orpheus-like enchanter of waves and dolphins with his music, points up the connotation. Orsino's "music," on the other hand, is a static well of emotion to which he allows his own rhetoric to submerge; Viola's is more essentially instrumental, effective, and convincing.[3]

The third scene of Act I completes the prologue by further equating the moral and physiological. Here we first encounter the world of what Malvolio calls "Sir Toby and the lighter people" (it is indeed true that there is none of Malvolio's element of "earth" in them). The continued joking about *dryness* that pervades the wit here in Olivia's house, both above and below stairs, is introduced here, in contrast to Olivia's floods of welling and self-indulgent tears. The idea behind the joking in this and the following scenes is that drinking and merriment will moisten and fulfill a dry nature. As Feste says later on, "Give the dry fool drink, then the fool is not dry." Toby's sanguine temperament and Aguecheek's somewhat phlegmatic one are here unveiled. They are never identified as such, however; and none of the wit that is turned on the associations of "humours," "elements," and "waters," though it runs throughout the play, ever refers to a motivating order in the universe, except insofar as Malvolio believes in it.

What is most important is that neither Feste, the feaster embodying not the spirit but the action of revelry, nor Malvolio, the ill-wisher (and the *bad appetite* as well), his polar opposite, appears in these introductory scenes. It is only upstairs in Olivia's house (I.v) that the action as such commences. The revels opens with Feste's exchange with Maria in which she attempts three times to insist on innocent interpretations of "well-hanged" and "points." But Feste is resolute in his ribaldry. Thus Olivia, momentarily voicing Malvolio's invariable position, calls Feste a "dry fool," and "dishonest"; Malvolio himself refers to him as a "barren rascal." From here on in it will be Feste who dances attendance on the revelry, singing, matching wit with Viola, and being paid by almost everyone for his presence. To a certain degree he remains outside the action, not participating in it because he represents its very nature; occasionally serving as a comic angel or messenger, he is nevertheless unmotivated by any appetite,

---

[3] See my own "Musica Mundana and Twelfth Night" in *Sound and Poetry,* ed. Northrop Frye (New York, 1957), pp. 55–82, for an extended treatment of the use of "speculative" and "practical" music in the play.

and is never sated of his fooling. His insights into the action are continuous, and his every remark is telling. "*Cucullus non facit monachum.* That's as much as to say I wear not motley in my brain." [4] Indeed, he does not, but more important is the fact that his robe and beard are not to make him a *real* priest later on. And neither he as Sir Thopas, nor Olivia as a "cloistress," nor Malvolio in his black suit or travestied virtue, nor the transvestite Viola is what he appears to be. No one will be revealed in his true dress until he has doffed his mask of feasting. And although neither Feste nor Malvolio will change in this respect, it is for completely opposite reasons that they will not do so.

Every character in the play, however, is granted some degree of insight into the nature of the others. It is almost as if everyone were masked with the black side of his vizard turned inwards; he sees more clearly past the *persona* of another than he can past his own. Valentine, for the Duke, comments on Olivia, as we have seen before. Even Malvolio is granted such an insight. Olivia asks him "What manner of man" Caesario is; unwittingly, his carping, over self-conscious and intellectualized answer cuts straight to the heart of Viola's disguise: "Not yet old enough for a man, nor young enough for a boy, as a squash is before 'tis a peascod, or a codling when 'tis almost an apple. 'Tis with him in standing water, between boy and man. He is very well-favored and he speaks very shrewishly. One would think his mother's milk were scarce out of him" (I.v.165–171).

The puns on "cod" and "codling" insist on being heard here, and as with the inadvertently delivered obscenity about Olivia's "great P's" and their source in the letter scene, Malvolio does not know what he is saying. The point is that Malvolio asserts, for an audience that knows the real facts, that Viola can scarcely be a male creature.

A more significant case of this hide-and-seek is Olivia's retort to Malvolio in the same scene: "O you are sick of self-love, Malvolio, and taste with a distempered appetite"; it provides the key to his physiological-moral nature. "Sick of self-love" means "sick with a moral infection called self-love," but it can also mean "already surfeited, or fed up with your own ego as an object of appetite." Malvolio's "distempered appetite" results from the fact that he alone is not possessed of a craving directed outward, towards some object on which it can surfeit and die; he alone cannot morally benefit from a period of self-indulgence. Actually this distemper manifests itself in terms of transitory desires on his part for status and for virtue, but these desires consume him in their fruitlessness; he is aware of the nature of neither of them. This is a brilliant analysis of the character of a melancholic, and Shakespeare's association of the melancholy, puritanic, and status-seeking characters in Malvolio throws considerable light on all of

---

[4] Cf. *Measure for Measure* (V.i.263), where Lucio refers in the identical words to the Duke disguised as Friar Lodowick.

them. The moral nature of the plot of *Twelfth Night* can be easily approached through the character of Malvolio, and this, I think, is what Lamb and his followers missed completely in their egalitarian sympathy for his being no "more than steward." For Malvolio's attachment to self-advancement is not being either aristocratically ridiculed or praised as an example of righteous bourgeois opposition to medieval hierarchies. In the context of the play's moral physiology, his disease is shown forth as a case of indigestion due to his self-love, the result of a perverted, rather than an excessive appetite.[5] In the world of feasting, the values of the commercial society outside the walls of the party go topsy-turvey: Feste is given money for making verbal fools of the donors thereof; everyone's desire is fulfilled in an unexpected way; and revellers are shown to rise through realms of unreality, disguise, and luxurious self-deception. We are seduced, by the revelling, away from seeing the malice in the plot to undo Malvolio. But whatever malice there is remains peculiarly just. It is only Malvolio who bears any ill will, and only he upon whom ill will can appear to be directed. He makes for himself a hell of the worldly heaven of festivity, and when Toby and Maria put him into darkness, into a counterfeit hell, they are merely representing in play a condition that he has already achieved.

The plot against Malvolio, then, is no more than an attempt to let him surfeit on himself, to present him with those self-centered, "time-pleasing" objects upon which his appetite is fixed. In essence, he is led to a feast in which his own vision of himself is spread before him, and commanded to eat it. The puritan concern with witchcraft and the satanic, and its associations of them with madness are carried to a logical extreme; and once Malvolio has been permitted to indulge in his self-interest by means of the letter episode, he is only treated as he would himself treat anyone whom he believed to be mad. His puritanism is mocked by allusions to his praying made by Toby and Maria; a priest (and a false, dissembling one at that, the answer to a puritan's prayer) is sent to him; and the implications of the darkness are eventually fulfilled as his prison becomes his hell.

It is interesting to notice how carefully Shakespeare analyzed another characteristic of the melancholic in his treatment of Malvolio. L. C. Knights has suggested[6] that the vogue of melancholy at the turn of the seventeenth century was occasioned to some degree by the actual presence in England of a large number of "*intellectuels en chômage*" (in Denis de Rougement's words), unemployed, university-trained men whose humanistic education had not fitted them for any suitable role in society. Malvolio is no patent and transparent uni-

---

[5] And Leslie Hotson has pointed out that his yellow stockings, as he later appears in them, are the true color of the Narcissus, as well as of the craven. See *The First Night of Twelfth Night* (London, 1954), p. 98 f.

[6] *Drama and Society in the Age of Jonson* (Manchester, 1936), pp. 315–332.

versity intellectual (like Holofernes, for example). He contrives, however, to over-rationalize his point (where the Duke will over-sentimentalize it) on almost every occasion. Even his first introduction of Viola, as has been seen before, is archly over-reasoned. His venture into exegesis of a text is almost telling.

It is not merely self-interest, I think, that colors the scrutiny of Maria's letter. His reading is indeed a close one: he observes that, after the first snatch of doggerel, "The numbers altered." But Malvolio is incapable of playing the party-game and guessing the riddle. Of "M,O,A,I doth sway my life," he can only say "And yet to crush this a little it would bow to me, for every one of these letters are in my name." He even avoids the reading that should, by all rights, appeal to him: Leslie Hotson has suggested that "M,O,A,I" probably stands for *Mare, Orbis, Aer,* and *Ignis,* the four elements to which Malvolio so often refers. Malvolio himself fails as a critic, following a "cold scent" that, as Fabian indicates, is "as rank as a fox" for him in that it tantalizes his ambition.

But he continues to aspire to scholarship. In order to let his tongue tang with arguments of state, he intends to "read politic authors." His intrusion on the scene of Toby's and Andrew's merry-making involves a most significant remark: "Is there no respect of persons, time, or place in you?", he asks. In other words, "Do you not observe even the dramatic unities in your revelling? Can you not apply even the values that govern things as frivolous as plays to your lives?" Coming from Malvolio, the ethical theorist, the remark feels very different from the remark made to Sir Toby by Maria, the practical moralist: "Aye, but you must confine yourself within the modest levels of order." Maria, presiding over the festivities, would keep things from getting out of hand. It is not only the spirit in which Malvolio's comment is uttered that accounts for this difference, however. I think that one of the implications is quite clearly the fact that Jonson's ordered, would-be-classic, but static and didactic comedy would disapprove of *Twelfth Night* as a moral play, and mistake its intention for a purely frivolous one.

The prank played on Malvolio is not merely an "interwoven" second story, but a fully developed double-plot. Like the Belmont episodes in *The Merchant of Venice,* it is a condensed representation of the action of the entire play. In *Twelfth Night,* however, it operates in reverse, to show the other side of the coin, as it were. For Malvolio there can be no fulfillment in "one self king." His story effectively and ironically underlines the progress towards this fulfillment in everybody else, and helps to delineate the limitations of the moral domain of the whole play. In contrast to Feste, who appears in the action at times as an abstracted spirit of revelry, Malvolio is a model of the sinner.

The whole play abounds in such contrasts and parallels of character, and the players form and regroup continually with respect to these, much in the manner of changing figurations in a suite of *branles*. Viola herself indulges in the festivities in a most delicate and (literally) charming way. She is almost too good a musician, too effective an Orpheus: "Heaven forbid my outside have not charmed her," she complains after her first encounter with Olivia. But as soon as she realizes that she is part of the game, she commits herself to it with redoubled force. If her "outside" is directed toward Olivia, her real identity and her own will are concentrated even more strongly on Orsino. In the most ironic of the love scenes she all but supplants Olivia in the Duke's affections. Orsino, glutting himself on his own version of romantic love, allows himself to make the most extravagant and self-deceptive statements about it:

> Come hither, boy. If ever thou shalt love,
> In the sweet pangs of it remember me;
> For such as I am all true lovers are,
> Unstaid and skittish in all motions else
> Save in the constant image of the creature
> That is beloved.
>
> (II.iv.15–20)

This skittishness, beneath the mask of the ravenous and constant bear, is obvious to Feste at least: "Now, the melancholy god protect thee, and the tailor make thy doublet of changeable taffeta, for thy mind is a very opal. I would have men of such constancy put to sea, that their business might be everything and their intent everywhere; for that's it that always makes a good voyage of nothing." (II.iv.75–80)

Orsino also gives us a curious version of the physiology of the passions on which the plot is based; it is only relatively accurate, of course, for he will be the last of the revellers to feel stuffed, to push away from him his heaping dish.

> There is no woman's sides
> Can bide the beating of so strong a passion
> As love doth give my heart, no woman's heart
> So big to hold so much. They lack retention.
> Alas, their love may be called appetite—
> No motion of the liver, but the palate—
> They suffer surfeit, cloyment and revolt.
> But mine is all as hungry as the sea
> And can digest as much.
>
> (II.iv.96–104)

Viola has been giving him her "inside" throughout the scene, and were he not still ravenous for Olivia's love he could see her for what she is: a woman with a constancy in love (for himself and her brother) that he can only imagine himself to possess. She is indeed an Allegory of Patience on some baroque tomb at this point. She is ironically distinguished from Olivia in that her "smiling at grief" is a disguising "outside" for her real sorrow, whereas Olivia's is a real self-indulgent pleasure taken at a grief outworn. It is as if Olivia had misread Scripture and taken the letter of "Blessed are they that mourn" for the spirit of it. Her grief is purely ceremonial.

The "lighter people," too, are engaged in carrying out the action in their own way, and they have more business in the play than merely to make a gull of Malvolio. Toby's huge stomach for food and drink parallels the Duke's ravenous capacity for sentiment. The drinking scene is in one sense the heart of the play. It starts out by declaring itself in no uncertain terms. "Does not our life consist of the four elements?" catechizes Sir Toby. "Faith, so they say," replies Andrew, "but I think it rather consists of eating and drinking." No one but Feste, perhaps, really knows the extent to which this is true, for Andrew is actually saying "We are not merely comic types, mind you, being manipulated by a dramatist of the humours. The essence of our lives lies in a movement from hunger to satiety that we share with all of nature."

When Toby and Andrew cry out for a love song, Feste obliges them, not with the raucous bawdy thing that one would expect, but instead, with a direct appeal to their actual hostess, Olivia. This is all the more remarkable in that it is made on behalf of everyone in the play. "O Mistress Mine" undercuts the Duke's overwhelming but ineffectual mouthings, Viola's effective but necessarily misdirected charming, and, of course, Aguecheek's absolute incompetence as a suitor. The argument is couched in purely naturalistic terms: "This feast will have to end, and so will all of our lives. You are not getting younger ('sweet and twenty' is the contemporaneous equivalent of 'sweet and thirty,' at least). Give up this inconstant roaming; your little game had better end in your marriage, anyway." The true love "that can sing both high and low" is Viola-Sebastian, the master-mistress of Orsino's and Olivia's passion. (Sebastian has just been introduced in the previous scene, and there are overtones here of his being invoked as Olivia's husband.) Sebastian has, aside from a certain decorative but benign courtly manner, no real identity apart from Viola. He is the fulfillment of her longing (for she has thought him dead) and the transformation into reality of the part she is playing in the *ludus amoris*. The prognostication is borne out by Sebastian's own remark: "You are betrothed both to a man and maid." He is himself characterized by an elegance hardly virile; and, finally, we must keep in mind the fact that Viola was played by a boy actor to begin with, and that Shakespeare's audience seemed to be always ready for an intricate irony of this kind.

But if Viola and Sebastian are really the same, "One face, one voice, one habit, and two persons, A natural perspective that is and is not," there is an interesting parallel between Viola and Aguecheek as well. Both are suitors for Olivia's hand: Andrew, ineffectively, for himself; Viola for Orsino, and (effectively) for Sebastian. Their confrontation in the arranged duel is all the more ironic in that Andrew is an effective pawn in Toby's game (Toby is swindling him), whereas Viola is an ineffective one in the Duke's (she is swindling him of Olivia's love).

Feste's other songs differ radically from "O Mistress Mine." He sings for the Duke a kind of languorous ayre, similar to so many that one finds in the songbooks.[7] It is aimed at Orsino in the very extravagance of its complaint. It is his own song, really, if we imagine him suddenly dying of love, being just as ceremoniously elaborate in his funeral instructions as he has been in his suit of Olivia. And Feste's bit of handy-dandy to Malvolio in his prison is a rough-and-tumble sort of thing, intended to suggest in its measures a scrap from a Morality, plainly invoking Malvolio in darkness as a devil in hell. Feste shows himself throughout the play to be a master of every convention of fooling.

If Feste's purpose is to serve as a symbol of the revels, however, he must also take a clear and necessary part in the all-important conclusion. *Twelfth Night* itself, the feast of the Epiphany, celebrates the discovery of the "True King" in the manger by the Wise Men. "Those wits," says Feste in Act I, Scene v, "that think they have thee [wit] do very oft prove fools, and I that am sure I lack thee may pass for a wise man." And so it is that under his influence the true Caesario, the "one self king," is revealed.[8] The whole of Act V might be taken, in connection with "the plot" in a trivial sense, to be the other *epiphany*, the perception that follows the *anagnorisis* or discovery of classic dramaturgy. But we have been dealing with the Action of *Twelfth Night* as representing the killing off of excessive appetite through indulgence of it, leading to the rebirth of the unencumbered self. The long final scene, then, serves to show forth the Caesario-King, and to unmask, discover, and reveal the fulfilled selves in the major characters.

The appearance of the priest (a real one, this time) serves more than the simple purpose of proving the existence of a marriage between Olivia and "Caesario." It is a simple but firm intrusion into the world of the play of a way of life that has remained outside of it so far. The straightforward solemnity of the priest's rhetoric is also something new; suggestions of its undivided purpose have appeared before only in Antonio's speeches. The priest declares that Olivia and her husband have been properly married:

> And all the ceremony of this compact
> Sealed in my function, by my testimony.
> Since when, my watch hath told me, toward my grave
> I have travelled but two hours.
>
> (V.i.163–166)

---

[7] The Rev. E. H. Fellowes, in *English Madrigal Verse* (Oxford, 1929), lists four different ayres with the conventional opening phrase, "Come away."

[8] For my interpretation of the last act I am indebted to Professor Roy W. Battenhouse's suggestions.

It is possible that the original performances had actually taken about two hours to reach this point. At any rate, the sombre acknowledgment of the passage of time in a real world is there. Antonio has prepared the way earlier in the scene; his straightforward confusion is that of the unwitting intruder in a masquerade who has been accused of mistaking the identities of two of the masquers.

That the surfeiting has gradually begun to occur, however, has become evident earlier. In the prison scene, Sir Toby has already begun to tire: "I would we were well rid of this knavery." He gives as his excuse for this the fact that he is already in enough trouble with Olivia, but such as this has not deterred him in the past. And, in the last scene, very drunk as he must be, he replies to Orsino's inquiry as to his condition that he hates the surgeon, "a drunken rogue." Self-knowledge has touched Sir Toby. He could not have said this earlier.

As the scene plays itself out, Malvolio alone is left unaccounted for. There is no accounting for him here, though; he remains a bad taste in the mouth. "Alas poor fool," says Olivia, "How have they baffled thee!" And thus, in Feste's words, "the whirligig of time brings in his revenges." Malvolio has become the fool, the "barren rascal." He leaves in a frenzy, to "be revenged," he shouts, "on the whole pack of you." He departs from the world of this play to resume a role in another, perhaps. His reincarnation might be as Middleton's De Flores, rather than even Jaques. His business has never been with the feasting to begin with, and now that it is over, and the revellers normalized, he is revealed as the true madman. He is "The Madly-Used Malvolio" to the additional degree that his own uses have been madness.

For Orsino and Viola the end has also arrived. She will be "Orsino's mistress and his fancy's queen." He has been surfeited of his misdirected voracity; the rich golden shaft, in his own words, "hath killed the flock of all affections else" that live in him. "Liver, brain and heart" are indeed all supplied; for both Olivia and himself, there has been fulfillment in "one self king." And, lest there be no mistake, each is to be married to a Caesario or king. Again, "Liver, brain and heart" seems to encompass everybody: Toby and Maria are married, Aguecheek chastened, etc.

At the end of the scene, all exit. Only Feste, the pure fact of feasting, remains. His final song is a summation of the play in many ways at once. Its formal structure seems to be a kind of quick rehearsal of the Ages of Man. In youth, "A foolish thing was but a toy": the fool's bauble, emblematic of both his *membrum virile* and his trickery, is a trivial fancy. But in "man's estate," the bauble represents a threat of knavery and thievery to respectable society, who shuts its owner out of doors. The "swaggering" and incessant drunkenness of the following strophes bring Man into prime and dotage, respectively. Lechery, trickery, dissembling, and drunkenness, inevitable and desperate in mundane existence, however, are just those activities which, mingled together in a world of feasting, serve to purge Man of the desire for them. The wind and the rain accompany him throughout his life, keeping him indoors with "dreams and imaginations" as a boy, pounding and drenching him unmercifully, when he is locked out of doors, remaining eternal and inevitable throughout his pride in desiring to perpetuate himself. The wind and the rain are the most desperate of elements, that pound the walls and batter the roof of the warm house that shuts them out, while, inside it, the revels are in progress. Only after the party is ended can Man face them without desperation.

It is the metaphor of the rain that lasts longest, though, and it recapitulates the images of water, elements and humours that have pervaded the entire play. Feste himself, who tires of nothing, addresses Viola: "Who you are and what you would are out of my welkin—I might say 'element' but the word is overworn." He adroitly comments on Malvolio's line "Go to; I am not of your element" by substituting a Saxon word for a Latin one. The additional association of the four elements with the humours cannot be overlooked. It is only Malvolio, of course, who uses the word "humour" with any seriousness: "And then to have the humour of State," he muses, as he imagines himself "Count Malvolio." Humours are also waters, however. And *waters,* or fluids of all kinds, are continually being forced on our attention. Wine, tears, seawater, even urine, are in evidence from the first scene on, and they are always being metaphorically identified with one another. They are all fluids, bathing the world of the play in possibilities for change as the humours do the body. Feste's answer to Maria in the prison scene has puzzled many editors; if we realize, however, that Feste is probably hysterically laughing at what he has just been up to, "Nay, I'm for all waters" may have the additional meaning that he is on the verge of losing control of himself. He is "for all waters" primarily in that he represents the fluidity of revelling celebration. And finally, when all is done, "The rain it raineth every day," and Feste reverts to gnomic utterance in a full and final seriousness. Water is rain that falls to us from Heaven. The world goes on. Our revels now are ended, but the actors solidify into humanity, in this case. "But that's all one, our play is done / And we'll strive to please you every day."

III

In this interpretation of *Twelfth Night,* I have in no sense meant to infer that Malvolio is to be identified as Ben Jonson, or that the play functioned in any systematic way in the war of the theatres. There are, of course, a number of propitious coincidences: Marston's *What You Will,* coming some six or seven years after *Twelfth Night,* devotes much effort to lampooning Jonson. What could have been meant by the title, however, as well as Shakespeare's real intention in his subtitle, remains obscure. Perhaps they both remain as the first part of some forgotten proverb to the effect that what you will (want) may come to you in an unexpected form. Perhaps they are both merely throwaway comments to the effect that the play is really "what you may call it." (It has been frequently suggested that it is a translation of Rabelais' "*Fay ce que vouldras.*") Then there is the dig, in *Every Man Out of His Humour,* at a comedy with a romantic (Italianate) plot more than vaguely resembling that of *Twelfth Night. Every Man Out* has been dated in 1599, but the idea that Shakespeare may have chosen just such a "romantic" story with which to oppose Jonson's comic theories is not inconceivable.

My point, however, is that *Twelfth Night* is opposed by its very nature to the kind of comedy that Jonson was not only writing, but advocating at the time; that is a moral comedy, representing human experience in terms of a fully dramatized metaphor rather than a static emblematic correspondence; and, finally, that it operates to refute the moral validity of comedy of humours in its insistence on the active metaphor of surfeiting the appetite, upon which the whole plot is constructed. It is only romantic in that it shares, with *As You Like It* (and with *Love's Labour's Lost,* too, for that matter), a hint of the world of transformation of the last plays. Its moral vision is as intense as that of the problem comedies.

IV

THE HISTORY PLAYS

THE SHAKESPEAREAN CONCEPTION OF HISTORY

The Henriad: Shakespeare's Major History Plays

Alvin B. Kernan

Taken together, Shakespeare's four major history plays, *Richard II*, *1 Henry IV*, *2 Henry IV*, and *Henry V* constitute an epic, *The Henriad*. Obviously these four plays are not an epic in the usual sense—there is no evidence that Shakespeare planned them as a unit—but they do have remarkable coherence and they possess that quality which in our time we take to be the chief characteristic of epic: a large-scale, heroic action, involving many men and many activities, tracing the movement of a nation or people through violent change from one condition to another. In *The Iliad* that action involves the wrath of Achilles and the misfortunes which it brought to the Achaeans before Troy. In *The Aeneid* the action is the transferal of the Empire of Troy to Latium. And in *Paradise Lost* the action is man's first disobedience and the fruit of that forbidden tree.

In *The Henriad*, the action is the passage from the England of Richard II to the England of Henry V. This dynastic shift serves as the supporting framework for a great many cultural and psychological transitions which run parallel to the main action, giving it body and meaning. In historical terms the movement from the world of Richard II to that of Henry V is the passage from the Middle Ages to the

---

First published in a shorter form in *The Yale Review*, Vol. LVIV, No. 1 (Fall, 1969).

Renaissance and the modern world. In political and social terms it is a movement from feudalism and hierarchy to the national state and individualism. In psychological terms it is a passage from a situation in which man knows with certainty who he is to an existential condition in which any identity is only a temporary role. In spatial and temporal terms it is a movement from a closed world to an infinite universe. In mythical terms the passage is from a garden world to a fallen world. In the most summary terms it is a movement from ceremony and ritual to history:

> The Renaissance was a moment when educated men were modifying a ceremonial conception of human life to create a historical conception. The ceremonial view, which assumed that names and meanings are fixed and final, expressed experience as pageant and ritual—pageant where the right names could march in proper order, or ritual where names could be changed in the right, the proper way. The historical view expresses life as drama. People in drama are not identical with their names, for they gain and lose their names, their status and meaning—and not by settled ritual: the gaining and losing of names, of meaning, is beyond the control of any set ritual sequence. . . . The people in [Shakespeare's] plays try to organize their lives by pageant and ritual, but the plays are dramatic precisely because the effort fails.[1]

It is by means of ceremony and ritual that the old kingdom is presented in the beginning of *The Henriad. Richard II* opens on a scene in which two furious peers, Mowbray and Hereford, confront and accuse one another of treason before their legitimate king. The place of judgment is the court itself, with all its ceremonial forms and symbols: crowns, trumpets, thrones, ranked retainers, robes of state and heraldic arms. This court, in its traditional setting with its ancient emblems and established procedures, repeats the pattern of innumerable former assemblies convoked for the same purpose, to absorb and reorder once again the disorderly elements in man and society.

When this ritual attempt fails, an even more solemn ritual is ordered, trial by combat. The ceremonial elements in I.iii are heavily emphasized: the combatant knights enter in the proper manner and take their assigned places in the lists. They make the expected speeches, and the marshal of the lists puts the formulaic questions to them.

> *The trumpets sound. Enter* BOLINGBROKE, DUKE OF HEREFORD, *appellant, in armour, and a* HERALD.
> KING RICHARD Marshal, ask yonder knight in arms,
> Both who he is and why he cometh hither
> Thus plated in habiliments of war;
> And formally, according to our law,

---

[1] C. L. Barber, *Shakespeare's Festive Comedy: A Study of Dramatic Form and Its Relation to Social Custom* (Princeton: Princeton University Press, 1959), p. 193.

Depose him in the justice of his cause.
MARSHAL What is thy name? and wherefore com'st thou hither
Before King Richard in his royal lists?
Against whom comest thou? and what's thy quarrel?
Speak like a true knight, so defend thee heaven!
BOLINGBROKE Harry of Hereford, Lancaster, and Derby,
Am I; who ready here do stand in arms
To prove, by God's grace and my body's valour,
In lists on Thomas Mowbray, Duke of Norfolk,
That he is a traitor, foul and dangerous,
To God of heaven, King Richard, and to me.
And as I truly fight, defend me heaven!
(*Richard II,* I.iii.26–41)

Here, and throughout the early acts of the play, traditional ways of acting and traditional values—the law, the sanctity of a knight's oath, established duty to God and king—reflected in the formulaic phrases, the conventional terms, and the orderly rhythms, control the violent passions, fury, fear, outrage, hatred, the lust for power, at work in Richard's England. The individual is submerged within the role imposed upon him by prescribed ways of thinking, acting, and speaking.

But, even as we admire, this old world is breaking up. The patriarchs of England—the seven sons of Edward II—are, like the twelve sons of Jacob, passing from the land, and with them their world passes. The sense of an ancient, more perfect world, fading from existence into memory is focused in John of Gaunt's comparison of England, as it was only yesterday, to another Eden:

This royal throne of kings, this scept'red isle,
This earth of majesty, this seat of Mars,
This other Eden, demi-paradise,
This fortress built by Nature for herself
Against infection and the hand of war,
This happy breed of men, this little world,
This precious stone set in the silver sea,
Which serves it in the office of a wall,
Or as a moat defensive to a house,
Against the envy of less happier lands;
This blessed plot, this earth, this realm, this England . . . .
(*Richard II,* II.i.40–50)

By III.iv when the "sea-walled garden" appears again, presided over by a gardener in "old Adam's likeness," it is full of weeds, the flowers choked, the trees unpruned, the hedges in ruin, the herbs eaten by caterpillars, and the great tree in its center dead.

What is passing in the course of *Richard II* is innocence, a sense of living in a golden world, and no one is more innocent than Richard himself. When Bolingbroke begins his rebellion, Richard confidently expects that God himself will send down soldiers to defend him and blast the usurper. The order of nature and the laws of men, he believes, guarantee his kingship:

> Not all the water in the rough rude sea
> Can wash the balm off from an anointed king;
> The breath of worldly men cannot depose
> The deputy elected by the Lord.
> For every man that Bolingbroke hath press'd
> To lift shrewd steel against our golden crown,
> God for his Richard hath in heavenly pay
> A glorious angel. Then, if angels fight,
> Weak men must fall; for heaven still guards the right.
> (*Richard II,* III.ii.54–62)

Richard, here and elsewhere in the play, manifests his belief in the conservative world view which has been variously called "The Great Chain of Being," "The Elizabethan World Picture," and "The Tudor Political Myth." This world view imaged the whole of creation, from God down to the meanest pebble, as being organized hierarchically, as a series of rungs in a ladder or links in a chain. Each category in turn mirrored the systematic arrangement of the whole, and its parts were distributed in descending order of authority, responsibility, and power. To act "naturally," to live in accordance with things as they are, was to accept your assigned place in society, controlled justly by the powers above and controlling justly those below entrusted to your care and authority. When man acted in a disorderly fashion, creating a disturbance within his own "little world" or microcosm, "Nature" quickly acted to right itself: all the other categories of being trembled sympathetically, the ripples spread through all creation, and the great powers began to react to restore order. This world view saw in all areas of life—religion, physics, psychology, government, zoology, and all social organizations—a reflection of the human dream of order, stability, harmony, coherence, and community. Life ideally lived was a dance or music.

Richard takes this great imaginative projection of human values for absolute fact, mistakes metaphor for science, and so believes that God will directly intervene in the coming battle and that the king's appearance in England will cause rebellion to disappear just as the rising of the sun (the "king" of the cosmos) banishes night and darkness. Like a child, he fails to distinguish human desire from actuality and therefore fails to understand that he cannot trust to "Nature" to maintain him as a king, simply because he *is* king. From the outset of the play powerful political and personal forces are at work undermining the social system, making a mockery of ritual and ceremony. Mowbray has been involved in graft and assassination for political purposes. Henry Hereford has been courting popularity with the common people, and he accuses Mowbray of treason knowing that he is innocent. His motive may be to embarrass Richard, who is himself deeply implicated in the murder of his uncle, Duke of Gloucester, the crime of which Mowbray is accused. Richard is violently jealous and suspicious of his cousin Hereford and uses the trial as an occasion for banishing him under the pretense of being merciful. Pressed by the perpetual need for money, Richard sells his right to gather taxes to profiteers. He neglects affairs of state to spend his time reveling with male favorites. Each of these acts indirectly undermines the order which Richard thinks immutable, and when upon John of Gaunt's death he seizes the banished Hereford's lands, he strikes a direct blow, as the Duke of York points out, against the great law of orderly succession on which his kingship rests:

> Take Hereford's rights away, and take from Time
> His charters and his customary rights;
> Let not to-morrow then ensue to-day;
> Be not thyself—for how art thou a king
> But by fair sequence and succession?
> (*Richard II,* II.i.95–99)

In general, Richard treats his kingdom and subjects in an arbitrary manner, and the play realizes his implication in his own destruction in the scene in which he uncrowns himself, names Bolingbroke his successor, and confesses the sins which brought him down. This is, of course, good political strategy for Bolingbroke, who, like modern dictators, realizes that nothing is so valuable to an uneasy ruler as his victim's public confession and admission of the justice of punishment. But the scene has another function. By uncrowning himself visibly, Richard is repeating and making manifest what he did earlier in the play when he worked so busily and blindly to destroy the values and rituals on which his kingship rested.

In *Paradise Lost* the results of the fall, Adam and Eve's disobedience to God, are immediate and spectacular: the earth tilts and the seasons become intemperate, the animals become vicious and prey on one another and on man, and man himself knows fear, anger, lust, and shame. What Milton presents on the scale of the universe, Shakespeare presents on the scale of the kingdom and the individual. Most immediately, Richard's disorders release a variety of other disorders on all levels of life. Richard having rebelled against the order which made and kept him king, Henry Bolingbroke immediately rebels against Richard. By the end of the play there is already another group of plotters planning to overthrow Henry. Throughout the three succeeding plays political scheming, plotting, raids on the commonwealth, and civil wars never cease. As one group of rebels dies, another group is already forming to take its place, each more desperate and violent than the last. Henry IV lives out his days facing one revolt after another, and even Henry V, whose reign in some ways is a restoration of political order, is still forced to deal with treasons which are "like / Another fall of man" (*Henry V,* II.ii.141–42).

As the old political order weakens, simple men like the good old Duke of York become confused and inept. His duty is, he knows, to his king; but who is his king? what to do if that duty now conflicts with other primary duties? The confusion in his mind is reflected in the confusion in his family. His son, the Duke of Aumerle, intrigues against the new king, and the Duchess of York tells her husband that his primary duty lies not to the King but to his own son. But the anguished York goes to the King to accuse his son of treason. This civil war within the family eventuates in an absurd scene in which the King hears York ask him to execute his son, while the Duchess of York asks the King for mercy and pleads against her own husband. The most serious matters have become a kind of mad joke. The disorder in York's family expands to the family of Henry, and by the end of the play we learn that Hal, the Prince of Wales, is already roistering in a tavern, defying his father, and using his power to break the law with impunity.

As the old order breaks up, a profound psychological confusion parallels the political confusion. In that Edenic world which Gaunt described and Richard destroyed, every man knew who he was. His religion, his family, his position in society, his assigned place in processions large and small, his coat of arms, his traditional duties, and even his clothing, which was then prescribed by sumptuary laws, told him who he was and what he should do and even gave him the formal language in which to express this socially-assigned self. But once, under the pressures of political necessity and personal desires, the old system is destroyed, the old identities go with it. Man then finds himself in the situation which Richard acts out in IV.i, the deposition scene. Richard is speaking, and when Northumberland attempts to break in with the exclamation "My lord," he responds with words which reveal how thoroughly shattered is his sense of the power of his name and the immutability of his identity as Richard Plantagenet, King of England:

> No lord of thine, thou haught insulting man,
> Nor no man's lord; I have no name, no title—
> No, not that name was given me at the font—
> But 'tis usurp'd. Alack the heavy day,
> That I have worn so many winters out,
> And know not now what name to call myself!
> (*Richard II,* IV.i.254–59)

Like the great actor he is, Richard cannot pass the opportunity to demonstrate visually the lesson he has learned. He calls for a looking glass, and holding it before his face he muses:

> No deeper wrinkles yet? Hath sorrow struck
> So many blows upon this face of mine
> And made no deeper wounds? O flatt'ring glass,

Like to my followers in prosperity,
Thou dost beguile me! Was this face the face
That every day under his household roof
Did keep ten thousand men? Was this the face
That like the sun did make beholders wink?
Is this the face which fac'd so many follies,
That was at last out-fac'd by Bolingbroke?
A brittle glory shineth in this face;
As brittle as the glory is the face;
[*He breaks the mirror.*]
(*Richard II,* IV.i.277–88)

Having already discovered that one's name can change rapidly in the world, Richard now becomes self-conscious, aware that the unchanged face he views in the glass squares with neither his greatly changed political condition nor his equally changed inner sense of himself.

Richard is not the first man in this play to discover that he no longer knows who he is. He has already forced the question of identity on Bolingbroke by banishing him from England and robbing him of his succession as Duke of Lancaster. Bolingbroke—whose names change rapidly: Hereford, Bolingbroke, Lancaster, and Henry IV—has understood the lesson well. Speaking to Bushy and Green, two of Richard's favorites, the man who had once confidently answered the question "What is thy name?" with the proud words "Harry of Hereford, Lancaster, and Derby / Am I," now tells the bitterness of banishment and the pain that comes from loss of those possessions and symbols which had heretofore guaranteed identity:

Myself—a prince by fortune of my birth,
Near to the King in blood, and near in love
Till you did make him misinterpret me—
Have stoop'd my neck under your injuries
And sigh'd my English breath in foreign clouds,
Eating the bitter bread of banishment,
Whilst you have fed upon my signories,
Dispark'd my parks and fell'd my forest woods,
From my own windows torn my household coat,
Raz'd out my imprese, leaving me no sign
Save men's opinions and my living blood
To show the world I am a gentleman.
(*Richard II,* III.i.16–27)

Man has not merely lost his true identity for a time; he has, once he abandoned the old hierarchies and rituals, broken into a strange, new existence where he is free to slide back and forth along the vast scale of being, coming to rest momentarily at various points, but never knowing for certain just who and what he is. John of Gaunt's awkward punning on his name as he lies dying suggests the pervasiveness of the feeling that names and the identities they carry are no longer real and permanent but only the roles of the moment. This fluctuation in identity is the basic rhythm of the play, and we feel it everywhere, in Richard's ever-changing moods, in Bolingbroke's rising fortunes and changing names, in Richard's decline from King of England to his last appearance on stage, a body borne in by his murderer. The pattern of up-down, of restless change in the self, appears in its most complete form in the great final speech Richard gives, sitting in the dungeon of Pomfret Castle, about to die, and trying desperately to understand himself and this strange world into which he has fallen. Richard began as a great and secure king, seated on a throne, sure of himself, surrounded by pomp, confirmed by ceremony, looking out over a world of light where everything in the universe was open and ordered. At the end of the play he is the isolated individual, solitary, sitting in a small circle of light, surrounded by darkness and by a flinty prison wall, uncertain of any reality or truth. Isolated, like some hero of Kafka, in a mysterious and a containing world, Richard takes the confusing and conflicting evidence which his mind offers him and attempts, by means of reason and the poetic power to construct analogies, to "hammer it out," to give it shape and form, to achieve some new coherence. The results are not comforting. As hard as he hammers, he can discover only endless mutability in the life of man and endless restlessness in his soul. All evidence is now ambiguous: Where the Bible promises innocence an easy salvation in one passage, "come little ones," turn the page and it speaks in tragic tones of the passage to the Kingdom of Heaven being as difficult as a camel's threading the eye of a needle. Man's powers at one moment seem infinite and he feels that he can "tear a passage through the flinty ribs / Of this hard world," but at the next moment he is the most helpless of creatures and can only comfort himself that many others have endured like misery. Fate forces new identities on him, but even in his own mind man can find no stability, and reality becomes theatrical, a playing of many roles in a constantly changing play:

> Thus play I in one person many people,
> And none contented. Sometimes am I king;
> Then treasons make me wish myself a beggar,
> And so I am. Then crushing penury
> Persuades me I was better when a king;
> Then am I king'd again; and by and by
> Think that I am unking'd by Bolingbroke,
> And straight am nothing. But whate'er I be,
> Nor I, nor any man that but man is,
> With nothing shall be pleas'd till he be eas'd
> With being nothing.
>
> (*Richard II,* V.v.31–41)

To accommodate the newly perceived paradoxical, shifting reality Richard changes from the formal, conventional style of the beginning of the play to a metaphysical style capable of handling irony and a reality in which the parts no longer mesh, capable of carrying deep, intense agitation and the passionate effort of thought.

The world continues to speak ambiguously to Richard in the form of two visitors. The first is a poor groom from his stables who, having seen the King before only from a distance, now risks his life to come to speak of sympathy and duty which alters not when it alteration finds. The second visitor is the murderer Exton, who has come to kill Richard in hopes of reward from Henry. Richard, having tried to define himself by means of poetry and failed, now takes the way of drama, and acts. He seizes a sword from one of Exton's thugs and strikes two of them down before being killed himself. And so he defines himself in a dramatic or historic—not a philosophical—way. He has never solved the question whether he is king or beggar, never found the meaning he hoped to have; but he has stumbled through experience to quite a different answer. He, like the rest of men, has no stable identity certified by the order of things immutable. He is instead tragic man, whose identity fluctuates between hero and victim, king and corpse; whose values are not guaranteed by anything but his own willingness to die for them; whose life is a painful and continuing process of change. Richard traces the way that all other characters in this world must follow in their turn.

Looking back on the lost past, the men of Henry IV's England see the "fall" occurring at that fatal moment when Richard threw down his warder, the symbol of his office and his duty, to stop for political reasons the ritual trial by combat between Bolingbroke and Mowbray. In *Richard II* the effects of that act are focused in the person of Richard and his passage into tragic existence. In the two parts of *Henry IV*, however, the effects are exploded to create an entire dramatic world and the many various characters who inhabit it. Richard's internal disorders and conflicting values grow into the increasingly bitter political and social disorders of a world racked by rebellion, strife, ambition, self-seeking, squabbling, and desperate attempts to hold things together. Richard's growing fear and awareness of the inevitable movement of time into an unknown future expand into polarities: a complete rejection of time (Falstaff) on one hand, and on the other an obsession with the limited amount of time available to man, and the necessity of using it as completely and efficiently as possible, which leads ultimately to a fearful vision of infinity. Richard's loss of certainty and his increasing inability to reconcile the contrary evidence of his own feelings and experiences enlarge into the murky confusion of history, the world of rumor, suspicion, and half-truth, where men making decisions of the utmost importance to themselves and to their country never really know the necessary facts. There may even be no definite answer to such crucial questions as, "Is the King's planned crusade genuine piety or political strategy?" "Is Hal really a riotous youth or is he only pretending to be a wastrel?" "Did Mortimer treasonously surrender his army to Glendower, and does Henry refuse to ransom him because he is a traitor or because he has a legal claim to the throne?" The kind of suspicion raised on suspicion, on which men must risk their lives in this world where truth is impossible to come by, is perfectly conveyed in the Earl of Worcester's lines in which he sketches out the path of reasoning which leads him to rebellion: he helped the King, the King can never forget this and will always fear that his former friends will think themselves not fully rewarded, and therefore they must always fear the king who may fear them:

> For, bear ourselves as even as we can,
> The King will always think him in our debt,
> And think we think ourselves unsatisfied,
> Till he hath found a time to pay us home.
> (*1 Henry IV,* I.iii.285–88)

As Richard's identity crumbles, he begins with increasing frequency to use images of the theater, of acting and role-playing, to reflect the growing gap between appearance and reality, and the instability of character. In the later plays, the impulse to theatricality, the sense of life as play and man as actor breaks into the open in repeated images of the theater, in numerous brief plays-within-the-play, in the conception of character and action. Playing becomes not only an instrument of deceit—Prince John's pretense that he will pardon the rebels if they lay down their arms—but also a means to truth—Hal's parodies of Hotspur's excessive energy and violence. Men in the world of *Henry IV* no longer take their identities as settled but assume that life is a succession of roles, played with skill and style to achieve a desired end. Hal plays the part of the prodigal son and the wastrel in order to appear better when he is settled as king; the Protean Falstaff plays a succession of roles for pleasure and profit.

Richard's discovery that man is a creature of infinite possibilities ranging all the way from dust to god, beggar to king, is also projected in the Henry plays into the wide and varied cast of characters, each of whom seems to be not a whole man but a fragment, some singular power inherent in human nature isolated and carried to its extreme. "Homo," may be, as Gadshill says, "a common name to all men" (*1 Henry IV,* II.i.92–93), but the adjective which should follow is constantly questioned. Does man to realize his humanity properly seek power? pleasure? learning? love? order? glory? Is the truly human setting the place of pleasure and fellowship, the Boar's Head Tavern in Eastcheap? the council table in the palace at Westminster? the desperate battlefields far to the north and west along the Scottish and the Welsh marches? Glendower's castle where old songs of love are played and the vast mysteries of the universe are discussed? These are the principal symbolic places in the Henry plays, the places in which man now works out, in a sudden surge of freedom and released energy, his destiny and his nature. Each of these symbolic places has a resident deity, a genius of the place, whose speeches and actions provide the best understanding of its attitudes and values.

The Glendower world, which focuses the values of magic, science, poetry and love, remains strangely peripheral, as if, despite the high value Shakespeare elsewhere places on these powers, they were not of fundamental importance in the great conflict. There is perhaps even a disqualifying sensitivity here, a tendency to withdraw from the power struggle, for when Hotspur—who also finds love trivial—offends Glendower by laughing at his magic, the Welshman simply withdraws his support and is not heard of again.

Falstaff presides over the tavern world, and when first seen this latter-day Bacchus is waking from a nap on a bench. Sitting up, stretching, he asks the Prince, "What time of day is it, lad?" The Prince, who has a supreme sense of time, realizes that Falstaff is the one character in this play to whom time, the sequence of irrecoverable moments, is totally meaningless.

> PRINCE Thou art so fat-witted with drinking of old sack, and unbuttoning thee after supper, and sleeping upon benches after noon, that thou hast forgotten to demand that truly which thou wouldest truly know. What a devil hast thou to do with the time of the day? Unless hours were cups of sack, and minutes capons, and clocks the tongues of bawds, and dials the signs of leaping-houses, and the blessed sun himself a fair hot wench in flame-coloured taffeta, I see no reason why thou shouldst be so superfluous to demand the time of the day.
>
> (*1 Henry IV,* I.ii.2–11)

The old knight is enormously fat, a walking version of the roast beef of Old England, given over entirely to epicurean pleasures. He never pays his debts; he is a liar, a thief, a drunkard, the very energy of disorder and lawlessness. For him a true man follows the pleasures of the belly and the bed, avoiding pain and labor whenever possible. He takes what he wants without worrying about property rights or morality. Such abstracts as honor, truth, duty, and honesty, those hard, painful virtues which he is always being exhorted to practice, seem to him patently ridiculous and self-defeating, and he is an adept at sliding around and under such claims. When trapped in some obvious lie or charged with some gross weakness of the flesh, he will, without regard for the restraints of logic, gaily change the subject, take up another pose, or make some such comment as "all's one for that." He is a master at staying alive and comfortable in an extremely difficult, dangerous, and potentially painful world.

Viewed from a sternly moral direction, Falstaff is a vice, a demi-devil, a tempter, a mere caterpillar of the commonwealth. When viewed from a more tolerant perspective Falstaff is an amusing and cunning old rogue, but still an obvious, slow-witted glutton and braggart, a victim of his own appetites and a figure of fun. But Falstaff meets these challenges more than halfway by asking continually the eternal comic questions: "What is so important about a well-run state? Why all this strange passion for this 'grinning honor,' this order and honesty, which cost so much pain and suffering?" These questions are usually asked indirectly, by means of parody and wit, and the shrewdness of mind and the style of execution are exquisite at points. For example, when he is urging Hal to join the robbery at Gadshill, and Hal protests that the Prince of Wales cannot become a common thief, Falstaff remarks quickly, "Thou cam'st not of the blood royal, if thou darest not stand for ten shillings." On the face of it he seems merely to be punning on the meaning of "royal," a type of coin. But there is an edge to this remark, which Hal apparently misses, for it remembers that that royal blood of England achieved its present eminence by means of robbery, not a little robbery such as the thieves are planning on Gadshill, but a big robbery in which all of England was taken.

While Falstaff is efficient in use of the rapier thrust of wit, his most masterful attacks are delivered by means of parody. When Hal seems to have bested him in a wit-combat, Falstaff shifts ground and plays the misled youth, the penitent determined to return to the paths of righteousness:

> Thou hast done much harm upon me, Hal—God forgive thee for it! Before I knew thee, Hal, I knew nothing; and now am I, if a man should speak truly, little better than one of the wicked. I must give over this life, and I will give it over. By the Lord, an I do not I am a villain! I'll be damn'd for never a king's son in Christendom.
>
> (*1 Henry IV*, I.ii.87–95)

To his appreciative audience this is no more than another of the Monsieur Remorse's self-beguilements or posturings. Given over entirely to the life of the flesh, he can still fool himself and try to fool others into believing that he is about to repent and care for his soul. But several features of the speech—its style, its obvious exaggeration, and its sly suggestion that true wickedness comes from the palace, not the tavern—combine to create behind the lines an eye-twinkling self-consciousness which is aware at once of how ridiculous is this pretense and yet how good a game it is. The speech is then self-parody, but it goes further, for Falstaff is also acting out the ridiculous pretenses of the rest of the world to holiness. Behind each of his pretenses—the royal king, the brave captain, the innocent child, the loyal knight, the penitent sinner—stands Falstaff himself, the old Adam, fat, red-nosed, slothful, and lecherous, a living low-burlesque of the establishment.

Each of Falstaff's parodies contains both the pretense of virtue (the pose) and what he takes to be human reality (himself), and as the play progresses he stages ever more pointed demonstrations of the gap between appearance and reality. On the eve of the great battle at Shrewsbury, Sir John, acting as draftmaster, has allowed all the healthy and prosperous to buy out and collected instead the poor, the battered, and the inept to assemble a remarkable regiment, "slaves as ragged as Lazarus in the painted cloth where the glutton's dogs licked his sores." As he marches this strange rout toward the battle, he encounters Hal and Westmoreland, banners flying, armor shining, horses snorting, filled with confidence and chivalry. These brave knights are astounded at the sight of such ridiculous soldiers, and Hal exclaims: "I did never see such pitiful rascals." Falstaff's reply contains a grimly realistic view of war and the function of the common soldier:

> Tut, tut; good enough to toss; food for powder, food for powder; they'll fill a pit as well as better: tush, man, mortal men, mortal men.
>
> (*1 Henry IV,* IV.ii.63–65)

War's reality has been paraded before war's pretenses. Falstaff's view that since the soldier's function is to be blown to pieces and fill a ditch, one man will do as well as another is proven by the events of the battle, in which only three of his men survive, and they so badly wounded that the rest of their lives will be spent begging. Falstaff's most famous use of this parody technique is, of course, his catechism, in which he compares the abstraction, honor, with the reality, the body of the honorable but dead Blunt, and draws some very common-sense conclusions about the durability of honor and its ability to set a leg or take away the pain of a wound.

Falstaff, and the tavern world which he personifies, is a most dangerous antagonist to any moral point of view, to any set of abstractions such as honor, duty, and country. His questions, so pointedly put, so beautifully dramatized, about what honor means, what a king really is, and what a nation does, are never satisfactorily answered in the play. He is always acting out some hilarious and penetrating truth about the establishment, and each time he asserts such a truth, he strengthens his own case for leading a pleasant, harmless life, asleep behind the arras after lunch, drinking a bottle of sack, and laughing and joking with a few witty friends about the foolishness of life as most sober-sided citizens lead it.

In the figure of Henry Percy, Hotspur, Shakespeare has constructed the exact opposite of Falstaff. If the old knight is all earth and water, the heavy elements, then Hotspur is all fire and air, the light and ascending elements. Where Falstaff seems all flesh and bones and body, Hotspur appears to lack a body and be all spirit. Where Falstaff, who always longs for a horse, is always forced by circumstances to walk—Hal steals his horse and later procures for him "a charge of foot"—Hotspur is fully alive only on the back of his horse. Where Falstaff refuses to have anything to do with time, Hotspur is always rushing forward to meet time, to outrun it. Falstaff's natural habitat is in the tavern before the fire; Percy's is on the battlefield. But the contrast between the two characters is best understood in terms of their distinct aims: where Falstaff always seeks pleasure, Hotspur always seeks fame, honor, *gloire*.

Scarcely aware of other people, never aware of their feelings, Hotspur is aimed like an arrow toward that mystical place where absolute honor is to be won. The farther away it is, the more difficult to arrive at, the more honor for the man who achieves it:

> By heaven, methinks it were an easy leap
> To pluck bright honour from the pale-fac'd moon;
> Or dive into the bottom of the deep,
> Where fathom-line could never touch the ground,
> And pluck up drowned honour by the locks;
> So he that doth redeem her thence might wear
> Without corrival all her dignities.
> (*1 Henry IV,* I.iii.201–07)

Honor, as Hotspur understands it, is no longer the honor of the medieval knight, of Roland or Galahad, achieved by humbling one's self and performing the difficult tasks imposed by one's God, one's feudal lord, or one's lady. It is instead the Renaissance thirst for individual fame, for immortality of reputation in a world where all else dies and is forgotten, and it possesses Hotspur utterly. Even his sleep is a restless, impatient dream of battle, which culminates in a breath-taking vision of Fame:

> And in thy face strange motions have appear'd,
> Such as we see when men restrain their breath
> On some great sudden hest.
> (*1 Henry IV,* II.iii.57–59)

Hotspur's life is a surging rush onward which endures no obstacles. He has no time for love or poetry or song, for grace or manners or political maneuvering. He prides himself on being honest, direct, bluntly straightforward. What his heart feels his lips speak. In a world of actors, he alone refuses to pretend, and his virtues lead him on to greatness and to death. His bluntness alerts his enemies, his honesty offends his allies, his impetuousness and courage lead him to charge a superior army. The thirst for fame is death-marked even before it dies on Shrewsbury Field. Its republican cry for liberty cries also for blood, "If we live, we live to tread on kings." It tastes the pleasure of the battle, feels the charge like a thunderbolt, is all on fire to hear that victims are coming to be offered to its god, "the fire-ey'd maid of smoky war." Honor covers a sensual delight in the nearness of death, death for the self and death for all others: "Doomsday is near; die all, die merrily" (*1 Henry IV,* IV.i.134).

A life and values which have so much death in them cannot endure for long, and Hotspur shortly dies at the hands of a more efficient and more durable force, embodied in the greatest of the Lancastrian kings, Prince Hal, later to be Henry V. As Hotspur dies, he glimpses, as Richard had earlier, the vast, infinite reaches of time where men briefly live, die, and are forgotten; where life and fame are but the fools of time; and where in some distant future even time itself gives way to some unthinkable emptiness:

> But thoughts, the slaves of life, and life, time's fool,
> And time, that takes survey of all the world,
> Must have a stop. O, I could prophesy,
> But that the earthy and cold hand of death
> Lies on my tongue. No, Percy, thou art dust
> And food for— [*Dies.*]
> (*1 Henry IV,* V.iv.81–86)

Hal's completion of Percy's thought, "for worms," suggests the extent to which he understands and shares this modern vision of the transience of man in the vastness of time and space.

It is the work of the politician to control and adjust such extremes as Hotspur's idealism and Falstaff's sensuality, which threaten civil order in the pursuit of what they take as the good. Superb politician though he may be, it is Henry IV's fate to spend his lifetime trying to order such contraries as these, and it is equally his fate never to succeed in doing so. All his skill and canniness cannot restrain the freedom, the individuality, and the energies he unleashed by usurping the throne and destroying the principle of traditional order that once kept such excesses in bounds. In seizing the throne from the weak and politically inept Richard, Henry sought his own advancement and perhaps even the good of the state (his motivation is never clear, even to himself), but the result is a life of anxiety and travail for him and for England. His life and reign are a great continuing irony: the politically effective king creates a disordered kingdom.

The irony begins to make itself felt from the moment of Henry's assuming the kingship. At the end of *Richard II,* the new king sits on the throne at Windsor Castle with a sense of security bred of his own efficiency and power. Giving Richard the last of his many names, Exton enters and offers his body as Henry's ultimate victory:

> Great King, within this coffin I present
> Thy buried fear. Herein all breathless lies
> The mightiest of thy greatest enemies,
> Richard of Bordeaux, by me hither brought.
> (*Richard II,* V.vi.30–33)

Without the slightest intention of doing so, Exton defines perfectly the problem which the body of Richard is going to constitute when he offers it to the King as "thy buried fear." Buried the body is in the ground; but the fear is also buried deep in the heart of Henry IV. Neither he nor his son will ever forget that their throne was secured by the murder of a king, and throughout their lives, even to the eve of the battle of Agincourt, they continue to make promises of expiation. The ghost of Richard will haunt them in another way as well, for the Lancastrian kings will always remember, will always have buried deep within them, the fear that what they have shown as possible, the murder of a king to seize a throne, abides as a dreadful example for others. The politically necessary act of king-killing is at once a success and a failure.

At what should have been the highest moment of Henry's triumph, this practical, efficient man begins to discover the tragic complexities of his being and his political situation. What are only hints in the closing scene of *Richard II* become obvious facts in the beginning of the first part of *Henry IV*. As the play opens, the King longs to undertake a crusade to the Holy Land to atone for the murder of Richard, but "dear expedience" has forced him to postpone this journey earlier and now is forcing him to delay it once more. Although he hopes that peace has come to England at last, even as he hopes word is brought of new disorders and barbarism on the far edges of the kingdom. The Welsh under the irregular and wild Glendower have defeated Henry's army, and after the battle the Welsh women mutilated the bodies in unspeakable ways. In the north, where Hotspur commands, the battle has been won against the Scot and Douglas, but the bodies were piled in high windrows oozing blood. The winning general, young Harry Hotspur, has now refused to surrender his prisoners to the King, whom he earlier helped to power. While the kingdom trembles and totters, Hal, the Prince of Wales, spends his time drinking in the tavern and rioting in the streets.

Throughout *Part I,* rebellion and disorder intensify, culminating in the battle at Shrewsbury, but even as the sounds of that battle die away, new rebels spring up and new armies march. As these internal disorders continue in *Part II* they become more savage and fierce until Northumberland, crying out in fury over the death of his son Hotspur, calls for chaos and universal death:

> Let heaven kiss earth! Now let not Nature's hand
> Keep the wild flood confin'd! Let order die!
> And let this world no longer be a stage
> To feed contention in a ling'ring act;
> But let one spirit of the first-born Cain
> Reign in all bosoms, that, each heart being set
> On bloody courses, the rude scene may end
> And darkness be the burier of the dead!
> (*2 Henry IV,* I.i.153–60)

As rebellion becomes more savage, so do the opposing political forces. In *Part I* the political maneuvering is adroit and skillful, but in *Part II* politics becomes a very dirty game indeed, and its full viciousness arrives when Henry's younger son, Prince John, tricks the rebels into dismissing their army by promising them an honest hearing and redress of grievances. But as soon as the rebel army has been disbanded, John orders all the rebellious lords off to execution. His explanation is the Machiavellian one that there is no need to keep faith with traitors, and after his "victory" he remarks piously, "God, and not we, have safely fought today." *The Prince,* not law and established duty, has become the guide to realistic politics.

As their leaders become more savage and more cynical, the ordinary Englishmen become, in the terms of the Archbishop of York, revolting animals, "beastly feeders," never satisfied with any ruler they have, always restlessly seeking change in government, willing to embark on any adventure. Having cheered Bolingbroke and rejoiced in the death of Richard, they are now dissatisfied with Henry and, howling like dogs to find and eat their vomit, go crying to the grave of Richard, which has become a shrine (*2 Henry IV,* I.iii.97–102).

Struggling with endless rebellions and increasing savagery, Henry IV comes at last to the place where Richard and Hotspur have already stood—where Adam and Eve stand in Books 11 and 12 of *Paradise Lost*—looking out on that vast span of time and change which swallows hope and obliterates the meaning of individual life:

> O God! that one might read the book of fate,
> And see the revolution of the times
> Make mountains level, and the continent,
> Weary of solid firmness, melt itself
> Into the sea; and other times to see
> The beachy girdle of the ocean
> Too wide for Neptune's hips; how chances mock,
> And changes fill the cup of alteration
> With divers liquors! O, if this were seen,
> The happiest youth, viewing his progress through,
> What perils past, what crosses to ensue,
> Would shut the book and sit him down and die.
> (*2 Henry IV,* III.i.45–56)

At the same time that he breaks into the vastness of time and space, the endlessness of change, man also discovers the iron law of historical necessity. Having rejected the old social restrictions of obedience, submission to tradition and ritual, and maintenance of assigned station and rank, having chosen freedom, men now begin to discover that freedom leads, ironically, to another kind of necessity, the tragic necessity of history, which forces you to endure the unsuspected consequences of what you are and what you have done. "The main chance of things" to come "in their seeds / And weak beginning lie intreasured," and just as Richard found himself surrounded by the stone walls of Pomfret dungeon, just as Hotspur followed fame to the point where he became food for worms, so Henry can only grimly meet what must be, the rebellion which follows endlessly from rebellion. The only possible virtue is dogged courage: "Are these things then necessities? / Then let us meet them like necessities" (*2 Henry IV*, III.i.92–93).

Near the end of *Part II* Henry at last receives the news he has waited for so long, the defeat of the last rebel army. But even as the news reaches him, he has a stroke and realizes that Fortune never comes "with both hands full," but writes "her fair words still in foulest letters." In the tragic world the past is never done with until you are dead, and even as Henry lies dying, the "polished perturbation" for which he has suffered so much lying beside him, Hal enters and, thinking his father dead, carries the crown away. The act is innocent, perhaps, but it re-enacts another crime in which the wish was also father to the thought and the crown was also taken from its rightful possessor before he was dead. That crown which glittered so attractively has become for Henry "a rich armour worn in heat of day, / That scald'st with safety," and so it will also be for the man who now carries it away.

Henry's experience is the experience of his world. If at first men felt an exhilarating release from the restraints of the old traditional order and realized in themselves newly-discovered potentialities of self, they now begin to discover that freedom and the individual life have their terrifying as well as their grander sides. Having confidently relied on themselves to make of life whatever they will it to be, they now begin to discover what it means to live without some of the ultimate comforts provided by the older system: without the grace and mercy of God, without an unchanging nature which continues to circle in its great patterns and manifest an order and meaning in the universe quite independent of the actions of men, without a stable society in which the individual man can achieve permanence and meaning by living the same life his father did and passing that life on to his children.

The continuing turmoil and suffering of the new world are intensified by the will to power and the incompatibility of its dominant energies. The sensualist, the idealist, and the politician, each seeks to be king, to control the kingdom, to become, as it were, the whole world. Each way of life challenges and is challenged by the others. This mutual antagonism is implicit in Percy's belief that he must have preeminent honor, "without co-rival," and in his contempt for the "sword and buckler" Prince of Wales. It is in Hal's and Falstaff's mocking scorn of Percy's bloodthirstiness, his reckless impatience, and his preference of his horse to his wife. It is in Falstaff's cynical awareness of the great world's hypocrisy and his continuing burlesques of its pretenses. It is in the King's contempt for the tavern world and his fear of the northern lords.

Out of these antagonisms rises the plot of the play. The politician seeks social order and stability but runs athwart the headlong search for honor and sensuality's absolute rejection of any kind of restraint. Sensuality and idealism in turn find that the social need for order imposes upon them limits which they cannot endure. At first the conflict is managed in terms of word-combats, such as Hotspur's angry argument with the King about the return of prisoners, and Falstaff's various parodies of the world of honor or of politics. Words issue into actions as the underworld disturbs the peace and ventures into the kingdom to rob and cheat. The desire for fame and honor finds no satisfaction in peaceful life and flares into open rebellion. The conflict intensifies as the play proceeds, and there is an inevitable drawing movement towards the north, where the King marches to encounter the opposing manifestations of will assembled under the banner of Hotspur. Politics and sensuality mix better than either does with idealism and its death-directedness, and Falstaff marches uneasily with the forces of order. Idealism, honor, and raw courage lack the sense and control needed for a world where only the fittest survive, and Hotspur's body, with the strange wound in his thigh, is borne off on the back of Falstaff. Falstaff's quick opportunism, raw common sense, and cat-footed sense of survival; and the politician's hard, clear objectivity, practicality, and ability to control passions are the virtues which survive.

Despite all the disorders of *1 Henry IV*, life there has a saving vitality, exuberance, and even joy—so much so that it is impossible really to regret the loss of the stability and ceremonial order of the older, more peaceful world which lies behind. The release of energy and the exhilarating effects of freedom—the positive side of the transition from the Middle Ages to the Renaissance—are so attractive that disorder seems almost a small price to pay for the wit and pleasure in life of Falstaff, the fiery idealism and high courage of the knight Harry Percy, the political skill and masterful strategy of statesmen like Henry IV and the Earl of Worcester. The vast possibilities of human nature and the mind of man come into view, and men begin to discover what they and their world are really like. As in *Paradise Lost,* the first experience of disobeying God, satisfying appetite, and eating of the tree of knowledge is hot and pleasurable. But as in Milton, so in *2 Henry IV* men soon learn that knowledge is knowledge of good *and* evil. The first joy of power and pleasure soon passes and the previously hidden side of freedom begins to turn into view. Justice Shallow and his cousin Silence sitting talking of the old days that are gone and agreeing that "Death is certain" set the tone of this darkening world. The Boar's Head Tavern, formerly the center of wit and pleasure, now has an ugly quality about it. It is openly a brothel, run by Mistress Quickly, whose name takes on a new significance; and we learn that Pistol and Doll Tearsheet have killed one of the customers. The jokes have lost their cutting edge, and the characters seem to be wearily imitating their successes at wit in *Part I.* True honor and military virtue seem to have died with Hotspur, existing now only in their grotesque forms: in Prince John, who finds it unnecessary for a man of honor to be honorable with rebels, and in the crazed pimp and bully, Pistol, raving about glory and conquest in a jumble of fantastic language picked up in the theater listening to the heroic rant of such figures as Marlowe's Tamburlaine.

The pleasure principle and common sense may be more durable

than Hotspur's idealism, but Falstaff also has his fatal necessities, which begin to appear prominently in *Part II*. He appears first reeling drunk, having just voided, and throughout the play his flesh reacts with illnesses and pain, gout and pox, to the excesses of pleasure, food, drink, sex. There are flashes here and there of the old Falstaff, but even his wit is blunted by a growing sense of self-satisfaction and sentimentality. As the old King sickens and Hal nears the throne, Falstaff begins to taste power and his imperial ambitions take open shape. His will to power has always been in the background of such actions as robbing the crown tax money, playing the king, and joking about the office he would hold when Hal assumed the throne; but he now displays an unconcerned insolence towards authority, mocks the Chief Justice in the streets, and cheats openly. As he begins to take himself more and more seriously, Falstaff turns philosopher, carrying his previously unexamined, amoral sense of life as pleasure to its inevitable and unpleasant extreme, a universal rule of dog-eat-dog: "If the young dace be a bait for the old pike, I see no reason in the law of nature but I may snap at [the gullible Justice Shallow]."

His moment comes, as it does to all the others. Upon hearing of the death of King Henry, Falstaff pauses only long enough to borrow a thousand pounds from Justice Shallow before riding hard toward London and his king, shouting the ominous words "The laws of England are at my commandment. Blessed are they that have been my friends; and woe to my Lord Chief Justice!" In most matters Falstaff is a skeptic, but there remains a fatal innocence in this fascinating old man, who now expects that his old companion, Hal, will greet him with open arms and the tavern and the palace will at last become one. As Falstaff steps out from the crowd towards the coronation train with all its symbols of the power of England, he opens his arms and cries: "God save thy Grace, King Hal; my royal Hal! . . . God save thee, my sweet boy!" The mistake in identity is surprising for a man so adept at playing roles and changing masks to suit the need of the moment. It is not Hal who replies but King Henry V, the mirror of all Christian kings:

> I know thee not, old man. Fall to thy prayers.
> How ill white hairs become a fool and jester!
> I have long dreamt of such a kind of man,
> So surfeit-swell'd, so old, and so profane;
> But, being awak'd, I do despise my dream. . . .
> Presume not that I am the thing I was. . . .
> (*2 Henry IV*, V.v.48–57)

And so Falstaff, who long ago had been page to Thomas Mowbray, is also banished and comes to that vision of nothingness to which so many have preceded him. His understanding of where he is takes the form of a simple acceptance of a duty he has earlier steadfastly refused to acknowledge, the necessity of paying debts: "Master Shallow, I owe you a thousand pound." We never see the knight again. He retires to the Boar's Head to die early in *Henry V* with a broken heart, calling for sack, babbling of green fields, and swearing still that women are devils incarnate. Ambition should be made of sterner stuff, as another Shakespearean character says; but while pleasure, wit, and good-natured common sense may lack the restraint and calculation needed in the long struggle for survival and power, their absence impoverishes, as does the death of Hotspur's frankness, courage, and idealism. The England which is made by killing Richard, Hotspur, and Falstaff is a more orderly but a less vital and less honest realm. And yet their deaths were certain, guaranteed by the very excess of their own virtue and by their own narrow interpretation of reality. The banishment of Falstaff and the destruction of wit and pleasure do not teach a moral lesson but present a tragic necessity. Henry V is not here making a wrong choice but simply instrumenting the inevitable triumph of politics over pleasure. If he is Falstaff's executioner, as he was Hotspur's, then both Falstaff and Hotspur made that execution inevitable. If the gain of order achieved by their deaths is at the same time a loss of energy, pleasure, common sense, and selfless dedication to the ideal, that is the nature of existence East of Eden, where every gain is loss and every good an evil.

Politics and statecraft, the passion for order, ultimately triumph in the competition for rule. The genius of the palace and council table is finally not Henry IV but his son Hal, Henry V, and he alone escapes the decline into despair, and death. As others sicken he grows stronger, and as others make fatal mistakes he becomes ever more sure and certain in his actions. Critics have seen Hal as the ideal prince undergoing a process of education. Not a cold and careful schemer like his father, Hal, we are told, moves easily between the world of the flesh in the tavern and the world of honor on the battlefield. He excels in both ways of life and has in addition the ability to act with the temperance, prudence, and good sense necessary to the politician. His position at Shrewsbury Field standing between the body of Hotspur, whom he has killed, and the supposed body of Falstaff, playing dead in order to live, is thus an emblematic presentation of his situation in *The Henriad*. In other words, passing through a series of trials, Hal comes to be not only the ideal king but the ideal man, the only total man in a world where all the rest of the characters are possessed by a single great energy or virtue. As such he becomes the hero-king restoring life to a dying land, removing the curse of Richard's murder from the kingdom.

There is much evidence to support these ethical and mythic readings, but Shakespeare complicates the situation enormously by his realistic portrayal of character. There is from the beginning something cold, withdrawn, and impersonal, even icily calculating, about Hal. He jokes, drinks, and joins in the fun of the tavern world, holds long conversations with the hostess and her servants, but he seems to be *in,* not *of,* this lower world. Though he may enjoy the company of Falstaff and his gang, he is fully aware of a very practical, political reason for being here, and he regards his boon companions with a hard awareness of their worth:

> I know you all, and will awhile uphold
> The unyok'd humour of your idleness;
> Yet herein will I imitate the sun,
> Who doth permit the base contagious clouds
> To smother up his beauty from the world,
> That, when he please again to be himself,
> Being wanted, he may be more wond'red at
> By breaking through the foul and ugly mists
> Of vapours that did seem to strangle him.
> If all the year were playing holidays,
> To sport would be as tedious as to work;
> But when they seldom come, they wish'd-for come,
> And nothing pleaseth but rare accidents.
> So, when this loose behaviour I throw off
> And pay the debt I never promised,
> By how much better than my word I am,
> By so much shall I falsify men's hopes;
> And, like bright metal on a sullen ground,
> My reformation, glitt'ring o'er my fault,
> Shall show more goodly and attract more eyes
> Than that which hath no foil to set it off.
> I'll so offend to make offence a skill,
> Redeeming time when men think least I will.
> (*1 Henry IV,* I.ii.188–210)

There is something grim about the phrase "I know you all," and something even grimmer about the adjective "unyok'd," suggesting an ethic in which only those things harnessed and made to draw are worthwhile. Furthermore, Hal has a very modern sense of the people's love of change, the value of a political "image," and the mechanics of constructing one. Henry IV created his political image by appearing only rarely before the people but always acting with the utmost affability and kindness to all. Hal's strategy, however, is to appear like a roisterer and a wastrel in order that expectations will be low and any achievements whatsoever as a ruler will seem magnificent by comparison. His strategy works perfectly, and in *Henry V* the Archbishop expresses the wonder of the King's knowledge and ability (*Henry V,* I.i.38–59). Hal never seems to lose sight of the fact that he is preparing to be king of England, and each of his schemes works, each of his predictions is fulfilled. After Falstaff has played the king, Hal surveys him critically and finds that this is no king, and so Falstaff stands down and Hal plays the role with all the sternness, the rhetoric, the authority of true majesty. Falstaff, innocently thinking this is only a merry jape, takes the part of the penitent prince and uses the occasion to put in a good word for himself:

FALSTAFF . . . . No, my good lord: banish Peto, banish Bardolph, banish Poins; but, for sweet Jack Falstaff, kind Jack Falstaff, true Jack Falstaff, valiant Jack Falstaff—and therefore more valiant, being, as he is, old Jack Falstaff—banish not him thy Harry's company, banish not him thy Harry's company. Banish plump Jack, and banish all the world.

PRINCE I do, I will.

(*1 Henry IV,* II.iv.521–29)

In that "I do, I will," we hear the voice of the future and see the coronation at Westminster, where a great king proves his ability to rule himself and others by the words addressed to an old rogue standing with open arms: "I know thee not, old man."

Hal's view of honor is equally detached and his calculations for achieving it are as precise as his management of the world of pleasure. He can be the chivalric knight, the man of honor, as well as he can be the tavern roisterer. But his parodies of the kind of honor which kills a dozen Scots before breakfast and complains of the quiet life suggest an objective view; and his completion of Hotspur's dying sentence, "Food for worms," measures the ultimate value of this kind of honor as coolly as the words "I do, I will" sum up Falstaff's future. Hal values honor, however, knows that a king must have it, and he has a plan for acquiring it. When Henry IV berates his son for a wasted life, contrasting him unfavorably with Hotspur, Hal replies that he intends to become the very chief of honor on some battlefield where his features will be covered all in blood—a sign which will, he says, mark him as his father's true son—and where he will tear honor from Hotspur's heart:

Percy is but my *factor,* good my lord,
To *engross* up glorious deeds on my behalf;
And I will call him to *so strict account*
That he shall *render* every glory up,
Yea, even the *slightest* worship of his time,
Or I will tear the *reckoning* from his heart.
(*1 Henry IV,* III.ii.147–52, italics mine)

The bookkeeping imagery here suggests a view of honor as a negotiable commodity, not the insubstantial ideal of Chaucer's "very, perfect, gentle knight," nor the Renaissance gentleman's honor achieved by a life of unremitting gentleness, of duty, of service, and of manners, nor Hotspur's fame that must be sought steadfastly in hard and difficult places through a lifetime of honesty and courage and dedication. Percy is wrong about honor and Hal is, as usual, precisely correct. He kills Hotspur in battle, acquires his honor, which in time becomes the honor of the king and the pride of the national state he rules. Private virtues become national virtues in *The Henriad,* even as the absolute individuals become Englishmen.

Though the Prince's bent is clearly political, his attitude toward the exercise of power and the rights of succession is remarkably clear-eyed and basic. When the old king on his deathbed tries to explain that the agonizing complexities resulting from his illegal seizure of the throne may continue to haunt his heir, Hal is rather surprised. His right to the crown is, he feels, absolute, and he intends to allow no questioning:

> My gracious liege,
> You won it, wore it, kept it, gave it me;
> Then plain and right must my possession be;
> Which I with more than with a common pain
> 'Gainst all the world will rightfully maintain.
> (*2 Henry IV,* IV.v.221–25)

This modern view of succession and kingship, which is as direct and practical as Hal's view of honor, is a world away from that mystical theory of legitimacy and the king's sacred involvement with God and the order of the cosmos which Richard took for granted.

A great production sets the playing style and the interpretation of a play for a generation. The ruling version of *Henry V* in our time has been the Laurence Olivier film with its hearts-of-oak and roast-beef-of-old-England tone. It is the story of bluff and hearty King Hal, swaggering his way across France, wooing in good foursquare English words the shy, but delighted, Princess of France, twirling his crown and tossing it on the back of his throne, roaring defiance to the gift of tennis balls from the degenerate French dauphin, giving great battlefield speeches about St. Crispin's Day, and exhorting the troops to close up the breaches in the wall with their English dead. It is the great swish of the arrows from the longbows of the sturdy English yeomanry—the first national army—which scythe down the gorgeously caparisoned but clumsy chivalry of France—the last feudal army—charging across the field at Agincourt. It is England becoming Britain as the hero-king unites his people and draws into his order the Welshman Fluellen, the Irishman Macmorris, and the Scot Captain Jamy, the violent and cantankerous representatives of those savage border lands where his predecessors fought so many barbarous battles. It is a land united as one man which marshals a democratic modern army to attack and defeat France; it roots out traitors with almost miraculous knowledge of their treason; it hangs thieves and looters without hesitation. It is, as Canterbury describes it, in an epic simile drawn from *The Aeneid,* a kingdom like the beehive where the "singing masons" build "roofs of gold," and the justice delivers "o'er to executors pale / The lazy yawning drone." Such rebellious elements as remain —traitorous peers and a gang of cutthroats and thieves at the Boar's Head who go to France "to suck, to suck, the very blood to suck"—the King handles with remarkable ease.

Henry V has the public virtues of a great king, magnanimity, courage, resourcefulness, energy, efficiency, and a great public presence. At the same time, certain private traits seen in him earlier—flat practicality, hard objectivity, a lack of complexity amounting almost to insensitivity, a sense of the uses of a public image, and a definite coldness—persist and contribute much to his political efficiency, even while raising questions about him as a man.

As *Henry V* opens, the Bishop of Ely and the Archbishop of Canterbury tell us that Parliament has proposed to expropriate church lands, but the King has not yet committed himself on the issue. Canterbury has offered a deal: if Henry will block the bill, the clergy will provide him with a great deal of money to support his proposed expedition to France. Rather than give a direct answer, Henry has asked the Archbishop what he thinks about the English king's rights to the throne of France,

> The severals and unhidden passages
> Of his true titles to some certain dukedoms,
> And generally to the crown and seat of France,
> Deriv'd from Edward, his great-grandfather.
> (*Henry V,* I.i.86–89)

Taking up the hint, the Church is now here, in the persons of Canterbury and Ely, to interpret Henry's French title for him. Before the Archbishop begins to speak Henry charges him most solemnly to speak nothing but certain truth, for a war between great nations and the deaths of many men hang upon his words. Happily for Canterbury, Hal's title to the throne of France is "as clear as is the summer's sun," but the proof he offers is an incredible jumble of ancient geography, the customs of the primitive Germans, the workings of something called the Salic Law prohibiting females from ruling in central Europe, and other obscure pedantries. The King, still not clear about his title, or wishing to declare himself again, asks plainly, "May I with right and conscience make this claim?" When reassured once more, all doubt dies and Henry determines to seize France as his right or obliterate it:

> Now are we well resolv'd; and, by God's help
> And yours, the noble sinews of our power,
> France being ours, we'll bend it to our awe,
> Or break it all to pieces;
> (*Henry V,* I.ii.222–25)

Nothing more is heard about the expropriation of church lands. It would be most interesting to hear either Falstaff or Hotspur comment on these speeches and events, but their voices are no longer heard in Henry V's England. What Hal's thoughts are it is impossible to say—his motives are always as obscure as his father's—but it is also impossible to forget the dying Henry IV's advice to his son, "to busy giddy minds with foreign quarrels."

This is not the only occasion on which there is something puzzling about Hal's motives, on which it is possible to see him acting as both the hero-king and a subtle politician. Hal, in III.iii, has brought his army across the sea to the walls of Harfleur. The town at first resists siege, but the citizens then decide that there is no hope and ask for a parley. As the parley begins, Hal turns on the citizens and storms at them for defending their town so long and putting themselves and their dependents in such danger. Furthermore, if the town continues to resist he will batter it to pieces and burn it to ashes. His soldiers inflamed by battle will break loose into the town "with conscience wide as hell" to murder, rape, and pillage. "What is it to me," the King shouts again and again, if these dreadful things happen? What responsibility do I have if these animals run lusting for blood through your streets, since it is you, the citizens of Harfleur, who by your stubbornness endanger your people? The repeated rhetorical question, "What is it to me," with its implicit answer, "nothing," sounds very strange in this context. Considering the brutalities that he is describing, it should be a great deal, and how does he think this army got across the English Channel and arrived before the walls of Harfleur? Who was it who assembled such cutthroats as Pistol and Nym and brought them to France "to suck, to suck, the very blood to suck"? The very question by which the King disclaims responsibility, ironically forces a more profound consideration of the matter.

I offer one more example of this kind of thing. Shortly after the terrified Harfleur surrenders, the King rides by his army, and Fluellen tells him that no one has been lost in the recent battle except a man executed for looting a church, "one Bardolph, if your Majesty know the man; his face is all bubukles, and whelks, and knobs, and flames o' fire; and his lips blows at his nose, and it is like a coal of fire, sometimes plue and sometimes red." This same Bardolph is the only one of Falstaff's gang who has survived all three Henry plays, and Hal has enjoyed with Falstaff and Poins many a joke about that great red nose in which the fire is at last out. But the King's only response is "We would have all such offenders so cut off." He then goes on to use the occasion to issue general orders to the army prohibiting looting, "for when lenity and cruelty play for a kingdom the gentler gamester is the soonest winner."

Whether Henry's reaction expresses indifference, forgetfulness, or an all-demanding sense of duty, it is impossible to say. His motives again escape us, but we can see that while there seems to be a thinness of personal feeling, there is at the same time a sure political sense of what is required of a king and the leader of a great army engaged in the conquest of a kingdom. This ambivalence emerges again and again, to reach full statement at last on the night before the battle of Agincourt. The King puts aside his public role, covering himself with a dark cloak, and walks in the night among the army. He comes to the campfire, flickering in the darkness like Richard's candlelight in Pomfret dungeon, of three ordinary English soldiers, John Bates, Alexander Court, and Michael Williams. The soldiers are face to face on the eve of the battle with those fundamental questions which so many others have faced in *The Henriad,* and they voice these questions in a most simple way—a way which contrasts powerfully with the pedantic language of the Archbishop of Canterbury which launched this army on the French adventure and with the heroic rhetoric which exhorts the army to go once more into the breach. The soldiers are frightened about dying and worried about their families and their own souls. Is the cause for which they fight a just one? If it is not, what happens to the soul of a man who dies hating and killing other men? How can a man reconcile his duty to his king and his duty as a Christian?

> But if the cause be not good, the King himself hath a heavy reckoning to make when all those legs and arms and heads, chopp'd off in a battle, shall join together at the latter day and cry all "We died at such a place"—some swearing, some crying for a surgeon, some upon their wives left poor behind them, some upon the debts they owe, some upon their children rawly left. I am afeard there are few die well that die in a battle; for how can they charitably dispose of anything when blood is their argument? Now, if these men do not die well, it will be a black matter for the King that led them to it; who to disobey were against all proportion of subjection.
>
> (*Henry V,* IV.i.133–45)

Harry Plantagenet responds as authority must respond: The King's cause *is* just, and his quarrel honorable, and therefore the men are absolved of any responsibility before God for shedding blood. But, almost as if in doubt, he goes on to argue that "the King is not bound to answer the particular endings of his soldiers" because he did not intend their deaths when he brought them to France. Here again, as before Harfleur, he is raising the questions he intends to avoid: Whether he intended death or not, he did bring his subjects to France, where they may die, and surely he bears some responsibility. And he continues to avoid the full question of responsibility by arguing that many of the soldiers carry mortal sins upon their souls and that therefore if they die in battle the King bears no responsibility for their damnation: "Every subject's duty is the king's, but every subject's soul is his own." But this really does not answer Williams' objection that every man who dies in battle dies in sin trying to murder his fellow men, and he is doing so because his king has brought him to this place and ordered him to fight. It is impossible to forget in this discussion of the justice of the cause the doubtful way in which the French war began.

In this brief scene in the middle of darkness on the edge of a great battle, Michael Williams has faced for himself and his king the most fundamental questions about his responsibility as ruler and as man.

But Henry does not answer the questions, either because he does not understand them or because no ruler of a state can ever answer such questions.

The actions and the speeches of King Henry V produce a curious ambiguity. On one hand he is the hero-king, the restorer of England's glory, and the efficient manager of the realm; but he is at the same time, it would appear, a cunning Machiavel, a cynical politician, a man lacking in moral depth, perhaps even a limited intelligence. Our difficulties in understanding the King are intensified by the almost total absence from the play of speeches in which Henry speaks as a private man, directly revealing his own feelings. He lives in the full glare of public life, and even those usually private activities such as wooing a wife are carried out on the great stage of the world. Nor does his language yield insights into the depths of self of the kind found in the language of Richard II, Falstaff, Hotspur. Instead, Henry uses a political and heroic rhetoric whose brightly polished surface allows no penetration.

Faced with the absence of motives, critics have resolved the problem by judging Henry according to their particular moral bias and concluding that he is either a good and efficient ruler who sacrifices himself for the good of the state, or a hypocritical and cunning politician who relentlessly seizes every opportunity to extend and consolidate his power. We must, however, take Henry as Shakespeare gives him to us: a man who has no private personal self, but only a public character, a character which is supremely, unerringly political, which chooses without hesitation that course of action which will make the kingdom function efficiently, balance the divisive powers within, and strengthen the ruler's grasp on the body politic. This type of man is not unknown to Shakespeare's or our own time. Historians have been guessing for centuries about Elizabeth I's motives for not marrying—hatred of men because of her father's treatment of her mother? ingrown virginity? pelvic malformation? unhappy love affair in youth? —but whatever Elizabeth's reasons, her constant hesitation was a political masterpiece. To have married a Protestant would have caused her Catholic subjects to despair and set Catholic Europe against her. To have married a Catholic would have driven her Protestant subjects to rebellion and alienated England from the growing Protestant powers in Europe. So long as she remained unmarried, but always considering marriage, she could prevent, even among the proud lords in her own court, that polarization of power which would have meant civil and world war.

Our own age shares with Shakespeare some understanding of political man, and the following description of an American politician is a perfect description, even down to the small details, of Henry V:

> He is a totally political man, clever but not thoughtful, calculating more than reflective. He appears at once sentimental and

> ruthless, thin-skinned and imperious, remarkably attuned to public moods and utterly expert at the "game" of political maneuver. He is all of a piece, seemingly monolithic, not only completely *in* but totally *of* politics. Upon the devices and costs of political manipulation he is capable of looking with some irony, but toward the idea of the manipulation itself and the kind of life it entails he shows no irony whatever.[2]

No one would agree more completely than Henry V that political man "is the role," that "the person [is] the function." As he turns away from the bitter encounter with his soldiers around the campfire, draws back from the tragic place where Richard, Hotspur, Falstaff, and Henry IV looked and died, Henry pauses alone in the darkness and asks himself the question Richard had so long ago answered so confidently: "What is a king?" Even here his speech is still rhetoric rather than poetry; and rather than revealing a self, it is as if some vague memory of a real self were sadly contemplating its final disappearance into a role, into ceremony:

> No, thou proud dream,
> That play'st so subtly with a king's repose,
> I am a king that find thee; and I know
> 'Tis not the balm, the sceptre, and the ball,
> The sword, the mace, the crown imperial,
> The intertissued robe of gold and pearl,
> The farced title running fore the king,
> The throne he sits on, nor the tide of pomp
> That beats upon the high shore of this world—
> No, not all these, thrice gorgeous ceremony,
> Not all these, laid in bed majestical,
> Can sleep so soundly as the wretched slave
> Who, with a body fill'd and vacant mind,
> Gets him to rest, cramm'd with distressful bread;
> (*Henry V,* IV.i.253–66)

But having seen the person fade into the political function, the King turns away from tragic knowledge and returns to his tent and to his role to become the conqueror of France, the greatest of the English kings, the husband of Katherine, and the father of Henry VI.

Henry reverses the path taken by Richard II, who believed that kingship and rule were his reality but discovered under the battering of circumstance that he was only a mortal man:

> You have but mistook me all this while.
> I live with bread like you, feel want,
> Taste grief, need friends; subjected thus,
> How can you say to me I am a king?
> (*Richard II,* III.ii.174–77)

---

[2] Irving Howe, "I'd Rather Be Wrong," *New York Review of Books* (June 17, 1965), p. 3.

At the other end of the cycle, the King who has known from the beginning that he is a man playing king—"Yet herein will I *imitate* the sun"—discovers, however briefly, the claims of his humanity, only to turn away and lock himself forever into the role. *The Henriad* traces in its kings a great paradox: Necessity forces man out of role into reality—necessity forces man back out of reality into role. The movement is much like that of *The Aeneid,* where the establishment of New Troy and, eventually, Augustan order requires the absorption of the man Aeneas into the role of the founder of Rome, and the destruction of such turbulent energies as Dido and Turnus. In both the Roman and English epics the even balance of loss and gain creates finally a tone of great sadness inextricably mixed with great triumph.

The world of Henry V with its state rituals and ceremony looks much like a restoration of the English Eden, ordered, prosperous, and united under a hero-king. But under the surface all is changed. In Richard's feudal kingdom society was organized and life lived in accordance with the great unchanging patterns of order, mutual support, and hierarchy, which were believed to govern all the created world. In Henry's national state, life is shifting and fluid, and action is taken not because it is morally, unchangeably right, but because it will bring about the desired result. Identity is now no longer God-given but only a role within which an individual is imprisoned by political necessity. The restored English garden, the beehive state, is superimposed on the ruined garden of France, a weed-filled, untilled wildness (*Henry V,* V.ii.30–62). Man no longer confidently expects the future to repeat the past but stands on the edge of great vistas of time and lives in the historical process of endless change. What was small and coherent is now vast and tends to fragmentation, what was unchanging is now in ceaseless flux, what was real is now acted, and what was external and certain is now internalized and ambiguous.

The Henriad is a brief but fairly accurate history of the reigns of Richard II, Henry IV, and Henry V. But the chronicle of the wars of succession between York and Lancaster is only the outward form of an action tracing the great psychological, social, and political shifts from the medieval to the modern world. Below the level of these great cultural shifts, however, a still more fundamental plot exists and gives to the plays much of their energy and perpetual fascination.

In the beginning there is a king, Richard II, and a society which believe like the child that the world is all of a piece, from the clod of earth up to God Himself. Man cannot be distinguished from world, for all parts of the indivisible universe move in sympathy with all other parts. God watches benevolently over this world overseeing the endless operation of justice and right. But man is at the center of this rich and brilliant universe. He trusts the authorities and traditions that he has inherited and assumes that nothing will ever change from the way it is.

Then, the knowledge of death, the conflicting pressures of reality, and the more violent passions—hate, blood-lust, the will to power—erupt and break up the old certainties. When the earthly king calls for help to the heavenly king there is not even the whisper of an answer. Feelings of isolation in great darkness grow. Certainty of identity is lost and the vastnesses of eternity and infinity are glimpsed. Man is driven inward upon himself, becomes self-conscious, as he realizes that there is a world "out there" which does not conform to his will or imagination. Confused, the old innocence dies with Richard II.

Life fragments, new energies are released, and many new possibilities of life appear: pleasure, politics, honor, war, poetry, and magic. The individual is no longer limited to "what he is" but is free to experiment and act out many parts. Prince Hal—shrewd and reality-oriented—now replaces Richard as the central figure in the psychic journey. At first he rejects the authority figures, the king, the father, the law, to live a life of pleasure and self-indulgence in the tavern, taking Falstaff as a father temporarily. He turns from the flesh to the spirit and seeks to find himself on the battlefield and in the search for honor and fame. In both tavern and battlefield, however, he "keeps his wits about him" and avoids the total involvement with these ultimately unrealistic extremes, both of which have death implicit in them.

In the end, the Prince kills wild idealism, Hotspur, and banishes unlimited pleasure, Falstaff, to return to his true father in spirit and person. With the death of the father, the Prince assumes the burdens of rule and takes up the adult role of trying to order and "make the world work." In the process of becoming a ruler his personal self, the essential "I," is lost forever as the man disappears into the role his work demands.

V

THE ELIZABETHAN TRAGEDIES

THE EARLIER TRAGIC FORM AND SUBJECT MATTER

Form and Formality in "Romeo and Juliet"

Harry Levin

"Fain would I dwell on form—", says Juliet from her window to Romeo in the moonlit orchard below,

> Fain would I dwell on form—fain, fain deny
> What I have spoke; but farewell compliment!
> (II.ii.88–89)[1]

Romeo has just violated convention, dramatic and otherwise, by overhearing what Juliet intended to be a soliloquy. Her cousin, Tybalt, had already committed a similar breach of social and theatrical decorum in the scene at the Capulets' feast, where he had also recognized Romeo's voice to be that of a Montague. There, when the lovers first met, the dialogue of their meeting had been formalized into a sonnet, acting out the conceit of his lips as pilgrims, her hand as a shrine, and his kiss as a culminating piece of stage-business, with an encore after an additional quatrain: "You kiss by th' book" (I.v.112). Neither had known the identity of the other; and each, upon finding it out, responded with an ominous exclamation coupling love and death (120, 140). The formality of their encounters was framed by the ceremonious

---

From *Shakespeare Quarterly,* Vol. XI, No. 1 (Winter, 1960). Reprinted by permission of Harry Levin and the Shakespeare Association of America, Inc.

[1] Line-references are to the separate edition of G. L. Kittredge's text (Boston, 1940).

character of the scene, with its dancers, its masquers, and—except for Tybalt's stifled outburst—its air of old-fashioned hospitality. "We'll measure them a measure", Benvolio had proposed; but Romeo, unwilling to join the dance, had resolved to be an onlooker and carry a torch (I.iv.10). That torch may have burned symbolically, but not for Juliet; indeed, as we are inclined to forget with Romeo, he attended the feast in order to see the dazzling but soon eclipsed Rosaline. Rosaline's prior effect upon him is all that we ever learn about her; yet it has been enough to make Romeo, when he was presented to us, a virtual stereotype of the romantic lover. As such, he has protested a good deal too much in his preliminary speeches, utilizing the conventional phrases and standardized images of Elizabethan eroticism, bandying generalizations, paradoxes, and sestets with Benvolio, and taking a quasi-religious vow which his introduction to Juliet would ironically break (I.ii.92–97). Afterward this role has been reduced to absurdity by the humorous man, Mercutio, in a mock-conjuration evoking Venus and Cupid and the inevitable jingle of "love" and "dove" (II.i.10). The scene that follows is actually a continuation, marked in neither the Folios nor the Quartos, and linked with what has gone before by a somewhat eroded rhyme.

'Tis in vain
To seek him here that means not to be found,

Benvolio concludes in the absence of Romeo (41, 42). Whereupon the latter, on the other side of the wall, chimes in:

He jests at scars that never felt a wound.
(II.ii.1)

Thus we stay behind, with Romeo, when the masquers depart. Juliet, appearing at the window, does not hear his descriptive invocation. Her first utterance is the very sigh that Mercutio burlesqued in the foregoing scene: "Ay, me!" (II.ii.25). Then, believing herself to be alone and masked by the darkness, she speaks her mind in sincerity and simplicity. She calls into question not merely Romeo's name but—by implication—all names, forms, conventions, sophistications, and arbitrary dictates of society, as opposed to the appeal of instinct directly conveyed in the odor of a rose. When Romeo takes her at her word and answers, she is startled and even alarmed for his sake; but she does not revert to courtly language.

I would not for the world they saw thee here,

she tells him, and her monosyllabic directness inspires the matching cadence of his response:

And but thou love me, let them find me here.
(77, 79)

She pays incidental tribute to the proprieties with her passing suggestion that, had he not overheard her, she would have dwelt on form, pretended to be more distant, and played the not impossible part of the captious beloved. But farewell compliment! Romeo's love for Juliet will have an immediacy which cuts straight through the verbal embellishment that has obscured his infatuation with Rosaline. That shadowy creature, having served her Dulcinea-like purpose, may well be forgotten. On the other hand, Romeo has his more tangible foil in the person of the County Paris, who is cast in that ungrateful part which the Italians call *terzo incòmodo,* the inconvenient third party, the unwelcome member of an amorous triangle. As the official suitor of Juliet, his speeches are always formal, and often sound stilted or priggish by contrast with Romeo's. Long after Romeo has abandoned his sonneteering, Paris will pronounce a sestet at Juliet's tomb (V.iii. 11–16). During their only colloquy, which occurs in Friar Laurence's cell, Juliet takes on the sophisticated tone of Paris, denying his claims and disclaiming his compliments in brisk stichomythy. As soon as he leaves, she turns to the Friar, and again—as so often in intimate moments—her lines fall into monosyllables:

> O, shut the door! and when thou hast done so,
> Come weep with me—past hope, past cure, past help!
> (IV.i.44–45)

Since the suit of Paris is the main subject of her conversations with her parents, she can hardly be sincere with them. Even before she met Romeo, her consent was hedged in prim phraseology:

> I'll look to like, if looking liking move.
> (I.iii.97)

And after her involvement she becomes adept in the stratagems of mental reservation, giving her mother equivocal rejoinders and rousing her father's anger by chopping logic (III.v.69–205). Despite the intervention of the Nurse on her behalf, her one straightforward plea is disregarded. Significantly Lady Capulet, broaching the theme of Paris in stiffly appropriate couplets, has compared his face to a volume:[2]

> This precious book of love, this unbound lover,
> To beautify him only lacks a cover.
> The fish lives in the sea, and 'tis much pride
> The fair without the fair within to hide.
> (I.iii.89–90)

---

[2] On the long and rich history of this trope, see the sixteenth chapter of E. R. Curtius, *European Literature and the Latin Middle Ages,* tr. W. R. Trask (New York, 1953).

That bookish comparison, by emphasizing the letter at the expense of the spirit, helps to lend Paris an aspect of unreality; to the Nurse, more ingenuously, he is "a man of wax" (76). Later Juliet will echo Lady Capulet's metaphor, transferring it from Paris to Romeo:

> Was ever book containing such vile matter
> So fairly bound?
> (III.ii.83–84)

Here, on having learned that Romeo has just slain Tybalt, she is undergoing a crisis of doubt, a typically Shakespearian recognition of the difference between appearance and reality. The fair without may not cover a fair within, after all. Her unjustified accusations, leading up to her rhetorical question, form a sequence of oxymoronic epithets: "Beautiful tyrant, fiend angelical, . . . honorable villain!" (75–79) W. H. Auden, in a recent comment on these lines,[3] cannot believe they would come from a heroine who had been exclaiming shortly before: "Gallop apace, you fiery-footed steeds. . . !" Yet Shakespeare has been perfectly consistent in suiting changes of style to changes of mood. When Juliet feels at one with Romeo, her intonations are genuine; when she feels at odds with him, they should be unconvincing. The attraction of love is played off against the revulsion from books, and coupled with the closely related themes of youth and haste, in one of Romeo's long-drawn-out leavetakings:

> Love goes toward love as schoolboys from their books;
> But love from love, towards school with heavy looks.
> (II.ii.157–58)

The school for these young lovers will be tragic experience. When Romeo, assuming that Juliet is dead and contemplating his own death, recognizes the corpse of Paris, he will extend the image to cover them both:

> O give me thy hand,
> One writ with me in sour misfortune's book!
> (V.iii.82)

It was this recoil from bookishness, together with the farewell to compliment, that animated *Love's Labour's Lost,* where literary artifice was so ingeniously deployed against itself, and Berowne was taught—by an actual heroine named Rosaline—that the best books were women's eyes. Some of Shakespeare's other early comedies came even

[3] In the paper-bound Laurel Shakespeare, ed. Francis Fergusson (New York, 1958), p. 26.

closer to adumbrating certain features of *Romeo and Juliet:* notably, *The Two Gentlemen of Verona,* with its locale, its window scene, its friar and rope, its betrothal and banishment, its emphasis upon the vagaries of love. Shakespeare's sonnets and erotic poems had won for him the reputation of an English Ovid. *Romeo and Juliet,* the most elaborate product of his so-called lyrical period, was his first successful experiment in tragedy.[4] Because of that very success, it is hard for us to realize the full extent of its novelty, though scholarship has lately been reminding us of how it must have struck contemporaries.[5] They would have been surprised, and possibly shocked, at seeing lovers taken so seriously. Legend, it had been heretofore taken for granted, was the proper matter for serious drama; romance was the stuff of the comic stage. Romantic tragedy—"*an excellent conceited Tragedie of Romeo and Juliet*", to cite the title-page of the First Quarto—was one of those contradictions in terms which Shakespeare seems to have delighted in resolving. His innovation might be described as transcending the usages of romantic comedy, which are therefore very much in evidence, particularly at the beginning. Subsequently, the leading characters acquire together a deeper dimension of feeling by expressly repudiating the artificial language they have talked and the superficial code they have lived by. Their formula might be that of the anti-Petrarchan sonnet:

> Foole said My muse to mee, looke in thy heart and write.[6]

An index of this development is the incidence of rhyme, heavily concentrated in the First Act, and its gradual replacement by a blank verse which is realistic or didactic with other speakers and unprecedentedly limpid and passionate with the lovers. "Love has no need of euphony", the eminent Russian translator of the play, Boris Pasternak, has commented. "Truth, not sound, dwells in its heart." [7]

Comedy set the pattern of courtship, as formally embodied in a dance. The other *genre* of Shakespeare's earlier stagecraft, history, set the pattern of conflict, as formally embodied in a duel. *Romeo and Juliet* might also be characterized as an anti-revenge play, in which hostile emotions are finally pacified by the interplay of kindlier ones. Romeo sums it up in his prophetic oxymorons:

---

[4] H. B. Charlton, in his British Academy lecture for 1939, "*Romeo and Juliet*" *as an Experimental Tragedy,* has considered the experiment in the light of Renaissance critical theory.

[5] Especially F. M. Dickey, *Not Wisely But Too Well: Shakespeare's Love Tragedies* (San Marino, 1957), pp. 63–88.

[6] Sir Philip Sidney, *Astrophel and Stella,* ed. Albert Feuillerat (Cambridge, 1922), p. 243.

[7] Boris Pasternak, "Translating Shakespeare", tr. Manya Harari, *The Twentieth Century,* CLXIV, 979 (September, 1958), p. 217.

> Here's much to do with hate, but more with love.
> Why then, O brawling love! O loving hate!
> O anything, of nothing first create!
>
> (I.i.162–64)

And Paris, true to type, waxes grandiose in lamenting Juliet:

> O love! O life! not life, but love in death!
>
> (IV.v.58)

Here, if we catch the echo from Hieronimo's lament in *The Spanish Tragedy,*

> O life! no life, but lively form of death,

we may well note that the use of antithesis, which is purely decorative with Kyd, is functional with Shakespeare. The contrarieties of his plot are reinforced on the plane of imagery by omnipresent reminders of light and darkness,[8] youth and age, and many other antitheses subsumed by the all-embracing one of Eros and Thanatos, the *leitmotif* of the *Liebestod,* the myth of the tryst in the tomb. This attraction of ultimate opposites—which is succinctly implicit in the Elizabethan ambiguity of the verb *to die*—is generalized when the Friar rhymes "womb" with "tomb", and particularized when Romeo hails the latter place as "thou womb of death" (I.iii.9, 10; V.iii.45). Hence the "extremities" of the situation, as the Prologue to the Second Act announces, are tempered "with extreme sweet" (14). Those extremes begin to meet as soon as the initial prologue, in a sonnet disarmingly smooth, has set forth the feud between the two households, "Where civil blood makes civil hands unclean" (4). Elegant verse yields to vulgar prose, and to an immediate riot, as the servants precipitate a renewal—for the third time—of their masters' quarrel. The brawl of Act I is renewed again in the *contretemps* of Act III and completed by the swordplay of Act V. Between the street-scenes, with their clashing welter of citizens and officers, we shuttle through a series of interiors, in a flurry of domestic arrangements and family relationships. The house of the Capulets is the logical center of action, and Juliet's chamber its central sanctum. Consequently, the sphere of privacy encloses Acts II and IV, in contradistinction to the public issues raised by the alternating episodes. The temporal alternation of the play, in its accelerating continuity, is aptly recapitulated by the impatient rhythm of Capulet's speech:

> Day, night, late, early,
> At home, abroad, alone, in company,
> Waking or sleeping . . .
>
> (III.v.177–79)

---

[8] Caroline Spurgeon, *Shakespeare's Imagery and What It Tells Us* (New York, 1936), pp. 310–316.

The alignment of the *dramatis personae* is as symmetrical as the antagonism they personify. It is not without relevance that the names of the feuding families, like the Christian names of the hero and heroine, are metrically interchangeable (though "Juliet" is more frequently a trochee than an amphimacer). Tybalt the Capulet is pitted against Benvolio the Montague in the first street-fight, which brings out—with parallel stage-directions—the heads of both houses restrained by respective wives. Both the hero and heroine are paired with others, Rosaline and Paris, and admonished by elderly confidants, the Friar and the Nurse. Escalus, as Prince of Verona, occupies a superior and neutral position; yet, in the interchange of blood for blood, he loses "a brace of kinsmen", Paris and Mercutio (V.iii.295). Three times he must quell and sentence the rioters before he can pronounce the final sestet, restoring order to the city-state through the lovers' sacrifice. He effects the resolution by summoning the patriarchal enemies, from their opposite sides, to be reconciled. "Capulet, Montague," he sternly arraigns them, and the polysyllables are brought home by monosyllabics:

> See what a scourge is laid upon your hate
> That heaven finds means to kill your joys with love.
> (291–93)

The two-sided counterpoise of the dramatic structure is well matched by the dynamic symmetry of the antithetical style. One of its peculiarities, which surprisingly seems to have escaped the attention of commentators, is a habit of stressing a word by repeating it within a line, a figure which may be classified in rhetoric as a kind of *ploce*. I have cited a few examples incidentally; let me now underline the device by pointing out a few more. Thus Montague and Capulet are accused of forcing their parties

> To wield old partisans in hands as old,
> Cank'red with peace, to part your cank'red hate.
> (I.i.100, 102)

This double instance, along with the wordplay on "cank'red," suggests the embattled atmosphere of partisanship through the halberds; and it is further emphasized in Benvolio's account of the fray:

> Came more and more, and fought on part and part.
> (122)

The key-words are not only doubled but affectionately intertwined, when Romeo confides to the Friar:

> As mine on hers, so hers is set on mine.
> (II.iii.59)

Again, he conveys the idea of reciprocity by declaring that Juliet returns "grace for grace and love for love" (86). The Friar's warning hints at poetic justice:

> These violent delights have violent ends.
> (II.vi.9)

Similarly Mercutio, challenged by Tybalt, turns "point to point", and the Nurse finds Juliet—in *antimetabole*—"Blubb'ring and weeping, weeping and blubbering" (III.ii.165; iii.87). Statistics would prove illusory, because some repetitions are simply idiomatic, grammatical, or—in the case of old Capulet or the Nurse—colloquial. But it is significant that the play contains well over a hundred such lines, the largest number being in the First Act and scarcely any left over for the Fifth.

The significance of this tendency toward reduplication, both stylistic and structural, can perhaps be best understood in the light of Bergson's well-known theory of the comic: the imposition of geometrical form upon the living data of formless consciousness. The stylization of love, the constant pairing and counter-balancing, the *quid pro quo* of Capulet and Montague, seem mechanical and unnatural. Nature has other proponents besides the lovers, especially Mercutio their fellow victim, who bequeathes his curse to both their houses. His is likewise an ironic end, since he has been as much a satirist of "the new form" and Tybalt's punctilio in duelling "by the book of arithmetic" as of "the numbers that Petrarch flowed in" and Romeo's affectations of gallantry (II.iv.34, 38; III.i.104). Mercutio's interpretation of dreams, running counter to Romeo's premonitions, is naturalistic, not to say Freudian; Queen Mab operates through fantasies of wish-fulfilment, bringing love to lovers, fees to lawyers, and tithe-pigs to parsons; the moral is that desires can be mischievous. In his repartee with Romeo, Mercutio looks forward to their fencing with Tybalt; furthermore he charges the air with bawdy suggestions that—in spite of the limitations of Shakespeare's theatre, its lack of actresses and absence of close-ups—love may have something to do with sex, if not with lust, with the physical complementarity of male and female.[9] He is abetted, in that respect, by the malapropistic garrulity of the Nurse, Angelica, who is naturally bound to Juliet through having been her wet-nurse, and who has lost the infant daughter that might have been Juliet's age. None the less, her crotchety hesitations are contrasted with Juliet's youthful ardors when the Nurse acts as go-between for Romeo. His counsellor, Friar Laurence, makes a measured entrance with his sententious couplets

---

[9] Coleridge's persistent defense of Shakespeare against the charge of gross language does more credit to that critic's high-mindedness than to his discernment. The concentrated ribaldry of the gallants in the street (II.iv) is deliberately contrasted with the previous exchange between the lovers in the orchard.

on the uses and abuses of natural properties, the medicinal and poisonous effects of plants:

> For this, being smelt, with that part cheers each part;
> Being tasted, slays all senses with the heart.
> (II.iii.25, 26)

His watchword is "Wisely and slow", yet he contributes to the grief at the sepulcher by ignoring his own advice, "They stumble that run fast" (94).[10] When Romeo upbraids him monosyllabically,

> Thou canst not speak of that thou doest not feel,

it is the age-old dilemma that separates the generations: *Si jeunesse savait, si vieillesse pouvait* (III.iii.64). Banished to Mantua, Romeo has illicit recourse to the Apothecary, whose shop—envisaged with Flemish precision—unhappily replaces the Friar's cell, and whose poison is the sinister counterpart of Laurence's potion.

Against this insistence upon polarity, at every level, the mutuality of the lovers stands out, the one organic relation amid an overplus of stylized expressions and attitudes. The naturalness of their diction is artfully gained, as we have noticed, through a running critique of artificiality. In drawing a curtain over the consummation of their love, Shakespeare heralds it with a prothalamium and follows it with an epithalamium. Juliet's "Gallop apace, you fiery-footed steeds", reversing the Ovidian *"lente currite, noctis equi"*, is spoken "alone" but in breathless anticipation of a companion (III.ii.1). After having besought the day to end, the sequel to her solo is the duet in which she begs the night to continue. In the ensuing *débat* of the nightingale and the lark, a refinement upon the antiphonal song of the owl and the cuckoo in *Love's Labour's Lost,* Romeo more realistically discerns "the herald of the morn" (III.v.6). When Juliet reluctantly agrees, "More light and light it grows", he completes the paradox with a doubly reduplicating line:

> More light and light—more dark and dark our woes!
> (35, 36)

The precariousness of their union, formulated arithmetically by the Friar as "two in one" (II.vi.37), is brought out by the terrible loneliness of Juliet's monologue upon taking the potion:

> My dismal scene I needs must act alone.
> (IV.iii.19)

---

[10] This is the leading theme of the play, in the interpretation of Brents Stirling, *Unity in Shakespearian Tragedy: The Interplay of Themes and Characters* (New York, 1956), pp. 10–25.

Her utter singleness, as an only child, is stressed by her father and mourned by her mother:

> But one, poor one, one poor and loving child.
> (v.46)

Tragedy tends to isolate where comedy brings together, to reveal the uniqueness of individuals rather than what they have in common with others. Asking for Romeo's profession of love, Juliet anticipates: "I know thou wilt say 'Ay' " (II.ii.90). That monosyllable of glad assent was the first she ever spoke, as we know from the Nurse's childish anecdote (I.iii.48). Later, asking the Nurse whether Romeo has been killed, Juliet pauses self-consciously over the pun between "Ay" and "I" or "eye":

> Say thou but 'I,'
> And that bare vowel 'I' shall poison more
> Than the death-darting eye of cockatrice.
> I am not I, if there be such an 'I';
> Or those eyes shut that make thee answer 'I.'
> If he be slain, say 'I'; or if not, 'no.'
> Brief sounds determine of my weal or woe.
> (III.ii.45–51)

Her identification with him is negated by death, conceived as a shut or poisoning eye, which throws the pair back upon their single selves. Each of them dies alone—or, at all events, in the belief that the other lies dead, and without the benefit of a recognition-scene. Juliet, of course, is still alive; but she has already voiced her death-speech in the potion scene. With the dagger, her last words, though richly symbolic, are brief and monosyllabic:

> This is thy sheath; there rest, and let me die.
> (V.iii.170)

The sense of vicissitude is re-enacted through various gestures of staging; Romeo and Juliet experience their exaltation "alot" on the upper stage; his descent via the rope is, as she fears, toward the tomb (III.v.56).[11] The antonymous adverbs *up* and *down* figure, with increasing prominence, among the brief sounds that determine Juliet's woe (e.g., V.ii.209–10). The overriding pattern through which she and Romeo have been trying to break—call it Fortune, the stars, or what you will—ends by closing in and breaking them; their private world disappears, and we are left in the social ambiance again. Capu-

---

[11] One of the more recent and pertinent discussions of staging is that of Richard Hosley, "The Use of the Upper Stage in *Romeo and Juliet*", *Shakespeare Quarterly,* V, 4 (Autumn, 1954), 371–379.

let's house has been bustling with preparations for a wedding, the happy ending of comedy. The news of Juliet's death is not yet tragic because it is premature; but it introduces a peripety which will become the starting point for *Hamlet.*

> All things that we ordained festival
> Turn from their office to black funeral—

the old man cries, and his litany of contraries is not less poignant because he has been so fond of playing the genial host:

> Our instruments to melancholy bells,
> Our wedding cheer to a sad burial feast;
> Our solemn hymns to sullen dirges change;
> Our bridal flowers serve for a buried corse;
> And all things change them to the contrary.
> (IV.v.84–90)

His lamentation, in which he is joined by his wife, the Nurse, and Paris, reasserts the formalities by means of what is virtually an operatic quartet. Thereupon the music becomes explicit, when they leave the stage to the Musicians, who have walked on with the County Paris. Normally these three might play during the *entr'acte,* but Shakespeare has woven them into the dialogue terminating the Fourth Act.[12] Though their art has the power of soothing the passions and thereby redressing grief, as the comic servant Peter reminds them with a quotation from Richard Edward's lyric *In Commendacion of Musicke,* he persists in his query: "Why 'silver sound'?" (131) Their answers are those of mere hirelings, who can indifferently change their tune from a merry dump to a doleful one, so long as they are paid with coin of the realm. Yet Peter's riddle touches a deeper chord of correspondence, the interconnection between discord and harmony, between impulse and discipline. "Consort", which can denote a concert or a companionship, can become the fighting word that motivates the unharmonious pricksong of the duellists (III.i.48). The "sweet division" of the lark sounds harsh and out of tune to Juliet, since it proclaims that the lovers must be divided (v.29). Why "silver sound"? Because Romeo, in the orchard, has sworn by the moon

> That tips with silver all these fruit-tree tops.
> (II.i.108)

---

[12] Professor F. T. Bowers reminds me that inter-act music was probably not a regular feature of public performance when *Romeo and Juliet* was first performed. Some early evidence for it has been gathered by T. S. Graves in "The Act-Time in Elizabethan Theatres", *Studies in Philology,* XII, 3 (July, 1915), 120–124—notably contemporary sound cues, written into a copy of the Second Quarto and cited by Malone. But if—as seems likely—such practices were exceptional, then Shakespeare was innovating all the farther.

Because Shakespeare, transposing sights and sounds into words, has made us imagine

> How silver-sweet sound lovers' tongues by night,
> Like softest music to attending ears!
> (167–68)

"Julius Caesar"

Maynard Mack

. . . I think the place we may want to begin is with I.ii; for here, as in the first witch scene in *Macbeth,* most of the play to come is already implicit. We have just learned from scene i of Caesar's return in triumph from warring on Pompey's sons, we have seen the warm though fickle adulation of the crowd and the apprehension of the tribunes; now we are to see the great man himself. The procession enters to triumphal music; with hubbub of a great press of people; with young men stripped for the ceremonial races, among them Antony; with statesmen in their togas: Decius, Cicero, Brutus, Cassius, Casca; with the two wives Calpurnia and Portia; and, in the lead, for not even Calpurnia is permitted at his side, the great man. As he starts to speak, an expectant hush settles over the gathering: what does the great man have on his mind?

> CAESAR Calpurnia.
> CASCA Peace, ho! Caesar speaks.
> CAESAR Calpurnia.
> CALPURNIA Here, my lord.
> CAESAR Stand you directly in Antonius' way
> When he does run his course. Antonius.
> ANTONY Caesar, my lord?
> CAESAR Forget not, in your speed, Antonius,
> To touch Calpurnia; for our elders say,
> The barren, touched in this holy chase,
> Shake off their sterile curse.
> ANTONY I shall remember:
> When Caesar says, "Do this," it is perform'd.

From *Essays on the Teaching of English,* ed. Edward J. Gordon and Edward S. Noyes. Published by Appleton-Century-Crofts under the auspices of the National Council of Teachers of English. Reprinted with the permission of the National Council of Teachers of English and Maynard Mack.

What the great man had on his mind, it appears, was to remind his wife, in this public place, that she is sterile; that there is an old tradition about how sterility can be removed; and that while of course he is much too sophisticated to accept such a superstition himself—it is "our elders" who say it—still, Calpurnia had jolly well better get out there and get tagged, or else!

Then the procession takes up again. The hubbub is resumed, but once more the expectant silence settles as a voice is heard.

> SOOTHSAYER Caesar!
> CAESAR Ha! Who calls?
> CASCA Bid every noise be still; peace yet again!
> CAESAR Who is it in the press that calls on me?
> I hear a tongue shriller than all the music
> Cry "Caesar!" Speak. Caesar is turn'd to hear.
> SOOTHSAYER Beware the ides of March.
> CAESAR What man is that?
> BRUTUS A soothsayer bids you beware the ides of March.
> CAESAR Set him before me; let me see his face.
> CASSIUS Fellow, come from the throng; look upon Caesar.
> CAESAR What say'st thou to me now? Speak once again.
> SOOTHSAYER Beware the ides of March.
> CAESAR He is a dreamer. Let us leave him. Pass.

It is easy to see from even these small instances, I think, how a first-rate dramatic imagination works. There is no hint of any procession in Plutarch, Shakespeare's source. "Caesar," says Plutarch, "*sat* to behold." There is no mention of Calpurnia in Plutarch's account of the Lupercalian race, and there is no mention anywhere of her sterility. Shakespeare, in nine lines, has given us an unforgettable picture of a man who would like to be emperor, pathetically concerned that he lacks an heir, and determined, even at the cost of making his wife a public spectacle, to establish that this is owing to no lack of virility in him. The first episode thus dramatizes instantaneously the oncoming theme of the play: that a man's will is not enough; that there are other matters to be reckoned with, like the infertility of one's wife, or one's own affliction of the falling sickness which spoils everything one hoped for just at the instant when one had it almost in one's hand. Brutus will be obliged to learn this lesson too.

In the second episode the theme develops. We see again the uneasy rationalism that everybody in this play affects; we hear it reverberate in the faint contempt—almost a challenge—of Brutus' words as he turns to Caesar: "A soothsayer bids you beware the ides of March." Yet underneath, in the soothsayer's presence and his sober warning, Shakespeare allows us to catch a hint of something else, something far more primitive and mysterious, from which rationalism in this play keeps trying vainly to cut itself away: "He is a dreamer. Let us leave him. Pass." Only we in the audience are in a position to see that the dreamer has foretold the path down which all these reasoners will go to that fatal encounter at the Capitol.

Meantime, in these same two episodes, we have learned something about the character of Caesar. In the first, it was the Caesar of human frailties who spoke to us, the husband with his hopeful superstition. In the second, it was the marble superman of state, impassive, impervious, speaking of himself in the third person: "Speak! Caesar is turn'd to hear." He even has the soothsayer brought before his face to repeat the message, as if he thought that somehow, in awe of the marble presence, the message would falter and dissolve: how can a superman need to beware the ides of March?

We hardly have time to do more than glimpse here a man of divided selves, when he is gone. But in his absence, the words of Cassius confirm our glimpse. Cassius' description of him exhibits the same duality that we had noticed earlier. On the one hand, an extremely ordinary man whose stamina in the swimming match was soon exhausted, who, when he had a fever once in Spain, shook and groaned like a sick girl, who even now, as we soon learn, is falling down with epilepsy in the market place. On the other hand, a being who has somehow become a god, who "bears the palm alone," who "bestrides the narrow world / Like a colossus." When the procession returns, no longer festive now, but angry, tense, there is the same effect once more. Our one Caesar shows a normal man's suspicion of his enemies, voices some shrewd human observations about Cassius, says to Antony, "Come on my right hand, for this ear is deaf." Our other Caesar says, as if he were suddenly reminded of something he had forgotten, "I rather tell thee what is to be fear'd / Than what I fear, for always I am Caesar."

Wherever Caesar appears hereafter, we shall find this singular division in him, and nowhere more so than in the scene in which he receives the conspirators at his house. Some aspects of this scene seem calculated for nothing else than to fix upon our minds the superman conception, the Big Brother of Orwell's *1984,* the great resonant name echoing down the halls of time. Thus at the beginning of the scene:

> the things that threatened me
> Ne'er look'd but on my back; when they shall see
> The face of Caesar, they are vanished.

And again later:

> danger knows full well
> That Caesar is more dangerous than he:
> We are two lions litter'd in one day,
> And I the elder and more terrible.

And again still later: "Shall Caesar send a lie?" And again: "The cause is in my will: I will not come." Other aspects, including his concern about Calpurnia's dream, his vacillation about going to the senate house, his anxiety about the portents of the night, plainly mark out his human weaknesses. Finally, as is the habit in this Rome, he puts the irrational from him that his wife's intuitions and her dream embody; he accepts the rationalization of the irrational that Decius skillfully manufactures, and, as earlier at the Lupercalia, hides from himself his own vivid sense of forces that lie beyond the will's control by attributing it to her:

> How foolish do your fears seem now, Calpurnia!
> I am ashamed I did yield to them.
> Give me my robe, for I will go.

So far in our consideration of the implications of I.ii, we have been looking only at Caesar, the title personage of the play, and its historical center. It is time now to turn to Brutus, the play's tragic center, whom we also find to be a divided man—"poor Brutus," to use his own phrase, "with himself at war." The war, we realize as the scene progresses, is a conflict between a quiet, essentially domestic and loving nature, and a powerful integrity expressing itself in a sense of honorable duty to the commonweal. This duality in Brutus seems to be what Cassius is probing at in his long disquisition about the mirror. The Brutus looking into the glass that Cassius figuratively holds up to him, the Brutus of this moment, now, in Rome, is a grave studious private man, of a wonderfully gentle temper, as we shall see again and again later on, very slow to passion, as Cassius' ill-concealed disappointment in having failed to kindle him to immediate response reveals, a man whose sensitive nature recoils at the hint of violence lurking in some of Cassius' speeches, just as he has already recoiled at going on with Caesar to the market place, to witness the mass hysteria of clapping hands, sweaty nightcaps, and stinking breath. This is the present self that looks into Cassius' mirror.

The image that looks back out, that Cassius wants him to see, the potential Brutus, is the man of public spirit, worried already by the question of Caesar's intentions, the lineal descendant of an earlier Brutus who drove a would-be monarch from the city, a man whose body is visibly stiffening in our sight at each huzza from the Forum, and whose anxiety, though he makes no reply to Cassius' inflammatory language, keeps bursting to the surface: "What means this shouting? I do fear the people / Choose Caesar for their king." The problem at the tragic center of the play, we begin to sense, is to be the tug of private versus public, the individual versus a world he never made, any citizen anywhere versus the selective service greetings that history is always mailing out to each of us. And this problem is to be traversed by that other tug this scene presents, of the irrational versus the rational, the destiny we think we can control versus the destiny that sweeps all before it.

Through I.ii, Brutus' public self, the self that responds to these selective service greetings, is no more than a reflection in a mirror, a mere anxiety in his own brain, about which he refuses to confide, even to Cassius. In II.i, we see the public self making further headway. First, there is Brutus' argument with himself about the threat of Caesar, and in his conclusion that Caesar must be killed we note how far his private self—he is, after all, one of Caesar's closest friends—has been invaded by the self of public spirit. From here on, the course of the invasion accelerates. The letter comes, tossed from the public world into the private world, into Brutus' garden, and addressing, as Cassius had, that public image reflected in the mirror: "Brutus, thou sleep'st: awake and see thyself." Then follows the well-known brief soliloquy (which Shakespeare was to expand into the whole play of *Macbeth*), showing us that Brutus' mind has moved on now from the phase of decision to the inquietudes that follow decision:

> Between the acting of a dreadful thing
> And the first motion, all the interim is
> Like a phantasma, or a hideous dream.

What is important to observe is that these lines stress once again the gulf that separates motive from action, that which is interior in man and controllable by his will from that which, once acted, becomes independent of him and moves with a life of its own. This gulf is a no man's land, a phantasma, a hideous dream.

Finally, there arrives in such a form that no audience can miss it the actual visible invasion itself, as this peaceful garden quiet is broken in on by knocking, like the knocking of fate in Beethoven's fifth symphony, and by men with faces hidden in their cloaks. Following this, a lovely interlude with Portia serves to emphasize how much the private self, the private world has been shattered. We have something close to discord here—as much of a discord as these very gentle people are capable of—and though there is a reconciliation at the end and Brutus' promise to confide in her soon, this division in the family is an omen. So is that knock of the latecomer, Caius Ligarius, which reminds us once again of the intrusions of the public life. And when Ligarius throws off his sick man's kerchief on learning that there is an honorable exploit afoot, we may see in it an epitome of the whole scene, a graphic visual renunciation, like Brutus', of the private good to the public; and we may see this also in Brutus' own exit a few lines later, not into the inner house where Portia waits for him, but out into the thunder and lightning of the public life of Rome. It is perhaps significant that at our final view of Portia, two scenes later, she too stands outside the privacy of the house, her mind wholly occupied with thoughts of what is happening at the Capitol, and trying to put on a public self for Brutus' sake: "Run, Lucius, and commend me to my lord: / Say I am merry. . . ."

Meantime, up there by the Capitol, the tragic center and the historical center meet. The suspense is very great as Caesar, seeing the Soothsayer in the throng, reminds him that the ides of March are come, and receives in answer, "Ay, Caesar, but not gone." More suspense as Artemidorus presses forward with the paper that we know contains a full discovery of the plot. Decius, apprehensive, steps quickly into the breach with another paper, a petition from Trebonius. More suspense still as Popilius sidles past Cassius with the whisper, "I wish your enterprise today may thrive," and then moves on to Caesar's side, where he engages him in animated talk. But they detect no tell-tale change in Caesar's countenance; Trebonius steps into his assignment and takes Antony aside; Metellus Cimber throws himself at Caesar's feet; Brutus gives the signal to "press near and second him," and Caesar's "Are we all ready?" draws every eye to Caesar's chair. One by one they all kneel before this demigod—an effective tableau which gives a coloring of priest-like ritual to what they are about to do. Caesar is to bleed, but, as Brutus has said, they will sublimate the act into a sacrifice:

> Let's kill him boldly but not wrathfully;
> Let's carve him as a dish fit for the gods,
> Not hew him as a carcass fit for hounds.

Everything in the scene must underscore this ceremonial attitude, in order to bring out the almost fatuous cleavage between the spirit of this enterprise and its bloody purpose.

The Caesar that we are permitted to see while all this ceremony is preparing is almost entirely the superman, for obvious reasons. To give a color of justice to Brutus' act and so to preserve our sense of his nobility even if we happen to think the assassination a mistake, as an Elizabethan audience emphatically would, Caesar has to appear in a mood of super-humanity at least as fatuous as the conspirators' mood of sacrifice. Hence Shakespeare makes him first of all insult Metellus Cimber: "If thou dost bend and pray and fawn for him, / I spurn thee like a cur"; then comment with intolerable pomposity, and, in fact, blasphemy, on his own iron resolution, for he affects to be immovable even by prayer and hence superior to the very gods. Finally, Shakespeare puts into his mouth one of those supreme arrogances that will remind us of the destroying *hybris* which makes men mad in order to ruin them. "Hence!" Caesar cries, "Wilt thou lift up Olympus?" It is at just this point, when the colossus Caesar drunk with self-love is before us, that Casca strikes. Then they all strike, with a last blow that brings out for the final time the other, human side of this double Caesar: "Et tu, Brute?"

And now this little group of men has altered history. The representative of the evil direction it was taking toward autocratic power lies dead before them. The direction to which it must be restored becomes emphatic in Cassius' cry of "Liberty, freedom, and enfranchisement." Solemnly, and again like priests who have just sacrificed a victim, they kneel together and bathe their hands and swords in Caesar's blood. Brutus exclaims:

> Then walk we forth, even to the market place;
> And waving our red weapons o'er our heads,
> Let's all cry, "Peace, freedom, and liberty!"

If the conjunction of those red hands and weapons with this slogan is not enough to bring an audience up with a start, the next passage will be, for now the conspirators explicitly invoke the judgment of history on their deed. On the stages of theatres the world over, so they anticipate, this lofty incident will be re-enacted, and

> So oft as that shall be,
> So often shall the knot of us be call'd
> The men that gave their country liberty.

We, the audience, recalling what actually did result in Rome—the civil wars, the long line of despotic emperors—cannot miss the irony of their prediction, an irony that insists on our recognizing that this effort to control history is going to fail. Why does it fail?

One reason why is shown us in the next few moments. The leader of this assault on history is, like many another reformer, a man of high idealism, who devoutly believes that the rest of the world is like himself. It was just to kill Caesar—so he persuades himself—because he was a great threat to freedom. It would not have been just to kill Antony, and he vetoed the idea. Even now, when the consequence of that decision has come back to face him in the shape of Antony's servant, kneeling before him, he sees no reason to reconsider it. There are good grounds for what they have done, he says; Antony will hear them, and be satisfied. With Antony, who shortly arrives in person, he takes this line again:

> Our reasons are so full of good regard
> That were you, Antony, the son of Caesar
> You should be satisfied.

With equal confidence in the rationality of man, he puts by Cassius' fears of what Antony will do if allowed to address the people: "By your pardon; I will myself into the pulpit first / And show the reason of our Caesar's death." Here is a man so much a friend of Caesar's that he is still speaking of him as "our Caesar," so capable of rising to what he takes to be his duty that he has taken on the leadership of those who intend to kill him, so trusting of common decency that he expects the populace will respond to reason, and Antony to the obligation laid on him by their permitting him to speak. At such a man, one hardly knows whether to laugh or cry.

The same mixture of feelings is likely to be stirring in us as Brutus speaks to the people in III.ii. As everybody knows, this is a speech in what used to be called the great liberal tradition, the tradition that assumed, as our American founding fathers did, that men in the mass are reasonable. It has therefore been made a prose oration, spare and terse in diction, tightly patterned in syntax so that it requires close attention, and founded, with respect to its argument, on three elements: the abstract sentiment of duty to the state (because he endangered Rome, Caesar had to be slain); the abstract sentiment of political justice (because he was ambitious, Caesar deserved his fall); and the moral authority of the man Brutus. As long as that moral authority is concretely before them in Brutus' presence, the populace is impressed. But since they are not trained minds, and only trained minds respond accurately to abstractions, they do not understand the content of his argument at all, as one of them indicates by shouting, "Let him be Caesar!" What moves them is the obvious sincerity and the known integrity of the speaker; and when he finishes, they are ready to carry him off on their shoulders on that account alone, leaving Antony a vacant Forum. The fair-mindedness of Brutus is thrilling but painful to behold as he calms this triumphal surge in his favor, urges them to stay and hear Antony, and then, in a moment very impressive dramatically as well as symbolically, walks off the stage, alone. We see then, if we have not seen before, the first answer to the question why the attack on history failed. It was blinded, as it so often has been, by the very idealism that impelled it.

When Antony takes the rostrum, we begin to get a second answer. It has been said by somebody that in a school for demagogues this speech should be the whole curriculum. Antony himself describes its method when he observes in the preceding scene, apropos of the effect of Caesar's dead body on the messenger from Octavius, "Passion, I see, is catching." This is a statement that cannot be made about reason, as many a school teacher learns to his cost. I have not time at my disposal to do anything like justice to Antony's speech, but I should like to make the following summary points.

First, Brutus formulates from the outset positive propositions about Caesar and about his own motives, on no other authority than his own. Because of his known integrity, Brutus can do this. Antony takes the safer alternative of concealing propositions in questions, by which the audience's mind is then guided to conclusions which seem its own:

> He hath brought many captives home to Rome,
> Whose ransoms did the general coffers fill:
> Did this in Caesar seem ambitious?
>
> . . .
>
> You all did see that on the Lupercal
> I thrice presented him a kingly crown,
> Which he did thrice refuse: was this ambition?

How well Shakespeare knew his crowds can be seen in the replies to Antony. Brutus, appealing to their reason, was greeted with wild outbursts of uncomprehending emotion: "Let him be Caesar!" Antony appeals only to their emotions and their pockets, but now they say, "Methinks there is much reason in his sayings," and chew upon it seriously.

Second, Antony stirs up impulses and then thwarts them. He appeals to their curiosity and their greed in the matter of the will, but then he doesn't come clean on it. In the same manner, he stirs up their rage against the conspirators, yet always pretends to hold them back: "I fear I wrong the honorable men / Whose daggers have stabb'd Caesar; I do fear it." Third, and this is largely the technical means by which he accomplishes the stirring up, his speech is baited with irony. The passage just quoted is a typical specimen. So is the famous refrain, "For Brutus is an honorable man." Now the rhetorical value of irony is that it stimulates the mind to formulate the contrary, that is, the intended meaning. It stimulates what the psychologists of propaganda nowadays call the assertive factor. "Are you the one man in seven who shaves daily?" "Did your husband forget to kiss you this morning?" The advertiser's technique is not, of course, ironical, but it illustrates the effect.

Finally, Antony rests his case, not, like Brutus, on abstractions centering in the state and political justice, but on emotions centering in the individual listener. The first great crescendo of the speech, which culminates in the passage on Caesar's wounds, appeals first to pity and then to indignation. The second one, culminating in the reading of Caesar's will, appeals first to curiosity and greed and then to gratitude. The management of the will is particularly cunning: it is an item more concrete than any words could be, an actual tantalizing document that can be flashed before the eye, after the manner of the senator mentioned in my preamble. It is described, at first vaguely, as being of such a sort that they would honor Caesar for it. Then, closer home, as something which would show "how Caesar lov'd you." Then, with an undisguised appeal to self-interest, as a testament that will make them his "heirs." The emotions aroused by this news enable Antony to make a final test of his ironical refrain about the "honorable men," and finding the results all that he had hoped, he can come down now among the crowd as one of them, and appeal directly to their feelings by appealing to his own: "If you have tears to shed, prepare to shed them now."

The success of this direct appeal to passion can be seen at its close. Where formerly we had a populace, now we have a mob. Since it is a mob, its mind can be sealed against any later seepage of rationality back into it by the insinuation that reasoning is always false anyway—simply a surface covering up private grudges, like the "reason" they have heard from Brutus; whereas from Antony himself, the plain blunt friend of Caesar, they are getting the plain blunt truth and (a favorite trick of politicians) only what they already know to be the truth.

But also, since it is a mob and therefore will eventually cool off, it must be called back one final time to hear the will. Antony no longer needs this as an incentive to riot; the mingled rage and pity he has aroused will take care of that. But when the hangover comes, and you are remembering how that fellow looked swaying a little on the rope's end, with his eyes bugging out and the veins knotted at his temples, then it is good to have something really reasonable to cling to, like seventy-five drachmas (or even thirty pieces of silver) and some orchards along a river.

At about this point, it becomes impossible not to see that a second reason for the failure of the attack on history is what it left out of account—what all these Romans from the beginning, except Antony, have been trying to leave out of account: the phenomenon of feeling, the nonrational factor in men, in the world, in history itself—of which this blind infuriated mob is one kind of exemplification. Too secure in his own fancied suppression of the subrational, Brutus has failed altogether to reckon with its power. Thus he could seriously say to Antony in the passage I quoted earlier: Antony, even if you were "the son of Caesar / You should be satisfied," as if the feeling of a son for a murdered father could ever be "satisfied" by reasons. And thus, too, he could walk off the stage alone, urging the crowd to hear Antony, the very figure of embodied "reason," unaware that only the irrational is catching.

Meantime, the scene of the mob tearing Cinna the Poet to pieces simply for having the same name as one of the conspirators (III.iii) gives us our first taste of the chaos invoked by Antony when he stood alone over Caesar's corpse. And as we consider that prediction and this mob, we are bound to realize that there is a third reason why the attack on history failed. As we have seen already, history is only partly responsive to noble motives, only partly responsive to rationality. Now we see—what Shakespeare hinted in the beginning with those two episodes of Calpurnia and the soothsayer—that it is only partly responsive to human influence of any sort. With all their reasons, the conspirators and Caesar only carried out what the soothsayer foreknew. There is, in short, a determination in history, whether we call it natural or providential, which at least *helps* to shape our ends, "rough hew them how we will." One of the names of that factor in this play is Caesarism. Brutus put the point, all unconsciously, in that scene when the conspirators were gathered at his house. He said:

> We all stand up against the spirit of Caesar:
> And in the spirit of men there is no blood:
> O that we could come by Caesar's spirit,
> And not dismember Caesar! But, alas,
> Caesar must bleed for it.

Then Caesar did bleed for it; but his spirit, as Brutus' own remark should have told him, proved to be invulnerable. It was only set free by his assassination, and now, as Antony says, "ranging for revenge,

. . . Shall in these confines with a monarch's voice / Cry 'Havoc' and let slip the dogs of war."

The rest of the play, I think, is self-explanatory. It is clear all through Acts IV and V that Brutus and Cassius are defeated before they begin to fight. Antony knows it and says so at V.i. Cassius knows it too. Cassius, an Epicurean in philosophy, and therefore one who has never heretofore believed in omens, now mistrusts his former rationalism: he suspects there may be something after all in those ravens, crows, and kites that wheel overhead. Brutus too mistrusts *his* rationalism. As a Stoic, his philosophy requires him to repudiate suicide, but he admits to Cassius that if the need comes he will repudiate philosophy instead. This, like Cassius' statement, is an unconscious admission of the force of unreason in human affairs, an unreason that makes its presence felt again and again during the great battle. Cassius, for instance, fails to realize that Octavius "Is overthrown by noble Brutus' power," becomes the victim of a mistaken report of Titinius' death, runs on his sword crying, "Caesar, thou art reveng'd," and is greeted, dead, by Brutus, in words that make still clearer their defeat by history: "O Julius Caesar, thou art mighty yet! / Thy spirit walks abroad, and turns our swords / In our own proper entrails." In the same vein, when it is Brutus' turn to die, we learn that the ghost of Caesar has reappeared, and he thrusts the sword home, saying, "Caesar, now be still."

To come then to a brief summary. Though I shouldn't care to be dogmatic about it, it seems clear to me that Shakespeare's primary theme in *Julius Caesar* has to do with the always ambiguous impact between man and history. During the first half of the play, what we are chiefly conscious of is the human will as a force in history—men making choices, controlling events. Our typical scenes are I.ii, where a man is trying to make up his mind; or II.i, where a man first reaches a decision and then, with his fellows, lays plans to implement it; or II.ii, where we have Decius Brutus persuading Caesar to decide to go to the senate house; or III.i and ii, where up through the assassination, and even up through Antony's speech, men are still, so to speak, impinging on history, moulding it to their conscious will.

But then comes a change. Though we still have men in action trying to mould their world (or else we would have no play at all), one senses a real shift in the direction of the impact. We begin to feel the insufficiency of noble aims, for history is also consequences; the insufficiency of reason and rational expectation, for the ultimate consequences of an act in history are unpredictable, and usually, by all human standards, illogical as well; and finally, the insufficiency of the human will itself, for there is always something to be reckoned with that is nonhuman and inscrutable—Nemesis, Moira, Fortuna, the Parcae, Providence, Determinism: men have had many names for it, but it is always there. Accordingly, in the second half of the play, our typical scenes are those like III.iii, where Antony has raised something that is no longer under his control; or like IV.i, where we see men acting as if, under the control of expediency or necessity or call it what you will, they no longer had wills of their own but prick down the names of nephews and brothers indiscriminately for slaughter; or like IV.iii and all the scenes thereafter, where we are constantly made to feel that Cassius and Brutus are in the hands of something bigger than they know.

In this light, we can see readily enough why it is that Shakespeare gave Julius Caesar that double character. The human Caesar who has human ailments and is a human friend is the Caesar that can be killed. The marmoreal Caesar, the everlasting Big Brother—the Napoleon, Mussolini, Hitler, Franco, Peron, Stalin, Kruschev, to mention only a handful of his more recent incarnations—that Caesar is the one who must repeatedly be killed but never dies, because he is in you, and you, and you, and me. Every classroom is a Rome, and there is no reason for any pupil, when he studies *Julius Caesar,* to imagine that this is ancient history.

Hamlet: The Prince or the Poem?

C. S. Lewis

A critic who makes no claim to be a true Shakespearian scholar and who has been honoured by an invitation to speak about Shakespeare to such an audience as this, feels rather like a child brought in at dessert to recite his piece before the grown-ups. I have a temptation to furbish up all my meagre Shakespearian scholarship and to plunge into some textual or chronological problem in the hope of seeming, for this one hour, more of an expert than I am. But it really wouldn't do. I should not deceive you: I should not even deceive myself. I have therefore decided to bestow all my childishness upon you.

And first, a reassurance. I am not going to advance a new interpretation of the character of Hamlet. Where great critics have failed I could not hope to succeed; it is rather my ambition (a more moderate one, I trust) to understand their failure. The problem I want to consider today arises in fact not directly out of the Prince's character nor even

---

From *Proceedings of the British Academy XXVIII.* Published by Oxford University Press. Reprinted by permission of Oxford University Press.

directly out of the play, but out of the state of criticism about the play.

To give anything like a full history of this criticism would be beyond my powers and beyond the scope of a lecture; but, for my present purposes, I think we can very roughly divide it into three main schools or tendencies. The first is that which maintains simply that the actions of Hamlet have not been given adequate motives and that the play is so far bad. . . . In our own time Mr Eliot has taken this view: *Hamlet* is rather like a film on which two photographs have been taken—an unhappy superposition of Shakespeare's work 'upon much cruder material'. The play 'is most certainly an artistic failure'. If this school of critics is right, we shall be wasting our time in attempting to understand why Hamlet delayed. The second school, on the other hand, thinks that he did not delay at all but went to work as quickly as the circumstances permitted. . . . This position has been brilliantly defended in modern times. In the third school or group I include all those critics who admit that Hamlet procrastinates and who explain the procrastination by his psychology. Within this general agreement there are, no doubt, very great diversities. Some critics, such as Hallam, Sievers, Raleigh, and Clutton Brock, trace the weakness to the shock inflicted upon Hamlet by the events which precede, and immediately follow, the opening of the play; others regard it as a more permanent condition; some extend it to actual insanity, others reduce it to an almost amiable flaw in a noble nature. This third group, which boasts the names of Richardson, Goethe, Coleridge, Schlegel, and Hazlitt, can still, I take it, claim to represent the central and, as it were, orthodox line of *Hamlet* criticism.

Such is the state of affairs; and we are all so accustomed to it that we are inclined to ignore its oddity. In order to remove the veil of familiarity I am going to ask you to make the imaginative effort of looking at this mass of criticism as if you had no independent knowledge of the thing criticized. Let us suppose that a picture which you have not seen is being talked about. The first thing you gather from the vast majority of the speakers—and a majority which includes the best art critics—is that this picture is undoubtedly a very great work. The next thing you discover is that hardly any two people in the room agree as to what it is a picture of. Most of them find something curious about the pose, and perhaps even the anatomy, of the central figure. One explains it by saying that it is a picture of the raising of Lazarus, and that the painter has cleverly managed to represent the uncertain gait of a body just recovering from the stiffness of death. Another, taking the central figure to be Bacchus returning from the conquest of India, says that it reels because it is drunk. A third, to whom it is self-evident that he has seen a picture of the death of Nelson, asks with some temper whether you expect a man to look quite normal just after he has been mortally wounded. A fourth maintains that such crudely representational canons of criticism will never penetrate so profound a work, and that the peculiarities of the central figure really reflect the content of the painter's subconsciousness. Hardly have you had time to digest these opinions when you run into another group of critics who denounce as a pseudo-problem what the first group has been discussing. According to this second group there is nothing odd about the central figure. A more natural and self-explanatory pose they never saw and they cannot imagine what all the bother is about. At long last you discover—isolated in a corner of the room, somewhat frowned upon by the rest of the company, and including few reputable *connoisseurs* in its ranks—a little knot of men who are whispering that the picture is a villainous daub and that the mystery of the central figure merely results from the fact that it is out of drawing.

Now if all this had really happened to any one of us, I believe that our first reaction would be to accept, at least provisionally, the third view. Certainly I think we should consider it much more seriously than we usually consider those critics who solve the whole *Hamlet* problem by calling *Hamlet* a bad play. At the very least we should at once perceive that they have a very strong case against the critics who admire. 'Here is a picture,' they might say, 'on whose meaning no two of you are in agreement. Communication between the artist and the spectator has almost completely broken down, for each of you admits that it has broken down as regards every spectator except himself. There are only two possible explanations. Either the artist was a very bad artist, or you are very bad critics. In deference to your number and your reputation, we choose the first alternative; though, as you will observe, it would work out to the same result if we chose the second.' As to the next group—those who denied that there was anything odd about the central figure—I believe that in the circumstances I have imagined we should hardly attend to them. A natural and self-explanatory pose in the central figure would be rejected as wholly inconsistent with its observed effect on all the other critics, both those who thought the picture good and those who thought it bad.

If we now return to the real situation, the same reactions appear reasonable. There is, indeed, this difference, that the critics who admit no delay and no indecision in Hamlet have an opponent with whom the corresponding critics of the picture were not embarrassed. The picture did not answer back. But Hamlet does. He pronounces himself a procrastinator, an undecided man, even a coward: and the ghost in part agrees with him. This, coupled with the more general difficulties of their position, appears to me to be fatal to their view. If so, we are left with those who think the play bad and those who agree in thinking it good and in placing its goodness almost wholly in the character of the hero, while disagreeing as to what that character is. Surely the devil's advocates are in a very strong position. Here is a play so dominated by one character that '*Hamlet* without the Prince' is a by-word. Here are critics justly famed, all of them for their sensibility, many of them for their skill in catching the finest shades of human passion and pursuing motives to their last hiding-places. Is it really credible that the greatest of dramatists, the most powerful painter of men, offering to such an audience his consummate portrait of a man should produce something which, if any one of them is right, all the rest have in some degree failed to recognize? Is this the sort of thing that happens? Does the meeting of supremely creative with supremely receptive imagination usually produce such results? Or is it not far easier to say that Homer nods, and Alexander's shoulder drooped, and Achilles' heel was vulnerable, and that Shakespeare, for once, either in haste, or over-reaching himself in unhappy ingenuity, has brought forth an abortion?

Yes. Of course it is far easier. 'Most certainly,' says Mr Eliot, 'an artistic failure.' But is it 'most certain'? Let me return for a moment to my analogy of the picture. In that dream there was one experiment we did not make. We didn't walk into the next room and look at it for ourselves. Supposing we had done so. Suppose that at the first glance all the cogent arguments of the unfavourable critics had dried on our lips, or echoed in our ears as idle babble. Suppose that looking on the picture we had found ourselves caught up into an unforgettable intensity of life and had come back from the room where it hung haunted for ever with the sense of vast dignities and strange sorrows and teased with thoughts beyond the reaches of our souls'—would not this have reversed our judgement and compelled us, in the teeth of *a priori* probability, to maintain that on one point at least the orthodox critics were in the right? 'Most certainly an artistic failure.' All argument is for that conclusion—until you read or see *Hamlet* again. And when you do, you are left saying that if this is failure, then failure is better than success. We want more of these 'bad' plays. From our first childish reading of the ghost scenes down to those golden minutes which we stole from marking examination papers on *Hamlet* to read a few pages of *Hamlet* itself, have we ever known the day or the hour when its enchantment failed? That castle is part of our own world. The affection we feel for the Prince, and, through him, for Horatio, is like a friendship in real life. The very turns of expression—half-lines and odd connecting links—of this play are worked into the language. It appears, said Shaftesbury in 1710, 'most to have affected English hearts and has perhaps been oftenest acted'. It has a taste of its own, an all-pervading relish which we recognize even in its smallest fragments, and which, once tasted, we recur to. When we want that taste, no other book will do instead. It may turn out in the end that the thing is not a complete success. This compelling quality in it may coexist with some radical defect. But I doubt if we shall ever be able to say, sad brow and true maid, that it is 'most certainly' a failure. Even if the proposition that it has failed were at last admitted for true, I can think of few critical truths which most of us would utter with less certainty, and with a more divided mind.

It seems, then, that we cannot escape from our problem by pronouncing the play bad. On the other hand, the critics, mostly agreeing to place the excellence of it in the delineation of the hero's character, describe that character in a dozen different ways. If they differ so much as to the kind of man whom Shakespeare meant to portray, how can we explain their unanimous praise of the portrayal? I can imagine a sketch so bad that one man thought it was an attempt at a horse and another thought it was an attempt at a donkey. But what kind of sketch would it have to be which looked like a *very good* horse to some, and like a *very good* donkey to others? The only solution which occurs to me is that the critics' delight in the play is not in fact due to the delineation of Hamlet's character but to something else. If the picture which you take for a horse and I for a donkey, delights us both, it is probable that what we are both enjoying is the pure line, or the colouring, not the delineation of an animal. If two men who have both been talking to the same woman agree in proclaiming her conversation delightful, though one praises it for its ingenuous innocence and the other for its clever sophistication, I should be inclined to conclude that her conversation has played very little part in the pleasure of either. I should suspect that the lady was nice to look at. . . .

A good way of introducing you to my experience of *Hamlet* will be to tell you the exact point at which anyone else's criticism of it begins to lose my allegiance. It is a fairly definite point. As soon as I find anyone treating the ghost merely as the means whereby Hamlet learns of his father's murder—as soon as a critic leaves us with the impression that some other method of disclosure (the finding of a letter or a conversation with a servant) would have done very nearly as well—I part company with that critic. After that, he may be as learned and sensitive as you please; but his outlook on literature is so remote from mine that he can teach me nothing. Hamlet for me is no more separable from his ghost than Macbeth from his witches, Una from her lion, or Dick Whittington from his cat. The Hamlet formula, so to speak, is not 'a man who has to avenge his father' but 'a man who has been given a task by a ghost'. Everything else about him is less important than that. If the play did not begin with the cold and darkness and sickening suspense of the ghost scenes it would be a radically different play. If, on the other hand, only the first act had survived, we should have a very tolerable notion of the play's peculiar quality. I put it to you that everyone's imagination here confirms mine. What is against me is the abstract pattern of motives and characters which we build up as critics when the actual flavour or tint of the poetry is already fading from our minds.

This ghost is different from any other ghost in Elizabethan drama—for, to tell the truth, the Elizabethans in general do their ghosts very vilely. It is permanently ambiguous. Indeed the very word 'ghost', by putting it into the same class with the 'ghosts' of Kyd and Chapman, nay by classifying it at all, puts us on the wrong track. It is 'this thing', 'this dreaded sight', an 'illusion', a 'spirit of health or goblin damn'd', liable at any moment to assume 'some other horrible form' which reason could not survive the vision of. Critics have disputed whether Hamlet is sincere when he doubts whether the apparition is his father's ghost or not. I take him to be perfectly sincere. He believes while the thing is present: he doubts when it is away. Doubt, uncertainty, bewilderment to almost any degree, is what the ghost creates not only in Hamlet's mind but in the minds of the other characters. Shakespeare does not take the concept of 'ghost' for granted, as other dramatists had done. In his play the appearance of the spectre means a breaking down of the walls of the world and the germination of thoughts that cannot really be thought: chaos is come again.

This does not mean that I am going to make the ghost the hero, or the play a ghost story—though I might add that a very good ghost story would be, to me, a more interesting thing than a maze of motives. I have started with the ghost because the ghost appears at the beginning of the play not only to give Hamlet necessary information but also, and even more, to strike the note. From the platform we pass to the court scene and so to Hamlet's first long speech. There are ten lines of it before we reach what is necessary to the plot: lines about the melting of flesh into a dew and the divine prohibition of self-slaughter. We have a second ghost scene after which the play itself, rather than the hero, goes mad for some minutes. We have a second soliloquy on the theme 'to die . . . to sleep'; and a third on 'the witching time of night, when churchyards yawn'. We have the King's effort to pray and Hamlet's comment on it. We have the ghost's third appearance. Ophelia goes mad and is drowned. Then comes the comic relief, surely the strangest comic relief ever written—comic relief beside an open grave, with a further discussion of suicide, a detailed inquiry into the rate of decomposition, a few clutches of skulls, and then 'Alas, poor Yorick!' On top of this, the hideous fighting in the grave; and then, soon, the catastrophe. . . .

In a sense, the subject of *Hamlet* is death. I do not mean by this that most of the characters die, or even that life and death are the stakes they play for; that is true of all tragedies. I do not mean that we rise from the reading of the play with the feeling that we have been in cold, empty places, places 'outside', *nocte tacentia late,* though that is true. Before I go on to explain myself let me say that here, and throughout my lecture, I am most deeply indebted to my friend Mr Owen Barfield. I have to make these acknowledgements both to him and to other of my friends so often that I am afraid of their being taken for an affectation. But they are not. The next best thing to being wise oneself is to live in a circle of those who are: that good fortune I have enjoyed for nearly twenty years.

The sense in which death is the subject of *Hamlet* will become apparent if we compare it with other plays. Macbeth has commerce with Hell, but at the very outset of his career dismisses all thought of the life to come. For Brutus and Othello, suicide in the high tragic manner is escape and climax. For Lear death is deliverance. For Romeo and

Antony, poignant loss. For all these, as for their author while he writes and the audience while they watch, death is the end: it is almost the frame of the picture. They think of dying: no one thinks, in these plays, of *being dead*. In Hamlet we are kept thinking about it all the time, whether in terms of the soul's destiny or of the body's. Purgatory, Hell, Heaven, the wounded name, the rights—or wrongs—of Ophelia's burial, and the staying-power of a tanner's corpse: and beyond this, beyond all Christian and all Pagan maps of the hereafter, comes a curious groping and tapping of thoughts, about 'what dreams may come'. It is this that gives to the whole play its quality of darkness and of misgiving. Of course there is much else in the play: but nearly always, the same groping. The characters are all watching one another, forming theories about one another, listening, contriving, full of anxiety. The world of *Hamlet* is a world where one has lost one's way. The Prince also has no doubt lost his, and we can tell the precise moment at which he finds it again. 'Not a whit. We defy augury. There's a special providence in the fall of a sparrow. If it be now, 'tis not to come: if it be not to come, it will be now: if it be not now, yet it will come: the readiness is all: since no man has aught of what he leaves, what is't to leave betimes?'

If I wanted to make one more addition to the gallery of Hamlet's portraits I should trace his hesitation to the fear of death; not to a physical fear of dying, but a fear of being dead. And I think I should get on quite comfortably. Any serious attention to the state of being dead, unless it is limited by some definite religious or anti-religious doctrine, must, I suppose, paralyse the will by introducing infinite uncertainties and rendering all motives inadequate. Being dead is the unknown x in our sum. Unless you ignore it or else give it a value, you can get no answer. But this is not what I am going to do. Shakespeare has not left in the text clear lines of causation which would enable us to connect Hamlet's hesitations with this source. I do not believe he has given us data for any portrait of the kind critics have tried to draw. To that extent I agree with Hanmer, Rümelin, and Mr Eliot. But I differ from them in thinking that it is a fault.

For what, after all, is happening to us when we read any of Hamlet's great speeches? We see visions of the flesh dissolving into a dew, of the world like an unweeded garden. We think of memory reeling in its 'distracted globe'. We watch him scampering hither and thither like a maniac to avoid the voices wherewith he is haunted. Someone says 'Walk out of the air', and we hear the words 'Into my grave' spontaneously respond to it. We think of being bounded in a nut-shell and king of infinite space: but for bad dreams. There's the trouble, for 'I am most dreadfully attended'. We see the picture of a dull and muddy-mettled rascal, a John-a-dreams, somehow unable to move while ultimate dishonour is done him. We listen to his fear lest the whole thing may be an illusion due to melancholy. We get the sense of sweet relief at the words 'shuffled off this mortal coil' but mixed with the bottomless doubt about what may follow then. We think of bones and skulls, of women breeding sinners, and of how some, to whom all this experience is a sealed book, can yet dare death and danger 'for an egg-shell'. But do we really enjoy these things, do we go back to them, because they show us Hamlet's character? Are they, from *that* point of view, so very interesting? Does the mere fact that a young man, literally haunted, dispossessed, and lacking friends, should feel thus, tell us anything remarkable? Let me put my question in another way. If instead of the speeches he actually utters about the firmament and man in his scene with Rosencrantz and Guildenstern Hamlet had merely said, 'I don't seem to enjoy things the way I used to,' and talked in that fashion throughout, should we find him interesting? I think the answer is 'Not very.' It may be replied that if he talked commonplace prose he would reveal his character less vividly. I am not so sure. He would certainly have revealed *something* less vividly; but would that something be himself? It seems to me that 'this majestical roof' and 'What a piece of work is a man' give me primarily an impression not of the sort of person he must be to lose the estimation of things but of the things themselves and their great value; and that I should be able to discern, though with very faint interest, the same condition of loss in a personage who was quite unable so to put before me what he was losing. And I do not think it true to reply that he would be a different character if he spoke less poetically. This point is often misunderstood. We sometimes speak as if the characters in whose mouths Shakespeare puts great poetry were poets: in the sense that Shakespeare was depicting men of poetical genius. But surely this is like thinking that Wagner's Wotan is the dramatic portrait of a baritone? In opera song is the medium by which the representation is made and not part of the thing represented. The actors sing; the dramatic personages are feigned to be speaking. The only character who sings dramatically in *Figaro* is Cherubino. Similarly in poetical drama poetry is the medium, not part of the delineated characters. While the actors speak poetry written for them by the poet, the dramatic personages are supposed to be merely talking. If ever there is occasion to *represent* poetry (as in the play scene from *Hamlet*), it is put into a different metre and strongly stylized so as to prevent confusion.

I trust that my conception is now becoming clear. I believe that we read Hamlet's speeches with interest chiefly because they describe so well a certain spiritual region through which most of us have passed and anyone in his circumstances might be expected to pass, rather than because of our concern to understand how and why this particular man entered it. I foresee an objection on the ground that I am thus really admitting his 'character' in the only sense that matters and that all characters whatever could be equally well talked away by the method I have adopted. But I do really find a distinction. When I read about Mrs Proudie I am not in the least interested in seeing the world from her point of view, for her point of view is not interesting; what does interest me is precisely the sort of person she was. In *Middlemarch* no reader wants to see Casaubon through Dorothea's eyes; the pathos, the comedy, the value of the whole thing is to understand Dorothea and see how such an illusion was inevitable for her. In Shakespeare himself I find Beatrice to be a character who could not be thus dissolved. We are interested not in some vision seen through her eyes, but precisely in the wonder of her being the girl she is. A comparison of the sayings we remember from her part with those we remember from Hamlet's brings out the contrast. On the one hand, 'I wonder that you will still be talking, Signior Benedick', 'There was a star danced and under that I was born', 'Kill Claudio'; on the other, 'The undiscovered country, from whose bourne no traveller returns', 'Use every man after his desert, and who should 'scape whipping?', 'The rest is silence.' Particularly noticeable is the passage where Hamlet professes to be describing his own character. 'I am myself indifferent honest, but yet I could accuse me of such things that it were better my mother had not borne me: I am very proud, revengeful, ambitious'. It is, of course, possible to devise some theory which explains these self-accusations in terms of character. But long before we have done so the real significance of the lines has taken possession of our imagination for ever. 'Such fellows as I' does not mean 'such fellows as Goethe's Hamlet, or Coleridge's Hamlet, or any Hamlet': it means *men*—creatures shapen in sin and conceived in iniquity—and the vast, empty visions of them 'crawling between earth and heaven' is what really counts and really carries the burden of the play.

It is often cast in the teeth of the great critics that each in painting *Hamlet* has drawn a portrait of himself. How if they were right? I would go a long way to meet Beatrice or Falstaff or Mr Jonathan Oldbuck or Disraeli's Lord Monmouth. I would not cross the room to meet Hamlet. It would never be necessary. He is always where I am. The method of the whole play is much nearer to Mr Eliot's own method in poetry than Mr Eliot suspects. Its true hero is man—haunted man—man with his mind on the frontier of two worlds, man unable either quite to reject or quite to admit the supernatural, man struggling to get something done as man has struggled from the beginning, yet incapable of achievement because of his inability to understand either himself or his fellows or the real quality of the universe which has produced him. To be sure, some hints of more particular motives for Hamlet's delay are every now and then fadged up to silence our questions, just as some show of motives is offered for the Duke's temporary abdication in *Measure for Measure*. In both cases it is only scaffolding or machinery. To mistake these mere *succedanea* for the real play and to try to work them up into a coherent psychology is the great error. I once had a whole batch of School Certificate answers on the 'Nun's Priest's Tale' by boys whose form-master was apparently a breeder of poultry. Everything that Chaucer had said in describing Chauntecleer and Pertelote was treated by them simply and solely as evidence about the precise breed of these two birds. And, I must admit, the result was very interesting. They proved beyond doubt that Chauntecleer was very different from our modern specialized strains and much closer to the Old English 'barn-door fowl'. But I couldn't help feeling that they had missed something. I believe our attention to Hamlet's 'character' in the usual sense misses almost as much.

Perhaps I should rather say that it *would* miss as much if our behaviour when we are actually reading were not wiser than our criticism in cold blood. The critics, or most of them, have at any rate kept constantly before us the knowledge that in this play there is greatness and mystery. They were never entirely wrong. Their error, in my view, was to put the mystery in the wrong place—in Hamlet's motives rather than in that darkness which enwraps Hamlet and the whole tragedy and all who read or watch it. It is a mysterious play in the sense of being a play about mystery. Mr Eliot suggests that 'more people have thought *Hamlet* a work of art because they found it interesting, than have found it interesting because it is a work of art'. When he wrote that sentence he must have been very near to what I believe to be the truth. This play is, above all else, *interesting*. But artistic failure is not in itself interesting, nor often interesting in any way: artistic success always is. To interest is the first duty of art; no other excellences will even begin to compensate for failure in this, and very serious faults will be covered by this, as by charity. The hypothesis that this play interests by being good and not by being bad has therefore the first claim on our consideration. The burden of proof rests on the other side. Is not the fascinated interest of the critics most naturally explained by supposing that this is the precise effect the play was written to produce? They may be finding the mystery in the wrong place; but the fact that they can never leave *Hamlet* alone, the continual groping, the sense, unextinguished by over a century of failures, that we have here something of inestimable importance, is surely the best evidence that the real and lasting mystery of our human situation has been greatly depicted.

The kind of criticism which I have attempted is always at a disadvantage against either historical criticism or character criticism. Their vocabulary has been perfected by long practice, and the truths with which they are concerned are those which we are accustomed to handle in the everyday business of life. But the things I want to talk about have no vocabulary and criticism has for centuries kept almost complete silence on them. I make no claim to be a pioneer. Professor Wilson Knight (though I disagree with nearly everything he says in detail), Miss Spurgeon, Miss Bodkin, and Mr Barfield are my leaders. But those who do not enjoy the honours of a pioneer may yet share his discomforts. One of them I feel acutely at the moment. I feel certain that to many of you the things I have been saying about *Hamlet* will appear intolerably sophisticated, abstract, and modern. And so they sound when we have to put them into words. But I shall have failed completely if I cannot persuade you that my view, for good or ill, has just the opposite characteristics—is naïve and concrete and archaic. I am trying to recall attention from the things an intellectual adult notices to the things a child or a peasant notices—night, ghosts, a castle, a lobby where a man can walk four hours together, a willow-fringed brook and a sad lady drowned, a graveyard and a terrible cliff above the sea, and amidst all these a pale man in black clothes (would that our producers would ever let him appear!) with his stockings coming down, a dishevelled man whose words make us at once think of loneliness and doubt and dread, of waste and dust and emptiness, and from whose hands, or from our own, we feel the richness of heaven and earth and the comfort of human affection slipping away.

"Troilus and Cressida"

Robert Ornstein

After the melancholy deeps of *Hamlet, Troilus and Cressida* and *Measure for Measure* seem strange interludes of mockery and denigration, retreats from the tragedy of evil to the comedy of vice. They are problems if not problem plays, "un-Shakespearean" in temper and viewpoint, ambiguous in characterization. They seem to turn ideals of chivalry, justice, and mercy seamy side out. The lecher leers over the virgin's shoulder; the romantic idealist falls in love with a whore; one touch of nature in the loins makes the whole world kin. But they are not so much comical satires as dialectical dramas in the manner of *Byron's Conspiracy;* like Chapman's play they approach the issues of tragedy ironically and analytically, and thus engage the intellect more than the imagination. If by comparison to the *Iliad* and the medieval gestes of Troy, *Troilus* seems a mockery of heroism, it is not contemptuous of the virtues which men sacrifice at the altar of war. Behind the joke of Achilles' cowardice and Pandarus' aching bones lies a serious study of man's aspiration towards the ideal in love and war.

In *Troilus* Shakespeare explores the paradoxical truth that war and lechery—the most primitive human activities—have from the dawn of

---

From Robert Ornstein, *The Moral Vision of Jacobean Tragedy,* the University of Wisconsin Press, 1960. Reprinted by permission of the copyright owners, the Regents of the University of Wisconsin.

civilization excited man's highest poetic faculties. The heroic legend immortalizes the conflicting dualities of man's nature and poses the central problem of his quest for ideal values. Chained to the earth by animal desires, condemned by mortality to the tyranny of time, man nevertheless hungers for a dedication that will give permanent significance to his life. Even in the savagery of war he learns some final truth about his humanity; even in untimely death he satisfies a hunger for experience that might otherwise be unfulfilled. Religion and philosophy escape the oppression of time by postulating eternal metaphysical values. The chivalric ideal challenges time with an appropriate recklessness by exalting the transitory qualities of youth, beauty, and strength and by placing its absolutes within the realm of mortality. By sophisticating primitive impulses with ceremonial ritual, it heightens and glorifies the sensation of life that flames in the brief orgiastic pleasures of love and war. It finds its eternity in the ecstatic moments of sexual possession and military conquest, the ancient complementary proofs of manhood and virility.

The Homeric myth tells of a decade of slaughter for the possession of a beautiful woman; the analytic intellect seeks a more realistic and complex motive for human sacrifice. It cannot believe that men died for the sake of a faithless woman, especially after years of futile, senseless struggle. Logic insists that ultimately both sides must have despised Helen. And thus Diomedes speaks for the Greeks:

> She's bitter to her country. Hear me, Paris:
> For every false drop in her bawdy veins
> A Grecian's life hath sunk; for every scruple
> Of her contaminated carrion weight
> A Troyan hath been slain. Since she could speak,
> She hath not given so many good words breath
> As for her Greeks and Troyans suff'red death.
> (IV.i.68–74)

Hector expresses the same thought with greater courtesy when he pleads:

> Let Helen go.
> Since the first sword was drawn about this question,
> Every tithe soul 'mongst many thousand dismes
> Hath been as dear as Helen. I mean, of ours.
> If we have lost so many tenths of ours
> To guard a thing not ours nor worth to us
> (Had it our name) the value of one ten,
> What merit's in that reason which denies
> The yielding of her up?
> (II.ii.17–25)

Here is the wearisome condition of warring mankind: two great civilizations locked in mortal combat for the sake of a woman whom neither side desires, corrupted and enervated by seven years of futile struggle but still unwilling to sacrifice the principle of honor for which the war is being fought.

The conflict between Trojan and Greek has many analogues in Shakespeare's drama. It is foreshadowed by the opposition between Richard and Bolingbroke and Hotspur and Hal, and it is recalled by the dichotomy of Egypt and Rome in *Antony and Cleopatra.* On one side is a decaying world of chivalry, courtly and romantic, softened by feminine influence and refined in sensibility. On the other side is a purely masculine, realistic world of soldiery and empire, pragmatic in its values, uncritical of its goals, concerned only with the attainment of power. The character of Troilus expresses the doomed, tainted nobility of a highly sophisticated yet immature civilization. He unites the impetuous valor of Hotspur and the romantic ardor of the inexperienced Romeo; he is the hero of medieval saga and the lover of the Renaissance sonnet cycles. His restless spirit protests the dullness of life; he shares Hotspur's contempt for wariness and for niggling calculations of profit and loss—for the *quid pro quo* by which reason determines the value of things. Like Chapman's early heroes, he would subjugate the material world to his poetic imagination. He speaks for the individual will against the restrictions and decorums of society.

The result of Troilus' romanticism is philosophical anarchy, but his ideal of honor is consistent in its premises. He has no illusions about the value of Helen; indeed, he actually exults in her soilure because it bears witness to the ideality of Troy's chivalric adventure. If the possession of a faithless drab were the goal of battle, then the cause would be worthless; but Helen is merely a symbol of the real issue. The Greeks do not want her; they seek to impose their will on Troy, and honor demands that the chivalric will be free and unconquered. Moreover the real enemy is not the Greek soldier but stagnation, the rusting of unused strength and vitality. Even if Helen is not worth the spilling of a single drop of blood, she is nevertheless

> a theme of honour and renown,
> A spur to valiant and magnanimous deeds,
> Whose present courage may beat down our foes,
> And fame in time to come canonize us.
> (II.ii.199–202)

To the romantic ego, man is the measurer of all things; nothing has value except as he treasures it. Against the realist's credo that the value of an object is its selling price (what other men will pay for it), Troilus sets forth the romantic ideal that the only significant values are those intangibles which a man will not sell at the price of his own life.

Hector protests the complete subjectivity of Troilus' idealism. He pleads for objective criteria of judgment, for a recognition of the absolute, "natural" values which reason determines and which inhere in the customs of society. Whereas Troilus sweeps aside moral considerations as irrelevant, Hector argues the immorality of keeping Helen:

> Nature craves
> All dues rend'red to their owners. Now
> What nearer debt in all humanity
> Than wife is to the husband? If this law
> Of nature be corrupted through affection,
> And that great minds, of partial indulgence
> To their benumbed wills, resist the same,
> There is a law in each well-ord'red nation
> To curb those raging appetites that are
> Most disobedient and refractory.
> If Helen then be wife to Sparta's king
> (As it is known she is), these moral laws
> Of nature and of nations speak aloud
> To have her back return'd. Thus to persist
> In doing wrong extenuates not wrong,
> But makes it much more heavy.
> (II.ii.173–88)

Here is the voice of sanity and reason but not necessarily of objective judgment. If value does not dwell in the "particular will," then it does not dwell either in general opinion. The mere accumulation of subjective judgments does not, as Montaigne noted, create objective values, nor does the stamp of custom approve what is "natural." Once the question of values is raised, it is legitimate to ask, "What is reason but as 'tis valu'd?" Actually Hector is more of a romanticist than Troilus; he would be the Red Cross Knight, the chivalric defender of rational ideals. Troilus sees more realistically that honor and reason lead in opposite directions:

> Nay, if we talk of reason,
> Let's shut our gates and sleep. Manhood and honour
> Should have hare hearts, would they but fat their thoughts
> With this cramm'd reason. Reason and respect
> Make livers pale and lustihood deject.
> (II.ii.46–50)

If it is "mad idolatry / To make the service greater than the god, it is the only idolatry appropriate to the god of war. For how many military causes were worth the waste and misery which they entailed? There is rarely a "reason" for war except for the loathsome truth which honor hides, that men want to fight.

It is a measure of Troy's corruption that the *débat* between Hector and Troilus is purely theoretical, a courtly charade that ends with Hector's announcement that he has sent his personal challenge to the Greeks. The Trojan heroes not only hold their honors dearer than their lives but dearer also than the lives of thousands of defenseless countrymen. Because there is no "cause" for battle, their dedication to honor is in fact a dedication to personal vanity. And yet there is a terrible innocence in Troilus' self-deception. By making theoretical abstractions out of his egoistic desires, he assumes that he has elevated them above the materialism of life and turned the "performance of his heaving spleen" into a metaphysical value. He is scornful of ordinary getting and spending but he chaffers for honor on the battlefield by selling other men's lives. Exalting the individual judgment over vulgar opinion, he nevertheless takes as his absolute the "immortal" reputation that rests on the giddy props of other men's memories. By refusing to calculate the cost of the war because honor is at stake, he discards as worthless the very Trojan lives his valor protects. Actually he is not an intellectual anarchist because he recognizes as valid only his own subjective conclusions.

Troilus is Shakespeare's most subtle study of narcissistic infatuation. The defense of a slut and the worship of a wanton suffice as mirrors to reflect his image as a chivalric lover. He is not gulled by Cressida's pose of modesty, nor is she a hypocrite. She is a daughter of the game which men would have her play and for which they despise her. She sees beneath the ceremonies of courtly love the commerce of desire in which all selling prices are artificial and the pleasure of possession unequal to the thrill of anticipation. More realist than sensualist, more wary and weary than wanton, she is alone in Troy and defenseless among the Greeks. Like Troilus she believes that women are as they are valued, but she is too experienced to place a value on her affections that is different from her worth in men's eyes. To Troilus she is the Lesbia of the sonnets, but the rest of Troy assesses her at a lower rate. And she sees from her treatment by Diomedes and the other Greeks that her price has fallen still further. Having lost Troilus except for the nightly "visitations" which will satisfy his appetite, she sells when she can—she is not for all markets.

To view Cressida's infidelity as a cynical traducement of the ideal of courtly love is to miss the larger commentary which Shakespeare makes upon the masculine ego. The brutal casualness with which Diomedes "wins" his lady satisfies more frankly and grossly the same impulse that lies behind Troilus' romanticism. The worshipping of a courtly mistress and the moaning anguish of an unrequited lover are poses that enhance the value of sexual possession. They afford an opportunity for self-dramatization; they enable the "refined" sensibility to prolong by anticipation the transient ecstasy of sexual union. What are women but as they are valued *by men?* Troy would not sell Helen, its theme of honor, for the price of survival, but it barters Cressida for a single prisoner. The noble Hector uses Andromache's beauty and chastity as the subject of his martial brag but when she begs him to avoid the fatal battle, he rudely thrusts her away and orders her into the palace. When his honor is at pawn, he owes a higher obligation to his enemy than to his wife.

Even as Troilus intellectualizes the chivalric code of Troy, Ulysses exemplifies the pragmatic realism of the Greeks. Astute, ruthless, cunning, he is Shakespeare's ultimate characterization of the politician, whose art is the manipulation of other men's ambitions and desires. Like the Trojans, the Greek leaders hold a council of state, but they are not concerned with the value of the war, only with a strategy that will bring it to a swift and successful conclusion. Seven years of futile bloodletting have eroded the Grecian spirit. Dissension, envy, and discontent have destroyed martial discipline and sapped the will to victory. Achilles lies in his tent, enamored of a Trojan woman, jeering at his leaders. The pompous Agamemnon lacks the qualities of leadership, and Menelaus, the cuckold, is universally despised. Although superior in force of arms, the Greek army is impotent and incapable of storming the gates of Troy.

Ulysses assesses the situation shrewdly. This is no time to probe the ulcer of a worthless cause. The demoralized Greeks must be distracted from the sordid circumstances of the war by a contemplation of metaphysical harmonies; the illusion of common counsel must be obtained by reference to abstract assumptions on which all men agree. Although Ulysses requires no soaring lecture on order and degree to diagnose the disease which rots the Grecian spirit, we detect no trace of irony or hypocrisy in his magnificent and oft-quoted speech. After all, this is the kind of abstract idealism which does not commit the realist to any particular course or code of action, and which comfortably reaffirms Ulysses' position in the Greek hierarchy against Thersites' cynicism and Achilles' rebellious pride. Because his idealism lies outside the realm of political action, he can at one time describe the universal order of nature and at another time remind Achilles that one touch of nature makes the whole world kin in frailty and giddiness. He can speak of the correspondence between the microcosm of the state and the macrocosm of the universe and then remark that honor, degree, and high estate in the little world of man rest upon ephemeral opinion.

We expect from the experienced and clear-sighted Ulysses a truly objective assessment of value. We find, however, that Ulysses has no opinions of his own on the worth of glory, honor, war, and love. He is an expert critic of other men's opinions; his most penetrating observations are on the vagaries of mob psychology:

> Let not virtue seek
> Remuneration for the thing it was!
> For beauty, wit,
> High birth, vigour of bone, desert in service,
> Love, friendship, charity, are subjects all
> To envious and calumniating Time.
> One touch of nature makes the whole world kin,
> That all with one consent praise new-born gauds,
> Though they are made and moulded of things past,
> And give to dust that is a little gilt
> More laud than gilt o'erdusted.
>
> (III.iii.169–79)

Without illusion, the realist is a connoisseur of other men's illusions; indeed, their illusions are the only realities with which he is actively concerned, the only ones on which he bases his calculations. If there are permanent and intrinsic values, they do not enter into or influence the course of political maneuver. Trapped in the same circumstances that corrupt Achilles and Troilus, Ulysses maintains his intellectual clarity by withholding all judgment except on the practical issues of war and state. Thus in a way his poised rational objectivity is more subversive of values than Troilus' impetuous romanticism. He is the Shakespearean analogue of Warwick in *St. Joan:* the urbane, civilized statesman, free from dangerous enthusiasms or prejudices, who is capable of instigating atrocities because he recognizes only political necessities.

Ulysses' policy brings Troy to its appointed doom. As in the "Henriad" and in *Antony and Cleopatra,* the realist defeats the romanticist, the politician vanquishes the chevalier, the masculine world of ambition and empire subjugates the more feminine world of courtly ceremony. In *Troilus,* however, the pattern of events seems too overtly dialectical; intellectual analysis robs the heroic fable of its inherent pathos. The waste of beauty, youth, and valor does not achieve personal and poignant significance in the fates of Hector and Troilus because they exist as characters only to exemplify a thesis. They are actors in an intellectual drama whose meaning they never comprehend; they are doomed by circumstances and by the tainted values of the civilization which they lead to destruction. Because the burden of redeeming a worthless cause rests on their shoulders, they grow more and more infatuated with honor, until the pursuit of a "goodly armour" leads Hector into the cowardly ambush by which Achilles regains his "reputation." The Greeks are equally driven by "necessity." Although Ulysses correctly diagnoses the disease of pride and emulation that infects Agamemnon's army, he dares not cure the disease because there is no other incentive to heroic action than the thirst for reputation. Universal law may demand that pride be checked, but political necessity demands that arrogance, envy, and stupidity be intensified and exploited. Sold like merchandise, the bartered Cressida becomes a Grecian drab because the difference between a courtly mistress and a common stale lies not in what men desire of her but how they treat her. The most exquisite courtesan of the *ancien régime* would have become the local trollop in an obscure army camp; for while an aristocratic courtier will pay with words, vows, and deeds for the faith of his mistress, the less refined soldier will pay a smaller price for a more temporary gratification.

Troilus' romantic ideal demands that Cressida be faithful; his self-esteem demands that she be true to *him.* As he watches her submit too easily and coyly to Diomedes, his ego is more deeply wounded than his heart; he suffers without illumination:

> This she? No, this is Diomed's Cressida!
> If beauty have a soul, this is not she;
> If souls guide vows, if vows be sanctimonies,
> If sanctimony be the gods' delight,
> If there be rule in unity itself—
> This is not she. O madness of discourse,
> That cause sets up with and against itself!
> Bifold authority! where reason can revolt
> Without perdition, and loss assume all reason
> Without revolt: this is, and is not, Cressid!
> Within my soul there doth conduce a fight
> Of this strange nature, that a thing inseparate
> Divides more wider than the sky and earth;
> And yet the spacious breadth of this division
> Admits no orifex for a point as subtle
> As Ariachne's broken woof to enter.
> Instance, O instance! strong as Pluto's gates:
> Cressid is mine, tied with the bonds of heaven.
> Instance, O instance! strong as heaven itself:
> The bonds of heaven are slipp'd, dissolv'd, and loos'd.
> (V.ii.137–56)

Troilus is not disillusioned; he projects his inner confusion into a law of universal chaos and would have us believe that because *his* vanity is stricken the bonds of heaven are slipped. If he were a more consistent philosopher, he would realize that he has no reason to complain, for if the individual mind sets the value of all things, then Diomedes is entitled to his estimate of Cressida's worth and she to her estimate of Troilus' affections.

Out of the sordidness of Cressida's infidelity, however, a new romantic cause is born. Another soiled woman becomes the theme of chivalric honor and the cause for senseless struggle. Now Troilus rages after Diomedes; now Diomedes assumes a courtly pose and dedicates Troilus' horse to his whore. The tables turn, the charade of chivalry approaches burlesque, but one touch of nature still makes the world kin. When Hector dies the charade ends: the appetite for glory reverts to a primitive bloodlust, for chivalry is a luxury which only the winner can afford. Refusing to calculate the cost of Hector's death lest it destroy the Trojan will to combat, Troilus has no reason to fight except for the savage impulse to kill. And after he and Ulysses have commented on the frailty of affection, it is only fitting that Pandarus should have his chance to speak. Naturally Pandarus is disappointed with Troilus' ingratitude. Even a bawd has feelings, and though he derived a vicarious pleasure from trading in flesh, his negotiations for Troilus were more selfless and "innocent" than the heroic idealism that doomed Troy.

The comic complaints of a syphilitic bawd end the play on a note of derision that seems to vindicate Thersites' scabrous cynicism. Yet the total impression of *Troilus* is hardly nihilistic. It is a depressing play, not because it establishes the futility of man's search for ideal values but because it is a sociological and psychological analysis of decadent values. Like Ulysses, Shakespeare is concerned here only with the nature of man's illusions, not with the essential worth of his ideals. The gestes of Troy do not mock the selfless dedication of Cordelia and Kent; however, they provide an ironic gloss for the chivalric gesture that costs Edmund his victory and his life.

VI

TRAGIC FORM AND THE JACOBEAN TRAGEDIES

THE STRUCTURE OF THE LATER TRAGEDIES

The Jacobean Shakespeare: Some Observations on the Construction of the Tragedies

Maynard Mack

This chapter aims at being a modest supplement (I cannot too much stress the adjective) to A. C. Bradley's pioneering analysis of the construction of Shakespearean tragedy, the second of his famous lectures, published some fifty-five years ago. Bradley's concern was with what would probably today be called the clearer outlines of Shakespearean practice—the management of exposition, conflict, crisis, catastrophe; the contrasts of pace and scene; the over-all patterns of rise-and-fall, variously modulated; the slackened tension after the crisis and Shakespeare's devices for countering this; and the faults.

Bradley is quite detailed about the faults. Sometimes, he says, there are too rapid shiftings of scene and *dramatis personae,* as in the middle section of *Antony and Cleopatra.* Sometimes there is extraneous matter, not required for plot or character development, like the player's speech in *Hamlet* about the murder of Priam, or Hamlet's advice later to the same player on speaking in the theater. Sometimes there are soliloquies too obviously expositional, as when Edgar disguises to become Poor Tom in *King Lear.* Or there is contradiction and incon-

From *Jacobean Theatre,* Stratford-upon-Avon Studies, Vol. I, ed. John Russell Brown and Bernard Harris. Reprinted by permission of Maynard Mack and Edward Arnold (Publishers), Ltd.

sistency, as the double time in *Othello*. Or flatulent writing: "obscure, inflated, tasteless," or "pestered with metaphors." Or "gnomic" insertions, like the Duke's couplet interchange with Brabantio in *Othello,* used "more freely than, I suppose, a good playwright now would care to do." And finally, to make an end, there is too often sacrificing of dramatic appropriateness to get something said that the author wants said. Thus the comments of the Player King and Claudius on the instability of human purpose arise because Shakespeare "wishes in part simply to write poetry, and partly to impress on the audience thoughts which will help them to understand, not the player-king nor yet King Claudius, but Hamlet himself." These failings, Bradley concludes, belong to an art of drama imperfectly developed, which Shakespeare inherited from his predecessors and acquiesced in, on occasion, from "indifference or want of care."

Though Bradley's analysis is still the best account we have of the outward shape of Shakespearean tragedy, a glance at his list of faults and, especially, his examples reminds us that a vast deal of water has got itself under the critical bridges since 1904. It is not simply that most of the faults he enumerates would no longer be regarded as such, but would, instead, be numbered among the characteristic practices of Shakespearean dramaturgy, even at its most triumphant. Still more striking is the extent to which our conception of the "construction" of the tragedies has itself changed. The matters Bradley described have not ceased to be important—far from it: several of our current interpreters, one feels, would benefit if, like Bottom of Master Mustardseed, they were to desire him "of more acquaintance." Still, it is impossible not to feel that Bradley missed something—that there is another kind of construction in Shakespeare's tragedies than the one he designates, more inward, more difficult to define, but not less significant. This other structure is not, like his, generated entirely by the interplay of plot and character. Nor is it, on the other hand, though it is fashionable nowadays to suppose so, ultimately a verbal matter. It is poetic, but it goes well beyond what in certain quarters today is called (with something like a lump in the throat) "the poetry." Some of its elements arise from the playwright's visualizing imagination, the consciousness of groupings, gestures, entrances, exits. Others may even be prior to language, in the sense that they appear to belong to a paradigm of tragic "form" that was consciously or unconsciously part of Shakespeare's inheritance and intuition as he worked.

At any rate, it is into this comparatively untraveled and uncharted territory of inward structure that I should like to launch a few tentative explorations. I shall occasionally look backward as far as *Julius Caesar* (1599), *Richard II* (1595–1600), and even *Romeo and Juliet* (1595–6); but in the main I shall be concerned with the tragedies of Shakespeare's prime, from *Hamlet* (1600–1) to *Coriolanus* (1607–8). In these seven or eight years, Shakespeare's golden period, he consolidated a species of tragic structure that for suggestiveness and flexibility has never been matched.[1] I do not anticipate being able to return with a map of this obscure terrain. I hope only to convince better travelers that there is something out there to be known.

First, the hero. The Shakespearean tragic hero, as everybody knows, is an overstater. His individual accent will vary with his personality, but there is always a residue of hyperbole. This, it would seem, is for Shakespeare the authentic tragic music, mark of a world where a man's reach must always exceed his grasp and everything costs not less than everything.

> Wert thou as far
> As that vast shore wash'd with the farthest sea,
> I would adventure for such merchandise.
> (*Romeo and Juliet,* II.ii.82)

> 'Swounds, show me what thou'lt do:
> Woo't weep? woo't fight? woo't fast? woo't tear thyself?
> Woo't drink up eisel? eat a crocodile
> I'll do't.
> (*Hamlet,* V.i.297)

> Nay, had she been true,
> If heaven would make me such another world
> Of one entire and perfect chrysolite,
> I'ld not have sold her for it.
> (*Othello,* V.ii.140)

> Death, traitor! nothing could have subdued nature
> To such a lowness but his unkind daughters.
> (*King Lear,* III.iv.72)

> Will all great Neptune's ocean wash this blood
> Clean from my hand?
> (*Macbeth,* II.ii.60)

> I, that with my sword
> Quarter'd the world, and o'er green Neptune's back
> With ships made cities, . . .
> (*Antony and Cleopatra,* IV.xiv.57)

> I go alone,
> Like to a lonely dragon, that his fen
> Makes fear'd and talk'd of more than seen.
> (*Coriolanus,* IV.i.29)

---

[1] The flexibility of the structure is witnessed by the amazing differences between the tragedies, of which it is, however, the lowest common multiple. In my discussion, I shall necessarily take the differences between the tragedies for granted and stress simply the vertebrate characteristics they share.

This idiom is not, of course, used by the hero only. It is the language he is dressed in by all who love him, and often by those who do not:

> This was the noblest Roman of them all: . . .
> His life was gentle, and the elements
> So mix'd in him that Nature might stand up
> And say to all the world "This was a man!"
> (*Julius Caesar,* V.v.68)

> The courtier's, soldier's, scholar's, eye, tongue, sword;
> The expectancy and rose of the fair state,
> The glass of fashion and the mold of form,
> The observed of all observers, . . .
> (*Hamlet,* III.i.159)

> Can he be angry? I have seen the cannon,
> When it hath blown his ranks into the air,
> And, like the devil, from his very arm
> Puff'd his own brother:—and can he be angry?
> (*Othello,* III.iv.134)

> On the Alps
> It is reported thou didst eat strange flesh,
> Which some did die to look on.
> (*Antony and Cleopatra,* I.iv.66)

> Let me twine
> Mine arms about that body, where against
> My grainèd ash an hundred times hath broke,
> And scarr'd the moon with splinters.
> (*Coriolanus,* IV.v.112)

But by whomever used, it is a language that depends for its vindication—for the redemption of its paper promises into gold—upon the hero, and any who stand, heroically, where he does. It is the mark of his, and their, commitment to something beyond "the vast waters / Of the petrel and the porpoise," as Mr. Eliot has it in *East Coker,* a commitment to something—not merely death—which shackles accidents and bolts up change and palates no dung whatever.

Thus the hyperbole of tragedy stands at the opposite end of a tonal scale from the hyperbole of comedy, which springs from and nourishes detachment:

> When I was about thy years, Hal, I was not an eagle's talon in the waist; I could have crept into any alderman's thumb-ring.
> (*1 Henry IV,* II.iv.362)

> O, she misused me past the endurance of a block! an oak but with one green leaf on it would have answered her; my very visor began to assume life, and scold with her.
> (*Much Ado About Nothing,* II.i.246)

> He has a son, who shall be flayed alive; then 'nointed over with honey, set on the head of a wasp's nest; then stand till he be three quarters and a dram dead; then recovered again with aqua-vitae or some other hot infusion; then, raw as he is, and in the hottest day prognostication proclaims, shall he be set against a brick-wall, the sun looking with a southward eye upon him, where he is to behold him with flies blown to death.
>
> (*The Winter's Tale,* IV.iv.811)

Comic overstatement aims at being preposterous. Until it becomes so, it remains flat. Tragic overstatement, on the other hand, aspires to be believed, and unless in some sense it is so, remains bombast.

Besides the hyperbolist, in Shakespeare's scheme of things, there is always the opposing voice, which belongs to the hero's foil. As the night the day, the idiom of absoluteness demands a vocabulary of a different intensity, a different rhetorical and moral wave length, to set it off. This other idiom is not necessarily understatement, though it often takes the form of a deflating accent and very often involves colloquialism—or perhaps merely a middling sort of speech—expressive of a suppler outlook than the hero's, and of other and less upsetting ways of encountering experience than his hyperbolic, not to say intransigent, rigorism. " 'Twere to consider too curiously to consider so," says Horatio of Hamlet's equation between the dust of Alexander and a bunghole, and this enunciates perfectly the foil's role. There is no tragedy in him because he does not consider "curiously"; there are always more things in earth and heaven than are dreamt of in his philosophy.

Each of the Shakespearean tragedies contains at least one personage to speak this part, which is regularly assigned to someone in the hero's immediate entourage—servitor, wife, friend. In *Romeo and Juliet,* it is of course Mercutio, with his witty resolution of all love into sex. In *Julius Caesar,* it is Cassius, whose restless urgent rhythms, full of flashing images, swirl about Brutus's rounder and abstracter speech, like dogs that bay the moon:

> BRUTUS I do believe that these applauses are
> For some new honors that are heap'd on Caesar.
> CASSIUS Why, man, he doth bestride the narrow world
> Like a Colossus, and we petty men
> Walk under his huge legs and peep about
> To find ourselves dishonorable graves.
>
> (I.ii.133)

In the famous forum speeches, this second voice is taken over temporarily by Antony, and there emerges a similar but yet more powerful contrast between them. Brutus's prose—in which the actuality of the assassination is intellectualized and held at bay by the strict patterns of an obtrusively formal rhetoric, almost as though corporal death were transubstantiated to "a ballet of bloodless categories"—gives way to Antony's sinewy verse about the "honorable men," which draws the deed, and its consequence the dead Caesar, ever closer till his own vengeful emotions are kindled in the mob.

In *Hamlet,* the relation of foil to hero undergoes an unusual adaptation. Here, since the raciest idiom of the play belongs to the hero himself, the foil, Horatio, is given a quite conventional speech, and, to make the contrast sharper (Hamlet being of all the heroes the most voluble), as little speech as may be. Like his stoicism, like his "blood and judgment"—

so well commingled,
That they are not a pipe for fortune's finger
To sound what stop she please—
(III.ii.74)

Horatio's "Here, sweet lord," "O, my dear lord," "Well, my lord" are, presumably (as the gentleman in *Lear* says of Cordelia's tears), "a better way" than Hamlet's self-lacerating virtuosities and verbosities. But of course we do not believe this and are not meant to: who would be Horatio if he could be Hamlet?

Plainly, this is one of the two questions that all the tragic foils exist to make us ask (the other we shall come to presently). Who, for instance, would be Enobarbus, clear-sighted as he is, in preference to Antony? His brilliant sardonic speech, so useful while he can hold his own career and all about him in the comic focus of detachment, withers in the face of his engagement to ultimate issues, and he dies speaking with imagery, accent, and feeling which are surely meant to identify him at the last with the absoluteness of the heroic world, the more so since his last syllables anticipate Cleopatra's:

Throw my heart
Against the flint and hardness of my fault;
Which, being dried with grief, will break to powder,
And finish all foul thoughts. O Antony,
Nobler than my revolt is infamous,
Forgive me in thine own particular;
But let the world rank me in register
A master-leaver and a fugitive:
O Antony! O Antony!
(IV.ix.15)

Such unequivocal judgments are a change indeed on the part of one who could earlier rally cynically with Menas about "two thieves kissing" when their hands meet.

King Lear is given two foils. The primary one is obviously the Fool, whose rhymes and riddles and jets of humor in the first two acts set off both the old king's brooding silences and his massively articulated longer speeches when aroused. But in the storm scenes, and occasionally elsewhere, one is almost as keenly conscious of the relief into which Lear's outrageous imprecations are thrown by the mute devoted patience of his servant Kent. For both foils—and this of course is their most prominent function as representatives of the opposing voice—the storm itself is only a storm, to be stoically endured, in the one case, and, in the other, if his master would but hear reason, eschewed:

> O nuncle, court holy-water in a dry house is better than this rain-water out o' door. Good nuncle, in, ask thy daughters' blessing: . . .
>
> (III.ii.10)

Doubtless the Fool does not wish to be taken quite *au pied de la lettre* in this—his talk is always in the vein of the false daughters', his action quite other. But neither for him nor for Kent does facing the thunder have any kind of transcendent meaning. In Lear's case, it has; the thunder he hears is like the thunder heard over Himavant in *The Waste Land;* it has what the anthropologists call "mana"; and his (and our) consuming questions are what it means—and if it means—and whose side it is on.

In my view, the most interesting uses of the opposing voice occur in *Macbeth* and *Othello.* In *Macbeth,* Shakespeare gives it to Lady Macbeth, and there was never, I think, a more thrilling tragic counterpoint set down for the stage than that in the scene following the murder of Duncan, when her purely physical reading of what has happened to them both is met by his metaphysical intuitions. His "noise" to her is just the owl screaming and the crickets' cry. The voice of one crying "sleep no more" is only his "brain-sickly" fear. The blood on his hands is what "a little water clears us of." "Consider it not so deeply," she says at one point, with an echo of Horatio in the graveyard. "These deeds must not be thought / After these ways." But in the tragic world, which always opens on transcendence, they must; and this she herself finds before she dies, a prisoner to the deed, endlessly washing the damned spot that will not out. "What's done cannot be undone" is a language that like Enobarbus she has to learn.

Othello's foil of course is Iago, about whose imagery and speech there hangs, as recent commentators have pointed out, a constructed air, an ingenious, hyperconscious generalizing air, essentially suited to one who, as W. H. Clemen has said, "seeks to poison . . . others with his images" (*The Development of Shakespeare's Imagery,* p. 122). Yet Iago's poison does not work more powerfully through his images than through a corrosive habit of abstraction applied in those unique relations of love and faith where abstraction is most irrelevant and most destructive. Iago has learned to "sickly o'er" the central and irreducible individual with the pale cast of class and kind:

Blessed fig's end! The wine she drinks is made of grapes. . . .
(II.i.251)

These Moors are changeable in their wills. . . . If sanctimony and a frail vow betwixt an erring barbarian and a supersubtle Venetian be not too hard for my wits . . .
(I.iii.342–43, 350–53)

Come on, come on; you are pictures out of doors,
Bells in your parlors, wildcats in your kitchens,
Saints in your injuries, devils being offended,
Players in your housewifery, and housewives in your beds.
(II.i.108)

I know our country disposition well;
In Venice they do let heaven see the pranks
They dare not show their husbands.
(III.iii.201)

Othello's downfall is signaled quite as clearly when he drifts into this rationalized dimension—

O curse of marriage,
That we can call these delicate creatures ours,
And not their appetites—
(III.iii.267)

leaving behind his true vernacular, the idiom of "My life upon her faith!", as when his mind fills with Iago's copulative imagery. Shakespeare seems to have been well aware that love (especially such love as can be reflected only in the union of a black man with a white woman, East with West) is the mutual knowing of uniqueness:

Reason, in itself confounded,
Saw division grow together,
To themselves yet either neither,
Simple were so well compounded,

That it cried, How true a twain
Seemeth this concordant one!
Love hath reason, reason none,
If what parts can so remain.

Whereupon it made this threne
To the phoenix and the dove,
Co-supremes and stars of love,
As chorus to their tragic scene.
(*The Phoenix and the Turtle,* l. 41)

And also that there are areas of experience where, as a great saint once said, one must first believe in order that one may know.

To one who should ask why these paired voices seem to be essential ingredients of Shakespearean tragedy, no single answer can, I think, be given. They occur partly, no doubt, because of their structural utility, the value of complementary personalities in a work of fiction being roughly analogous to the value of thesis and antithesis in a discursive work. Partly too, no doubt, because in stage performance, the antiphonal effects of the two main vocabularies, strengthened by diversity in manner, costume, placing on the stage, supply variety of mood and gratify the eye and ear. But these are superficial considerations. Perhaps we come to something more satisfactory when we consider that these two voices apparently answer to reverberations which reach far back in the human past. *Mutatis mutandis,* Coriolanus and Menenius, Antony and Enobarbus, Macbeth and Lady Macbeth, Lear and his Fool, Othello and Iago, Hamlet and Horatio, Brutus and Cassius, Romeo and Mercutio exhibit a kind of duality that is also exhibited in Oedipus and Jocasta (as well as Creon), Antigone and Ismene, Prometheus and Oceanus, Phaedra and her nurse—and also, in many instances in Greek tragedy, by the protagonist and the chorus.

If it is true, as can be argued, that the Greek chorus functions in large measure as spokesman for the values of the community, and the first actor, in large measure, for the passionate life of the individual, we can perhaps see a philosophical basis for the long succession of opposing voices. What matters to the community is obviously accommodation—all those adjustments and resiliences that enable it to survive; whereas what matters to the individual, at least in his heroic mood, is just as obviously integrity—all that enables him to remain an *individual,* one thing not many. The confrontation of these two outlooks is therefore a confrontation of two of our most cherished instincts, the instinct to be resolute, autonomous, free, and the instinct to be "realistic," adaptable, secure. If it is also true, as I think most of us believe, that tragic drama is in one way or other a record of man's affair with transcendence (whether this be defined as gods, God, or, as by Malraux, the human "fate," which men must "question" even if they cannot control), we can see further why the hero must have an idiom—such as hyperbole—that establishes him as moving to measures played above, or outside, our normal space and time. For the *reductio ad absurdum* of the tragic confrontation is the comic one, exemplified in Don Quixote and his Sancho, where the comedy arises precisely from the fact that the hero only *imagines* he moves to measures above and outside our normal world; and where, to the extent that we come to identify with his faith, the comedy slides towards pathos and even the tragic absolute.

These considerations, however, remain speculative. What is not in doubt is that dramaturgically the antiphony of two voices and two vocabularies serves Shakespeare well, and in one of its extensions gives rise to a phenomenon as peculiar and personal to him as his signature. Towards the close of a tragic play, or if not towards the close, at the climax, will normally appear a short scene or episode (sometimes more than one) of spiritual cross purposes: a scene in which the line of tragic speech and feeling generated by commitment is crossed by an alien speech and feeling very much detached. Bradley, noting such of these episodes as are "humorous or semi-humorous," places them among Shakespeare's devices for sustaining interest after the crisis, since their introduction "affords variety and relief, and also heightens by contrast the tragic feelings." Another perceptive critic has noted that though such scenes afford "relief," it is not by laughter. "We return for a moment to simple people, a gravedigger, a porter, a countryman, and to the goings on of every day, the feeling for bread and cheese, and when we go back to the high tragic mood we do so with a heightened sense that we are moving in a world fully realized" (F. P. Wilson, *Elizabethan and Jacobean,* p. 122). To such comments, we must add another. For the whole effect of these episodes does not come simply from variety, or from the juxtaposition of bread and cheese with the high tragic mood, though these elements are certainly present in it.

It arises, in the main, I think, from the fact that Shakespeare here lays open to us, in an especially poignant form, what I take to be the central dialogue of tragic experience. It is a dialogue of which the Greek dialogue of individual with community, the seventeenth-century dialogue of soul with body, the twentieth-century dialogue of self with soul are perhaps all versions in their different ways: a dialogue in which each party makes its case in its own tongue, incapable of wholly comprehending what the other means. And Shakespeare objectifies it for us on his stage by the encounter of those by whom, "changed, changed utterly," a terrible beauty has been born, with those who are still players in life's casual comedy. Hamlet and the gravediggers, Desdemona and Emilia, Cleopatra and the clown afford particularly fine examples of Shakespeare's technique in this respect.

In the first instance, the mixture of profoundly imaginative feelings contained in Hamlet's epitaph for Yorick—

> I knew him, Horatio: a fellow of infinite jest, of most excellent fancy; he hath borne me on his back a thousand times; and now, how abhorred in my imagination it is! my gorge rises at it. Here hung those lips that I have kissed I know not how oft. Where be your gibes now? your gambols? your songs? your flashes of merriment, that were wont to set the table on a roar? Not one now, to mock your own grinning? quite chap-fallen? Now get you to my lady's chamber, and tell her, let her paint an inch thick, to this favor she must come; make her laugh at that—
>
> (V.i.203)

is weighed over against the buffoon literalism of the clown—

HAMLET What man dost thou dig it for?
FIRST CLOWN For no man, sir.
HAMLET What woman, then?
FIRST CLOWN For none, neither.
HAMLET Who is to be buried in 't?
FIRST CLOWN One that was a woman, sir; but, rest her soul, she's dead—

(V.i.141)

and against his uncompromising factualism too, his hard dry vocabulary of detachment, without overtones, by which he cuts his métier down to a size that can be lived with:

> I'faith, if he be not rotten before he die, . . . he will last you some eight year or nine year: a tanner will last you nine year. (V.i.180)

But in this scene Hamlet's macabre thoughts are not allowed to outweigh the clown. A case is made for factualism and literalism. Horatio is seen to have a point in saying it is to consider too curiously to consider as Hamlet does. A man must come to terms with the graveyard; but how long may he linger in it with impunity, or allow it to linger in him? Such reckonings the opposing voice, whether spoken by the primary foil or by another, is calculated to awake in us: this is the second kind of question that it exists to make us ask.

In a sense, then, the implicit subject of all these episodes is the predicament of being human. They bring before us the grandeur of man's nature, which contains, potentially, both voices, both ends of the moral and psychic spectrum. They bring before us the necessity of his choice, because it is rarely given to him to go through any door without closing the rest. And they bring before us the sadness, the infinite sadness of his lot, because, short of the "certain certainties" that tragedy does not deal with, he has no sublunar way of knowing whether defiant "heroism" is really more to be desired than suppler "wisdom." The alabaster innocence of Desdemona's world shines out beside the crumpled bedsitters of Emilia's—

DESDEMONA Wouldst thou do such a deed for all the world?
EMILIA Why, would not you?
DESDEMONA No, by this heavenly light!
EMILIA Nor I neither by this heavenly light; I might do't as well i' the dark.
DESDEMONA Wouldst thou do such a deed for all the world?
EMILIA The world's a huge thing: it is a great price
For a small vice.
DESDEMONA In troth, I think thou wouldst not.
EMILIA In troth, I think I should . . . who would not make her husband a cuckold to make him a monarch? I should venture purgatory for 't.

DESDEMONA Beshrew me, if I would do such a wrong
For the whole world.

EMILIA Why, the wrong is but a wrong i' the world; and having the world for your labor, 'tis a wrong in your own world, and you might quickly make it right.

DESDEMONA I do not think there is any such woman—
(IV.iii.65)

but the two languages never, essentially, commune—and, for this reason, the dialogue they hold can never be finally adjudicated.

The same effect may be noted in Cleopatra's scene with the countryman who brings her the asps. Her exultation casts a glow over the whole scene of her death. But her language when the countryman has gone would not have the tragic resonance it has, if we could not hear echoing between the lines the gritty accents of the opposing voice:

Give me my robe, put on my crown; I have
Immortal longings in me.

Truly, I have him: but I would not be the party that should desire you to touch him, for his biting is immortal; those that do die of it do seldom or never recover.

The stroke of death is as a lover's pinch,
Which hurts, and is desired.

I heard of one of them no longer than yesterday: a very honest woman, but something given to lie; as a woman should not do, but in the way of honesty: how she died of the biting of it, what pain she felt.

Peace, peace!
Dost thou not see my baby at my breast,
That sucks the nurse asleep?
(V.ii.283–313)

Give it nothing, I pray you, for it is not worth the feeding.
(V.ii.245–71)

The "worm"—or "my baby"; the Antony Demetrius and Philo see—or the Antony whose face is as the heavens; the "small vice" of Emilia—or the deed one would not do for the whole world; the skull knocked about the mazzard by a sexton's spade—or the skull which "had a tongue in it and could sing once": these are incommensurables, which human nature nevertheless must somehow measure, reconcile, and enclose.

We move now from "character" to "action," and to the question: what happens in a Shakespearean tragedy? Bradley's traditional categories—exposition, conflict, crisis, catastrophe, etc.—give us one side of this, but, as we noticed earlier, largely the external side, and are in any case rather too clumsy for the job we try to do with them. They apply as well to potboilers of the commercial theater as to serious works of art, to prose as well as poetic drama. What is worse, they are unable to register the unique capacity of Shakespearean dramaturgy to hint, evoke, imply, and, in short, by indirections find directions out. The nature of some of Shakespeare's "indirections" is a topic we must explore before we can hope to confront the question posed above with other terms than Bradley's.

To clarify what I mean by indirection, let me cite an instance from *King Lear*. Everybody has noticed, no doubt, that Lear's Fool (apart from being the King's primary foil) gives voice during the first two acts to notations of topsi-turviness that are not, one feels, simply his own responses to the inversions of order that have occurred in family and state, but a reflection of the King's; or, to put the matter another way, the situation is so arranged by Shakespeare that we are invited to apply the Fool's comments to Lear's inner experience, and I suspect that most of us do so. The Fool thus serves, to some extent, as a screen on which Shakespeare flashes, as it were, readings from the psychic life of the protagonist, possibly even his subconscious life, which could not otherwise be conveyed in drama at all. Likewise, the Fool's *idée fixe* in this matter, his apparent obsession with one idea (often a clinical symptom of incipient insanity) is perhaps dramatic shorthand, and even sleight-of-hand, for goings-on in the King's brain that only occasionally bubble to the surface in the form of conscious apprehensions: "O let me not be mad, not mad sweet heaven." "O fool, I shall go mad." Conceivably, there may even be significance in the circumstance that the Fool does not enter the play as a speaking character till after King Lear has behaved like a fool, and leaves it before he is cured.

Whatever the truth of this last point, the example of the Fool in Lear introduces us to devices of play construction and ways of recording the progress of inward "action," which, though the traditional categories say nothing about them, are a basic resource of Shakespeare's playwriting, and nowhere more so than in the tragedies. We may now consider a few of them in turn.

First, there are the figures, like the Fool, some part of whose consciousness, as conveyed to us at particular moments, seems to be doing double duty, filling our minds with impressions analogous to those which we may presume to be occupying the conscious or unconscious mind of the hero, whether he is before us on the stage or not. A possible example may be Lady Macbeth's sleepwalking scene. Macbeth is absent at this juncture, has gone "into the field"—has not in fact been visible during two long scenes and will not be visible again till the next scene after this. In the interval, the slaying at Macduff's castle and the conversations between Malcolm and Macduff keep him before us in his capacity as tyrant, murderer, "Hell-kite," seen from the outside. But Lady Macbeth's sleepwalking is, I think, Shakespeare's device for keeping him before us in his capacity as tragic hero and sufferer. The "great perturbation in nature" of which the doctor whispers ("to receive at once the benefit of sleep, and do the effects of watching"), the "slumbery agitation," the "thick-coming fancies / That keep her from her rest": these, by a kind of poetical displacement, we may apply to him as well as to her; and we are invited to do so by the fact that from the moment of the first murder all the play's references to sleep, and its destruction, have had reference to Macbeth himself. We are, of course, conscious as we watch the scene, that this is Lady Macbeth suffering the metaphysical aspects of murder that she did not believe in; we may also be conscious that the remorse pictured here tends to distinguish her from her husband, who for some time has been giving his "initiate fear" the "hard use" he said it lacked, with dehumanizing consequences. Yet in some way the pity of this situation suffuses him as well as her, the more so because in every word she utters his presence beside her is supposed; and if we allow this to be true, not only will Menteith's comment in the following scene—

> Who then shall blame
> His pester'd senses to recoil and start,
> When all that is within him does condemn
> Itself for being there—
>
> (V.ii.22)

evoke an image of suffering as well as retribution, but we shall better understand Macbeth's striking expression, at his next appearance, in words that we are almost bound to feel have some reference to himself, of corrosive griefs haunting below the conscious levels of the mind:

> Canst thou not minister to a mind diseased,
> Pluck from the memory a rooted sorrow,
> Raze out the written troubles of the brain
> And with some sweet oblivious antidote
> Cleanse the stuff'd bosom of that perilous stuff
> Which weighs upon the heart?
>
> (V.iii.40)

Such speeches as this, and as Lady Macbeth's while sleepwalking—which we might call umbrella speeches, since more than one consciousness may shelter under them—are not uncommon in Shakespeare's dramaturgy, as many critics have pointed out. *Lear* affords the classic examples: in the Fool, as we have seen, and also in Edgar. Edgar's speech during the storm scenes projects in part his role of Poor Tom, the eternal outcast; in part, Edmund (and also Oswald), the vicious servant, self-seeking, with heart set on lust and proud array; possibly in part, Gloucester, whose arrival with a torch the Fool appropriately announces (without knowing it) in terms related to Edgar's themes: "Now a little fire in a wide field were like an old lecher's heart"; and surely, in some part too, the King, for the chips and tag-ends of Edgar's speech reflect, as if from Lear's own mind, not simply mental disintegration, but a strong sense of a fragmented moral order: "Obey thy parents; keep thy word justly; swear not; commit not with man's sworn spouse. . . ."

But in my view, the most interesting of all the umbrella speeches in the tragedies is Enobarbus's famous description of Cleopatra in her barge. The triumvirs have gone offstage, Antony to have his first view of Octavia. When we see him again, his union with Octavia will have been agreed on all parts (though not yet celebrated), and he will be saying to her, with what can hardly be supposed to be insincerity:

> My Octavia,
> Read not my blemishes in the world's report:
> I have not kept my square; but that to come
> Shall all be done by the rule. Good night, dear lady.
> (II.iii.4)

Then the soothsayer appears, reminds Antony that his guardian angel will always be overpowered when Caesar's is by, urges him to return to Egypt; and Antony, left alone after the soothsayer has gone, meditates a moment on the truth of the pronouncement and then says abruptly:

> I will to Egypt:
> And though I make this marriage for my peace,
> I' the east my pleasure lies.
> (II.iii.38)

There is plainly a piece of prestidigitation here. It is performed in part by means of the soothsayer's entry, which is evidently a kind of visual surrogate for Antony's own personal intuition. ("I see it in my motion, have it not in my tongue," the soothsayer says, when asked for the reasons he wishes Antony to return; and that is presumably the way Antony sees it too: in his "motion," i.e., involuntarily, intuitively.) But a larger part is played by Enobarbus's account of Cleopatra. Between the exit of the triumvirs and the reappearance of Antony making unsolicited promises to Octavia, this is the one thing that intervenes. And it is the only thing that needs to. Shakespeare has made it so powerful, so colored our imaginations with it, that we understand the promises of Antony, not in the light in which he understands them as he makes them, but in the riotous brilliance of Enobarbus's evocation of Cleopatra. The psychic gap, in Antony, between "My Octavia" and "Good night, dear lady," on the one hand, and "I will to Egypt," on the other, is filled by a vision, given to us, of irresistible and indeed quasi-unearthly power, of which the soothsayer's intuition is simply a more abstract formulation. Here again, by indirection, Shakespeare finds direction out.

Not all mirror situations in the tragedies involve reflection of another consciousness. Some, as is well known, emphasize the outlines of an action by recapitulating it, as when Edgar's descent to Poor Tom and subsequent gradual re-ascent to support the gored state echoes the downward and upward movement in the lives of both King Lear and Gloucester; or as when Enobarbus's defection to, and again from, the bidding of his practical reason repeats that which Antony has already experienced, and Cleopatra will experience (at least in one way of understanding Act V) between Antony's death and her own. *Hamlet,* complex in all respects, offers an unusually complex form of this. The three sons, who are, in various senses, all avengers of dead fathers, are all deflected, temporarily, from their designs by the maneuvers of an elder (Claudius for Laertes and Hamlet; the King of Norway, inspired by Claudius, for Fortinbras), who in two cases is the young man's uncle. There are of course important differences between these three young men which we are not to forget; but with respect to structure, the images in the mirror are chiefly likenesses. Hamlet, outmaneuvered by Claudius, off to England to be executed, crosses the path of Fortinbras, who has also been outmaneuvered by Claudius (working through his uncle), and is off to Poland to make mouths at the invisible event, while at the same moment Laertes, clamoring for immediate satisfaction in the King's palace, is outmaneuvered in his turn. Likewise, at the play's end, all three young men are "victorious," in ways they could hardly have foreseen. The return of Fortinbras, having achieved his objective in Poland, to find his "rights" in Denmark achieved without a blow, is timed to coincide with Hamlet's achieving his objective in exposing and killing the King, and Laertes' achieving his objective of avenging his father's death on Hamlet. When this episode is played before us in the theater, there is little question, to my way of thinking, but that something of the glow and martial upsurge dramatized in Fortinbras's entrance associates itself to Hamlet, even as Fortinbras's words associate Hamlet to a soldier's death. Meantime, Laertes, who has been trapped by the King and has paid with his life for it, gives us an alternative reflection of the Prince, which is equally a part of the truth.

Fortinbras's arrival at the close of *Hamlet* is an instance of an especially interesting type of mirroring to be found everywhere in Shakespeare's work—the emblematic entrance, and exit. Sometimes such exits occur by death, as the death of Gaunt, who takes a sacramental view of kingship and nation, in *Richard II,* at the instant when Richard has destroyed, by his personal conduct and by "farming" his realm, the sacramental relationships which make such a view possible to maintain. Gaunt has to die, we might say, before a usurpation like his son's can even be imagined; and it is, I take it, not without significance that the first word of Bolingbroke's return comes a few seconds after we have heard (from the same speaker, Northumberland) that Gaunt's tongue "is now a stringless instrument." Something similar, it seems clear, occurs with the death of Mamillius in *The Winter's Tale*. Sickening with his father's sickening mind, Mamillius dies in the instant that his father repudiates the message of the oracle; and though, in the end, all else is restored to Leontes, Mamillius is not.

In the tragedies, emblematic entrances and exits assume a variety of forms, ranging from those whose significance is obvious to those where it is uncertain, controversial, and perhaps simply a mirage. One entrance whose significance is unmistakable occurs in the first act of *Macbeth,* when Duncan, speaking of the traitor Cawdor, whom he has slain, laments that there is no art to find the mind's construction in the face, just as the new Cawdor, traitor-to-be, appears before him. Equally unmistakable is the significance of the King's exit, in the first scene of *Lear,* with the man who like himself has put externals first. "Come, noble Burgundy," he says, and in a pairing that can be made profoundly moving on the stage, the two men go out together.

But what are we to say of Antony's freedman Eros, who enters for the first time (at least by name) just before his master's suicide and kills himself rather than kill Antony. This is all from his source, Plutarch's life of Antony; but why did Shakespeare include it? Did Eros's name mean something to him? Are we to see here a shadowing of the other deaths for love, or not? And the carrying off of Lepidus, drunk, from the feast aboard Pompey's galley. Does this anticipate his subsequent fate? and if it does, what does the intoxication signify which in this scene all the great men are subject to in their degree? Is it ordinary drunkenness; or is it, like the drunkenness that afflicts Caliban, Trinculo, and Stephano in *The Tempest,* a species of self-intoxication, Shakespeare's subdued comment on the thrust to worldly power? Or again, what of the arrival of the players in *Hamlet?* Granted their role in the plot, does Shakespeare make no other profit from them? Are such matters as the speech on Priam's murder and the advice on acting interesting excrescences, as Bradley thought, or does each mirror something that we are to appropriate to our understanding of the play: in the first instance, the strange confederacy of passion and paralysis in the hero's mind,[2] in the second, the question that tolls on all sides through the castle at Elsinore: when is an act not an "act"? [3]

These are questions to which it is not always easy to give a sound answer. The ground becomes somewhat firmer underfoot, I think, if we turn for a concluding instance to Bianca's pat appearances in *Othello.* R. B. Heilman suggests that in rushing to the scene of the

---

[2] See an important comment on this by H. Levin, in *Kenyon Review* (1950), pp. 273–96.

[3] I have touched on this point in *Tragic Themes in Western Literature,* ed. C. Brooks (1953).

night assault on Cassio, when she might have stayed safely within doors, and so exposing herself to vilification as a "notable strumpet," Bianca acts in a manner "thematically relevant, because Othello has just been attacking Desdemona as a strumpet"—both "strumpets," in other words, are faithful (*Magic in the Web,* p. 180). Whether this is true or not, Bianca makes two very striking entrances earlier, when in each case she may be thought to supply in living form on the stage the prostitute figure that Desdemona has become in Othello's mind. Her second entrance is notably expressive. Othello here is partially overhearing while Iago rallies Cassio about Bianca, Othello being under the delusion that the talk is of Desdemona. At the point when, in Othello's mental imagery, Desdemona becomes the soliciting whore—"she tells him how she plucked him to my chamber"—Bianca enters in the flesh, and not only enters, but flourishes the magic handkerchief, now degenerated, like the love it was to ensure, to some "minx's," some "hobbyhorse's" token, the subject of jealous bickering. In the theater, the emblematic effect of this can hardly be ignored.[4]

Further types of mirroring will spring to every reader's mind. The recapitulation of a motif, for instance, as in the poisoning episodes in *Hamlet*. *Hamlet* criticism has too much ignored, I think, the fact that a story of poisoning forms the climax of the first act, a mime and "play" of poisoning the climax of the third, and actual poisoning, on a wide scale, the climax of the fifth. Surely this repetition was calculated to keep steady for Shakespeare's Elizabethan audiences the political and moral bearings of the play? We may say what we like about Hamlet's frailties, which are real, but we can hardly ignore the fact that in each of the poisoning episodes the poisoner is the King. The King, who ought to be like the sun, giving warmth, radiance, and fertility to his kingdom, is actually its destroyer. The "leperous distilment" he pours into Hamlet's father's ear, which courses through his body with such despatch, has coursed just as swiftly through the body politic, and what we see in Denmark as a result is a poisoned kingdom, containing one corruption upon another of Renaissance ideals: the "wise councilor," who is instead a tedious windbag; the young "man of honor," who has no trust in another's honor, as his advice to his sister shows, and none of his own, as his own treachery to Hamlet shows; the "friends," who are not friends but spies; the loved one, the "mistress," who proves disloyal (a decoy, however reluctant, for villainy), and goes mad—through poison also, "the poison of deep grief"; the mother and Queen, who instead of being the guardian of the kingdom's matronly virtues has set a harlot's blister on love's forehead and made marriage vows "as false as dicers' oaths"; and the Prince, the

[4] Another emblematic entrance is the first entrance of the soothsayer in *Julius Caesar;* see "The Teaching of Drama," *Essays on the Teaching of English,* ed. E. J. Gordon and E. S. Noyes (1960).

"ideal courtier," the Renaissance man—once active, energetic, now reduced to anguished introspection; a glass of fashion, now a sloven in antic disarray; a noble mind, now partly unhinged, in fact as well as seeming; the observed of all observers, now observed in a more sinister sense; the mold of form, now capable of obscenities, cruelty, even treachery, mining below the mines of his school friends to hoist them with their own petard. All this, in one way or another, is the poison of the King, and in the last scene, lest we miss the point, we are made to see the spiritual poison become literal and seize on all those whom it has not already destroyed.

> a Prince's Court
> Is like a common Fountaine, whence should flow
> Pure silver-droppes in generall: But if't chance
> Some curs'd example poyson't neere the head,
> Death, and diseases through the whole land spread.

The lines are Webster's, but they state with precision one of the themes of Shakespeare's play.

Finally, in the tragedies as elsewhere in Shakespeare, we have the kinds of replication that have been specifically called "mirror scenes," [5] or (more in Ercles' vein) scenes of "analogical probability." [6] The most impressive examples here are frequently the opening scenes and episodes. The witches of *Macbeth,* whose "foul is fair" and battle that is "won *and* lost" anticipate so much to come. The "great debate" in *Antony and Cleopatra,* initiated in the comments of Philo and the posturings of the lovers, and reverberating thereafter within, as well as around, the lovers till they die. The watchmen on the platform in *Hamlet,* feeling out a mystery—an image that will re-form in our minds again and again as we watch almost every member of the *dramatis personae* engage in similar activity later on. The technique of manipulation established at the outset of *Othello,* the persuading of someone to believe something he is reluctant to believe and which is not true in the sense presented—exemplified in Iago's management of both Roderigo and Brabantio, and prefiguring later developments even to the detail that the manipulator operates by preference through an instrument.

Lear offers perhaps the best of all these instances. Here the "Nature" of which the play is to make so much, ambiguous, double-barreled, is represented in its normative aspect in the hierarchies on the stage before us—a whole political society from its *primum mobile,* the great King, down to lowliest attendant, a whole family society from father down

---

[5] By H. T. Price, in *Joseph Quincy Adams Memorial Studies,* ed. J. McManaway (1948), pp. 101 ff.

[6] See P. J. Aldus, *Shakespeare Quarterly* (1955), pp. 397 ff. Aldus deals suggestively with the opening scene of *Julius Caesar.*

through married daughters and sons-in-law to a third daughter with her wooers—and, in its appetitive aspect, which Edmund will formulate in a few moments, in the overt self-will of the old King and the hidden self-will, the "plighted cunning," of the false daughters. As the scene progresses, in fact, we can see these hierarchies of the normative nature, which at first looked so formidable and solid, crumble away in the repudiation of Cordelia, the banishment of Kent, the exit of Lear and Burgundy, till nothing is left standing on the stage but Nature red in tooth and claw as the false daughters lay their heads together.

I have dwelt a little on these effects of "indirection" in the tragedies because I believe that most of us as playgoers are keenly conscious of their presence. I have perhaps described them badly, in some instances possibly misconceived them; but they are not my invention; this kind of thing has been pointed to more and more widely during the past fifty years by reputable observers. In short, these effects, in some important sense, are "there." And if they are, the question we must ask is, Why? What are they for? How are they used?

I return then to the query with which this section began: what *does* happen in a Shakespearean tragedy? Is it possible to formulate an answer that will, while not repudiating the traditional categories so far as they are useful, take into account the matters we have been examining? In the present state of our knowledge I am not convinced that this is possible: we have been too much concerned in this century with the verbal, which is only part of the picture. Nevertheless, I should like to make a few exploratory gestures.

Obviously the most important thing that happens in a Shakespearean tragedy is that the hero follows a cycle of change, which is, in part, psychic change. And this seems generally to be constituted in three phases. During the first phase, corresponding roughly to Bradley's exposition, the hero is delineated. Among other things, he is placed in positions that enable him to sound the particular timbre of his tragic music:

> Not so, my lord; I am too much i' the sun.
> (*Hamlet,* I.ii.67)

> Seems, madam! nay, it is; I know not "seems."
> (I.ii.76)

> My father's brother, but no more like my father
> Than I to Hercules.
> (I.ii.152)

> My fate cries out,
> And makes each petty artery in this body
> As hardy as the Nemean lion's nerve.
> (I.iv.81)

Chiming against this we are also permitted to hear the particular timbre of the opposing voice, spoken by the foil as well as others:

> If it be,
> Why seems it so particular with thee?
> (I.ii.74)

> For what we know must be and is as common
> As any the most vulgar thing to sense,
> Why should we in our peevish opposition
> Take it to heart?
> (I.ii.98)

> What if it tempt you toward the flood, my lord,
> Or to the dreadful summit of the cliff
> That beetles o'er his base into the sea,
> And there assume some other horrible form,
> Which might deprive your sovereignty of reason
> And draw you into madness?
> (I.iv.69)

From now on, as we saw, these are the differing attitudes towards experience that will supply the essential dialogue of the play.

The second phase is much more comprehensive. It contains the conflict, crisis, and falling action—in short, the heart of the matter. Here several interesting developments occur. The one certain over-all development in this phase is that the hero tends to become his own antithesis. We touched on this earlier in the case of Hamlet, in whom "the courtier's, soldier's, scholar's, eye, tongue, sword" suffer some rather savage violations before the play is done. Likewise, Othello the unshakable, whose original composure under the most trying insults and misrepresentations almost takes the breath away, breaks in this phase into furies, grovels on the floor in a trance, strikes his wife publicly. King Lear, "the great image of authority" both by temperament and position, becomes a helpless crazed old man crying in a storm, destitute of everything but one servant and his Fool. Macbeth, who would have "holily" what he would have "highly," who is too full of the milk of human kindness to catch the nearest way, whose whole being revolts with every step he takes in his own revolt—his hair standing on end, his imagination filling with angels "trumpet-tongued," his hands (after the deed) threatening to pluck out his own eyes—turns into the numbed usurper, "supped full with horrors," who is hardly capable of responding even to his wife's death. The development is equally plain in Antony and Coriolanus. "The greatest prince o' th' world, / The noblest," finds his greatness slipped from him, and his nobility debased to the ignominy of having helpless emissaries whipped. The proud and upright Coriolanus, patriot soldier, truckles in the market place for votes, revolts to the enemy he has vanquished, carries war against his own flesh and blood.

This manner of delineating tragic "action," though it may be traced here and there in other drama, seems to be on the whole a property of the Elizabethans and Jacobeans. Possibly it springs from their concern with "whole" personalities on the tragic stage, rather than as so often with the ancients and Racine, just those aspects of personality that guarantee the *dénouement*. In any case, it seems to have become a consistent feature of Shakespeare's dramaturgy, and beautifully defines the sense of psychological alienation and uprootedness that tragic experience in the Elizabethan and Jacobean theater generally seems to embrace. Its distinctively tragic implications stand out the more when we reflect that psychic change in comedy (if indeed comedy can be said to concern itself with psychic change at all) consists in making—or in showing—the protagonist to be more and more what he always was.[7]

In this second phase too, either as an outward manifestation of inward change, or as a shorthand indication that such change is about to begin or end, belong the tragic journeys. Romeo is off to Mantua, Brutus to the Eastern end of the Roman world, Hamlet to England, Othello to Cyprus, Lear and Gloucester to Dover, Timon to the cave, Macbeth to the heath to revisit the witches, Antony to Rome and Athens, Coriolanus to Antium.[8] Such journeys, we rightly say, are called for by the plots. But perhaps we should not be wrong if we added that Shakespearean plotting tends to call for journeys, conceivably for discernible reasons. For one thing, journeys can enhance our impression that psychological changes are taking place, either by emphasizing a lapse of time, or by taking us to new settings, or by both. I suspect we register such effects subconsciously more often than we think.

Furthermore, though it would be foolish to assign to any of the journeys in Shakespeare's tragedies a precise symbolic meaning, several of them have vaguely symbolic overtones—serving as surrogates either for what can never be exhibited on the stage, as the mysterious processes leading to psychic change, which cannot be articulated into speech, even soliloquy, without losing their formless instinctive character; or for the processes of self-discovery, the learning processes—a function journeys fulfill in many of the world's best-known stories (the *Aeneid*, the *Divine Comedy*, *Tom Jones*, etc.) and in some of Shakespeare's comedies. Hamlet's abortive journey to England is possibly an instance of the first category. After his return, and particularly after what he tells us of his actions while at sea, we are not surprised if he appears, spiritually, a changed man. Lear's and Gloucester's journey to Dover is perhaps an instance of the second category, leading as it does through suffering to insight and reconciliation.

During the hero's journey, or at any rate during his over-all progress in the second phase, he will normally pass through a variety of mirror-

---

[7] I have elaborated this point in an introduction to Fielding's *Joseph Andrews* (1948).

[8] These are merely samples; other journeys occur that I have not named here.

ing situations of the sort formerly discussed (though it will be by us and not him that the likeness in the mirror is seen). In some of these, the hero will be confronted, so to speak, with a version of his own situation, and his failure to recognize it may be a measure of the nature of the disaster to ensue. Coriolanus, revolted from Rome and now its enemy, meets himself in Aufidius's embrace in Antium. Hamlet meets himself in Fortinbras as the latter marches to Poland, but does not see the likeness—only the differences. Lear goes to Goneril's and there meets, as everyone remembers, images of his own behavior to Cordelia. Thrust into the night, he meets his own defenselessness in Edgar, and is impelled to pray. Encountering in Dover fields, both Lear and Gloucester confront in each other an extension of their own experience: blindness that sees and madness that is wise. Macbeth revisits the witches on the heath and finds there (without recognizing them) not only the emblems of his death and downfall to come but his speciousness and duplicity. Antony encounters in Enobarbus's defection his own; and possibly, in Pompey, his own later muddled indecision between "honor" and *Realpolitik*. Othello hears the innocent Cassio set upon in the dark, then goes to re-enact that scene in a more figurative darkness in Desdemona's bedroom. Sometimes, alternatively or additionally, the hero's way will lie through quasi-symbolic settings or situations. The heath in both *Macbeth* and *King Lear* is infinitely suggestive, even if like all good symbols it refuses to dissipate its *Dinglichkeit* in meaning. The same is true of the dark castle platform in Hamlet, and the graveyard; of the cliff at Dover and Gloucester's leap; of the "monument," where both Antony and Cleopatra die; and of course, as many have pointed out, of the night scenes, the storm, the music, the changes of clothing, the banquets. So much in Shakespeare's tragedies stands on the brink of symbol that for this reason, if no other, the usual terms for describing their construction and mode of action need reinforcement.

After the hero has reached and passed through his own antithesis, there comes a third phase in his development that is extremely difficult to define. It represents a recovery of sorts; in some cases, perhaps even a species of synthesis. The once powerful, now powerless king, will have power again, but of another kind—the kind suggested in his reconciliation with Cordelia and his speech beginning "Come, let's away to prison"; and he will have sanity again, but in a mode not dreamed of at the beginning of the play. Or, to take Othello's case, it will be given the hero to recapture the faith he lost,[9] to learn that the pearl really was richer than all his tribe, and to execute quite another order of justice than the blinkered justice meted out to Cassio and the blind injustice meted out to Desdemona. Or again, to shift to Antony, the man who has so long been thrown into storms of rage and recrimina-

[9] This point is well made in Helen Gardner's *The Noble Moor* (1956).

tion by the caprices of his unstable mistress receives the last of them without a murmur of reproach, though it has led directly to his death, and dies in greater unison with her than we have ever seen him live.

I believe that some mark of this nature is visible in all the tragedies. Coriolanus, "boy" though he is and in some ways remains, makes a triumphant choice (detract from his motives as we may), and he knows what it is likely to cost. Moreover, he refuses the way of escape that lies open if he should return now with Volumnia and Vergilia to Rome. "I'll not to Rome, I'll back with you," he tells Aufidius, "and pray you / Stand to me in this cause." The young man who, after this, dies accused of treachery—by Aufidius's treachery, and the suggestibility of the crowd, as slippery in Corioli as Rome—cannot be thought identical in all respects with the young man who joined Menenius in the play's opening scene. He is that young man, but with the notable difference of his triumphant choice behind him; and there is bound to be more than a military association in our minds when the Second Lord of the Volscians, seeking to quell the mob, cries, "The man is noble, and his fame folds in / This orb o' th' earth"; and again too when the First Lord exclaims over his body, "Let him be regarded / As the most noble corse that ever herald / Did follow to his urn." Even the monster Macbeth is so handled by Shakespeare, as has been often enough observed, that he seems to regain something at the close—if nothing more, at least some of that *élan* which made him the all-praised Bellona's bridegroom of the play's second scene; and everything Macbeth says, following Duncan's death, about the emptiness of the achievement, the lack of posterity, the sear, the yellow leaf, deprived of "that which should accompany old age, / As honor, love, obedience, troops of friends," affords evidence that the meaning of his experience has not been lost on him.

To say this, I wish to make it clear, is not to say that the Shakespearean tragic hero undergoes an "illumination," or, to use the third term of K. Burke's sequence, a Mathema or perception.[10] This is a terminology that seems to me not very useful to the discussion of tragedy as Shakespeare presents it. It is sufficient for my purposes to say simply that the phase in which we are conscious of the hero as approaching his opposite is followed by a final phase in which we are conscious of him as exhibiting one or more aspects of his original, or —since these may not coincide—his better self: as in the case of Antony's final reunion with Cleopatra, and Coriolanus's decision not to sack Rome. Whether we then go on to give this phenomenon a specific spiritual significance, seeing in it the objective correlative of "perception" or "illumination," is a question that depends, obviously, on a great many factors, more of them perhaps situated in our own individual philosophies than in the text, and, so, likely to lead us away from

[10] *A Grammar of Motives* (1945), pp. 38 ff.

Shakespeare rather than towards him. Clearly if Shakespeare wished us to engage in this activity, he was remiss in the provision of clues. Even in *King Lear,* the one play where some sort of regeneration or new insight in the hero has been universally acknowledged, the man before us in the last scene—who sweeps Kent aside, rakes all who have helped him with grapeshot ("A plague upon you, murderers, traitors all. I might have saved her . . ."), exults in the revenge he has exacted for Cordelia's death, and dies self-deceived in the thought she still lives —this man is one of the most profoundly human figures ever created in a play; but he is not, certainly, the Platonic idea laid up in heaven, or in critical schemes, of regenerate man.

I have kept to the end, and out of proper order, the most interesting of all the symbolic elements in the hero's second phase. This is his experience of madness. One discovers with some surprise, I think, how many of Shakespeare's heroes are associated with this disease. Only Titus, Hamlet, Lear, and Timon, in various senses, actually go mad; but Iago boasts that he will make Othello mad, and in a way succeeds; Antony, after the second defeat at sea, is said by Cleopatra to be

> more mad,
> Than Telamon for his shield; the boar of Thessaly
> Was never so emboss'd;
> (IV.xiii.2)

Caithness in *Macbeth* tells us that some say the king is mad, while "others, that lesser hate him, / Do call it valiant fury"; Romeo, rather oddly, enjoins Paris at Juliet's tomb to

> be gone; live, and hereafter say,
> A madman's mercy bade thee run away.
> (V.iii.66)

Even Brutus, by the Antony of *Antony and Cleopatra,* is said to have been "mad."

What (if anything), one wonders, may this mean? Doubtless a sort of explanation can be found in Elizabethan psychological lore, which held that the excess of any passion approached madness, and in the general prevalence, through Seneca and other sources, of the adage: *Quos vult perdere Jupiter dementat prius.*[11] Furthermore, madness, when actually exhibited, was dramatically useful, as Kyd had shown. It was arresting in itself, and it allowed the combination in a single figure of tragic hero and buffoon, to whom could be accorded the license of the allowed fool in speech and action.

---

[11] ["Whom Jupiter wishes to destroy he first makes mad."]

Just possibly, however, there was yet more to it than this, if we may judge by Shakespeare's sketches of madness in Hamlet and King Lear. In both these, madness is to some degree a punishment or doom, corresponding to the adage. Lear prays to the heavens that he may not suffer madness, and Hamlet asks Laertes, in his apology before the duel, to overlook his conduct, since "you must needs have heard, how I am punish'd / With a sore distraction." It is equally obvious, however, that in both instances the madness has a further dimension, as insight, and this is true also of Ophelia. Ophelia, mad, is able to make awards of flowers to the King and Queen which are appropriate to frailties of which she cannot be supposed to have conscious knowledge. For the same reason, I suspect we do not need Dover Wilson's radical displacement of Hamlet's entry in II.ii, so as to enable him to overhear Polonius.[12] It is enough that Hamlet wears, even if it is for the moment self-assumed, the guise of the madman. As such, he can be presumed to have intuitive unformulated awarenesses that reach the surface in free (yet relevant) associations, like those of Polonius with a fishmonger, Ophelia with carrion. Lear likewise is allowed free yet relevant associations. His great speech in Dover fields on the lust of women derives from the designs of Goneril and Regan on Edmund, of which he consciously knows nothing. Moreover, both he and Hamlet can be privileged in madness to say things—Hamlet about the corruption of human nature, and Lear about the corruption of the Jacobean social system (and by extension about all social systems whatever), which Shakespeare could hardly have risked apart from this license. Doubtless one of the anguishes of being a great artist is that you cannot tell people what they and you and your common institutions are really like —when viewed absolutely—without being dismissed as insane. To communicate at all, you must acknowledge the opposing voice; for there always is an opposing voice, and it is as deeply rooted in your own nature as in your audience's.

Just possibly, therefore, the meaning of tragic madness for Shakespeare approximated the meaning that the legendary figure of Cassandra (whom Shakespeare had in fact put briefly on his stage in the second act of *Troilus and Cressida*) has held for so many artists since his time. Cassandra's madness, like Lear's and Hamlet's—possibly, also, like the madness *verbally* assigned to other Shakespearean tragic heroes —contains both punishment and insight. She is doomed to know, by a consciousness that moves to measures outside our normal space and time; she is doomed never to be believed, because those to whom she speaks can hear only the opposing voice. With the language of the god Apollo sounding in her brain, and the incredulity of her fellow mortals ringing in her ears, she makes an ideal emblem of the predicament of the Shakespearean tragic hero, caught as he is between the absolute

---

[12] *What Happens in "Hamlet"* (1935), pp. 103 ff.

and the expedient. And by the same token, of the predicament of the artist—Shakespeare himself, perhaps—who, having been given the power to see the "truth," can convey it only through poetry—what we commonly call a "fiction," and dismiss.

In all these matters, let me add in parenthesis, we would do well to extend more generously our inferences about Shakespeare to the Jacobean playwrights as a group. Some of us have been overlong content with a view of Jacobean tragedy as naïve as those formerly entertained of Restoration comedy, eighteenth-century literature, and modern poetry. But a whole generation of writers does not become obsessed by the sexual feuding of cavalier and citizen, or rhetorical "rules" and social norms, or abrupt images and catapulting rhythms, or outrageous stories of incest, madness, brutality, and lust, because the poetic imagination has suddenly gone "frivolous," or "cold," or "eccentric," or "corrupt." Such concerns respond to spiritual needs, however dimly apprehended, and one of the prime needs of Jacobean writers, as the intelligible and on the whole friendly universe of the Middle Ages failed around them, was quite evidently to face up to what men are or may be when stripped to their naked humanity and mortality, and torn loose from accustomed moorings. Flamineo's phrase in *The White Devil*—"this busy trade of life"—offered as a passing summary of the play's monstrous burden of blood and madness:

> This busy trade of life appears most vain,
> Since rest breeds rest, where all seek pain by pain—

is characteristically understated and ironic, like Iago's "Pleasure and action make the hours seem short." The creators of Iago and Flamineo, and all the responsible writers of Jacobean tragedy along with them, knew perfectly well that it was not in fact the "trade," or habitude, of life to which they held up art's mirror, but life "on the stretch," nature at its farthest reach of possibility. They were fascinated by violence because they were fascinated by the potencies of the human will: its weaknesses, triumphs, delusions, corruptions, its capacities for destruction and regeneration, its residual dignity when, all else removed, man stood at his being's limit; and because they knew that in violence lay the will's supreme test, for aggressor and sufferer alike.

Whatever the themes of individual plays, therefore, the one pervasive Jacobean theme tends to be the undertaking and working out of acts of will, and especially (in that strongly Calvinistic age) of acts of self-will. This is surely the reason why, in Clifford Leech's happy phrase, these writers know so little of heaven, so much of hell; and why, to one conversant with their work so many products of the century to come seem like fulfillments of ancient prophecy: Milton's Satan and his "God"—the philosophy embodied in *Leviathan*—even, perhaps, the clash of the Civil Wars and the cleavage in the English spirit reaching from Cavalier and Puritan to Jacobite and Whig and well beyond. At the very beginning of the century, these writers had got hold of the theme that was to exercise it in all departments, political, economic, religious, cultural, till past its close, the problem of anarchic will; and so decisive, so many-sided is their treatment of this problem that even in Milton's massive recapitulation of it in *Paradise Lost* the issue seems sometimes to be losing in vitality what it has gained in clarity, to be fossilizing and becoming formula. The utterances of *his* white devil have more resonance but less complexity and immediacy of feeling than those of Vittoria Corombona, Bosola, Macbeth, or Beatrice Vermandero; and some of them bear a perilous resemblance to the posturings of Restoration heroic tragedy, where the old agonies are heard from still, but now clogged, and put through paces like captive giants in a raree show.

However this may be, I return at the end to the proposition I set out with: there is a lot about the construction of a Shakespearean tragic "action" that we still do not know. My own attempts to get towards it in this chapter are fumbling and may be preposterous: even to myself they sound a little like Bottom's dream. But the interesting thing about Bottom's dream, from my point of view, is that, though he found he was an ass all right, the Titania he tried to tell about was real.

SHAKESPEARE'S LATER TRAGEDIES

"Othello": An Introduction

Alvin B. Kernan

When Shakespeare wrote *Othello,* about 1604, his knowledge of human nature and his ability to dramatize it in language and action were at their height. The play offers, even in its minor characters, a number of unusually full and profound studies of humanity: Brabantio, the sophisticated, civilized Venetian senator, unable to comprehend that his delicate daughter could love and marry a Moor, speaking excitedly of black magic and spells to account for what his mind cannot understand; Cassio, the gentleman-soldier, polished in manners and gracious in bearing, wildly drunk and revealing a deeply rooted pride in his ramblings about senior officers being saved before their juniors; Emilia, the sensible and conventional waiting woman, making small talk about love and suddenly remarking that though she believes adultery to be wrong, still if the price were high enough she would sell—and so, she believes, would most women. The vision of human nature which the play offers is one of ancient terrors and primal drives—fear of the unknown, pride, greed, lust—underlying smooth, civilized surfaces—the noble senator, the competent and well-mannered lieutenant, the conventional gentlewoman.

The contrast between surface manner and inner nature is even more pronounced in two of the major characters. "Honest Iago" conceals beneath his exterior of the plain soldier and blunt, practical man of

---

the world a diabolism so intense as to defy rational explanation—it must be taken like lust or pride as simply a given part of human nature, an anti-life spirit which seeks the destruction of everything outside the self. Othello appears in the opening acts as the very personification of self-control, of the man with so secure a sense of his own worth that nothing can ruffle the consequent calmness of mind and manner. But the man who has roamed the wild and savage world unmoved by its terrors, who has not changed countenance when the cannon killed his brother standing beside him, this man is still capable of believing his wife a whore on the slightest of evidence and committing murders to revenge himself. In Desdemona alone do the heart and the hand go together: she is what she seems to be. Ironically, she alone is accused of pretending to be what she is not. Her very openness and honesty make her suspect in a world where few men are what they appear, and her chastity is inevitably brought into question in a world where every other major character is in some degree touched with sexual corruption.

Most criticism of *Othello* has concerned itself with exploring the depths of these characters and tracing the intricate, mysterious operations of their minds. I should like, however, to leave this work to the individual reader and to the critical essays printed at the back of this volume in order to discuss, briefly, what might be called the "gross mechanics" of the play, the larger patterns in which events and characters are arranged. These patterns are the context within which the individual characters are defined, just as the pattern of a sentence is the context which defines the exact meaning of the individual words within it.

Othello is probably the most neatly, the most formally constructed of Shakespeare's plays. Every character is, for example, balanced by another similar or contrasting character. Desdemona is balanced by her opposite, Iago; love and concern for others at one end of the scale, hatred and concern for self at the other. The true and loyal soldier Cassio balances the false and traitorous soldier Iago. These balances and contrasts throw into relief the essential qualities of the characters. Desdemona's love, for example, shows up a good deal more clearly in contrast to Iago's hate, and vice versa. The values of contrast are increased and the full range of human nature displayed by extending these simple contrasts into developing series. The essential purity of Desdemona stands in contrast to the more "practical" view of chastity held by Emilia, and her view in turn is illuminated by the workaday view of sensuality held by the courtesan Bianca, who treats love, ordinarily, as a commodity. Or, to take another example, Iago's success in fooling Othello is but the culmination of a series of such betrayals that includes the duping of Roderigo, Brabantio, and Cassio. Each duping is the explanatory image of the other, for in every case Iago's method and end are the same: he plays on and teases to life some hitherto controlled and concealed dark passion in his victim. In each case he seeks in some way the same end, the symbolic murder of

Desdemona, the destruction in some form of the life principle of which she is the major embodiment.

These various contrasts and parallelisms ultimately blend into a larger, more general pattern that is the central movement of the play. We can begin to see this pattern in the "symbolic geography" of the play. Every play, or work of art, creates its own particular image of space and time, its own symbolic world. The outer limits of the world of *Othello* are defined by the Turks—the infidels, the unbelievers, the "general enemy" as the play calls them—who, just over the horizon, sail back and forth trying to confuse and trick the Christians in order to invade their dominions and destroy them. Out beyond the horizon, reported but unseen, are also those "anters vast and deserts idle" of which Othello speaks. Out there is a land of "rough quarries, rocks, and hills whose heads touch heaven" inhabited by "cannibals that each other eat" and monstrous forms of men "whose heads grow beneath their shoulders." On the edges of this land is the raging ocean with its "high seas, and howling winds," its "guttered rocks and congregated sands" hidden beneath the waters to "enclog the guiltless keel."

Within the circle formed by barbarism, monstrosity, sterility, and the brute power of nature lie the two Christian strongholds of Venice and Cyprus. Renaissance Venice was known for its wealth acquired by trade, its political cunning, and its courtesans; but Shakespeare, while reminding us of the tradition of the "supersubtle Venetian," makes Venice over into a form of *The City,* the ageless image of government, of reason, of law, and of social concord. Here, when Brabantio's strong passions and irrational fears threaten to create riot and injustice, his grievances are examined by a court of law, judged by reason, and the verdict enforced by civic power. Here, the clear mind of the Senate probes the actions of the Turks, penetrates through their pretenses to their true purposes, makes sense of the frantic and fearful contradictory messages which pour in from the fleet, and arranges the necessary defense. Act I, Scene iii—the Senate scene—focuses on the magnificent speeches of Othello and Desdemona as they declare their love and explain it, but the lovers are surrounded, guarded, by the assembled, ranked governors of Venice, who control passions that otherwise would have led to a bloody street brawl and bring justice out of what otherwise would have been riot. The solemn presence and ordering power of the Senate would be most powerfully realized in a stage production, where the senators would appear in their rich robes, with all their symbols of office, seated in ranks around several excited individuals expressing such primal passions as pride of race, fear of dark powers, and violent love. In a play where so much of the language is magnificent, rich, and of heroic proportions, simpler statements come to seem more forceful; and the meaning of *The City* is perhaps nowhere more completely realized than in Brabantio's brief, secure answer to the first fearful cries of theft and talk of copulating animals that Iago and Roderigo send up from the darkness below his window:

What tell'st thou me of robbing? This is Venice;
My house is not a grange.
(I.i.102–03)

Here then are the major reference points on a map of the world of *Othello:* out at the far edge are the Turks, barbarism, disorder, and amoral destructive powers; closer and more familiar is Venice, *The City,* order, law, and reason. Cyprus, standing on the frontier between barbarism and *The City,* is not the secure fortress of civilization that Venice is. It is rather an outpost, weakly defended and far out in the raging ocean, close to the "general enemy" and the immediate object of his attack. It is a "town of war yet wild" where the "people's hearts [are] brimful of fear." Here passions are more explosive and closer to the surface than in Venice, and here, instead of the ancient order and established government of *The City,* there is only one man to control violence and defend civilization—the Moor Othello, himself of savage origins and a converted Christian.

The movement of the play is from Venice to Cyprus, from *The City* to the outpost, from organized society to a condition much closer to raw nature, and from collective life to the life of the solitary individual. This movement is a characteristic pattern in Shakespeare's plays, both comedies and tragedies: in *A Midsummer Night's Dream* the lovers and players go from the civilized, daylight world of Athens to the irrational, magical wood outside Athens and the primal powers of life represented by the elves and fairies; Lear moves from his palace and secure identity to the savage world of the heath where all values and all identities come into question; and everyone in *The Tempest* is shipwrecked at some time on Prospero's magic island, where life seen from a new perspective assumes strange and fantastic shapes. At the other end of this journey there is always some kind of return to *The City,* to the palace, and to old relationships, but the nature of this return differs widely in Shakespeare's plays. In *Othello* the movement at the end of the play is back toward Venice, the Turk defeated; but Desdemona, Othello, Emilia, and Roderigo do not return. Their deaths are the price paid for the return.

This passage from Venice to Cyprus to fight the Turk and encounter the forces of barbarism is the geographical form of an action that occurs on the social and psychological levels as well. That is, there are social and mental conditions that correspond to Venice and Cyprus, and there are forces at work in society and in man that correspond to the Turks, the raging seas, and "cannibals that each other eat."

The exposure to danger, the breakdown and the ultimate reestablishment of society—the parallel on the social level to the action on the geographical level—is quickly traced. We have already noted that the Venetian Senate embodies order, reason, justice, and concord, the binding forces that hold *The City* together. In Venice the ancient laws and the established customs of society work to control violent men and violent passions to ensure the safety and well-being of the individual and the group. But there are anarchic forces at work in the city, which threaten traditional social forms and relationships, and all these forces center in Iago. His discontent with his own rank and his determination to displace Cassio endanger the orderly military hierarchy in which the junior serves his senior. He endangers marriage, the traditional form for ordering male and female relationships, by his own unfounded suspicions of his wife and by his efforts to destroy Othello's marriage by fanning to life the darker, anarchic passions of Brabantio and Roderigo. He tries to subvert the operation of law and justice by first stirring up Brabantio to gather his followers and seek revenge in the streets; and then when the two warlike forces are met, Iago begins a quarrel with Roderigo in hopes of starting a brawl. The nature of the antisocial forces that Iago represents are focused in the imagery of his advice to Roderigo on how to call out to her father the news of Desdemona's marriage. Call, he says,

> with like timorous [frightening] accent and dire yell
> As when, by night and negligence, the fire
> Is spied in populous cities.
>
> (I.i.72–74)

Fire, panic, darkness, neglect of duty—these are the natural and human forces that destroy great cities and turn their citizens to mobs.

In Venice, Iago's attempts to create civic chaos are frustrated by Othello's calm management of himself and the orderly legal proceedings of the Senate. In Cyprus, however, society is less secure—even as the island is more exposed to the Turks—and Othello alone is responsible for finding truth and maintaining order. Here Iago's poison begins to work, and he succeeds at once in manufacturing the riot that he failed to create in Venice. Seen on stage, the fight on the watch between Cassio and Montano is chaos come again: two drunken officers, charged with the defense of the town, trying to kill each other like savage animals, a bedlam of voices and shouts, broken, disordered furniture, and above all this the discordant clamor of the "dreadful" alarm bell—used to signal attacks and fire. This success is but the prologue for other more serious disruptions of society and of the various human relationships that it fosters. The General is set against his officer, husband against wife, Christian against Christian, servant against master. Justice becomes a travesty of itself as Othello—using legal terms such as "It is the *cause*"—assumes the offices of accuser, judge, jury, and executioner of his wife. Manners disappear as the Moor strikes his wife publicly and treats her maid as a procuress. The brightly lighted Senate chamber is now replaced with a dark Cyprus street where Venetians cut one another down and men are murdered from behind. This anarchy finally gives way in the last scene, when Desdemona's faith is proven, to a restoration of order and an execution of justice on the two major criminals.

What we have followed so far is a movement expressed in geographical and social symbols from Venice to a Cyprus exposed to attack, from *The City* to barbarism, from Christendom to the domain of the Turks, from order to riot, from justice to wild revenge and murder, from truth to falsehood. It now remains to see just what this movement means on the level of the individual in the heart and mind of man. Of the three major characters, Desdemona, Othello, and Iago, the first and the last do not change their natures or their attitudes toward life during the course of the play. These two are polar opposites, the antitheses of each other. To speak in the most general terms, Desdemona expresses in her language and actions an innocent, unselfish love and concern for others. Othello catches her very essence when he speaks of her miraculous love, which transcended their differences in age, color, beauty, and culture:

> She loved me for the dangers I had passed,
> And I loved her that she did pity them.
> (I.iii.166–67)

This love in its various forms finds expression not only in her absolute commitment of herself to Othello, but in her gentleness, her kindness to others, her innocent trust in all men, her pleas for Cassio's restoration to Othello's favor; and it endures even past death at her husband's hands, for she comes back to life for a moment to answer Emilia's question, "who hath done this deed?" with the unbelievable words,

> Nobody—I myself. Farewell.
> Commend me to my kind lord. O, farewell!
> (V.ii.123–24)

Iago is her opposite in every way. Where she is open and guileless, he is never what he seems to be; where she thinks the best of everyone, he thinks the worst, usually turning to imagery of animals and physical functions to express his low opinion of human nature; where she seeks to serve and love others, he uses others to further his own dark aims and satisfy his hatred of mankind; where she is emotional and idealistic, he is icily logical and cynical. Desdemona and Iago are much more complicated than this, but perhaps enough has been said to suggest the nature of these two moral poles of the play. One is a life force that strives for order, community, growth, and light. The other is an anti-life force that seeks anarchy, death, and darkness. One is the foundation of all that men have built in the world, including *The City;* the other leads back toward ancient chaos and barbarism.

Othello, like most men, is a combination of the forces of love and hate, which are isolated in impossibly pure states in Desdemona and Iago. His psychic voyage from Venice to Cyprus is a passage of the soul and the will from the values of one of these characters to those of the other. This passage is charted by his acceptance and rejection of one or the other. He begins by refusing to have Iago as his lieutenant, choosing the more "theoretical" though less experienced Cassio. He marries Desdemona. Though he is not aware that he does so, he expresses the full meaning of this choice when he speaks of her in such suggestive terms as "my soul's joy" and refers to her even as he is about to kill her, as "Promethean heat," the vital fire that gives life to the world. Similarly, he comes to know that all that is valuable in life depends on her love, and in the magnificent speech beginning, "O now, forever / Farewell the tranquil mind" (III.iii.344–45), he details the emptiness of all human activity if Desdemona be proved false. But Iago, taking advantage of latent "Iagolike" feelings and thoughts in Othello, persuades him that Desdemona is only common clay. Othello then gives himself over to Iago at the end of III.iii, where they kneel together to plan the revenge, and Othello says, "Now art thou my lieutenant." To which Iago responds with blood-chilling simplicity, "I am your own forever." The full meaning of this choice is expressed, again unconsciously, by Othello when he says of Desdemona,

> Perdition catch my soul
> But I do love thee! and when I love thee not,
> Chaos is come again.
>
> (III.iii.90–92)

The murder of Desdemona acts out the final destruction in Othello himself of all the ordering powers of love, of trust, of the bond between human beings.

Desdemona and Iago then represent two states of mind, two understandings of life, and Othello's movement from one to the other is the movement on the level of character and psychology from Venice to Cyprus, from *The City* to anarchy. His return to *The City* and the defeat of the Turk is effected, at the expense of his own life, when he learns *what* he has killed and executes himself as the only fitting judgment on his act. His willingness to speak of what he has done—in contrast to Iago's sullen silence—is a willingness to recognize the meaning of Desdemona's faith and chastity, to acknowledge that innocence and love do exist, and that therefore *The City* can stand, though his life is required to validate the truth and justice on which it is built.

Othello offers a variety of interrelated symbols that locate and define in historical, natural, social, moral, and human terms those qualities of being and universal forces that are forever at war in the universe and between which tragic man is always in movement. On one side there are Turks, cannibals, barbarism, monstrous deformities of nature, the brute force of the sea, riot, mobs, darkness, Iago, hatred, lust, concern for the self only, and cynicism. On the other side there are Venice, *The City,* law, senates, amity, hierarchy, Desdemona, love, concern for others, and innocent trust. As the characters of the play act and speak, they bring together, by means of parallelism and metaphor, the various forms of the different ways of life. There is, for example, a meaningful similarity in the underhanded way Iago works and the ruse by which the Turks try to fool the Venetians into thinking they are bound for Rhodes when their object is Cyprus. Or, there is again a flash of identification when we hear that the reefs and shoals that threaten ships are "ensteeped," that is, hidden under the surface of the sea, as Iago is hidden under the surface of his "honesty." But Shakespeare binds the various levels of being more closely together by the use of imagery that compares things on one level of action with things on another. For example, when Iago swears that his low judgment of all female virtue "is true, or else I am a Turk" (II.i.113), logic demands, since one woman, Desdemona, *is* true and chaste, that we account him "a Turk." He is thus identified with the unbelievers, the Ottoman Turks, and that Asiatic power, which for centuries threatened Christendom, is shown to have its social and psychological equivalent in Iago's particular attitude toward life. Similarly, when Othello sees the drunken brawl on the watchtower, he exclaims,

> Are we turned Turks, and to ourselves do that
> Which heaven hath forbid the Ottomites?
> (II.iii.169–70)

At the very time when the historical enemy has been defeated, his fleet providentially routed by the great storm, his characteristics—drunken loss of control, brawling over honor, disorder—begin to conquer the island only so recently and fortuitously saved. The conquest continues, and the defender of the island, Othello, convinced of Desdemona's guilt, compares his determination to revenge himself to "the Pontic Sea, / Whose icy current and compulsive course / Nev'r keeps retiring ebb" (III.iii.450–52). The comparison tells us that in his rage and hatred he has become one with the savage seas and the brute, amoral powers of nature that are displayed in the storm scene at the beginning of Act II. But most important is Othello's identification of himself at the end of the play as the "base Judean" who "threw a pearl away richer than all his tribe." The more familiar Quarto reading is "base Indian," but both words point toward the barbarian who fails to recognize value and beauty when he possesses it—the primitive savage who picks up a pearl and throws it away not knowing its worth; or the Jews (Judas may be specifically meant) who denied and crucified another great figure of love, thinking they were dealing with only a troublesome rabble-rouser. A few lines further on Othello proceeds to the final and absolute identification of himself with the infidel. He speaks of a "malignant and a turbaned Turk" who "beat a Venetian and traduced the state," and he then acknowledges that he is that Turk by stabbing himself, even as he once stabbed the other unbeliever.

So he ends as both the Turk and the destroyer of the Turk, the infidel and the defender of the faith.

When Iago's schemes are at last exposed, Othello, finding it impossible for a moment to believe that a *man* could have contrived such evil, stares at Iago's feet and then says sadly, "but that's a fable." What he hopes to find when he looks down are the cloven hoofs of the devil, and had they been there he would have been an actor in a morality play, tempted beyond his strength, like many a man before him, by a supernatural power outside himself. In some ways I have schematized *Othello* as just such a morality play, offering an allegorical journey between heaven and hell on a stage filled with purely symbolic figures. This is the kind of abstraction of art toward which criticism inevitably moves, and in this case the allegorical framework is very solidly there. But Othello does not see the cloven hoofs when he looks down; he sees a pair of human feet at the end of a very human body; and he is forced to realize that far from living in some simplified, "fabulous" world where evil is a metaphysical power raiding human life from without, he dwells where evil is somehow inextricably woven with good into man himself. On his stage the good angel does not return to heaven when defeated, but is murdered, and her body remains on the bed, "cold, cold." He lives where good intentions, past services, psychic weaknesses, and an inability to see through evil cannot excuse an act, as they might in some simpler world where more perfect justice existed. In short, Othello is forced to recognize that he lives in a tragic world, and he pays the price for having been great enough to inhabit it.

Here is the essence of Shakespeare's art, an ability to create immediate, full, and total life as men actually live and experience it; and yet at the same time to arrange this reality so that it gives substance to and derives shape from a formal vision of all life that comprehends and reaches back from man and nature through society and history to cosmic powers that operate through all time and space. His plays are both allegorical and realistic at once; his characters both recognizable men and at the same time devils, demigods, and forces in nature. I have discussed only the more allegorical elements in *Othello,* the skeleton of ideas and formal patterns within which the characters must necessarily be understood. But it is equally true that the exact qualities of the abstract moral values and ideas, their full reality, exist only in the characters. It is necessary to know that Desdemona represents one particular human value, love or charity, in order to avoid making such mistakes as searching for some tragic flaw in her which would justify her death. But at the same time, if we would know what love and charity *are* in all their fullness, then our definition can only be the actions, the language, the emotions of the character Desdemona. She is Shakespeare's word for love. If we wish to know not just the obvious fact that men choose evil over good, but *why* they do so, then we must look both analytically and feelingly at all the evidence that the world offers for believing that Desdemona is false and at all the biases in Othello's mind that predispose him to believe such evidence. Othello's passage from Venice to Cyprus, from absolute love for Desdemona to extinguishing the light in her bedchamber, and to the execution of himself, these are Shakespeare's words for tragic man.

"King Lear" or "Endgame"

Jan Kott

> KING LEAR Dost thou call me fool, boy?
> FOOL All thy other titles thou hast given away; that thou wast born with.
> (*King Lear,* I.iv.)

> We are all born mad. Some remain so.
> (*Waiting for Godot,* II)

I

The attitude of modern criticism to *King Lear* is ambiguous and somehow embarrassed. Doubtless *King Lear* is still recognized as a masterpiece, beside which even *Macbeth* and *Hamlet* seem tame and pedestrian. *King Lear* is compared to Bach's *Mass in B Minor,* to Beethoven's *Fifth* and *Ninth* Symphonies, to Wagner's *Parsifal,* Michelangelo's *Last Judgement,* or Dante's *Purgatory* and *Inferno.* But at the same time *King Lear* gives one the impression of a high mountain that everyone admires, yet no one particularly wishes to climb. It is as if the play had lost its power to excite on the stage and in reading; as if it were out of place in our time, or, at any rate, had no place in the modern theatre. But the question is: what is modern theatre?

The apogee of *King Lear's* theatrical history was reached no doubt in the romantic era. *King Lear* fit the romantic theatre perfectly; but only conceived as a melodrama, full of horrors, and dealing with a

---

tragic king, deprived of his crown, conspired against by heaven and earth, nature and men. Charles Lamb might well laugh at early nineteenth-century performances in which a miserable old man wandered about the stage bare-headed, stick in hand, in an artificial storm and rain. But the theatre was soon to attain the full power of illusion. Diorama, scene changes effected by means of new stage machinery without bringing the curtain down, made it possible suddenly, almost miraculously to transform a Gothic castle into a mountainous region, or a blood-red sunset into a stormy night. Lightning and thunder, rain and wind, seemed like the real thing. It was easy for the romantic imagination to find its favourite landscape: gloomy castles, hovels, deserted spots, mysterious and awe-inspiring places, towering rocks gleaming white in the moonlight. *King Lear* was also in keeping with the romantic style of acting, since it offered scope for the sweeping gestures, terrifying scenes, and violent soliloquies, loudly delivered, so popular with Kean and his school. The actor's task was to demonstrate the blackest depths of the human soul. Lear's and Gloucester's unhappy fate was to arouse pity and terror, to shock the audience. And so it did. Suffering purified Lear and restored his tragic greatness. Shakespeare's *King Lear* was the "black theatre" of romanticism.

Then came the turn of historical, antiquarian and realistic Shakespeare. Stage designers were sent to Rome to copy features of the Forum for sets to *Julius Caesar*. Crowds of extras were dressed in period costume. Copies were made of medieval dress, Renaissance jewelry, Elizabethan furniture. Sets became more and more solid and imposing. The stage was turned into a large exhibition of historical props. A balcony had to be a real balcony; a palace, a real palace; a street, a real street. Real trees were substituted for the old painted landscape.

At that time attempts were made to set *King Lear* also in a definite historical period. With the help of archeologists Celtic burial places were reconstructed on the stage. Lear became an old druid. Theatrical machinery was more and more perfect, so that storm, wind and rain could drown the actors' voices more and more effectively. As a result of the odd marriage between new and perfected theatre techniques and archeological reconstruction of a Celtic tomb, only the plot remained of Shakespeare's play. In such a theatre Shakespeare was indeed out of place: he was untheatrical.

The turn of the century brought a revolution in Shakespearean studies. For the first time his plays began to be interpreted through the theatre of his time. A generation of scholars was busy patiently recreating the Elizabethan stage, style of acting and theatrical traditions. Granville-Barker in his famous *Prefaces to Shakespeare* showed, or at least tried to show, how *Lear* must have been played at the Globe. The return to the so-called "authentic" Shakespeare began. From now on the storm was to rage in Lear's and Gloucester's breasts rather than on the stage. The trouble was, however, that the demented old man, tearing his long white beard, suddenly became ridiculous. He should have been tragic, but he no longer was.

Nearly all Shakespeare's expositions have an amazing speed and directness in the way conflicts are shown and put into action and the whole tone of the play is set. The exposition of *King Lear* seems preposterous if one is to look for psychological verisimilitude in it. A great and powerful king holds a competition of rhetoric among his daughters, as to which one of them will best express her love for him, and makes the division of his kingdom depend on its outcome. He does not see or understand anything: Regan's and Goneril's hypocrisy is all too evident. Regarded as a person, a character, Lear is ridiculous, naive and stupid. When he goes mad, he can arouse only compassion, never pity and terror.

Gloucester, too, is naive and ridiculous. In the early scenes he seems a stock character from a comedy of manners. Robert Speaight compares him to a gentleman of somewhat old-fashioned views who strolls on a Sunday along St. James's Street complete with bowler hat and umbrella.[1] Nothing about him hints at the tragic old man whose eyes will be gouged out. It is true that Polonius in *Hamlet* is also a comic figure, who later is stabbed to death. But his death is grotesque, too, while Lear and Gloucester are to go through immense sufferings.

Producers have found it virtually impossible to cope with the plot of *King Lear*. When realistically treated, Lear and Gloucester were too ridiculous to appear tragic heroes. If the exposition was treated as a fairy tale or legend, the cruelty of Shakespeare's world, too, became unreal. Yet the cruelty of *Lear* was to the Elizabethans a contemporary reality, and has remained real since. But it is a philosophical cruelty. Neither the romantic, nor the naturalistic theatre was able to show that sort of cruelty; only the new theatre can. In this new theatre there are no characters, and the tragic element has been superseded by grotesque. Grotesque is more cruel than tragedy.

The exposition of *King Lear* is as absurd, and as necessary as the arrival at Güllen of multi-millionairess Claire Zachanassian and her entourage, including a new husband, a couple of eunuchs, a large coffin, and a tiger in a cage in Dürrenmatt's *Visit*. The exposition of *King Lear* shows a world that is to be destroyed.

Since the end of the eighteenth century no dramatist has had a greater impact on European drama than Shakespeare. But the theatres in which Shakespeare's plays have been produced were in turn influenced by contemporary plays. Shakespeare has been a living influence in so far as contemporary plays, through which his dramas were interpreted, were a living force themselves. When Shakespeare is dull and dead on the stage, it means that not only the theatre but also the plays written in that particular period are dead. This is one of the reasons why Shakespeare's universality has never dated.

[1] See R. Speaight, *Nature in Shakespearian Tragedy*, London, 1955.

The book devoted to "Shakespeare and the new drama" has not yet been written. Perhaps it is too early for such a book to appear. But it is odd how often the word "Shakespearean" is uttered when one speaks about Brecht, Dürrenmatt, or Beckett. These three names stand, of course, for three different kinds of theatrical vision, and the word "Shakespearean" means something different in relation to each of them. It may be invoked to compare with Dürrenmatt's full-bloodedness, sharpness, lack of cohesion, and stylistic confusion; with Brecht's epic quality; or with Beckett's new *Theatrum mundi.* But every one of these three kinds of drama and theatre has more similarities to Shakespeare and medieval morality plays than to nineteenth-century drama, whether romantic, or naturalistic. Only in this sense can the new theatre be called anti-theatre.

A striking feature of the new theatre is its grotesque quality. Despite appearances to the contrary, this new grotesque has not replaced the old drama and the comedy of manners. It deals with problems, conflicts and themes of tragedy such as: human fate, the meaning of existence, freedom and inevitability, the discrepancy between the absolute and the fragile human order. Grotesque means tragedy re-written in different terms. Maurice Regnault's statement: "the absence of tragedy in a tragic world gives birth to comedy" is only seemingly paradoxical. Grotesque exists in a tragic world. Both the tragic and the grotesque vision of the world are composed as it were of the same elements. In a tragic and grotesque world, situations are imposed, compulsory and inescapable. Freedom of choice and decision are part of this compulsory situation, in which both the tragic hero and the grotesque actor must always lose their struggle against the absolute. The downfall of the tragic hero is a confirmation and recognition of the absolute; whereas the downfall of the grotesque actor means mockery of the absolute and its desecration. The absolute is transformed into a blind mechanism, a kind of automaton. Mockery is directed not only at the tormentor, but also at the victim who believed in the tormentor's justice, raising him to the level of the absolute. The victim has consecrated his tormentor by recognizing himself as victim.

In the final instance tragedy is an appraisal of human fate, a measure of the absolute. The grotesque is a criticism of the absolute in the name of frail human experience. That is why tragedy brings catharsis, while grotesque offers no consolation whatsoever. "Tragedy," wrote Gorgias of Leontium, "is a swindle in which the swindler is more just than the swindled, and the swindled wiser than the swindler." One may travesty this aphorism by saying that grotesque is a swindle in which the swindled is more just than the swindler, and the swindler wiser than the swindled. Claire Zachanassian in Dürrenmatt's *Visit* is wiser than Anton Schill, but he is more just than she is. Schill's death, like Polonius's death in *Hamlet,* is grotesque. Neither Schill, nor the inhabitants of Güllen are tragic heroes. The old lady with her artificial breasts, teeth and limbs is not a goddess; she hardly even exists, she might almost have been invented. Schill and the people of Güllen find themselves in a situation in which there is no room for tragedy, but only for grotesque. "Comedy," writes Ionesco in his *Expérience du théâtre,* "is a feeling of absurdity, and seems more hopeless than tragedy; comedy allows no way out of a given situation." [2]

The tragic and the grotesque worlds are closed, and there is no escape from them. In the tragic world this compulsory situation has been imposed in turn by the Gods, Fate, the Christian God, Nature, and History that has been endowed with reason and inevitability.

On the other side, opposed to this arrangement, there was always man. If Nature was the absolute, man was unnatural. If man was natural, the absolute was represented by Grace, without which there was no salvation. In the world of the grotesque, downfall cannot be justified by, or blamed on, the absolute. The absolute is not endowed with any ultimate reasons; it is stronger, and that is all. The absolute is absurd. Maybe that is why the grotesque often makes use of the concept of a mechanism which has been put in motion and cannot be stopped. Various kinds of impersonal and hostile mechanisms have taken the place of God, Nature and History, found in the old tragedy. The notion of absurd mechanism is probably the last metaphysical concept remaining in modern grotesque. But this absurd mechanism is not transcendental any more in relation to man, or at any rate to mankind. It is a trap set by man himself into which he has fallen.

The scene of tragedy has mostly been a natural landscape. Raging nature witnessed man's downfall, or—as in *King Lear*—played an active part in the action. Modern grotesque usually takes place in the midst of civilization. Nature has evaporated from it almost completely. Man is confined to a room and surrounded by inanimate objects. But objects have now been raised to the status of symbols of human fate, or situation, and perform a similar function to that played in Shakespeare by forest, storm, or eclipse of the sun. Even Sartre's hell is just a vast hotel consisting of rooms and corridors, beyond which there are more rooms and more corridors. This hell "behind closed doors" does not need any metaphysical aids.

Ionesco's hell is arranged on similar lines. A new tenant moves into an empty flat. Furniture is brought in. There is more and more furniture. Furniture surrounds the tenant on all sides. He is surrounded already by four wardrobes but more are brought in. He has been closed in by furniture. He can no longer be seen. He has been brought down to the level of inanimate objects and has become an object himself.

In Beckett's *Endgame* there is a room with a wheelchair and two dustbins. A picture hangs face to the wall. There is also a staircase, a telescope and a whistle. All that remains of nature is sand in the dustbins, a flea, and the part of man that belongs to nature: his body.

---

[2] E. Ionesco, "*Expérience du théâtre,*" *Nouvelle Revue Française,* February 1958.

HAMM Nature has forgotten us.
CLOV There's no more nature.
HAMM No more nature! You exaggerate.
CLOV In the vicinity.
HAMM But we breathe, we change! We lose our hair, our teeth! Our bloom! Our ideals!
CLOV Then she hasn't forgotten us.

(p. 16)[3]

It can easily be shown how, in the new theatre, tragic situations become grotesque. Such a classic situation of tragedy is the necessity of making a choice between opposing values. Antigone is doomed to choose between human and divine order; between Creon's demands, and those of the absolute. The tragedy lies in the very principle of choice by which one of the values must be annihilated. The cruelty of the absolute lies in demanding such a choice and in imposing a situation which excludes the possibility of a compromise, and where one of the alternatives is death. The absolute is greedy and demands everything; the hero's death is its confirmation.

The tragic situation becomes grotesque when both alternatives of the choice imposed are absurd, irrelevant or compromising. The hero has to play, even if there is no game. Every move is bad, but he cannot throw down his cards. To throw down the cards would also be a bad move.

It is this situation that Dürrenmatt's Romulus finds himself in. He is the last emperor of a crumbling empire. He will not alter the course of history. History has made a fool of him. He can either die in a spectacular fashion, or lie on his bed and wait to be butchered. He can surrender, compose speeches, or commit suicide. In his position as the last Roman emperor, every one of these solutions is compromising and ridiculous. History has turned Romulus into a clown, and yet demands that he treat her seriously. Romulus has only one good move to make: consciously to accept the part of a clown and play it to the end. He can breed chickens. In this way the historical inevitability will have been made a fool of. The absolute will have been flouted.

Antigone is a tragedy of choice, *Oedipus* a tragedy of "unmerited guilt" and destiny. The gods loyally warn the protagonist that fate has destined him to be a patricide and his own mother's husband. The hero has full freedom of decision and action. The gods do not interfere; they just watch and wait until he makes a mistake. Then they punish him. The gods are just, and punish the hero for a crime he has indeed committed, and only after he has committed it. But the protagonist had to commit a crime. Oedipus wanted to cheat fate, but did

---

[3] All quotations from Beckett are given in the author's own translation. Page references in quotations from *Endgame* and *Act Without Words* apply to the Faber & Faber edition of 1958.

not and could not escape it. He fell into a trap, made his mistake, killed his father and married his mother. What is to happen will happen.

The tragedy of Oedipus may, perhaps, be posed as a problem belonging to the theory of game. The game is just, i.e. at the outset both partners must have the same chances of losing or winning, and both must play according to the same rules. In its game with Oedipus fate does not invoke the help of the gods, does not change the laws of nature. Fate wins its game without recourse to miracles.

The game must be just, but at the same time must be so arranged that the same party always wins; so that Oedipus always loses.

Let us imagine an electronic computer, which plays chess and calculates any number of moves in advance. A man must play chess with an electronic computer, cannot leave or break the game, and has to lose the game. His defeat is just, because it is effected according to the rules of the game; he loses because he has made a mistake. But he could not have won.

A man losing the chess game with an electronic computer, whom he himself has fed with combinatorial analysis and rules, whom he himself has "taught" to play, is not a tragic hero any more. If he plays that chess game from the moment he was born until he dies, and if he has to lose, he will at most be the hero of a tragi-grotesque. All that is left of tragedy is the concept of "unmerited guilt", the inevitable defeat, and unavoidable mistake. But the absolute has ceased to exist. It has been replaced by the absurdity of the human situation.

The absurdity does not consist in the fact that manmade mechanisms are in certain conditions stronger, and even wiser, than he. The absurdity consists in the fact that they create a compulsory situation by forcing him to a game in which the probability of his total defeat constantly increases. The Christian view of the end of the world, with the Last Judgement and its segregation of the just and the unjust, is pathetic. The end of the world caused by the big bomb is spectacular, but grotesque just the same. Such an end of the world is intellectually unacceptable, whether to Christians or to Marxists. It would be a silly ending.

The comparison between fate's game with Oedipus, and a game of chess with an electronic computer, is not precise enough. An automatic device to play chess, even if it could compute any number of moves, need not win all the time. It would simply more often win than lose. But among automatic devices that really exist one could find a much better example. There is a machine for a game similar to tossing coins for "heads or tails". I put a coin on the table the way I like, with "heads" or "tails" on top. The machine does not see the coin, but it is to make out how I have put it. If it gives the right answer, it wins. I inform the machine whether it has given the right answer. I put the coin again, and so on. After a time the machine begins to win by giving the right answers more and more often. It has memorized and learned my system; it has deciphered me as it were. It foresees that after three "heads" I will put two "tails". I change the system, and play using a different method. The blind machine learns this one too, and begins to win again. I am endowed with free will and have the freedom of choice. I can put "heads" or "tails". But in the end, like Oedipus, I must lose the game.

There is a move by which I do not lose. I do not put the coin on the table, I do not choose. I simply toss it. I have given up the system, and left matters to chance. Now the machine and I have even chances. The possibility of win and loss, of "heads" or "tails" is the same. It amounts to fifty-fifty. The machine wanted me to treat it seriously, to play rationally with it, using a system, a method. But I do not want to. It is I who have now seen through the machine's method.

The machine stands for fate, which acts on the principle of the law of averages. In order to have even chances with fate I must become fate myself; I must chance my luck; act with a fifty-fifty chance. A man who, when playing with the machine, gives up his free will and freedom of choice, adopts an attitude to fate similar to that which Dürrenmatt's Romulus adopted with regard to historical necessity. Instead of putting the coin with "heads" on top a hundred times in succession, or "heads" and "tails" in turn, or two "tails" after ten "heads", he would just toss the coin up. That kind of man most certainly is not a tragic hero. He has adopted a clownish attitude to fate. Romulus is such a man.

In modern tragedy fate, gods and nature have been replaced by history. History is the only frame of reference, the final authority to accept or reject the validity of human actions. It is unavoidable and realizes its ultimate aims; it is objective "reason", as well as objective "progress". In this scheme of things history is a theatre with actors, but without an audience. No one watches the performance, for everybody is taking part. The script of this grand spectacle has been composed in advance and includes a necessary epilogue, which will explain everything. But, as in the *commedia dell' arte,* the text has not been written down. The actors improvise and only some of them foresee correctly what will happen in the following acts. In this particular theatre the scene changes with the actors; they are constantly setting it up and pulling it down again.

Actors are often wrong, but their mistakes have been foreseen by the scenario. One might even say that mistakes are the basis of the script, and that it is thanks to them that the action unfolds. History contains both the past and the future. Actors from previous scenes keep coming back, repeating old conflicts, and want to play parts that are long since over. They needlessly prolong the performance and have to be removed from the stage. They arrived too late. Other actors have arrived too early and start performing a scene from the next act, without noticing that the stage is not yet ready for them. They want to speed up the performance, but this cannot be done: every act has to be performed in its proper order. Those who arrive too early are also removed from the stage.

It is these parts that nineteenth-century philosophy and literature considered tragic. For Hegel the tragic heroes of history were those who came too late. Their reasons were noble but one-sided. They had been correct in the previous era, in the preceding act. If they continue to insist on them, they must be crushed by history. La Vendée was for Hegel an example of historical tragedy. Count Henry in Krasiński's *Undivine Comedy* is a Hegelian tragic hero.

Those who came too early, striving in vain to speed up the course of history, are also history's tragic heroes. Their reasons, too, are one-sided; they will become valid only at the next historical phase, in the succeeding act. They failed to understand that freedom is only the conscious recognition of necessity. Consequently they were annihilated by historical necessity, which solves only those problems that are capable of solution. The Paris Commune is an example of this kind of historical tragedy. Pancrace in *Undivine Comedy* is a tragic hero of history thus conceived.

The gotesque mocks the historical absolute, as it has mocked the absolutes of gods, nature and destiny. It does so by means of the so-called "barrel of laughs", a popular feature of any fun-fair: a score or more of people try to keep their balance while the upturned barrel revolves round its axis. One can only keep one's balance by moving on the bottom of the barrel in the opposite direction to, and with the same speed as, its movement. This is not at all easy. Those who move too fast or too slow in relation to the barrel's movement are bound to fall. The barrel brings them up, then they roll downwards trying desperately to cling to the moving floor. The more violent their gestures and their grip on the walls, the more difficult it is for them to get up, and the funnier they look.

The barrel is put in motion by a motor, which is transcendental in relation to it. However, one may easily imagine a barrel that is set in motion by the people inside it: by those who manage to preserve their balance and those who fall over. A barrel like this would be immanent. Its movements would, of course, be variable: sometimes it would revolve in one direction, sometimes in the other. It would be even more difficult to preserve one's balance in a barrel like this: one would have to change step all the time, move forward and backward, faster or slower. In such an immanent barrel many more people would fall over. But neither those who fall because they move too fast, nor those who fall because they move too slow, are tragic heroes. They are just grotesque. They will be grotesque even if there is no way out of this immanent barrel. The social mechanism shown in most of Adamov's plays is very much like the barrel of laughs.

The world of tragedy and the world of grotesque have a similar structure. Grotesque takes over the themes of tragedy and poses the same fundamental questions. Only its answers are different. This dispute about the tragic and grotesque interpretations of human fate reflects the everlasting conflict of two philosophies and two ways of thinking; of two opposing attitudes defined by the Polish philosopher Leszek Kołakowski as the irreconcilable antagonism between the priest and the clown. Between tragedy and grotesque there is the same conflict for or against such notions as eschatology, belief in the absolute, hope for the ultimate solution of the contradiction between the moral order and every-day practice. Tragedy is the theatre of priests, grotesque is the theatre of clowns.

This conflict between two philosophies and two types of theatre becomes particularly acute in times of great upheavals. When established values have been overthrown, and there is no appeal, to God, Nature, or History, from the tortures inflicted by the cruel world, the clown becomes the central figure in the theatre. He accompanies the exiled trio—the king, the nobleman and his son—on their cruel wanderings through the cold endless night which has fallen on the world; through the "cold night" which, as in Shakespeare's *King Lear,* "will turn us all to fools and madmen."

II

After his eyes have been gouged out, Gloucester wants to throw himself over the cliffs of Dover into the sea. He is led by his own son, who feigns madness. Both have reached the depths of human suffering; the top of "the pyramid of suffering", as Juliusz Słowacki has described *King Lear.* But on the stage there are just two actors, one playing a blind man, the other playing a man who plays a madman. They walk together.

> GLOUCESTER When shall I come to th' top of that same hill?
> EDGAR You do climb up it now. Look how we labour.
> GLOUCESTER Methinks the ground is even.
> EDGAR Horrible steep.
> Hark, do you hear the sea?
> GLOUCESTER No, truly.
>
> (IV.vi)

It is easy to imagine this scene. The text itself provides stage directions. Edgar is supporting Gloucester; he lifts his feet high pretending to walk uphill. Gloucester, too, lifts his feet, as if expecting the ground to rise, but underneath his foot there is only air. This entire scene is written for a very definite type of theatre, namely pantomime.

This pantomime only makes sense if enacted on a flat and level stage.

Edgar feigns madness, but in doing so he must adopt the right gestures. In its theatrical expression this is a scene in which a madman leads a blind man and talks him into believing in a non-existing mountain. In another moment a landscape will be sketched in. Shakespeare often creates a landscape on an empty stage. A few words, and the diffused, soft afternoon light at the Globe changes into night, evening, or morning. But no other Shakespearean landscape is so exact, precise and clear as this one. It is like a Breughel painting thick with people, objects and events. A little human figure hanging halfway down the cliff is gathering samphire. Fishermen walking on the beach are like mice. A ship seems a little boat, a boat is floating like a buoy.

It is this abyss of Shakespeare's imagination that Słowacki makes the hero of his *Kordian* look into:

> Come! Here, on the top stand still. Your head will whirl,
> When you cast your eyes on the abyss below your feet.
> Crows flying there half-way no bigger are than beetles.
> And there, too, someone is toiling, gathering weed.
> He looks no bigger than a human head.
> And there on the beach the fishermen seem like ants . . .

This veristic and perspective landscape created on an empty stage is not meant to serve as part of the decor, or to replace the non-existent settings. Slowacki understood perfectly the dramatic purpose of this scene:

> Oh, Shakespeare! Spirit! You have built a mountain
> Higher than that created by God.
> For you have talked of an abyss to a man blind . . .

The landscape is now just a score for the pantomime. Gloucester and Edgar have reached the top of the cliff. The landscape is now below them.

> Give me your hand. You are now within a foot
> Of th' extreme verge. For all beneath the moon
> Would I not leap upright.
>
> (*King Lear,* IV.vi)

In Shakespeare's time the actors probably put their feet forward through a small balustrade above the apron-stage, immediately over the heads of the "groundlings". But we are not concerned here with an historical reconstruction of the Elizabethan stage. It is the presence and importance of the mime that is significant. Shakespeare is stubborn. Gloucester has already jumped over the precipice. Both actors are at the foot of a non-existent cliff. The same landscape is now above them. The mime continues.

> GLOUCESTER But have I fall'n, or no?
> EDGAR From the dread summit of this chalky bourn.
> Look up a-height. The shrill-gorg'd lark so far
> Cannot be seen or heard. Do but look up.
>
> (IV.vi)

The mime creates a scenic area: the top and bottom of the cliff, the precipice. Shakespeare makes use of all the means of anti-illusionist theatre in order to create a most realistic and concrete landscape. A landscape which is only a blind man's illusion. There is perspective in it, light, men and things, even sounds. From the height of the cliff the sea cannot be heard, but there is mention of its roar. From the foot of the cliff the lark cannot be heard, but there is mention of its song. In this landscape sounds are present by their very absence: the silence is filled with them, just as the empty stage is filled with the mountain.

The scene of the suicidal leap is also a mime. Gloucester kneels in a last prayer and then, in accordance with tradition of the play's English performances, falls over. He is now at the bottom of the cliff. But there was no height; it was an illusion. Gloucester knelt down on an empty stage, fell over and got up. At this point disillusion follows.[4]

The non-existent cliff is not meant just to deceive the blind man. For a short while we, too, believed in this landscape and in the mime. The meaning of this parable is not easy to define. But one thing is clear: this type of parable is not to be thought of outside the theatre, or rather outside a certain kind of theatre. In narrative prose Edgar could, of course, lead the blind Gloucester to the cliffs of Dover, let him jump down from a stone and make him believe that he was jumping from the top of a cliff. But he might just as well lead him a day's journey away from the castle and make him jump from a stone on any heap of sand. In film and in prose there is only the choice between a real stone lying in the sand and an equally real jump from the top of a chalk cliff into the sea. One cannot transpose Gloucester's suicide attempt to the screen, unless one were to film a stage performance. But in the naturalistic, or even stylized theatre, with the precipice painted or projected onto a screen, Shakespeare's parable would be completely obliterated.

The stage must be empty. On it a suicide, or rather its symbol, has been performed. Mime is the performance of symbols. In Ionesco's *Le tueur sans gages* the Architect, who is at the same time the commissioner of police, shows Berenger round the *Cité Radieuse*. On an empty stage Berenger sniffs at non-existent flowers and taps non-existent walls. The Radiant City exists and does not exist, or rather it has existed always and everywhere. And that is why it is so terrifying. Similarly, the Shakespearean precipice at Dover exists and does not exist. It is the abyss, waiting all the time. The abyss, into which one can jump, is everywhere.

By a few words of dialogue Shakespeare often turned the platform

---

[4] Compare the analysis of this scene in G. Wilson Knight's most original study of the grotesque elements in *King Lear* (treated somewhat differently from in my essay): " 'King Lear' and the Comedy of the Grotesque," in *The Wheel of Fire*, London, 1957.

stage, the inner stage, or the gallery into a London street, a forest, a palace, a ship, or a castle battlement. But these were always real places of action. Townspeople gathered outside the Tower, lovers wandered through the forest, Brutus murdered Caesar in the Forum. The white precipice at Dover performs a different function. Gloucester does not jump from the top of the cliff, or from a stone. For once, in *King Lear,* Shakespeare shows the paradox of pure theatre. It is the same theatrical paradox that Ionesco uses in his *Le tueur sans gages.*

In the naturalistic theatre one can perform a murder scene, or a scene of terror. The shot may be fired from a revolver or a toy pistol. But in the mime there is no difference between a revolver and a toy pistol: in fact neither exists. Like death, the shot is only a performance, a parable, a symbol.

Gloucester, falling over on flat, even boards, plays a scene from a great morality play. He is no longer a court dignitary whose eyes have been gouged out because he showed mercy to the banished king. The action is no longer confined to Elizabethan or Celtic England. Gloucester is Everyman, and the stage becomes the medieval *Theatrum mundi.* A Biblical parable is now enacted; the one about the rich man who became a beggar, and the blind man who recovered his inner sight when he lost his eyes. Everyman begins his wanderings through the world. In medieval mystery plays also the stage was empty, but in the background there were four mansions, four gates representing Earth, Purgatory, Heaven and Hell. In *King Lear* the stage is empty throughout: there is nothing, except the cruel earth, where man goes on his journey from the cradle to the grave. The theme of *King Lear* is an enquiry into the meaning of this journey, into the existence or non-existence of Heaven and Hell.

From the middle of Act II to the end of Act IV, Shakespeare takes up a Biblical theme. But this new *Book of Job* or a new Dantean *Inferno* was written towards the close of the Renaissance. In Shakespeare's play there is neither Christian Heaven, nor the heaven predicted and believed in by humanists. *King Lear* makes a tragic mockery of all eschatologies: of the heaven promised on earth, and the Heaven promised after death; in fact—of both Christian and secular theodicies; of cosmogony and of the rational view of history; of the gods and the good nature, of man made in "image and likeness". In *King Lear* both the medieval and the Renaissance orders of established values disintegrate. All that remains at the end of this gigantic pantomime, is the earth—empty and bleeding. On this earth, through which tempest has passed leaving only stones, the King, the Fool, the Blind Man and the Madman carry on their distracted dialogue.

The blind Gloucester falls over on the empty stage. His suicidal leap is tragic. Gloucester has reached the depths of human misery; so has Edgar, who pretends to be mad Tom in order to save his father. But the pantomime performed by actors on the stage is grotesque, and has something of a circus about it. The blind Gloucester who has climbed a non-existent height and fallen over on flat boards, is a clown. A philosophical buffoonery of the sort found in modern theatre has been performed.

> Whistle from left wing.
> He (the man) does not move.
> He looks at his hands, looks round for scissors, sees them, goes and picks them up, starts to trim his nails, stops, runs his finger along blade of scissors, goes and lays them on small cube, turns aside, opens his collar, frees his neck and fingers it.
> The small cube is pulled up and disappears in flies, carrying away rope and scissors.
> He turns to take scissors, sees what has happened.
> He turns aside, reflects.
> He goes and sits down on big cube.
> The big cube is pulled from under him. He falls. The big cube is pulled up and disappears in flies.
> He remains lying on his side, his face towards auditorium, staring before him.
>
> (*Act Without Words,* pp. 59–60)

The *Act Without Words* closes Beckett's *Endgame,* providing as it were its final interpretation. Remaining vestiges of characters, action and situation have been further reduced here. All that remains is one situation acting as a parable of universal human fate. A total situation. Man has been thrown onto the empty stage. He tries to escape into the wings, but is kicked back. From above a tree with some leaves, a jug of water, tailoring scissors, and some cubes are pulled down on ropes. The man tries to hide in the shade of the leaves, but the tree is pulled up. He tries to catch hold of the jug, but it rises into the air. He attempts suicide, but this, too, proves impossible. "The bough folds down against trunk." (p. 59) The man sits down and thinks. The jug and the tree appear again. The man does not move.

In this ending to *Endgame* the forces external to man—gods, fate, world—are not indifferent, but sneering and malicious. They tempt him all the time. These forces are stronger than he. Man must be defeated and cannot escape from the situation that has been imposed on him. All he can do is to give up; refuse to play blindman's buff. Only by the possibility of refusal can he surmount the external forces.

It is easy to see how close to the Bible this parable is, even in its metaphors: palm, its shadow, water. The force above and beyond man is strongly reminiscent of the Old Testament God. This is also a *Book of Job,* but without an optimistic ending.

This new *Book of Job* is shown in buffo, as a circus pantomime. *Act Without Words* is performed by a clown. The philosophical parable may be interpreted as tragedy or grotesque, but its artistic expression is grotesque only. Gloucester's suicide attempt, too, is merely a circus somersault on an empty stage. Gloucester's and Edgar's situation is tragic, but it has been shown in pantomime, the classic expression of buffoonery. In Shakespeare clowns often ape the gestures of kings and heroes, but only in *King Lear* are great tragic scenes shown through clowning.

It is not only the suicide mime that is grotesque. The accompanying dialogue is also cruel and mocking. The blind Gloucester kneels and prays:

> O you mighty gods!
> This world I do renounce, and, in your sights
> Shake patiently my great affliction off.
> If I could bear it longer, and not fall
> To quarrel with your great opposeless wills,
> My snuff and loathed part of nature should
> Burn itself out. If Edgar live, O, bless him!
> (IV.vi)

Gloucester's suicide has a meaning only if the gods exist. It is a protest against undeserved suffering and the world's injustice. This protest is made in a definite direction. It refers to eschatology. Even if the gods are cruel, they must take this suicide into consideration. It will count in the final reckoning between gods and man. Its sole value lies in its reference to the absolute.

But if the gods, and their moral order in the world, do not exist, Gloucester's suicide does not solve or alter anything. It is only a somersault on an empty stage. It is deceptive and unsuccessful on the factual, as well as on the metaphysical plane. Not only the pantomime, but the whole situation is then grotesque. From the beginning to the end. It is waiting for a Godot who does not come.

> ESTRAGON Why don't we hang ourselves?
> VLADIMIR With what?
> ESTRAGON You haven't got a bit of rope?
> VLADIMIR No.
> ESTRAGON Then we can't.
> VLADIMIR Let's go.
> ESTRAGON Wait, there's my belt.
> VLADIMIR It's too short.
> ESTRAGON You could hang on to my legs.
> VLADIMIR And who'd hang on to mine?
> ESTRAGON True.
> VLADIMIR Show all the same. (*Estragon loosens the cord that holds up his trousers which, much too big for him, fall about his ankles. They look at the cord.*) It might do at a pinch. But is it strong enough?
> ESTRAGON We'll soon see. Here.
> (*They each take an end of the cord and pull. It breaks. They almost fall.*)
> VLADIMIR Not worth a curse.
> (*Waiting for Godot*. II)

Gloucester did fall, and he got up again. He made his suicide attempt, but he failed to shake the world. Nothing has changed. Edgar's comment is ironical:

> . . . Had he been where he thought,
> By this had thought been past.
> (IV.vi)

If there are no gods, suicide makes no sense. Death exists in any case. Suicide cannot alter human fate, but only accelerate it. It ceases to be a protest. It is a surrender. It becomes the acceptance of [the] world's greatest cruelty—death. Gloucester has finally realized:

> . . . Henceforth I'll bear
> Affliction till it do cry out itself
> 'Enough, enough,' and die.
> (IV.vi)

And once again, in the last act:

> No further, sir. A man may rot even here.
> (V.ii)

After his grotesque suicide the blind Gloucester talks to the deranged Lear. Estragon and Vladimir carry on a very similar conversation, interrupted by the despairing cries of the blind Pozzo, who has fallen down and cannot get up. Pozzo would find it easiest to understand Gloucester:

> . . . one day I went blind, one day we'll go deaf, one day we were born, one day we shall die . . . They give birth astride of a grave, the light gleams an instant, then it's night once more.
> (*Waiting for Godot,* II)

Shakespeare had said as much, in fewer words:

> . . . Men must endure
> Their going hence, even as their coming hither;
> Ripeness is all.
> (V.ii)

But it was Ionesco who put it most briefly of all, in his *Le tueur sans gages:* "We shall all die, this is the only serious alienation."

III

The theme of *King Lear* is the decay and fall of the world. The play opens like the Histories, with the division of the realm and the king's abdication. It also ends like the Histories, with the proclamation of a new king. Between the prologue and the epilogue there is a civil war. But unlike the Histories and Tragedies, in *King Lear* the world is not healed again. In *King Lear* there is no young and resolute Fortinbras to ascend the throne of Denmark; no cool-headed Octavius to become Augustus Caesar; no noble Malcolm to "give to our tables meat, sleep to our nights." In the epilogues to the Histories and Tragedies the new monarch invites those present to his coronation. In *King Lear* there will be no coronation. There is no one whom Edgar can invite to it. Everybody has died or been murdered. Gloucester was right when he said: "This great world / Shall so wear out to naught." Those who have survived—Edgar, Albany and Kent—are, as Lear has been, just "ruin'd piece[s] of nature".

Of the twelve major characters half are just and good, the other half, unjust and bad. It is a division as consistent and abstract as in a morality play. But this is a morality play in which every one will be destroyed: noble characters along with base ones, the persecutors with the persecuted, the torturers with the tortured. Vivisection will go on until the stage is empty. The decay and fall of the world will be shown on two levels, on two different kinds of stage, as it were. One of these may be called Macbeth's stage, the other, Job's stage.

Macbeth's stage is the scene of crime. At the beginning there is a nursery tale of two bad daughters and one good daughter. The good daughter will die hanged in prison. The bad daughters will also die, but not until they have become adulterers, and one of them also a poisoner and murderess of her husband. All bonds, all laws, whether divine, natural or human, are broken. Social order, from the kingdom to the family, will crumble into dust. There are no longer kings and subjects, fathers and children, husbands and wives. There are only huge Renaissance monsters, devouring one another like beasts of prey. Everything has been condensed, drawn in broad outlines, characters are hardly marked. The history of the world can do without psychology and without rhetoric. It is just action. These violent sequences are merely an illustration and an example, and perform the function of a black, realistic counterpart to "Job's stage".

For it is Job's stage that constitutes the main scene. On it the ironic, clownish morality play on human fate will be performed. But before that happens, all the characters must be uprooted from their social positions and pulled down, to final degradation. They must reach rock-bottom. The downfall is not merely a philosophical parable, as Gloucester's leap over the supposed precipice is. The theme of downfall is carried through by Shakespeare stubbornly, consistently and is repeated at least four times. The fall is at the same time physical and spiritual, bodily and social.

At the beginning there was a king with his court and ministers. Later, there are just four beggars wandering about in a wilderness, exposed to raging winds and rain. The fall may be slow, or sudden.

Lear has at first a retinue of a hundred men, then fifty, then only one. Kent is banished by one angry gesture of the king. But the process of degradation is always the same. Everything that distinguishes a man—his titles, social position, even name—is lost. Names are not needed any more. Every one is just a shadow of himself; just a man.

> KING LEAR Doth any here know me? This is not Lear.
> Doth Lear walk thus? speak thus?
>
> . . . .
>
> Who is it that can tell me who I am?
> FOOL Lear's shadow.
>
> (I.iv)

And once more the same question, and the same answer. The banished Kent returns in disguise to his king.

> KING LEAR How now? What art thou?
> KENT A man, sir.
>
> (I.iv)

A naked man has no name. Before the morality commences, every one must be naked. Naked like a worm.

> Then Job arose, and rent his mantle, and shaved his head, and fell down upon the ground, and worshipped.
>
> And said, Naked came I out of my mother's womb, and naked shall return thither.
>
> (*Book of Job,* I.20–21)

Biblical imagery in this new *Book of Job* is no mere chance. Edgar says that he will with his "nakedness outface / The winds and persecutions of the sky." (II.iii) This theme returns obstinately, and with an equal consistency:

> I' th' last night's storm I such a fellow saw,
> Which made me think a man a worm.
>
> (IV.i)

A downfall means suffering and torment. It may be a physical or spiritual torment, or both. Lear will lose his wits; Kent will be put in the stocks; Gloucester will have his eyes gouged out and will attempt suicide. For a man to become naked, or rather to become nothing but man, it is not enough to deprive him of his name, social position and character. One must also maim and massacre him both morally and physically. Turn him—like King Lear—into a "ruin'd piece of nature", and only then ask him who he is. For it is the new Renaissance Job who is to judge the events on "Macbeth's stage".

A Polish critic, Andrzej Falkiewicz, has observed this process of maiming and mutilating man, not in Shakespeare, but in modern literature and drama.[5] He compares it to the peeling of an onion. One takes off the husk, and then peels the layers of onion one by one. Where does an onion end and what is in its core? The blind man is a man, the madman is a man, the doting old man is a man. Man and nothing but man. A nobody, who suffers, tries to give his suffering a meaning or nobility, who revolts or accepts his suffering, and who must die.

> O gods! Who is't can say 'I am at the worst'?
> I am worse than e'er I was.
>
> . . . .
>
> And worse I may be yet. The worst is not
> So long as we can say 'This is the worst.'
>
> (IV.i)

Vladimir and Estragon talk to each other in a very similar fashion. They gibber, but in that gibber there are remnants of the same eschatology:

> . . . We came crying hither; . . .
>
> . . . .
>
> When we are born, we cry that we are come
> To this great stage of fools.
>
> (IV.vi)

The world is real, and the shoe really pinches. Suffering is also real. But the gesture with which the ruin of a man demands that his pinching shoe be taken off is ridiculous. Just as ridiculous as blind Gloucester's somersault on the flat empty stage.

The Biblical Job, too, is the ruin of a man. But this ruin constantly talks to God. He curses, imprecates, blasphemes. Ultimately he admits that God is right. He has justified his sufferings and ennobled them. He included them in the metaphysical and absolute order. The *Book of Job* is a theatre of the priests. Whereas in both Shakespearean and Beckettian *Endgames* the *Book of Job* is performed by clowns. But here, too, the gods are invoked throughout by all the characters; by Lear, Gloucester, Kent, even Albany:

> KING LEAR By Jupiter, I swear no!
> KENT By Juno, I swear ay!
>
> (II.iv)

At first gods have Greek names. Then they are only gods, great and terrifying judges high above, who are supposed to intervene sooner or

---

[5] A. Falkiewicz, "Theatrical Experiment of the Fifties," *Dialog*, No. 9, 1959 (in Polish).

later. But the gods do not intervene. They are silent. Gradually the tone becomes more and more ironical. The ruin of a man invoking God is ever more ridiculous. The action becomes more and more cruel, but at the same time assumes a more and more clownish character:

> By the kind gods, 'tis most ignobly done
> To pluck me by the beard.
>
> (III.vii)

Defeat, suffering, cruelty have a meaning even when gods are cruel. Even then. It is the last theological chance to justify suffering. The Biblical Job knew about it well when he called on God:

> If the scourge slay suddenly, he will laugh at the trial of the innocent.
>
> (*Book of Job,* IX.23)

From the just God, one can still appeal to the unjust God. Says Gloucester after his eyes have been gouged out:

> As flies to wanton boys are we to th' gods.
> They kill us for their sport.
>
> (IV.i)

But as long as gods exist, all can yet be saved:

> Hearken unto this, O Job: stand still, and consider the wondrous works of God.
>
> (*Book of Job,* XXXVII.14)

The Bible is Beckett's favourite reading. After all, the passage sounds like the dialogue in *Endgame:*

> CLOV They said to me, Here's the place, raise your head and look at all that beauty. That order! They said to me, Come now you're not a brute beast, think upon these things and you'll see how all becomes clear. And simple! They said to me, What skilled attention they get, all these dying of their wounds.
>
> HAMM Enough!
>
> CLOV I say to myself—sometimes, Clov, you must learn to suffer better than that if you want them to weary of punishing you. I say to myself—sometimes, Clov, you must be their better then if you want them to let you go—one day.
>
> (pp. 50–51)

Clov is a clown, but he is more unhappy than Hamm. Clov's gabble is still eschatological, just as Lucky's in *Waiting for Godot.* In this dialogue of "human ruins" Hamm alone has realized the folly of all suffering. He has one reply to make to eschatology: "Take it easy . . .

Peace to our . . . arses". Both couples: Pozzo who has been made blind, and Lucky who has been made dumb, on the one hand, Hamm who cannot get up, and Clov who cannot sit down, on the other, have been taken from the Endgame of *King Lear:*

> KING LEAR Read.
> GLOUCESTER What, with the case of eyes?
>
> . . . .
>
> KING LEAR What, art mad? A man may see how the world goes with no eyes. Look with thine ears.
>
> (IV.vi)

These are Biblical parables. The blind see clearly, madmen tell the truth. After all, they are all mad. "There are four of them"—writes Camus—"one by profession, one by choice, two by the suffering they have been through. They are four torn bodies, four unfathomable faces of the same fate." [6] The Fool accompanies Lear on the cold night of madness; Edgar takes the blind Gloucester through a grotesque suicide. Lear's invocations on the gods are countered by the Fool's scatological jokes; Gloucester's prayers by Edgar's clownish demonology:

> Frateretto calls me, and tells me Nero is an angler in the lake of darkness. Pray, innocent, and beware the foul fiend. . . . The foul fiend bites my back. . . . Purr! the cat is gray.
>
> (III.vi)

But Edgar's demonology is no more than a parody, a travesty of contemporary Egyptian dream books and books on witchcraft; a great and brutal gibe, in fact. He gibes at himself, at Job, conversing with God. For above "Job's stage", there is in *King Lear* only "Macbeth's stage". On it people murder, butcher and torture one another, commit adultery and fornication, divide kingdoms. From the point of view of a Job who has ceased to talk to God, they are clowns. Clowns who do not yet know they are clowns.

> KING LEAR . . . Come, come, I am a king;
> My masters, know you that?
> GENTLEMAN You are a royal one, and we obey you.
> KING LEAR Then there's life in't. Nay, an you get it, you shall get it by running. Sa, sa, sa, sa!
>
> (IV.vi)

The zero hour has come. Lear has come to understand it at last. Just as blind Hamm came to understand everything, although he was

---

[6] A. Camus, *Le Mythe de Sisyphe,* Paris, 1942.

bound to his wheel-throne. And Pozzo, when he turned blind and fell over his sand-filled bags:

> POZZO I woke up one fine day as blind as Fortune . . .
> VLADIMIR And when was that?
> POZZO I don't know . . . Don't question me! The blind have no notion of time. The things of time are hidden from them too.
> (*Waiting for Godot,* II)

And this is how King Lear ends his final frantic tirade:

> No rescue? What, a prisoner? I am even
> The natural fool of fortune.
> (IV.vi)

In a moment he will run off the stage. Before that happens he will ask for his pinching shoe to be taken off. He is clown now, so he can afford to do this. On "Job's stage" four clowns have performed the old medieval *sotie* about the decay and fall of the world. But in both Shakespearean and Beckettian *Endgames* it is the modern world that fell; the Renaissance world, and ours. Accounts have been settled in a very similar way.

IV

The original clown was Harlequin. There is something in him of an animal, a faun and a devil. That is why he wears a black mask. He rushes about and seems to transform himself into different shapes. The laws of space and time do not seem to apply to him. He changes his guises in a flash and can be in several places at once. He is a demon of movement. In Goldoni's play *The Servant of Two Masters,* as produced by the Piccolo Teatro of Milan, Harlequin, sitting on the brim of a wooden platform, plucked a hair from his head, lengthened or shortened it, pulled it through his ears, or put it on his nose and kept it rigid in the air. Harlequin is a prestidigitator. He is servant who really does not serve anybody and jockeys everybody away. He sneers at merchants and lovers, at marquesses and soldiers. He makes fun of love and ambition, of power and money. He is wiser than his masters, although he seems only to be more clever. He is independent, because he has realized that the world is simply folly.

Puck from *A Midsummer Night's Dream* is a popular goblin of English folklore, a Robin Goodfellow. But he is also the Harlequin of the Renaissance *commedia dell' arte*. He, too, is a quick-change artist, a prestidigitator and producer of the comedy of errors. He confuses the couples of lovers and causes Titania to caress an ass's head. In fact, he makes them all ridiculous, Titania and Oberon no less than

Hermia and Lysander, Helena and Demetrius. He exposes the folly of love. He is accident, fate, chance. Chance happens to be ironical, though it does not know about it itself. Puck plays practical jokes. He does not know what he has done. That is why he can turn somersaults on the stage, just as Harlequin does.

Buffoonery is a philosophy and a profession at the same time. Touchstone and Feste are professional clowns. They wear jesters' attire, and are in service of the prince. They have not ceased to be Harlequins and are not above pantomime. But they do not produce the performance any more; they do not even take part in it, but merely comment on it. That is why they are jeering and bitter. The position of a jester is ambiguous and abounds in internal contradictions, arising from the discrepancy between profession and philosophy. The profession of a jester, like that of an intellectual, consists in providing entertainment. His philosophy demands of him that he tell the truth and abolish myths. The Fool in *King Lear* does not even have a name, he is just a Fool, pure Fool. But he is the first fool to be aware of the fool's position:

> FOOL Prithee, nuncle, keep a schoolmaster that can teach thy fool to lie. I would fain learn to lie.
>
> KING LEAR An you lie, sirrah, we'll have you whipp'd.
>
> FOOL I marvel what kin thou and thy daughters are. They'll have me whipp'd for speaking true; thou'lt have me whipp'd for lying; and sometimes I am whipp'd for holding my peace. I had rather be any kind o'thing than a fool! And yet I would not be thee, nuncle. Thou hast pared thy wit o' both sides and left nothing i'th' middle.
>
> (I.iv)

A fool who has recognized himself for a fool, who has accepted the fact that he is only a jester in the service of the prince, ceases to be a clown. But the clown's philosophy is based on the assumption that every one is a fool; and the greatest fool is he who does not know he is a fool: the prince himself. That is why the clown has to make fools of others; otherwise he would not be a clown. The clown is subject to alienations because he is a clown, but at the same time he cannot accept the alienation; he rejects it when he becomes aware of it. The clown has the social position of the bastard, as described many times by Sartre. The bastard is a bastard for as long as he accepts his bastard's position and regards it as inevitable. The bastard ceases to be a bastard when he does not consider himself a bastard any more. But at this point the bastard must abolish the division into bastards and legitimate offspring. He then enters into opposition against the foundations of social order, or at least exposes them. Social pressures want to limit the Clown to his part of a clown, to pin the label "clown" on him. But he does not accept this part. On the contrary: he constantly pins that label on others:

KING LEAR Dost thou call me fool, boy?
FOOL All thy other titles thou hast given away; that thou wast born with.
KENT This is not altogether fool, my lord.
FOOL No, faith; lords and great men will not let me. If I had a monopoly out, they would have part on't. And ladies too, they will not let me have all the fool to myself; they'll be snatching. (I.iv)

This is the opening of the "clowns' play", performed on "Job's stage". In his very first scene, the Fool offers Lear his fool's cap. For buffoonery is not only a philosophy, it is also a kind of theatre. To us it is the most contemporary aspect of *King Lear.* Only it has to be seen and interpreted properly. For this reason one must reject all the romantic and naturalistic accessories; the opera and melodrama about the old man who, driven out by his daughters, wanders about bareheaded in a storm and goes mad as a result of his misfortunes. But, as in the case of Hamlet, there is method in this madness. Madness in *King Lear* is a philosophy, a conscious cross-over to the position of the Clown. Leszek Kołakowski writes:

> The Clown is he who, although moving in high society, is not part of it, and tells unpleasant things to everybody in it; who disputes everything regarded as evident. He would not be able to do all this, if he were part of that society himself; then he could at most be a drawing-room scandalizer. The Clown must stand aside and observe the good society from outside, in order to discover the non-evidence of evidence, and non-finality of its finality. At the same time he must move in good society in order to get to know its sacred cows, and have occasion to tell the unpleasant things. . . . The philosophy of Clowns is the philosophy that in every epoch shows up as doubtful what has been regarded as most certain; it reveals contradictions inherent in what seems to have been proven by visual experience; it holds up to ridicule what seems obvious common sense, and discovers truth in the absurd.[7]

Let us now turn to *King Lear:*

FOOL Give me an egg, nuncle, and I'll give thee two crowns.
KING LEAR What two crowns shall they be?
FOOL Why, after I have cut the egg i' th' middle and eat up the meat, the two crowns of the egg. When thou clovest thy crown i' th' middle and gav'st away both parts, thou bor'st thine ass on thy back o'er the dirt. . . . Now thou art an O without a figure. I am better than thou art now: I am a fool, thou art nothing. (I.iv)

---

[7] L. Kołakowski, "The Priest and the Clown—Reflections on Theological Heritage in Modern Thinking" (in Polish) *Twórczość,* No. 10, 1959, pp. 82–83.

After the crown had been torn off his head, Richard II asked for a mirror. He cast a look, and broke the mirror. He saw in the mirror his own unchanged face; the same that had belonged to a king. This amazed him. In *King Lear* the degradation occurs gradually, step by step. Lear divided his kingdom and gave away his power, but wanted to remain a king. He believed that a king could not cease to be a king, just as the sun could not cease to shine. He believed in pure majesty, in the pure idea of kingship. In historical dramas royal majesty is deprived of its sacred character by a stab of the dagger, or by the brutal tearing off of the crown from a living king's head. In *King Lear* it is the Fool who deprives majesty of its sacredness.

Lear and Gloucester are adherents of eschatology; they desperately believe in the existence of absolutes. They invoke the gods, believe in justice, appeal to laws of nature. They have fallen off "Macbeth's stage", but remain its prisoners. Only the Fool stands outside "Macbeth's stage", just as he has stood outside "Job's stage". He is looking from the outside and does not follow any ideology. He rejects all appearances, of law, justice, moral order. He sees brute force, cruelty and lust. He has no illusions and does not seek consolation in the existence of natural or supernatural order, which provides for the punishment of evil and reward of good. Lear, insisting on his fictitious majesty, seems ridiculous to him. All the more ridiculous because he does not see how ridiculous he is. But the Fool does not desert his ridiculous, degraded king, and accompanies him on his way to madness. The Fool knows that the only true madness is to regard this world as rational. The feudal order is absurd and can be described only in terms of the absurd. The world stands upside down:

> When usurers tell their gold i' th' field,
> And bawds and whores do churches build:
> Then shall the realm of Albion
> Come to great confusion.
> Then comes the time, who lives to see't,
> That going shall be us'd with feet.
>
> (III.ii)

Hamlet escaped into madness not only to confuse informers and deceive Claudius. Madness to him was also a philosophy, a criticism of pure reason, a great, ironic clearing of accounts with the world, which has left its orbit. The Fool adopts the language Hamlet used in the scenes in which he feigned madness. There is nothing left in it now of Greek and Roman rhetoric, so popular in the Renaissance; nothing left of the cold and noble Senecan indifference to the inevitable destiny. Lear, Gloucester, Kent, Albany, even Edmund still use rhetoric. The Fool's language is different. It abounds in Biblical travesties and inverted medieval parables. One can find in it splendid baroque surrealist expressions, sudden leaps of imagination, condensations and epitomes, brutal, vulgar and scatological comparisons. His rhymes are like limericks. The Fool uses dialectics, paradox and the absurd kind of humour. His language is that of our modern grotesque. The same grotesque that exposes the absurdity of apparent reality and of the absolute by means of a great and universal *reductio ad absurdum.*

> KING LEAR O me, my heart, my rising heart! But down!
> FOOL Cry to it, nuncle, as the cockney did to the eels when she put 'em i' th' paste alive. She knapp'd 'em o' th' coxcombs with a stick and cried 'Down, wantons, down!' 'Twas her brother that, in pure kindness to his horse, buttered his hay.
> (II.iv)

The Fool appears on the stage when Lear's fall is only beginning. He disappears by the end of Act III. His last words are: "And I'll go to bed at noon." He will not be seen or heard again. A clown is not needed any more. King Lear has gone through the school of clown's philosophy. When he meets Gloucester for the last time, he will speak the Fool's language and look at "Macbeth's stage" the way the Fool has looked at it: "They told me I was everything. 'Tis a lie—I am not ague-proof." (IV.vi)

The Naked Babe and the Cloak of Manliness

Cleanth Brooks

The debate about the proper limits of metaphor has perhaps never been carried on in so spirited a fashion as it has been within the last twenty-five years. The tendency has been to argue for a much wider extension of those limits than critics like Dr. Johnson, say, were willing to allow—one wider even than the Romantic poets were willing to allow. Indeed, some alarm has been expressed of late, in one quarter or another, lest John Donne's characteristic treatment of metaphor be taken as the type and norm, measured against which other poets must, of necessity, come off badly. Yet, on the whole, I think that it must be

---

conceded that the debate on metaphor has been stimulating and illuminating—and not least so with reference to those poets who lie quite outside the tradition of metaphysical wit.

Since the "new criticism," so called, has tended to center around the rehabilitation of Donne, and the Donne tradition, the latter point, I believe, needs to be emphasized. Actually, it would be a poor rehabilitation which, if exalting Donne above all his fellow poets, in fact succeeded in leaving him quite as much isolated from the rest of them as he was before. What the new awareness of the importance of metaphor—if it is actually new, and if its character is really that of a freshened awareness—what this new awareness of metaphor results in when applied to poets other than Donne and his followers is therefore a matter of first importance. Shakespeare provides, of course, the supremely interesting case.

But there are some misapprehensions to be avoided at the outset. We tend to associate Donne with the self-conscious and witty figure—his comparison of the souls of the lovers to the two legs of the compass is the obvious example. Shakespeare's extended figures are elaborated in another fashion. They are, we are inclined to feel, spontaneous comparisons struck out in the heat of composition, and not carefully articulated, self-conscious conceits at all. Indeed, for the average reader the connection between spontaneity and seriously imaginative poetry is so strong that he will probably reject as preposterous any account of Shakespeare's poetry which sees an elaborate pattern in the imagery. He will reject it because to accept it means for him the assumption that the writer was not a fervent poet but a preternaturally cold and self-conscious monster.

Poems are certainly not made by formula and blueprint. One rightly holds suspect a critical interpretation that implies that they are. Shakespeare, we may be sure, was no such monster of calculation. But neither, for that matter, was Donne. Even in Donne's poetry, the elaborated and logically developed comparisons are outnumbered by the abrupt and succinct comparisons—by what T. S. Eliot has called the "telescoped conceits." Moreover, the extended comparisons themselves are frequently knit together in the sudden and apparently uncalculated fashion of the telescoped images; and if one examines the way in which the famous compass comparison is related to the rest of the poem in which it occurs, he may feel that even this elaborately "logical" figure was probably the result of a happy accident.

The truth of the matter is that we know very little of the various poets' methods of composition, and that what may seem to us the product of deliberate choice may well have been as "spontaneous" as anything else in the poem. Certainly, the general vigor of metaphor in the Elizabethan period—as testified to by pamphlets, sermons, and plays—should warn us against putting the literature of that period at the mercy of our own personal theories of poetic composition. In any case, we shall probably speculate to better advantage—if speculate we must—-on the possible significant interrelations of image with image rather than on the possible amount of pen-biting which the interrelations may have cost the author.

I do not intend, however, to beg the case by oversimplifying the relation between Shakespeare's intricate figures and Donne's. There are most important differences; and, indeed, Shakespeare's very similarities to the witty poets will, for many readers, tell against the thesis proposed here. For those instances in which Shakespeare most obviously resembles the witty poets occur in the earlier plays or in *Venus and Adonis* and *The Rape of Lucrece;* and these we are inclined to dismiss as early experiments—trial pieces from the Shakespearean workshop. We demand, quite properly, instances from the great style of the later plays.

Still, we will do well not to forget the witty examples in the poems and earlier plays. They indicate that Shakespeare is in the beginning not too far removed from Donne, and that, for certain effects at least, he was willing to play with the witty comparison. Dr. Johnson, in teasing the metaphysical poets for their fanciful conceits on the subject of tears, might well have added instances from Shakespeare. One remembers, for example, from *Venus and Adonis:*

> O, how her eyes and tears did lend and borrow!
> Her eyes seen in her tears, tears in her eye;
> Both crystals, where they view'd each other's sorrow. . . .

Or, that more exquisite instance which Shakespeare, perhaps half-smiling, provided for the King in *Love's Labor's Lost:*

> So sweet a kiss the golden sun gives not
> To those fresh morning drops upon the rose,
> As thy eye-beams, when their fresh rays have smote
> The night of dew that on my cheeks down flows:
> Nor shines the silver moon one half so bright
> Through the transparent bosom of the deep,
> As does thy face through tears of mine give light:
> Thou shin'st in every tear that I do weep,
> No drop but as a coach doth carry thee:
> So ridest thou triumphing in my woe.
> Do but behold the tears that swell in me,
> And they thy glory through my grief will show:
> But do not love thyself—then thou wilt keep
> My tears for glasses, and still make me weep.

But Berowne, we know, at the end of the play, foreswears all such

> Taffeta phrases, silken terms precise,
> Three-piled hyperboles, spruce affectation,
> Figures pedantical. . . .

in favor of "russet yeas and honest kersey noes." It is sometimes assumed that Shakespeare did the same thing in his later dramas, and certainly the epithet "taffeta phrases" does not describe the great style of *Macbeth* and *Lear*. Theirs is assuredly of a tougher fabric. But "russet" and "honest kersey" do not describe it either. The weaving was not so simple as that.

The weaving was very intricate indeed—if anything, *more* rather than *less* intricate than that of *Venus and Adonis,* though obviously the pattern was fashioned in accordance with other designs, and yielded other kinds of poetry. But in suggesting that there is a real continuity between the imagery of *Venus and Adonis,* say, and that of a play like *Macbeth,* I am glad to be able to avail myself of Coleridge's support. I refer to the remarkable fifteenth chapter of the *Biographia.*

There Coleridge stresses not the beautiful tapestry work—the purely visual effect—of the images, but quite another quality. He suggests that Shakespeare was prompted by a secret dramatic instinct to realize, in the imagery itself, that "constant intervention and running comment by tone, look and gesture" ordinarily provided by the actor, and that Shakespeare's imagery becomes under this prompting "a series and never broken chain . . . always vivid and, because unbroken, often minute. . . ." Coleridge goes on, a few sentences later, to emphasize further "the perpetual activity of attention required on the part of the reader, . . . the rapid flow, the quick change, and the playful nature of the thoughts and images."

These characteristics, Coleridge hastens to say, are not in themselves enough to make superlative poetry. "They become proofs of original genius only as far as they are modified by a predominant passion; or by associated thoughts or images awakened by that passion; or when they have the effect of reducing multitude to unity, or succession to an instant; or lastly, when a human and intellectual life is transferred to them from the poet's own spirit."

Of the intellectual vigor which Shakespeare possessed, Coleridge then proceeds to speak—perhaps extravagantly. But he goes on to say: "In Shakespeare's *poems,* the creative power and the intellectual energy wrestle as in a war embrace. Each in its excess of strength seems to threaten the extinction of the other."

I am tempted to gloss Coleridge's comment here, perhaps too heavily, with remarks taken from Chapter XIII where he discusses the distinction between the Imagination and the Fancy—the modifying and creative power, on the one hand, and on the other, that "mode of Memory" . . . "blended with, and modified by . . . Choice." But if in *Venus and Adonis* and *The Rape of Lucrece* the powers grapple "in a war embrace," Coleridge goes on to pronounce: "At length, in the *Drama* they were reconciled, and fought each with its shield before the breast of the other."

It is a noble metaphor. I believe that it is also an accurate one, and that it comprises one of the most brilliant insights ever made into the nature of the dramatic poetry of Shakespeare's mature style. If it is accurate, we shall expect to find, even in the mature poetry, the "never broken chain" of images, "always vivid and, because unbroken, often minute," but we shall expect to find the individual images, not mechanically linked together in the mode of Fancy, but organically related, modified by "a predominant passion," and mutually modifying each other.

T. S. Eliot has remarked that "The difference between imagination and fancy, in view of [the] poetry of wit, is a very narrow one." If I have interpreted Coleridge correctly, he is saying that in Shakespeare's greatest work, the distinction lapses altogether—or rather, that one is caught up and merged in the other. As his latest champion, I. A. Richards, observes: "Coleridge often insisted—and would have insisted still more often had he been a better judge of his reader's capacity for misunderstanding—that Fancy and Imagination are not exclusive of, or inimical to, one another."

I began by suggesting that our reading of Donne might contribute something to our reading of Shakespeare, though I tried to make plain the fact that I had no design of trying to turn Shakespeare into Donne, or—what I regard as nonsense—of trying to exalt Donne above Shakespeare. I have in mind specifically some such matter as this: that since the *Songs and Sonets* of Donne no less than *Venus and Adonis,* requires a "perpetual activity of attention . . . on the part of the reader from the rapid flow, the quick change, and the playful nature of the thoughts and images," the discipline gained from reading Donne may allow us to see more clearly the survival of such qualities in the later style of Shakespeare. And, again, I have in mind some such matter as this: that if a reading of Donne has taught us that the "rapid flow, the quick change, and the playful nature of the thoughts and images"—qualities which we are all too prone to associate merely with the fancy—can, on occasion, take on imaginative power, we may, thus taught, better appreciate details in Shakespeare which we shall otherwise dismiss as merely fanciful, or, what is more likely, which we shall simply ignore altogether.

With Donne, of course, the chains of imagery, "always vivid" and "often minute" are perfectly evident. For many readers they are all too evident. The difficulty is not to prove that they exist, but that, on occasion, they may subserve a more imaginative unity. With Shakespeare, the difficulty may well be to prove that the chains exist at all. In general, we may say, Shakespeare has made it relatively easy for his admirers to choose what they like and neglect what they like. What he gives on one or another level is usually so magnificent that the reader finds it easy to ignore other levels.

Yet there are passages not easy to ignore and on which even critics with the conventional interests have been forced to comment. One of these passages occurs in *Macbeth,* Act I, Scene vii, where Macbeth compares the pity for his victim-to-be, Duncan, to

> a naked new-born babe,
> Striding the blast, or heaven's cherubim, hors'd
> Upon the sightless couriers of the air . . .

The comparison is odd, to say the least. Is the babe natural or supernatural—an ordinary, helpless baby, who, as newborn, could not, of course, even toddle, much less stride the blast? Or is it some infant Hercules, quite capable of striding the blast, but, since it is powerful and not helpless, hardly the typical pitiable object?

Shakespeare seems bent upon having it both ways—and, if we read on through the passage—bent upon having the best of both worlds; for he proceeds to give us the option: pity is like the babe "or heaven's cherubim" who quite appropriately, of course, do ride the blast. Yet, even if we waive the question of the legitimacy of the alternative (of which Shakespeare so promptly avails himself), is the cherubim comparison really any more successful than is the babe comparison? Would not one of the great warrior archangels be more appropriate to the scene than the cherub? Does Shakespeare mean for pity or for fear of retribution to be dominant in Macbeth's mind?

Or is it possible that Shakespeare could not make up his own mind? Was he merely writing hastily and loosely, and letting the word "pity" suggest the typically pitiable object, the babe naked in the blast, and then, stirred by the vague notion that some threat to Macbeth should be hinted, using "heaven's cherubim"—already suggested by "babe"—to convey the hint? Is the passage vague or precise? Loosely or tightly organized? Comments upon the passage have ranged all the way from one critic's calling it "pure rant, and intended to be so" to another's laudation: "Either like a mortal babe, terrible in helplessness; or like heaven's angel-children, mighty in love and compassion. This magnificent passage . . ."

An even more interesting, and perhaps more disturbing passage in the play is that in which Macbeth describes his discovery of the murder:

> Here lay Duncan,
> His silver skin lac'd with his golden blood;
> And his gash'd stabs look'd like a breach in nature
> For ruin's wasteful entrance: there, the murderers,
> Steep'd in the colors of their trade, their daggers
> Unmannerly breech'd with gore. . . .

It is amusing to watch the textual critics, particularly those of the eighteenth century, fight a stubborn rear-guard action against the acceptance of "breech'd." Warburton emended "breech'd" to "reech'd"; Johnson, to "drench'd"; Seward, to "hatch'd." Other critics argued that the *breeches* implied were really the handles of the daggers, and that, accordingly, "breech'd" actually here meant "sheathed." The Variorum page witnesses the desperate character of the defense, but the position has had to be yielded, after all. *The Shakespeare Glossary* defines "breech'd" as meaning "covered as with breeches," and thus leaves the poet committed to a reading which must still shock the average reader as much as it shocked that nineteenth-century critic who pronounced upon it as follows: "A metaphor must not be far-fetched nor dwell upon the details of a disgusting picture, as in these lines. There is little, and that far-fetched, similarity between *gold lace* and *blood,* or between *bloody daggers* and *breech'd legs*. The slightness of the similarity, recalling the greatness of the dissimilarity, disgusts us with the attempted comparison."

The two passages are not of the utmost importance, I dare say, though the speeches (of which each is a part) are put in Macbeth's mouth and come at moments of great dramatic tension in the play. Yet, in neither case is there any warrant for thinking that Shakespeare was not trying to write as well as he could. Moreover, whether we like it or not, the imagery is fairly typical of Shakespeare's mature style. Either passage ought to raise some qualms among those who retreat to Shakespeare's authority when they seek to urge the claims of "noble simplicity." They are hardly simple. Yet it is possible that such passages as these may illustrate another poetic resource, another type of imagery which, even in spite of its apparent violence and complication, Shakespeare could absorb into the total structure of his work.

Shakespeare, I repeat, is not Donne—is a much greater poet than Donne; yet the example of his typical handling of imagery will scarcely render support to the usual attacks on Donne's imagery—for, with regard to the two passages in question, the second one, at any rate, is about as strained as Donne is at his most extreme pitch.

Yet I think that Shakespeare's daggers attired in their bloody breeches can be defended as poetry, and as characteristically Shakespearean poetry. Furthermore, both this passage and that about the newborn babe, it seems to me, are far more than excrescences, mere extravagances of detail: each, it seems to me, contains a central symbol of the play, and symbols which we must understand if we are to understand either the detailed passage or the play as a whole.

If this be true, then more is at stake than the merit of the quoted lines taken as lines. (The lines as constituting mere details of a larger structure could, of course, be omitted in the acting of the play without seriously damaging the total effect of the tragedy—though this argument obviously cuts two ways. Whole scenes, and admittedly fine scenes, might also be omitted—have in fact *been* omitted—without quite destroying the massive structure of the tragedy.) What is at stake is the whole matter of the relation of Shakespeare's imagery to the total structures of the plays themselves.

I should like to use the passages as convenient points of entry into the larger symbols which dominate the play. They *are* convenient because, even if we judge them to be faulty, they demonstrate how obsessive for Shakespeare the symbols were—they demonstrate how far the conscious (or unconscious) symbolism could take him.

If we see how the passages are related to these symbols, and they to the tragedy as a whole, the main matter is achieved; and having seen this, if we still prefer "to wish the lines away," that, of course, is our privilege. In the meantime, we may have learned something about Shakespeare's methods—not merely of building metaphors—but of encompassing his larger meanings.

One of the most startling things which has come out of Miss Spurgeon's book on Shakespeare's imagery is her discovery of the "old clothes" imagery in *Macbeth*. As she points out: "The idea constantly recurs that Macbeth's new honours sit ill upon him, like a loose and badly fitting garment, belonging to someone else." And she goes on to quote passage after passage in which the idea is expressed. But, though we are all in Miss Spurgeon's debt for having pointed this out, one has to observe that Miss Spurgeon has hardly explored the full implications of her discovery. Perhaps her interest in classifying and cataloguing the imagery of the plays has obscured for her some of the larger and more important relationships. At any rate, for reasons to be given below, she has realized only a part of the potentialities of her discovery.

Her comment on the clothes imagery reaches its climax with the following paragraphs:

> And, at the end, when the tyrant is at bay at Dunsinane, and the English troops are advancing, the Scottish lords still have this image in their minds. Caithness sees him as a man vainly trying to fasten a large garment on him with too small a belt:
>
> He cannot buckle his distemper'd cause
> Within the belt of rule;
>
> while Angus, in a similar image, vividly sums up the essence of what they all have been thinking ever since Macbeth's accession to power:
>
> now does he feel his title
> Hang loose about him, like a giant's robe
> Upon a dwarfish thief.

This imaginative picture of a small, ignoble man encumbered and degraded by garments unsuited to him, should be put against the view emphasized by some critics (notably Coleridge and Bradley) of the likeness between Macbeth and Milton's Satan in grandeur and sublimity.

Undoubtedly Macbeth . . . is great, magnificently great . . . But he could never be put beside, say, Hamlet or Othello, in nobility of nature; and there *is* an aspect in which he is but a poor, vain, cruel, treacherous creature, snatching ruthlessly over the dead bodies of kinsman and friend at place and power he is utterly unfitted to possess. It is worth remembering that it is thus that Shakespeare, with his unshrinking clarity of vision, repeatedly *sees* him.

But this is to make primary what is only one aspect of the old-clothes imagery! And there is no warrant for interpreting the garment imagery as used by Macbeth's enemies, Caithness and Angus, to mean that *Shakespeare* sees Macbeth as a poor and somewhat comic figure.

The crucial point of the comparison, it seems to me, lies not in the smallness of the man and the largeness of the robes, but rather in the fact that—whether the man be large or small—these are not *his* garments; in Macbeth's case they are actually stolen garments. Macbeth is uncomfortable in them because he is continually conscious of the fact that they do not belong to him. There is a further point, and it is one of the utmost importance; the oldest symbol for the hypocrite is that of the man who cloaks his true nature under a disguise. Macbeth loathes playing the part of the hypocrite—and actually does not play it too well. If we keep this in mind as we look back at the instances of the garment images which Miss Spurgeon has collected for us, we shall see that the pattern of imagery becomes very rich indeed. Macbeth says in Act I:

> The Thane of Cawdor lives: why do you dress me
> In borrow'd robes?

Macbeth at this point wants no honors that are not honestly his. Banquo says in Act I:

> New honors come upon him,
> Like our strange garments, cleave not to their mold,
> But with the aid of use.

But Banquo's remark, one must observe, is not censorious. It is indeed a compliment to say of one that he wears new honors with some awkwardness. The observation becomes ironical only in terms of what is to occur later.

Macbeth says in Act I:

> He hath honor'd me of late; and I have bought
> Golden opinions from all sorts of people,
> Which would be worn now in their newest gloss,
> Not cast aside so soon.

Macbeth here is proud of his new clothes: he is happy to wear what he has truly earned. It is the part of simple good husbandry not to throw aside these new garments and replace them with robes stolen from Duncan.

But Macbeth has already been wearing Duncan's garments in anticipation, as his wife implies in the metaphor with which she answers him:

> Was the hope drunk,
> Wherein you dress'd yourself?

(The metaphor may seem hopelessly mixed, and a full and accurate analysis of such mixed metaphors in terms of the premises of Shakespeare's style waits upon some critic who will have to consider not only this passage but many more like it in Shakespeare.) For our purposes here, however, one may observe that the psychological line, the line of the basic symbolism, runs on unbroken. A man dressed in a drunken hope is garbed in strange attire indeed—a ridiculous dress which accords thoroughly with the contemptuous picture that Lady Macbeth wishes to evoke. Macbeth's earlier dream of glory has been a drunken fantasy merely, if he flinches from action now.

But the series of garment metaphors which run through the play is paralleled by a series of masking or cloaking images which—if we free ourselves of Miss Spurgeon's rather mechanical scheme of classification —show themselves to be merely variants of the garments which hide none too well his disgraceful self. He is consciously hiding that self throughout the play.

"False face must hide what the false heart doth know," he counsels Lady Macbeth before the murder of Duncan; and later, just before the murder of Banquo, he invokes night to "Scarf up the eye of pitiful day."

One of the most powerful of these cloaking images is given to Lady Macbeth in the famous speech in Act I:

> Come, thick night,
> And pall thee in the dunnest smoke of hell,
> That my keen knife see not the wound it makes,
> Nor heaven peep through the blanket of the dark,
> To cry, "Hold, Hold!"

I suppose that it is natural to conceive the "keen knife" here as held in her own hand. Lady Macbeth is capable of wielding it. And in this interpretation, the imagery is thoroughly significant. Night is to be doubly black so that not even her knife may see the wound it makes. But I think that there is good warrant for regarding her "keen knife" as Macbeth himself. She has just, a few lines above, given her analysis of Macbeth's character as one who would "not play false, / And yet [would] wrongly win." To bring him to the point of action, she will have to "chastise [him] with the valor of [her] tongue." There is good reason, then, for her to invoke night to become blacker still—to pall itself in the "dunnest smoke of hell." For night must not only screen the deed from the eye of heaven—conceal it at least until it is too late for heaven to call out to Macbeth "Hold, Hold!" Lady Macbeth would have night blanket the deed from the hesitant doer. The imagery thus repeats and reinforces the substance of Macbeth's anguished aside uttered in the preceding scene:

> Let not light see my black and deep desires;
> The eye wink at the hand; yet let that be
> Which the eye fears, when it is done, to see.

I do not know whether "blanket" and "pall" qualify as garment metaphors in Miss Spurgeon's classification: yet one is the clothing of sleep, and the other, the clothing of death—they are the appropriate garments of night; and they carry on an important aspect of the general clothes imagery. It is not necessary to attempt to give here an exhaustive list of instances of the garment metaphor; but one should say a word about the remarkable passage in II.iii.

Here, after the discovery of Duncan's murder, Banquo says

> And when we have our naked frailties hid,
> That suffer in exposure, let us meet,
> And question this most bloody piece of work—

that is, "When we have clothed ourselves against the chill morning air, let us meet to discuss this bloody piece of work." Macbeth answers, as if his subconscious mind were already taking Banquo's innocent phrase, "naked frailties," in a deeper, ironic sense:

> Let's briefly put on manly readiness. . . .

It is ironic; for the "manly readiness" which he urges the other lords to put on, is, in his own case, a hypocrite's garment: he can only pretend to be the loyal, grief-stricken liege who is almost unstrung by the horror of Duncan's murder.

But the word "manly" carries still a further ironic implication: earlier, Macbeth had told Lady Macbeth that he dared

> do all that may become a man;
> Who dares do more is none.

Under the weight of her reproaches of cowardice, however, he *has* dared do more, and has become less than a man, a beast. He has already laid aside, therefore, one kind of "manly readiness" and has assumed another: he has garbed himself in a sterner composure than that which he counsels to his fellows—the hard and inhuman "manly readiness" of the resolved murderer.

The clothes imagery, used sometimes with emphasis on one aspect of it, sometimes on another, does pervade the play. And it should be evident that the daggers "breech'd with gore"—though Miss Spurgeon does not include the passage in her examples of clothes imagery—represent one more variant of this general symbol. Consider the passage once more:

> Here lay Duncan,
> His silver skin lac'd with his golden blood;
> And his gash'd stabs look'd like a breach in nature
> For ruin's wasteful entrance: there, the murderers,
> Steep'd in the colors of their trade, their daggers
> Unmannerly breech'd with gore. . . .

The clothes imagery runs throughout the passage; the body of the king is dressed in the most precious of garments, the blood royal itself; and the daggers too are dressed—in the same garment. The daggers, "naked" except for their lower parts which are reddened with blood, are like men in "unmannerly" dress—men, naked except for their red breeches, lying beside the red-handed grooms. The figure, though vivid, is fantastic; granted. But the basis for the comparison is *not* slight and adventitious. The metaphor fits the real situation on the deepest levels. As Macbeth and Lennox burst into the room, they find the daggers wearing, as Macbeth knows all too well, a horrible masquerade. They have been carefully "clothed" to play a part. They are not honest daggers, honorably naked in readiness to guard the king, or, "mannerly" clothed in their own sheaths. Yet the disguise which they wear will enable Macbeth to assume the robes of Duncan—robes to which he is no more entitled than are the daggers to the royal garments which they now wear, grotesquely.

The reader will, of course, make up his own mind as to the value of the passage. But the metaphor in question, in the light of the other garment imagery, cannot be dismissed as merely a strained ingenuity, irrelevant to the play. And the reader who *does* accept it as poetry will probably be that reader who knows the play best, not the reader who knows it slightly and regards Shakespeare's poetry as a rhetoric more or less loosely draped over the "content" of the play.

And now what can be said of pity, the "naked new-born babe"? Though Miss Spurgeon does not note it (since the governing scheme of her book would have hardly allowed her to see it), there are, by the way, a great many references to babes in this play—references which occur on a number of levels. The babe appears sometimes as a character, such as Macduff's child; sometimes as a symbol, like the crowned babe and the bloody babe which are raised by the witches on the occasion of Macbeth's visit to them; sometimes, in a metaphor, as in the passage under discussion. The number of such references can hardly be accidental; and the babe turns out to be, as a matter of fact, perhaps the most powerful symbol in the tragedy.

But to see this fully, it will be necessary to review the motivation of the play. The stimulus to Duncan's murder, as we know, was the prophecy of the Weird Sisters. But Macbeth's subsequent career of bloodshed stems from the same prophecy. Macbeth was to have the crown, but the crown was to pass to Banquo's children. The second part of the prophecy troubles Macbeth from the start. It does not oppress him, however, until the crown has been won. But from this point on, the effect of the prophecy is to hurry Macbeth into action and more action until he is finally precipitated into ruin.

We need not spend much time in speculating on whether Macbeth, had he been content with Duncan's murder, had he tempted fate no further, had he been willing to court the favor of his nobles, might not have died peaceably in bed. We are dealing, not with history, but with a play. Yet, even in history the usurper sometimes succeeds; and he sometimes succeeds on the stage. Shakespeare himself knew of, and wrote plays about, usurpers who successfully maintained possession of the crown. But, in any case, this much is plain: the train of murders into which Macbeth launches aggravates suspicions of his guilt and alienates the nobles.

Yet, a Macbeth who could act once, and then settle down to enjoy the fruits of this one attempt to meddle with the future would, of course, not be Macbeth. For it is not merely his great imagination and his warrior courage in defeat which redeem him for tragedy and place him beside the other great tragic protagonists: rather, it is his attempt to conquer the future, an attempt involving him, like Oedipus, in a desperate struggle with fate itself. It is this which holds our imaginative sympathy, even after he has degenerated into a bloody tyrant and has become the slayer of Macduff's wife and children.

To sum up, there can be no question that Macbeth stands at the height of his power after his murder of Duncan, and that the plan—as outlined by Lady Macbeth—has been relatively successful. The road turns toward disaster only when Macbeth decides to murder Banquo. Why does he make this decision? Shakespeare has pointed up the basic motivation very carefully:

> Then prophet-like,
> They hail'd him father to a line of kings.
> Upon my head they plac'd a fruitless crown,
> And put a barren scepter in my gripe,
> Thence to be wrench'd with an unlineal hand,
> No son of mine succeeding. If't be so,
> For Banquo's issue have I fil'd my mind;
> For them the gracious Duncan have I murder'd;
> Put rancors in the vessel of my peace
> Only for them; and mine eternal jewel
> Given to the common enemy of man,
> To make them kings, the seed of Banquo kings!

Presumably, Macbeth had entered upon his course from sheer personal ambition. Ironically, it is the more human part of Macbeth—his desire to have more than a limited personal satisfaction, his desire to found a line, his wish to pass something on to later generations—which prompts him to dispose of Banquo. There is, of course, a resentment against Banquo, but that resentment is itself closely related to Macbeth's desire to found a dynasty. Banquo, who has risked nothing, who has remained upright, who has not defiled himself, will have kings for children; Macbeth, none. Again, ironically, the Weird Sisters who have given Macbeth, so he has thought, the priceless gift of knowledge of the future, have given the real future to Banquo.

So Banquo's murder is decided upon, and accomplished. But Banquo's son escapes, and once more, the future has eluded Macbeth. The murder of Banquo thus becomes almost meaningless. This general point may be obvious enough, but we shall do well to note some of the further ways in which Shakespeare has pointed up the significance of Macbeth's war with the future.

When Macbeth, at the beginning of Scene vii, Act I, contemplates Duncan's murder, it is the future over which he agonizes:

> If it were done, when 'tis done, then 'twere well
> It were done quickly; if the assassination
> Could trammel up the consequence, and catch
> With his surcease success; that but this blow
> Might be the be-all and the end-all here. . . .

But the continuum of time cannot be partitioned off; the future is implicit in the present. There is no net strong enough to trammel up the consequence—not even in this world.

Lady Macbeth, of course, has fewer qualms. When Macbeth hesitates to repudiate the duties which he owes Duncan—duties which, by some accident of imagery perhaps—I hesitate to press the significance—he has earlier actually called "children"—Lady Macbeth cries out that she is willing to crush her own child in order to gain the crown:

> I have given suck, and know
> How tender 'tis to love the babe that milks me;
> I would, while it was smiling in my face,
> Have pluck'd my nipple from his boneless gums
> And dash'd the brains out, had I so sworn as you
> Have done to this.

Robert Penn Warren has made the penetrating observation that all of Shakespeare's villains are rationalists. Lady Macbeth is certainly of their company. She knows what she wants; and she is ruthless in her consideration of means. She will always "catch the nearest way." This is not to say that she ignores the problem of scruples, or that she is ready to oversimplify psychological complexities. But scruples are to be used to entangle one's enemies. One is not to become tangled in the mesh of scruples himself. Even though she loves her husband and though her ambition for herself is a part of her ambition for him, still she seems willing to consider even Macbeth at times as pure instrument, playing upon his hopes and fears and pride.

Her rationalism is quite sincere. She is apparently thoroughly honest in declaring that

> The sleeping and the dead
> Are but as pictures; 'tis the eye of childhood
> That fears a painted devil. If he do bleed,
> I'll gild the faces of the grooms withal,
> For it must seem their guilt.

For her, there is no moral order: *guilt* is something like *gilt*—one can wash it off or paint it on. Her pun is not frivolous and it is deeply expressive.

Lady Macbeth abjures all pity; she is willing to unsex herself; and her continual taunt to Macbeth, when he falters, is that he is acting like a baby—not like a man. This "manhood" Macbeth tries to learn. He is a dogged pupil. For that reason he is almost pathetic when the shallow rationalism which his wife urges upon him fails. His tone is almost one of puzzled bewilderment at nature's unfairness in failing to play the game according to the rules—the rules which have applied to other murders:

> the time has been,
> That, when the brains were out, the man would die,
> And there an end; but now they rise again. . . .

Yet, after the harrowing scene, Macbeth can say, with a sort of dogged weariness:

> Come, we'll to sleep. My strange and self-abuse
> Is the initiate fear that wants hard use:
> We are yet but young in deed.

Ironically, Macbeth is still echoing the dominant metaphor of Lady Macbeth's reproach. He has not yet attained to "manhood"; that *must* be the explanation. He has not yet succeeded in hardening himself into something inhuman.

Tempted by the Weird Sisters and urged on by his wife, Macbeth is thus caught between the irrational and the rational. There is a sense, of course, in which every man is caught between them. Man must try to predict and plan and control his destiny. That is man's fate; and the struggle, if he is to realize himself as a man, cannot be avoided. The question, of course, which has always interested the tragic dramatist involves the terms on which the struggle is accepted and the protagonist's attitude toward fate and toward himself. Macbeth in his general concern for the future is typical—is Every Man. He becomes the typical tragic protagonist when he yields to pride and *hybris*. The occasion for temptation is offered by the prophecy of the Weird Sisters. They offer him knowledge which cannot be arrived at rationally. They offer a key—if only a partial key—to what is otherwise unpredictable. Lady Macbeth, on the other hand, by employing a ruthless clarity of perception, by discounting all emotional claims, offers him the promise of bringing about the course of events which he desires.

Now, in the middle of the play, though he has not lost confidence and though, as he himself says, there can be no turning back, doubts have begun to arise; and he returns to the Weird Sisters to secure unambiguous answers to his fears. But, pathetically and ironically for Macbeth, in returning to the Weird Sisters, he is really trying to impose rationality on what sets itself forth plainly as irrational: that is, Macbeth would force a rigid control on a future which, by definition—by the very fact that the Weird Sisters already know it—stands beyond his manipulation.

It is because of his hopes for his own children and his fears of Banquo's that he has returned to the witches for counsel. It is altogether appropriate, therefore, that two of the apparitions by which their counsel is revealed should be babes, the crowned babe and the bloody babe.

For the babe signifies the future which Macbeth would control and cannot control. It is the unpredictable thing itself—as Yeats has put it magnificently, "The uncontrollable mystery on the bestial floor." It is the one thing that can justify, even in Macbeth's mind, the murders which he has committed. Earlier in the play, Macbeth had declared that if the deed could "trammel up the consequence," he would be willing to "jump the life to come." But he cannot jump the life to come. In his own terms he is betrayed. For it is idle to speak of jumping the life to come if one yearns to found a line of kings. It is the babe that betrays Macbeth—his own babes, most of all.

The logic of Macbeth's distraught mind, thus, forces him to make war on children, a war which in itself reflects his desperation and is a confession of weakness. Macbeth's ruffians, for example, break into Macduff's castle and kill his wife and children. The scene in which the innocent child prattles with his mother about his absent father, and then is murdered, is typical Shakespearean "fourth act" pathos. But the pathos is not adventitious; the scene ties into the inner symbolism of the play. For the child, in its helplessness, defies the murderers. Its defiance testifies to the force which threatens Macbeth and which Macbeth cannot destroy.

But we are not, of course, to placard the child as The Future in a rather stiff and mechanical allegory. *Macbeth* is no such allegory. Shakespeare's symbols are richer and more flexible than that. The babe signifies not only the future; it symbolizes all those enlarging purposes which make life meaningful, and it symbolizes, furthermore, all those emotional and—to Lady Macbeth—irrational ties which make man more than a machine—which render him human. It signifies pre-eminently the pity which Macbeth, under Lady Macbeth's tutelage, would wean himself of as something "unmanly." Lady Macbeth's great speeches early in the play become brilliantly ironical when we realize that Shakespeare is using the same symbol for the unpredictable future that he uses for human compassion. Lady Macbeth is willing to go to any length to grasp the future: she would willingly dash out the brains of her own child if it stood in her way to that future. But this is to repudiate the future, for the child is its symbol.

Shakespeare does not, of course, limit himself to the symbolism of the child: he makes use of other symbols of growth and development, notably that of the plant. And this plant symbolism patterns itself to reflect the development of the play. For example, Banquo says to the Weird Sisters, early in the play:

> If you can look into the seeds of time,
> And say which grain will grow and which will not,
> Speak then to me. . . .

A little later, on welcoming Macbeth, Duncan says to him:

> I have begun to plant thee, and will labor
> To make thee full of growing.

After the murder of Duncan, Macbeth falls into the same metaphor when he comes to resolve on Banquo's death. The Weird Sisters, he reflects, had hailed Banquo as

> . . . father to a line of kings.
> Upon my head they placed a fruitless crown,
> And put a barren scepter in my gripe. . . .

Late in the play, Macbeth sees himself as the winter-stricken tree:

> I have liv'd long enough: my way of life
> Is fall'n into the sear, the yellow leaf. . . .

The plant symbolism, then, supplements the child symbolism. At points it merges with it, as when Macbeth ponders bitterly that he has damned himself

> To make them kings, the seed of Banquo kings!

And, in at least one brilliant example, the plant symbolism unites with the clothes symbolism. It is a crowning irony that one of the Weird Sisters' prophecies on which Macbeth has staked his hopes is fulfilled when Birnam Wood comes to Dunsinane. For, in a sense, Macbeth is here hoist on his own petard. Macbeth, who has invoked night to

"Scarf up the tender eye of pitiful day," and who has, again and again, used the "false face" to "hide what the false heart doth know," here has the trick turned against him. But the garment which cloaks the avengers is the living green of nature itself, and nature seems, to the startled eyes of his sentinels, to be rising up against him.

But it is the babe, the child, that dominates the symbolism. Most fittingly, the last of the prophecies in which Macbeth has placed his confidence, concerns the child: and Macbeth comes to know the final worst when Macduff declares to him that he was not "born of woman" but was from his "mother's womb / Untimely ripp'd." The babe here has defied even the thing which one feels may reasonably be predicted of him—his time of birth. With Macduff's pronouncement, the unpredictable has broken through the last shred of the net of calculation. The future cannot be trammeled up. The naked babe confronts Macbeth to pronounce his doom.

The passage with which we began this essay, then, is an integral part of a larger context, and of a very rich context:

> And pity, like a naked new-born babe,
> Striding the blast, or heaven's cherubim, hors'd
> Upon the sightless couriers of the air,
> Shall blow the horrid deed in every eye,
> That tears shall drown the wind.

Pity is like the naked babe, the most sensitive and helpless thing; yet, almost as soon as the comparison is announced, the symbol of weakness begins to turn into a symbol of strength; for the babe, though newborn, is pictured as "Striding the blast" like an elemental force—like "heaven's cherubim, hors'd / Upon the sightless couriers of the air." We can give an answer to the question put earlier: is Pity like the human and helpless babe, or powerful as the angel that rides the winds? It is both; and it is strong because of its very weakness. The paradox is inherent in the situation itself; and it is the paradox that will destroy the overbrittle rationalism on which Macbeth founds his career.

For what will it avail Macbeth to cover the deed with the blanket of the dark if the elemental forces that ride the winds will blow the horrid deed in every eye? And what will it avail Macbeth to clothe himself in "manliness"—to become bloody, bold, and resolute,—if he is to find himself again and again, viewing his bloody work through the "eye of childhood / That fears a painted devil"? Certainly, the final and climactic appearance of the babe symbol merges all the contradictory elements of the symbol. For, with Macduff's statement about his birth, the naked babe rises before Macbeth as not only the future that eludes calculation but as avenging angel as well.

The clothed daggers and the naked babe—mechanism and life—instrument and end—death and birth—that which should be left bare and clean and that which should be clothed and warmed—these are facets of two of the great symbols which run throughout the play. They are not the only symbols, to be sure; they are not the most obvious symbols: darkness and blood appear more often. But with a flexibility which must amaze the reader, the image of the garment and the image of the babe are so used as to encompass an astonishingly large area of the total situation. And between them—the naked babe, essential humanity, humanity stripped down to the naked thing itself, and yet as various as the future—and the various garbs which humanity assumes, the robes of honor, the hypocrite's disguise, the inhuman "manliness" with which Macbeth endeavors to cover up his essential humanity—between them, they furnish Shakespeare with his most subtle and ironically telling instruments.

VII

THE LATE PLAYS AND THE ROMANCES

THE LAST OF THE GREAT TRAGEDIES

"Antony and Cleopatra": A Shakespearian Adjustment

John Danby

At each stage in his development Shakespeare displays a surprising capacity for renewal. Let us assume that *Antony and Cleopatra* comes after *King Lear,* that it goes with *Coriolanus,* and that both it and *Coriolanus* immediately precede the so-called 'last period'. Between *Antony and Cleopatra* and the plays that have gone before there is no obvious connection in theme or technique. At the same time, only Plutarch links it with *Coriolanus*. Nothing in it would normally prepare us for *Cymbeline* or *The Winter's Tale* to follow. This apparent isolation is one of the main obstacles to a correct focus on the play. There seems to be a break in the internal continuity of the Shakespearian series—a continuity of series which stretches, I think, from *Henry VI* to *King Lear* at least, and which could possibly be extended to include *Timon:* though here again there is something of a lesion, and special factors, external to the 'inner biography' of Shakespeare as a playwright, might have to be invoked to explain all that is happening. *Timon,* however, it might be granted, is the aftermath of *King Lear*. Can the same be said about *Antony and Cleopatra?*

From John Danby, *Elizabethan and Jacobean Poets*. Reprinted by permission of Faber and Faber, Ltd.

I

To describe the swiftness of *Antony and Cleopatra* we need to draw on the imagery of the cinema. There is more cinematic movement, more panning, tracking, and playing with the camera, more mixing of shots than in any other of Shakespeare's tragedies. At the same time the technique is always under deliberate, almost cool, control. *Antony and Cleopatra* has none of the haphazardies of *Pericles* nor any of the plot-imposed vagaries of the last period. The technique is inwardly related to the meaning Shakespeare has to express. What is indicated is not enervation or indifference, but rather what Coleridge recognized as 'giant power,' an 'angelic strength'.

The swift traverse of time and space has often been commented upon. There is also the mixing. Egypt is called up vividly in Rome by Enobarbus's descriptions. Rome is always felt as a real presence in Egypt. On the frontiers of Empire Ventidius discusses what repercussions his victories will have on the people at staff-headquarters. Equally the present is interpenetrated by the past. Antony's past, particularly, is always powerfully put before us:

> Antony,
> Leave thy lascivious wassails. When thou once
> Wast beaten from Modena, where thou slew'st
> Hirtius and Pansa, consuls, at thy heels
> Did famine follow, whom thou fought'st against
> Though daintily brought up, with patience more
> Than savages could suffer; thou didst drink
> The stale of horses, and the gilded puddle
> Which beasts would cough at; thy palate then did deign
> The roughest berry on the rudest hedge;
> Yea, like the stag, when snow the pasture sheets,
> It is reported thou didst eat strange flesh,
> Which some did die to look on.
>
> (I.iv.55–68)

So, too, is Cleopatra's:

> I found you as a morsel cold upon
> Dead Caesar's trencher; nay, you were a fragment
> Of Cneius Pompey's; besides what hotter hours,
> Unregister'd in vulgar fame, you have
> Luxuriously pick'd out.
>
> (III.ix.116–20)

The hinterland of the quarrels that alternately divide and bring together again the triumvirate is constantly being suggested, troubles, truces, and manoeuvres that go back (like Cleopatra's love-affairs) to Julius Caesar's days. In no other of his plays is Shakespeare at such pains to suggest the stream of time past and its steady course through the present. In the public world of Roman affairs this is especially so. In the other world of Cleopatra the same suggestion of perspective always frames what is said and done. Is Antony merely the last of a long succession of such lovers? Or is this affair singular and unique as all love-affairs claim to be? Not enough weight has been given in recent assessments of the play to the ambiguity which invests everything in Egypt equally with all things in Rome. Yet this ambiguity is central to Shakespeare's experience in the play. If it is wrong to see the 'mutual pair' as a strumpet and her fool, it is also wrong to see them as a Phoenix and a Turtle.

In addition to the swiftness and the variety of the impacts, and the interpenetration of the parts of time and space as they mix in the speech of the people immediately before us, there is also the added burden which Shakespeare's 'giant power' of compelling presentation imposes. The effects are at once those of a rapid impressionism and a careful lapidary enrichment. Each figure, however minor, has its moment when it comes up into the brilliant foreground light—the Soothsayer with his 'infinite book of secrecy', the Old Man wishing 'much joy o' the worm', Enobarbus describing the barge on the Nile, Lepidus asking 'What manner o' thing is your crocodile?' Ventidius giving once for all the field-officer's view of the higher-ups, the Eunuch and the game of billiards, Dolabella, Octavia, even Fulvia whom we never see: the canvas seems covered with Constable's snow.

Another feature of Shakespeare's technique which makes for the impression of uniqueness might be pointed to here. Shakespeare seems to be innovating also in methods of character-portrayal. Some of the stage conventions, as described by Miss Bradbrook, do not seem to apply. Which, for example, are we to believe—what Caesar says about Antony after he is dead, or what he says about him, and his conduct towards him, while he is alive? What was Fulvia's 'character', about whom we have such conflicting reports? Throughout the play we are forced by Shakespeare himself not to take comment at its face value. Judgments are more personal here than elsewhere. Goneril and Regan discussing their father's condition are reliable judges. Caesar, Antony, Enobarbus, the soldiers Demetrius and Philo, are not—or not to the same extent. Judgment knits itself back into character as it might do in Ibsen, and character issues from a mutable and ambiguous flux of things. Antony's momentary *agnorisis* can be generalized to cover the whole play:

> Sometimes we see a cloud that's dragonish;
> A vapour sometimes like a bear or lion,
> A tower'd citadel, a pendant rock,
> A forked mountain, or blue promontory,
> With trees upon't, that nod unto the world
> And mock our eyes with air: thou hast seen these signs;
> They are black vespers pageants . . .

That which is now a horse, even with a thought
The rack dislimns, and makes it indistinct
As water is in water . . .
My good knave, Eros, now thy captain is
Even such a body: here I am Antony,
Yet cannot hold this visible shape, my knave.
(IV.xii.2–14)

There is something deliquescent in the reality behind the play. It is a deliquescence to the full display of which each judgment, each aspect pointed to, and each character, is necessary, always provided that no single one of these is taken as final. The proportion of comment and judgment on the central characters is higher in *Antony and Cleopatra* than anywhere else in Shakespeare. This further underlines its uniqueness and the difficulties of coming by an adequate final assessment. Antony and Cleopatra are presented in three ways. There is what is said about them; there is what they say themselves; there is what they do. Each of these might correspond to a different 'level' of response. Each is in tension against the others. Each makes its continuous and insistent claim on the spectator for judgment in his own right. The pigments vividly opposed to each other on the canvas have to mix in the spectator's eye.

Underlying, however, the bewildering oscillations of scene, the overlapping and pleating of different times and places, the co-presence of opposed judgments, the innumerable opportunities for radical choice to intervene, there is, I think, a deliberate logic. It is this which gives the play its compact unity of effect and makes its movement a sign of angelic strength rather than a symptom of febrility. It is the logic of a peculiarly Shakespearian dialectic. Opposites are juxtaposed, mingled, married; then from the very union which seems to promise strength dissolution flows. It is the process of this dialectic—the central process of the play—which we must trace if we wish to arrive anywhere near Shakespeare's meaning.

II

The first scene opens with Philo's comment on the 'dotage' of his general:

those his goodly eyes
That o'er the files and musters of the war
Have glow'd like plated Mars: now bend, now turn
The office and devotion of their view
Upon a tawny front; his captain's heart,
Which in the scuffles of great fights hath burst
The buckles on his breast, reneges all temper,
And is become the bellows and the fan
To cool a gipsy's lust.
(I.i.2–10)

Nothing more has time to be said. Antony and Cleopatra themselves appear. Their first words express the essence of romantic love, a tacit contradiction of all that Philo seems to have just suggested:

> CLEOPATRA If it be love indeed, tell me how much.
> ANTONY There's beggary in the love that can be reckon'd.
> CLEOPATRA I'll set a bourn how far to be belov'd.
> ANTONY Then must thou needs find out new heaven, new earth.
>
> (I.i.14–17)

Again immediately, an attendant announces the arrival of news from Rome. The atmosphere of the Egyptian court changes. We see the opposite effects of the intrusion on the two it most concerns. Antony will not hear the messengers. Cleopatra insists that he shall. Antony is taunted with a wicked caricature of what the news might be, and of the relation in which he stands to Rome. Yet the version is sufficiently like to make Antony blush—from anger, or shame, or both:

> Your dismission
> Is come from Caesar; therefore hear it, Antony,
> Where's Fulvia's process? Caesar's would I say? both?
> Call in the messengers. As I am Egypt's queen,
> Thou blushest, Antony, and that blood of thine
> Is Caesar's homager; else so thy cheek pays shame
> When shrill-tongued Fulvia scolds.
>
> (I.i.26–32)

Antony's reaction is to pitch his romantic vows higher still, asserting his independence of Rome in terms that should leave no doubt as to where he stands:

> Let Rome in Tiber melt, and the wide arch
> Of the rang'd empire fall! Here is my space.
> Kingdoms are clay; our dungy earth alike
> Feeds beast as man: the nobleness of life
> Is to do thus; when such a mutual pair
> And such a twain can do't, in which I bind
> On pain of punishment, the world to weet
> We stand up peerless.
>
> (I.i.33–40)

This again has all the ring of absolute and heroic self-committal. Cleopatra's reply, however, is typical both of herself and of the ambivalence that runs through everything in the play:

> Excellent falsehood!
> Why did he marry Fulvia and not love her?
> I'll seem the fool I am not; Antony
> Will be himself.
>
> (I.i.40–43)

Her first words might be oxymoron or plain disbelief. The next call up the vista of Antony's past, with its broken pledges and unconscious insincerities—if they were no more. Her last words are highly ambiguous and turn the whole situation upside-down: she is the helpless creature wilfully blinding and deceiving herself, Antony is the self-contained and calculating manipulator of her weaknesses. In replying, Antony is like the man innocent of ju-jutsu who thinks he is pushing when really he is being pulled:

> But stirr'd by Cleopatra.
> Now, for the love of Love and her soft hours,
> Let's not confound the time with conference harsh . . .
> . . . What sport tonight?
>
> (I.i.43–47)

Shakespeare gives the operative lines a subtle falsity of note that could equally indicate hearty play-acting, slightly awkward self-consciousness, or wilful evasion. Cleopatra's answer is realistic and comes with a new urgency:

> Hear the ambassadors.
>
> (I.i.48)

It drives Antony also to something we can recognize as more fully himself—something that is perceptive and tinged with the masterful as well as the reckless:

> Fie, wrangling queen!
> Whom everything becomes, to chide, to laugh,
> To weep; whose every passion fully strives
> To make itself in thee fair and admir'd.
> No messenger, but thine; and all alone,
> Tonight we'll wander through the streets and note
> The qualities of people. Come, my queen;
> Last night you did desire it: speak not to us.
>
> (I.i.48–55)

This is not only Antony's view of Cleopatra's character, and a reliable account of what she is really like. It is also an expression of the deliquescent reality at the heart of the play which incarnates itself most completely in the persons of the hero and heroine. After Antony's speech, with this two-fold authority it bears, the comment of the soldiers seems peculiarly limited and out of place:

> DEMETRIUS Is Caesar with Antonius priz'd so slight?
> PHILO Sir, sometimes when he is not Antony,
> He comes too short of that great property

Which still should go with Antony.
DEMETRIUS I am full sorry
That he approves the common liar, who
Thus speaks of him at Rome; but I will hope
Of better deeds tomorrow.

(I.i.56–62)

It serves to remind us, however, of the world that stands around the lovers, the world of the faithful soldier who can only understand the soldierly, the world of 'the common liar' that enjoys the unpleasant 'truth', the world, too, of Rome and Caesar that is radically opposed to the world of Egypt and Cleopatra.

The first scene is only slightly more than sixty lines long. Yet it is sufficient to illustrate all the main features of the play we have pointed to, and extensive enough to set up the swinging ambivalence—the alternatives and ambiguities constantly proposed to choice—which will govern and control our whole reaction to the play. There is the speed and oscillation, the interpenetration of Rome and Egypt and of present and past. Above all there is the dialectic marriage of the contraries and their dissolution through union. The jealousy of Cleopatra towards Fulvia, the outrage of Caesar to Antony's *amour propre*—these negative repulsions can serve to hold the mutual pair together as firmly as positive attractions. Antony and Cleopatra are opposed to the world that surrounds and isolates them. In this isolation their union seems absolute, infinite, and self-sufficient. Yet the war of the contraries pervades the love, too. In coming together they lapse, slide, and fall apart unceasingly.

The outstanding achievement of the first scene is the way in which it begins with the soldiers' condemnation and returns us at the end to the same thing—allowing for this side eighteen lines out of the sixty-two. Yet at the end we are no longer satisfied as to the adequacy of what Demetrius and Philo say. Not that what they say has been disproved by what we have seen of Antony and Cleopatra. They are and they remain a strumpet and her fool. To have any judgment at all is to choose, apparently, either the judgment of the soldiers' at the beginning of the scene or the lovers' own self-assessment that immediately follows it. (Coleridge chose the former; Dr. Sitwell and Mr. Wilson Knight take the latter.) To entertain either judgment, however, is not enough. The deliquescent truth is neither in them nor between them, but contains both. *Antony and Cleopatra* is Shakespeare's critique of judgment.

Scene i played out romantic love and lovers' quarrels on a lofty stage. It also gave the sharp local comment of the soldiery. Scene ii takes the theme of love below-stairs and changes key. It also gives the universal comment of the Soothsayer, with its suggestion that everything is already decided, the tragedy is in the nature of things, now is already over, the future past, the present always:

> In nature's infinite book of secrecy
> A little can I read . . .
> I make not but foresee. . . .
> You have seen and prov'd a fairer former fortune
> Than that which is to approach.
>
> (I.ii.11–36)

In place of the 'romance' of love, Charmian, Iras, and Alexas give the 'reality'. The reality in this case is a strong succession of rich, powerful, and adequate males:

> Let me be married to three kings in a forenoon, and widow them all; let me have a child at fifty to whom Herod of Jewry may do homage; find me to marry with Octavius Caesar, and companion me with my mistress.

It reads like a parody of Cleopatra's aspirations, just as the women's bickering and teasing of Alexas mimics Cleopatra's handling of Antony:

> Alexas—come, his fortune, his fortune. O! let him marry a woman that cannot go, sweet Isis, I beseech thee; and let her die too, and give him a worse; and let worse follow worse, till the worst of all follow him laughing to his grave, fifty-fold a cuckold!

This seems a nightmare version of Antony's fate—the reflection in a distorting mirror of the thoughts and feelings that course through Antony after Cleopatra's desertion in the disastrous sea-fight.

The group is interrupted in its fortune-telling by the entry of Cleopatra. She is looking for Antony. Her remarks prepare us for the different mood about to establish itself:

> Saw you my lord? . . .
> He was disposed to mirth; but on the sudden
> A Roman thought hath struck him.
>
> (I.ii.86–91)

Antony is heard approaching. Cleopatra immediately goes off. Now that he is coming she will refuse to see him.

When Antony appears he is surrounded by the messengers from Rome and immersed in Roman affairs. He veers savagely to the point of view both of the soldiers in the first scene and 'the common liar' in Rome. Throughout the play this is what marks him off from Cleopatra and makes him a more complex meeting-ground for the opposites than even she is herself. He can understand and respond to the appeal of Rome as much as he can understand and respond to Egypt:

> Speak to me home, mince not the general tongue;
> Name Cleopatra as she's called in Rome;

> Rail thou in Fulvia's phrase; and taunt my faults
> With such full licence as both truth and malice
> Have power to utter. O! then we bring forth weeds
> When our quick winds lie still; and our ills told us
> Is as our earing. Fare thee well awhile . . .
> These strongly Egyptian fetters I must break,
> Or lose myself in dotage.
>
> (I.ii.113–26)

The second messenger brings news of Fulvia's death. It is characteristic of the play that what is hated during life should find favour once it is dead. Later in this scene that is reported to be the case with Pompey in the popular reaction to him:

> our slippery people—
> Whose love is never link'd to the deserver
> Till his deserts are past—begin to throw
> Pompey the great and all his dignities
> Upon his son.
>
> (I.ii.198–202)

This is what happens, too, in Antony's case when, once he is dead, Octavius sings his praises. It also happens when Cleopatra is thought to have committed suicide and Antony flings from vituperation to acclamation almost without pausing. It happens now with Fulvia. Antony says:

> There's a great spirit gone! Thus did I desire it:
> What our contempts do often hurl from us
> We wish it ours again; the present pleasure,
> By revolution lowering, does become
> The opposite of itself: she's good being gone.
> The hand could pluck her back that shov'd her on.
> I must from this enchanting queen break off.
>
> (I.ii.131–37)

Typically, when he joins the general, Enobarbus summons all the counter-arguments. To leave Egypt would be to kill Cleopatra. 'She is cunning,' Antony says, 'past man's thought.' 'Alack, sir, no,' Enobarbus rejoins,

> her passions are made of nothing but the finest part of pure love. We cannot call her winds and waters sighs and tears; they are greater storms and tempests than almanacs can report: this cannot be cunning in her; if it be, she makes a shower of rain as well as Jove.
>
> (I.ii.156–62)

Even if we read Enobarbus's words as irony, the double-irony that works by virtue of the constant ambivalence in the play still turns them back to something approaching the truth: and Cleopatra's real distress and anxiety over Antony's departure have already cut through the scene like a knife. The ding-dong continues:

> ANTONY Would I had never seen her!
> ENOBARBUS O, sir! you had then left unseen a wonderful piece of work.
> ANTONY Fulvia is dead.
> ENOBARBUS Sir?
> ANTONY Fulvia is dead.
> ENOBARBUS Fulvia?
> ANTONY Dead.
> ENOBARBUS Why, sir, give the gods a thankful sacrifice . . . this grief is crown'd with consolation; your old smock brings forth a new petticoat.
>
> (I.ii.163–81)

Antony, however, has made up his mind to go back to Rome.

Antony does go back to Rome—but not in the mood and not with the motives of thorough-going reformation in which he remains at the end of Scene ii. In Scene iii the alchemy of the Shakespearian process is further at work. It works to make Antony do the thing resolved upon but for reasons the very opposite of those which led him to the resolve. The scene of his departure is chosen for Cleopatra's most sincere avowal. Having tormented Antony beyond all bearing she suddenly breaks off with:

> Courteous lord, one word.
> Sir, you and I must part, but that's not it;
> Sir, you and I have loved, but there's not it;
> That you know well: something it is I would—
> O my oblivion is a very Antony
> And I am all forgotten.
>
> (I.iii.86–91)

Antony's final words in the scene almost catch the very idiom of *The Phoenix and the Turtle:*

> Let us go. Come.
> Our separation so abides and flies,
> That thou, residing here, go'st yet with me,
> And I, hence fleeting, here remain with thee.
> Away!
>
> (I.iii.101–05)

It is, so to speak, the honeymoon of the contraries—only possible while the lovers are apart.

III

The first three scenes show how pervasive is that quality in technique and vision which we have called the Shakespearian 'dialectic'. It comes out in single images, it can permeate whole speeches, it governs the build-up inside each scene, it explains the way one scene is related to another. The word 'dialectic', of course, is unfortunately post-Hegelian. The thing we wish to point to, however, in using the word, is Shakespearian. In *Antony and Cleopatra* Shakespeare needs the opposites that merge, unite, and fall apart. They enable him to handle the reality he is writing about—the vast containing opposites of Rome and Egypt, the World and the Flesh.

Rome is the sphere of the political. Shakespeare uses the contraries (long before Blake) to give some sort of rational account of the irrationals there involved. The common people, for example, is 'the common liar'. Antony has already noted that its love is 'never link'd to the deserver till his deserts are past'. Caesar, too, has his own cold knowledge of the same fact:

> It hath been taught us from the primal state
> That he which is was wished until he were;
> And the ebb'd man, ne'er loved till ne'er worth love,
> Comes dear'd by being lack'd. This common body,
> Like to the vagabond flag upon the stream,
> Goes to and back, lackeying the varying tide,
> To rot itself with motion.
>
> (I.iv.41–47)

The great men, however, behave exactly as they say the commons do, too. With Antony, Fulvia becomes dear'd by being lack'd. In Caesar's case it is the same. The threat of Pompey makes him suddenly appreciate the grandeur of Antony's leadership, courage, and endurance. The magnanimous praise of Antony in Act V is only possible because Antony by then is dead. The law is general: judgment is a kind of accommodation to the irrational on reason's part:

> men's judgments are
> A parcel of their fortunes, and things outward
> Do draw the inward quality after them,
> To suffer all alike.
>
> (III.ix.31–34)

Even soldierly 'honour' is rooted in the ambiguous. When Pompey's man mentions his treacherous scheme for disposing of all Pompey's rivals at one blow (the rivals are also Pompey's guests on board ship), Pompey exclaims:

> Ah, this thou should'st have done
> And not have spoken on't. In me 'tis villainy;
> In thee 't had been good service. Thou must know
> 'Tis not my profit that does lead mine honour;
> Mine honour it. Repent that e'er thy tongue

> Hath so betray'd thine act; being done unknown,
> I should have found it afterwards well done,
> But must condemn it now.
>
> (II.vii.80–87)

The law is general because it reflects the nature of the terrene world —the tidal swing of the opposites on which all things balance in a motion that rots them away.

The self-destruction of things that rot with the motion which their own nature and situation dictate is almost obsessive with Shakespeare throughout the play. The political world is the manipulation of the common body they despise by the great men whom the commons can never love until they are safely rid of them. The pattern which remains constant in all the possible groupings is that of open conflict alternating with diseased truce, neither of them satisfactory:

> Equality of two domestic powers
> Breeds scrupulous faction. The hated, grown to strength,
> Are newly grown to love. . . .
> And quietness, grown sick of rest, would purge
> By any desperate change.
>
> (I.iii.47–54)

Compacts between the great men merely represent the temporary sinking of lesser enmities in front of greater:

> lesser enmities give way to greater.
> Were't not that we stand up against them all
> 'Twere pregnant they should square amongst themselves.
>
> (II.i.43–45)

Pompey's is a correct appreciation. It is because of him that Octavius and Antony are reconciled. They will rivet the alliance by means of Antony's marriage to Caesar's sister. Enobarbus knows automatically that this union is a certain way of making conflict ultimately inevitable.

> you shall find the bond that seems to tie their friendship together
> will be the very strangler of their amity.
>
> (II.vi.128–30)

Octavia is one of Shakespeare's minor triumphs in the play, beautifully placed in relation to the main figures and the tenor of their meaning. Her importance is apt to be overlooked unless her careful positioning is noted. Her presence gives a symmetrical form to the main relations of the play. Octavia is the opposite of Cleopatra as Antony is the opposite of Caesar. She is woman made the submissive tool of Roman policy where Cleopatra always strives to make the political subservient to her. (It is the thought of being led in triumph by Caesar as much as the thought of Antony's death which finally decides Cleopatra for suicide.) Where Caesar and Cleopatra are simple and opposite, Octavia—like Antony—is a focal point for the contraries. There is nothing in her as a 'character-study' to account for the effect her presence has. It is rather that she is transparent to the reality behind the play and one of its least mistakable mediators. On the occasions when she appears herself, or when mention is made of her, it is the interfluent life of this reality rather than the personality of its vehicle which fills the scene.

Her first entry is significant. It comes immediately after the triumvirate and Pompey have made their pact. We have just heard the following satiric account of Lepidus's behaviour—and Lepidus, like Octavia, has to stand between the two demi-Atlases:

> AGRIPPA 'Tis a noble Lepidus.
> ENOBARBUS A very fine one. O! how he loves Caesar.
> AGRIPPA Nay, but how dearly he adores Mark Antony.
> ENOBARBUS Caesar? Why, he's the Jupiter of men!
> AGRIPPA What's Antony? the god of Jupiter.
> ENOBARBUS Spake you of Caesar? How, the nonpareil!
> AGRIPPA O Antony! O thou Arabian bird!
> (III.ii.6–12)

Then the triumvirate and Octavia come on. Octavia stirs Antony deeply. But the imagery in which his vision of her is clothed carries us past the person described to the 'varying tide' by which everything in the play is moved:

> Her tongue will not obey her heart, nor can
> Her heart obey her tongue; the swan's down feather
> That stands upon the swell of the full tide
> And neither way inclines.
> (III.ii.47–50)

Octavia never escapes from her position midway between the contraries that maintain and split the world. With Antony away in Athens, her brother first falls on Pompey then finds a pretext to destroy Lepidus. He is now ready to mount his attack on the last remaining rival, his 'competitor in top of all design'. Hearing of it, Octavia cries:

> A more unhappy lady,
> If this division chance, ne'er stood between,
> Praying for both parts. . . .
> . . . Husband win, win brother,
> Prays and destroys the prayer; no midway
> 'Twixt these extremes at all.
> (III.iv.12–20)

Octavia's is the alternative plight to Cleopatra's for womanhood in the play. The choice is merely between alternative methods of destruction—either at one's own hands, or through the agency of the process.

The 'swan's down feather', like the 'vagabond flag', can only swing on the tide until it rots with motion.

Rome is the world of politics and policy. Its supreme term is Octavius Caesar himself. He, like Octavia, must be brought into relation with the pattern which he helps in part to define. Half his significance is lost if he is seen only as a 'character'. In Octavius's case we have aids external to the play which help towards a clear focus on what Shakespeare intends by him. He falls recognizably into Shakespeare's studies of the 'politician'—the series that begins with Richard III and continues down through Edmund.

Octavius is a notable development in the figure which started as a machiavel pure and simple. Shakespeare now betrays no sign of alarm, no hint of revulsion or rejection, almost no trace of emotion in putting him into a story. He is taken completely for granted. He has arrived and he will stay. He is part of the structure of things. He is 'Rome'. In matters of politics and policy it is obvious that only the politicians count: and politics is one half of life. The politician is a perfectly normal person. Given all his own way he would doubtless bring—as Octavius is certain his triumphs eventually will bring—a 'universal peace'. To be normal like him, of course, and to enjoy the peace he offers, two conditions are necessary. First, one must sacrifice the other half of life; then, one must be prepared to make complete submission. By the time Shakespeare comes to depict Octavius he has refined away all the accidentals from the portrait—the diabolism, the rhetoric, the elaborate hypocrisy, the perverse glamour: everything but the essential deadliness and inescapability. Octavius marks an advance on Goneril and Regan. He shares their impatience with tavern and brothel. He has no share in the lust which entraps even them. We might almost doubt whether Octavius has any personal appetite at all, even the lust for power. His plan to lead Cleopatra in triumph has the appearance of a desire for personal satisfaction, but it is more likely that it fits into an impersonal wish on Caesar's part to subdue all things to Rome. Caesar, of course, is Rome—but a kind of impersonal embodiment. He is more like a cold and universal force than a warm-blooded man. He is the perfect commissar, invulnerable as no human being should be. Egypt has no part in his composition.

Caesar has the deceitfulness of the machiavel, but he plays his cards without any flourish. He can rely on his opponents to undo themselves: they are more complicated than he. He puts the deserters from Antony in the van of his own battle:

> Plant those that are revolted in the van,
> That Antony may seem to spend his fury
> Upon himself.
>
> (IV.vi.9–11)

The strength and weakness of those ranged against him constitute Caesar's fifth column. The opposition will rot away or eat the sword it fights with.

It is in the last act that Egypt and Rome confront each other singly, the duplicity of Caesar pitted against the duplicity of Cleopatra. There is no doubt as to who shall survive the contest. The tension is maintained throughout the fifth act only by the doubt left in the spectator's mind right up to the end as to which way Cleopatra will jump: will she accept submission or will she take her own life? The whole play has prepared us for just this doubt. In a sense, whichever way the decision goes it is immaterial. The point of the play is not the decisions taken but the dubieties and ambivalences from which choice springs—the barren choice that only hastens its own negation. Rome, from the nature of things, can admit no compromise. Egypt, equally, can never submit to its contrary. So Cleopatra kills herself.

Cleopatra has been loved by recent commentators not wisely but too well. As Caesar impersonates the World, she, of course, incarnates the Flesh. Part of Shakespeare's sleight of hand in the play—his trickery with our normal standards and powers of judgment—is to construct an account of the human universe consisting of only these two terms. There is no suggestion that the dichotomy is resolvable: unless we are willing to take the delusions of either party as a resolution, the 'universal peace' of Caesar, the Egypt-beyond-the-grave of Antony and Cleopatra in their autotoxic exaltations before they kill themselves.

Cleopatra is the Flesh, deciduous, opulent, and endlessly renewable:

> she did make defect perfection . . .
> Age cannot wither her, nor custom stale
> Her infinite variety; other women cloy
> The appetites they feed, but she makes hungry
> Where most she satisfies; for vilest things
> Become themselves in her, that the holy priests
> Bless her when she is riggish.
>
> (II.ii.239–48)

The Flesh is also the female principle. Cleopatra is Eve, and Woman:

> No more but e'en a woman, and commanded
> By such poor passion as the maid that milks
> And does the meanest chares.
>
> (IV.xiii.73–75)

She is also Circe:

> Let witchcraft join with beauty, lust with both!
>
> (II.i.22)

Shakespeare gives Cleopatra everything of which he is capable except his final and absolute approval. Cleopatra is not an Octavia, much less a Cordelia. The profusion of rich and hectic colour that surrounds her is the colour of the endless cycle of growth and decay, new greenery on old rottenness, the colour of the passions, the wild flaring of life as it burns itself richly away to death so that love of life and greed for death become indistinguishable:

> there is mettle in death which commits some loving act upon
> her, she hath such a celerity in dying.
>
> (I.ii.152–54)

The strength of the case Shakespeare puts against her is undeniable. The soldiers, and Caesar, and Antony when the consciousness of Rome speaks through him, are right, as far as they go. The strength of the case for her is that it is only Rome that condemns her. And Egypt is a force as universal as Rome—as hot as the other is cold, as inevitably self-renewing as the other is inescapably deadly. And the only appeal that can be made in the play is from Egypt to Rome, from Rome to Egypt. And neither of these is final, because between them they have brought down Antony, the 'man of men'.

For the tragedy of *Antony and Cleopatra* is, above all, the tragedy of Antony. His human stature is greater than either Cleopatra's or Caesar's. Yet there is no sphere in which he can express himself except either Rome or Egypt, and to bestride both like a Colossus and keep his balance is impossible. The opposites play through Antony and play with him, and finally destroy him. To Caesar (while Antony is in Egypt, and alive) he is:

> A man who is the abstract of all faults
> That all men follow.
>
> (I.iv.9–10)

To Cleopatra he appears instead a 'heavenly mingle':

> Be'st thou sad or merry,
> The violence of either thee becomes,
> So it does no man else.
>
> (I.v.59–61)

When she sees him returning safe from the battlefield she cries:

> O infinite virtue! Com'st thou smiling from
> The world's great snare uncaught?
>
> (IV.viii.17–18)

After he is dead she remembers him as a kind of Mars:

> His face was as the heavens, and therein stuck
> A sun and moon, which kept their course, and lighted
> This little O, the earth . . .
> His legs bestrid the ocean; his rear'd arm
> Crested the world; his voice was propertied

As all the tuned spheres, and that to friends;
But when he meant to quail and shake the orb,
He was as rattling thunder. For his bounty,
There was no winter in't, an autumn 'twas
That grew the more by reaping; his delights
Were dolphin-like, they show'd his back above
The element they lived in; in his livery
Walk'd crowns and crownets, realms and islands were
As plates dropped from his pocket . . .
. . . Nature wants stuff
To vie strange forms with fancy, yet t'imagine
An Antony were nature's piece 'gainst fancy,
Condemning shadows quite.
(V.ii.79–99)

This, of course, is again the past catching fire from the urgent needs of the present, flaring in memory and imagination as it never did in actuality. Antony is nothing so unambiguous as this. The most judicious account of him is that of Lepidus when he is replying to Caesar's strictures:

I must not think there are
Evils enow to darken all his goodness:
His faults in him seem as the spots of heaven,
More fiery by night's blackness; hereditary
Rather than purchased, what he cannot change
Than what he chooses.
(I.iv.10–15)

Here the ambiguities of the play's moral universe get their completest expression: faults shine like stars, the heaven is black, the stars are spots. Ambivalence need go no further.

IV

The earlier criticism of *Antony and Cleopatra* tended to stress the downfall of the soldier in the middle-aged infatuate. More recent criticism has seen the play as the epiphany of the soldier in the lover, and the reassurance of all concerned that death is not the end. In the view that has been put forward here neither of these is right. The meaning of *Antony and Cleopatra* is in the Shakespearian 'dialectic'—in the deliquescent reality that expresses itself through the contraries.

Antony and Cleopatra swims with glamour. Once we lose sight of the controlling structure of the opposites which holds the play together we are at the mercy of any random selection from its occasions. And occasions abound—moments, opinions, moods, speeches, characters, fragments of situation, forked mountains and blue promontories, imposed upon us with all the force of a 'giant power'. It is, then, eminently understandable that critics should succumb like Antony or hold aloof like Demetrius and Philo.

The Roman condemnation of the lovers is obviously inadequate. The sentimental reaction in their favour is equally mistaken. There is no so-called 'love-romanticism' in the play. The flesh has its glory and passion, its witchery. Love in *Antony and Cleopatra* is both these. The love of Antony and Cleopatra, however, is not asserted as a 'final value'. The whole tenour of the play, in fact, moves in an opposite direction. Egypt is the Egypt of the biblical glosses: exile from the spirit, thraldom to the flesh-pots, diminution of human kindness. To go further still in sentimentality and claim that there is a 'redemption' motif in Antony and Cleopatra's love is an even more violent error. To the Shakespeare who wrote *King Lear* it would surely smack of blasphemy. The fourth and fifth acts of *Antony and Cleopatra* are not epiphanies. They are the ends moved to by that process whereby things rot themselves with motion—unhappy and bedizened and sordid, streaked with the mean, the ignoble, the contemptible. Shakespeare may have his plays in which 'redemption' is a theme (and I think he has), but *Antony and Cleopatra* is not one of them.

Antony and Cleopatra is an account of things in terms of the World and the Flesh, Rome and Egypt, the two great contraries that maintain and destroy each other, considered apart from any third sphere which might stand over against them. How is it related to the plays of the 'great period', the period which comes to an end with *King Lear?*

The clue is given, I think, in the missing third term. *Antony and Cleopatra* is the deliberate construction of a world without a Cordelia, Shakespeare's symbol for a reality that transcends the political and the personal and

> redeems nature from the general curse
> Which twain have brought her to.
> (*King Lear,* IV.vi.211–12)

One must call the construction deliberate, because after *King Lear* there can be no doubt that Shakespeare knew exactly where he was in these matters. Both *Antony and Cleopatra* and *Coriolanus* follow North's Plutarch without benefit of clergy. Both Antony and Coriolanus were cited by the sixteenth-century moralists as notable examples of heathen men who lacked patience—the one committing suicide, the other rebelling against his country. In *Antony and Cleopatra* suicide is the general fate of those who wish to die. Cleopatra gives the audience a conscious reminder of the un-Christian ethos involved:

> All's but naught;
> Patience is sottish, and impatience does
> Become a dog that's mad: then is it sin
> To rush into the secret house of death
> Ere death dare come to us?
> (IV.xiii.78–82)

The Christian world-view in Shakespeare's time turned round a number of conceptions which were covered by the Elizabethans in their examination of the meanings of 'Nature'. The theme of 'Nature' runs through the whole of *Macbeth, King Lear,* and *Timon.* Its absence from *Antony and Cleopatra* suggests Shakespeare's satisfaction that for him the theme is exhausted. He is inwardly free now to look at a classical story, deliberately excise the Christian core of his thought, and make up his account of what then remains over.

This explains the effect, I think, of *Antony and Cleopatra.* Freedom from the compulsive theme of the Natures, the conscious security gained from having given it final expression, enabled Shakespeare to handle something new and something which was bound to be intrinsically simpler. Part of the energy absorbed in grappling with theme now bestows itself on technique. *Antony and Cleopatra* gives the impression of being a technical *tour de force* which Shakespeare enjoyed for its own sake.

The excision also explains, I think, the tone of the play—the sense of ripe-rottenness and hopelessness, the vision of self-destruction, the feeling of strenuous frustration and fevered futility, that which finds its greatest expression in Antony's speech before he gives himself his death-blow:

> Now
> All length is torture; since the torch is out,
> Lie down and stray no further. Now all labour
> Mars what it does; yea, very force entangles
> Itself with strength; seal then, and all is done.
> (IV.xii.45–49)

The excision, finally, explains what might be regarded as a diminution of scope in *Antony and Cleopatra.* (We are, of course, only comparing Shakespeare with himself.) The theme of Rome and Egypt, however, is simpler than the theme of 'Nature', the trick of using the contraries (again, for Shakespeare) relatively an easy way of organizing the universe. It is unusual, at any rate, for Shakespeare to rely on one trick so completely as he seems to do in *Antony and Cleopatra.* At times we are almost tempted to believe he has fallen a victim of habitual mannerism.

One last comment might be made. We referred at the beginning of this chapter to Shakespeare's surprising capacity for self-renewal. *Antony and Cleopatra* is not the aftermath of Lear in any pejorative sense. There is something in it that is new and exciting and profound. Shakespeare remained still the youngest as the greatest of his contemporaries. In *Antony and Cleopatra* he is making his own adjustments to the new Jacobean tastes. The play is Shakespeare's study of Mars and Venus—the presiding deities of Baroque society, painted for us again and again on the canvasses of his time. It shows us Virtue, the root of the heroic in man, turned merely into *virtu,* the warrior's art, and both of them ensnared in the world, very force entangling itself with strength. It depicts the 'man of men' soldiering for a cynical Rome or whoring on furlough in a reckless Egypt. It is the tragedy of the destruction of man, the creative spirit, in perverse war and insensate love—the two complementary and opposed halves of a discreating society.

THE ROMANCES

The Last Plays of Shakespeare

D. A. Traversi

Though *Antony and Cleopatra*—with *Coriolanus*—is the last of the great tragedies, it does not represent the last stage in the artist's development. It was followed by a series of plays, written apparently between 1608 and 1611 (*Pericles, Cymbeline, The Winter's Tale,* and *The Tempest*), which are closely related to one another in theme and represent an effort to give artistic form to a new symbolic conception. At the heart of each of these plays, present in various forms but clearly responding to a definite continuity of purpose, lies an organic relationship between breakdown and reconstruction, the divisions created in the most intimate human bonds (and more especially in the unity of the family) by the action of time and passion and the final healing of these divisions. Near the opening of each play—even in *Cymbeline,* where the treatment of the central theme is partially obscured—a father loses his offspring through the excess of his own passion-driven folly; the main action is devoted, though again with less than complete clarity in *Cymbeline,* to the suffering and remorse which follow from this mutual estrangement, and—at the end of the play—the lost child (properly a daughter whose name has clear symbolic associations: Marina in *Pericles,* Perdita in *The Winter's Tale,* and Miranda in *The Tempest*) is restored to her father's blessing and becomes an instrument of reconciliation. In these plots the harmonizing theme first attempted in *King Lear,* and there broken by the prevailing tragic emotion, produces a symbolic conception of drama completely removed from realism and scarcely paralleled in English literature.

From *The Age of Shakespeare,* ed. Boris Ford. Reprinted by permission of Penguin Books, Ltd.

It is important to realize from the first that the type of symbolism to be observed in these comedies, far from representing an imposition of abstract conceptions, is above all a natural extension of the qualities of Shakespeare's mature verse. This is already apparent in the type of poetry normally associated with Cordelia in the later scenes of *King Lear,* of which the Gentleman's account of her sorrow is perhaps especially typical. As he puts it:

> . . . patience and sorrow strove
> Who should express her goodliest. You have seen
> Sunshine and rain at once: her smiles and tears
> Were like a better way: those happy smilets
> That play'd on her ripe lip seem'd not to know
> What guests were in her eyes: which parted thence
> As pearls from diamonds dropp'd. In brief,
> Sorrow would be a rarity most beloved,
> If all could so become it.
>
> (IV.iii)

The logic of this passage is clearly not that of factual description. Few of the comparisons used to convey the quality of the queen's grief have any direct visual connexion with the scene described: 'sunshine and rain', 'ripe lip', 'guests', 'pearls', and 'diamonds' are all connected with one another and with Cordelia less as visible attributes than as expressions of the sense of value, conveyed through intimations of richness and fertility, which they impart. It is this sense, pervadingly present, which imposes unity upon apparently conflicting elements. The struggle between the queen and her passions is a strife between two emotions—'patience' and 'sorrow'—equally natural and worthy, each contributing, beyond the conflict, to a 'goodly' expression of her nature. Her behaviour, in fact, is so normal in its spontaneity that it reflects the balance of nature in 'sunshine' and 'rain', leading up to the single harmonious effect which presents itself as 'a better way', an indication of possible redemption; and this, in turn, causes us to feel no surprise when 'happy smilets' make their appearance, just after, as indicative of Cordelia's mood. 'Sunshine and rain', moreover, by a different thread of imagery, leads directly to the suggestion, in 'ripe', of the maturing crops, and 'guests' hints at the bounty which expresses itself in hospitality; and the prevailing sense of the whole passage is gathered up in the further phrase 'pearls from diamonds dropp'd'. These are 'rarities', and sorrow itself thus borne is less a tragic manifestation of weakness than a rarity enriching human nature, part of a harmony calling for its external manifestation less in continued exposure to suffering than in the symbol of healing reconciliation.

Poetry of this type, indeed, naturally calls for a parallel development of the normal conceptions of dramatic plot. To the exigencies of verse freed from the narrower limitations of realism, action fittingly responds by becoming itself fully symbolic, an extension or extra vehicle of the poetry. The symbolic form, indeed, is attempted in *King Lear,* and maintains itself with overpowering poignancy for the duration of the scene (IV.vii) in which Cordelia kneels for the blessing of her newly awakened father and receives from him, in return, his request for forgiveness. Not until the final comedies, however, is this symbolic conception of plot consistently extended to cover whole plays; and even there the development of a fresh conception of the relationship between verse and its dramatic vehicle was not achieved in a single stage. The first experiment in the new form, *Pericles, Prince of Tyre,* is perhaps best regarded as the work of an inferior author in which Shakespeare detected the presence, beneath obvious inequalities, of a significant symbolic pattern and to which he contributed, at moments of special interest, the expression of his own highly personal conceptions. If this be a true account of the play —and there are moments when the separation of the primitive foundations from the distinctively Shakespearian passages is admittedly difficult to maintain[1]—we can regard Pericles, when the play opens, as embarked upon a pilgrimage in search of true happiness; his appeal before Antiochus (I.i) is to the 'gods that made me man and sway in love', who have inflamed in his breast the desire 'to taste the fruit of yon celestial tree', and his reaction to the King's ambiguous warning is an affirmation of deepened moral understanding:

> Antiochus, I thank thee, who hath taught
> My frail mortality to know itself.

Driven by the discovery of hidden evil to abandon his first dream of felicity, Pericles is exposed to a variety of experiences which, crudely expressed as they often are, can be interpreted as representing various stages in moral growth. The anger of the tyrant, aroused by the discovery of his incestuous secret, obliges him to leave his kingdom, exposing him first to penury and then to a storm which, as in so many of Shakespeare's later plays, reflects the hero's subjection to tragedy. In the storm, and through the action of three Fishermen, he recovers the armour bequeathed to him by his father, an incident (II.i) itself capable of bearing a symbolic interpretation; and, once more clothed in it as his defence, he wins in tournament the hand of Thaisa, daughter of Simonides of Pentapolis. With the consummation of their marriage the first part of a play so far remarkably uneven, not to say imperfect, is complete.

The rest of the tragedy brings us, beyond all reasonable doubt, into contact with Shakespeare's first attempt to develop the theme of symbolic reconciliation which is our main concern. With Pericles

---

[1] The argument against divided authorship in both *Pericles* and *Cymbeline* has been most forcibly stated by G. Wilson Knight in *The Crown of Life* (1947) and elsewhere.

exposed to a storm at sea which he expressly ascribes to the will of the 'gods' (III.i), and with the death, on board ship and in childbirth, of his wife, the true sense of the action at last becomes clear. Thaisa, dying through exposure to the elements, bequeaths her husband on her death-bed a living continuation of herself ('this piece of your dead queen'), and Pericles hails the event in words in which stress and calm, tragedy and following peace, are significantly blended:

> Now, mild may be thy life!
> For a more blustrous birth had never babe:
> Quiet and gentle thy conditions! for
> Thou art the rudeliest welcome to this world
> That ever was prince's[2] child. Happy what follows!
> Thou hast as chiding a nativity
> As fire, air, water, earth and heaven can make,
> To herald thee from the womb.
>
> (III.i)

The balance of contrasted images here is at once unmistakably Shakespearian, a product of the same imagination as that which conceived Cordelia's regal grief, and an indication of the point reached at this stage in the symbolic pattern. Pericles prays that the 'mildness' of his daughter's life may compensate for the unprecedented 'blustrous' conditions of her birth, the future hope of a 'quiet and gentle' environment for the 'rudeliest welcome' to the world which she has undergone at the moment of her begetting. Behind the more superficial aspects of this prayer for peace lies the characteristic Shakespearian intuition of subsistent continuity, the sense that birth and death, tempest and following calm, are in reality related aspects of a single process to which the elements themselves—'fire, air, water', and even 'earth and heaven'—are, in their universal presence, witnesses. Thus imaginatively supported and given poetic substance, the episode, which at once looks back to the sufferings of Pericles in his pilgrimage (of which it is the consummation) and anticipates the birth of a new and deeper understanding, becomes the pivot or turning-point of the whole action.

The rest of *Pericles,* indeed, simply develops in highly individual poetic terms the conception thus introduced into the action. It is essentially in terms of the poetry that the symbolic plan is given life, artistic validity. The new-born child grows into Pericles' daughter Marina, who is left by her father with Cleon at Tarsus and exposed through the jealousy of Dionyza to tragedy in the brothel-scenes (IV. ii.v.vi) which—inferior though they are in sentiment and execution—clearly belong, like so much else that fails to give full satisfaction in this play, to the developing pattern. Thaisa, meanwhile, whom her

[2] 'princess'? The text is in doubt here.

husband thinks dead, is cast ashore at Ephesus and restored to life by the beneficent wisdom of Cerimon 'to make the world twice rich' (III.ii). The time to restore her to her husband, however, has not yet come. Before this can be, Pericles himself has to complete a long period of exposure to sorrow until Marina is ready to play her part as the instrument of reconciliation; the resurrection of Thaisa needs to be balanced by the moral rebirth of Pericles, itself brought about by the child of his own blood. When the time is at last ripe (V.i), the restoration of harmony is conveyed step by step through a subtle blend of dramatic action and poetic imagery. Pericles appears on board ship, curtained from the sight of onlookers and so cut off, in a sense, from a world which he has decided in his sorrow to abandon. Marina, still unaware that she is in her father's presence, goes in to him to exercise her healing gifts and, quickened by a sense whose true meaning is still hidden from him, he breaks into renewed speech and finally salutes her in terms that carry yet a step further the spirit of poetic symbolism in which all this part of the play is steeped:

> I am great with woe, and shall deliver weeping.
> My dearest wife was like this maid, and such a one
> My daughter might have been: my queen's square brows;
> Her stature to an inch; as wand-like straight;
> As silver-voic'd; her eyes as jewel-like,
> And cas'd as richly; in pace another Juno;
> Who starves the ears she feeds, and makes them hungry,
> The more she gives them speech.
>
> (V.i)

Pericles' opening words, balanced between contrary emotions, indicate fittingly that his past grief has been, spiritually speaking, fertile and introduce once more the birth-theme with which so much of the play is steeped. The physical birth in the tempest is, in fact, at last opening into its counterpart in the spiritual order. What is in process of being born, under the revival of poignant past memories, is now expressed as a new vision of humanity restored to a stature almost divine. In the healing figure of Marina are re-born the 'square brows' of Thaisa, her perfect carriage, her 'silver voice' and 'jewel-like' eyes (the epithets, with their indication of infinite riches, recall those formerly used to indicate the quality of Cordelia's royal grief) and, above all, the 'pace' of Juno, the queen of the gods; and to round off the transforming splendour of the description, her utterance is such that it gives sustenance without surfeit (she 'starves the ears she feeds') and, as it nourishes her hearers, makes them 'hungry' for further speech. Almost all the recurrent themes of Shakespeare's symbolic imagery are here gathered together into a vision of life re-born, exalted in 'grace'.

The conclusion of the play is simply a rounding-off, in the light of this reborn splendour and in terms of imagery superbly rich and tender, of the dramatic situation. Pericles, having persuaded himself that the girl before him is indeed, in spite of the veneration she has roused in him, 'flesh and blood', asks her to explain the significance of her name; she replies with the revelation, full of meaning in its double associations of past suffering and providential preservation, that she was 'born at sea'. From this discovery to the declaration of her mother's death is but a step, a step, however, which leads in turn to the full overflow of Pericles' pent-up emotions and, at last, to the explicit statement of the central symbol:

> O, come hither,
> Thou that begett'st him that did thee beget;
> Thou that wast born at sea, buried at Tarsus,
> And found at sea again!
>
> (V.i)

Pericles, 'reborn' to life, a second time 'begotten' through the saving action of his own daughter, now puts on 'fresh garments' and calls for the music that is, here as in all these final plays, the expression of harmony restored. Thus clad, and after his sorrow has been, like Lear's, soothed in sleep, he makes his way to the temple at Ephesus to be restored to the wife whom he had lost. The restoration takes place to the echo, repeated for the last time, of the two basic conceptions of the play: that of the organic relationship that unites birth and death, both related to their origin in exposure to the elements—

> . . . did you not name a tempest,
> A birth, and death?—

and that of the sacred continuity of the family, re-created in the sea and now restored in the flesh to be given its full religious sanction:

> Look, who kneels here! Flesh of thy flesh, Thaisa:
> Thy burden at the sea, and call'd Marina
> For she was yielded there.

With filial love once more responding, by kneeling, to paternal blessing, the family unity temporarily shattered by tempest and the action of time is restored in deepened understanding and enriched by spiritual splendour.

The second play of this period, *Cymbeline,* though without the disconcerting crudities of the early scenes of *Pericles,* is in some ways a less interesting piece. More closely connected with the fashionable dramatic convention of the moment, which called for sentiment and a glorification of the simple life on lines popularized by John Fletcher, it none the less shows Shakespeare attempting—with partial success—to use these conventions for his own purposes. The theme of loss and reconciliation, though less clearly defined than in *Pericles,* is present in the new story. Cymbeline loses his children, Guiderius and Arviragus, whose place at court falls to Cloten through the machinations of his twice-married queen; they are exposed for long years to the simplicities, crude but noble, of the primitive life under the charge of the banished Belarius, and finally return to their father's embrace. Thus restored to civilized life, they bring with them the virtues of barbaric honesty which are henceforth to be integrated into the order of true courtliness.

That order is introduced into the play, and related in turn to the master-theme of loss and gain, through yet another story of division and exposure to trial, that of Imogen and Posthumus. In the treatment of this second action, which derives equally with the first from Cymbeline's primary error of judgement in his second marriage, Shakespeare's language comes to life in a way that distinguishes the play decisively from the sentimental conceptions of Fletcher. The clash of loyalties occasioned by Imogen's forced betrothal to Cloten is given a definite universality of context in the opening words of the play:

> . . . our bloods
> No more obey the heavens than our courtiers
> Still seem as does the king.

Against the background of concord which thus relates the observation of courtly 'degree' to the operation of the 'heavens', the arbitrary act of the monarch, occasioned by the blindness of the passion that binds him to his second wife, produces in his subjects an underlying sense of profound disquiet. First indicated, perhaps, indirectly in 'seem', it is openly expressed a little later in the First Gentleman's assertion that

> . . . not a courtier,
> Although they wear their faces to the bent
> Of the king's looks, hath a heart that is not
> Glad at the thing they scowl at.

The linguistic quality of this passage, with its suggestion in 'wear their faces' of the masking of true sentiment and the conflict of natural feeling and duty implied in the contrast between 'glad' and 'scowl at', indicates the prevailing state of moral dislocation. The opening invocation of harmony serves as background to a condition, if not of open rebellion, at least of profound uneasiness. This uneasiness, implying as it does a disturbance of the bond which binds individual conduct to the functioning of the cosmic order, has its part to play in the complete conception. The return to normality through the integration of natural simplicity and true courtly virtue, and the subordination of both to a higher loyalty, is the true theme of *Cymbeline.*

In accordance with this general plan, Imogen's repudiation of the uncouth pretensions of Cloten, whose supposed courtliness can only be acceptable to Cymbeline's passion-distorted vision, implies her choice of a superior conception of humanity, at once supremely natural and deeply civilized. This conception inspires the opening description of Posthumus, whom the king formerly endowed with

> . . . all the learnings that his time
> Could make him the receiver of; which he took,
> As we do air, fast as 't was minist'red;
> And in's spring became a harvest; liv'd in court—
> Which rare it is to do—most prais'd, most lov'd;
> A sample to the youngest; to th' more mature
> A glass that feated them; and to the graver
> A child that guided dotards.
>
> (I.i)

The virtues thus celebrated in Posthumus are those of true courtliness, fostered by a 'learning' imbibed as naturally as air and proceeding, in the normal course of youthful development, to its spontaneous 'harvest'. In a world in which true virtue is indeed rare, he has become an example to all ages and conditions, a mirror of the finer human qualities which Imogen, in loving him, has appreciated at their proper worth.

The 'rarity' of this example, indeed, is emphasized first by contrast with the aristocratic pretensions of Cloten—a court parody of the truly 'natural' man, enslaved to the prompting of his own passions—and later by the success which attends the cynical intrigues of Iachimo. To the latter, apparently dispassionate but in reality enslaved to his own sensuality, true virtue is inconceivable. In his attack upon Imogen, the overflow of physical imagery, product of

> . . . the cloyed will,
> That satiate yet unsatisfied desire, that tub
> Both fill'd and running,
>
> (I.vi)

is at once intense and deeply repellent; this is a speaker to whose cynical intelligence passion seems sterile, even disgusting, but to whom no limiting conception of value is conceivable as a check to the senseless operations of desire. It is his resentment against the physical embodiment of such a conception in Imogen that causes him to intrigue against her chastity. She repels, easily enough, his direct assault, but is powerless to meet the guile by which he steals from her in sleep the 'proof' of his conquest; and as a result of her defencelessness she is faced, not only with the passionate resentment of her father, but with the anger of the disillusioned Posthumus.

At this point, and as a result of their common expulsion from the so-called civilized world, the story of the two lovers meets that of the lost sons of Cymbeline in a common exposure to 'nature'. They, in their discussion with their father (III.iii), balance a realization of the advantages of the simple life against their sense of its limitations; on the one hand:

> Haply this life is best,
> If quiet life be best,

on the other, Arviragus acknowledges himself to be 'beastly' and feels his limitations as a prison:

> . . . our cage
> We make a quire, as doth the prison'd bird,
> And sing our bondage freely.

Simplicity has limitations of its own, freedom under conditions of primitive life involves the 'bondage' of the higher, specifically civilized faculties. These will only be awakened in Cymbeline's sons when they are restored to free loyalty and to a proper relationship with the father they have lost.

The theme thus indicated is scarcely consistently developed in the play. It seems clear, however, that the 'death' of Imogen (IV.ii) is part of the symbolism of the conception. It implies a certain liberation, fittingly expressed in the dirge over her dead body:

> Fear no more the frown o' th' great,
> Thou art past the tyrant's stroke,
> (IV.ii)

and to it corresponds the captivity of Posthumus and the tone of his meditations in prison:

> Most welcome, bondage! for thou art a way,
> I think, to liberty.
> (V.iv)

Both, in their spirit of tempered acceptance, are proper preludes to the battle in which Posthumus and the sons of Cymbeline alike find their proper place, fighting against the foreign invader in the orbit of patriotism and in devotion, respectively, to their king and father. The play ends on the familiar note of reconciliation, coupled with an ample gesture of thanksgiving. To the Soothsayer's declaration of the relevance of supernatural purpose:

> The fingers of the pow'rs above do tune
> The harmony of this peace—

Cymbeline, restored to true self-knowledge and to his position as royal symbol of unity, replies with a gesture of forgiveness and a final offering of thanks:

> Laud we the gods;
> And let our crooked smokes climb to their nostrils
> From our blest altars.
>
> (V.v)

In this vision of consecration to a unifying purpose, the personal issues of the play, the love of Imogen for Posthumus maintained through trials and the integration of natural simplicity with the civilized graces, find in subjection to Cymbeline, as father and king, their proper sublimation.

To pass from *Pericles* and *Cymbeline* to *The Winter's Tale* is to leave the field of experiment for that of finished achievement. The play is less, in fact, an ordinary 'comedy', even of the type of *Twelfth Night* or *A Midsummer Night's Dream,* than a construction approaching the *ballet* form, a strictly formal creation in which music plays an important though subsidiary part, and in which the main effects are achieved by the use of subtly interrelated poetic imagery. Its plot is perfectly adjusted to the new symbolic technique, and it is useful—if only to get away from the idea of realistic drama—to see its various stages as the successive movements, differing in feeling and tempo, which go to make up the unity of a symphony. In accordance with this conception, the 'first movement' would deal with the tragic break-up of existing unity through the passionate folly of one man. Leontes and Polixenes, respectively kings of Sicily and Bohemia (here clearly countries of the imagination), open the play as life-long friends; but from the moment of their first appearance, their friendship contains seeds of division. Their 'affection', as we are told in Camillo's opening remarks, 'cannot choose but branch now', and they have 'shook hands, as over a vast; and embrac'd, as it were, from the ends of opposed winds'. The threat of tragedy thus veiled in the apparent celebration of their unity soon takes shape in the passionate, jealous conviction of Leontes that Polixenes has replaced him in the affections of his wife Hermione.

This division, which Shakespeare makes no attempt to render psychologically probable, is clearly not to be explained in terms of mere realism. It is, in a very real sense, symbolic, indicative of a possibility universally present in the human make-up, and its nature is made clear in the course of Polixenes' account of the foundations upon which his friendship with Leontes had rested. 'We were', he exclaims,

> Two lads that thought there was no more behind
> But such a day to-morrow as to-day,

And to be boy eternal . . .
We were as twinn'd lambs that did frisk i' th' sun,
And bleat the one at th' other; we knew not
The doctrine of ill-doing, no, nor dream'd
That any did.

(I.ii)

The friendship between the two kings, which dates from childhood, has rested, in other words, on the youthful state of innocence; based on a sentimental ignoring of the reality of time, it originally assumed that it was possible to remain 'boy eternal'. The realities of human nature, however, make this impossible. Boyhood is necessarily a state of transition. Time corrupts those unprepared to oppose its action with a corresponding moral effort, and youthful innocence, left to itself, falls fatally under the shadow of the 'doctrine of ill-doing'. Only through a conscious reaction to tragedy, and the consequent acceptance of deeper experience, can this idyllic state of childlike acceptance grow into an independent, conscious maturity.

In particular, and as a potent factor in separating the mature man from his childhood, time brings a capacity for sensual passion which may be good, if it leads to its natural fulfilment in the creative unity of the family, or evil and destructive, in the form of egoism and its consequences, jealousy overcoming all restraint of reason. In Leontes, it is the evil impulse which comes to the surface, destroying his friendship with Polixenes and leading him to turn upon his saintly wife Hermione with animal intensity of feeling. His sexual passion, in other words, thrusts reason aside, expressing itself in phrases as intense as they are broken and incoherent:

It is a bawdy planet, that will strike
Where 't is predominant . . .

(I.ii)

No barricado for a belly . . .

(I.ii)

I have drunk, and seen the spider.

(II.i)

Like Othello, Leontes refuses to listen to the restraining advice of those around him; his refusal is an essential part of his symbolic function as incarnation of the spirit of unreason. Moved by it, he condemns his new-born child, first to death, then to abandonment, and his wife to prison without pausing to wait—so sure is he in his madness of the justice of his proceeding—for the sentence, previously invoked, of the divine oracle. That sentence, when it comes, proves Hermione to have been innocent; but meanwhile she has died—or so

Leontes believes—of grief, his son has been lost, and his friendship with Polixenes has been shattered beyond all apparent remedy. The first movement of destruction and disintegration is complete with Leontes' broken confession of guilt: 'Apollo's angry; and the heavens themselves / Do strike at my injustice' (III.ii).

The 'second movement', although very short, contains the turning-point which is, in all these plays, an essential feature of the symbolic structure. It opens (III.iii) in a storm which carries on, symbolically speaking, the idea of the divine displeasure and is treated, poetically, in a manner that recalls *Pericles.* As in the earlier play, the evocation of tempest serves as a background to the idea of birth; when the peasant who has witnessed the hurricane describes the drowning of a ship's crew in the angry seas, his father replies by showing in his arms a newly found child—the child, in fact, of Leontes—adding, in words that echo a similarly crucial utterance in *Pericles,* 'thou mettest with things dying, I with things newborn'. The significance of the discovery thus placed at the centre of the play is abundantly clear. The child, born of Leontes' imperfect passion, has none the less no share in the responsibility for his sin; born in tempest and looking forward to future calm, she connects the tragic past with the restored harmony of the future and becomes the instrument of reconciliation.

Before this reconciliation can begin to take shape in the 'third' movement, however, we have to pass over sixteen years. Leontes' daughter then reappears as Perdita (like Marina before her, symbolically named) and meets Florizel, the disguised son of Polixenes, at the rustic sheep-shearing organized by her supposed 'father', the shepherd who discovered her as a baby in the storm. Their love, according to the prevailing pattern of these comedies, is to be the means of reconciling their estranged parents; but the time is not yet ripe for this resolution, because their feeling for one another is still too youthful and immature, still insufficiently tempered by contact with reality. In one of the most revealing speeches of the play, Perdita, as she offers her pastoral flowers to Florizel, describes her feeling for him in terms of Spring, flowering after the long winter of discontent:

> O Proserpina,
> For the flowers now, that, frighted, thou let'st fall
> From Dis's waggon! daffodils,
> That come before the swallow dares, and take
> The winds of March with beauty; violets, dim
> But sweeter than the lids of Juno's eyes
> Or Cytherea's breath; pale primroses,
> That die unmarried, ere they can behold
> Bright Phoebus in his strength,—a malady
> Most incident to maids; bold oxlips and
> The crown imperial.
>
> (IV.iv)

Beautiful as the speech is and for all its conclusiveness as a sign that the spring of reconciliation has dawned, the love it expresses still lacks the necessary maturity which only experience can provide. The emphasis laid, in the imagery, upon Spring, that is upon birth, inexperience, virginity, is subtly balanced by an implicit sense of death; the flowers to which Perdita refers are 'pale' and 'dim'; they 'die unmarried', in unfulfilled promise, having failed to 'behold Phoebus in his strength'. Like the friendship of Polixenes and Leontes, this is an emotion which, in so far as it is unprepared to meet the challenge implied in the passage of time, is destined to die.

Florizel's reply in turn expresses, with at least equal beauty, a similar desire to live outside time, to hold up the course of mutability in a way that is ultimately impossible. When he says to Perdita:

> . . . when you do dance, I wish you
> A wave o' th' sea, that you might ever do
> Nothing but that,

his emotion, though expressed in language and rhythm that are perfect in their very simplicity, is still nostalgic, still an attempt to evade the pressure of mutability, to escape from the problems presented by maturity into a permanent dream of first love. The conclusion is, inevitably, the same as that implied in Perdita's speech. The meeting of the lovers is a sign that Spring has been born, indeed, out of Winter tragedy; but Spring needs still to pass over into the Summer which is its fulfilment, otherwise it must, in the very nature of things, wither. In terms of the dramatic action which concerns us, the spring-like beauty of this love is not yet mature; in order to become so, it needs to be reinforced by the deeply spiritual penitence of Leontes. That is why, at this moment of idyllic celebration, Polixenes enters to cast across it the shadow of aged, impotent anger, taking away his son, threatening Perdita with torture, and falling himself into something very like Leontes' sin. A final meeting at the court of Sicilia must precede the final reconciliation.

Enough has been said to show that this great pastoral scene plays a far more important part in the symbolic structure of *The Winter's Tale* than would appear if we regard it as no more than a splendid piece of decorative make-believe. Besides developing, in terms of highly subtle poetry, the theme of spiritual integration analysed above, it also introduces into the developing pattern a note of special relevance, so to call it, already experimented with in *Cymbeline*. In pastoral Bohemia, as in primitive Britain, there exists a powerful contrast between court sophistication and the simple life. Perdita is especially forthright on this subject. When Polixenes, with his sneering description of her as 'worthy enough a herdsman', accuses her of enticing Florizel to debase himself and threatens her with torture, her reply is a frank acceptance of the implied challenge:

> I was not much afeard; for once or twice
> I was about to speak, and tell him plainly,
> The selfsame sun that shines upon his court
> Hides not his visage from our cottage, but
> Looks on alike.
>
> (IV.iv)

Once again, however, Shakespeare's aim is not contrast but integration. The good life is not to be fully attained in pastoral abstraction, although many of its elements may be present in this idyllic form: nor is court life, if by that we mean a civilized social existence subject to natural loyalties and based on the recognition of the deepest ties of blood, necessarily corrupt or debased. The virtues of the one need to be infused into the graces of the other; that is why, when all the characters of the play converge upon Leontes' court for the final clarification before 'the queen's picture', a subsidiary place is found (V.ii) for the Shepherd and Clown who, by the very fact of their having discovered and reared Perdita, have their own claim to participation in the complete pattern. Before this, their last appearance before Leontes' palace, it is true that they have been unmercifully scarified by Autolycus—who represents in this play something very like the forces of wayward human anarchy, and whom Shakespeare throws in, as it were, with an inconsequential but profoundly human gesture, lest his conception should seem too perfectly, abstractly balanced—but the fact remains that they *do* arrive, and that the Clown's gently ironic comment on social pretensions—'So we wept—and there was the first gentleman-like tears that ever we shed'—throws, from its particular angle of simplicity, a light of its own upon the entire situation.

The final resolution, towards which the whole play has been tending, is the work of the fourth and last 'movement'. We return, after a gap of sixteen years, to Leontes, whose courtiers have been urging him to marry again. The bond of wedlock, and its fulfilment in the shape of heirs, is repeatedly stressed as an essential factor in *The Winter's Tale*. The sanctity of Hermione has been from the first closely bound-up with reverence for her motherhood; this connexion was most intimately expressed in the spirit of the comments on her pregnancy made by her two attendant Ladies to the young Mamillius:

> FIRST LADY The queen your mother rounds apace . . .
> SECOND LADY She is spread of late
> Into a *goodly* bulk; *good time* encounter her.
>
> (II.i)

The adjectives underline the presence in Hermione of a beneficent and creative fertility. Now, in the arguments addressed to Leontes by his courtiers, the natural fulfilment of the marriage-tie is associated with the royal craving for an heir. Leontes' own attitude is a delicate blend of apparently contrary emotions. Bound by 'saint-like sorrow', a repentance for past errors which the memory of Hermione's virtue keeps alive in him, he none the less shares the universal desire for an *heir* as fulfilment, as manifestation of the natural fertility of which his sin has deprived him. These two strains of feeling are, indeed, bound together by the supreme fact of his situation. The child he so intensely desires can only be born of Hermione, whom he believes to be dead: can only, therefore, be the very daughter whom, in his past folly, he condemned to die.

At last, however, Leontes has repented enough. The final expiation of his past error coincides with the concentration of the whole action at his court. Florizel and Perdita, fleeing before the displeasure of Polixenes, seek refuge from the latter's prejudice at another and wiser court, and all is ready for the final reconciliation. At this point, the utterly unrealistic *ballet* quality of the play is more than ever apparent. Leontes, in the presence of all the chief actors in the fable, is placed by the faithful Paulina before the life-like 'statue' of Hermione, which gradually comes to life by a process which corresponds, in its harmonious majesty, to the definitive birth of a new life out of the long Winter of penance and suffering. The statue seems to live, it breathes, is warm; it tortures Leontes with the revival of past memories, but with the poignancy of a sorrow that he now desires to hold, to make eternal. Deluded, as he still believes, into thinking that the 'statue' has the appearance of life, he exclaims:

> Make me to think so twenty years together!
> No settled senses of the world can match
> The pleasure of that madness.
>
> (V.iii)

Finally, as though in answer to his prayer, the 'statue' comes to life, and Leontes and Hermione, restored to one another after sixteen years of sorrow and separation, once more embrace. Florizel and Perdita kneel, like Cordelia and Marina before them, to receive the blessing which Leontes, now restored to his wife, is at last ready to give to his daughter, also found again; while Polixenes, entering upon this scene of joy and reconciliation, completes it by consenting to her marriage with Florizel. In this way, the children's love heals the divisions introduced by passion into the original friendship of the fathers, and Winter has passed at last through Spring into the Summer of gracious consummation and fulfilment.

Shakespeare's last unquestioned play, *The Tempest—Henry VIII,* sometimes considered to be of later date, is scarcely a work of the first order, and we may reasonably admit the collaboration of John Fletcher in the writing of it[3]—is also concerned with reconciliation.

---

[3] For a contrary view see, again, G. Wilson Knight's *The Crown of Life,* where great importance is attached to the play in the author's interpretation of the Shakespearian pattern.

Unlike *The Winter's Tale,* however, it telescopes the complete process of estrangement, suffering, and restored harmony by viewing the earlier stages as past history and concentrating almost exclusively upon the final, resolutive stage in the full development. To do this it takes us away from ordinary life to a magic island on which the normal laws of nature are suspended. Prospero, undisputed master of the island, controls it entirely through the ministration of the spirits whom he has learned to master, and lives with his daughter Miranda —who has no clear memory of any other life—in a state of idyllic simplicity. This change of emphasis, however, should not blind us to the fact that *The Tempest* is as closely connected as *The Winter's Tale* with the passions and conflicts of normal living. The whole point of the early scenes of *The Tempest* is that this abstraction from common reality cannot last. Just as much as the characters in *The Winter's Tale,* those of *The Tempest* are faced with the universal human necessity for maturing; and their attainment of maturity implies at some stage the loss of their original state of innocence, though, as the play proceeds to show, they may find it again—backed this time by a full experience—at the end of their development.

The state of innocence is, even on Prospero's island, a precarious one. He himself, of course, is only there as a result of the envy and ambition of his brother Antonio, and we must not believe that the conditions of a full and civilized life are to be found within its narrow limits. His position, indeed, has been caused by definite and clearly stated deficiencies in the practical order. His trust and neglect of the proper ends of worldly government, as stated by him to Miranda (I.ii), recall those of the Duke in *Measure for Measure* (a person with whom he shows no few points of contact) in opening the way for the entry of evil into his domains. Prospero, in fact, has not been able, any more than Shakespeare's more obviously tragic characters, to avoid the existence and development of evil. As always, he is faced by a passion-born excrescence implicit in the nature of things, the effects of which are inevitably disruptive; but though evil impulse of this kind is as clearly present in *The Tempest* as in any of the earlier plays, Prospero is differentiated from Shakespeare's tragic heroes by holding in his hands the weapon of contemplative wisdom, and with it an assurance that, with the help of destiny (more explicitly objectivized than anywhere else in the plays), evil can be mastered. It is his possession of this weapon, and not any state of abstraction from reality, that makes him less the victim of internal passion and external circumstance than a quasi-divine controlling force guiding the action of those around him in accordance with his own superior understanding.

When the play opens, Prospero knows that the time has come for the reconciliation of past divisions and for the entry into what is to be, in a very real sense, a fuller life. The reconciliation, however, must be genuine and complete, made with a full knowledge of what evil, as a destructive force undermining 'degree' to fulfil its own selfish ends, can do. As a first step Miranda, who, as Prospero's daughter, has an essential part to play in the coming reconciliation, must be awakened to the implications of full maturity. To do this, and at the same time to create the conditions without which reconciliation would be impossible, Prospero uses his magic power to raise a tempest—itself symbolically associated, as we have by now learned to expect, with the stress of tragedy—in order to bring together on his idyllic island all those who have formerly wronged him. By so doing, he deliberately introduces into his domain suffering and ambition, evils hitherto unknown there but which will themselves, in due course, be mastered and become instruments of reconciliation; for suffering and the exposure to evil bring with them, when confronted by a corresponding moral effort, self-knowledge (as in *King Lear*), and a maturity without which reconciliation would be a false, idyllic simplification.

It is not surprising, in view of this conception, that the early part of the play should be largely devoted to a careful analysis of the motives of the newcomers and to a distinction between their various degrees of guilt. The least reprehensible is seen to be Alonso, who, although in part responsible for Prospero's banishment, is now sorry for his past acts and overcome by the loss—as he believes—of his son Ferdinand. When confronted with the condemnation of the disguised Ariel, he alone among the conspirators expressly recognizes his responsibility and associates his treatment of Prospero with his present bereavement:

> . . . the thunder,
> That deep and dreadful organ-pipe, pronounc'd
> The name of Prosper: it did bass my trespass.
> Therefore my son i' th' ooze is bedded.
> (III.iii)

Alonso, indeed, with his readiness to deplore the past and his ability to receive the healing visitation of slumber (II.i), plays in *The Tempest,* though in a minor key, something of the part of Leontes in *The Winter's Tale;* his sufferings, culminating in the storm which has separated him from his son, have brought repentance to him, and he in turn will be accordingly forgiven, included in the final pattern of reconciliation.

Not all the evil brought to the island, however, can be thus reduced to conformity. Evil, here as always in Shakespeare, consists in the determination of selfish men, inspired by one or other of the human passions to the exclusion of the remaining elements in a balanced existence, to break the bonds of unity and conscience through following self-interest to anarchy. As such, it is represented on the island by Sebastian and Antonio, who are moved by a spirit of ruthless egoism. It is worth noting that they are themselves carefully distinguished. Sebastian is the less guilty of the two. Possessing the germs of wickedness in his character, he yet needs someone more forceful, more conscious of the true nature of his desires, to rouse them into activity; he is, in his own words, 'standing water', and the action of his more determined companion is needed to teach him 'how to flow' (II.i). Antonio, on the other hand, belongs to a longer and more sinister line of Shakespearian villains, and reminds us, as Prospero's brother, of the illegitimate Edmund who plotted with such terrible consequences against his half-brother in *King Lear;* possessed of the same critical, destructive intelligence, he applies it with the same limited, partial understanding in disregard of all natural bonds to achieve the selfish purposes which are the only end his reason can propose to him. Conscience, despised by him in vigorous, self-confident speech as less than a 'kibe', is a 'deity' for which he can find no place in the order of things; 'three inches' of 'obedient steel', and nothing more, stand between him and the attainment of his designs on Milan. The spirits of Iago, Lady Macbeth, and Edmund assert themselves for the last time in the words of a courtier who, having dispossessed his brother, is prepared to eliminate his king.

Apart from Antonio and Sebastian, degenerate representatives of the courtly, sophisticated order and the principal actors in the island conspiracy, there remain only the drunken sailors, Stephano and Trinculo, whose actions are based on a combination of gross vulgarity and venial sin, and very little more. Their anarchic instincts are less the result of reasoning, the privilege of their supposed 'betters', than the product of drink, which obliterates in them the true sense of their situation and releases them, in their own conception, from the obligations which normally bind them to their masters and fellowmen. On the island, however, these two essentially commonplace beings are brought into touch, not with the simple, noble savage who peoples undiscovered islands in the imagination of courtly theorists like Gonzalo, but with the *true* sources of energy in the natural man. Caliban, the offspring of a witch but himself uncorrupted by civilization, is a strange mixture of the poetical and the absurd, the pathetic and the savagely evil. No one can doubt his essential superiority, as a creature of sensibility, to Stephano and Trinculo. Unlike them, he possesses a genuine and distinctive poetic note, which expresses itself repeatedly in appreciation of the natural beauties around him; but, no less than they, he is forced, with the break-up of the original simplicity of the island under Prospero's earlier unquestioned rule, to choose between his spiritual and his animal nature. Both have so far been held in unity by a superior power, respectively encouraged and curbed by the rule of Prospero; but now, with the original balance upset by the invasion of alien forces, one or the other must take control. It is at this point (II.ii) that Caliban meets Stephano and Trinculo with their bottle, and, lacking any true god to worship although the primitive instinct for adoration is strong in him, he falls at their feet. The drunken sailor becomes, in his eyes, 'a brave god', bearing 'celestial liquors'; and this god in turn corrupts him by encouraging his undeveloped notions of liberty, which bring him finally into servitude, not now to Prospero, but to the bottle-bearing drunkard whose feet he is moved to kiss. Last of all, through the release, under the pretext of his newly acquired 'freedom', of the animal instincts which have always been a part of his nature, Caliban balances the designs of Sebastian and Antonio upon Alonso with his own plot to murder Prospero.

The true purpose of *The Tempest* is now beginning to emerge from our analysis. Once more, as so often in Shakespeare, the problem of liberty is set at the centre of the play. The degeneration of Caliban when exposed to the influence of the outside world shows that liberty can easily lead to a state of enslavement to evil; the only means by which this danger can be avoided involves an acceptance of the idea of service freely given to a superior conception of good. Nevertheless—and here we are brought perhaps a step further than in any other play—to recognize good, and the order which naturally proceeds from it, is to accept it as an integral part of the natural order of the universe, and therefore as objectively guaranteed. For this reason, Prospero is more than a good man with an unusual degree of insight into moral realities; he is the instrument of a destiny which is concerned to bring together the diverse characters and situations described in *The Tempest,* for only in relation to an objective conception of the operations of destiny can all the conflicting anarchies let loose upon the island by his own permission be judged.

There is a decisive moment in the play when the voice of Destiny, elsewhere implied with varying degrees of firmness, is allowed to speak openly. Ariel's great speech addressed to Alonso and his guilty companions before he deprives them of the enchanted banquet that has just been set before them is, in fact, nothing less than the keystone upon which the structure of the whole play rests:

> You are three men of sin, whom destiny,
> That hath to instrument this lower world,
> And what is in't, the never-surfeited sea
> Hath caused to belch up you; and, on this island,
> Where man doth not inhabit, you 'mongst men
> Being most unfit to live . . .
> But remember
> (For that's my business to you) that you three
> From Milan did supplant good Prospero,
> Expos'd unto the sea (which hath requit it)
> Him and his innocent child; for which foul deed,
> The pow'rs delaying, not forgetting, have
> Incens'd the seas and shores, yea, all the creatures,
> Against your peace. Thee of thy son, Alonso,
> They have bereft; and do pronounce by me
> Ling'ring perdition (worse than any death

Can be at once) shall step by step attend
You and your ways, whose wraths to guard you from,
Which here, in this most desolate isle, else falls
Upon your heads, is nothing but heart's sorrow
And a clear life ensuing.

(III.iii)

Here at last—rather even than in any speech of Prospero's—is an explicit statement of what *The Tempest* is about. Perhaps for the first time in Shakespeare's work the voice of Destiny delivers itself directly in judgment. The sea, to which Prospero and Miranda were exposed by their enemies, has performed once more the same function, at once destroying and preserving, as in *Pericles* and *The Winter's Tale;* but it has done this in a way not directly foreseen in the earlier plays, by bringing the criminals, through Prospero's own action, to judgement. By shifting the whole symbolic process of breakdown and restoration to its last stage, and looking back upon its genesis and development as things already substantially complete, Shakespeare has, in a sense, limited the scope of his action; but he has also saved himself from a repetition of effects already achieved and opened the way to a new kind of play. The very essence of this new conception lies in Ariel's call upon the conspirators for repentance as a necessary prelude to salvation. Unless their sojourn on this 'most desolate isle' has taught them the evil and folly of their ways, unless it has shown them the necessity for true 'heart's sorrow' and 'a clear life' to follow, their doom is, spiritually speaking, certain. For it is in the nature of unbridled passion, as Shakespeare had already presented it in his great tragedies, to lead its victims to self-destruction; and *The Tempest,* with its insistence upon notions of penance and amendment that can only follow from the acceptance of such a personal, spiritual conception of Destiny as is here for the first time placed squarely and unambiguously at the centre of the play, is conceived as nothing less than a counterpoise to this tragic process of ruin.

The Tempest, then, is no mere romantic idyll or piece of poetic fancy. Since Destiny, according to its central assertion, is real and there is a life-giving order sanctioned by it, reconciliation can truly be born from the bitterness of tragic experience. The instruments of this reconciliation are, as always, the children of the fathers whom passion originally divided. Miranda, awakened by Prospero to human realities and exposed by him to a symbolic process of trial, marries Ferdinand, whom she first saw in her naïve state of innocence as a vision proceeding from a 'brave new world' of her own circumscribed imagination, but whom she has come in the course of the play to love as a man. Once more, the children restore the parents to harmony and the 'brave new world' itself is seen as an ennobling vision of love in the light of an enriched experience.

As in *Pericles* and *The Winter's Tale* the whole symbolic action is rounded off by a specifically religious gesture. In the words of the faithful Gonzalo at the moment of consummation, the gods are invoked to 'crown' the new-born vision of humanity with an appropriate symbol of royalty: the 'gods' who have unfolded the whole plot through its various stages and brought it at last to its harmonious conclusion. The crown that they bestow is, in effect, a sign of the 'second', the redeemed and 'reasonable' life which has at last been given to the protagonists of the play through their experiences on the island. As Gonzalo puts it:

> In one voyage
> Did Claribel her husband find at Tunis,
> And Ferdinand, her brother, found a wife
> *Where he himself was lost;* Prospero his dukedom
> In a poor isle; *and all of us ourselves*
> *When no man was his own.*
>
> (V.i)

In the light of these lines, the whole action—the loss no less than the finding, the separations no less than the reunions—is clearly seen to be a closely woven texture of symbolic elements. Recognized as such, it grows vastly into a significance that rounds off our understanding of the whole play. To the very last, Shakespeare is careful to balance his construction with a characteristic sense of the relativity of all our feelings and speculations; Prospero has already set against the prevailing sense of order and harmony his reference to 'the baseless fabric' of our vision, and at the end Stephano and Trinculo, representatives—like Autolycus before them—of the irreducible human element that defies incorporation into any pattern, are left, neither condoned nor very seriously condemned, to the island which Prospero and his group are leaving for re-entry into a full civilized existence. These reservations, however, do not affect the general scope of the conception, which is harmonizing and inclusive. For it is at this point, if anywhere, that the pattern of *The Tempest*—and with it the whole design initiated in the historical plays and carried through the tragedies to this last symbolic integration—is substantially complete.

A 9
B 0
C 1
D 2
E 3
F 4
G 5
H 6
I 7
J 8